PLAYFAIR
CRICKET ANNUAL 2008

61st edition
EDITED BY BILL FRINDALL
All statistics by the Editor unless otherwise stated

Preface	2
Acknowledgements	3
Duckworth/Lewis – A Brief Explanation	4
2008 Season	
England v New Zealand – Series Records	6
England v South Africa – Series Records	8
New Zealand and South Africa Registers	10
County Register, 2007 Championship ~~Averages~~ and Records	11
What is a Kolpak Registration?	127
Umpires – ECB Lists and ICC Eli~~te~~	128
2007 Season	
University and Touring Team Reg~~isters~~	
Statistical Highlights	
First-Class Averages	
LV County Championship	
NatWest Limited-Overs Internat~~ional~~	
Friends Provident Trophy	
Benson & Hedges Cup	
Ireland and Scotland Registers	
NatWest PRO 40 League	
Twenty20 Cup	
Minor Counties Championship and Averages	5
Second XI Championship	/8
Cricketer of the Year Awards	179
Current Career Records	
First-Class Cricket	180
Limited-Overs Internationals	201
Test Matches	214
Leading Current Players	224
Limited-Overs 'List A' Cricket	225
Cricket Records	
First-Class Cricket	234
Oxbridge Match Results and Records	243
Limited-Overs Internationals	245
Twenty20 Internationals	255
Women's Test Cricket	259
Test Matches	263
Test Match Scores and England Series Averages – May 2007 to December 2007	276
Leading Test Aggregates 2007	305
Test Match Championship Schedule	306
2008 Fixtures	
Second XI	307
Minor Counties	309
Principal Matches	312
England U-19, England Women's Internationals and MCC UCCE Challenge	318
Fillers/Miscellaneous	
County Benefits 2008	16
County Caps Awarded 2007	103
Scoring of No-Balls and Wides 2008	174
Fielding Chart	319

PREFACE

These notes are being written after the opening day's play of the First Test between New Zealand and England. Most of the host team donned white clothing for the first time in three months and their strongest eleven had been ravaged by the lure of Indian dollars. The full impact of the Packer-style war between a frustrated television mogul and the Indian Board struck home only after New Zealand Cricket terminated the contract of their world-class fast bowler, Shane Bond, after initially agreeing to his joining the rebel Indian Cricket League (ICL).

Then came the astonishing multi-million dollar auction of players in the 'official' Indian Premier League. The Indian Board was excessively tardy in embracing the 20-over format but, following the outstanding success of the inaugural world Twenty20 competition in South Africa last September, it swiftly formed the IPL in direct competition to the rebel version. This was readily given the seal of approval by an International Cricket Council mindful of the overwhelming financial muscle of the Indian Board and ever eager to supplement its own coffers.

Twenty20 cricket was the brainchild of an ECB employee and astonished its many detractors by the popularity and vast attendances attracted by its inaugural county competition in 2003. When asked what he thought of this format, Trevor Bailey responded sardonically with 'Everyone makes mistakes'. For those who find limited-overs cricket tedious in the extreme because of its immense bias towards batsmen, formulaic predictability and hideous coloured clothing, the shorter format has two major advantages. It removes the 30-over graveyard shift that forms the centre of the 50-over game and it leaves a considerable part of the day in which to do something useful. It is perhaps proof of the ever-dwindling human attention span that has introduced mini versions to several major sports, that Twenty20 has become cricket's cash cow.

Because of the lack of public support for Test cricket in New Zealand, the current series is being staged on smaller grounds such as Hamilton and Napier instead of at the vast rugby mausoleums in Auckland and Christchurch. Significantly, New Zealand's women cricketers no longer play Test matches.

Although only a handful of English players have joined the ICL and none were considered by the IPL because its 2008 programme clashed with the county season, the 'Indian mutiny' could dramatically affect this summer's county season. Just as this edition was going to press with the County Register section sealed, the ECB announced that any overseas registrations who had joined the ICL would be banned from county cricket unless they received written approval from their national boards. As Pakistan has already banned their ICL signatories from all domestic cricket, this probably means that Sussex may have to seek a hat-trick of championship titles without the considerable services of their ace leg-spinner, Mushtaq Ahmed.

This will be good news for their competitors, especially Surrey who, through some unfathomable whim of the England selectors, look certain to have the uninterrupted services of Mark Ramprakash. How they can continue to overlook an fit, quick-footed, run-hungry batsman who has uniquely averaged over 100 in successive seasons beggars belief. He needs just three first-class hundreds to become the 25th member of the Hundred Hundreds Club.

Two former Surrey champions (and boyhood heroes) will reach equally notable landmarks this summer. Arthur McIntyre and Sir Alec Bedser, currently the two oldest living England cricketers, will celebrate their 90th birthdays on 14 May and 4 July respectively. Many Happy Returns to you both.

BILL FRINDALL
Highbrook, Hamilton, New Zealand
6 March 2008

ACKNOWLEDGEMENTS
AND THANKS

HEADLINE
David Wilson (Editorial Director)
Rhea Halford (Editorial Assistant)
John Skermer (proofs)

LETTERPART
Lorraine Byfield
Chris Leggett
Caroline Leggett

CAREER RECORDS
Philip Bailey
Cricket Archive
Robin Abrahams
Andrew Roberts

ECB
Alan Fordham

COUNTY SCORER/STATISTICIANS
John Brown (Derbyshire)
Brian Hunt (Durham)
Tony Choat (Essex)
Andrew Hignell (Glamorgan)
Keith Gerrish Gloucestershire)
Tony Weld (Hampshire)
Jack Foley (Kent)
Alan West (Lancashire)
Graham York (Leicestershire)
Don Shelley (Middlesex)
Tony Kingston (Northamptonshire)
Gordon Stringfellow (Nottinghamshire)
Gerry Stickley (Somerset)
Mike Charman (Sussex)
Keith Booth (Surrey)
David Wainwright (Warwickshire)
Neil Smith (Worcestershire)
Roy Wilkinson (Yorkshire)

UNIVERSITIES
Ray Markham (Cambridge)
Graeme Fowler (Durham)
Margaret Folwell (Loughborough)
Neil Harris (Oxford)

TASTATS
Ric Finlay
David Fitzgerald

OVERSEAS
Rajesh Kumar (India)
Andrew Samson (South Africa)
Cheryl Styles (New Zealand)
Charlie Wat (Australia)

COUNTY ADMINISTRATIONS
Tom Sears (Derbyshire)
Ellen Johnson (Durham)
Greg Lansdowne (Essex)
Caryl Watkin (Glamorgan)
Lizzie Allen (Gloucestershire)
Tim Tremlett (Hampshire)
Carolyn Dunne (Kent)
Diana Lloyd (Lancashire)
Elaine Pickering (Leicestershire)
Emma Channon (Middlesex)
David Capel (Northamptonshire)
Mick Newell (Nottinghamshire)
Sally Donoghue (Somerset)
Stephen Howes (Surrey)
Simon Dyke (Sussex)
Keith Cook (Warwickshire)
Steve Rhodes (Worcestershire)
James Buttler (Yorkshire)

DUCKWORTH/LEWIS – A BRIEF EXPLANATION

The Duckworth/Lewis (D/L) method has been around now for 10 years and it is generally accepted as being a very fair method for resetting targets in interrupted one-day matches. However, ask a typical cricket fan as to how the calculations are done and the fallback excuse of not being good at maths at school is frequently trotted out. But if you can work out how much tax you have to pay on your net income then D/L calculations are well within your grasp.

You may well have heard that the D/L method is based on the idea of resources – these are the combination of wickets and overs that a team has for their innings. However, it's not just the numbers of these that matter; it is also their relative value – wickets and overs have different relative importance as an innings progresses. For example, having lots of wickets in hand without overs left in which to use them is of little value, just as if lots of overs remain they have little value if there are no wickets left with which to use them. In conducting their innings, teams need to manage these twin resources in order to maximise the total they set or maximise their chances of winning the match. Through some neat behind-the-scenes mathematics and statistical analysis of hundreds of matches, Duckworth and Lewis have produced a table that represents the average percentages remaining of their twin resources of a 50-over innings. In the extract of the table supplied you will see that teams start with all 50 overs and 10 wickets – and therefore 100% of their resources. As an innings progresses a team receives its overs, loses its wickets and thereby consumes its resources. The table works always in overs left – in that way it can be used for matches that are shorter than 50 overs – and tells us what percentage of their combined resources remains.

Wickets lost:	0	2	4	6	9
Overs remaining:-					
50	100.0	85.1	62.7	34.9	4.7
40	89.3	77.8	59.5	34.6	4.7
30	75.1	67.3	54.1	33.6	4.7
25	66.5	60.5	50.0	32.6	4.7
20	56.6	52.4	44.6	30.8	4.7
10	32.1	30.8	28.3	22.8	4.7
5	17.2	16.8	16.1	14.3	4.6

Suppose that a team have batted for 45 overs and have lost 6 wickets. With 5 overs left, for 6 wickets lost the table shows they have 14.3% of their resources remaining. If their innings is now terminated, these resources are lost and they have had available for their innings 100–14.3 = 85.7% resources compared with the 100% for a complete 50-over innings.

These figures came into play in a crucial Group match of the 2003 World Cup in South Africa. Against the host nation, Sri Lanka scored 268 in their 100% resources of 50 overs. Rain began to fall and abandonment looked likely at the end of the 45th over of South Africa's innings. Charts of the D/L method were consulted and the relevant figure was obtained through the comparative resources of the two teams. The calculation was 268×85.7/100=229.676. This meant that in order to win SA needed to reach 230 by the end of the 45th over if the match were abandoned. A score of 229 would be the score to tie.

How would South Africa know this? You will have seen the D/L par-score displayed on scoreboards. These numbers come from the par-score sheet that is distributed during the interval to team camps, match officials and the media. The par-score is given for the end of every one of the combinations of overs left and wickets lost (and even on a ball-by-ball basis). This sheet is clearly labelled as the score needed to tie. In the World Cup match the SA camp told the batsmen, Boucher and Klusener, that they needed to get to 229 by the end of the over. Thanks to a six from Boucher off the penultimate ball of the over, they achieved this – and to avoid losing his wicket, which would have raised the par-score, Boucher blocked the last ball. Play was duly abandoned at the end of the over but the dismay in the SA camp was palpable when it was finally realised that the 229 the batsmen had been told to score was in fact the score to *tie* and not to *win* the match. So a tie it was and the misreading of the clear information available led to the elimination of the host nation from the tournament.

Whenever a stoppage occurs within an innings, the table provides the information by which to calculate the resources lost. Suppose that there are 20 overs left with only 4 wickets down and a stoppage reduces the innings by 10 overs so there are now only 10 overs left on the resumption. You will see from the table that the team went off with 44.6% resources left and came back with 28.3% left. The stoppage would have cost them 44.6–28.3 = 16.3% of their resources so that they would have available 100–16.3 = 83.7% resources for their innings if there are no more stoppages (but if there are, the resources available are further reduced in the same way) and, in most cases, the target comes from reducing the first innings score in proportion to the resources available as in the World Cup example.

Sometimes teams start with fewer than 50 overs either due to a shorter match competition, such as the Pro40 or Twenty20, or due to a delayed start. For a 25-over innings, for instance, teams start with 66.5% resources compared with a 50-over innings. Although they have half the overs they still have all 10 wickets and therefore more than half their resources – the table says about two-thirds compared with 50-over innings. Any loss of overs would reduce this further in the same way and using the same figures as in the table.

So you see that it really is simple to calculate targets following interruptions during the second innings. The method is simply to adjust the first innings score in proportion to the resources available to the two teams – rounding up to win and one fewer to tie.

A distinctive feature of the D/L method compared with previous methods of adjusting targets is that it compensates the team batting first for stoppages within their innings – their batting strategy has been based on the full 50 overs and so to have it curtailed is usually a disadvantage. The D/L method usually sets an enhanced target, that is, a target which is quite a few runs more than the team batting first scored. This has the effect of compensating them for the unexpected shortening of the first innings and the advantage that the team batting second have from knowing in advance of their shorter innings.

How this is achieved, together with further detailed descriptions of the Duckworth/Lewis method and some frequently asked questions, can be found at the Cricinfo website: www.cricinfo.com/db/ABOUT_CRICKET/RAIN_RULES/ and a booklet is available from Acumen Books at www.acumenbooks.co.uk/ducklew.htm.

Although rain is usually the cause of stoppages and D/L adjusted targets, interruptions have occurred for several other causes including sandstorms, snow, floodlight failures, crowd disturbances and, on a few occasions, due to the sun!

Cases at the higher levels of the game usually run to 80-100 per year and total well over 800 since the method's first use on 1st January 1997 in which England lost to Zimbabwe when they would have won by the old, unfair average run-rate method.

There have been some advances in the methodology since January 1997. With higher totals being more prevalent, teams need to score a bigger percentage of their runs in the earlier stages of their innings than those suggested by the standard tables. Consequently, higher scores lead to the need for the table to be adjusted and this needs the computer to do the calculations. Whereas what is now known as the Standard Edition, using a single table of resources as described here, is used at lower levels of the game where computers aren't necessary or available, the higher levels of the game now use the more advanced computerised version called the Professional Edition. In this edition, the computer in effect produces a different table of resources for every match, but thereafter the calculations are the same as described here.

ENGLAND v NEW ZEALAND

SERIES RECORDS
1929-30 to 2004

HIGHEST INNINGS TOTALS

England	in England	567-8d		Nottingham	1994
	in New Zealand	593-6d		Auckland	1974-75
New Zealand	in England	551-9d		Lord's	1973
	in New Zealand	537		Wellington	1983-84

LOWEST INNINGS TOTALS

England	in England	126		Birmingham	1999
	in New Zealand	64		Wellington	1977-78
New Zealand	in England	47		Lord's	1958
	in New Zealand	26		Auckland	1954-55

HIGHEST MATCH AGGREGATE　　1445 for 33 wickets　　Lord's　　2004
LOWEST MATCH AGGREGATE　　390 for 30 wickets　　Lord's　　1958

HIGHEST INDIVIDUAL INNINGS

England	in England	310*	J.H.Edrich	Leeds	1965
	in New Zealand	336*	W.R.Hammond	Auckland	1932-33
New Zealand	in England	206	M.P.Donnelly	Lord's	1949
	in New Zealand	222	N.J.Astle	Christchurch	2001-02

HIGHEST AGGREGATE OF RUNS IN A SERIES

England	in England	469	(av 78.16)	L.Hutton	1949
	in New Zealand	563	(av 563.00)	W.R.Hammond	1932-33
New Zealand	in England	462	(av 77.00)	M.P.Donnelly	1949
	in New Zealand	341	(av 85.25)	C.S.Dempster	1929-30

RECORD WICKET PARTNERSHIPS – ENGLAND

1st	223	G.Fowler (105)/C.J.Tavaré (109)	The Oval	1983
2nd	369	J.H.Edrich (310*)/K.F.Barrington (163)	Leeds	1965
3rd	245	J.Hardstaff jr (114)/W.R.Hammond (140)	Lord's	1937
4th	266	M.H.Denness (181)/K.W.R.Fletcher (216)	Auckland	1974-75
5th	242	W.R.Hammond (227)/L.E.G.Ames (103)	Christchurch	1932-33
6th	281	G.P.Thorpe (200*)/A.Flintoff (137)	Christchurch	2001-02
7th	149	A.P.E.Knott (104)/P.Lever (64)	Auckland	1970-71
8th	246	L.E.G.Ames (137)/G.O.B.Allen (122)	Lord's	1931
9th	163*	M.C.Cowdrey (128*)/A.C.Smith (69*)	Wellington	1962-63
10th	59	A.P.E.Knott (49)/N.Gifford (25*)	Nottingham	1973

RECORD WICKET PARTNERSHIPS – NEW ZEALAND

1st	276	C.S.Dempster (136)/J.E.Mills (117)	Wellington	1929-30
2nd	241	J.G.Wright (116)/A.H.Jones (143)	Wellington	1991-92
3rd	210	B.A.Edgar (83)/M.D.Crowe (106)	Lord's	1986
4th	155	M.D.Crowe (143)/M.J.Greatbatch (68)	Wellington	1987-88
5th	180	M.D.Crowe (142)/S.A.Thomson (69)	Lord's	1994
6th	141	M.D.Crowe (115)/A.C.Parore (71)	Manchester	1994
7th	117	D.N.Patel (99)/C.L.Cairns (61)	Christchurch	1991-92
8th	104	D.A.R.Moloney (64)/A.W.Roberts (66*)	Lord's	1937
9th	118	J.V.Coney (174*)/B.L.Cairns (64)	Wellington	1983-84
10th	118	N.J.Astle (222)/C.L.Cairns (23*)	Christchurch	2001-02

BEST INNINGS BOWLING ANALYSIS

England	in England	7- 32	D.L.Underwood	Lord's	1969
	in New Zealand	7- 47	P.C.R.Tufnell	Christchurch	1991-92
New Zealand	in England	7- 74	B.L.Cairns	Leeds	1983
	in New Zealand	7-143	B.L.Cairns	Wellington	1983-84

BEST MATCH BOWLING ANALYSIS

England	in England	12-101	D.L.Underwood	The Oval	1969
	in New Zealand	12- 97	D.L.Underwood	Christchurch	1970-71
New Zealand	in England	11-169	D.J.Nash	Lord's	1994
	in New Zealand	10-100	R.J.Hadlee	Wellington	1977-78

HIGHEST AGGREGATE OF WICKETS IN A SERIES

England	in England	34	(av 7.47)	G.A.R.Lock	1958
	in New Zealand	19	(av 19.00)	D.Gough	1996-97
		19	(av 19.84)	A.R.Caddick	2001-02
New Zealand	in England	21	(av 26.61)	R.J.Hadlee	1983
	in New Zealand	15	(av 19.53)	R.O.Collinge	1977-78
		15	(av 24.73)	R.J.Hadlee	1977-78

RESULTS SUMMARY
ENGLAND v NEW ZEALAND – IN ENGLAND

	Tests	Series			Lord's			The Oval			Manchester			Leeds			Birmingham			Nottingham		
		E	NZ	D	E	NZ	D	E	NZ	D	E	NZ	D	E	NZ	D	E	NZ	D	E	NZ	D
1931	3	1	–	2	–	–	1	1	–	–	–	–	1									
1937	3	1	–	2	–	–	1	1	–	–	1	–	–									
1949	4	–	–	4	–	–	1				–	–	1	–	–	1				–	–	1
1958	5	4	–	1	1	–	–				1	–	–	1	–	–	1	–	–			
1965	3	3	–	–	1	–	–				1	–	–							1	–	–
1969	3	2	–	1	1	–	–	1	–	–										–	–	1
1973	3	2	–	1	1	–	–				1	–	–				1	–	–			
1978	3	3	–	–	1	–	–	1	–	–				1	–	–						
1983	4	3	1	–	1	–	–							1	–	–	1	–	–			
1986	3	–	1	2	1	–	–				–	–	1							–	1	–
1990	3	1	–	2	–	–	1	1	–	–				–	–	1						
1994	3	1	–	2	–	1	–				–	–	1				1	–	–			
1999	4	1	2	1	–	1	–	1	–	–				–	1	–	1	–	–			
2004	3	3	–	–	1	–	–				1	–	–				1	–	–			
	47	25	4	18	6	1	7	4	–	–	2	–	4	4	1	1	4	–	–	5	1	2

ENGLAND v NEW ZEALAND – IN NEW ZEALAND

	Tests	Series			Christchurch			Wellington			Auckland			Dunedin		
		E	NZ	D	E	NZ	D	E	NZ	D	E	NZ	D	E	NZ	D
1929-30	4	1	–	3	1	–	–	–	–	1	–	–	2	–	–	–
1932-33	2	–	–	2	–	–	1				–	–	1			
1946-47	1	–	–	1				–	–	1						
1950-51	2	1	–	1	–	–	1	1	–	–						
1954-55	2	2	–	–	1	–	–	1	–	–						
1958-59	2	1	–	1				1	–	–	–	–	1			
1962-63	3	3	–	–	1	–	–	1	–	–	1	–	–			
1965-66	3	–	–	3	–	–	1	–	–	1	–	–	1			
1970-71	2	1	–	1	1	–	–				–	–	1			
1974-75	2	1	–	1	1	–	–				1	–	–			
1977-78	3	1	1	1				–	–	1	1	–	–	–	1	–
1983-84	3	–	1	2	1	–	–				–	–	1			
1987-88	3	–	–	3				–	–	1	–	–	1	–	–	1
1991-92	3	2	–	1	1	–	–				1	–	–			
1996-97	3	2	–	1	1	–	–				1	–	–			
2001-02	3	1	1	1				1	–	–	–	1	–	1	–	–
	41	16	3	22	8	1	6	3	1	5	4	1	10	1	–	1
Totals	88	41	7	40												

ENGLAND v SOUTH AFRICA
SERIES RECORDS

1888-89 to 2004-05

Key to grounds: Durban – [1]Lord's, [2]Kingsmead; Johannesburg – [1]Old Wanderers,
[2]Ellis Park, [3]Wanderers.

HIGHEST INNINGS TOTALS

England	in England	604-9d	The Oval	2003
	in South Africa	654-5	Durban[2]	1938-39
South Africa	in England	682-6d	Lord's	2003
	in South Africa	572-7	Durban[2]	1999-00

LOWEST INNINGS TOTALS

England	in England	76	Leeds	1907
	in South Africa	92	Cape Town	1898-99
South Africa	in England	30	Birmingham	1924
	in South Africa	30	Port Elizabeth	1895-96

HIGHEST MATCH AGGREGATE   1981 for 35 wickets   Durban[2]   1938-39
LOWEST MATCH AGGREGATE   378 for 30 wickets   The Oval   1912

HIGHEST INDIVIDUAL INNINGS

England	in England	219	M.E.Trescothick	The Oval	2003
	in South Africa	243	E.Paynter	Durban[2]	1938-39
South Africa	in England	277	G.C.Smith	Birmingham	2003
	in South Africa	275	G.Kirsten	Durban[2]	1999-00

HIGHEST AGGREGATE OF RUNS IN A SERIES

England	in England	753	(av 94.12)	D.C.S.Compton	1947
	in South Africa	656	(av 72.88)	A.J.Strauss	2004-05
South Africa	in England	714	(av 79.33)	G.C.Smith	2003
	in South Africa	625	(av 69.44)	J.H.Kallis	2004-05

RECORD WICKET PARTNERSHIPS – ENGLAND

1st	359	L.Hutton (158)/C.Washbrook (195)	Johannesburg[2]	1948-49
2nd	280	P.A.Gibb (120)/W.J.Edrich (219)	Durban[2]	1938-39
3rd	370	W.J.Edrich (189)/D.C.S.Compton (208)	Lord's	1947
4th	197	W.R.Hammond (181)/L.E.G.Ames (115)	Cape Town	1938-39
5th	237	D.C.S.Compton (163)/N.W.D.Yardley (99)	Nottingham	1947
6th	206*	K.F.Barrington (148*)/J.M.Parks (108*)	Durban[2]	1964-65
7th	115	J.W.H.T.Douglas (119)/M.C.Bird (61)	Durban[1]	1913-14
8th	154	C.W.Wright (71)/H.R.Bromley-Davenport (84)	Johannesburg[1]	1895-96
9th	99	A.Flintoff (95)/S.J.Harmison (6*)	The Oval	2003
10th	92	C.A.G.Russell (111)/A.E.R.Gilligan (39*)	Durban[2]	1922-23

RECORD WICKET PARTNERSHIPS – SOUTH AFRICA

1st	338	G.C.Smith (277)/H.H.Gibbs (179)	Birmingham	2003
2nd	257	G.C.Smith (259)/G.Kirsten (108)	Lord's	2003
3rd	319	A.Melville (189)/A.D.Nourse (149)	Nottingham	1947
4th	214	H.W.Taylor (121)/H.G.Deane (93)	The Oval	1929
5th	192	G.Kirsten (275)/M.V.Boucher (108)	Durban[2]	1999-00
6th	171	J.H.B.Waite (113)/P.L.Winslow (108)	Manchester	1955
7th	123	H.G.Deane (73)/E.P.Nupen (69)	Durban[2]	1927-28
8th	150	G.Kirsten (130)/M.Zondeki (59)	Leeds	2003
9th	137	E.L.Dalton (117)/A.B.C.Langton (73*)	The Oval	1935
10th	103	H.G.Owen-Smith (129)/A.J.Bell (26*)	Leeds	1929

BEST INNINGS BOWLING ANALYSIS

England	in England	9- 57	D.E.Malcolm	The Oval	1994
	in South Africa	9- 28	G.A.Lohmann	Johannesburg[1]	1895-96
South Africa	in England	7- 65	S.J.Pegler	Lord's	1912
	in South Africa	9-113	H.J.Tayfield	Johannesburg[3]	1956-57

BEST MATCH BOWLING ANALYSIS

England	in England	15- 99	C.Blythe	Leeds	1907
	in South Africa	17-159	S.F.Barnes	Johannesburg[1]	1913-14
South Africa	in England	10- 87	P.M.Pollock	Nottingham	1965
	in South Africa	13-192	H.J.Tayfield	Johannesburg[3]	1956-57

HIGHEST AGGREGATE OF WICKETS IN A SERIES

England	in England	34	(av 8.29)	S.F.Barnes	1912
	in South Africa	49	(av 10.93)	S.F.Barnes	1913-14
South Africa	in England	33	(av 19.78)	A.A.Donald	1998
	in South Africa	37	(av 17.18)	H.J.Tayfield	1956-57

RESULTS SUMMARY
ENGLAND v SOUTH AFRICA – IN ENGLAND

		Series			Lord's			Leeds			The Oval			Birmingham			Manchester			Nottingham		
	Tests	E	SA	D	E	SA	D	E	SA	D	E	SA	D	E	SA	D	E	SA	D	E	SA	D
1907	3	1	-	2			1	1					1									
1912	3	3	-	-	1			1			1											
1924	5	3	-	2	1			1					1	1					1			
1929	5	2	-	3			1	1					1			1	1					
1935	5	-	1	4		1				1			1						1			1
1947	5	3	-	2	1			1					1				1					1
1951	5	3	1	1	1					1	1						1				1	
1955	5	3	2	-	1				1		1							1		1		
1960	5	3	-	2	1								1	1					1	1		
1965	3	-	1	2			1						1								1	
1994	3	1	1	1		1				1	1											
1998	5	2	1	2		1		1								1			1	1		
2003	5	2	2	1		1			1		1					1				1		
57		26	9	22	6	4	3	6	2	3	5	-	7	2	-	3	3	1	4	4	2	2

ENGLAND v SOUTH AFRICA – IN SOUTH AFRICA

		Series			Port Elizabeth			Cape Town			Johannesburg			Durban			Pretoria		
	Tests	E	SA	D	E	SA	D	E	SA	D	E	SA	D	E	SA	D	E	SA	D
1888-89	2	2	-	-	1			1											
1891-92	1	1	-	-				1											
1895-96	3	3	-	-	1			1			1								
1898-99	2	2	-	-				1			1								
1905-06	5	1	4	-				1	1			3							
1909-10	5	2	3	-				1	1		1	1			1				
1913-14	5	4	-	1	1						2			1		1			
1922-23	5	2	1	2				1				1	1	1		1			
1927-28	5	2	2	1				1			1	1			1	1			
1930-31	5	-	1	4						1		1	1			2			
1938-39	5	1	-	4						1			2	1		1			
1948-49	5	2	-	3	1					1			2	1					
1956-57	5	2	2	1		1		1			1	1				1			
1964-65	5	1	-	4			1			1			2	1					
1995-96	5	-	1	4			1		1				1			1			1
1999-00	5	1	2	2			1		1			1				1	1		
2004-05	5	2	1	2	1				1		1					1			1
73		28	17	28	5	1	3	9	5	4	8	9	9	5	2	10	1	-	2
Totals 130		54	26	50															

TOURING TEAMS REGISTER 2008

Neither New Zealand nor South Africa had selected their 2008 touring teams at the time of going to press. The following players who had represented those teams in Test matches since 1 September 2006 were still available for selection:-

NEW ZEALAND.

Full Names	Birthdate	Birthplace	Team	Type	F-C Debut
BELL, Matthew David	25.02.77	Dunedin	Wellington	RHB/OB	1993-94
BOND, Shane Edward	07.06.75	Christchurch	Canterbury	RHB/RF	1996-97
CUMMING, Craig Derek	31.08.75	Timaru	Otago	RHB/RSM	1995-96
FLEMING, Stephen Paul	01.04.73	Christchurch	Wellington	LHB/RSM	1991-92
FRANKLIN, James Edward Charles	07.11.80	Wellington	Wellington	LHB/LFM	1998-99
FULTON, Peter Gordon	01.02.79	Christchurch	Canterbury	RHB/RM	2000-01
GILLESPIE, Mark Raymond	17.10.79	Wanganui	Wellington	RHB/RFM	1999-00
HOW, Jamie Michael	19.05.81	New Plymouth	C Districts	RHB/RM	2000-01
McCULLUM, Brendon Barrie	27.09.81	Dunedin	Otago	RHB/WK	1999-00
MARTIN, Christopher Stewart	10.12.74	Christchurch	Canterbury	RHB/RFM	1997-98
MASON, Michael James	27.08.74	Carterton	C Districts	RHB/RFM	1997-98
MILLS, Kyle David	15.03.79	Auckland	Auckland	RHB/RFM	1998-99
O'BRIEN, Iain Edward	10.07.76	Lower Hutt	Wellington	RHB/RM	2000-01
ORAM, Jacob David Philip	28.07.78	Palmerston North	C Districts	LHB/RM	1997-98
PAPPS, Michael Hugh William	02.07.79	Christchurch	Canterbury	RHB/WK	1998-99
PATEL, Jeetan Shashi	07.11.80	Wellington	Wellington	RHB/OB	1999-00
SINCLAIR, Mathew Stuart	09.11.75	Katherine, Australia	C Districts	RHB/RM	1995-96
STYRIS, Scott Bernard	10.07.75	Brisbane, Australia	N Districts	RHB/RMF	1994-95
TAYLOR, Luteru Ross Poutoa Lote	08.03.84	Lower Hutt	C Districts	RHB/OB	2002-03
TUFFEY, Daryl Raymond	11.06.78	Milton	N Districts	RHB/RFM	1996-97
VETTORI, Daniel Luca	27.01.79	Auckland	N Districts	RHB/SLA	1996-97
VINCENT, Lou	11.11.78	Warkworth	Auckland	RHB/WK	1997-98

SOUTH AFRICA

Full Names	Birthdate	Birthplace	Team	Type	F-C Debut
AMLA, Hasim Mahomed	31.03.83	Durban	Dolphins	RHB/RM	1999-00
BOTHA, Johan	02.05.82	Johannesburg	Warriors	RHB/OB	2000-01
BOUCHER, Mark Verdon	03.12.76	East London	Warriors	RHB/WK	1995-96
De VILLIERS, Abraham Benjamin	17.02.84	Pretoria	Titans	RHB/WK	2003-04
DIPPENAAR, Henrik Human ('Boeta')	14.06.77	Kimberley	Eagles	RHB/OB	1995-96
GIBBS, Herschelle Herman	23.02.74	Cape Town	Cape Cobras	RHB/RM	1990-91
HARRIS, Paul Lee	02.11.78	Salisbury, Rhodesia	Titans	RHB.SLA	1998-99
KALLIS, Jacques Henry	16.10.75	Cape Town	Cape Cobras	RHB/RFM	1993-94
McKENZIE, Neil Douglas	24.11.75	Johannesburg	Lions	RHB/RM	1994-95
MORKEL, Morne	06.10.84	Vereeniging	Titans	LHB/RFM	2003-04
NEL, Andre	15.07.77	Germiston	Titans	RHB/RFM	1996-97
NTINI, Makhaya	06.07.77	Mdingi	Warriors	RHB/RF	1995-96
POLLOCK, Shaun Maclean	16.07.73	Port Elizabeth	Dolphins	RHB/RFM	1991-92
PRINCE, Ashwell Gavin	28.05.77	Port Elizabeth	Cape Cobras	LHB	1995-96
SMITH, Graeme Craig	01.02.81	Johannesburg	Cape Cobras	LHB/OB	1999-00
STEYN, Dale Willem	27.06.83	Phalaborwa	Titans	RHB/RF	2003-04

THE FIRST-CLASS COUNTIES REGISTER, RECORDS AND 2007 AVERAGES

Career statistics are to the end of the 2007 season.
Test Match and LOI career bests have been updated to 1 February and 19 January 2008 respectively.

ABBREVIATIONS – General

*	not out/unbroken partnership	IT20	International Twenty20
b	born	l-o	limited-overs
BB	Best innings bowling analysis	LOI	Limited-Overs Internationals
Cap	Awarded 1st XI County Cap	Tests	Official Test Matches
f-c	first-class	F-c Tours	Overseas tours involving first-class
HS	Highest Score		appearances

Awards

PCA 2007   Professional Cricketer's Association Player of 2007
Wisden 2006   One of *Wisden Cricketers' Almanack's* Five Cricketers of 2006
YC 2007   Cricket Writers' Club Young Cricketer of 2007

ECB Competitions

BHC	Benson & Hedges Cup (1972-2002)
CC	LV County Championship
CGT	Cheltenham & Gloucester Trophy (2001-06)
FPT	Friends Provident Trophy
NL	National League (1999-2005)
NWT	NatWest Trophy (1981-2000)
P40	NatWest PRO 40 League
SL	Sunday League (1969-98)
T20	Twenty20 Competition

Education

ARU	Anglia Ruskin University
BHS	Boys' High School
C	College
CFE	College of Further Education
CHE	College of Higher Education
CS	Comprehensive School
GS	Grammar School
HS	High School
I	Institute
IHE	Institute of Higher Education
RGS	Royal Grammar School
S	School
SFC	Sixth Form College
SM	Secondary Modern School
SS	Secondary School
TC	Technical College
T(H)S	Technical (High) School
U	University
UMIST	University of Manchester Institute of Science and Technology
UWIC	University of Wales Institute, Cardiff

Playing Categories

LBG	Bowls right-arm leg-breaks and googlies
LF	Bowls left-arm fast
LFM	Bowls left-arm fast-medium
LHB	Bats left-handed
LM	Bowls left-arm medium pace

LMF	Bowls left-arm medium fast
OB	Bowls right-arm off-breaks
RF	Bowls right-arm fast
RFM	Bowls right-arm fast-medium
RHB	Bats right-handed
RM	Bowls right-arm medium pace
RMF	Bowls right-arm medium-fast
RSM	Bowls right-arm slow-medium
SLA	Bowls left-arm leg-breaks
SLC	Bowls left-arm 'Chinamen'
WK	Wicket-keeper

Teams (see also p 140)

ACT	Australian Capital Territory
ADBP	Agricultural Development Bank of P
B	Bangladesh
CD	Central Districts
EP	Eastern Province
FS	Free State
GW	Griqualand West
HK	Hong Kong
K	Kenya
KRL	Khan Research Laboratories
NBP	National Bank of Pakistan
ND	Northern Districts
NSW	New South Wales
NT	Northern Transvaal
NW	North West
(O)FS	(Orange) Free State
PIA	Pakistan International Airlines
PNSC	Pakistan National Shipping Corp
PTC	Pakistan Telecommunication Co
Q	Queensland
REDCO	Really Efficient Development Co
SAU	South African Universities
Tas	Tasmania
UP	Uttar Pradesh
Vic	Victoria
WA	Western Australia
WAPDA	Water & Power Development Auth.
WP	Western Province

DERBYSHIRE

Formation of Present Club: 4 November 1870
Inaugural First-Class Match: 1871
Colours: Chocolate, Amber and Pale Blue
Badge: Rose and Crown
County Champions: (1) 1936
Gillette/NatWest/C&G/FP Trophy Winners: (1) 1981
Benson and Hedges Cup Winners: (1) 1993
Pro 40/National League (Div 1) Winners: (0); best – 4th (Div 2) 2002
Sunday League Winners: (1) 1990
Twenty20 Cup Winners: (0) best – Quarter-Finalist 2005.

Chief Executive: Tom Sears, County Cricket Ground, Nottingham Road, Derby DE21 6DA • Tel: 01332 383211/388101 • Fax: 01332 290251 • Email: post@derbyshireccc.com • Web: www.derbyshireccc.com

Director of Cricket: J.E.Morris. **Captain**: R.Clarke. **Vice-Captain**: tba. **Overseas Players**: D.P.M.D.Jayawardena and C.J.L.Rogers. **2008 Beneficiary**: S.D.Stubbings. **Head Groundsman**: Neil Godrich. **Scorer**: John M.Brown. ‡ New registration. ^{NQ} Not qualified for England.

BIRCH, Daniel John (Kimberley CS, Nottingham), b Nottingham 21 Jan 1981. Son of J.D.Birch (Nottinghamshire 1973-88). 6'3". LHB, RM. Debut (Derbyshire) 2007, scoring 130 v CU (Cambridge), including 122* before lunch. HS 130 (*see above*). CC HS 95 v Glos (Derby) 2007 – on Championship debut. LO HS 60 v Lancs (Derby) 2007 (FPT). T20 HS 8.

BORRINGTON, Paul Michael (Repton S; Chellarton S; Loughborough U), b Nottingham 24 May 1988. Son of A.J.Borrington (Derbyshire 1971-80). 5'10". RHB, OB. Derbyshire 2005-07 (summer contract). HS 50 v Northants (Derby) 2007.

CLARE, Jonathan Luke (St Theodore's HS), b Burnley, Lancs 14 Jun 1986. 6'4". RHB, RMF. Debut (Derbyshire) 2007. HS 22 v Northants (Derby) 2007. BB 5-90 v Notts (Chesterfield) 2007 – on debut. LO HS 12 v Durham (Chesterfield) 2007 (P40). LO BB 3-44 v Middlesex (Lord's) 2007 (P40).

‡CLARKE, Rikki (Broadwater SS; Godalming C), b Orsett, Essex 29 Sep 1981. 6'4". RHB, RFM. Surrey 2002-07, scoring 107* v CU (Cambridge) on debut; cap 2005. MCC 2006. Joins Derbyshire 2008 as captain. YC 2002. **Tests**: 2 (2003-04); HS 55 and BB 2-7 v B (Chittagong) 2003-04. **LOI**: 20 (2003 to 2006); HS 39 v P (Lord's) 2006; BB 2-28 v B (Dhaka) 2003-04. F-c Tours: WI 2003-04, 2005-06; SL 2002-03 (ECB Acad), 2004-05; B 2003-04. 1000 runs (1): 1027 (2006). HS 214 Sy v Somerset (Guildford) 2006. BB 4-21 Sy v Leics (Leicester) 2003. LO HS 98* Sy v Derbys (Derby) 2002 (NL). LO BB 4-49 Sy v Warwks (Birmingham) 2005 (NL). T20 HS 79*. T20 BB 3-11.

DEAN, Kevin James (Leek HS; Leek CFE), b Derby 16 Oct 1975. 6'5". LHB, LMF. Debut (Derbyshire) 1996; cap 1998; benefit 2006. MCC 2002. HS 54* v Worcs (Derby) 2002. 50 wkts (2): most – 83 (2002). BB 8-52 v Kent (Canterbury) 2000. 2 hat-tricks (1998, 2000). LO HS 16* v Glamorgan (Cardiff) 1998 (SL) and 16* v Middlesex (Derby) 2002 (NL). LO BB 5-32 v Glos (Derby) 1996 (SL). T20 HS 8*. T20 BB 2-14.

‡**DOSHI, Nayan** Dilip (King Alfred S, London), b Nottingham 6 Oct 1978. Son of D.R.Doshi (Bengal, Notts, Warwks, Saurashtra, and India 1968-69 to 1986). 6'4". RHB, SLA. Saurashtra 2001-02 to date. Surrey 2004-07; cap 2006. Buckinghamshire 2001. 50 wkts (1): 51 (2006). HS 37 Saurashtra v Vidarbha (Rajkot) 2005-06. UK HS 33 Sy v Notts (Oval) 2005. BB 7-110 (10-183 match) Sy v Sussex (Hove) 2004. LO HS 38* Saurashtra v Baroda (Bombay) 2001-02. LO BB 5-30 Sy v Derbys (Chesterfield) 2006 (P40). T20 HS 1*. T20 BB 4-22.

‡**NOHINDS, Wavell** Wayne (Camperdown HS), b Kingston, Jamaica 7 Sep 1976. 6'0". LHB, RM. Jamaica 1995-96 to date. Joins Derbyshire 2008 as Kolpak registration. **Tests** (WI): 45 (1999-00 to 2005-06); HS 213 v SA (Georgetown) 2004-05; BB 3-79 v SA (Johannesburg) 2003-04. **LOI** (WI): 114 (1999 to 2006-07); HS 127* v Z (Harare) 2003-04; BB 3-24 v E (Oval) 2004. F-c Tours (WI): A 2000-01, 2005-06; SA 1997-98, 2003-04; NZ 1999-00; I 1998-99, 2002-03; P (Sharjah) 2001-02; Z 2001, 2003-04; B 1998-99, 2002-03. HS 213 (*see Tests*). BB 3-9 WI B v Jamaica (Montego Bay) 2000-01. LO HS 127* (*see LOI*). LO BB 4-35 WI v Zim A (Kwekwe) 2003-04. IT20 14. T20 HS 44*.

HUNTER, Ian David (Fyndoune Community C, Sacriston; New C, Durham), b Durham City 11 Sep 1979. 6'2". RHB, RMF. Durham 2000-03. Derbyshire debut 2004. HS 65 Du v Northants (Northampton) 2002. De HS 48 v Somerset (Taunton) 2006. BB 5-63 v Du (Chester-le-St) 2005. LO HS 39 Du v Leics (Leicester) 2002 (BHC). LO BB 4-29 Du v Essex (Ilford) 2000 (NL). T20 HS 25*. T20 BB 3-26.

‡**NOJAYAWARDENA, Denagamage Proboth Mahela** De Silva (Nalanda C, Colombo), b Colombo, Sri Lanka 27 May 1977. 5'9". RHB, RM. Sinhalese SC 1996-97 to date. North Central Province 2003-04 to 2004-05. *Wisden* 2006. **Tests** (SL): 93 (1997 to 2007-08, 19 as captain); HS 374 v SA (Colombo) 2006; BB 2-32 v P (Galle) 2000-01. **LOI** (SL): 255 (1997-98 to 2007-08, 55 as captain); HS 128 v I (Sharjah) 2000-01; BB 2-56 v K (Southampton) 1999. F-c Tours (SL) (C=captain): E 1998, 2002, 2006C; A 2004, 2007-08C; SA 1997-98, 2000-01, 2002-03; WI 2003; NZ 2004-05, 2006-07C; I 1997-98, 2005-06; P 1998-99, 1999-00, 2000-01, 2002-03, 2004-05; Z 1999-00, 2004; B 1998-99, 2005-06C. 1000 runs (0+2); most 1426 (2001-02). HS 374 (*see Tests*). BB 5-72 Sinhalese v Colts (Colombo) 1996-97. LO HS 128 (*see LOI*). LO BB 3-25 Sinhalese v Sebastianites (Colombo) 1998-99. IT20 HS 65. T20 HS 65. T20 BB 2-22.

‡**JONES, Edward** Peter, b Stoke-on-Trent, Staffs 23 Oct 1989. RHB, RMF. Derbyshire 2nd XI 2007. Summer contract – awaiting 1st XI debut.

KLOKKER, Frederik Andreas (Hindsholm S), b Odense, Denmark 13 Mar 1983. LHB, WK. Warwickshire (1 match) 2006. Derbyshire (2 matches) 2007 (match contract). Denmark (not f-c) 1999-00 to 2005. MCC YC 2002-05. HS 100* De v CU (Cambridge) 2007 – on Derbyshire debut. CC HS 40 Wa v Sussex (Hove) 2006. LO HS 138* Denmark v USA (Armagh) 2005.

LUNGLEY, Tom (St John Houghton SS; SE Derbyshire C), b Derby 25 Jul 1979. 6'1". LHB, RM. Debut (Derbyshire) 2000; cap 2007. HS 47 v Warwks (Derby) 2001. 50 wkts (1): 59 (2007). BB 5-20 v Leics (Derby) 2007. LO HS 45 v Essex (Chelmsford) 2001 (NL). LO BB 4-28 v Essex (Derby) 2001 (NL). T20 HS 25. T20 BB 4-11.

NEEDHAM, Jake (Nottingham Bluecoat S, Aspley), b Portsmouth, Hants 30 Sep 1986. 6'1". RHB, OB. Debut (Derbyshire) 2005. HS 48 v Notts (Chesterfield) 2007. BB 3-92 v Essex (Derby) 2007. LO HS 42 and BB 2-36 v Somerset (Taunton) 2007 (P40). T20 HS 0*.

PAGET, Christopher David (Repton S; Van Mildert C, Durham), b Stafford 2 Nov 1987. 6'0". RHB, OB. Debut (Derbyshire) 2004 (summer contract). No f-c appearances 2005-07. Durham UCCE 2007. HS 46 DU v Lancs (Durham) 2007. De HS 7. BB 3-63 De v WI (Derby) 2004. CC BB – . LO HS 3 and BB 1-48 v Durham (Chesterfield) 2007 (P40).

PATEL Akhil (Kimberley CS, Nottingham), b Nottingham 18 Jun 1990. Younger brother of S.R.Patel (*see NOTTINGHAMSHIRE*). 5'10". LHB, SLC. Debut (Derbyshire) 2007 (summer contract). Awaiting CC debut. HS 31 v CU (Cambridge) 2007 – on debut.

PIPE, David **James** (Queensbury S, Bradford), b Bradford, Yorks 16 Dec 1977. 5'11". RHB, WK. Worcestershire 1998-2005. Derbyshire debut 2006; cap 2007. HS 133* v Essex (Chelmsford) 2007. LO HS 83 v Leics (Leicester) 2007 (FPT). Held 8 catches Wo v Herts (Hertford) 2001 (CGT) to equal 1-o record. T20 HS 29*.

POYNTON, Thomas (John Taylor HS, Barton-under-Needwood; Repton S), b Burton upon Trent, Staffs 25 Nov 1989. 5'10". RHB, WK. Debut (Derbyshire) 2007 (summer contract). HS 2 v Glamorgan (Derby) 2007. LO HS – . T20 HS 3.

REDFERN, Daniel James (Adam's GS, Newport, Shropshire), b Shrewsbury, Shropshire 18 Apr 1990. 5'9". LHB, OB. Debut (Derbyshire) 2007 (summer contract). HS 51 v Northants (Derby) 2007. BB 1-7. LO HS 32 v Kent (Derby) 2007 (P40).

^NQ^**ROGERS, Christopher** John Llewellyn (Wesley C, Perth; Curtin U, Perth), b St George, Sydney, Australia 31 Aug 1977. Son of W.J.Rogers (NSW 1968-69 to 1969-70). 5'10". LHB, LBG. W Australia 1998-99 to date. Derbyshire 2004. Leicestershire 2005. Northamptonshire 2006. Shropshire 2003. Wiltshire 2005. **Tests** (A): 1 (2007-08); HS 15 v I (Perth) 2007-08 – on debut. 1000 runs (1+1): most – 1360 (2006). HS 319 Nh v Glos (Northampton) 2006. De HS 156 v Durham (Derby) 2004. BB 1-16 Nh v Leics (Northampton) 2006. LO HS 117* WA v Q (Perth) 2003-04. BB 2-22 Nh v Durham (Northampton) 2006. T20 HS 35.

‡**SADLER, John** Leonard (St Thomas A'Beckett S, Sandal), b Dewsbury, Yorks 19 Nov 1981. 5'11". LHB, LBG. Leicestershire 2003-07. 1000 runs (1): 1024 (2006). HS 145 Le v Surrey (Leicester) 2003 and 145 Le v Sussex (Hove) 2003. BB 1-5 v Middlesex (Southgate) 2007. LO HS 113* Le v Derbys (Leicester) 2007 (FPT). LO BB 1-33 Le v Yorks (Leeds) 2007 (FPT). T20 HS 73.

SAFFELL, Oliver Henry James (De Lisle S, Loughborough; Derby U), b Derby 16 Jul 1986. 6'1". RHB, RMF. Debut (Derbyshire) 2007 (match contract). Awaiting CC debut. HS 35* and BB 3-37 v CU (Cambridge) 2007 – on debut.

^NQ^**SMITH, Gregory** Marc (St Stithins C), b Johannesburg, South Africa 20 Apr 1983. 5'9". RHB, RM/OB. Debut (SA Academy) 2003-04. Griqualand West 2003-04. Derbyshire debut 2006 (Kolpak registration). HS 86 v Glos (Derby) 2006. BB 3-31 v Middlesex (Southgate) 2007. LO HS 88 v Kent (Derby) 2007 (P40). LO BB 3-19 v Scotland (Edinburgh) 2007 (FPT). T20 HS 79.

STUBBINGS, Stephen David (Frankston HS, Aus; Swinburne U, Aus), b Huddersfield, Yorks 31 Mar 1978. 6'3". LHB, OB. Debut (Derbyshire) 1997; cap 2001; benefit 2008. 1000 runs (3): most 1126 (2005). HS 151 v Somerset (Taunton) 2005. LO HS 110 v Northants (Northampton) 2006 (CGT). T20 HS 57.

WAGG, Graham Grant (Ashlawn S, Rugby), b Rugby, 28 Apr 1983. 6'0". RHB, LM. Warwickshire 2002-04; contract terminated after ECB imposed a 15-month ban, expiring 1 Jan 2006, for taking cocaine. Derbyshire debut 2006; cap 2007. F-c Tour (Eng A): I 2003-04. HS 94 v Surrey (Derby) 2006. 50 wkts (1): 53 (2007). BB 6-38 v Somerset (Taunton) 2006. LO HS 45 Eng A v Karnataka (Bangalore) 2003-04 and 45 v Yorks (Derby) 2007. LO BB 4-36 v Scotland (Edinburgh) 2007 (FPT). T20 HS 27. T20 BB 3-24.

WHITE, Wayne Andrew (John Port S, Etwall; Nottingham Trent U), b Derby 22 Apr 1985. 6'2". RHB, RMF. Debut (Derbyshire) 2005. HS 19* Surrey (Derby) 2006. BB 5-87 v Northants (Northampton) 2007. LO HS 25 v Somerset (Taunton) 2007 (P40). LO BB 1-23 (P40).

‡**WHITELEY, Ross** Andrew (Repton S), b Sheffield, Yorks 13 Sep 1988. RHB, WK. Derbyshire 2nd XI 2006-07. Summer contract – awaiting 1st XI debut.

RELEASED/RETIRED
(Having made a County 1st XI appearance in 2007)

ADNAN, Mohammad **Hassan** SYED (M.A.O. College, Lahore), b Lahore, Pakistan 15 May 1974. 5'10". RHB, OB. Islamabad 1994-95, 2000-01. WAPDA 1997-98 to 2004-05 (as an overseas player 2002-03 to 2004-05). Gujranwala 1997-98 to 1998-99. Lahore 2003-04. Played 49 f-c matches in Pakistan before his Derbyshire debut in 2004. Span. 1000 runs (1): 1380 (2004). HS 191 v Somerset (Taunton) 2005. BB 1-4 (CC). LO HS 113* v NZ (Derby) 2004. LO BB 2-13 v Leics (Derby) 2004 (NL). T20 HS 54. T20 BB 1-18.

BALLANCE, G.S. – *see YORKSHIRE.*

NQ**BIRT, Travis** Rodney (Sale Catholic C), b Sale, Victoria, Australia 9 Dec 1981. 5'11". LHB, RM. Tasmania 2004-05 to date. Australia A 2006. Derbyshire 2006-07. 1000 runs (1): 1059 (2006). HS 181 De v Glos (Bristol) 2006. BB 1-24 De v Surrey (Oval) 2006. LO HS 145 Tas v S Aus Hobart) 2004-05. LO BB 2-15 De v Glos (Derby) 2006 (P40). T20 HS 40.

BOTHA, A.G. – *see WARWICKSHIRE.*

CUSDEN, Simon Mark James (Simon Langton GS, Canterbury), b Canterbury 21 Feb 1985. 6'5". RHB, RFM. Kent 2004-06. Derbyshire 2007. HS 14 and De BB 2-67 v CU (Cambridge) 2007 – his only match for Derbyshire. BB 4-68 K v Northants (Canterbury) 2004. LO HS 3 (NL). LO BB 1-29 (NL).

NQ**DIGHTON, Michael** Gray (Kent Senior HS, Perth, Australia), b Toowoomba, Queensland, Australia 24 Apr 1976. 6'4". RHB, RMF. W Australia 1997-98 to 1999-00. Tasmania 2001-02 to date. Derbyshire 2007 (Kolpak registration). HS 182* WA v Q (Perth) 1999-00. De HS 68 v Middlesex (Southgate) 2007 – on UK debut. De BB 2-47 De v Essex (Derby) 2007. LO HS 146* Tas v NSW (Sydney) 2007-08. LO BB 2-46 De v Kent (Derby) 2007 (P40). T20 HS 111. T20 BB 6-25.

NQ**HARVEY, Ian** Joseph (Wonthaggi TC), b Wonthaggi, Victoria, Australia 10 Apr 1972. 5'10". RHB, RMF. Victoria 1993-94 to 2004-05. Gloucestershire 1999-2003, 2006; cap 1999. Yorkshire 2004-05. Cape Cobras 2005-06. Derbyshire 2007 (Kolpak registration) scoring 136 v Essex (Chelmsford) on debut. *Wisden* 2003. **LOI** (A): 73 (1997-98 to 2004); HS 48* v WI (Kingston) 2003; BB 4-16 v B (Darwin) 2003. F-c Tour: NZ 1994-95 (Aus Academy). HS 209* Y v Somerset (Leeds) 2005. De HS 153 v Somerset (Taunton) 2007. BB 8-101 Aus A v SA A (Adelaide) 2002-03. UK BB 6-19 (10-32 match) Gs v Sussex (Hove) 2000. De BB 1-14. Hat-trick (Victoria 2001-02). LO HS 112 Gs v Somerset (Taunton) 2006 (CGT). LO BB 5-19 Gs v Northants (Bristol) 2000 (NL). T20 HS 109. T20 BB 3-28.

HODGKINSON, Richard (Kirkby Centre CS; West Notts C), b Mansfield 9 Dec 1983. 6'5". RHB, RFM. Nottinghamshire staff 2003-05 (no f-c appearances). Derbyshire (1 match) 2007. HS 6 v Notts (Nottingham) 2007. LO HS 0 Nt v Worcs (Worcester) 2005. LO BB 2-36 Notts CB v Oxon (Oxford) 2001.

NO**KATICH, Simon** Mathew (Trinity C, WA; U of WA), b Middle Swan, Midland, W Australia 21 Aug 1975. 6'0". LHB, SLC. W Australia 1996-97 to 2001-02. NSW 2002-03 to date. Durham 2000; cap 2000. Yorkshire 2002 (one match). Hampshire 2003-05; cap 2003. Derbyshire 2007; captain/cap 2007. **Tests** (A): 23 (2001 to 2005-06); HS 125 v I (Sydney) 2003-04; BB 6-65 v Z (Sydney) 2003-04. **LOI** (A): 45 (2000-01 to 2006-07); 107* v SL (Brisbane) 2005-06. IT20 (A): 3 (2004-05 to 2005-06); HS 39. F-c Tours (A): E 2001, 2005; NZ 2004-05; I 2004-05; SL 1999-00, 2003-04. 1000 runs (3+3): most – 1301 (2003-04). HS 306 NSW v Q (Sydney) 2007-08. UK HS 221 v Somerset (Taunton) 2007. BB 7-130 NSW v Vic (Melbourne) 2002-03. UK BB 4-21 H v Northants (Southampton) 2003. LO HS 136* NSW v Vic (Bowral) 2003-04. LO BB 3-21 Aus A v SA (Adelaide) 2001-02. T20 HS 59*.

NO**RANKIN, W.B.** – *see WARWICKSHIRE*.

TAYLOR, C.R. – *see YORKSHIRE*.

WESTON, William Philip Christopher (Durham S), b Durham City 16 Jun 1973. Brother of R.M.S.Weston (Durham, Derbyshire and Middlesex 1995-2003); Son of M.P.Weston (Durham; England RFU). 6'3". LHB, LM. Worcestershire 1991-2002; cap 1995. Gloucestershire 2003-06; cap 2004. Derbyshire 2007. F-c Tours (Wo): Z 1993-94, 1996-97. 1000 runs (4); most – 1389 (1996). HS 205 Wo v Northants (Northampton) 1997. De HS 38 v Notts (Chesterfield) 2007. BB 2-39 Wo v P (Worcester) 1992. CC BB (Gs) 1-8. LO HS 134 Wo v Derbys (Derby) 2001 (NL). LO BB (Wo) 1-2 (SL). T20 HS 73*.

G.Welch left the staff, without making a County 1st XI appearance in 2007, and has joined Essex as seam bowling coach.

COUNTY BENEFITS AWARDED FOR 2008

Derbyshire	S.D.Stubbings
Durham	–
Essex	–
Glamorgan	D.L.Hemp
Gloucestershire	C.M.Spearman
Hampshire	J.P.Crawley
Kent	M.J.Walker
Lancashire	M.B.Loye
Leicestershire	J.N.Snape (Testimonial)
Middlesex	O.A.Shah
Northamptonshire	J.F.Brown
Nottinghamshire	A.J.Harris
Somerset	M.E.Trescothick
Surrey	M.R.Ramprakash (Testimonial)
	W.H. ('Bill') Gordon (Testimonial)
Sussex	R.S.C.Martin-Jenkins
Warwickshire	M.J.Powell
Worcestershire	–
Yorkshire	M.J.Hoggard

DERBYSHIRE 2007

RESULTS SUMMARY

	Place	Won	Lost	Tied	Drew	No Result
LV County Championship (2nd Division)	6th	3	5		8	
All First-Class Matches		3	5		9	
Friends Provident Trophy (North Conference)	8th	2	6			1
NatWest Pro40 League (2nd Division)	8th	1	7			
Twenty/20 Cup (North Division)	6th		4			4

LV COUNTY CHAMPIONSHIP AVERAGES

BATTING AND FIELDING

Cap		M	I	NO	HS	Runs	Avge	100	50	Ct/St
2007	S.M.Katich	13	23	6	221	1284	75.52	3	8	9
–	T.R.Birt	13	24	1	162	884	38.43	2	5	22
2007	D.J.Pipe	14	21	5	133*	577	36.06	2	1	42/4
–	J.Needham	3	5	2	48	104	34.66	–	–	1
–	M.G.Dighton	7	14	1	68	418	32.15	–	2	10
2007	G.G.Wagg	15	21	4	82	530	31.17	–	4	7
2001	S.D.Stubbings	15	29	2	128	788	29.18	2	2	6
–	C.R.Taylor	4	6	–	96	168	28.00	–	2	4
–	D.J.Redfern	4	6	1	51	134	26.80	–	1	5
2004	A.G.Botha	14	19	1	101	410	22.77	1	2	11
2004	M.Hassan Adnan	10	19	2	63	379	22.29	–	2	5
–	G.M.Smith	11	18	2	74	356	22.25	–	3	4
–	D.J.Birch	3	6	–	95	106	17.66	–	1	1
–	W.P.C.Weston	9	15	–	38	198	13.20	–	–	5
–	W.A.White	3	5	–	19	59	11.80	–	–	2
2007	T.Lungley	15	21	6	30*	169	11.26	–	–	5
1998	K.J.Dean	10	12	6	16	46	7.66	–	–	2
–	W.B.Rankin	3	4	1	5	5	1.66	–	–	3

Also batted: P.M.Borrington (1 match) 15, 14 (2 ct); J.L.Clare (2) 20, 0, 22; I.J.Harvey (2) 136, 0*, 153 (4 ct); R.Hodgkinson (1) 6; I.D.Hunter (1) 1*; F.A.Klokker (1) 23, 48; T.Poynton (2) 0, 0, 2 (3 ct).

BOWLING

	O	M	R	W	Avge	Best	5wI	10wM
J.L.Clare	49.2	10	203	10	20.30	5- 90	1	–
T.Lungley	435.5	106	1555	59	26.35	5- 20	3	–
K.J.Dean	267	80	659	23	28.65	5- 24	1	–
A.G.Botha	479.5	117	1464	51	28.70	6-101	3	–
W.B.Rankin	76.3	11	292	10	29.20	4- 41	–	–
G.G.Wagg	492	94	1785	53	33.67	5-119	2	–
G.M.Smith	203.1	49	656	18	36.44	3- 31	–	–
Also bowled:								
J.Needham	63.2	12	209	6	34.83	3- 92	–	–
W.A.White	76	13	367	9	40.77	5- 87	1	–

T.R.Birt 3.3-0-26-0; M.G.Dighton 41-4-133-4; I.J.Harvey 30-5-116-2; R.Hodgkinson 10-0-75-0; I.D.Hunter 46-9-130-3; S.M.Katich 38-4-144-2; D.J.Redfern 19-3-70-2; W.P.C.Weston 2-1-12-0.

The First-Class Averages (pp 140–158) give the records of Derbyshire players in all first-class county matches (Derbyshire's other opponents being Cambridge UCCE), with the exception of A.G.Botha, who played two matches for Warwickshire and whose full Derbyshire first-class figures are as above.

DERBYSHIRE RECORDS

FIRST-CLASS CRICKET

Highest Total	For 801-8d		v	Somerset	Taunton	2007
	V 662		by	Yorkshire	Chesterfield	1898
Lowest Total	For 16		v	Notts	Nottingham	1879
	V 23		by	Hampshire	Burton upon T	1958
Highest Innings	For 274	G.A.Davidson	v	Lancashire	Manchester	1896
	V 343*	P.A.Perrin	for	Essex	Chesterfield	1904

Highest Partnership for each Wicket

1st	322	H.Storer/J.Bowden	v	Essex	Derby	1929
2nd	417	K.J.Barnett/T.A.Tweats	v	Yorkshire	Derby	1997
3rd	316*	A.S.Rollins/K.J.Barnett	v	Leics	Leicester	1997
4th	328	P.Vaulkhard/D.Smith	v	Notts	Nottingham	1946
5th	302*†	J.E.Morris/D.G.Cork	v	Glos	Cheltenham	1993
6th	212	G.M.Lee/T.S.Worthington	v	Essex	Chesterfield	1932
7th	258	M.P.Dowman/D.G.Cork	v	Durham	Derby	2000
8th	198	K.M.Krikken/D.G.Cork	v	Lancashire	Manchester	1996
9th	283	A.Warren/J.Chapman	v	Warwicks	Blackwell	1910
10th	132	A.Hill/M.Jean-Jacques	v	Yorkshire	Sheffield	1986

† 346 runs were added for this wicket in two separate partnerships

Best Bowling	For 10- 40	W.Bestwick	v	Glamorgan	Cardiff	1921
(Innings)	V 10- 45	R.L.Johnson	for	Middlesex	Derby	1994
Best Bowling	For 17-103	W.Mycroft	v	Hampshire	Southampton	1876
(Match)	V 16-101	G.Giffen	for	Australians	Derby	1886

Most Runs – Season	2165	D.B.Carr	(av 48.11)	1959
Most Runs – Career	23854	K.J.Barnett	(av 41.12)	1979-98
Most 100s – Season	8	P.N.Kirsten		1982
Most 100s – Career	53	K.J.Barnett		1979-98
Most Wkts – Season	168	T.B.Mitchell	(av 19.55)	1935
Most Wkts – Career	1670	H.L.Jackson	(av 17.11)	1947-63
Most Career W-K Dismissals	1304	R.W.Taylor	(1157 ct; 147 st)	1961-84
Most Career Catches in the Field	563	D.C.Morgan		1950-69

LIMITED-OVERS CRICKET

Highest Total	FPT	365-3		v	Cornwall	Derby	1986
	P40	304-3		v	Kent	Maidstone	2005
	T20	195-8		v	Yorkshire	Leeds	2005
Lowest Total	FPT	79		v	Surrey	The Oval	1967
	P40	61		v	Hampshire	Portsmouth	1990
	T20	98		v	Lancs	Manchester	2005
Highest Innings	FPT	173*	M.J.Di Venuto	v	Derbys CB	Derby	2000
	P40	141*	C.J.Adams	v	Kent	Chesterfield	1992
	T20	83	J.Moss	v	Yorks	Leeds	2005
Best Bowling	FPT	8-21	M.A.Holding	v	Sussex	Hove	1988
	P40	6- 7	M.Hendrick	v	Notts	Nottingham	1972
	T20	4-13	T.Lungley	v	Notts	Derby	2003

18

DURHAM

Formation of Present Club: 23 May 1882
Inaugural First-Class Match: 1992
Colours: Navy Blue, Yellow and Maroon
Badge: Coat of Arms of the County of Durham
County Champions: (0); best – 2nd (Div 1) 2007
Gillette/NatWest/C&G/FP Trophy Winners: (1) 2007
Benson and Hedges Cup Winners: (0); best –
Quarter-Finalist 1998, 2000, 2001
Pro 40/National League (Div 1) Winners: (0); best – 1st
(Div 2) 2007
Sunday League Winners: (0); best – 7th 1993
Twenty20 Cup Winners: (0); best – 4th in Group 2004

Chief Executive: David Harker, County Ground, Riverside, Chester-le-Street, Co Durham DH3 3QR • Tel: 0191 387 1717 • Fax: 0191 387 1616 • Email: marketing@durham ccc.co.uk • Web: www.durhamccc.co.uk

Director of Cricket: G.Cook. **Captain**: D.M.Benkenstein. **Vice-Captain**: P.D.Colling-wood. **Overseas Player**: S.Chanderpaul. **2008 Beneficiary**: none. **Head Groundsman**: David Measor. **Scorer**: Brian Hunt. ‡ New registration. NQ Not qualified for England.

Durham initially awarded caps immediately after their players joined the staff but revised this policy in 1998, again capping players on merit, past 'awards' having been nullified. Durham abolished both their capping and 'awards' systems after the 2005 season.

NQ**BENKENSTEIN, Dale Martin** (Durban HS; Michaelhouse HS), b Salisbury, Rhodesia 9 Jun 1974. Son of M.M.Benkenstein (Rhodesia, Natal B 1970-71 to 1980-81); brother of twins B.R. (Natal B 1993-94) and B.N. Benkenstein (Natal B, GW 1994-95 to 1996-97). 5'9". RHB, RM/OB. Natal/KwaZulu-Natal 1993-94 to 2003-04. Dolphins 2004-05 to date. MCC 2004. British passport. Durham debut/cap 2005; captain 2006 to date. **LOI** (SA): 23 (1998-99 to 2002-03); HS 69 v WI (Cape Town) 1998-99; BB 3-5 v K (Colombo) 2002-03. F-c Tours (SA A): WI 2000; NZ 1998-99 (SA); SL 1995 (SA U-24), 1998. 1000 (3); most – 1500 (2006). HS 259 KZ-Natal v Northerns (Durban) 2001-02. Du HS 162* v Derby (Chester-le-St) 2005. BB 4-16 Dolphins v Warriors (Durban) 2005-06. Du 4-29 v Northants (Northampton) 2005. LO HS 107* Natal v North West (Fochville) 1997-98. LO BB 4-16 v Surrey (Chester-le-St) 2005. T20 HS 56*. T20 BB 3-10.

NQ**BREESE, Gareth Rohan** (Wolmer's BHS, Kingston; Kingston U of Technology, Jamaica), b Montego Bay, Jamaica 9 Jan 1976. 5'7". RHB, OB. Jamaica 1995-96 to 2005-06; captain/overseas player 2003-04 to 2005-06. British passport (Welsh father). Durham debut 2004; cap 2005. **Tests** (WI): 1 (2002-03); HS 5 and BB 2-108 v I (Madras) 2002-03. F-c Tours (WI): E 2002 (WI A); I 2002-03. HS 165* v Somerset (Taunton) 2004. BB 7-60 Jamaica v Barbados (Bridgetown) 2000-01. Du BB 5-41 (10-151 match) v Yorks (Scarborough) 2004 – scored 35 and 68 to complete match double. LO HS 68* v Notts (Chester-le-St) 2007 (FPT). LO BB 5-49 v Worcs (Chester-le-St) 2007 (FPT). T20 HS 24*. T20 BB 4-14.

NQCHANDERPAUL, Shivnarine (Unity Village SS), b Unity Village, Demerara, Guyana 16 Aug 1974. 5'6". LHB, LB. Guyana 1991-92 to 2005-06. Durham 2007. **Tests** (WI): 107 (1993-94 to 2007-08, 14 as captain); HS 203* v SA (Georgetown) 2004-05; BB 1-2 v A (Adelaide) 1996-97. **LOI** (WI): 224 (1994-95 to 2007-08, 16 as captain); HS 150 v SA (E London) 1998-99; BB 3-18 v I (Sharjah) 1997-98. F-c Tours (WI) (C=Captain): E 1995, 2000, 2004, 2007; A 1995-96, 1996-97, 2000-01, 2005-06C; SA 1998-99, 2003-04, 2007-08; NZ 1994-95, 1999-00, 2005-06C; I 1994-95, 2002-03; P 1997-98, 2001-02 (Sharjah), 2006-07; SL 2005C; Z 2001, 2003-04; B 1999-00, 2002-03; K 2001. 1000 runs (1+1): most – 1107 (2004-05). HS 303* Guyana v Jamaica (Kingston) 1995-96. Du HS 81 v Surrey (Chester-le-St) 2007. BB 4-48 Guyana v Leeward Is (Basseterre) 1992-93. LO HS 150 (*see LOI*). LO BB 4-22 Guyana v Trinidad (Hampton Court) 1995-96. IT20 HS 41. T20 HS 41.

NQCLAYDON, Mitchell Eric (Westfield Sports HS, Sydney), b Fairfield, NSW, Australia 25 Nov 1982. 6'4". LHB, RMF. Yorkshire 2005-06. Durham debut 2007. HS 38 Y v Durham (Chester-le-St) 2006. Du HS 14* v Yorks (Chester-le-St) 2007. BB 3-26 v DU (Durham) 2006. CC BB 1-42 Y v Durham (Chester-le-St) 2007. LO HS 9 Y v Worcs (Worcester) 2006 (CGT). LO BB 2-41 Y v Derbys (Leeds) 2006 (CGT). T20 HS 12*. T20 BB 2-6.

COETZER, Kyle James (Aberdeen GS), b Aberdeen, Scotland 14 Apr 1984. 5'11". RHB, RM. Debut (Durham) 2004. Scotland 2004. HS 153* v DU (Durham) 2007. CC HS 142 v Warwks (Chester-le-St) 2007. LO HS 76 v Surrey (Guildford) 2007 (P40). T20 HS 1.

COLLINGWOOD, Paul David (Blackfyne CS; Derwentside C), b Shotley Bridge 26 May 1976. 5'11". RHB, RMF. Debut (Durham) 1996 v Northants (Chester-le-St) taking wicket of D.J.Capel with his first ball before scoring 91 and 16; cap 1998; benefit 2007. MBE 2005. *Wisden* 2007. **ECB central contract 2007-08. Tests**: 30 (2003-04 to 2007-08); HS 206 v A (Adelaide) 2006-07; BB 2-24 v I (Oval) 2007. **LOI**: 141 (2001 to 2007-08, 20 as captain); HS 120* v A (Melbourne) 2006-07; BB 6-31 v B (Nottingham) 2005 – first to score a hundred (112*) and take six wickets in same LOI. F-c Tours: A 2006-07; WI 2003-04; I 2005-06; P 2005-06; SL 2003-04, 2007-08. 1000 runs (2); most – 1120 (2005), inc six hundreds (Du record). HS 206 (*see Tests*). Du HS 190 v SL (Chester-le-St) 2002 and 190 v Derbys (Derby) 2005. BB 5-52 v Somerset (Stockton) 2005. LO HS 120* (*see LOI*). LO BB 6-31 (*see LOI*). IT20 HS 79. IT20 BB 4-22. T20 HS 79. T20 BB 4-22.

DAVIES, Anthony Mark (Northfield CS, Billingham; Stockton SFC), b Stockton-on-Tees 4 Oct 1980. 6'3". RHB, RMF. Debut (Durham) 2002; cap 2005. Nottinghamshire 2007 (on loan). HS 62 v Somerset (Stockton) 2005. 50 wkts (1): 50 (2004). BB 7-59 Notts v Northants (Nottingham) 2007. Du BB 6-32 v Worcs (Chester-le-St) 2005. LO HS 31* v Warwks (Chester-le-St) 2002 (NL). LO BB 4-13 v Sussex (Chester-le-St) 2001 (NL). T20 HS 6. T20 BB 2-14.

NQDi VENUTO, Michael James (St Virgil's C; Hobart), b Hobart, Australia 12 Dec 1973. 6'0". LHB, RM/LBG. Tasmania 1991-92 to 2007-08. Sussex 1999; cap 1999. Derbyshire 2000-06; cap 2000; appointed captain for 2004 but missed entire season – back surgery. Durham 2007, carrying his bat for 155* v Worcs (Worcester) on debut. Italian passport 2008. **LOI** (A): 9 (1996-97 to 1997-98); HS 89 v SA (Johannesburg) 1996-97. F-c Tours: Z 1995-96 (Tas); Scotland/Ireland 1998 (Aus A). 1000 runs (7): most – 1538 (2002). HS 230 De v Northants (Derby) 2002. Du HS 204* v Kent (Chester-le-St) 2007. BB 1-0 Tas v Q (Brisbane) 1999-00. UK BB 1-3 Sx v Somerset (Taunton) 1999. LO HS 173* v Derbys CB (Derby) 2000 (NWT). LO BB 1-10 Tas v Q (Hobart) 1995-96. T20 HS 95*. T20 BB 3-19.

EVANS, Luke (St Aidan's S, Sunderland), b Sunderland 26 Apr 1987. 6'7". RHB, RMF. Debut (Durham) 2007 – awaiting CC debut. HS 1 and BB 2-39 v SL A (Chester-le-St) 2007.

GIDMAN, William Robert Simon (Wycliffe C; Berkshire C of Agriculture), b High Wycombe, Bucks 14 Feb 1985. Younger brother of A.P.R.Gidman (*see GLOUCESTER-SHIRE*). 6'2". LHB, RM. Debut (Durham) 2007 (awaiting CC debut). MCC YC 2004-06. HS 8 and BB 3-37 v SL A (Chester-le-St) 2007. HS LO 12 Gs CB v Surrey CB (Bristol) 2002.

GODDARD, Lee James (Batley GS; Huddersfield TC; Loughborough U), b Dewsbury, Yorks 22 Oct 1982. 5'10". RHB, WK. Loughborough UCCE 2003. Derbyshire 2004, 2006. Durham 2007. HS 91 De v Surrey (Derby) 2006. Du HS 52 v SL A (Chester-le-St) 2007. LO HS 36 De v Kent (Canterbury) 2006 (P40). T20 HS – .

HARMISON, Ben William (Ashington HS), b Ashington, Northumb 9 Jan 1986. Younger brother of S.J.Harmison. 6'5". LHB, RMF. Debut (Durham) 2006, scoring 110 v Oxford UCCE (Oxford). Scored 105 in his second match (v West Indies A) to emulate A.Fairbairn (Middlesex 1947) in scoring hundreds in first two f-c matches, those matches being in England. HS 110 (*see above*). BB 2-29 v Warwks (Chester-le-St) 2007. LO HS 57 v Notts (Chester-le-St) 2006 (P40). LO BB 1-8 v Yorks (Chester-le-St) 2007 (P40). T20 HS 5.

HARMISON, Stephen James (Ashington HS), b Ashington, Northumb 23 Oct 1978. Elder brother of B.W.Harmison. 6'4". RHB, RF. Debut (Durham) 1996; cap 1999. Lions 2007-08. MCC 2007. *Wisden* 2004. MBE 2005. **ECB central contract 2007-08. Tests**: 55 (2002 to 2007-08); HS 42 v SA (Cape Town) 2004-05 – first No. 11 to top-score for England; BB 7-12 (9-73 match) v WI (Kingston) 2003-04. **LOI**: 46 (2002-03 to 2006-07); HS 13* v NZ (Chester-le-St) 2003; BB 5-33 v A (Bristol) 2005; hat-trick v I (Nottingham) 2004. F-c Tours: A 2002-03, 2005-06 (RW), 2006-07; SA 1998-99 (Eng A), 2004-05; WI 2003-04; I 2005-06; P 2005-06; SL 2007-08; Z 1998-99 (Eng A); B 2003-04. HS 42 (*see Tests*). Du HS 36 v Kent (Canterbury) 1998. 50 wkts (4); most – 64 (1999). BB 7-12 (*see Tests*). Du BB 6-52 (9-84 match) v Lancs (Manchester) 2005. Hat-trick v Worcs (Chester-le-St) 2005. LO HS 17 v Lancs (Manchester) 2006 (CGT). LO BB 5-33 (*see LOI*). IT20 HS – . IT20 BB 1-13. T20 HS 5. T20 BB 2-27.

IQBAL, Moneeb Mohammed (Hillhead HS; Anniesland C, Glasgow), b Glasgow, Scotland 28 Feb 1986. Brother-in-law of Mohammad Ramzan (Pakistan &etc 1986-87 to 2003-04). RHB, LB. Debut (Durham) 2006 (no appearances 2007). Development contract. HS 20 and CC BB 2-57 v Kent (Stockton) 2006. BB 4-36 v OU (Oxford) 2006.

KILLEEN, Neil (Greencroft CS; Derwentside C; Teesside U), b Shotley Bridge 17 Oct 1975. 6'2". RHB, RMF. Debut (Durham) 1995; cap 1999; benefit 2006. MCC 1999-2000. Tour (MCC) B 1999-00. HS 48 v Somerset (Chester-le-St) 1995. 50 wkts (1): 58 (1999). BB 7-70 v Hants (Chester-le-St) 2003. LO HS 32 v Middlesex (Lord's) 1996 (SL). LO BB 6-31 v Derbys (Derby) 2000 (NL). T20 HS 17*. T20 BB 4-7.

‡**NOMcKENZIE, Neil** Douglas (King Edward VII HS; Rand Afrikaans U), b Johannesburg, South Africa 24 Nov 1975. 5'9½". Son of K.A.McKenzie (N-E Transvaal and Transvaal 1966-67 to 1986-87). RHB, RM. Transvaal/Gauteng 1994-95 to 1998-99. Northerns 1999-00 to 2003-04. Lions 2004-05 to date. Somerset 2007 (Kolpak registration). **Tests** (SA): 42 (2000 to 2007-08); HS 120 v NZ (Port Elizabeth) 2000-01. **LOI** (SA): 59 (1999-00 to 2003-04): HS 131* v K (Cape Town) 2001-02. F-c Tours (SA): E 2003; A 2001-02; WI 2000-01; NZ 2003-04; P 2003-04; SL 2000; Z 2001-02, 2004 (SA A); B 2003. HS 182 South Africa v NZ (Potchefstroom) 2007-08. UK HS 105* SA v Kent (Canterbury) 2003. CC HS 84 Sm v Glamorgan (Taunton) 2007. BB 2-13 Lions v Eagles (Kimberley) 2007-08. LO HS 131* (*see LOI*). LO BB 2-19 Gauteng v GW (Kimberley) 1997-98. IT20 HS – . T20 HS 85*.

‡**MAHOMED, Uzair** (Woodhouse Grove S, Leeds), b Johannesburg, South Africa 20 Aug 1987. 5'8". RHB, OB. Durham Academy and 2nd XI 2005-07. Development contract – awaiting 1st XI debut. Northumberland 2005.

MUCHALL, Gordon James (Durham S), b Newcastle upon Tyne, Northumb 2 Nov 1982. 6'0". Elder brother of P.B.Muchall. RHB, RM. Northumberland 1999. Debut (Durham) 2002; cap 2005. F-c Tours (ECB Acad): SL 2002-03. HS 219 v Kent (Canterbury) 2006. BB 3-26 v Yorks (Leeds) 2003. LO HS 101* v Yorks (Leeds) 2005 (NL). LO BB 1-15 (NL). T20 HS 64*. T20 BB 1-8.

MUCHALL, Paul Bernard (Durham S), b Newcastle upon Tyne, Northumb 17 Mar 1987. Younger brother of G.J.Muchall. RHB, RM. Development contract – awaiting 1st XI debut. Northumberland 2006-07.

MUSTARD, Philip (Usworth CS), b Sunderland 8 Oct 1982. 5'11". LHB, WK. Debut (Durham) 2002. **LOI:** 10 (2007-08): HS 83 v NZ (Napier) 2007-08. HS 130 v Kent (Canterbury) 2006. LO HS 108 v Northants (Northampton) 2007 (FPT). T20 HS 67*.

ONIONS, Graham (St Thomas More RC S, Blaydon), b Gateshead 9 Sep 1982. 6'1". RHB, RMF. Debut (Durham) 2004. MCC 2007. HS 41 v Yorks (Leeds) 2007. 50 wkts (1): 54 (2006). BB 8-101 v Warwks (Birmingham) 2007. LO HS 11 v Notts (Chester-le-St) 2006 (P40). LO BB 3-39 v Derbys (Derby) 2005 (NL). T20 HS 31. T20 BB 3-25.

PARK, Garry Terence (Eshowe HS, Natal; Anglia Ruskin U), b Empangeni, Zululand, South Africa 19 Apr 1983. 5'7". RHB, WK, RM. Cambridge UCCE 2003-05. Debut (Durham) 2006. Cambridgeshire 2005. HS 100* v Yorks (Leeds) 2006. LO HS 33 v Derbys (Chester-le-St) 2007 (FPT). T20 HS 25*.

PLUNKETT, Liam Edward (Nunthorpe SS; Teesside Tertiary C), b Middlesbrough, Yorks 6 Apr 1985. 6'3". RHB, RFM. Debut (Durham) 2003. Dolphins 2007-08. **Tests:** 9 (2005-06 to 2007); HS 44* v WI (Leeds) 2007; BB 3-17 v SL (Birmingham) 2006. **LOI:** 27 (2005-06 to 2007); HS 56 v P (Lahore) 2005-06; BB 3-24 v A (Sydney) 2006-07. F-c Tours: I 2005-06; P 2006. HS 74* v Somerset (Stockton) 2005. 50 wkts (2): most – 51 (2005). BB 6-74 v Hants (Chester-le-St) 2004. LO HS 56 (*see LOI*). LO BB 4-15 v Essex (Chester-le-St) 2007 (FPT). IT20 HS – . IT20 BB 1-37. T20 HS 8. T20 BB 2-18.

SCOTT, Gary Michael (Hetton CS), b Sunderland 21 Jul 1984. 6'0". RHB, OB. Debut (Durham) 2001 – youngest Durham f-c debutant (17y 19d), 2005. No appearances 2007. HS 133 v OU (Oxford) 2006. CC HS 77 v Yorks (Leeds) 2006. BB 2-39 v Warwks (Chester-le-St) 2006. LO HS 100 Durham CB v Herefords (Darlington) 2002 (CGT). LO BB 2-24 v Warwks (Birmingham) 2006 (P40). T20 HS 31. T20 BB 3-27.

SMITH, William Rew (Bedford S; Collingwood C, Durham), b Luton, Beds 28 Sep 1982. 5'9". RHB, OB. Nottinghamshire 2002-06. Durham UCCE 2003-05; captain 2004-05. British U 2004-05. Durham debut 2007. Notts 2nd XI debut 1999 when aged 16y 309d. Bedfordshire 1999-2002. HS 156 DU v Somerset (Taunton) 2005, sharing opening partnership of 304 with A.J.Maiden. CC HS 141 Nt v Middlesex (Lord's) 2006. Du HS 105 v DU (Durham) 2007. BB 3-34 DU v Leics (Leicester) 2005. CC BB 1-5 v Lancs (Chester-le-St) 2007. LO HS 103 v Worcs (Chester-le-St) 2007 (FPT). T20 HS 55. T20 BB 1-31.

STONEMAN, Mark Daniel (Whickham CS), b Newcastle upon Tyne, Northumb 26 Jun 1987. 5'11". LHB, RM. Debut (Durham) 2007. HS 101 v Sussex (Chester-le-St) 2007.

^NQ**THORP, Callum** David (Servite C, Tuart Hill, Perth), b Mount Lawley, Perth, Australia 11 Feb 1975. 6'3". British passport (English parents). RHB, RMF. W Australia 2002-03 to 2003-04. Durham debut 2005. HS 75 and BB 6-55 (11-97 match) v Hants (Southampton) 2006. LO HS 52 v B (Chester-le-Street) 2005. LO BB 6-17 v Scotland (Edinburgh) 2006 (CGT). T20 HS 13. T20 BB 2-32.

^NQ**WISEMAN, Paul** John (Auckland IT), b Takapuna, Auckland, New Zealand 4 May 1970. 6'1". RHB, OB. Auckland 1991-92 to 1992-93. Otago 1994-95 to 2000-01. Canterbury 2001-02 to 2005-06. Durham debut 2006. **Tests** (NZ): 25 (1998 to 2004-05); HS 36 v SA (Hamilton) 2003-04; BB 5-82 v SL (Colombo) 1997-98 – on debut. **LOI** (NZ): 15 (1997-98 to 2003); HS 16 v SL (Colombo) 1998; BB 4-45 v Z (Nairobi) 2000-01. Tours (NZ): A 2004-05 (NZ Acad), 2004-05 (NZ A); I 1999-00, 2003-04; SL 1998, 2003, 2005-06 (NZ A); Z 1997-98, 2000-01; B 2004-05. HS 130 Canterbury v ND (Hamilton) 2005-06. UK HS 44 v Surrey (Oval) 2007. BB 9-13 Canterbury v CD (Christchurch) 2004-05. UK BB 5-65 v Hants (Chester-le-St) 2007. LO HS 65* Canterbury v Auckland (Christchurch) 2001-02. LO BB 4-45 (*see LOI*). T20 HS 0. T20 BB 2-20.

RELEASED/RETIRED
(Having made a County 1st XI appearance in 2007)

GIBSON, Ottis Delroy (Ellerslie SS), b Sion Hill, Bridgetown, Barbados 16 Mar 1969. 6'2". RHB, RFM. Barbados 1990-91 to 1997-98. Border 1992-93 to 1994-95. Glamorgan 1994-96; cap 1994. Griqualand West 1998-99 to 1999-00. Gauteng 2000-01. Leicestershire 2004-05; cap 2004. Durham 2006-07. Staffordshire 2001. PCA 2007. **Tests** (WI): 2 (1995 to 1998-99); HS 37 v SA (Cape Town) 1998-99; BB 2-81 v E (Lord's) 1995. **LOI** (WI): 15 (1995 to 1996-97); HS 52 v A (Brisbane) 1995-96; BB 5-40 v SL (Perth) 1995-96. F-c Tours (WI): E 1995; A 1995-96; SA 1997-98 (WI A), 1998-99; SL 1996-97 (WI A). HS 155 Du v Yorks (Leeds) 2006. 50 wkts (3): most – 80 (2007). BB 10-47 (12-100 match) Du v Hants (Chester-le-St) 2007. LO HS 102* Staffs v Northumb (Jesmond) 2001 (CGT). LO BB 5-19 Border v GW (Kimberley) 1992-93. T20 HS 22. T20 BB 2-20. Appointed ECB Bowling Coach.

^NQ**STYRIS, Scott** Bernard (Hamilton BHS), b Brisbane, Australia 10 Jul 1975. 5'10". RHB, RMF. Northern Districts 1994-95 to 2004-05. Middlesex 2005-06; cap 2006. Auckland 2005-06. Durham 2007. **Tests** (NZ): 29 (2002 to 2007-08); HS 170 v SA (Auckland) 2003-04; BB 3-28 v I (Wellington) 2002-03. **LOI** (NZ): 141 (1999-00 to 2007-08); HS 141 v SL (Bloemfontein) 2002-03; BB 6-25 v WI (Port-of-Spain) 2002. F-c Tours (NZ): E 2000 (NZ A), 2004; A 2004-05; SA 2000-01, 2005-06, 2007-08; WI 2002; I 2003-04; SL 2002-03; Z 2005; B 2004-05. HS 212* ND v Otago (Hamilton) 2001-02. BB 6-32 ND v Otago (Gisborne) 1999-00. UK HS 133 and UK BB 6-71 v Lancs (Lord's) 2006. Du HS 48 and Du BB 2-56 v Lancs (Chester-le-St) 2007 – on Du debut. LO HS 141 (*see LOI*). LO BB 6-25 (*see LOI*). IT20 HS 66. IT20 BB 2-33. T20 HS 73*. T20 BB 3-25.

DURHAM 2007

RESULTS SUMMARY

	Place	Won	Lost	Tied	Drew	No Result
LV County Championship (1st Division)	2nd	7	5		4	
All First-Class Matches		8	6		4	
Friends Provident Trophy (North Conference)	**Winners**	9	2			
NatWest Pro40 League (2nd Division)	**1st**	6	2			
Twenty/20 Cup (North Division)	5th	1	4			3

LV COUNTY CHAMPIONSHIP AVERAGES
BATTING AND FIELDING

Cap†		M	I	NO	HS	Runs	Avge	100	50	Ct/St
	M.J.Di Venuto	13	25	5	204*	1329	66.45	3	9	21
2005	D.M.Benkenstein	16	28	5	117	1278	55.56	3	8	5
	S.Chanderpaul	4	7	1	81	224	37.33	–	2	4
	K.J.Coetzer	12	22	1	142	688	32.76	1	2	12
	O.D.Gibson	15	23	2	71	578	27.52	–	4	6
	P.Mustard	16	29	2	76	701	25.96	–	4	62/3
2005	G.J.Muchall	10	18	1	66	433	25.47	–	4	7
	M.D.Stoneman	7	13	–	101	313	24.07	1	1	2
	S.B.Styris	5	10	–	48	210	21.00	–	–	1
	B.W.Harmison	8	14	2	101	251	20.91	1	1	5
	W.R.Smith	10	19	–	48	397	20.89	–	–	5
	P.J.Wiseman	12	18	5	44	256	19.69	–	–	6
	L.E.Plunkett	11	17	3	59*	275	19.64	–	2	9
2005	G.R.Breese	9	16	1	53	132	18.85	–	1	5
	G.Onions	11	14	4	41	163	16.30	–	–	2
	C.D.Thorp	2	4	1	30*	40	13.33	–	–	–
1999	S.J.Harmison	6	9	3	30	74	12.33	–	–	1
2005	A.M.Davies	9	12	4	21	67	8.37	–	–	5

Also batted: M.E.Claydon (1 match) 14*; P.D.Collingwood (1 – cap 1998) 0, 58 (1 ct); G.T.Park (2) 0, 61, 15. N.Killeen (1 – cap 1999) did not bat.

BOWLING

	O	M	R	W	Best	5wI	10wM
S.J.Harmison	174.1	39	524	32	6- 87	3	–
O.D.Gibson	479.5	103	1660	80	10- 47	4	3
A.M.Davies	238.4	68	658	24	4- 48	–	–
P.J.Wiseman	269.3	47	915	31	5- 65	1	–
L.E.Plunkett	323.3	70	1139	38	5-105	1	–
G.Onions	319.1	64	1181	36	8-101	2	–

Also bowled: C.D.Thorp   47.4   10   163   6   3- 51   –   –
D.M.Benkenstein 59-11-202-2;   G.R.Breese   47-4-196-0;   M.E.Claydon   28-0-139-0;
S.Chanderpaul 8-3-23-0;   P.D.Collingwood 17-4-39-0;   B.W.Harmison 50.2-6-268-3;
N.Killeen 18-2-69-0; W.R.Smith 7-0-38-1; S.B.Styris 51-7-217-4.
† Durham abolished their capping system after 2005.

The First-Class Averages (pp 140–158) give the records of Durham players in all first-class county matches (Durham's other opponents being Durham UCCE and Sri Lanka A), with the exception of S.Chanderpaul and P.D.Collingwood, whose full county figures are as above, and:

A.M.Davies 10-12-4-21-67-8.37-0-0-5ct. 259.4-73-734-26-28.23-4/18-0-0.
S.J.Harmison 7-11-3-30-91-11.37-0-0-1ct. 184.1-40-578-34-17.00-6/87-3-0.
G.Onions 12-16-5-41-191-17.36-0-0-3ct. 345.1-68-1286-39-32.97-8/101-2-0.
L.E.Plunkett 12-19-4-59*-310-20.66-0-2-9ct. 354.5-80-1215-43-28.25-5/105-1-0.

DURHAM RECORDS

FIRST-CLASS CRICKET

Highest Total	For 645-6d		v	Middlesex	Lord's	2002
	V 810-4d		by	Warwicks	Birmingham	1994
Lowest Total	For 67		v	Middlesex	Lord's	1996
	V 56		by	Somerset	Chester-le-St[2]	2003
Highest Innings	For 273	M.L.Love	v	Hampshire	Chester-le-St[2]	2003
	V 501*	B.C.Lara	for	Warwicks	Birmingham	1994

Highest Partnership for each Wicket

1st	334*	S.Hutton/M.A.Roseberry	v	Oxford U	Oxford	1996
2nd	258	J.J.B.Lewis/M.L.Love	v	Notts	Chester-le-St	2001
3rd	205	G.Fowler/S.Hutton	v	Yorkshire	Leeds	1993
4th	250	P.D.Collingwood/D.M.Benkenstein	v	Derbys	Derby	2005
5th	222	D.M.Benkenstein/G.R.Breese	v	Middlesex	Lord's	2006
6th	249	G.J.Muchall/P.Mustard	v	Kent	Canterbury	2006
7th	315	D.M.Benkenstein/O.D.Gibson	v	Yorkshire	Leeds	2006
8th	134	A.C.Cummins/D.A.Graveney	v	Warwicks	Birmingham	1994
9th	127	D.G.C.Ligertwood/S.J.E.Brown	v	Surrey	Stockton	1996
10th	103	M.M.Betts/D.M.Cox	v	Sussex	Hove	1996

Best Bowling	For 10- 47	O.D.Gibson	v	Hampshire	Chester-le-St[2]	2007
(Innings)	V 9- 36	M.S.Kasprowicz	for Glamorgan	Cardiff		2003
Best Bowling	For 14-177	A.Walker	v	Essex	Chelmsford	1995
(Match)	V 13-110	M.S.Kasprowicz	for Glamorgan	Chester-le-St[2]		2003

Most Runs – Season	1536	W.Larkins	(av 37.46)		1992
Most Runs – Career	7854	J.J.B.Lewis	(av 31.41)		1997-2006
Most 100s – Season	6	P.D.Collingwood			2005
Most 100s – Career	14	J.E.Morris			1994-99
	14	P.D.Collingwood			1996-2005
Most Wkts – Season	80	O.D.Gibson	(av 20.75)		2007
Most Wkts – Career	518	S.J.E.Brown	(av 28.30)		1992-2002
Most Career W-K Dismissals	194	M.P.Speight	(189 ct; 5 st)		1997-2001
Most Career Catches in the Field	117	P.D.Collingwood			1996-2007

LIMITED-OVERS CRICKET

Highest Total	FPT	332-4	v	Worcs	Chester-le-St[2]	2007
	P40	319-3	v	Worcs	Worcester	2004
	T20	180-4	v	Notts	Chester-le-St[2]	2005
Lowest Total	FPT	82	v	Worcs	Chester-le-St[1]	1968
	P40	72	v	Warwicks	Birmingham	2002
	T20	98	v	Yorks	Chester-le-St[2]	2006
Highest Innings	FPT	132 M.A.Gough	v	Wales MC	Cardiff	2002
	P40	131* W.Larkins	v	Hampshire	Portsmouth	1994
	T20	67* P.Mustard	v	Derbyshire	Chester-le-St[2]	2006
Best Bowling	FPT	7-32 S.P.Davis	v	Lancashire	Chester-le-St[1]	1983
	P40	6-31 N.Killeen	v	Derbyshire	Derby	2000
	T20	4- 7 N.Killeen	v	Leics	Leicester	2004

[1] Chester-le-Street CC (Ropery Lane) [2] Riverside Ground

25

ESSEX

Formation of Present Club: 14 January 1876
Inaugural First-Class Match: 1894
Colours: Blue, Gold and Red
Badge: Three Seaxes above Scroll bearing 'Essex'
County Champions: (6) 1979, 1983, 1984, 1986, 1991, 1992
Gillette/NatWest/C&G/FP Trophy Winners: (2) 1985, 1997
Benson and Hedges Cup Winners: (2) 1979, 1998
Pro 40/National League (Div 1) Winners: (2) 2005, 2006
Sunday League Winners: (3) 1981, 1984, 1985
Twenty20 Cup Winners: (0); best – Semi-Finalist 2006

Chief Executive: David E.East, County Ground, New Writtle Street, Chelmsford CM2 0PG • Tel: 01245 252420 • Fax: 01245 254030 • Email: administration.essex@ecb.co.uk • Web: www.essexcricket.org.uk

First Team Coach: A.P.Grayson. **Batting Coach**: G.A.Gooch. **Seam Bowling Coach**: G.Welch. **Captain**: M.L.Pettini. **Vice-Captain**: J.S.Foster. **Overseas Player**: Danish Kaneria. **2008 Beneficiary**: none. **Head Groundsman**: Stuart Kerrison. **Scorer**: A.E. (Tony) Choat. ‡ New registration. NQ Not qualified for England.

AHMED, Jahid Sheikh (St Peter's HS, Burnham-on-Crouch; East London U), b Chelmsford 20 Feb 1986. 5'11". RHB, RMF. Debut (Essex) 2005. MCC YC 2004. HS 14* v Worcs (Worcester) 2005 – on debut. BB 2-41 v Middlesex (Chelmsford) 2007. LO HS 1* v Hants (Southampton) 2007 (P40). LO BB 4-32 v SL (Chelmsford) 2006. T20 HS – . T20 BB 1-25.

BOPARA, Ravinder Singh (Brampton Manor S; Barking Abbey Sports C), b Newham, London 4 May 1985. 5'8". RHB, RMF. Debut (Essex) 2002; cap 2005. MCC 2006. **Tests**: 3 (2007-08); HS 34 v SL (Kandy) 2007-08 – on debut; BB 1-39 v SL (Galle) 2007-08. **LOI**: 21 (2006-07 to 2007-08); HS 52 v SL (N Sound, Antigua) 2006-07. BB 2-43 v Canada (Gros Islet, St Lucia) 2006-07. F-c Tour: SL 2007-08. HS 229 v Northants (Chelmsford) 2007. BB 5-75 v Surrey (Chelmsford) 2006. LO HS 101* v Ireland (Dublin) 2007 (FPT). LO BB 3-13 v Hants (Chelmsford) 2007 (FPT). T20 HS 83. T20 BB 3-18.

CHAMBERS, Maurice Anthony (Homerton TC; Sir George Monoux C), b Port Antonio, Jamaica 14 Sep 1987. 6'3". RHB, RFM. Debut (Essex) 2005. No f-c appearances 2006-07 – stress fracture of the back. MCC YC 2004. HS 2* and BB 1-73 v Derbys (Chelmsford) 2005 – on debut.

CHOPRA, Varun (Ilford County HS), b Barking 21 Jun 1987. 6'1". RHB, LB. Debut (Essex) 2006. HS 106 v Glos (Chelmsford) 2006 – on CC debut. LO HS 102 v Middlesex (Chelmsford) 2007 (FPT). T20 HS 5.

COOK, Alastair Nathan (Bedford S), b Gloucester 25 Dec 1984. 6'3". LHB, OB. Debut (Essex) 2003; cap 2005. MCC 2004-07. Essex 2nd XI debut 2000 when aged 15y 235d. England U-19 captain 2003-04. YC 2005. **ECB central contract 2007-08. Tests**: 24 (2005-6 to 2007-08); HS 127 v P (Manchester) 2006. Scored 60 and 104* v I (Nagpur) 2005-06 on debut. Third, after D.G.Bradman and S.R.Tendulkar, to score seven Test hundreds before his 23rd birthday. Second, after M.A.Taylor, to score 1000 runs in the calendar year of his debut. **LOI**: 21 (2006 to 2007-08); HS 102 v I (Southampton) 2007. F-c Tours: A 2006-07; WI 2005-06 (Eng A); I 2005-06; SL 2004-05 (Eng A), 2007-08. 1000 runs (3); most – 1466 (2005). HS 195 v Northants (Northampton) 2005. Scored 214 v Australians (Chelmsford) 2005 in 2-day non-f-c match. BB 3-13 v Northants (Chelmsford) 2005. LO HS 125 v Surrey (Croydon) 2007 (FPT). IT20 HS 15. T20 HS 15.

NQDANISH Parabha Shanker **KANERIA** (St Patrick's HS; Government Islamia C), b Karachi, Pakistan 16 Dec 1980. 6'1". Cousin of Anil Dalpat (Pakistan) and second Hindu to represent Pakistan. RHB, LBG. Debut (PNSC) 1998-99. Karachi Whites/Blues/Harbour 1998-99 to 2004-05. Habib Bank 2000-01 to date. Essex 2004-05, 2007; cap 2004. **Tests** (P): 51 (2000-01 to 2007-08); HS 29 v E (Leeds) 2006; BB 7-77 v B (Dhaka) 2001-02. **LOI** (P): 18 (2001-02 to 2006-07); HS 6*; BB 3-31 v NZ (Dambulla) 2003. F-c Tours (P): E 2006; A 2004-05; SA 2006-07; NZ 2004-05; NZ 2003-04; I 2004-05, 2007-08; SL 2001 (Pak A), 2005-06; B 2001-02; K 2000 (Pak A). HS 65 v Notts (Nottingham) 2007. 50 wkts (2+1); most – 74 (2007). BB 7-39 Karachi Whites v Gujranwala (Karachi) 2000-01. UKBB 7-65 (13-186 match) v Yorks (Chelmsford) 2004. LO HS 33* v Sussex (Arundel) 2007 (FPT). LO BB 5-21 Habib Bank v Customs (Karachi) 2005-06. T20 HS 5. T20 BB 4-31.

NQFLOWER, Grant William (St George's C), b Salisbury, Rhodesia 20 Dec 1970. 5'10". Younger brother of A Flower (Mashonaland, Essex, S Australia and Zimbabwe 1986-87 to 2006). RHB, SLA. Debut (Zimbabwe) 1989-90. Mashonaland U-24/Young Mashonaland 1993-94 to 1995-96. Mashonaland 1994-95 to 2003-04. MCC 1996-97. Leicestershire 2002 (one match); cap 2002. Essex debut/cap 2005 (Kolpak registration). **Tests** (Z): 67 (1992-93 to 2003-04); HS 201* v P (Harare) 1994-95 sharing with A.Flower in fourth-wicket partnership of 269, the highest stand between brothers in Test cricket; BB 4-41 (8-104 match) v B (Chittagong) 2001-02. **LOI** (Z): 219 (1992-93 to 2003-04, 1 as captain); HS 142* v B (Bulawayo) 2000-01; BB 4-32 v K (Dhaka) 1998-99. F-c Tours (Z): E 1990, 2000; A 1994-95; SA 1999-00; WI 1999-00; NZ 1995-96, 1997-98, 2000-01; I 1992-93, 2000-01, 2001-02; P 1993-94, 1996-97, 1998-99; SL 1996-97, 1997-98, 2001-02; B 2001-02. HS 243* Mashonaland v Matabeleland (Harare) 1996-97. UK HS 203 v Northants (Chelmsford) 2007. BB 7-31 Z v Lahore (Lahore) 1998-99. UK BB 4-66 Le v Warwks (Birmingham) 2002. Ex BB 3-28 v Glos (Bristol) 2006. LO HS 148* Mashonaland v Midlands (Kwekwe) 2002-03. LO BB 4-32 (see LOI). T20 HS 40. T20 BB 3-20.

FOSTER, James Savin (Forest S, Snaresbrook; Collingwood S, Durham U), b Whipps Cross 15 Apr 1980. 6'0". RHB, WK. British U 2000-01. Essex debut 2000; cap 2001. Durham UCCE 2001. MCC 2004. **Tests**: 7 (2001-02 to 2002-03); HS 48 v I (Bangalore) 2001-02. **LOI**: 11 (2001-02); HS 13 v I (Bombay) 2001-02. F-c Tours: A 2002-03; WI 2000-01 (Eng A); NZ 2001-02; I 2001-02. 1000 runs (1): 1037 (2004). HS 212 v Leics (Chelmsford) 2004. LO HS 69* v Hants (Chelmsford) 2007 (FPT). T20 HS 62*.

‡GALLIAN, Jason Edward Riche (Pittwater House S, Sydney; Keble C, Oxford), b Manly, Sydney, Australia 25 Jun 1971. Qualified for England 1994. 6'0". RHB, RM. Lancashire 1990-97, taking wicket of D.A.Hagan (OU) with his first ball; cap 1994. Oxford U 1992-93; blue 1992-93; captain 1993. Combined U 1992-93. Nottinghamshire 1998-2007; cap 1998; captain 1998 (part) to 2004; benefit 2005. Captained Australia YC v England YC 1989-90, scoring 158* in 1st 'Test'. **Tests**: 3 (1995 to 1995-96); HS 28 v SA (Pt Elizabeth) 1995-96. F-c Tours: A 1996-97 (Eng A); WI 1995-96 (La); SA 1995-96 (part); I 1994-95 (Eng A); P 1995-96 (Eng A). 1000 runs (6); most – 1220 (2005). HS 312 La v Derbys (Manchester) 1996 (record score at Old Trafford). BB 6-115 La v Surrey (Southport) 1996. LO HS 134 La v Notts (Manchester) 1995 (BHC). LO BB 5-15 La v Minor C (Leek) 1995 (BHC). T20 HS 62

‡MASTERS, David Daniel (Fort Luton HS; Mid Kent CHE), b Chatham, Kent 22 Apr 1978. Son of K.D.Masters (Kent 1983-84). 6'4". RHB, RMF. Kent 2000-02. Leicestershire 2003-07; cap 2007. Middlesex 2008. HS 119 Le v Sussex (Hove) 2003. BB 6-27 K v Durham (Tunbridge Wells) 2000. LO HS 39 Le v Glos (Cheltenham) 2006 (P40). LO BB 5-20 K v Durham (Maidstone) 2002 (NL). T20 HS 7. T20 BB 3-7.

‡MICKELBURGH, Jaik Charles (Bungay HS), b Norwich, Norfolk 30 Mar 1990. RHB, RM. Norfolk 2007. Essex 2nd XI debut aged 16 years 160 days. Awaiting 1st XI debut.

MIDDLEBROOK, James Daniel (Pudsey Crawshaw S), b Leeds, Yorks 13 May 1977. 6'1". RHB, OB. Yorkshire 1998-2001. Essex debut 2002; cap 2003. HS 127 v Middlesex (Lord's) 2007. 50 wkts (1): 56 (2003). BB 6-123 v Kent (Chelmsford) 2003. Hat-trick 20. LO HS 47 v Worcs (Worcester) 2004 (CGT). LO BB 4-27 v Somerset (Taunton) 2006 (CGT). T20 HS 43. T20 BB 3-25.

NAPIER, Graham Richard (The Gilberd S, Colchester), b Colchester 6 Jan 1980. 5'9½". RHB, RM. Debut (Essex) 1997; cap 2003. MCC 2004. F-c Tour (Eng A): I 2003-04. HS 125 v Notts (Chelmsford) 2007. BB 5-56 v Derbys (Derby) 2004. LO HS 79 Essex CB v Lancs CB (Chelmsford) 2000 (NWT). LO BB 6-29 v Worcs (Chelmsford) 2001 (NL). T20 HS 38. T20 BB 3-13.

PALLADINO, Antonio Paul (Cardinal Pole SS; Anglia Polytechnic U), b Tower Hamlets, London 29 Jun 1983. 6'0". RHB, RMF. Cambridge UCCE 2003-05. Essex debut 2003. HS 41 v Notts (Nottingham) 2004. BB 6-41 v Kent (Canterbury) 2003. LO HS 16 Essex CB v Essex (Chelmsford) 2003. LO BB 3-32 v Glamorgan (Chelmsford) 2003 (NL). T20 HS 1*. T20 BB 2-3.

PETTINI, Mark Lewis (Comberton Village C; Hills Road SFC, Cambridge; Cardiff U), b Brighton, Sussex 7 Aug 1983. RHB, RM. 5'10". Debut (Essex) 2001; cap 2006; captain 2007 (part) to date. MCC 2005. 1000 runs (1): 1218 (2006). HS 208* v Derbys (Chelmsford) 2006. LO 103* v Middlesex (Chelmsford) 2007 (FPT). T20 HS 60.

PHILLIPS, Timothy James (Felsted S; St Hild & St Bede C, Durham U), b Cambridge 13 Mar 1981. 6'1". LHB, SLA. Essex 1999, 2001-02, 2005 to date; cap 2006. Durham UCCE 2001-02. HS 89 v Worcs (Worcester) 2005. BB 5-41 v Derbys (Chelmsford) 2006. LO HS 24* v Lancs (Manchester) 2005 (CGT). LO BB 5-34 v Lancs (Chelmsford) 2006 (P40). T20 HS 31. T20 BB 2-11.

[NQ]**Ten DOESCHATE, Ryan** Neil (Fairbairn C; Cape Town U), b Port Elizabeth, South Africa 30 Jun 1980. 5'10½". RHB, RMF. Debut (Essex) 2003; cap 2006. EU passport – Dutch ancestry. Holland 2005 to date. **LOI** (H): 11 (2006 to 2006-07); HS 109* v Bermuda (Nairobi) 2006-07; BB 4-31 v Canada (Nairobi) 2006-07. F-c Tours (H): SA 2006-07; K 2005-06; Ireland 2005; HS 259* and BB 6-20 (9-112 match) Holland v Canada (Pretoria) 2006. Ex HS 148 v Glamorgan (Chelmsford) 2007. Ex BB 5-143 v Surrey (Croydon) 2006. LO HS 109* (see LOI). LO BB 5-50 v Glos (Bristol) 2007 (FPT). T20 HS 49*. T20 BB 2-27.

TUDOR, Alex Jeremy (St Mark's S, Hammersmith; City of Westminster C), b West Brompton, London 23 Oct 1977. 6'5". RHB, RF. Surrey 1995-2004; cap 1999. Essex debut 2005. YC 1999. **Tests**: 10 (1998-99 to 2002-03); HS 99* v NZ (Birmingham) 1999 – record score by an England 'night-watchman'; BB 5-44 v A (Nottingham) 2001. **LOI**: 3 (2002); HS 6; BB 2-30 v I (Oval) 2002. F-c Tours: A 1998-99, 2002-03; SA 1999-00; WI 2000-01 (Eng A); P 2000-01. HS 144 v Derbys (Chelmsford) 2006. BB 7-48 Sy v Lancs (Oval) 2000. Ex BB 5-67 v Somerset (Southend) 2006. LO HS 56 Sy v Lancs (Croydon) 2004 (NL). LO BB 4-26 Sy v Hants (Oval) 2000 (NL).

WESTFIELD, Mervyn Simon (Barking C), b Romford 5 May 1988. 6'1". RHB, RFM. Debut (Essex) 2005. HS 32 v and BB 4-72 v Somerset (Southend) 2006. LO HS 4* (P40). LO BB – .

WESTLEY, Thomas (Linton Village C; Hills Road SFC), b Cambridge 13 March 1989. 6'2". RHB, OB. Debut (Essex) 2007. MCC 2007. Essex 2nd XI debut 2004 when aged 15 years 88 days. Cambridgeshire 2005. HS 72 v Somerset (Chelmsford) 2007. BB 1-24 MCC v SL A (Arundel) 2007. Ex BB – . LO HS 36 v Worcs (Chelmsford) 2007 (P40).

‡**WHEATER, Adam** (Millfield S), b Whipps Cross 13 Feb 1990. RHB, WK. Essex 2nd XI debut when aged 16 years 190 days.

‡**WRIGHT, Christopher** Julian Clement (Eggars S, Alton; Anglia Ruskin U), b Chipping Norton, Oxon 14 Jul 1985. 6'3". RHB, RFM. Cambridge UCCE 2004-05. Middlesex 2004-07. Tamil Union 2005-06. HS 76 CU v Essex (Cambridge) 2005. CC HS 42 M v Kent (Lord's) 2006. BB 2-21 M v Glamorgan (Swansea) 2007. LO HS 21* M v Somerset (Lord's) 2007 (FPT). LO BB 3-21 Tamil Union v Singha (Colombo) 2005-06. T20 HS 1*. T20 BB 2-24.

RELEASED/RETIRED
(Having made a County 1st XI appearance in 2007)

NQ**BICHEL, Andrew** John (Laidley HS; Laidley, Queensland), b Laidley, Queensland, Australia 27 Aug 1970. RHB, RFM. 5'11". Queensland 1992-93 to date. Worcestershire 2001-02, 2004; cap 2001. Hampshire 2005. Essex 2006-07; cap 2007. **Tests** (A): 19 (1996-97 to 2003-04); HS 71 v WI (Bridgetown) 2002-03; BB 5-60 v WI (Melbourne) 2000-01. **LOI** (A): 67 (1996-97 to 2003-04); HS 64 v NZ (Pt Elizabeth) 2002-03; BB 7-20 v E (Pt Elizabeth) 2002-03. F-c Tours (A): E 1997; SA 1996-97, 2001-02; WI 1998-99, 2002-03; P 2002-03 (in Sharjah); Scotland 1998 (Aus A). HS 148 Ex v Notts (Chelmsford) 2007. 50 wkts (1+3): most – 66 (2001). BB 9-93 (10-131 match) Wo v Glos (Worcester) 2002. Ex BB 7-36 v Derbys (Derby) 2007. LO HS 100 Wo v Glamorgan (Cardiff) 2001 (BHC). LO BB 7-20 (*see LOI*). T20 HS 58*. T20 BB 4-23.

HOLLIOAKE, Adam John (St Joseph's C, Sydney; St Patrick's C, Ballarat; St George's C, Weybridge; Surrey Tutorial C), b Melbourne, Australia 5 Sep 1971. RHB, RMF. Surrey 1993-2004, scoring 13 and 123 v Derbys (Ilkeston) on debut; cap 1995; captain 1997-2003; benefit 2004. Qualified for England 1992. Essex (T20 only) 2007. *Wisden* 2002. Retired after 2004 season. **Tests**: 4 (1997 to 1997-98); HS 45 and BB 2-31 v A (Nottingham) 1997 – on debut. **LOI**: 35 (1996 to 1999, 14 as captain); HS 83* v SA (Dhaka) 1998-99; BB 4-23 v P (Birmingham) 1996 – on debut. F-c Tours: A 1996-97 (Eng A – captain); WI 1997-98. 1000 runs (2); most – 1522 (1996). HS 208 v Leics (Oval) 2002. BB 5-62 v Glam (Swansea) 1998. Awards: CGT 2; BHC 1. LO HS 117* v Sussex (Hove) 2002 (CGT). LO BB 6-17 v Kent (Canterbury) 2003 (NL). T20 HS 65*. T20BB 5-21.

IRANI, Ronald Charles (Smithills CS, Bolton), b Leigh, Lancs 26 Oct 1971. 6'3". RHB, RMF. Lancashire 1990-93. Essex 1994-2007; cap 1994; captain 2000-07 (*part*); benefit 2003. **Tests**: 3 (1996 to 1999); HS 41 v I (Lord's) 1996; BB 1-22. Took wicket of M.Azharuddin with his fifth ball in Test cricket. **LOI**: 31 (1996 to 2002-03); HS 53 and BB 5-26 v I (Oval) 2002. F-c Tours: NZ 1996-97, 1999-00 (Eng A); P 1995-96 (Eng A); Z 1996-97; B 1999-00 (Eng A). 1000 runs (7); most – 1202 (2005). HS 218 v Glamorgan (Chelmsford) 2007. 50 wkts (1): 51 (1999). BB 6-71 v Notts (Nottingham) 2002. LO HS 158* v Glamorgan (Chelmsford) 2004 (NL). LO BB 5-26 (*see LOI*). T20 HS 100*.

McGARRY, Andrew Charles (King Edward VI GS, Chelmsford; SE Essex C of Arts & Technology, Southend), b Basildon 8 Nov 1981. 6'5". RHB, RFM. Essex 1999-2003, 2007. Suffolk 2004-06. HS 11* v CU (Cambridge) 2002. CC HS 10 v Leics (Leicester) 2007. BB 5-27 v CU (Cambridge) 2003. CC BB 3-29 v Worcs (Chelmsford) 2000. LO HS 1 (NL). LO BB 2-20 v Surrey (Colchester) 2000 (NL).

RELEASED/RETIRED continued on p 41

ESSEX 2007

RESULTS SUMMARY

	Place	Won	Lost	Tied	Drew	No Result
LV County Championship (2nd Division)	4th	6	4		6	
All First-Class Matches		6	4		7	
Friends Provident Trophy (South Conference)	Semi-Finalist	6	3			1
NatWest Pro40 League (1st Division)	9th	1	4	1		2
Twenty/20 Cup (South Division)	4th	3	4			1

LV COUNTY CHAMPIONSHIP AVERAGES

BATTING AND FIELDING

Cap		M	I	NO	HS	Runs	Avge	100	50	Ct/St
1994	R.C.Irani	4	6	2	218	465	116.25	2	–	4
2005	R.S.Bopara	10	16	2	229	849	60.64	3	3	4
2007	A.J.Bichel	8	12	4	148	482	60.25	2	2	7
2005	A.N.Cook	3	5	–	136	294	58.80	2	–	2
2003	G.R.Napier	9	9	2	125	306	43.71	1	1	4
2006	R.N.ten Doeschate	15	22	2	148	845	42.25	3	3	10
2005	G.W.Flower	10	15	1	203	557	39.78	2	–	17
2001	J.S.Foster	15	23	1	204	827	37.59	1	5	31/5
2003	J.D.Middlebrook	16	23	6	127	560	32.94	1	3	14
–	V.Chopra	15	25	3	86	597	27.13	–	4	14
–	T.Westley	4	6	1	72	131	26.20	–	1	3
2006	M.L.Pettini	16	26	1	86*	567	22.68	–	6	17
2004	Danish Kaneria	13	16	1	65	216	14.40	–	1	1
–	A.J.Tudor	10	13	3	35	112	11.20	–	–	3
2006	T.J.Phillips	9	13	–	68	144	11.07	–	1	4
–	A.P.Palladino	7	8	2	18	51	8.50	–	–	1
–	A.Nel	4	5	1	10	19	4.75	–	–	–

Also batted: J.S.Ahmed (2 matches) 7*, 7, 0* (2 ct); A.C.McGarry (3) 10, 5* (1 ct); M.J.Saggers (2) 2*; M.S.Westfield (1) 4*.

BOWLING

	O	M	R	W	Avge	Best	5wI	10wM
A.J.Bichel	217.4	43	842	41	20.53	7-36	3	1
Danish Kaneria	560.5	124	1643	74	22.20	7-95	7	1
M.J.Saggers	81.0	20	244	10	24.40	5-39	1	–
A.P.Palladino	106.5	30	350	12	29.16	4-44	–	–
A.J.Tudor	174.2	42	602	17	35.41	3-29	–	–
A.Nel	122.2	31	391	10	39.10	3-62	–	–
J.D.Middlebrook	341.5	62	1020	24	42.50	4-53	–	–
R.S.Bopara	130.2	23	496	11	45.09	3-60	–	–
Also bowled:								
T.J.Phillips	70	11	244	6	40.66	3-28	–	–
G.R.Napier	140.1	28	560	8	70.00	3-55	–	–
R.N.ten Doeschate	113.3	18	528	7	75.42	1-13	–	–

J.S.Ahmed 25-4-129-3; V.Chopra 5-0-25-0; A.N.Cook 1-0-6-0; G.W.Flower 16-5-54-1; A.C.McGarry 39.1-9-142-2; M.S.Westfield 13-1-64-0.

The First-Class Averages (pp 140–158) give the records of Essex players in all first-class county matches (Essex's other opponents being Cambridge UCCE), with the exception of A.N.Cook and M.J.Saggers, whose full Essex first-class figures are as above, and:

R.S.Bopara 11-17-2-229-931-62.06-3-4-4ct. 130.2-23-496-11-45.09-3/60-0-0.

T.Westley 5-7-2-72-177-35.40-0-1-3ct. Did not bowl.

ESSEX RECORDS

FIRST-CLASS CRICKET

Highest Total	For 761-6d		v	Leics	Chelmsford	1990
	V 803-4d		by	Kent	Brentwood	1934
Lowest Total	For 30		v	Yorkshire	Leyton	1901
	V 14		by	Surrey	Chelmsford	1983
Highest Innings	For 343*	P.A.Perrin	v	Derbyshire	Chesterfield	1904
	V 332	W.H.Ashdown	for	Kent	Brentwood	1934

Highest Partnership for each Wicket

1st	316	G.A.Gooch/P.J.Prichard	v	Kent	Chelmsford	1994
2nd	403	G.A.Gooch/P.J.Prichard	v	Leics	Chelmsford	1990
3rd	347*	M.E.Waugh/N.Hussain	v	Lancashire	Ilford	1992
4th	314	Salim Malik/N.Hussain	v	Surrey	The Oval	1991
5th	316	N.Hussain/M.A.Garnham	v	Leics	Leicester	1991
6th	206	J.W.H.T.Douglas/J.O'Connor	v	Glos	Cheltenham	1923
	206	B.R.Knight/R.A.G.Luckin	v	Middlesex	Brentwood	1962
7th	261	J.W.H.T.Douglas/J.Freeman	v	Lancashire	Leyton	1914
8th	263	D.R.Wilcox/R.M.Taylor	v	Warwicks	Southend	1946
9th	251	J.W.H.T.Douglas/S.N.Hare	v	Derbyshire	Leyton	1921
10th	218	F.H.Vigar/T.P.B.Smith	v	Derbyshire	Chesterfield	1947

Best Bowling	For 10- 32	H.Pickett	v	Leics	Leyton	1895
(Innings)	V 10- 40	E.G.Dennett	for	Glos	Bristol	1906
Best Bowling	For 17-119	W.Mead	v	Hampshire	Southampton	1895
(Match)	V 17- 56	C.W.L.Parker	for	Glos	Gloucester	1925

Most Runs – Season	2559	G.A.Gooch	(av 67.34)	1984
Most Runs – Career	30701	G.A.Gooch	(av 51.77)	1973-97
Most 100s – Season	9	J.O'Connor		1929, 1934
	9	D.J.Insole		1955
Most 100s – Career	94	G.A.Gooch		1973-97
Most Wkts – Season	172	T.P.B.Smith	(av 27.13)	1947
Most Wkts – Career	1610	T.P.B.Smith	(av 26.68)	1929-51
Most Career W-K Dismissals	1231	B.Taylor	(1040 ct; 191 st)	1949-73
Most Career Catches in the Field	519	K.W.R.Fletcher		1962-88

LIMITED-OVERS CRICKET

Highest Total	FPT	386-5		v	Wiltshire	Chelmsford	1988
	P40	316-4		v	Glamorgan	Chelmsford	2004
	T20	196-6		v	Sussex	Chelmsford	2006
Lowest Total	FPT	57		v	Lancashire	Lord's	1996
	P40	69		v	Derbyshire	Chesterfield	1974
	T20	99		v	Kent	Chelmsford	2007
Highest Innings	FPT	144	G.A.Gooch	v	Hampshire	Chelmsford	1990
	P40	176	G.A.Gooch	v	Glamorgan	Southend	1983
	T20	100*	R.C.Irani	v	Sussex	Hove	2006
Best Bowling	FPT	5- 8	J.K.Lever	v	Middlesex	Westcliff	1972
		5- 8	G.A.Gooch	v	Cheshire	Chester	1995
	P40	8-26	K.D.Boyce	v	Lancashire	Manchester	1971
	T20	4-20	S.A.Brant	v	Kent	Maidstone	2004

GLAMORGAN

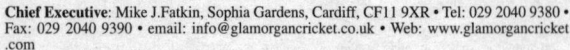

Formation of Present Club: 6 July 1888
Inaugural First-Class Match: 1921
Colours: Blue and Gold
Badge: Gold Daffodil
County Champions: (3) 1948, 1969, 1997
Gillette/NatWest/C&G/FP Trophy Winners: (0); best – Finalist 1977
Benson and Hedges Cup Winners: (0); best – Finalist 2000
Pro 40/National League (Div 1) Winners: (2) 2002, 2004
Sunday League Winners: (1) 1993
Twenty20 Cup Winners: (0); best – Semi-Finalist 2004

Chief Executive: Mike J.Fatkin, Sophia Gardens, Cardiff, CF11 9XR • Tel: 029 2040 9380 • Fax: 029 2040 9390 • email: info@glamorgancricket.co.uk • Web: www.glamorgancricket.com

Cricket Manager: M.P.Maynard. **Director of Player Development**: S.L.Watkin. **Captain**: D.L.Hemp. **Vice-Captain**: none. **Overseas Player**: J.N.Gillespie. **2008 Beneficiary**: D.L.Hemp. **Head Groundsman**: Len Smith. **Scorer**: Dr Andrew K.Hignell. ‡ New registration. NQ Not qualified for England.

BRAGG, William David (Rougemont S, Newport; UWIC), b Newport, Monmouthshire 24 Oct 1986. 5'9". LHB, WK. Debut (Glamorgan) 2007. Wales MC 2004-06. HS 24 v Somerset (Taunton) 2007 – on debut. LO HS 41* Wales MC v Notts (Swansea) 2005.

COSKER, Dean Andrew (Millfield S), b Weymouth, Dorset 7 Jan 1978. 5'11". RHB, SLA. Debut (Glamorgan) 1996; cap 2000. F-c Tours (Eng A): SA 1998-99, SL 1997-98; Z 1998-99, K 1997-98. HS 52 v Glos (Bristol) 2005. BB 6-140 v Lancs (Colwyn Bay) 1998. LO HS 39* v Hants (Swansea) 2007 (FPT). LO BB 5-54 v Essex (Chelmsford) 2003 (NL). T20 HS 10*. T20 BB 3-18.

CROFT, Robert Damien Bale (St John Lloyd Catholic CS, Llanelli; Neath Tertiary C; W Glamorgan IHE), b Morriston, Swansea 25 May 1970. 5'10½". RHB, OB. Debut (Glamorgan) 1989; cap 1992; benefit 2000; captain 2003 (*part*) to 2006 (*part*). MCC 1996. **Tests**: 21 (1996 to 2001); HS 37* v SA (Manchester) 1998; BB 5-95 v NZ (Christchurch) 1996-97. **LOI**: 50 (1996 to 2001); HS 32 v SL (Perth) 1998-99; BB 3-51 v SA (Oval) 1998. F-c Tours: A 1998-99; SA 1993-94 (Eng A), 1995-96 (Gm); WI 1991-92 (Eng A), 1997-98; NZ 1996-97; SL 2000-01, 2003-04; Z 1990-91 (Gm), 1994-95 (Gm), 1996-97 (Gm). HS 143 v Somerset (Taunton) 1995. 50 wkts (9); most – 76 (1996). BB 8-66 (14-169 match) v Warwks (Swansea) 1992. LO HS 143 v Lincs (Lincoln) 2004 (CGT). LO BB 6-20 v Worcs (Cardiff) 1994 (SL). T20 HS 62*. T20 BB 3-32.

‡DALRYMPLE, James William Murray (Radley C; St Peter's C, Oxford), b Nairobi, Kenya 21 Jan 1981. 5'11". RHB, OB. Oxford UCCE/U 2001-03; captain 2002; blue 2001-02-03. British U 2001-02. Middlesex 2001-07; cap 2004. **LOI**: 27 (2006 to 2006-07); HS 67 v SL (Lord's) 2006; BB 2-5 v I (Jaipur) 2006-07. F-c Tour (Eng A): WI 2005-06. HS 244 M v Surrey (Oval) 2004. BB 5-49 OU v CU (Cambridge) 2003. CC BB 4-53 M v Hants (Southgate) 2005. LO HS 107 M v Glamorgan (Lord's) 2004 (CGT). LO BB 4-14 M v Essex (Southgate) 2001 (NL). IT20 HS 32. IT20 BB 1-10. T20 HS 61. T20 BB 2-8.

‡NOGILLESPIE, Jason Neil (Cabra C, Adelaide), b Darlinghurst, Sydney, Australia 19 April 1975. 6'5". RHB, RFM. S Australia 1994-95 to date. Yorkshire 2006-07; cap 2007. *Wisden* 2001. **Tests** (A): 71 (1996-97 to 2005-06); HS 201* v Ind (Chittagong) 2005-06 (as a night-watchman in probably his final Test innings); BB 7-37 v E (Leeds) 1997. **LOI** (A); 97 (1996 to 2005); HS 44* v WI (Adelaide) 2004-05; BB 5-22 v P (Nairobi) 2002. F-c Tours (A): E 1997, 2001, 2005; SA 1996-97, 2001-02; WI 1998-99, 2002-03; NZ 2004-05; I 2000-01, 2004-05; P 2007-08 (Aus A); SL 1999, 2002-03 (v P), 2003-04; B 2005-06; Scotland/Ireland 1998 (Aus A). HS 201* (*see Tests*). UK HS 123* Y v Surrey (Oval) 2007, sharing in Yorkshire record 9th wicket partnership of 246 with T.T.Bresnan. 50 wkts (0+1): 51 (1995-96). BB 8-50 S Aus v NSW (Sydney) 2001-02. UK BB 7-37 A v E (Leeds) 1997. CC BB 6-37 v Durham (Chester-le-St) 2006. LO HS 44* (see LOI). LO BB 5-22 (see LOI). IT20 HS 24. IT20 BB 1-49. T20 HS 24. T20 BB 2-19.

GRANT, Richard Neil (Cefn Saeson CS; Neath Port Talbot C), b Neath 5 Jun 1984. 5'10". RHB, RM. Debut (Glamorgan) 2005. HS 79 v Northants (Colwyn Bay) 2007. BB 1-7 v Somerset (Taunton) 2007. LO HS 45 v Kent (Cardiff) 2006 (CGT). LO BB 2-21 v West Indies A (Ebbw Vale) 2006. T20 HS 77. T20 BB 4-38.

HARRIS, James Alexander Russell (Pontardulais CS; Gorseinon C), b Morriston 16 May 1990. 6'0". RHB, RFM. Debut (Glamorgan) 2007 – aged 16 years 351 days – youngest Glamorgan player to take a first-class wicket. Glamorgan 2nd XI debut 2005 when aged 14 years 353 days. Wales MC 2005-07. HS 87* v Notts (Swansea) 2007. BB 7-66 (12-118) v Glos (Bristol) 2007 – youngest (17 years 3 days) to take 10 wickets in any CC match. LO HS 5 (*thrice*). LO BB 2-57 v Glos (Colwyn Bay) 2007 (FPT).

HARRISON, David Stuart (W Monmouth CS; Usk C, Pontypool), b Newport, Monmouthshire 30 Jul 1981. Elder brother of A.J.Harrison (Glamorgan 2005-06); son of S.C.Harrison (Glamorgan 1971-77). 6'4". RHB, RMF. Debut (Glamorgan) 1999; cap 2006. No appearances 2007. MCC 2005. HS 88 v Essex (Chelmsford) 2004. 50 wkts (1): 57 (2004). BB 5-48 v Somerset (Swansea) 2004. LO HS 37* and LO BB 5-26 v Yorks (Leeds) 2002 (NL). T20 HS 4. T20 BB 2-17.

HEMP, David Lloyd (Olchfa CS; Millfield S; W Glamorgan C; Birmingham U), b Hamilton, Bermuda 8 Nov 1970. UK resident since 1976. 6'0". LHB, RM. Glamorgan 1991-96, 2002 to date; cap 1994; captain 2006 (*part*) to date; benefit 2007. Warwickshire 1997-2001; cap 1997. Bermuda 2006-07. Free State (List A only) 1997-98. Wales (MC) 1992-93. **LOI** (Bermuda): 20 (2006-07 to 2007-08); HS 76* v I (Port-of-Spain) 2006-07; BB 1-25 v K (Mombasa) 2006-07 – on debut. F-c Tours (Bermuda): SA 1995-96 (Gm), 2006-07; I 1994-95 (Eng A); Z 1994-95 (Gm); K 2006-07, 2007-08; UAE 2007-08. 1000 runs (6); most – 1452 (1994). HS 247* Bermuda v Holland (Pretoria) 2006-07. CC HS 186* Wa v Worcs (Birmingham) 2001. Gm HS 171* v Kent (Canterbury) 2005. BB 3-23 v South Africa A (Cardiff) 1996. CC BB 2-29 Wa v Glos (Birmingham) 2000. LO HS 121 v Comb U (Cardiff) 1995 (BHC). LO BB 4-32 Wa v Minor C (Lakenham) 1998 (BHC). T20 HS 74.

MAYNARD, Thomas Lloyd (Millfield S; Whitchurch HS, Cardiff), b Cardiff 25 Mar 1989. Son of M.P.Maynard (Glamorgan and England 1985-2005). 6'3". RHB, OB. Wales MC 2006-07. HS 18 v Derbys (Cardiff) 2007. BB – . LO HS 71 v Glos (Colwyn Bay) 2007 (FPT). T20 HS 11.

O'SHEA, Michael Peter (Barry CS; Millfield S), b Cardiff 4 Sep 1987. 5'11". RHB, OB. Debut (Glamorgan) 2005; no f-c appearances 2006. Wales MC 2005. HS 24 v Kent (Canterbury) 2005. LO HS 49 v Durham (Chester-le-St) 2007 (P40). LO BB 2-37 v Hants (Swansea) 2007 (FPT).

OWEN, William Thomas (Prestatyn HS; UWIC), b St Asaph, Flintshire 2 Sep 1988. 6'0". RHB, RMF. Debut (Glamorgan) 2007. Wales MC 2007. HS – v Glos (Cardiff) 2007 – only 1st XI appearance.

POWELL, Michael John (Crickhowell SS; Pontypool CFE), b Abergavenny, Monmouthshire 3 Feb 1977. 6'1". RHB, OB, occ WK. Debut (Glamorgan) 1997 scoring 200* v OU (Oxford); cap 2000. 1000 runs (5): most – 1327 (2006). HS 299 v Glos (Cheltenham) 2006 – record score for Glamorgan in England. BB 2-39 v OU (Oxford) 1999. CC BB – . LO HS 91* v Leics (Cardiff) 2003 (NL). LO BB 1-26 (CGT). T20 HS 68*.

REES, Gareth Peter (Coedcae CS; Bath U), b Swansea 8 Apr 1985. 6'1". LHB, LM. Wales MC 2003-05. Debut (Glamorgan) 2006. HS 109 v Derbys (Cardiff) 2007. LO HS 63 v Durham (Chester-le-St) 2007 (P40).

‡**SHANTRY, Adam** John (Priory S; Shrewsbury SFC), b Bristol 13 Nov 1982. 6'2½". Son of B.K.Shantry (Gloucestershire 1978-79). LHB, LFM. Northamptonshire 2003-04. Warwickshire debut 2006-07. Shropshire 2001. HS 38* Nh v Somerset (Northampton) 2003 – on CC debut (also took 3-8 including 3 wkts in 5 balls). BB 5-49 Wa v West Indies A (Birmingham) 2006. CC BB 4-31 Wa v Sussex (Hove) 2007. LO HS 15 Nh CB v Yorks CB (Northampton) 2002 (CGT). LO BB 5-37 Nh v NZ (Northampton) 2004. T20 HS – . T20 BB – .

TUDGE, Kyle Daniel (Monmouth S; UWIC), b Newport 19 Mar 1987. 5'10". RHB, SLA. Debut (Glamorgan) 2006. Summer contract. MCC YC 2004-06. Wales MC 2004-07. HS 4 and BB – v Worcs (Colwyn Bay) 2006. LO HS 4 and BB – Wales MC v Notts (Swansea) 2005 (CGT).

WALLACE, Mark Alexander (Crickhowell HS), b Abergavenny, Monmouthshire 19 Nov 1981. 5'9". LHB, WK. Debut (Glamorgan) 1999; cap 2003. F-c Tour (ECB Acad): SL 2002-03. HS 128 v Glos (Bristol) 2007. LO HS 48 v Suffolk (Bury St Edmunds) 2005 (CGT). T 20 HS 35*.

WATERS, Huw Thomas (Llantaram CS; Monmouth S), b Cardiff 26 Sep 1986. 6'2". RHB, RMF. Debut (Glamorgan) 2005. Wales MC 2004-07. HS 34 v Kent (Canterbury) 2005. BB 5-86 v Somerset (Taunton) 2006. LO HS 8 v Hants (Swansea) 2007 (FPT). LO BB 3-47 v Durham (Chester-le-St) 2007 (P40).

WATKINS, Ryan Edward (Pontllanfraith CS; Cross Keys TC), b Abergavenny, Monmouthshire 9 Jun 1983. 6'0". LHB, RM. Debut (Glamorgan) 2005. Wales MC 2004-06. HS 87 v Essex (Cardiff) 2006. BB 4-40 v Worcs (Worcester) 2006. LO HS 39 v Derbys (Derby) 2007 (P40). LO BB 2-25 v Warwks (Colwyn Bay) 2006 (P40). T20 HS 6*. T20 BB 3-33.

WHARF, Alexander George (Buttershaw Upper S; Thomas Danby C), b Bradford, Yorks 4 Jun 1975. 6'5". RHB, RMF. Yorkshire 1994-97. Nottinghamshire 1998-99. Glamorgan debut 2000, scoring 100* v OU (Oxford); cap 2000. **LOI:** 13 (2004 to 2004-05): HS 9; BB 4-24 v Z (Harare) 2004-05. F-c Tour (Eng A): WI 2005-06. HS 128* v Glos (Bristol) 2007. 50 wkts (1): 52 (2003). BB 6-59 v Glos (Bristol) 2005. LO HS 72 v Lancs (Manchester) 2004 (NL). LO BB 6-5 v Kent (Cardiff) 2004 (NL). T20 HS 19. T20 BB 4-39.

‡**WOOD, Matthew** James (Shelley HS & SFC), b Huddersfield, Yorks 6 Apr 1977. 5'9". RHB, OB. Yorkshire 1997-2007; cap 2001. MCC 1999-00. F-c Tour (MCC): B 1999-00. 1000 runs (4): most – 1432 (2003). HS 207 Y v Somerset (Taunton) 2003. BB 1-4 Y v Somerset (Leeds) 2003. LO HS 160 Y v Devon (Exmouth) 2004 (CGT). LO BB 3-45 Y v Cambs (March) 2003 (CGT). T20 HS 96*. T20 BB 1-11.

WRIGHT, Ben James (Cowbridge CS), b Preston, Lancs 5 Dec 1987. 5'9". RHB, RM. Debut (Glamorgan) 2006. HS 108 v Leics (Leicester) 2007. BB 1-14 v Essex (Chelmsford) 2007. LO HS 61 v Middlesex (Lord's) 2007 (FPT). LO BB – . T20 HS 35*.

CHERRY, Daniel David (Tonbridge S; U of Wales, Swansea), b Newport, Monmouthshire 7 Feb 1980. 5'9". LHB, RM. Glamorgan 1998-2007. HS 226 v Middlesex (Southgate) 2005. LO HS 42 v Middlesex (Lord's) 2005 (NL). LO BB 1-26 (P40). T20 HS 43*. T20 BB 2-6.

DAVIES, Andrew Philip (Dwr-y-Felin CS; Christ C, Brecon), b Neath 7 Nov 1976. 5'11". LHB, RMF. Glamorgan 1995-2007; cap 2007. Wales (MC). HS 54 v Somerset (Taunton) 2007. BB 5-79 v Worcs (Cardiff) 2002. LO HS 27 v Surrey (Oval) 2007 (P40). LO BB 5-19 v Lincs (Sleaford) 2002 (CGT). T20 HS 11. T20 BB 3-17.

[NO]**ELLIOTT, Matthew** Thomas Gray (Kyabram Secondary C; La Trobe U), b Chelsea, Victoria, Australia 28 Sep 1971. 6'3". LHB, LM/SLC. Victoria 1992-93 to 2004-05. Glamorgan 2000, 2004-05, 2007; cap 2000. Yorkshire 2002. S Australia 2005-06 to date. *Wisden* 1997. **Tests** (A): 21 (1996-97 to 2004); HS 199 v E (Leeds) 1997. **LOI** (A): 1 (1997); HS 1 v E (Lord's) 1997. F-c Tours (A): E 1995 (Young A), 1997; SA 1996-97; WI 1998-99. 1000 runs (3+5); most − 1429 (2003-04). HS 203 v Tasmania (Melbourne) 1995-96. UK HS 199 (*see Tests*). CC HS 177 v Sussex (Colwyn Bay) 2000. BB 3-68 Vic Q (Melbourne) 2004-05. UK BB 1-23 A v Hants (Southampton) 1995. LO HS 156 v Dorset (Bournemouth) 2000 (NWT). T20 HS 52*.

JONES, S.P. − *see* WORCESTERSHIRE.

[NO]**MAHER, James** Patrick (St Augustine's C, Cairns), b Innisfail, Queensland, Australia 27 Feb 1974. LHB, RM. Queensland 1993-94 to date. Glamorgan 2001, 2003, 2007; cap 2001. Durham 2005-06. **LOI** (A): 26 (1997-98 to 2003-04); HS 95 v SA (Pretoria) 2001-02. F-c Tour (A): WI 2002-03. 1000 (1+2): most − 1194 (2001-02). HS 223 Q v Vic (Brisbane) 2005-06. Gm HS 217 v Essex (Cardiff) 2001. BB 3-11 Q v WA (Perth) 1995-96. UK BB − . LO HS 187 Q v WA (Brisbane) 2003-04. LO BB 3-29 Gm v Surrey (Croydon) 2003 (NL). T20 HS 59.

PENG GILLENDER, **Nicky** (Newcastle upon Tyne RGS), b Newcastle upon Tyne, Northumb 18 Sep 1982. 6'2". RHB, OB. Durham 2000-05; cap 2001. Glamorgan 2006-07. HS 158 Du v Durham UCCE (Chester-le-St) 2003. CC HS 133 Du v Glamorgan (Cardiff) 2003. Scored 98 Du v Surrey (Chester-le-St) on debut. Gm HS 65 v Notts (Swansea) 2007. LO HS 121 Du v Worcs (Worcester) 2001 (NL). T20 HS 49.

SHINGLER, Aaron Craig (Pontardulais CS; Gorseinon TC; UWIC), b Aldershot, Hants 7 Aug 1987. 6'5". RHB, RFM. Glamorgan 2nd XI debut aged 16 years 271 days. Summer contract − awaiting f-c debut. Wales MC 2004-07. LOI for England U-19 v Bangladesh U-19 at Savar 2005-06.

[NO]**WRIGHT, Damien** Geoffrey (Terrigal HS, NSW), b Casino, NSW, Australia 25 Jul 1975. 6'1". RHB, RFM. Tasmania 1997-98 to 2006-07. Scotland 2001 (CGT). Northamptonshire 2003, 2005. Withdrew from 2004 overseas player contract with Derbyshire because of a knee injury. Glamorgan 2007. HS 111 Tas v Vic (Hobart) 2004-05. UK HS 85 Nh v Worcs (Worcester) 2005. 50 wkts (1): 53 (2005). BB 8-60 Nh v Yorks (Leeds) 2005. Gm HS 1 and BB 3-60 v Middlesex (Swansea) 2007. LO HS 55 Scotland v Middlesex CB (Southgate) 2001 (CGT). LO BB 5-37 Nh v Notts (Northampton) 2005 (NL). T20 HS 38*. T20 BB 3-17.

A.J.Harrison left the staff without making a County 1st XI appearance in 2007.

GLAMORGAN 2007

RESULTS SUMMARY

	Place	Won	Lost	Tied	Drew	No Result
LV County Championship (2nd Division)	9th	1	9		5	1
All First-Class Matches		2	9		5	1
Friends Provident Trophy (South Conference)	9th		6			3
NatWest Pro40 League (2nd Division)	9th		7			1
Twenty/20 Cup (Midlands/West Wales Division)	6th	1	4			3

LV COUNTY CHAMPIONSHIP AVERAGES
BATTING AND FIELDING

Cap		M	I	NO	HS	Runs	Avge	100	50	Ct/St
2000	M.T.G.Elliott	3	5	–	95	251	50.20	–	2	3
2000	M.J.Powell	5	9	2	64	293	41.85	–	4	3
2007	A.P.Davies	6	11	5	54	219	36.50	–	1	3
2000	A.G.Wharf	14	25	3	128*	626	28.45	2	1	7
1994	D.L.Hemp	14	24	–	97	675	28.12	–	5	8
–	R.N.Grant	8	13	–	79	350	26.92	–	2	1
1992	R.D.B.Croft	15	25	2	115	569	24.73	1	1	10
–	G.P.Rees	10	18	–	109	429	23.83	2	2	8
2003	M.A.Wallace	15	26	–	128	572	22.00	2	–	37/6
–	B.J.Wright	10	17	2	108	327	21.80	1	1	11
–	N.Peng	3	6	–	65	111	18.50	–	1	2
2001	J.P.Maher	8	15	–	55	252	16.80	–	1	9
–	J.A.R.Harris	9	14	2	87*	196	16.33	–	1	4
–	D.D.Cherry	6	11	–	48	179	16.27	–	–	3
2002	S.P.Jones	4	7	1	39	86	14.33	–	–	–
–	W.D.Bragg	2	4	–	24	51	12.75	–	–	–
–	R.E.Watkins	7	12	–	30	144	12.00	–	–	3
–	H.T.Waters	10	16	8	33	87	10.87	–	–	4
2000	D.A.Cosker	10	16	2	30	137	9.78	–	–	2

Also batted: T.L.Maynard (2 matches) 15, 18, 2; M.P.O'Shea (2) 10, 0; D.G.Wright (1) 0, 1 (1 ct). W.T.Owen (1) did not bat.

BOWLING

	O	M	R	W	Avge	Best	5wI	10wM
J.A.R.Harris	247.5	53	811	33	24.57	7-66	2	1
R.D.B.Croft	562.1	80	1748	53	32.98	6-44	5	1
D.A.Cosker	277	48	878	26	33.76	5-69	1	–
A.G.Wharf	283.5	24	1192	31	38.45	4-77	–	–
H.T.Waters	201.3	31	741	15	49.40	4-76	–	–
Also bowled:								
R.E.Watkins	76.3	11	331	6	55.16	4-89	–	–
A.P.Davies	111	16	477	7	68.14	3-70	–	–

D.D.Cherry 2-0-5-0; R.N.Grant 11.4-0-78-2; S.P.Jones 89-13-290-1; T.L.Maynard 2-0-18-0;
W.T.Owen 8-0-37-0; B.J.Wright 22-0-89-2; D.G.Wright 16.4-0-60-3.

The First-Class Averages (pp 140–158) give the records of Glamorgan players in all
first-class county matches (Glamorgan's other opponents being Oxford UCCE).

GLAMORGAN RECORDS

FIRST-CLASS CRICKET

Highest Total	For 718-3d			v	Sussex	Colwyn Bay	2000
	V 712			by	Northants	Northampton	1998
Lowest Total	For 22			v	Lancashire	Liverpool	1924
	V 33			by	Leics	Ebbw Vale	1965
Highest Innings	For 309*	S.P.James		v	Sussex	Colwyn Bay	2000
	V 322*	M.B.Loye		for	Northants	Northampton	1998

Highest Partnership for each Wicket

1st	374	M.T.G.Elliott/S.P.James	v	Sussex	Colwyn Bay	2000
2nd	252	M.P.Maynard/D.L.Hemp	v	Northants	Cardiff	2002
3rd	313	D.E.Davies/W.E.Jones	v	Essex	Brentwood	1948
4th	425*	A.Dale/I.V.A.Richards	v	Middlesex	Cardiff	1993
5th	264	M.Robinson/S.W.Montgomery	v	Hampshire	Bournemouth	1949
6th	230	W.E.Jones/B.L.Muncer	v	Worcs	Worcester	1953
7th	211	P.A.Cottey/O.D.Gibson	v	Leics	Swansea	1996
8th	202	D.Davies/J.J.Hills	v	Sussex	Eastbourne	1928
9th	203*	J.J.Hills/J.C.Clay	v	Worcs	Swansea	1929
10th	143	T.Davies/S.A.B.Daniels	v	Glos	Swansea	1982

Best Bowling	For 10- 51	J.Mercer	v	Worcs	Worcester	1936
(Innings)	V 10- 18	G.Geary	for	Leics	Pontypridd	1929
Best Bowling	For 17-212	J.C.Clay	v	Worcs	Swansea	1937
(Match)	V 16- 96	G.Geary	for	Leics	Pontypridd	1929

Most Runs – Season	2276	H.Morris	(av 55.51)		1990
Most Runs – Career	34056	A.Jones	(av 33.03)		1957-83
Most 100s – Season	10	H.Morris			1990
Most 100s – Career	54	M.P.Maynard			1985-2005
Most Wkts – Season	176	J.C.Clay	(av 17.34)		1937
Most Wkts – Career	2174	D.J.Shepherd	(av 20.95)		1950-72
Most Career W-K Dismissals	933	E.W.Jones	(840 ct; 93 st)		1961-83
Most Career Catches in the Field	656	P.M.Walker			1956-72

LIMITED-OVERS CRICKET

Highest Total	FPT	429	v	Surrey	The Oval	2002
	P40	305-6	v	Worcs	Cardiff	2001
	T20	206-6	v	Somerset	Taunton	2006
Lowest Total	FPT	76	v	Northants	Northampton	1968
	P40	42	v	Derbyshire	Swansea	1979
	T20	113	v	Warwicks	Birmingham	2003
Highest Innings	FPT	162* I.V.A.Richards	v	Oxfordshire	Swansea	1993
	P40	155* J.H.Kallis	v	Surrey	Pontypridd	1999
	T20	116* I.J.Thomas	v	Somerset	Taunton	2004
Best Bowling	FPT	5-13 R.J.Shastri	v	Scotland	Edinburgh	1988
	P40	7-16 S.D.Thomas	v	Surrey	Swansea	1998
	T20	4-38 R.N.Grant	v	Worcs	Worcester	2005

GLOUCESTERSHIRE

Formation of Present Club: 1871
Inaugural First-Class Match: 1870
Colours: Blue, Gold, Brown, Silver, Green and Red
Badge: Coat of Arms of the City and County of Bristol
County Champions (since 1890): (0); best – 2nd 1930, 1931, 1947, 1959, 1969, 1986
Gillette/NatWest/C&G/FP Trophy Winners: (5) 1973, 1999, 2000, 2003, 2004
Benson and Hedges Cup Winners: (3) 1977, 1999, 2000
Pro 40/National League (Div 1) Winners: (1) 2000
Sunday League Winners: (0); best – 2nd 1988
Twenty20 Cup Winners: (0); best – Finalist 2007

Chief Executive: Tom E.M.Richardson, County Ground, Nevil Road, Bristol BS7 9EJ • Tel: 0117 910 8000 • Fax: 0117 924 1193 • Email: info@glosccc.co.uk • Web: www.glosccc.co.uk

Head Coach: *tba*. **Captain**: J.Lewis. **Vice-Captain**: A.P.R.Gidman. **Overseas Player**: M.J.North. **2008 Beneficiary**: C.M.Spearman. **Head Groundsman**: Sean Williams. **Scorer**: Keith T.Gerrish. ‡ New registration.  Not qualified for England.

Gloucestershire revised their capping policy in 2004 and now award players with their County Caps when they make their first-class debut.

ADSHEAD, Stephen John (Bridley Moor HS, Redditch), b Redditch 29 Jan 1980. 5'9". RHB, WK. Herefordshire 1999. Leicestershire 2000 (one non-CC match). Worcestershire 2003 (2 matches). Gloucestershire debut/cap 2005. HS 148* v Surrey (Oval) 2005. LO HS 77* Shropshire v Northumb (Oswestry) 2003 (CGT). T20 HS 81.

ALI, Kadeer (Handsworth GS), b Moseley, Birmingham 7 Mar 1983. 6'1". Brother of M.M.Ali (*see WORCESTERSHIRE*), cousin of Kabir Ali (*see WORCESTERSHIRE*). RHB, RM/LB. Worcestershire 2000-04. Gloucestershire debut/cap 2005. F-c Tour (Eng A): I 2003-04. HS 145 v Northants (Northampton) 2006. BB 1-4 v Glamorgan (Bristol) 2005. LO HS 114 v Hants (Southampton) 2007 (P40). LO BB 1-4 Wo v Worcs CB (Worcester) 2003 (CGT). T20 HS 53.

BANERJEE, Vikram (King Edward's S, Birmingham; Downing C, Cambridge), b Bradford, Yorks 20 Mar 1984. 6'0". LHB, SLA. Cambridge UCCE/U 2004-06; blue 2004-05-06. Gloucestershire debut/cap 2006. HS 29 CU v OU (Cambridge) 2005. Gs HS 11* v Northants (Northampton) 2007 and 11* v Essex (Southend) 2007. BB 4-38 v Northants (Gloucester) 2007.

BROWN, David Owen (Queen Elizabeth's GS, Blackburn; Collingwood C, Durham), b Burnley, Lancs 8 Dec 1982. Younger brother of M.J.Brown (*see HAMPSHIRE*). RHB, RM. 6'0". Durham UCCE 2003-05. British U 2005. Gloucestershire debut/cap 2006. HS 77 DU v Leics (Leicester) 2005. Gs HS 43 v Derbyshire (Derby) 2007. BB 2-25 v Northants (Gloucester) 2007. LO HS 63* v Surrey (Bristol) 2006 (CGT) – on debut. LO BB 3-29 v Glamorgan (Colwyn Bay) 2007 (FPT). T20 HS 36. T20 BB 1-11.

FISHER, Ian Douglas (Beckfoot GS, Bingley; Thomas Danby C, Leeds), b Bradford, Yorks 31 Mar 1976. 5'10½". LHB, SLA. Yorkshire 1995-96 (Y in Zim) to 2001. Gloucestershire debut 2002; cap 2004. F-c Tour: Z 1995-96 (Y). HS 103* v Essex (Gloucester) 2002. BB 5-30 (10-123 match) v Durham (Bristol) 2003. LO HS 37* Glamorgan (Colwyn Bay) 2007 (FPT). LO BB 3-18 v Northants (Northampton) 2004 (NL). T20 HS 9*. T20 BB 4-22.

38

GIDMAN, Alex Peter Richard (Wycliffe C), b High Wycombe, Bucks 22 Jun 1981. Elder brother of W.R.S.Gidman (*see DURHAM*). 6'3". RHB, RM. Debut (Gloucestershire) 2002; cap 2004. MCC YC 2001. MCC 2004, 2007. Otago 2007-08. F-c Tours (Eng A): SL 2004-05. Appointed captain of Eng A tour to India 2003-04 but withdrew because of hand injury. 1000 runs (3); most – 1244 (2006). HS 142 v Surrey (Bristol) 2005. BB 4-47 v Glamorgan (Cardiff) 2005. LO HS 88* v Warwks (Bristol) 2007 (P40). LO BB 5-42 Eng A v Bangladesh A (Mirpur) 2006-07. T20 HS 61. T20 BB 1-2.

‡GITSHAM, Matthew Thomas, b Truro, Cornwall 1 Feb 1982. RHB, LB. Somerset Cricket Board 1999-2001. Buckinghamshire 2006. Gloucestershire 2nd XI 2007. LO HS 15 v Somerset CB v Wales MC (North Perrott) 2001 (CGT).

GREENIDGE, Carl Gary (Lodge S and St Michael S, Barbados; Heathcote S, Chingford; W Hatch HS; City of Westminster C), b Basingstoke, Hants 20 Apr 1978. Son of C.Gordon Greenidge (Hampshire, Barbados and West Indies 1970-92). 5'10". RHB, RMF. MCC YC 1998. Surrey 1999-2000. Northamptonshire 2002-04. Gloucestershire debut/cap 2005. HS 46 Nh v Derbys (Derby) 2002. Gs HS 27 v Derbys (Derby) 2007. 50 wkts (1): 53 (2002). BB 6-40 Nh v Durham (Chester-le-St) 2002. Gs BB 5-54 v Leics (Leicester) 2007. LO HS 29 v Glamorgan (Colwyn Bay) 2007 (FPT). LO BB 4-15 v Ireland (Dublin) 2007 (FPT). T20 HS 20. T20 BB 3-15.

HARDINGES, Mark Andrew (Malvern C; Bath U), b Gloucester 5 Feb 1978. 6'1". RHB, RMF. Debut (Gloucestershire) 1999; cap 2004. British U 2000. HS 172 v OU (Oxford) 2002. CC HS 107* v Essex (Chelmsford) 2006. BB 5-51 v Kent (Maidstone) 2005. LO HS 111* v Lancs (Manchester) 2005 (NL). LO BB 4-19 v Salop (Shrewsbury) 2002 (CGT). T20 HS 94*. T20 BB 3-18.

HODNETT, Grant Phillip (Durban Preparatory HS; Northwood HS), b Johannesburg, South Africa 17 Aug 1982. 6'4". RHB, LB. Debut (Gloucestershire) 2005; cap 2005. HS 168 v Derbys (Bristol) 2007. LO HS 50 v Somerset (Bristol) 2007 (FPT).

NOIRELAND, Anthony John (Plumtree HS), b Masvingo, Zimbabwe 30 Aug 1984. RHB, RM. Midlands 2002-03 to 2004-05. Gloucestershire debut/cap 2007 (Kolpak registration). **LOI** (Z): 26 (2005-06 to 2006-07); HS 8* v K (Bulawayo) 2005-06; BB 3-41 v B (Harare) (twice) – 2006 and 2006-07. HS 15 Midlands v Matabeleland (Kwekwe) 2002-03. Gs HS 10* v Glamorgan (Bristol) 2007. BB 7-36 Zimbabwe A v Bangladesh A (Mirpur) 2006-07. Gs BB 3-39 v Leics (Bristol) 2007. LO HS 17 Midlands v Matabeleland (Harare) 2005-06. LO BB 4-16 Zimbabwe A v Kenya (Harare) 2005-06. IT20 HS 2*. IT20 BB 1-33. T20 HS 8*. T20 BB 3-10.

KIRBY, Steven Paul (Elton HS; Bury C), b Ainsworth, nr Bolton, Lancs 4 Oct 1977. 6'3½". RHB, RFM. Leicestershire staff 1998 – no f-c appearances. Yorkshire 2001-04, debut as sub for M.J.Hoggard (England duty) taking 7-50; cap 2003. Gloucestershire debut/cap 2005. F-c Tour (Eng A): I 2003-04 (*part*). HS 57 Y v Hants (Leeds) 2002. Gs HS 37 v Northants (Northampton) 2007. 50 wkts (1): 67 (2003). BB 8-80 (13-154 match) Y v Somerset (Taunton) 2003. Gs BB 5-41 v Essex (Southend) 2007. LO HS 15 Y v Leics (Leicester) 2003 (NL). LO BB 5-36 v Middlesex (Lord's) 2007 (FPT). T20 HS 1*. T20 BB 2-15.

LEWIS, Jonathan (Churchfields S, Swindon; Swindon C), b Aylesbury, Bucks 26 Aug 1975. 6'2". RHB, RMF. Debut (Gloucestershire) 1995; cap 1998; captain 2006 to date; benefit 2007. MCC 2005. Wiltshire 1993, 1995. Northamptonshire staff 1994. **Tests:** 1 (2006); HS 20 and BB 3-68 v SL (Nottingham) 2006. **LOI:** 13 (2005 to 2007); HS 17 v I (Leeds) 2007; BB 4-36 v A (Brisbane) 2006-07. F-c Tours (Eng A): WI 2000-01; SL 2004-05. HS 62 v Worcs (Cheltenham) 1999. 50 wkts (6); most – 74 (2003). BB 8-95 v Z (Gloucester) 2000. CC BB 7-38 (10-75 match) v Somerset (Bristol) 2006. Hat-trick 2000. LO HS 40 and LO BB 5-19 v Hants (Southampton) 2005 (NL). IT20 HS 1. IT20 BB 4-24. T20 HS 43. T20 BB 4-24.

NQMARSHALL, Hamish John Hamilton (Mahurangi C, Warkworth; King C, Auckland), b Warkworth, NZ 15 Feb 1979. Twin brother of J.A.H.Marshall (ND and NZ 1997-98 to date). 5'9". RHB, RM. N Districts 1998-99 to 2006-07. Gloucestershire debut 2006 (scoring 102 v Worcs on UK debut); cap 2006. Buckinghamshire 2003. **Tests** (NZ): 13 (2000-01 to 2005-06); HS 160 v SL (Napier) 2004-05. **LOI** (NZ): 65 (2003-04 to 2006-07); HS 101* v P (Faisalabad) 2003-04. F-c Tours (NZ): A 2004-05; SA 2000-01, 2005-06; Z 2005; B 2004-05. 1000 runs (1): 1218 (2006). HS 168 v Leics (Cheltenham) 2006. BB 1-6 ND v CD (Gisborne) 2006-07. Gs BB 1-9 v Leics (Leicester) 2007. LO HS 122 v Sussex (Hove) 2007 (P40). LO BB 1-14 ND v Otago (Dunedin) 2004-05. IT20 HS 8. T20 HS 100.

NQNORTH, Marcus James (Kent Street Sr HS), b Pakenham, Melbourne, Australia 28 Jul 1979. 6'1". LHB, OB. Debut (Aus Academy in Zim) 1998-99. W Australia 1999-00 to 2006-07. Durham 2004. Lancashire 2005. Derbyshire 2006. Gloucestershire debut/cap 2007. F-c Tours (Aus A): P 2005-06; Z 1998-99 (Aus Acad). 1000 runs (0+1): 1074 (2003-04). HS 239* WA v Vic (Perth) 2006-07. CC HS 219 Du v Glamorgan (Cardiff) 2004. Gs HS 109 v Northants (Gloucester) 2007. BB 4-16 Du v Durham UCCE (Chester-le-St) 2004 – on DU debut. CC BB 3-53 v Leics (Bristol) 2007. LO HS 134* WA v Q (Perth) 2004-05. LO BB 4-26 Durham CB v Bucks (Beaconsfield) 2001 (CGT). T20 HS 59. T20 BB 2-19.

‡NQPORTERFIELD, William Thomas Stuart, b Londonderry, Ireland 6 Sep 1984. LHB. Debut (Ireland) 2006. MCC 2007. F-c Tours (Ire): E 2007; Scot 2006; UAE 2006-07. LOI (Ire): 20 (2006 to 2007); HS 112* v Bermuda (Nairobi) 2006-07. HS 166 Ireland v Bermuda (Dublin) 2007. UK HS 54 Ireland v Canada (Leicester) 2007. LO HS 112* (*see LOI*).

RUDGE, William Douglas (Clifton C), b Southmead, Bristol 15 Jul 1983. 6'4". RHB, RM. Debut (Gloucestershire)/cap 2005. HS 15 v Surrey (Oval) 2005. BB 3-46 v Bangladesh A (Bristol) 2005 – on debut. CC BB 3-75 v Middlesex (Bristol) 2005. LO HS 4 and BB 2-1 v Sussex (Arundel) 2006 (CGT). T20 HS 1. T20 BB 3-37.

SNELL, Stephen David (Sandown HS), b Winchester, Hampshire 27 Feb 1983. 6'0". RHB, WK. Debut (Gloucestershire)/cap 2005. MCC YC 2002-04. HS 83* v Bangladesh A (Bristol) 2005 – on debut. CC HS 13 v Warwks (Birmingham) 2005. LO HS 17 v Glamorgan (Cardiff) 2005 (NL).

SPEARMAN, Craig Murray (Kelston HS, Auckland; Massey U, Palmerston North), b Auckland, New Zealand 4 Jul 1972. RHB. Auckland 1993-94 to 1994-95. Central Districts 1996-97 to 2003-04. Gloucestershire debut/cap 2002; benefit 2008. Qualified for England 2005. **Tests** (NZ): 19 (1995-96 to 2000-01); HS 112 v Z (Auckland) 1995-96. **LOI** (NZ): 51 (1995-96 to 2000-01); HS 86 v Z (Harare) 2000-01. F-c Tours (NZ): SA 2000-01; WI 1995-96; I 1999-00; P 1996-97; SL 1998; Z 1997-98, 2000-01. 1000 runs (3); most – 1462 (2004). HS 341 v Middlesex (Gloucester) 2004 – record Gloucestershire score. BB 1-37 CD v Wellington (New Plymouth) 1999-00. LO HS 153 v Warwks (Gloucester) 2003 (NL). T20 HS 88.

STAYT, Thomas Patrick (Lavington S, Market Lavington; St Augustine's C, Trowbridge; Exeter U), b Salisbury, Wilts 20 Jan 1986. 6'2". RHB, RMF. Debut (Gloucestershire); cap 2007. HS 6 v Middlesex (Bristol) 2007. BB 3-51 v Middlesex (Lord's) 2007 – on debut.

TAYLOR, Christopher Glyn (Colston's Collegiate S), b Southmead, Bristol 27 Sep 1976. 5'7". RHB, OB. Debut (Gloucestershire) 2000, scoring 104 v Middlesex – first to score a hundred at Lord's in a Championship match on his first-class debut; cap 2001; captain 2004-05. 1000 runs (1): 1077 (2004). HS 196 v Notts (Nottingham) 2001. BB 4-52 v Northants (Northampton) 2007. LO HS 93 v Warwks (Bristol) 2002 (BHC). LO BB 2-5 v Northants (Northampton) 2004 (NL). T20 HS 83.

THOMPSON, Jackson Gladwin (St Benedict's C; Gloucestershire U), b Nasik, Maharashtra, India 7 Feb 1986. LHB, OB. Debut (Gloucestershire); cap 2007. Oxfordshire 2007. HS 21 v Middlesex (Bristol) 2007 – on debut. LO HS 7 v Glamorgan (Colwyn Bay) 2007 (FPT).

RELEASED/RETIRED
(Having made a County 1st XI appearance in 2007)

NQEDMONDSON, Ben Matthew (Kirwan HS, Townsville; Ignatius Park C, Townsville), b Southport, Queensland, Australia 28 Sep 1978. 6'0½". LHB, RFM. W Australia 2003-04 to date. Denmark 2003. Gloucestershire debut/cap 2007. HS 18 v Northants (Northampton) 2007. BB 6-28 WA v Tas (Hobart) 2006-07. Gs BB 4-50 v Derbys (Bristol) 2007. LO HS 4 WA v Tas (Perth) 2006-07. LO BB 5-39 WA v S Aus (Perth) 2006-07. T20 HS 2*. T20 BB 4-14.

NQNOFFKE, A.A. – *see MIDDLESEX*.

D.A.Burton left the staff without making a County 1st XI appearance in 2007.

ESSEX RELEASED/RETIRED (continued from p 29)

NQNEL, Andre (Dr E.G.Jansen S, Boksburg), b Germiston, Transvaal, South Africa 15 Jul 1977. 6'4". RHB, RFM. Easterns 1996-97 to 2003-04. Northamptonshire 2003; cap 2003. Titans 2004-05. Essex 2005 (one match). **Tests** (SA): 34 (2001-02 to 2007-08); HS 34 v WI (Port Elizabeth) 2007-08; BB 6-32 (10-88 match) v WI (Bridgetown) 2004-05. **LOI** (SA): 70 (2000-01 to 2007-08); HS 30* v NZ (Port Elizabeth) 2007-08; BB 5-45 v B (Providence, Guyana) 2006-07. F-c Tours (SA): A 2005-06; WI 2000-01, 2004-05; NZ 2003-04; P 2003-04, 2007-08; SL 2006; Z 2001-02, 2007-08; Ireland/Scotland 1999 (SA Acad). HS 44 Easterns v FS (Benoni) 2000-01. UK/CC HS 42 Nh v Glamorgan (Cardiff) 2003. Ex HS 10 v Leics (Leicester) 2007. BB 6-25 Easterns v Gauteng (Johannesburg) 2001-02. UK/CC BB 5-47 Nh v Glos (Gloucester) 2003. BB 3-62 v Northants (Northampton) 2007. LO HS 30* (*see LOI*). LO BB 6-27 Easterns v GW (Benoni) 2000-01. IT20 HS 0*. IT20 BB 2-19. T20 HS 12. T20 BB 2-19.

A.Flower and S.D.Thomas left the staff without making a County 1st XI appearance in 2007.

GLOUCESTERSHIRE 2007

RESULTS SUMMARY

	Place	Won	Lost	Tied	Drew	No Result
LV County Championship (2nd Division)	7th	3	5		8	
All First-Class Matches		3	5		8	
Friends Provident Trophy (South Conference)	3rd	6	2			1
NatWest Pro40 League (1st Division)	6th	2	4			2
Twenty/20 Cup (Midlands/West Wales Division) Finalist	6	3			2	

LV COUNTY CHAMPIONSHIP AVERAGES
BATTING AND FIELDING

Cap		M	I	NO	HS	Runs	Avge	100	50	Ct/St
2007	M.J.North	5	10	–	109	565	56.50	3	2	4
2006	H.J.H.Marshall	13	21	1	123	817	40.85	3	3	9
2002	C.M.Spearman	11	17	–	110	688	40.47	2	3	15
2004	A.P.R.Gidman	16	27	4	130	912	39.65	3	4	9
2001	C.G.Taylor	15	23	4	112*	733	38.57	3	2	13
2005	G.P.Hodnett	15	25	1	168	886	36.91	2	6	8
2005	Kadeer Ali	16	28	1	140	903	33.44	2	4	8
2004	S.J.Adshead	13	18	1	99	447	26.29	–	3	28/2
2004	M.A.Hardinges	9	15	1	104	335	23.92	1	1	6
2007	A.A.Noffke	3	5	–	61	109	21.80	–	1	1
2006	D.O.Brown	3	6	–	43	92	15.33	–	–	2
1998	J.Lewis	8†	8	1	42*	91	13.00	–	–	2
2004	I.D.Fisher	3	6	–	41	67	11.16	–	–	2
2007	A.J.Ireland	3	5	3	10*	21	10.50	–	–	2
2005	S.P.Kirby	11	13	1	37	119	9.91	–	–	1
2005	C.G.Greenidge	8	11	1	27	95	9.50	–	–	3
2006	V.Banerjee	11	15	10	11*	46	9.20	–	–	3
2005	S.D.Snell	4	8	–	12	57	7.12	–	–	8
2007	B.M.Edmondson	5	6	2	18	28	7.00	–	–	2

Also batted: W.D.Rudge (1 match – cap 2005) 0, 3* (1 ct); T.P.Stayt (3 – cap 2007) 0, 6, 3* (2 ct); J.G.Thompson (1 – cap 2007) 11, 21.

BOWLING

	O	M	R	W	Avge	Best	5wI	10wM
A.A.Noffke	124.4	34	335	15	22.33	6-68	1	–
S.P.Kirby	312.4	73	961	41	23.43	5-41	3	1
C.G.Greenidge	183	28	752	28	26.85	5-54	1	–
C.G.Taylor	91	13	331	10	33.10	4-52	–	–
J.Lewis	150.1	33	472	12	39.33	5-41	1	–
V.Banerjee	348.5	57	1178	26	45.30	4-38	–	–
M.A.Hardinges	215	45	822	16	51.37	3-59	–	–
Also bowled:								
M.J.North	130	16	359	9	39.88	3-53		
A.J.Ireland	90	15	332	7	47.42	3-39		
B.M.Edmondson	103	12	446	9	49.55	4-50		
A.P.R.Gidman	152	25	548	8	68.50	1- 4		

D.O.Brown 38-8-140-2; I.D.Fisher 55-13-153-2; G.P.Hodnett 2.3-0-10-0; H.J.H.Marshall 19-1-81-2; W.D.Rudge 12-2-40-0; T.P.Stayt 59-9-218-4.

Gloucestershire played no fixtures outside the County Championship in 2007. The First-Class Averages (pp 140–158) give the records of their players in all first-class county matches, with the exception of A.P.R.Gidman, whose full county figures are as above.

Gloucestershire award caps on first-class debut.

†Full substitute in one match for C.G.Greenidge.

GLOUCESTERSHIRE RECORDS

FIRST-CLASS CRICKET

Highest Total	For 695-9d		v	Middlesex	Gloucester	2004
	V 774-7d		by	Australians	Bristol	1948
Lowest Total	For 17		v	Australians	Cheltenham	1896
	V 12		by	Northants	Gloucester	1907
Highest Innings	For 341	C.M.Spearman	v	Middlesex	Gloucester	2004
	V 319	C.J.L.Rogers	for	Northants	Northampton	2006

Highest Partnership for each Wicket

1st	395	D.M.Young/R.B.Nicholls	v	Oxford U	Oxford	1962
2nd	256	C.T.M.Pugh/T.W.Graveney	v	Derbyshire	Chesterfield	1960
3rd	336	W.R.Hammond/B.H.Lyon	v	Leics	Leicester	1933
4th	321	W.R.Hammond/W.L.Neale	v	Leics	Gloucester	1937
5th	261	W.G.Grace/W.O.Moberley	v	Yorkshire	Cheltenham	1876
6th	320	G.L.Jessop/J.H.Board	v	Sussex	Hove	1903
7th	248	W.G.Grace/E.L.Thomas	v	Sussex	Hove	1896
8th	239	W.R.Hammond/A.E.Wilson	v	Lancashire	Bristol	1938
9th	193	W.G.Grace/S.A.P.Kitcat	v	Sussex	Bristol	1896
10th	131	W.R.Gouldsworthy/J.G.Bessant	v	Somerset	Bristol	1923

Best Bowling	For	10-40	E.G.Dennett	v	Essex	Bristol	1906
(Innings)	V	10-66	A.A.Mailey	for	Australians	Cheltenham	1921
		10-66	K.Smales	for	Notts	Stroud	1956
Best Bowling	For	17-56	C.W.L.Parker	v	Essex	Gloucester	1925
(Match)	V	15-87	A.J.Conway	for	Worcs	Moreton-in-M	1914

Most Runs – Season	2860	W.R.Hammond	(av 69.75)		1933
Most Runs – Career	33664	W.R.Hammond	(av 57.05)		1920-51
Most 100s – Season	13	W.R.Hammond			1938
Most 100s – Career	113	W.R.Hammond			1920-51
Most Wkts – Season	222	T.W.J.Goddard	(av 16.80)		1937
	222	T.W.J.Goddard	(av 16.37)		1947
Most Wkts – Career	3170	C.W.L.Parker	(av 19.43)		1903-35
Most Career W-K Dismissals	1054	R.C.Russell	(950 ct; 104 st)		1981-2004
Most Career Catches in the Field	719	C.A.Milton			1948-74

LIMITED-OVERS CRICKET

Highest Total	FPT	401-7		v	Bucks	Wing	2003
	P40	344-6		v	Northants	Cheltenham	2001
	T20	227-4		v	Somerset	Bristol	2006
Lowest Total	FPT	82		v	Notts	Bristol	1987
	P40	49		v	Middlesex	Bristol	1978
	T20	128		v	Glamorgan	Cardiff	2005
Highest Innings	FPT	177	A.J.Wright	v	Scotland	Bristol	1997
	P40	153	C.M.Spearman	v	Warwicks	Gloucester	2003
	T20	100*	I.J.Harvey	v	Warwicks	Birmingham	2003
Best Bowling	FPT	6-21	C.A.Walsh	v	Kent	Bristol	1990
		6-21	C.A.Walsh	v	Cheshire	Bristol	1992
	P40	6-52	J.N.Shepherd	v	Kent	Bristol	1983
	T20	4-22	I.D.Fisher	v	Somerset	Bristol	2004

43

HAMPSHIRE

Formation of Present Club: 12 August 1863
Inaugural First-Class Match: 1864
Colours: Blue, Gold and White
Badge: Tudor Rose and Crown
County Champions: (2) 1961, 1973
Gillette/NatWest/C&G/FP Trophy Winners: (2) 1991, 2005
Benson and Hedges Cup Winners: (2) 1988, 1992
Pro 40/National League (Div 1) Winners: (0); best – 3rd 2004
Sunday League Winners: (3) 1975, 1978, 1986
Twenty20 Cup Winners: (0) – best Quarter-Finalist 2004

Chairman and CEO: Rod Bransgrove, The Rose Bowl, Botley Road, West End, Southampton SO30 3XH • Tel: 023 8047 2002 • Fax: 023 8047 2122 • Email: enquiries@rosebowlplc.com • Webs: www.rosebowlplc.com

Cricket Secretary and Director of Rose Bowl Plc: T.M.Tremlett. **First XI Manager/Coach**: V.P.Terry. **Captain**: S.K.Warne. **Vice-Captain**: tba. **Overseas Players**: S.E.Bond, S.K.Warne and S.R.Watson. **2008 Beneficiary**: J.P.Crawley. **Head Groundsman**: Nigel Gray. **Scorer**: A.E. (Tony) Weld. ‡ New registration. ᴺᑫ Not qualified for England.

ADAMS, James Henry Kenneth (Sherborne S; University C, London; Loughborough U), b Winchester 23 Sep 1980. 6'2". LHB, LM. British U 2002-04. Hampshire debut 2002; cap 2006. Loughborough UCCE 2003-04 – scoring 107 v Somerset (Taunton) on debut. Dorset 1998. 1000 runs (1): 1173 (2006). HS 262* v Notts (Nottingham) 2006. BB 2-16 v Durham (Chester-le-St) 2004. LO HS 40 v Glamorgan (Southampton) 2004 (NL). LO BB 1-34 v Essex (Chelmsford) 2007 (FPT). T20 HS 17*.

BALCOMBE, David John (St John's S, Leatherhead; St Hild & St Bede C, Durham), b City of London 24 Dec 1984. 6'4". RHB, RFM. Durham UCCE 2005-07. British U 2006. Hampshire 2007. HS 73 DU v Leics (Leicester) 2005. H HS 29 v Kent (Southampton) 2007. BB 5-112 DU v Durham (Durham) 2005. H BB 3-58 v Yorks (Leeds) 2007. LO HS 2 and BB – v Lancs (Manchester) 2007 (P40). T20 HS 3. T20 BB – .

BENHAM, Christopher Charles (Yately CS; Loughborough U), b Frimley, Surrey 24 Mar 1983. 6'1". RHB, RM/OB. Loughborough UCCE 2004. Hampshire debut 2004. HS 95 v Warwks (Southampton) 2006. LO HS 158 v Glamorgan (Southampton) 2006. T20 HS 59.

‡ᴺᑫBOND, Shane Edward (Papanui HS; Lincoln U), b Christchurch, NZ 7 Jun 1975. 6'2". RHB, RF. Canterbury 1996-97 to 2006-07. Warwickshire 2002. **Tests** (NZ): 17 (2001-02 to 2007-08); HS 41* v Z (Harare) 2005; BB 6-51 v Z (Bulawayo) 2005. **LOI** (NZ): 67 (2001-02 to 2006-07); HS 31* v I (Auckland) 2002-03; BB 6-19 v I (Bulawayo) 2005. F-c Tours (NZ): E 2004; A 2001-02; SA 2005-06, 2007-08; WI 2002; SL 2003; Z 2005-06. HS 100 Canterbury v ND (Christchurch) 2004-05. BB 6-51 (*see Tests*). CC HS 29* and BB 5-64 Wa v Somerset (Taunton) 2002. LO HS 40 Canterbury v Wellington (Christchurch) 2002-03. LO BB 6-19 (*see LOI*). IT20 HS 19. IT20 BB 2-12. T20 HS 28. T20 BB 2-12.

BROWN, Michael James (Queen Elizabeth GS, Blackburn; Collingwood C, Durham U), b Burnley, Lancs 9 Feb 1980. 6'0". Elder brother of D.O.Brown (*see GLOUCESTERSHIRE*). RHB, OB. Middlesex 1999-2003. Durham UCCE 2001-02. British U 2001-02. Hampshire debut 2004; cap 2007. 1000 runs (1): 1078 (2007). HS 133 v LU (Southampton) 2006. CC HS 126* v Durham (Chester-le-St) 2007. LO HS 76 v Glamorgan (Southampton) 2006 (CGT). T20 HS 35.

BURROWS, Thomas George (Reading GS; Southampton Solent U), b Wokingham, Berkshire 5 May 1985. 5'8". RHB, WK. Debut (Hampshire) 2005. Berkshire 2001-03. HS 42 v Kent (Canterbury) 2005 – on debut. LO HS 16 v West Indies A (Southampton) 2006. T20 HS – .

CARBERRY, Michael Alexander (St John Rigby Catholic C), b Croydon, Surrey 29 Sep 1980. 6'0". LHB, OB. Surrey 2001-02. Kent 2003-05. Hampshire debut/cap 2006. F-c Tour (Eng A): B 2006-07. 1000 runs (1): 1067 (2007). HS 192* v Warwks (Southampton) 2007. BB 2-85 v Durham (Chester-le-St) 2006. LO HS 88 v Surrey (Croydon) 2006 (CGT). LO BB (K) 1-21 (NL). T20 HS 90.

CRAWLEY, John Paul (Manchester GS; Trinity C, Cambridge), b Maldon, Essex 21 Sep 1971. Younger brother of M.A.Crawley (Oxford U, Lancs and Notts 1987-94) and P.M.Crawley (Cambridge U 1992). 6'1". RHB, RM, occ WK. Lancashire 1990-2001; cap 1994; captain 1999-2001. Cambridge U 1991-93; blue 1991-92-93; captain 1992-93. Hampshire debut/cap 2002; captain 2003; benefit 2007. YC 1994. **Tests**: 37 (1994 to 2002-03); HS 156* v SL (Oval) 1998. **LOI**: 13 (1994-95 to 1998-99); HS 73 v Z (Harare) 1996-97. F-c Tours: A 1994-95, 1998-99, 2002-03; SA 1993-94 (Eng A), 1995-96; WI 1995-96 (La), 1997-98, 2000-01 (Eng A); NZ 1996-97; Z 1996-97. 1000 runs (10); most – 1851 (1998). HS 311* v Notts (Southampton) 2005. BB 1-7 v Surrey (Oval) 2005. LO HS 114 La v Notts (Manchester) 1995 (BHC). T20 HS 23.

DAWSON, Liam Andrew (John Bentley S, Calne), b Swindon, Wilts 1 Mar 1990. 5'8". RHB, SLA. Debut (Hampshire) 2007. Wiltshire 2006-07. HS – v Yorks (Leeds) 2007 – only f-c match. LO HS 32 v Northants (Northampton) 2007 (P40). LO BB – .

NQ**ERVINE, Sean** Michael (Lomagundi C, Chinhoyi), b Harare, Zimbabwe 6 Dec 1982. Elder brother of C.R.Ervine (Midlands 2003-04 to 2004-05); son of R.M.Ervine (Rhodesia 1977-78); grandson of M.A.Den (Rhodesia 1935-36); nephew of N.B.Ervine (Rhodesia 1977-78) and G.M.Den (Rhodesia and Eastern Province 1963-64 to 1969-70). Irish passport. 6'2". LHB, RM. CFX Academy 2000-01 to 2001. Midlands 2001-02 to 2003-04. Hampshire debut/cap 2005 (Kolpak registration). Western Australia 2006-07. **Tests** (Z): 5 (2003 to 2003-04); HS 86 v B (Harare) 2003-04; BB 4-146 v A (Perth) 2003-04. **LOI** (Z): 42 (2001-02 to 2003-04); HS 100 v I (Adelaide) 2003-04; BB 3-29 v P (Sharjah) 2001-02. F-c Tours: E 2003; A 2003-04. HS 126 Midlands v Manicaland (Mutare) 2002-03. H HS 103* v Lancs (Manchester) 2007. BB 6-82 Midlands v Mashonaland (Kwekwe) 2002-03. H BB 5-60 v Glamorgan (Cardiff) 2005. LO HS 134* WA v S Aus (Adelaide) 2007-08. LO BB 5-50 v Glamorgan (Cardiff) 2005 (CGT). T20 HS 56*. T20 BB 3-18.

GRIFFITHS, David Andrew (Sandown HS, IOW), b Newport, IOW 10 Sep 1985. 6'1". LHB, RFM. Debut (Hampshire) 2006. HS 31* v Surrey (Southampton) 2007. BB 4-46 v Durham (Chester-le-St) 2007 – on CC debut. T20 HS 4*. T20 BB 3-13.

‡**HOWELL, Benny** Alexander Cameron (Oratory S), b Bridouc, France 5 Oct 1988. RHB, RM. Awaiting f-c debut. Hampshire 2nd XI 2005-07. Berkshire 2007.

LAMB, Gregory Arthur (Lomagundi C, Chinhoyi; Guildford C, Surrey), b Harare, Zimbabwe 4 Mar 1980. 5'11". RHB, RM/OB. Debut (ZCU President's XI) 1998-99. ZC/CFX Academy 1998-99 to 1999-00. Mashonaland 2000-01. Hampshire debut 2004 – no f-c appearances 2007. F-c Tour (Zim A): SL 1999-00. HS 100* CFX Academy v Manicaland (Mutare) 1999-00. H HS 94 v Derbys (Derby) 2004 – on UK debut. BB 7-73 CFX Academy v Midlands (Kwekwe) 1999-00. H BB 2-30 v Middlesex (Southgate) 2005. LO HS 100* v Northants (Southampton) 2005 (NL). LO BB 4-38 v Yorks (Leeds) 2006 (P40). T20 HS 67. T20 BB 4-28.

LATOUF, Kevin John (Millfield S; Barton Peveril C), b Pretoria, South Africa 7 Sep 1985. 5'10". RHB, RM. Debut (Hampshire) 2006. No 1st XI appearances 2007. HS 29 v LU (Southampton) 2006 – on debut. Awaiting CC debut. LO HS 25 v Surrey (Oval) 2005 (CGT) on 1st XI debut.

LUMB, Michael John (St Stithians C, Johannesburg), b Johannesburg, South Africa 12 Feb 1980. Son of R.G.Lumb (Yorkshire 1970-84); nephew of A.J.S.Smith (SAU and Natal 1972-73 to 1983-84). 6'0". LHB, RM. Yorkshire 2000-06; ECB qualified and CC debut 2001; cap 2003. Hampshire debut 2007. F-c Tour (Eng A): I 2003-04. 1000 runs (1): 1038 (2003). HS 144 Y v Middlesex (Southgate) 2006. H HS 89 v Kent (Southampton) 2007. BB 2-10 Y v Kent (Canterbury) 2001. H BB – . LO HS 108 v Sussex (Hove) 2007 (P40). T20 HS 84*. T20 BB 3-32.

MASCARENHAS, Adrian Dimitri (Trinity C, Perth, Australia), b Hammersmith, London 30 Oct 1977. 6'2". Resident in Australia 1979-96. RHB, RMF. Debut (Hampshire) 1996, taking 6-88 v Glamorgan (Southampton); took 16 wickets in first two CC matches; cap 1998; benefit 2007. Dorset 1996. **LOI**: 10 (2007 to 2007-08); HS 52 v I (Bristol) 2007; hit sixes off five successive balls from Yuvraj Singh v I (Oval) 2007; BB 3-23 v I (Lord's) 2007. HS 131 v Kent (Canterbury) 2006. 50 wkts (1): 56 (2004). BB 6-25 v Derbys (Southampton) 2004. LO HS 79 v Worcs (Southampton) 1999 (NL) and 79 v Kent (Canterbury) 2004 (NL). LO BB 5-27 v Glos (Southampton) 2002 (NL). IT20 HS 18*. IT20 BB 3-18. T20 HS 52. T20 BB 5-14.

‡**MORRIS, Richard** Kyle (Bradfield C; Loughborough U), b Newbury, Berkshire 26 Sep 1987. Younger brother of J.C.Morris (Durham UCCE and MCC 2005-07). 6'1". RHB, RMF. Loughborough UCCE 2006. Berkshire 2004. Hampshire 2nd XI 2005-07. HS 8 LU v Essex (Chelmsford) 2006 – on debut. BB 2-58 LU v Hants (Southampton) 2006.

PIETERSEN, Kevin Peter (Maritzburg C; Natal U), b Pietermaritzburg, South Africa 27 Jun 1980. British passport (English mother) – qualified for England Oct 2004. 6'4". RHB, OB. MBE 2005. *Wisden* 2005. Natal/KwaZulu-Natal 1997-98 to 1999-00. Nottinghamshire 2001-04; cap 2002. MCC 2004. Hampshire debut/cap 2005 (no f-c appearances 2006-07). **ECB central contract 2007-08. Tests**: 33 (2005 to 2007-08); HS 226 v WI (Leeds) 2007. BB 1-11. **LOI**: 69 (2004-05 to 2007-08); HS 116 v SA (Pretoria) 2004-05; scored 454 runs (av 151.33) in 7-match series, including fastest England 100 off 69 balls (E London), v SA 2004-05; BB 1-4. F-c Tours: A 2006-07; I 2003-04 (Eng A), 2005-06; P 2005-06; SL 2007-08. 1000 runs (3): most – 1546 (2003). HS 254* Nt v Middlesex (Nottingham) 2002. H HS 126 v Glamorgan (Southampton) 2005. BB 4-31 Nt v DU (Nottingham) 2003. CC BB 3-72 Nt v Hants (Nottingham) 2004. H BB – . LO HS 147 Nt v Somerset (Taunton) 2002 (NL). LO BB 3-14 Nt v Middlesex (Lord's 2004 (NL). IT20 HS 79. T20 HS 79. T20 BB 2-9.

POTHAS, Nic (King Edward VII S; Rand Afrikaans U), b Johannesburg 18 Nov 1973. ECB qualified – EU (Greek) passport. 6'3". RHB, WK, occ RM. Transvaal 1993-94 to 1996-97. Gauteng 1997-98 to 2000-01. Hampshire debut 2002; cap 2003. **LOI** (SA): 3 (2000-01); HS 24 v P (Singapore) 2000 – on debut. F-c Tours (SA): E 1996 (SA A); WI 2000 (SA A); SL 1998. HS 165 Gauteng v KZ-Natal (Johannesburg) 1998-99. H HS 146* v Worcs (Worcester) 2003. BB 1-16 v Middlesex (Lord's) 2006. Held 7 catches in an innings v Lancs (Manchester) 2006. LO HS 114* v Glamorgan (Cardiff) 2005 (CGT). T20 HS 59.

TAYLOR, Billy Victor (Bitterne Park S, Southampton), b Southampton, Hants 11 Jan 1977. Younger brother of J.L.Taylor (Wiltshire 1998 to 2002). 6'3". LHB, RMF. Sussex 1999-2003. Hampshire debut 2004; cap 2006. No f-c appearances 2007. Wiltshire 1996-98. HS 40 v Essex (Southampton) 2008. BB 6-32 v Middlesex (Southampton) 2006 (inc hat-trick). LO HS 21* Sx v Notts (Cleethorpes) 1999 (NL). LO BB 5-28 Sx v Middlesex (Lord's) 2002 (BHC). T20 HS 12*. T20 BB 2-9.

TOMLINSON, James Andrew (Harrow Way S, Andover; Cardiff U), b Winchester 12 Jun 1982. 6'1". LHB, LMF. British U 2002-03. Hampshire debut 2002. Wiltshire 2001. HS 23 v I (Southampton) 2002. CC HS 12* v Derbys (Derby) 2004. BB 6-63 v Derbys (Derby) 2003. LO HS 6 (NL). LO BB 4-47 v Glamorgan (Southampton) 2006 (CGT). T20 HS 5. T20 BB 1-20.

TREMLETT, Christopher Timothy (Thornden S, Chandler's Ford; Taunton's C, Southampton), b Southampton 2 Sep 1981. Son of T.M.Tremlett (Hampshire 1976-91); grandson of M.F.Tremlett (Somerset, CD and England 1947-60). 6'7". RHB, RMF. Debut (Hampshire) v NZ A (Portsmouth) 2000, taking wicket of M.H.Richardson with his first ball; cap 2004. Tests: 3 (2007); HS 25* v I (Oval) 2007; BB 3-12 v I (Nottingham) 2007. **LOI:** 8 (2005 to 2007); HS 19* v I (Birmingham) 2007; BB 4-32 v B (Nottingham) 2005 – on debut (hat-trick ball hit stump without dislodging bails). F-c Tour (ECB Acad): SL 2002-03. HS 64 v Glos (Southampton) 2005. BB 6-44 v Sussex (Hove) 2005. Hat-trick v Notts (Nottingham) 2005. LO HS 38* v Cheshire (Alderley Edge) 2004 (CGT). LO BB 4-25 v Essex (Southend) 2002 (NL). IT20 HS – . IT20 BB 2-45.T20 HS 13. T20 BB 3-12.

[NQ]**WARNE, Shane** Keith (Hampton HS; Mentone GS), b Upper Ferntree Gully, Melbourne, Australia 13 Sep 1969. 6'0". RHB, LBG. Victoria 1990-91 to 2006-07; captain 1997-98 to 1998-99. Hampshire 2000, 2004 to date; cap 2000; captain 2004 to date. *Wisden* 1993 (also one of *Five Cricketers of the Century*). **Tests** (A): 144 (1991-92 to 2006-07); HS 99 v NZ (Perth) 2001-02; BB 8-71 v E (Brisbane) 1994-95; hat-trick v E (Melbourne) 1994-95. **LOI** (A): 193 (1992-93 to 2002-03, 11 as captain); HS 55 v SA (Pt Elizabeth) 1993-94; BB 5-33 v WI (Sydney) 1996-97. F-c Tours (A): E 1993, 1997, 2001, 2005; SA 1993-94, 1996-97, 2001-02, 2005-06; WI 1994-95, 1998-99; NZ 1992-93, 1999-00; I 1997-98, 2000-01, 2004-05; P 1994-95, 2002-03 (in SL/Sharjah); SL 1992, 1999, 2003-04; Z 1991-92 (Aus B), 1999-00; B 2005-06. HS 107* v Kent (Canterbury) 2005 – maiden 100 in his 321st innings. 50 wkts (7+2); most – 87 (2005). BB 8-71 (*see Tests*). H BB 7-99 v Middlesex (Southampton) 2006. LO HS 55 (*see LOI*). LO BB 6-42 v Surrey (Croydon) 2006 (CGT). T20 HS 12. T20 BB 1-29.

[NQ]**WATSON, Shane** Robert (Ipswich GS), b Ipswich, Queensland, Australia 17 Jun 1981. 6'0". RHB, RFM. Tasmania 2000-01 to 2003-04. Hampshire 2004-05; cap 2005. Queensland 2004-05 to date. **Tests** (A): 2 (2004-05 to 2005-06); HS 31 v P (Sydney) 2004-05 – on debut; BB 1-25 v WI (Brisbane) 2005-06. **LOI** (A): 62 (2001-02 to 2006-07); HS 79 v I (Kuala Lumpur) 2006-07; BB 4-43 v WI (Kuala Lumpur) 2006-07. F-c Tours (Aus): SA 2001-02 scoring 100* in only innings; I 2004-05; P 2005-06 (Aus A). HS 203* v Warwks (Southampton) 2005. Scored 112* v Somerset (Southampton) 2004 on UK debut. BB 6-32 v Tas v Q (Hobart) 2001-02. H BB 2-33 v Kent (Southampton) 2005. LO HS 132 v Surrey (Oval) 2005 (CGT). LO BB 4-43 A v World XI (Melbourne) 2005-06. IT20 HS 4. IT20 BB 1-19. T20 HS 97*. T20 BB 3-30.

RELEASED/RETIRED
(Having made a County 1st XI appearance in 2007)

BRUCE, James Thomas Anthony (Eton C; St Hild & St Bede C, Durham U), b Hammersmith, London 17 Dec 1979. 6'1". RHB, RMF. Durham UCCE 2001-02. Hampshire 2003-07; cap 2006. Cumberland 2001. HS 32 v Surrey (Oval) 2007. BB 5-43 v Notts (Southampton) 2006. LO HS 19* v Essex (Southampton) 2006 (CGT). LO BB 4-18 v Glos (Southampton) 2006 (CGT). T20 HS 12. T20 BB 3-20.

RELEASED/RETIRED continued on p 60

HAMPSHIRE 2007

RESULTS SUMMARY

	Place	Won	Lost	Tied	Drew	No Result
LV County Championship (1st Division)	5th	5	3		8	
All First-Class Matches		5	3		8	
Friends Provident Trophy (South Conference)	Finalist	7	2	1		1
NatWest Pro40 League (1st Division)	4th	4	3			1
Twenty/20 Cup (South Division)	6th	1	4	1		2

LV COUNTY CHAMPIONSHIP AVERAGES

BATTING AND FIELDING

Cap		M	I	NO	HS	Runs	Avge	100	50	Ct/t
2006	M.A.Carberry	13	24	3	192*	1067	50.80	5	3	2
2003	N.Pothas	15	23	7	126*	750	46.87	1	5	38/6
2007	M.J.Brown	16	29	4	126*	1078	43.12	3	5	14
2006	J.H.K.Adams	11	20	1	110	773	40.68	1	5	10
2002	J.P.Crawley	15	27	5	113*	866	39.36	1	6	4
2004	C.T.Tremlett	6	8	4	62*	150	37.50	–	1	1
1998	A.D.Mascarenhas	10	16	2	90	489	34.92	–	3	2
2005	S.M.Ervine	7	10	2	103*	276	34.50	1	1	5
–	M.J.Lumb	16	25	–	89	775	31.00	–	8	13
–	C.C.Benham	9	14	–	76	312	22.28	–	1	10
2000	S.K.Warne	15	19	–	50	364	19.15	–	1	17
–	D.B.L.Powell	4	6	–	25	63	10.50	–	–	1
–	S.R.Clark	6	9	2	17	71	10.14	–	–	3
–	J.A.Tomlinson	5	4	2	9	19	9.50	–	–	1
–	D.A.Griffiths	5	8	3	31*	42	8.40	–	–	1
2006	J.T.A.Bruce	14	18	7	32	84	7.63	–	–	4
1992	S.D.Udal	5	8	1	17*	34	4.85	–	–	–

Also batted: D.J.Balcombe (2 matches) 29, 25; T.G.Burrows (1) 35 (4 ct). L.A.Dawson (1) did not bat.

BOWLING

	O	M	R	W	Avge	Best	5wI	10wM
D.B.L.Powell	102.3	22	343	15	22.86	4- 8	–	–
S.R.Clark	175.2	32	602	24	25.08	7- 82	1	–
S.K.Warne	438.1	56	1479	50	29.58	6- 83	5	1
J.T.A.Bruce	352.5	71	1199	39	30.74	5- 64	2	–
A.D.Mascarenhas	190	46	481	15	32.06	4- 33	–	–
S.D.Udal	150.1	25	469	14	33.50	4-138	–	–
D.A.Griffiths	100.3	9	411	12	34.25	4- 46	–	–
C.T.Tremlett	161.4	29	559	15	37.26	4- 47	–	–
J.A.Tomlinson	154.4	31	528	13	40.61	5- 78	1	–

Also bowled:

D.J.Balcombe	48.1	9	164	5	32.80	3- 58	–	–
S.M.Ervine	149.5	23	549	8	68.62	2- 48	–	–

J.H.K.Adams 40-8-137-3; M.A.Carberry 30-3-125-2; J.P.Crawley 2-0-22-0; M.J.Lumb 4-0-30-0.

Hampshire played no fixtures outside the County Championship in 2007. The First-Class Averages (pp 140–158) give the records of their players in all first-class county matches, with the exception of D.J.Balcombe, D.B.L.Powell and C.T.Tremlett, whose full county figures are as above, and K.P.Pietersen, whose seven first-class appearances were all for England.

HAMPSHIRE RECORDS

FIRST-CLASS CRICKET

Highest Total	For 714-5d		v	Notts	Southampton	2005
	V 742		by	Surrey	The Oval	1909
Lowest Total	For 15		v	Warwicks	Birmingham	1922
	V 23		by	Yorkshire	Middlesbrough	1965
Highest Innings	For 316	R.H.Moore	v	Warwicks	Bournemouth	1937
	V 303*	G.A.Hick	for	Worcs	Southampton	1997

Highest Partnership for each Wicket

1st	347	V.P.Terry/C.L.Smith	v	Warwicks	Birmingham	1987
2nd	321	G.Brown/E.I.M.Barrett	v	Glos	Southampton	1920
3rd	344	G.Brown/C.P.Mead	v	Yorkshire	Portsmouth	1927
4th	263	R.E.Marshall/D.A.Livingstone	v	Middlesex	Lord's	1970
5th	235	G.Hill/D.F.Walker	v	Sussex	Portsmouth	1937
6th	411	R.M.Poore/E.G.Wynyard	v	Somerset	Taunton	1899
7th	325	G.Brown/C.H.Abercrombie	v	Essex	Leyton	1913
8th	257	N.Pothas/A.J.Bichel	v	Glos	Cheltenham	2005
9th	230	D.A.Livingstone/A.T.Castell	v	Surrey	Southampton	1962
10th	192	H.A.W.Bowell/W.H.Livsey	v	Worcs	Bournemouth	1921

Best Bowling	For	9- 25	R.M.H.Cottam	v	Lancashire	Manchester	1965
(Innings)	V	10- 46	W.Hickton	for	Lancashire	Manchester	1870
Best Bowling	For	16- 88	J.A.Newman	v	Somerset	Weston-s-Mare	1927
(Match)	V	17-103	W.Mycroft	v	Derbyshire	Southampton	1876

Most Runs – Season	2854	C.P.Mead	(av 79.27)		1928
Most Runs – Career	48892	C.P.Mead	(av 48.84)		1905-36
Most 100s – Season	12	C.P.Mead			1928
Most 100s – Career	138	C.P.Mead			1905-36
Most Wkts – Season	190	A.S.Kennedy	(av 15.61)		1922
Most Wkts – Career	2669	D.Shackleton	(av 18.23)		1948-69
Most Career W-K Dismissals	700	R.J.Parks	(630 ct/70 st)		1980-92
Most Career Catches in the Field	629	C.P.Mead			1905-36

LIMITED-OVERS CRICKET

Highest Total	FPT	371-4		v	Glamorgan	Southampton	1975
	P40	353-8		v	Middlesex	Lord's	2005
	T20	225-2		v	Middlesex	Southampton	2006
Lowest Total	FPT	75		v	Essex	Chelmsford	2007
	P40	43		v	Essex	Basingstoke	1972
	T20	95		v	Essex	Chelmsford	2004
Highest Innings	FPT	177	C.G.Greenidge	v	Glamorgan	Southampton	1975
	P40	172	C.G.Greenidge	v	Surrey	Southampton	1987
	T20	97*	S.R.Watson	v	Kent	Southampton	2004
Best Bowling	FPT	7-30	P.J.Sainsbury	v	Norfolk	Southampton	1965
	P40	6-20	T.E.Jesty	v	Glamorgan	Cardiff	1975
	T20	5-14	A.D.Mascarenhas	v	Sussex	Hove	2004

KENT

Formation of Present Club: 1 March 1859
Substantial Reorganisation: 6 December 1870
Inaugural First-Class Match: 1864
Colours: Maroon and White
Badge: White Horse on a Red Ground
County Champions: (6) 1906, 1909, 1910, 1913, 1970, 1978
Joint Champions: (1) 1977
Gillette/NatWest/C&G/FP Trophy Winners: (2) 1967, 1974
Benson and Hedges Cup Winners: (3) 1973, 1976, 1978
Pro 40/National League (Div 1) Winners: (1) 2001
Sunday League Winners: (4) 1972, 1973, 1976, 1995
Twenty20 Cup Winners: (1): 2007

Chief Executive: Paul E.Millman, St Lawrence Ground, Canterbury, CT1 3NZ • Tel: 01227 456886 • Fax: 01227 762168 • Email: kent@ecb.co.uk • Web: www.kentccc.com

First XI Coach: G.Ford. **Captain**: R.W.T.Key. **Vice-Captain**: tba. **Overseas Player**: Yasir Arafat. **2008 Beneficiary**: M.J.Walker. **Head Groundsman**: Mike Grantham. **Scorer**: Jack C.Foley. ‡ New registration. ^NQ Not qualified for England.

‡^NQ**AZHAR MAHMOOD** SAGAR (F.G. No. 1 HS, Islamabad), b Rawalpindi, Pakistan 28 Feb 1975. 5'11". RHB, RFM. Islamabad 1993-94 to 1997-98, 2001-02 to 2006-07. United Bank 1995-96 to 1996-97. Rawalpindi 1998-99 to 2004-05. MCC 2001. PIA 2001-02. Surrey 2002-07; cap 2004. Habib Bank 2006-07. Joins Kent 2008 as British passport holder. **Tests** (P): 21 (1997-98 to 2001); HS 136 v SA (Johannesburg) 1997-98; BB 4-50 v E (Lord's) 2001. Scored 128* and 50* v SA (Rawalpindi) 1997-98 on debut. **LOI** (P): 143 (1996-97 to 2006-07); HS 67 v I (Adelaide) 1999-00; BB 6-18 v WI (Sharjah) 1999-00. F-c Tours (P): E 1997 (Pak A), 2001; A 1999-00; SA 1997-98; I 1998-99; SL 2000; Z 1997-98. HS 204* Sy v Middlesex (Oval) 2005. 50 wkts (0+1): 59 (1996-97). BB 8-61 Sy v Lancs (Oval) 2002. LO HS 101* Sy v Glamorgan (Oval) 2006 (CGT). LO BB 6-18 (*see LOI*). T20 HS 65*. T20 BB 4-20.

BLAKE, Alexander James (Hayes SS), b Farnborough 25 Jan 1989. 6'3". LHB, RMF. Kent (l-o) 2007 – awaiting f-c debut. LO HS 11* v Surrey (Canterbury) 2007 (P40). LO BB 1-25 v Glamorgan (Cardiff) 2007 (P40).

CHAMBERS, Dominic James (St Edmunds S; Canterbury C), b Canterbury 6 Jan 1984. 6'0". RHB, RMF. Debut (Kent) 2006. Awaiting CC debut – no f-c appearance 2007. HS 12 v CU (Cambridge) 2006.

COOK, Simon James (Matthew Arnold S), b Oxford 15 Jan 1977. 6'4". RHB, RMF. Middlesex 1999-2004; cap 2003. Kent debut 2005; cap 2007. HS 93* M v Notts (Lord's) 2001. K HS 71 v Yorks (Leeds) 2006. BB 8-63 M v Northants (Southend) 2002. K BB 6-35 v Sussex (Canterbury) 2007. LO HS 67* M v Durham (Lord's) 2003 (NL). LO BB 6-37 M v Leics (Leicester) 2004 (NL). T20 HS 25*. T20 BB 3-14.

DENLY, Joseph Liam (Chaucer TC), b Canterbury 16 Mar 1986. 6'0". RHB, LB. Debut (Kent) 2004. 1000 runs (1): 1003 (2007). HS 115* v Hants (Canterbury) 2007 – carried bat through innings of 199. BB 2-13 v Surrey (Canterbury) 2007. LO HS 102* v Ireland (Belfast) 2007 (FPT). T20 HS 63*.

NQDEXTER, Neil John (Northwood HS; Varsity C; U of South Africa), b Johannesburg, South Africa 21 Aug 1984. 6'0". RHB, RM. Debut (Kent) 2005. HS 131* v Notts (Canterbury) 2006. BB 2-40 v Lancs (Manchester) 2006. LO HS 135* v Glamorgan (Cardiff) 2006 (CGT). LO BB 3-17 v Leics (Canterbury) 2006 (P40). T20 HS 36. T20 BB 3-27.

DIXEY, Paul Garrod (King's S, Canterbury; Hatfield C, Durham), b Canterbury 2 Nov 1987. 5'8". RHB, WK. Debut (Kent) 2005; awaiting CC debut – no f-c appearances 2007. MCC 2007. Durham UCCE 2007. HS 25 DU v Notts (Durham) 2007. K HS 24 v Bangladesh A (Canterbury) 2005 – on debut. LO HS – v Sri Lanka A (Canterbury) 2007.

GOODMAN, James Elliot (St Olave's GS), b Farnborough 19 Nov 1990. 5'10". RHB, RM. Kent l-o debut 2007 – awaiting f-c debut. Kent 2nd XI 2006-07. LO HS – v Sri Lanka A (Canterbury) 2007.

ILES, James Alexander (Maidstone GS), b Chatham 11 Feb 1990. 6'4". RHB, RMF. Debut (Kent) 2006; no f-c appearances 2007; awaiting CC debut. HS – and BB 1-27 v CU (Cambridge) 2006. LO HS – and BB 1-27 v Sri Lanka A (Canterbury) 2007.

JONES, Geraint Owen (Harristown State HS, Toowoomba and MacGregor State HS, Brisbane, Australia), b Kundiawa, Papua New Guinea 14 Jul 1976. Welsh parents. 5'10". RHB, WK. Debut (Kent) 2001; cap 2003. MBE 2005. **Tests**: 34 (2003-04 to 2006-07); HS 100 v NZ (Leeds) 2004. **LOI**: 49 (2004 to 2006); HS 80 v Z (Bulawayo) 2004-05. F-c Tours: A 2006-07; SA 2004-05; WI 2003-04; I 2005-06; P 2005-06; SL 2003-04. HS 108* v Essex (Chelmsford) 2003. LO HS 80 (see LOI). IT20 HS 19. T20 HS 24*.

JOSEPH, Robert ('Robbie') Hartman (Sutton Vallence S; St Mary's C, Twickenham), b Antigua 20 Jan 1982. Resided in England since 1997. 6'1". RHB, RFM. Debut (First-Class Counties XI v NZ) 2000. Kent debut 2004. HS 36* v Sussex (Hove) 2007. BB 5-19 v Bangladesh A (Canterbury) 2005. CC BB 5-57 v Sussex (Canterbury) 2006. LO HS 15 v (Canterbury) 2005 (NL). LO BB 3-50 v Ireland (Belfast) 2007 (FPT).

NQKEMP, Justin Miles (Queens C; Port Elizabeth U), b Queenstown, Cape Province, South Africa 2 Oct 1977. Son of J.W.Kemp (Border 1975-76 to 1976-77); grandson of J.M.Kemp (Border 1947-48). RHB, RFM. E Province 1996-97 to 2002-03. Worcestershire 2003. Northerns 2003-04 to 2004-05. Titans 2004-05 to 2006-07. Kent 2005-06 (Kolpak registration 2008); cap 2006. Cape Cobras 2007-08. **Tests** (SA): 4 (2000-01 to 2005-06); HS 55 v A (Perth) 2005-06; BB 3-33 v SL (Pretoria) 2000-01 on debut. **LOI** (SA): 79 (2000-01 to 2007-08); HS 100* v I (Cape Town) 2006-07; BB 3-20 v I (Durban) 2001-02. F-c Tours (SA): A 2002-03 (SA A), 2005-06; WI 2000 (SA A), 2000-01; Z 1998-99 (SA Acad). HS 188 EP v North West (Port Elizabeth) 2000-01. CC HS 124* v Yorks (Canterbury) 2006. BB 6-56 EP v Border (Port Elizabeth) 2000-01. CC BB 5-48 Wo v Glamorgan (Cardiff) 2003 – on Worcs debut. K BB 3-53 v Middlesex (Lord's) 2005. LO HS 107* Northerns v GW (Centurion) 2003-04. LO BB 6-20 EP v FS (Port Elizabeth) 2000-01. IT20 HS 89*. IT20 BB – . T20 HS 89*. T20 BB 3-19.

KEY, Robert William Trevor (Colfe's S), b East Dulwich, London 12 May 1979. 6'1". RHB, RM/OB. Debut (Kent) 1998; cap 2001, captain 2006 to date. Wisden 2004. **Tests**: 15 (2002 to 2004-05); HS 221 v WI (Lord's) 2004. **LOI**: 5 (2003 to 2004); HS 19 v WI (Lord's) 2004. F-c Tours: A 2002-03; SA 1998-99 (Eng A), 2004-05; SL 2002-03 (ECB Acad); Z 1998-99 (Eng A). 1000 runs (5): most – 1896 (2004). HS 221 (see Tests). BB – . K HS 199 v Surrey (Oval) 2004. LO HS 114 v Notts (Nottingham) 2002 (NL). T20 HS 68*.

KHAN, Amjad (Skolenpa Duevej, Denmark), b Copenhagen, Denmark 14 Oct 1980. 6'0". RHB, RFM. Debut (Kent) 2001. Denmark 1998-2000. Qualified for England Dec 2006. Missed 2007 season following reconstructive knee surgery. HS 78 v Middlesex (Lord's) 2003. 50 wkts (2); most – 63 (2002). BB 6-52 v Yorks (Canterbury) 2002. LO HS 65* Denmark v Ireland (Harare) 1999-00. LO BB 4-26 v Leics (Leicester) 2003 (NL). T20 HS 15. T20 BB 3-11.

^{NQ}**McLAREN, Ryan** (Grey C, Bloemfontein; Free State U), b Kimberley, South Africa 9 Feb 1983. 6'4". Son of P.McLaren (GW 1977-78 to 1994-95). Nephew of Keith McLaren (GW 1971-72 to 1984-85). Cousin of A.P.McLaren (GW 1998-99 to date). LHB, RMF. Free State 2003-04 to 2004-05. Eagles 2004-05 to date. Kent debut 2007 (Kolpak registration); cap 2007. HS 140 Eagles v Warriors (Bloemfontein) 2005-06. K HS 54* v Durham (Canterbury) 2007. 50 wkts (1): 54 (2006-07). BB 8-38 Eagles v Cape Cobras (Stellenbosch) 2006-07. K BB 5-24 v Warwks (Canterbury) 2007. LO HS 78* v Somerset (Canterbury) 2007 (P40). LO BB 4-29 v Glamorgan (Canterbury) 2007 (FPT). T20 HS 46*. T20 BB 3-22.

NORTHEAST, Sam Alexander (Harrow S), b Ashford 16 Oct 1989. RHB, OB. Debut (Kent) 2007. HS 5 v Durham (Canterbury) 2007 – on debut. LO HS – v Sri Lanka A (Canterbury) 2007.

PARSONS, Thomas William (Maidstone GS; Rutherford Hall, Loughborough U), b Melbourne, Australia 2 May 1987. 6'3". RHB, RFM. Debut (Loughborough UCCE) 2007. Kent (l-o) 2007 – awaiting county f-c debut. HS 10 and BB 3-70 LU v Worcs (Worcester) 2007 – on debut. LO HS – and BB 2-41 v Sri Lanka A (Canterbury) 2007.

SAGGERS, Martin John (Springwood HS, King's Lynn; Huddersfield U), b King's Lynn, Norfolk 23 May 1972. 6'2". RHB, RMF. Durham 1996-98. Kent debut 1999; cap 2001. MCC 2004. Essex 2007 (on loan). Norfolk 1995-96. **Tests**: 3 (2003-04 to 2004); HS 1 and BB 2-29 v B (Chittagong) 2003-04 on debut. F-c Tour: B 2003-04. HS 64 v Worcs (Canterbury) 2004. 50 wkts (4): most – 83 (2002). BB 7-79 v Durham (Chester-le-St) 2000. LO HS 34* Minor C v Leics (Jesmond) 1996 (BHC). LO BB 5-22 v Glos (Canterbury) 2001 (NL). T20 HS 5. T20 BB 2-14.

STEVENS, Darren Ian (Hinckley C), b Leicester 30 Apr 1976. 5'11". RHB, RM. Leicestershire 1997-2004; cap 2002. MCC 2002. Kent debut/cap 2005. F-c Tour (ECB Acad): SL 2002-03. 1000 (1): 1277 (2005). HS 208 v Glamorgan (Canterbury) 2005. BB 4-36 v Yorks (Canterbury) 2006. LO HS 133 Le v Northumb (Jesmond) 2000 (NWT). LO BB 5-32 v Scotland (Edinburgh) 2005 (NL). T20 HS 69. T20 BB 4-14.

TREDWELL, James Cullum (Southlands Community CS, New Romney), b Ashford 27 Feb 1982. 6'0". LHB, OB. Debut (Kent) 2001; cap 2007. MCC 2004. F-c Tour (Eng A): I 2003-04 (captain). HS.116* v Yorks (Tunbridge Wells) 2007. BB 6-47 v Surrey (Canterbury) 2007. LO HS 88 v Surrey (Oval) 2007. LO BB 4-16 v Scotland (Canterbury) 2005 (NL). T20 HS 34. T20 BB 4-21.

^{NQ}**VAN JAARSVELD, Martin** (Warmbaths S; Pretoria U), b Klerksdorp, South Africa 18 Jun 1974. 6'2". RHB, OB. N Transvaal/Northerns 1994-95 to 2003-04. Northamptonshire 2004. Titans 2004-05 to date. Kent debut/cap 2005 (Kolpak registration) scoring 118 and 111 v Warwicks (Canterbury) – second player after C.W.G.Bassano (Derbyshire) to score two hundreds on a county debut. **Tests** (SA): 9 (2002-03 to 2004-05); HS 73 v WI (Johannesburg) 2003-04. **LOI** (SA): 11 (2002-03 to 2004); HS 45 v E (Birmingham) 2003; BB 1-0. Took wickets with his first and third balls in LOI. F-c Tours (SA): A 2002-03 (SA A); NZ 2003-04; I 2004-05; SL 1998-99 (SA A), 2004; Z 1998-99 (SA Acad). 1000 runs (3+1); most – 1268 (2001-02). HS 262* v Glamorgan (Cardiff) 2005. BB 2-17 v Hants (Southampton) 2007. LO HS 123 NT v EP (Pretoria) 1996-97. LO BB 3-43 v Sri Lanka A (Canterbury) 2007. T20 HS 76*. T20 BB 2-19.

WALKER, Matthew Jonathan (King's S, Rochester), b Gravesend 2 Jan 1974. Grandson of Jack Walker (Kent 1949). 5'8". LHB, RM. Debut (Kent) 1992-93 (Z tour); UK debut 1994; cap 2000; benefit 2008. F-c Tour: Z 1992-93 (K). 1000 runs (3); most 1419 (2006). HS 275* v Somerset (Canterbury) 1996. BB 2-21 v Middlesex (Canterbury) 2004. LO HS 117 v Warwks (Canterbury) 1997 (BHC). LO BB 4-24 v Yorks (Leeds) 2001 (NL). T20 HS 58*.

^{NQ}**YASIR ARAFAT** Satti (Gordon C, Rawalpindi), b Rawalpindi 12 Mar 1982. 5'9½". RHB, RMF. Rawalpindi 1997-98 to 2006-07. Pakistan Reserves 1999-00. KRL 2000-01 to date. National Bank 2005-06. Sussex 2006; cap 2006. Kent debut/cap 2007. Scotland (not f-c) 2004-05. **Tests** (P): 1 (2007-08); HS 44 and BB 5-161 v I (Bangalore) 2007-08 – on debut. **LOI** (P): 7 (1999-00 to 2006-07); HS 27 v SA (Chandigarh) 2006-07; BB 1-28. F-c Tours (P): I 2007-08; SL 2001 (Pak A), 2004-05 (Pak A). HS 122 v Sussex (Canterbury) 2007. 50 wkts (0+4); most – 91 (2001-02). BB 7-102 Rawalpindi v Sialkot (Sialkot) 2001-02. UK BB 5-63 K v Hants (Canterbury) 2007. LO HS 87 Rawalpindi v Bahawalpur (Karachi) 2000-01. LO BB 6-24 Pakistan A v England A (Colombo) 2004-05. IT20 HS 17, IT20 BB 1-31. T20 HS 49. T20 BB 4-21.

RELEASED/RETIRED
(Having made a County 1st XI appearance in 2007)

HALL, A.J. – *see NORTHAMPTONSHIRE.*

MALINGA, Separamadu **Lasith** SWARNAJITH, b Galle, Sri Lanka 28 Aug 1983. 5'8". RHB, RF. Galle 2001-02 to 2003-04. Nondescripts 2004-05 to 2006-07. Kent 2007. **Tests** (SL): 28 (2004 to 2007-08); HS 42* v A (Hobart) 2007-08; BB 5-65 v NZ (Wellington) 2006-07. **LOI** (SL): 44 (2004 to 2007-08); HS 15 v P (Colombo) 2005-06; BB 4-44 v E (Leeds) 2006. F-c Tours (SL): E 2006; A 2004, 2004-05; NZ 2003-04 (SL A), 2004-05, 2006-07; I 2003-04 (SL A), 2005-06; P 2004-05; B 2005-06. HS 42* (*see Tests*). K HS 12 and BB 1-40 v Surrey (Canterbury) 2007 – on Kent debut. BB 6-17 Galle v Police (Colombo) 2003-04. LO HS 23* Nondescripts v Moors (Colombo) 2006-07. LO BB 4-16 SL Emerging Players v India EP (Colombo) 2003-04. IT20 HS 27. IT20 BB 3-43. T20 HS 27. T20 BB 3-30.

^{NQ}**MORKEL, M.** – *see YORKSHIRE.*

PATEL, Minal Mahesh (Dartford GS; Erith TC), b Bombay, India 7 Jul 1970. 5'9". RHB, SLA. Kent 1989-2007; cap 1994; benefit 2004. MCC 1999-00, 2004. Central Districts 2005-06. **Tests**: 2 (1996); HS 27 and BB 1-101 v I (Nottingham) 1996. F-c Tours (Eng A): I 1994-95; B 1999-00 (MCC). HS 87 v Glamorgan (Cardiff) 2005. 50 wkts (4); most – 90 (1994). BB 8-96 v Lancs (Canterbury) 1994. LO HS 27* v Somerset (Canterbury) 2001 (CGT). LO BB 3-20 v Somerset (Taunton) 2006 (P40). T20 HS 8. T20 BB 4-26.

K.J.F.Jones left the staff without making a County 1st XI appearance in 2007.

KENT 2007

RESULTS SUMMARY

	Place	Won	Lost	Tied	Drew	No Result
LV County Championship (1st Division)	7th	3	5		7	1
All First-Class Matches		3	5		7	1
Friends Provident Trophy (South Conference)	4th	5	3			1
NatWest Pro40 League (2nd Division)	5th	5	3			
Twenty/20 Cup (South Division)	Winners	7	2	1		1

LV COUNTY CHAMPIONSHIP AVERAGES

BATTING AND FIELDING

Cap		M	I	NO	HS	Runs	Avge	100	50	Ct/St
–	R.H.Joseph	3	5	4	36*	60	60.00	–	–	2
2001	R.W.T.Key	15	25	3	182	1250	56.81	5	4	4
2005	M.van Jaarsveld	15	23	1	166	1011	45.95	5	3	17
–	N.J.Dexter	8	10	2	86	350	43.75	–	3	6
–	J.L.Denly	15	25	3	115*	902	41.00	2	5	9
2000	M.J.Walker	12	18	–	157	733	40.72	3	2	6
2005	D.I.Stevens	11	17	–	174	628	36.94	2	2	7
2003	G.O.Jones	15	21	3	106*	623	34.61	2	3	42/4
2007	Yasir Arafat	10	13	1	122	369	30.75	2	–	2
2005	A.J.Hall	7	10	1	77	264	29.33	–	2	6
2007	J.C.Tredwell	14	19	2	116*	454	26.70	1	2	11
2007	R.McLaren	15	18	5	54*	272	20.92	–	1	7
2007	S.J.Cook	12	14	5	50*	151	16.77	–	1	4
2001	M.J.Saggers	7	7	1	16	47	7.83	–	–	–

Also batted: S.L.Malinga (4 matches) 0, 12, 1*; S.A.Northeast (1) 5, 0; M.M.Patel (1 – cap 1994) 15, 52 (1 ct).

BOWLING

	O	M	R	W	Avge	Best	5wI	10wM
M.J.Saggers	156.4	36	463	19	24.36	5-43	1	–
R.McLaren	316	58	1079	44	24.52	5-24	1	–
D.I.Stevens	112.5	24	305	12	25.41	3-91	–	–
Yasir Arafat	238.5	44	882	27	32.66	5-63	1	–
S.J.Cook	242.4	58	740	22	33.63	6-35	1	–
J.C.Tredwell	415.3	76	1285	36	35.69	6-47	1	–
A.J.Hall	163	27	610	15	40.66	5-59	1	–

Also bowled:

| M.van Jaarsveld | 20.2 | 4 | 68 | 5 | 13.60 | 2-17 | | |
| J.L.Denly | 67.1 | 15 | 203 | 6 | 33.83 | 2-13 | | |

N.J.Dexter 13-0-72-1; G.O.Jones 0-2-14-0; R.H.Joseph 57-11-233-3; R.W.T.Key 7-0-33-0; S.L.Malinga 40-2-197-2; M.M.Patel 31-4-107-1; M.J.Walker 2-0-10-1.

Kent played no fixtures outside the County Championship in 2007. The First-Class Averages (pp 140–158) give their records in all first-class county matches, with the exception of J.L.Denly and M.J.Saggers, whose full first-class figures for Kent are as above.

KENT RECORDS

FIRST-CLASS CRICKET

Highest Total	For 803-4d		v	Essex	Brentwood	1934
	V 676		by	Australians	Canterbury	1921
Lowest Total	For 18		v	Sussex	Gravesend	1867
	V 16		by	Warwicks	Tonbridge	1913
Highest Innings	For 332	W.H.Ashdown	v	Essex	Brentwood	1934
	V 344	W.G.Grace	for	MCC	Canterbury	1876

Highest Partnership for each Wicket

1st	300	N.R.Taylor/M.R.Benson	v	Derbyshire	Canterbury	1991
2nd	366	S.G.Hinks/N.R.Taylor	v	Middlesex	Canterbury	1990
3rd	323	R.W.T.Key/M.van Jaarsveld	v	Surrey	Tunbridge W	2005
4th	368	P.A.de Silva/G.R.Cowdrey	v	Derbyshire	Maidstone	1995
5th	277	F.E.Woolley/L.E.G.Ames	v	New Zealand	Canterbury	1931
6th	315	P.A.de Silva/M.A.Ealham	v	Notts	Nottingham	1995
7th	248	A.P.Day/E.Humphreys	v	Somerset	Taunton	1908
8th	177	G.O.Jones/Yasir Arafat	v	Warwicks	Canterbury	2007
9th	171	M.A.Ealham/P.A.Strang	v	Notts	Nottingham	1997
10th	235	F.E.Woolley/A.Fielder	v	Worcs	Stourbridge	1909

Best Bowling	For 10- 30	C.Blythe	v	Northants	Northampton	1907
(Innings)	V 10- 48	C.H.G.Bland	for	Sussex	Tonbridge	1899
Best Bowling	For 17- 48	C.Blythe	v	Northants	Northampton	1907
(Match)	V 17-106	T.W.J.Goddard	for	Glos	Bristol	1939

Most Runs – Season	2894	F.E.Woolley	(av 59.06)	1928
Most Runs – Career	47868	F.E.Woolley	(av 41.77)	1906-38
Most 100s – Season	10	F.E.Woolley		1928
	10	F.E.Woolley		1934
Most 100s – Career	122	F.E.Woolley		1906-38
Most Wkts – Season	262	A.P.Freeman	(av 14.74)	1933
Most Wkts – Career	3340	A.P.Freeman	(av 17.64)	1914-36
Most Career W-K Dismissals	1253	F.H.Huish	(901 ct/352 st)	1895-1914
Most Career Catches in the Field	773	F.E.Woolley		1906-38

LIMITED-OVERS CRICKET

Highest Total	FPT	384-6	v	Berkshire	Finchampstead	1994
	P40	327-6	v	Leics	Canterbury	1993
	T20	186-6	v	Essex	Beckenham	2006
Lowest Total	FPT	60	v	Somerset	Taunton	1979
	P40	83	v	Middlesex	Lord's	1984
	T20	91	v	Surrey	The Oval	2006
Highest Innings	FPT	136*	C.L.Hooper	v	Berkshire	Finchampstead	1994
	P40	146	A.Symonds	v	Lancs	Tunbridge Wells	2004
	T20	112	A.Symonds	v	Middlesex	Maidstone	2004
Best Bowling	FPT	8-31	D.L.Underwood	v	Scotland	Edinburgh	1987
	P40	6- 9	R.A.Woolmer	v	Derbyshire	Chesterfield	1979
	T20	4-14	D.I.Stevens	v	Essex	Chelmsford	2007

LANCASHIRE

Formation of Present Club: 12 January 1864
Inaugural First-Class Match: 1865
Colours: Red, Green and Blue
Badge: Red Rose
County Champions (since 1890): (7) 1897, 1904, 1926, 1927, 1928, 1930, 1934
Joint Champions: (1) 1950
Gillette/NatWest/C&G/FP Trophy Winners: (7) 1970, 1971, 1972, 1975, 1990, 1996, 1998
Benson and Hedges Cup Winners: (4) 1984, 1990, 1995, 1996
Pro 40/National League (Div 1) Winners: (1) 1999.
Sunday League Winners: (4) 1969, 1970, 1989, 1998
Twenty20 Cup Winners: (0); best – Finalist 2005

Chief Executive: Jim Cumbes, Old Trafford, Manchester M16 0PX • Tel: 0161 282 4000 • Fax: 0161 282 4100 • Email: enquiries@lccc.co.uk • Web: www.lccc.co.uk

Cricket Manager/First XI Coach: M.Watkinson. **Captain**: S.G.Law. **Vice-Captain**: none. **Overseas Player**: B.J.Hodge. **2008 Beneficiary**: M.B.Loye. **Head Groundsman**: Peter Marron. **Scorer**: Alan West. ‡ New registration. NQ Not qualified for England.

ANDERSON, James Michael (St Theodore RC HS and SFC, Burnley), b Burnley 30 Jul 1982. 6'2". LHB, RFM. Debut (Lancashire) 2002; cap 2003. YC 2003. ECB central contract 2007-08. Tests: 20 (2003 to 2007-08); HS 21* v SA (Lord's) 2003; BB 5-42 v I (Lord's) 2007. LOI: 86 (2002-03 to 2007-08); HS 15 v A (Jaipur) 2006-07; BB 4-23 v I (Southampton) 2004. T20 HS 10. Hat-trick v P (Oval) 2003 – 1st for Eng in 373 LOI. F-c Tours: A 2006-07; SA 2004-05; WI 2003-04, 2005-06 (Eng A) (part); I 2005-06 (part); SL 2003-04, 2007-08. HS 37* v Durham (Manchester) 2005. 50 wkts (2); most – 60 (2005). BB 6-23 v Hants (Southampton) 2002. Hat-trick (Lancs) 2003. LO HS 15 (see LOI). LO BB 4-23 (see LOI). IT20 HS 1*. IT20 BB 2-24. T20 HS 16. T20 BB 2-24.

BROWN, Karl Robert (Hesketh Fletcher HS, Atherton), b Bolton 17 May 1988. 5'10". RHB, RMF. Debut (Lancashire) 2006. Awaiting CC debut. HS 32 v DU (Durham) 2006. BB – . LO HS 1 v Worcs (Manchester) 2007 (FPT).

CHAPPLE, Glen (West Craven HS; Nelson & Colne C), b Skipton, Yorks 23 Jan 1974. 6'1". RHB, RFM. Debut (Lancashire) 1992; cap 1994; benefit 2004. LOI: 1 (2006); HS 14 and BB – v Ireland (Belfast) 2006. F-c Tours (Eng A): A 1996-97; WI 1995-96 (La); I 1994-95. HS 155 v Somerset (Manchester) 2001. Scored 100 off 27 balls in contrived circumstances v Glamorgan (Manchester) 1993. 50 wkts (4); most – 55 (1994). BB 7-53 v Durham (Blackpool) 2007. LO HS 81* v Derbys (Manchester) 2002 (CGT). LO BB 6-18 v Essex (Lord's) 1996 (NWT). T20 HS 55*. T20 BB 2-13.

CHEETHAM, Steven Philip (Bury GS; Holy Cross SFC), b Oldham 5 Sep 1987. 6'5". RHB, RFM. Debut (Lancashire) 2007. Summer contract – awaiting CC debut. HS – and BB 1-44 v Durham U (Durham) 2007.

CHILTON, Mark James (Manchester GS; Durham U), b Sheffield, Yorks 2 Oct 1976. 6'3". RHB, RM. Debut (Lancashire) 1997; cap 2002. Durham U British U 1998. 1000 runs (1): 1154 (2003). HS 131 v Kent (Manchester) 2006. BB 1-1 (twice). LO HS 115 v Surrey (Croydon) 2004 (NL). LO BB 5-26 Brit U v Sussex (Cambridge) 1997 (BHC). T20 HS 38.

CORK, Dominic Gerald (St Joseph's C, Stoke-on-Trent; Newcastle CFE), b Newcastle-under-Lyme, Staffs 7 Aug 1971. 6'2". RHB, RFM. Derbyshire 1990-2003; cap 1993; captain 1998-2003; benefit 2001. Lancashire debut/cap 2004. *Wisden* 1995. PCA 1995. Staffordshire 1989-90. **Tests**: 37 (1995 to 2002); HS 59 v NZ (Auckland) 1996-97; BB 7-43 v WI (Lord's) 1995 – on debut (record England analysis by Test match debutant); hat-trick v WI (Manchester) 1995 – the first in Test history to occur in the opening over of a day's play. **LOI**: 32 (1992 to 2002-03); HS 31* v NZ (Napier) 1996-97; BB 3-27 v WI (Lord's) 1995. F-c Tours: A 1992-93 (Eng A), 1998-99; SA 1993-94 (Eng A), 1995-96; WI 1991-92 (Eng A); NZ 1996-97; I 1994-95 (Eng A); P 2000-01 (part). HS 200* De v Durham (Derby) 2000. La HS 154 v Durham (Manchester) 2006. 50 wkts (7); most – 90 (1995). BB 9-43 (13-93 match) De v Northants (Derby) 1995. Took 8-53 before lunch on his 20th birthday for De v Essex (Derby) 1991. 2 hat-tricks: 1994 and 1995 (*see Tests*). La BB 7-120 v Middlesex (Lord's) 2004. LO HS 93 De v Derbys CB (Derby) 2000 (NWT). LO BB 6-21 De v Glamorgan (Chesterfield) 1997 (SL). T20 HS 28. T20 BB 4-16.

CROFT, Steven John (Highfield HS, Blackpool; Myerscough C), b Blackpool 11 Oct 1984. 5'10". RHB, RMF. Debut (Lancashire) 2005. HS 65 v Sussex (Hove) 2007. BB 3-40 v Durham (Blackpool) 2007. LO HS 63 v Notts (Nottingham) 2007 (FPT). LO BB 4-59 v Sussex (Hove) 2006 (P40). T20 HS 49. T20 BB 2-10.

CROSS, Gareth David (Moorside S; Eccles C), b Bury 20 Jun 1984. 5'9". RHB, RMF, WK. Debut (Lancashire) 2005. HS 72 v Kent (Canterbury) 2006. LO HS 76 v Warwks (Birmingham) 2007 (P40). T20 HS 62.

‡[NO]**Du PLESSIS**, Francois, b Pretoria, South Africa 13 Jul 1984. RHB, LB. Northerns 2003-04 to 2005-06. Titans 2005-06 to date. Joins Lancashire (Kolpak registration) 2008. HS 156 Northerns v Gauteng (Johannesburg) 2005-06. BB 4-39 Northerns v Free State (Pretoria) 2004-05. LO HS 114 Northerns v EP (Pretoria) 2005-06. LO BB 4-47 Northerns v Easterns (Pretoria) 2005-06. T20 HS 76. T20 BB 2-26.

FLINTOFF, Andrew (Ribbleton Hall HS), b Preston 6 Dec 1977. 6'4". RHB, RF. Debut (Lancashire) 1995; cap 1998; benefit 2006. YC 1998. *Wisden* 2003. PCA 2004, 2005. MBE 2005. BBC Sports Personality of 2005. **ECB central contract 2007-08. Tests**: 66 (1998 to 2006-07, 11 as captain); HS 167 v WI (Birmingham) 2004; BB 5-58 v WI (Bridgetown) 2003-04. **LOI**: 112 (1998-99 to 2007, 14 as captain); HS 123 v WI (Lord's) 2004; BB 5-56 v I (Bristol) 2007. F-c Tours (Eng) (C=Captain): A 2002-03 (part), 2006-07C; SA 1998-99 (Eng A), 1999-00, 2004-05; WI 2003-04; NZ 2001-02; I 2001-02, 2005-06C; P 2000-01 (part), 2005-06; SL 1997-98 (Eng A), 2003-04; Z 1998-99 (Eng A); K 1997-98 (Eng A). HS 167 (*see Tests*). La HS 160 v Yorks (Manchester) 1999. BB 5-24 v Hants (Southampton) 1999. LO HS 143 (off 66 balls) v Essex (Chelmsford) 1999 (NL). LO BB 5-56 (*see LOI*). IT20 HS 31. IT20 BB 2-23. T20 HS 85. T20 BB 3-4.

[NO]**HODGE, Bradley** John (St Bede's C, Mentone; Deakin U), b Sandringham, Victoria, Australia 29 Dec 1974. 5'8". RHB, OB. Victoria 1993-94 to date. Durham 2002. Leicestershire 2003-04; cap 2003; captain 2004 (part). Lancashire debut 2005; cap 2006. **Tests** (A): 5 (2005-06); HS 203* v SA (Perth) 2005-06. **LOI** (A): 25 (2005-06 to 2007-08) HS 123 v Holland (Basseterre, St Kitts) 2006-07; BB 1-17 v Scotland (Basseterre) 2006-07. F-c Tours (A): I 2004-05; P 2005-06 (Aus A); Z 1998-99 (Aus Acad). 1000 runs (2+3); most 1548 (2004). HS 302* (Leics record) v Notts (Nottingham) 2003. La HS 161 v Middlesex (Lord's) 2006. BB 4-17 Aus A v WI (Hobart) 2000-01. CC BB 3-21 v Warwks (Birmingham) 2006. LO HS 164 Aus A v SA A (Perth) 2002-03. LO BB 5-28 Aus A v SA A (Canberra) 2002-03. IT20 HS 36. IT20 BB – . T20 HS 106. T20 BB 4-17.

HOGG, Kyle William (Saddleworth HS), b Birmingham, Warwks 2 Jul 1983. Son of W.Hogg (Lancashire and Warwickshire 1976-83; grandson of S.Ramadhin (Trinidad, Lancashire and West Indies 1949-50 to 1965). 6'4". LHB, RFM. Debut (Lancashire) 2001. Otago 2006-07. Worcestershire 2007 (on loan). Nottinghamshire 2007 (on loan). F-c Tour (ECB Acad): SL 2002-03. HS 71 Otago v CD (Napier) 2006-07. La HS 70 v Middlesex (Lord's) 2006. BB 5-48 v Leics (Manchester) 2002 – on CC debut. LO HS 41* v Glamorgan (Manchester) 2005 (NL). LO BB 4-20 v Hants (Southampton) 2002 (NL). T20 HS 27. T20 BB 2-10.

HORTON, Paul James (St Margaret's HS, Liverpool), b Sydney, Australia 20 Sep 1982. 5'10". RHB, RM. UK resident since 1997. Debut (Lancashire) 2003; cap 2007. 1000 runs (1): 1116 (2007). HS 152 v Hants (Manchester) 2007. LO HS 47 v Warwks (Birmingham) 2007 (P40). T20 HS 11.

KEEDY, Gary (Garforth CS), b Wakefield, Yorks 27 Nov 1974. 6'0". LHB, SLA. Yorkshire 1994 (one match). Lancashire debut 1995; cap 2000. F-c Tour: WI 1995-96 (La). HS 57 v Yorks (Leeds) 2002. 50 wkts (3): most – 72 (2004). BB 7-95 (14-227 match) v Glos (Manchester) 2004. LO HS 22 v Sri Lanka A (Liverpool) 2007. LO BB 5-30 v Sussex (Manchester) 2000 (NL). T20 HS 9*. T20 BB 3-25.

LAW, Stuart Grant (Craigslea State HS), b Herston, Brisbane, Australia 18 Oct 1968. 6'1". RHB, RM/LBG. Queensland 1988-89 to 2003-04; captain 1994-95 to 1996-97, 1999-00 to 2001-02. Essex 1996-2001; cap 1996. Lancashire debut/cap 2002; benefit 2007; captain 2008. *Wisden* 1997. PCA 1999. British Citizenship after 2004 season. Tests (A): 1 (1995-96); HS 54* v SL (Perth) 1995-96. LOI (A): 54 (1994-95 to 1998-99); HS 110 v Z (Hobart) 1994-95; BB 2-22 v P (Sydney) 1996-97. F-c Tours: E 1995 (Young A); Z 1991-92 (Aus B). 1000 runs (9+2); most – 1833 (1999). HS 263 Ex v Somerset (Chelmsford) 1999. La HS 236* v Warwks (Manchester) 2003. BB 5-39 Q v Tasmania (Brisbane) 1995-96. CC BB 3-27 Ex v Worcs (Chelmsford) 1997. La BB 1-24 v Yorks (Manchester) 2002. LO HS 163 Young A v Surrey (Oval) 1995. LO BB 5-26 Q v SL (Cairns) 1995-96. T20 HS 101.

LOYE, Malachy Bernhard (Moulton S), b Northampton 27 Sep 1972. 6'2". RHB, OB. Northamptonshire 1991-2002; cap 1994. PCA 1998. Lancashire debut 2003 – scoring 126 v Surrey (Oval) and 113 v Notts (Manchester) in his first two innings; cap 2003; benefit 2008. Auckland 2006-07. LOI: 7 (2006-07); HS 45 v A (Sydney) 2006-07. F-c Tours (Eng A): SA 1993-94, 1998-99; Z 1994-95 (Nh), 1998-99. 1000 runs (6); most – 1296 (2006). HS 322* Nh v Glamorgan (Northampton) 1998 – record Northants score until 2001. La HS 200 v Durham (Chester-le-St) 2005. BB 1-8 v Kent (Blackpool) 2003. LO HS 127 v Durham (Manchester) 2006 (CGT). T20 HS 100.

MAHMOOD, Sajid Iqbal (North C, Bolton), b Bolton 21 Dec 1981. 6'4". RHB, RF. Debut (Lancashire) 2002; cap 2007. MCC 2005. Tests: 8 (2006 to 2006-07); HS 34 and BB 4-22 v P (Leeds) 2006. LOI: 25 (2004 to 2006-07); HS 22* v P (Birmingham) 2006; BB 4-50 v SL (North Shore, Antigua) 2006-07. F-c Tours (Eng A): A 2006-07 (Eng); WI 2005-06; I 2003-04; SL 2004-05. HS 94 v Sussex (Manchester) 2004. BB 5-37 v DU (Durham) 2003. CC BB 5-52 v Sussex (Liverpool) 2006. LO HS 29 v Staffs (Stone) 2004 (CGT). LO BB 5-16 v Sri Lanka A (Liverpool) 2007. IT20 HS 0*. IT20 BB 1-34. T20 HS 21. T20 BB 1-17.

MARSHALL, Simon James (Birkenhead S; Pembroke C, Cambridge), b Arrowe Park, Wirral, Cheshire 20 Sep 1982. 6'3". RHB, LB. Cambridge U 2002-04; blue 2002-03-04. British U 2004. Lancashire debut 2005. Cheshire 2001-03. Hockey blue. HS 126* CU v OU (Cambridge) 2003. La HS 35* v OU (Oxford) 2005. CC HS 26* v Worcs (Manchester) 2005. BB 6-128 CU v Essex (Cambridge) 2002. La BB 2-23 v OU (Oxford) 2005 – on La debut. CC BB 1-8. LO HS 22 v Warwks (Manchester) 2007 (FPT). LO BB 3-36 v Durham (Manchester) 2006 (CGT) and 3-36 v Warwks (Birmingham) 2007 (P40). T20 HS 47. T20 BB 4-20.

MULLANEY, Steven John (St Mary's RC S, Astley), b Warrington, Cheshire 19 Nov 1986. 5'9". RHB, RM. Debut (Lancashire) 2006. Awaiting CC debut. HS 165* v DU (Durham) 2007. LO HS 12 v Notts (Nottingham) 2007 (FPT). LO BB 3-13 v Derbys (Derby) 2007 (FPT). T20 HS 5.

NEWBY, Oliver James (Ribblesdale HS; Myerscough C), b Blackburn 26 Aug 1984. 6'5". RHB, RMF. Debut (Lancashire) 2003. Nottinghamshire 2005 (on loan). HS 38* Nt v Kent (Nottingham) 2005 – on Notts debut. La HS 26 v Warwks (Manchester) 2007. BB 4-58 v Notts (Manchester) 2006. LO HS 7* (NL). LO BB 2-37 v Glos (Manchester) 2004 (NL). T20 HS 6*. T20 BB 2-34.

PARRY, Stephen David (Audenshaw HS), b Manchester 12 Jan 1986. 5'11". RHB, SLA. Debut (Lancashire) 2007 taking 5-23 v Durham UCCE (Durham). Awaiting CC debut. Cumberland 2005-06. HS – and BB 5-23 (*see above*).

SMITH, Thomas Christopher (Parkland HS, Chorley; Runshaw C, Leyland), b Liverpool 26 Dec 1985. 6'3". LHB, RMF. Debut (Lancashire) 2005. F-c Tour (Eng A): B 2006-07. HS 49 v Hants (Southampton) 2006. BB 4-57 v Yorks (Leeds) 2006. LO HS 30 v Notts (Nottingham) 2007 (FPT). BB 3-8 v Leics (Manchester) 2006 (CGT). T20 HS 21. T20 BB 3-15.

SUTCLIFFE, Iain John (Leeds GS; Queen's C, Oxford), b Leeds, Yorks 20 Dec 1974. 6'2". LHB, occ LB. Oxford U 1994-96; blue 1995-96; boxing blue 1993-94. Leicestershire 1995-2002; cap 1997. Combined/British U 1995-96. Lancashire debut/cap 2003. Northamptonshire 2007 (on loan). F-c Tour (Le): SA 1996-97. 1000 runs (3): most – 1088 (2002). HS 203 Le v Glamorgan (Cardiff) 2001. La HS 159 v Warwks (Blackpool) 2006. BB 2-21 OU v CU (Lord's) 1996. CC BB (Le) 1-7. La BB 1-11. LO HS 105* Le v Notts (Nottingham) 1998 (BHC). T20 HS 4.

SUTTON, Luke David (Millfield S; Durham U), b Keynsham, Somerset 4 Oct 1976. 5'11". RHB, WK. Somerset 1997-98. Derbyshire 2000-05; cap 2002; captain 2004-05. Lancashire debut 2006; cap 2007. HS 151* v Yorks (Manchester) 2006. LO HS 83 De v Lancs (Derby) 2003 (NL). T20 HS 61*.

RELEASED/RETIRED
(Having made a County 1st XI appearance in 2007)

NQJAYASURIYA, S.T. – *see WARWICKSHIRE*.

NQLAXMAN, Vangipurapu Venkata Sai ('VVS'), b Hyderabad, India 1 Nov 1974. 6'1". RHB, OB. Hyderabad 1992-93 to date. South Zone 1994-95 to 2006-07. Lancashire 2007. *Wisden* 2001. **Tests** (I): 90 (1996-97 to 2007-08); HS 281 v A (Calcutta) 2000-01; BB 1-2 v P (Calcutta) 2007-08. **LOI** (I): 86 (1997-98 to 2006-07); HS 131 v Z (Adelaide) 2003-04. F-c Tours (I): E 2002, 2007; A 1999-00, 2003-04, 2007-08; SA 1996-97, 2001-02, 2006-07; WI 1996-97, 2001-02, 2002-03 (Ind A – Capt), 2006; NZ 1998-99, 2002-03; P 2003-04, 2005-06; SL 1998-99; Z 2001, 2005-06; B 2004-05. 1000 runs (0+4): most – 1432 (1999-00). HS 353 v Hyderabad v Karnataka (Bangalore) 1999-00. La HS 103 v Warwks (Manchester) 2007. BB 3-11 Hyderabad v Railways (Delhi) 1999-00. LO HS 131 (*see LOI*). LO BB 2-42 Hyderabad v Tamil Nadu (Madras) 2000-01.

^{NQ}**MURALITHARAN, Muthiah** (St Anthony's C, Kandy), b Kandy, Sri Lanka 17 Apr 1972. 5'5". RHB, OB. Central Province 1989-90 to 2003-04. Tamil Union 1991-92 to 2003-04. Lancashire 1999 (taking 7-44 and 7-33 v Warwks at Southport on debut), 2001, 2005, 2007; cap 1999. Kent 2003; cap 2003. *Wisden* 1998. **Tests** (SL): 117 (1992-93 to 2007-08); HS 67 v I (Kandy) 2001-02; BB 9-51 (13-115 match) v Z (Kandy) 2001-02. **LOI** (SL): 289 (1993-94 to 2006-07); HS 27 v A (Sydney) 2005-06; BB 7-30 v I (Sharjah) 2000-01. F-c Tours (SL): E 1991, 1998, 2002, 2006; A 1995-96, 2005-06, 2007-08; SA 1992-93 (SL U-24), 1994-95, 1997-98, 2000-01, 2002-03; WI 1996-97, 2003; NZ 1994-95, 1996-97; I 1993-94, 1997-98, 2006-07; P 1995-96, 1999-00, 2001-02; Z 1994-95, 1999-00, 2004; B 2005-06. HS 67 (*see Tests*). La HS 28 v Sussex (Liverpool) 2007. 50 wkts (3+3); most – 96 (2003-04). Took 66 wkts in seven CC matches 1999. BB 9-51 (13-115 match) (*see Tests*). La BB 7-39 (11-61 match) v Derbys (Derby) 1999. Lo HS 27 (*see LOI*) and 27 v Scotland (Manchester) 2007 (FPT). LO BB 7-30 (*see LOI*). IT20 HS – . IT20 BB 2-27. T20 HS 9. T20 BB 4-18.

HAMPSHIRE RELEASED/RETIRED (continued from p 47)

^{NQ}**CLARK, Stuart** Rupert (Woolooware HS; Sydney U), b Caringbah, Sydney, Australia 28 Sep 1975. 6'5". RHB, RFM. NSW 1997-98 to date. Middlesex 2004-05. Hampshire 2007; cap 2007. **Tests** (A): 15 (2005-06 to 2007-08); HS 39 v E (Brisbane) 2006-07; BB 5-55 (9-89 match) v SA (Cape Town) 2005-06 – on debut. **LOI** (A): 28 (2005-06 to 2007-08); HS 16* v SA (Durban) 2005-06; BB 4-54 v NZ (Sydney) 2006-07. F-c Tours (A): SA 2005-06; P 2005-06 (Aus A); B 2005-06. HS 62 NSW v S Aus (Adelaide) 2006-07. UK HS 34 M v Northants (Northampton) 2004 – on UK debut. H HS 17 v Durham (Southampton) 2007. BB 8-58 NSW v WA (Perth) 2006-07, including hat-trick. UK BB 7-82 v Lancs (Southampton) 2007. Lo HS 26* M v Sussex (Hove) 2004 (NL). Lo BB 6-27 v Surrey (Southampton) 2007 (FPT). IT20 HS – . IT20 BB 4-20. T20 HS – . T20 BB 4-20.

^{NQ}**POWELL, Daren** Brent-Lyle (St Alban's S; St Elizabeth Technical HS), b Malvenn, St Elizabeth, Jamaica 15 Apr 1978. 6'0". RHB, RFM. Jamaica 2000-01 to 2006-07. Gauteng 2003-04. Derbyshire 2004. Hampshire 2007. **Tests** (WI): 25 (2002 to 2007-08); HS 36* v E (Lord's) 2007; BB 5-25 v SL (Kandy) 2005. **LOI** (WI): 34 (2002-03 to 2007-08); HS 48* v SA (St George's, Grenada) 2006-07; BB 4-27 v I (Cuttack) 2006-07. F-c Tours (WI): E 2002 (WI A), 2007; A 2005-06; SA 2007-08; NZ 2005-06; I 2002-03; P 2006-07; SL 2005; B 2002-03. HS 62 West Indies A v Durham (Chester-le-St) 2006. UK HS 36* (*see Tests*). H HS 25 v Surrey (Southampton) 2007. BB 6-49 v DU (Derby) 2004. CC BB 4-8 H v Worcs (Southampton) 2007. LO HS 48* (see LOI). LO BB 5-23 Jamaica v Trinidad (Discovery Bay, Jamaica) 2002-03. IT20 HS 1*. IT20 BB 1-6. T20 HS 1*. T20 BB 1-6.

STOKES, Mitchell Sam Thomas (Cranbourne S; Basingstoke TC), b Basingstoke 27 Mar 1987. 5'8". RHB, OB. Berkshire 2005. Hampshire (l-o) 2005. Awaiting f-c debut. LO HS 36 H v West Indies A (Southampton) 2006. LO BB – . T20 HS 62. T20 BB – .

UDAL, S.D. – *see MIDDLESEX*.

^{NQ}**VOGES, Adam** Charles (Edith Cowan U, Perth), b Perth, Australia 4 Oct 1979. 6'0". RHB, SLC. W Australia 2002-03 to date. Hampshire (l-o) 2007. **LOI** (A): 1 (2006-07); HS 16* v NZ (Hamilton) 2006-07 – on debut. F-c Tour (Aus A): P 2007-08. HS 180 WA v Tas (Hobart) 2007-08. BB 4-92 WA v S Aus (Adelaide) 2006-07. LO HS 100* WA v NSW (Sydney) 2004-05. LO BB 3-33 WA v Tas (Perth) 2007-08. IT20 HS 26. T20 HS 74*. T20 BB 2-4.

^{NQ}60

LANCASHIRE 2007

RESULTS SUMMARY

	Place	Won	Lost	Tied	Drew	No Result
LV County Championship (1st Division)	3rd	5	2		8	1
All First-Class Matches		6	2		8	1
Friends Provident Trophy (North Conference)	7th	3	5			1
NatWest Pro40 League (1st Division)	3rd	3	1			4
Twenty/20 Cup (North Division)	Semi-Finalist	4	2			4

LV COUNTY CHAMPIONSHIP AVERAGES

BATTING AND FIELDING

Cap		M	I	NO	HS	Runs	Avge	100	50	Ct/St
2002	S.G.Law	14	22	2	206	1277	63.85	3	9	17
–	V.V.S.Laxman	5	8	1	103	380	54.28	2	2	7
2007	P.J.Horton	13	23	2	152	1034	49.23	3	4	16
–	L.D.Sutton	15	19	3	111	587	36.68	1	2	42/2
2003	M.B.Loye	8	14	2	105*	427	35.58	1	1	5
2006	B.J.Hodge	8	13	2	156*	354	32.18	1	–	4
1998	A.Flintoff	3	4	–	61	128	32.00	–	1	4
–	T.C.Smith	6	6	2	44	119	29.75	–	–	4
1999	M.Muralitharan	8	7	5	28	58	29.00	–	–	1
2002	M.J.Chilton	14	24	2	115	616	28.00	1	2	7
2004	D.G.Cork	13	17	4	48*	329	25.30	–	–	4
1994	G.Chapple	12	16	1	88	338	22.53	–	2	4
–	S.J.Croft	10	17	2	65	323	21.53	–	2	11
2007	S.I.Mahmood	10	14	3	41	148	13.45	–	–	3
2003	I.J.Sutcliffe	3	6	–	57	75	12.50	–	1	5
2000	G.Keedy	10	9	5	9	34	8.50	–	–	3
–	O.J.Newby	8	8	1	26	48	6.85	–	–	1

Also batted: J.M.Anderson (6 matches† – cap 2003) 0, 0, 1 (1 ct); K.W.Hogg (1) 29;
S.T.Jayasuriya (1) 38.

BOWLING

	O	M	R	W	Avge	Best	5wI	10wM
M.Muralitharan	392.3	90	952	51	18.66	6- 72	5	–
G.Chapple	365.1	79	1027	47	21.85	7- 53	1	1
J.M.Anderson	171.1	40	569	18	31.61	5- 98	1	–
S.I.Mahmood	270.3	43	955	30	31.83	4- 21	–	–
O.J.Newby	148.4	20	594	18	33.00	3- 44	–	–
D.G.Cork	360.5	74	1011	30	33.70	3- 39	–	–
G.Keedy	272.5	55	813	24	33.87	5-159	–	–
Also bowled:								
A.Flintoff	34.5	10	120	5	24.00	3- 38	–	–
T.C.Smith	95.5	20	351	8	43.87	2- 47	–	–

M.J.Chilton 4-0-13-0; S.J.Croft 53-6-207-4; B.J.Hodge 2-0-5-0; K.W.Hogg 24-7-65-0;
S.T.Jayasuriya 4-0-10-1; S.G.Law 4-0-21-0; V.V.S.Laxman 5-1-15-0.

The First-Class Averages (pp 140–158) give the records of Lancashire players in all the
County's first-class matches (Lancashire's other opponents being Durham UCCE), with the
exception of J.M.Anderson, S.T.Jayasuriya and V.V.S.Laxman, whose full county figures are
as above, and:
   K.W.Hogg 2-2-0-30-59-29.50-0-0-0ct. 53-17-131-1-1/31-0-0.
   I.J.Sutcliffe 4-8-2-104*-194-32.33-1-1-5ct. Did not bowl.
   †Full substitute in three matches (for O.J.Newby (2) and T.C.Smith).

LANCASHIRE RECORDS

FIRST-CLASS CRICKET

Highest Total	For 863		v	Surrey	The Oval	1990
	V 707-9d		by	Surrey	The Oval	1990
Lowest Total	For 25		v	Derbyshire	Manchester	1871
	V 22		by	Glamorgan	Liverpool	1924
Highest Innings	For 424	A.C.MacLaren	v	Somerset	Taunton	1895
	V 315*	T.W.Hayward	for	Surrey	The Oval	1898

Highest Partnership for each Wicket

1st	368	A.C.MacLaren/R.H.Spooner	v	Glos	Liverpool	1903
2nd	371	F.B.Watson/G.E.Tyldesley	v	Surrey	Manchester	1928
3rd	364	M.A.Atherton/N.H.Fairbrother	v	Surrey	The Oval	1990
4th	358	S.P.Titchard/G.D.Lloyd	v	Essex	Chelmsford	1996
5th	360	S.G.Law/C.L.Hooper	v	Warwicks	Birmingham	2003
6th	278	J.Iddon/H.R.W.Butterworth	v	Sussex	Manchester	1932
7th	248	G.D.Lloyd/I.D.Austin	v	Yorkshire	Leeds	1997
8th	158	J.Lyon/R.M.Ratcliffe	v	Warwicks	Manchester	1979
9th	142	L.O.S.Poidevin/A.Kermode	v	Sussex	Eastbourne	1907
10th	173	J.Briggs/R.Pilling	v	Surrey	Liverpool	1885

Best Bowling	For 10-46	W.Hickton	v	Hampshire	Manchester	1870
(Innings)	V 10-40	G.O.B.Allen	for	Middlesex	Lord's	1929
Best Bowling	For 17-91	H.Dean	v	Yorkshire	Liverpool	1913
(Match)	V 16-65	G.Giffen	for	Australians	Manchester	1886

Most Runs – Season	2633	J.T.Tyldesley	(av 56.02)		1901
Most Runs – Career	34222	G.E.Tyldesley	(av 45.20)		1909-36
Most 100s – Season	11	C.Hallows			1928
Most 100s – Career	90	G.E.Tyldesley			1909-36
Most Wkts – Season	198	E.A.McDonald	(av 18.55)		1925
Most Wkts – Career	1816	J.B.Statham	(av 15.12)		1950-68
Most Career W-K Dismissals	925	G.Duckworth	(635 ct/290 st)		1923-38
Most Career Catches in the Field	556	K.J.Grieves			1949-64

LIMITED-OVERS CRICKET

Highest Total	FPT	381-3		v	Herts	Radlett	1999
	P40	310-7		v	Somerset	Taunton	2003
	T20	217-4		v	Surrey	The Oval	2005
Lowest Total	FPT	59		v	Worcs	Worcester	1963
	P40	68		v	Yorkshire	Leeds	2000
		68		v	Surrey	The Oval	2002
	T20	91		v	Derbyshire	Manchester	2003
Highest Innings	FPT	162*	A.R.Crook	v	Bucks	Wormsley	2005
	P40	143	A.Flintoff	v	Essex	Chelmsford	1999
	T20	101	S.G.Law	v	Yorkshire	Manchester	2005
Best Bowling	FPT	6-18	G.Chapple	v	Essex	Lord's	1996
	P40	6-25	G.Chapple	v	Yorkshire	Leeds	1998
	T20	4-16	D.G.Cork	v	Notts	Manchester	2006

LEICESTERSHIRE

Formation of Present Club: 25 March 1879
Inaugural First-Class Match: 1894
Colours: Dark Green and Scarlet
Badge: Gold Running Fox on Green Ground
County Champions: (3) 1975, 1996, 1998
Gillette/NatWest/C&G/FP Trophy Winners: (0); best –
Finalist 1992, 2001
Benson and Hedges Cup Winners: (0) 1972, 1975, 1985
Pro 40/National League (Div 1) Winners: (0); best – 2nd
2001
Sunday League Champions: (2) 1974, 1977
Twenty20 Cup Winners: (2) 2004, 2006

Chief Executive: David Smith, County Ground, Grace Road, Leicester LE2 8AD • Tel:
0871 282 1879 • Fax: 0871 282 1873 • Email: enquiries@leicestershireccc.co.uk • Web:
www.leicestershireccc.co.uk

Senior Coach: Tim Boon. **Head Coach/Academy Director**: Phil Whitticase. **Captain**:
P.A.Nixon. **Vice-Captain**: tba. **Overseas Players**: H.H.Dippenaar. **2008 Beneficiary**:
J.N.Snape (testimonial). **Head Groundsman**: Andy Whiteman. **Scorer**: Graham A.York.
‡ New registration. ^{NQ} Not qualified for England.

^{NQ}**ACKERMAN, Hylton** Deon (**'HD'**) (Rondebosch BHS), b Cape Town, South Africa
14 Feb 1973. 5'11". Son of H.M.Ackerman (Border, NE Transvaal, Northants, Natal, W
Province 1963-64 to 1981-82). RHB, RM. W Province 1993-94 to 2002-03. Gauteng
2003-04. Lions 2004-05. Cape Cobras 2005-06. Warriors 2006-07 to date. Tests (SA): 4 (1997-98): HS 57 v P (Durban)
1997-98 – on debut. F-c Tours (SA): E 1996 (SA A); A 1995-96 (WP); SL 1995 (SA U-24),
1998; Z 1996-97 (WP). 1000 runs (2+1); most – 1808 (2006). HS 309* v Glamorgan
(Cardiff) 2006. LO HS 114* v Sussex (Hove) 2005 (NL). T20 HS 87.

ALLENBY, James (Christ Church GS, Perth), b Perth, W Australia 12 Sep 1982. 6'0".
RHB, RM. Debut (Leicestershire) 2006. Western Australia (T20) 2006-07. HS 103* v Essex
(Leicester) 2006. BB 5-125 v Glos (Bristol) 2007 – his first five f-c wickets. LO HS 91* v
Middlesex (Lord's) 2007 (P40). LO BB 5-43 v Derbys (Leicester) 2007 (FPT). T20 HS 64.
T20 BB 2-22.

BOYCE, Matthew Andrew Golding (Oakham S; Nottingham U), b Cheltenham, Glos
13 Aug 1985. 5'9". LHB, RM. Debut (Leicestershire) 2006. HS 6 v P (Leicester) 2006. CC
HS 5 v Glos (Leicester) 2007. LO HS 36 v Surrey (Leicester) 2007 (P40).

CLIFF, Samuel James (Colonel Frank Seely S, Calverton, Notts), b Nottingham 3 Oct
1987. 6'2". RHB, RMF. Debut (Leicestershire) 2007. HS 11 v Northants (Leicester) 2007.
BB 1-28 v OU (Oxford) 2007 – on debut. CC BB – .

COBB, Joshua James (Oakham S), b Leicester 17 Aug 1990. 5'11½". Son of R.A.Cobb
(Leics and N Transvaal 1980-89). RHB, LB. Debut (Leicestershire) 2007. HS 21 v
Northants (Leicester) 2007 – on debut. BB – .

CUMMINS, Ryan Anthony Gilbert (Wallington CGS; Loughborough U), b Sutton, Surrey
14 Apr 1984. Great-grandson of G.M.Reay (Surrey 1913-23). 6'4". RHB, RM. Loughbor-
ough UCCE 2003-05. Leicestershire debut 2005. HS 34* v OU (Oxford) 2007. Le HS 26* v
Glos (Leicester) 2007. BB 5-60 v Northants (Leicester) 2007. LO HS 10 v Warwks
(Birmingham) 2007 (FPT). LO BB 2-14 v Durham (Chester-le-St) 2006 (CGT). T20 HS – .
T20 BB – .

‡**NQDIPPENAAR**, Hendrik Human (**'Boeta'**) (Grey C, Bloemfontein; UNISA), Kimberley, South Africa 14 Jun 1977. 5'10½". RHB, OB. Free State 1995-96 to 2003-04. Eagles 2004-05 to date. **Tests** (SA): 38 (1999-00 to 2006-07); HS 177* v B (Chittagong) 2002-03. **LOI** (SA): 101 (1999-00 to 2007); HS 125* v SL (Adelaide) 2005-06. F-c Tours (SA) (C=Captain): E 2003; A 2001-02; WI 1996-97 (FS), 2000-01, 2004-05; I 2004-05, 2007-08C (SA A); P 2003-04; SL 2004, 2006; Z 1999-00, 2001-02, 2007C (SA A); B 2003. 1000 runs (0+1): 1070 (1998-99). HS 250* Eagles v Warriors (Kimberley) 2006-07. BB – . LO HS 125* (see LOI). LO BB – . IT20 HS 1. T20 HS 35*.

GURNEY, Harry Frederick (Garendon HS; Loughborough GS; Leeds U), b Nottingham 25 Oct 1986. 6'2". RHB, LMF. Bradford/Leeds UCCE 2006-07 (not f-c). Debut (Leicestershire) 2007. HS 1 and BB 1-84 v Northants (Leicester) 2007.

NQHENDERSON, Claude William (Worcester HS), b Worcester, Cape Province South Africa 14 Jun 1972. Elder brother of J.M.Henderson (Boland, Transvaal, North West, Free Ste and Eagles 1994-95 to 2005-06). 6'1½". RHB, SLA. Boland 1990-91 to 1997-98. W Province 1998-99 to 2003-04. Leicestershire debut/cap 2004 (the first Kolpak registration). Lions 2006-07 to date. **Tests** (SA): 7 (2001-02 to 2002-03); HS 30 and BB 4-116 v A (Adelaide) 2001-02. **LOI** (SA): 4 (2001-02); HS – ; BB 4-17 v Z (Harare) 2001-02. F-c Tours (SA): A 2001-02; SL 1998 (SA A); Z 2001-02. HS 81 v Glos (Leicester) 2007. BB 7-57 Boland v EP (Paarl) 1994-95. Le BB 7-74 v Durham (Leicester) 2004. LO HS 45 Lions v Eagles (Johannesburg) 2006-07. LO BB 6-29 Boland v Easterns (Paarl) 1997-98. T20 HS 9*. T20 BB 3-26.

NQKRUGER, Garnett John-Peter (Gelvandale HS; Russel Road C), b Port Elizabeth, South Africa 5 Jan 1977. RHB, RMF. E Province 1997-98 to 2002-03. Gauteng 2003-04. Lions 2004-05 to date. Leicestershire debut 2007 (Kolpak registration). **LOI** (SA): 3 (2005-06); HS 0*; BB 1-43 v A (Brisbane) 2005-06 – on debut. F-c Tour (SA A): WI 2000-01; SL 2005-06; Z 2004. HS 58 South Africa A v Windward Is (Kingstown) 2000-01. Le HS 15 v Derbys (Leicester) 2007. BB 8-112 Lions v Dolphins (Durban) 2005-06. Le BB 5-62 v Glamorgan (Leicester) 2007. LO HS 20* EP v WP (Cape Town) 2002-03. LO BB 6-23 EP v NW (Port Elizabeth) 1999-00. IT20 HS 3. IT20 BB – . IT20 HS 12*. T20 BB 3-32.

‡**MALIK**, Muhammad **Nadeem**, (Wilford Meadows CS; Bilborough C), b Nottingham 6 Oct 1982. 6'5". RHB, RFM. Nottinghamshire 2001-03, 2007 – on loan. Worcestershire 2004-07. Notts 2nd XI debut 1999 when aged 16y 337d. HS 39* Wo v NZ (Worcester) 2004. CC HS 35 Wo v Glamorgan (Colwyn Bay) 2006. BB 5-57 Nt v Derbys (Nottingham) 2001. LO HS 11 Nt v Worcs (Nottingham) 2002 (NL). LO BB 4-42 Wo v Sussex (Worcester) 2004 (NL). T20 HS 3*. T20 BB 3-23.

NAIK, Jigar Kumar Hakumatrai (Rushey Mead SS; Gateway SFC; Nottingham Trent U; Loughborough U), b Leicester 10 Aug 1984. 6'2". RHB, OB. Debut (Leicestershire) 2006. Loughborough UCCE 2007. HS 15 LU v Yorks (Leeds) 2007. Le HS 15 and BB 1-58 v Middlesex (Southgate) 2007. BB 1-55 v West Indies A (Leicester) 2006. LO HS 1 Leics CB v Kent CB (Maidstone) 2002 (CGT). LO BB 3-24 v Glamorgan (Leicester) 2007 (P40).

NEW, Thomas James (Quarrydale S), b Sutton in Ashfield, Notts 18 Jan 1985. 5'10". LHB, RM, WK. Debut (Leicestershire) 2004. HS 125 v OU (Oxford) 2007. HS 98 v Glos (Bristol) 2007. BB 2-18 v Glos (Leicester) 2007. LO HS 68 v Northants (Oakham) 2006 (CGT).

NIXON, Paul Andrew (Ullswater HS, Penrith), b Carlisle, Cumberland 21 Oct 1970. 6'0". LHB, WK, occ RM. Leicestershire 1989-99, 2003 to date; cap 1994; benefit 2007; captain 2007 (part) to date. MCC 1999-00. Kent 2000-02; cap 2000. Cumberland 1987. **LOI**: 19 (2006-07); HS 49 v NZ (Perth) 2006-07. F-c Tours: SA 1996-97 (Le); I 1994-95 (Eng A); P 2000-01; B 1999-00 (MCC). 1000 runs (1): 1046 (1994). HS 144* v Northants (Northampton) 2006. LO HS 101 v Sri Lanka A (Galle) 1998-99. IT20 HS 65. T20 HS 65.

‡**POPE, Joel** Ian (Whitton S), b Ashford, Middlesex 23 Oct 1988. RHB, WK. MCC YC 2007. Awaiting 1st XI debut.

ROWE, Daniel Thomas (Archbishop McGrath S; Glamorgan U, Cardiff), b Ogwr, Glamorgan 22 Mar 1984. 6'0". RHB, RM. Debut (Leicestershire) 2006. Cardiff UCCE 2004-06 (not f-c). HS 85 v Essex (Leicester) 2007. BB 5-61 v OU (Oxford) 2007. CC BB 2-27 v Essex (Leicester) 2007. LO HS 2* v Scotland (Leicester) 2007 (FPT). LO BB 1-26 v Derbys (Leicester) 2006 (P40).

SNAPE, Jeremy Nicholas (Denstone C; Durham U), b Stoke-on-Trent, Staffs 27 Apr 1973. 5'8½". RHB, OB. Northamptonshire 1992-97. Combined U 1993-94. Gloucestershire 1999-2002; cap 1999. Leicestershire debut 2003; cap 2006; captain 2006-07 (*part*). No f-c appearances 2007. Limited-Overs contract 2008. **LOI**: 10 (2001-02 to 2002-03); HS 38 v I (Madras) 2001-02; BB 3-43 v Z (Bulawayo) 2001-02. F-c Tour: Z 1994-95 (Nh). HS 131 Gs v Sussex (Cheltenham) 2001. Le HS 90 v Derbys (Leicester) 2006. BB 5-65 Nh v Durham (Northampton) 1995. Le BB 3-108 v Surrey (Leicester) 2003. LO HS 104* Gs v Notts (Nottingham) 2001 (NL). LO BB 5-32 Nh v Leics (Northampton) 1997 (BHC). IT20 HS 7. IT20 BB – . T20 HS 47*. T20 BB 4-22 – took 3-6, including T20 hat-trick, v Yorks (Leicester) 2007.

RELEASED/RETIRED
(Registered players who made a County 1st XI appearance in 2007)

BROAD, S.C.J. – *see NOTTINGHAMSHIRE.*

FERRABY, Nicholas John (Oakham S; Loughborough U), b Market Harborough 31 May 1983. 6'0". RHB, RM. Leicestershire (List A) 2007. No f-c appearances. Leics 2nd XI 2000-07. Cambridgeshire 2006-07. LO HS 13* v Glamorgan (Leicester) 2007 (P40). LO BB – .

HARRISON, Paul William (Forest S and Collyer's C, Horsham; Loughborough U), b Cuckfield, Sussex 22 May 1984. 6'2". RHB, RM, WK. Loughborough UCCE 2004-06. Warwickshire 2005 (one non-CC match). British U 2006. Leicestershire debut 2006. HS 54 LU v Notts (Nottingham) 2005. Le HS 5 v West Indies A (Leicester) 2006. LO HS 61 v Yorks (Scarborough) 2006 (P40). T20 HS 26.

JACOBS, Arno (Hoer Volkskool; Potchefstroom U), b Potchefstroom, South Africa 13 Mar 1977. Younger brother of S.Jacobs (Transvaal/Gauteng 1987-88 to 1999-00). LHB, OB, WK. North West 1997-98 to 2002-03. E Province 2003-04. Warriors 2004-05 to date. Leicestershire 2007. Scotland (list A) 2007. Scored 112 on debut (NW v W Province B 1997-98). HS 197 NW v Border (Potchefstroom) 2001-02. Le HS 55 v Middlesex (Leicester) 2007. BB 1-2 Combined XI v Sri Lanka A (Potchefstroom) 1999-00. Le BB – . LO HS 118 and BB 2-22 NW v Easterns (Potchefstroom) 2002-03. T20 HS 45. T20 BB 5-26.

NQ**LANGEVELDT, Charl** Kenneth (Luckhoff SS), b Stellenbosch, South Africa 17 Dec 1974. RHB, RFM. Boland 1997-98 to 2002-03. Lions 2004-05 to 2006-07. Somerset 2005; cap 2005. Leicestershire 2007 (Kolpak registration). **Tests** (SA): 6 (2004-05 to 2005-06); HS 10 v WI (Georgetown) 2004-05; BB 5-46 v E (Cape Town) 2004-05 – on debut. **LOI** (SA): 53 (2001-02 to 2006-07); HS 12 v Pakistan (Lahore) 2007-08; BB 5-39 v SL (Providence, Guyana) 2006-07. F-c Tours (SA): A 2002-03 (SA A), 2005-06; WI 2000 (SA A), 2004-05; I 2007-08 (SA A); Z 1998 (SA Acad), 2004 (SA A), 2007-08 (SA A). HS 56 Boland v E Province (Port Elizabeth) 1999-00. UK HS 18* Sm v Leics (Taunton) 2005 – on UK debut. Le HS 10* and UK BB 4-41 v Essex (Leicester) 2007. BB 6-48 Lions v Titans (Potchefstroom) 2006-07. LO HS 33* S Africa v SL (Potchefstroom) 2002-03. LO BB 5-7 SA President's XI v B (Pietermaritzburg) 2000-01. IT20 HS 2. IT20 BB 2-14. T20 HS 2. T20 BB 2-14

[NQ]**MANSOOR AMJAD** (Quaid HS, Sialkot), b Sialkot, Pakistan 14 Dec 1987. 6'0". RHB, LBG. Zarai Taraqiati Bank 2003-04 to 2004-05. Sialkot 2004-05 to 2006-07. National Bank 2005-06 to date. Leicestershire 2006-07. F-c Tours (Pak A): I 2006-07 (Sialkot); Z 2005; K 2004. HS 122* NBP v Sialkot (Multan) 2005-06. Le HS 105* v Glamorgan (Leicester) 2007. BB 6-19 Pak A v Zim A (Harare) 2005. Le BB 3-16 v Derbys (Derby) 2007. LO HS 56 Sialkot v Rawalpindi (Karachi) 2006-07. LO BB 5-37 NBP v Service Industries (Faisalabad) 2005-06. T20 HS 23. T20 BB 2-28.

MASTERS, D.D. – *see ESSEX.*

MAUNDERS, John Kenneth (Ashford HS; Spelthorne C), b Ashford, Middlesex 4 Apr 1981. 5'10". LHB, RM. Middlesex 1999 (one non-CC match); 2nd XI debut aged 16 years 19 days. Leicestershire 2003-07. Registered by Shropshire 2008. HS 180 Le v Glos (Cheltenham) 2006. BB 4-15 Le v Worcs (Worcester) 2006. LO HS 109* Le v Derbys (Leicester) 2007 (FPT). LO BB 2-16 Le v Warwks (Birmingham) 2005 (CGT). T20 HS 10. T20 BB 2-14.

ROBINSON, Darren David John (Tabor HS, Braintree; Chelmsford CFE), b Braintree, Essex 2 Mar 1973. 5'10½". RHB, RMF. Essex 1993-2003; cap 1997. Leicestershire 2004-07; cap 2007; CC captain 2007 (*part*). 1000 runs (3): most – 1474 (2002). HS 200 Ex v NZ (Chelmsford) 1999. CC HS 175 Ex v Glos (Gloucester) 2002. Le HS 154 v Yorks (Leicester 2004). BB 1-7 Ex v Middlesex (Chelmsford) 2003. LO HS 137* Ex v Sussex (Hove) 1998 (BHC). LO BB 1-7 Ex v Middlesex (Chelmsford) 1997 (SL). T20 HS 41.

ROSENBERG, Marc Christopher (Kearnsney C, Durban; Loughborough U), b Johannesburg, South Africa 10 Feb 1982. 6'0". RHB, RM. Loughborough UCCE 2004. North West 2004-05. Leicestershire 2006-07. HS 86 North West v GW (Potchefstroom) 2004-05. UK HS 64* Le v Glos (Bristol) 2007 – on CC debut. BB 1-27 LU v Somerset (Taunton) 2004. Le BB – . LO HS 26 North West v GW (Potchefstroom) 2004-05. LO BB 3-17 North West v WP (Cape Town) 2004-05.

SADLER, J.L. – *see DERBYSHIRE.*

[NQ]**SINGH, Rudra** Pratap, b Rae Bareli, Uttar Pradesh, India 6 Dec 1985. RHB, LMF. Uttar Pradesh 2005-06 to 2006-07. Central Zone 2004-05. Leicestershire 2007; cap 2007. **Tests** (I): 11 (2005-06 to 2007-08); HS 30 v A (Perth) 2007-08; BB 5-59 v E (Lord's) 2007. **LOI** (I): 38 (2005-06 to 2007-08); HS 12* (twice); BB 4-35 v SL (Rajkot) 2005-06. F-c Tours (I): E 2007; A 2006 (Ind A), 2007-08; P 2005-06; B 2007. HS 41* I v Sussex (Hove) 2007. Le HS 25 v Notts (Nottingham) 2007. BB 5-33 UP v Maharashtra (Kolhapur) 2004-05. UK BB 5-59 (*see Tests*). Le BB 3-62 V Somerset (Leicester) 2007. LO HS 35 Central Zone v West Zone (Ahmedabad) 2006-07. LO BB 5-30 India A v UAE (Abu Dhabi) 2006. IT20 HS 1*. IT20 BB 4-13. T20 HS 4*. T20 BB 4-13.

TAYLOR, Jerome Everton (St Elizabeth Technical HS), b Aberdeen, St Elizabeth, Jamaica 22 Jun 1984. 5'10". RHB, RF. Jamaica 2002-03 to 2006-07. Leicestershire 2007. **Tests** (WI) 16 (2003 to 2007-08); HS 23* v E (Leeds) 2007; BB 5-50 v I (Kingston) 2006. **LOI** (WI): 39 (2003 to 2007-08): HS 13 v SL (Providence, Guyana) 2006-07; BB 5-48 v Z (Bulawayo) 2007-08. F-c Tours (WI): E 2007; SA 2007-08; NZ 2005-06; P 2006-07; Z 2003-04. HS 40 Le v Derbys (Leicester) 2007. BB 8-59 Jamaica v Trinidad (Port-of-Spain) 2002-03. Le BB 6-35 v Middlesex (Southgate) 2007. LO HS 22 v Derbys (Derby) 2007 (P40). LO BB 5-48 (*see LOI*). IT20 HS – . IT20 BB 3-6. T20 HS – . T20 BB 5-10.

WALKER, Nicholas Guy Eades (Haileybury Imperial Service C), b Enfield, Middlesex 7 Aug 1984. 6'2". RHB, RFM. Derbyshire 2004-2005. Leicestershire 2006-07. Hertfordshire 2001-03. HS 80 off 57 balls (4 sixes, 11 fours), the record score by a Derbyshire No. 11, adding 103 for 10th wicket with M.A.Sheikh, and took 5-68 v Somerset (Derby) 2004. Le HS 31 v Essex (Leicester) 2007. BB 5-59 v Somerset (Leicester) 2006. LO HS 43 De v Scotland (Derby) 2004 (NL). LO BB 4-26 v Somerset (Leicester) 2006 (P40). T20 HS 16*. T20 BB 3-19.

D.A.Stiff left the staff without making a County 1st XI appearance in 2007.

LEICESTERSHIRE 2007

RESULTS SUMMARY

	Place	Won	Lost	Tied	Drew	No Result
LV County Championship (2nd Division)	8th	2	8		5	1
All First-Class Matches		3	8		5	1
Friends Provident Trophy (North Conference)	6th	4	3			2
NatWest Pro40 League (2nd Division)	7th	3	4		1	
Twenty/20 Cup (North Division)	4th	2	1			5

LV COUNTY CHAMPIONSHIP AVERAGES
BATTING AND FIELDING

Cap		M	I	NO	HS	Runs	Avge	100	50	Ct/St
2007	S.C.J.Broad	5	6	2	91*	197	49.25	–	1	–
1994	P.A.Nixon	13	21	3	126	879	48.83	2	5	36/1
–	J.Allenby	15	25	4	93	731	34.80	–	5	13
–	T.J.New	15	28	3	98	832	33.28	–	8	13/1
2007	D.D.J.Robinson	8	14	1	122	407	31.30	1	1	5
–	Mansoor Amjad	9	13	2	105*	319	29.00	1	1	6
2005	H.D.Ackerman	15	26	–	153	723	27.80	3	1	15
–	A.Jacobs	5	8	2	55	156	26.00	–	1	2
–	J.K.Maunders	12	21	–	97	544	25.90	–	4	10
–	D.T.Rowe	4	5	1	85	103	25.75	–	1	–
2004	C.W.Henderson	9	12	–	81	301	25.08	–	1	2
–	C.K.Langeveldt	3	4	3	10*	25	25.00	–	–	–
–	N.G.E.Walker	8	11	5	31	143	23.83	–	–	4
–	J.E.Taylor	3	5	1	40	86	21.50	–	–	–
–	M.C.Rosenberg	6	7	1	64*	128	21.33	–	1	2
2007	D.D.Masters	11	16	2	46	242	17.28	–	–	1
–	J.L.Sadler	9	16	–	45	265	16.56	–	–	4
–	R.A.G.Cummins	4	8	2	26*	70	11.66	–	–	2
–	G.J.P.Kruger	4	4	–	15	28	7.00	–	–	1
2007	R.P.Singh	2	4	–	25	28	7.00	–	–	2

Also batted (1 match each): M.A.G.Boyce 5; S.J.Cliff 1*, 11; J.J.Cobb 2, 21; H.F.Gurney 1, 0*; J.K.H.Naik 15, 5* (2 ct).

BOWLING

	O	M	R	W	Avge	Best	5wI	10wM
D.D.Masters	327.4	89	924	41	22.53	6- 60	3	–
J.E.Taylor	72	14	287	12	23.91	6- 35	2	–
G.J.P.Kruger	85	16	324	13	24.92	5- 62	1	–
S.C.J.Broad	141	19	526	19	27.68	5- 67	1	–
R.A.G.Cummins	113.2	25	418	13	32.15	5- 60	1	–
N.G.E.Walker	171	27	777	18	43.16	4- 70	–	–
J.Allenby	207.2	41	660	14	47.14	5-125	1	–
Mansoor Amjad	161.2	17	645	12	53.75	3- 16	–	–
C.W.Henderson	295.3	60	935	17	55.00	5- 80	1	–
Also bowled:								
R.P.Singh	60.4	14	250	8	31.25	3- 62	–	–
C.K.Langeveldt	101.4	27	295	8	36.87	4- 41	–	–
D.T.Rowe	53	6	316	5	63.20	2- 27	–	–

S.J.Cliff 18-0-98-0; J.J.Cobb 9-0-44-0; H.F.Gurney 36-5-173-2; A.Jacobs 2-0-13-0; J.K.Maunders 41.5-3-184-1; J.K.H.Naik 19-3-58-1; T.J.New 28.1-4-168-4; P.A.Nixon 2-0-9-0; D.D.J.Robinson 8-0-50-1; M.C.Rosenberg 9.2-1-45-0; J.L.Sadler 12-2-89-1.

The First-Class Averages (pp 140–158) give the records of Leicestershire players in all first-class county matches (their other opponents being Oxford UCCE), with the exception of S.C.J.Broad, J.K.H.Naik, R.P.Singh and J.E.Taylor, whose full county figures are as above.

LEICESTERSHIRE RECORDS

FIRST-CLASS CRICKET

Highest Total	For	701-4d		v	Worcs	Worcester	1906
	V	761-6d		by	Essex	Chelmsford	1990
Lowest Total	For	25		v	Kent	Leicester	1912
	V	24		by	Glamorgan	Leicester	1971
		24		by	Oxford U	Oxford	1985
Highest Innings	For	309*	H.D.Ackerman	v	Glamorgan	Cardiff	2006
	V	341	G.H.Hirst	for	Yorkshire	Leicester	1905

Highest Partnership for each Wicket

1st	390	B.Dudleston/J.F.Steele	v	Derbyshire	Leicester	1979
2nd	289*	J.C.Balderstone/D.I.Gower	v	Essex	Leicester	1981
3rd	436*	D.L.Maddy/B.J.Hodge	v	L'boro UCCE	Leicester	2003
4th	290*	P.Willey/T.J.Boon	v	Warwicks	Leicester	1984
5th	322	B.F.Smith/P.V.Simmons	v	Notts	Worksop	1998
6th	284	P.V.Simmons/P.A.Nixon	v	Durham	Chester-le-St	1996
7th	219*	J.D.R.Benson/P.Whitticase	v	Hampshire	Bournemouth	1991
8th	172	P.A.Nixon/D.J.Millns	v	Lancashire	Manchester	1996
9th	160	R.T.Crawford/W.W.Odell	v	Worcs	Leicester	1902
10th	228	R.Illingworth/K.Higgs	v	Northants	Leicester	1977

Best Bowling	For	10- 18	G.Geary	v	Glamorgan	Pontypridd	1929
(Innings)	V	10- 32	H.Pickett	for	Essex	Leyton	1895
Best Bowling	For	16- 96	G.Geary	v	Glamorgan	Pontypridd	1929
(Match)	V	16-102	C.Blythe	for	Kent	Leicester	1909

Most Runs – Season	2446	L.G.Berry	(av 52.04)		1937
Most Runs – Career	30143	L.G.Berry	(av 30.32)		1924-51
Most 100s – Season	7	L.G.Berry			1937
	7	W.Watson			1959
	7	B.F.Davison			1982
Most 100s – Career	45	L.G.Berry			1924-51
Most Wkts – Season	170	J.E.Walsh	(av 18.96)		1948
Most Wkts – Career	2131	W.E.Astill	(av 23.18)		1906-39
Most Career W-K Dismissals	903	R.W.Tolchard	(794 ct/109 st)		1965-83
Most Career Catches in the Field	427	M.R.Hallam			1950-70

LIMITED-OVERS CRICKET

Highest Total	FPT	406-5		v	Berkshire	Leicester	1996
	P40	344-4		v	Durham	Chester-le-St	1996
	T20	221-3		v	Yorkshire	Leeds	2004
Lowest Total	FPT	56		v	Northants	Leicester	1964
	P40	36		v	Sussex	Leicester	1973
	T20	137		v	Derbyshire	Derby	2005
Highest Innings	FPT	201	V.J.Wells	v	Berkshire	Leicester	1996
	P40	154*	B.J.Hodge	v	Sussex	Horsham	2004
	T20	111	D.L.Maddy	v	Yorkshire	Leeds	2004
Best Bowling	FPT	6-16	C.M.Willoughby	v	Somerset	Leicester	2005
	P40	6-17	K.Higgs	v	Glamorgan	Leicester	1973
	T20	4-22	C.E.Dagnall	v	Notts	Leicester	2004
		4-22	J.N.Snape	v	Essex	Nottingham	2006

MIDDLESEX

Formation of Present Club: 2 February 1864
Inaugural First-Class Match: 1864
Colours: Blue
Badge: Three Seaxes
County Champions (since 1890): (10) 1903, 1920, 1921, 1947, 1976, 1980, 1982, 1985, 1990, 1993
Joint Champions: (2) 1949, 1977
Gillette/NatWest/C&G/FP Trophy Winners: (4) 1977, 1980, 1984, 1988
Benson and Hedges Cup Winners: (2) 1983, 1986
Pro 40/National League (Div 1) Winners: (0); best – 1st (Div 2) 2004
Sunday League Winners: (1) 1992
Twenty20 Cup Winners: (0); best – Quarter-Finalist 2005

Secretary: Vincent J.Codrington, Lord's Cricket Ground, London NW8 8QN • Tel: 020 7289 1300 • Fax: 020 7289 5831 • Email: enquiries@middlesexccc.com • Web: www.middlesex ccc.com

Head Coach: Toby A.Radford. **Assistant Coach**: Richard J.Scott. **Captain**: E.T.Smith. **Vice-Captain**: E.C.Joyce. **Overseas Players**: M.Kartik and A.A.Noffke. **2008 Beneficiary**: O.A.Shah. **Head Groundsman**: Mick Hunt. **Scorer**: Don K.Shelley. ‡ New registration. NQ Not qualified for England.

‡**BERG, Gareth** Kyle, b Cape Town, South Africa 18 Jan 1981. RHB, RMF. Western Province Academy (1999-00) and WP B (2001-02 to 2002-03. Northants 2nd XI 2004. Middlesex 2nd XI 2007. Kolpak registration. Awaiting f-c and List A debuts.

COMPTON, Nicholas Richard Denis (Harrow S), b Durban, South Africa 26 Jun 1983. 6'1". Son of R.Compton (Natal 1978-79 to 1980-81). Grandson of D.C.S.Compton (Middlesex, England, Holkar, Europeans, Commonwealth and Cavaliers 1936-1964); great-nephew of L.H.Compton (Middlesex 1938-56). RHB, OB. Debut (Middlesex) 2004; cap 2006. MCC 2007. F-c Tour (Eng A): B 2006-07. 1000 runs (1): 1315 (2006). HS 190 v Durham (Lord's) 2006. BB 1-94 v Sussex (Southgate) 2007. LO HS 110* v Sussex (Lord's) 2007 (FPT). LO BB - . T20 HS 50*.

‡**NQDe WET, Friedel** (Grenswag Hoerskool; Pretoria TC), b Durban, South Africa 26 Jun 1980. RHB, RFM. Northerns 2001-02 to 2002-03. North West 2004-05 to 2006-07. Lions 2005-06 to date. Joins Middlesex 2008 as Kolpak registration. F-c Tours (SA A): I 2007-08. HS 56 Lions v Titans (Pretoria) 2007-08. 50 wkts (0+1): 61 (2006-07). BB 7-61 Lions v Cape Cobras (Cape Town) 2005-06. LO HS 56* v NW v FS (Potchefstroom) 2005-06. LO BB 5-59 Lions v Eagles (Johannesburg) 2006-07. T20 HS 6. T20 BB 2-18.

EVANS, Daniel (Brierton CS, Hartlepool), b Hartlepool, Co Durham 24 Jul 1987. 6'5". RHB, RFM. Debut (Middlesex) 2007. Durham 2nd XI 2004-06. HS 7 v Essex (Chelmsford) 2007. BB 3-31 v Glos (Bristol) 2007.

FINN, Steven Thomas (Parmiter's S, Garston), b Watford, Herts 4 Apr 1989. 6'5½". RHB, RFM. Debut (Middlesex) 2005. HS 3 v Essex (Chelmsford) 2007. BB 4-51 v Glos (Bristol) 2007. LO HS 2 v Lancs (Lord's) 2007 (P40). LO BB 3-23 v Somerset (Taunton) 2007 (P40).

GODLEMAN, Billy Ashley (Islington Green S), b Islington, London 11 Feb 1989. 6'3". LHB, LB. Debut (Middlesex) 2005. HS 113* v Somerset (Taunton) 2007 – on CC debut. LO HS 18 v Hants (Southampton) 2007 (FPT). T20 HS 41.

‡**HOUSEGO, Daniel** Mark (Oratory S), b Windsor, Berkshire 12 Oct 1988. RHB, LB. Middlesex 2nd XI 2005-07. Berkshire 2006. Awaiting 1st XI debut.

JOYCE, Edmund Christopher (Presentation C, Bray, Co Wicklow; Trinity C, Dublin), b Dublin, Ireland 22 Sep 1978. 5'11". Brother of four Ireland cricketers: Augustine (2000), Dominick (2004-06), Cecilia (2001-07) and Isobel, her twin (1999-2007). LHB, RM. Ireland 1997-98. Middlesex debut 1999; cap 2002. Qualified for England 2005. MCC 2006. **LOI**: 17 (2006 to 2006-07); HS 107 v A (Sydney) 2006-07. F-c Tour (Eng A): WI 2005-06. 1000 runs (5); most 1668 (2005). HS 211 v Warwks (Birmingham) 2006. BB 2-34 v CU (Cambridge) 2004. CC BB 1-4 v Glamorgan (Cardiff) 2005. LO HS 115* Ireland v UAE (Belfast) 2005. LO BB 2-10 v Notts (Nottingham) 2003 (NL). IT20 HS 1. T20 HS 31.

NQKARTIK, Murali (educated in New Delhi), b Madras, India 11 Sep 1976. 6'0". LHB, SLA. Railways 1996-97 to date. Central Zone 1997-98 to 2006-07. Lancashire 2005-06. Middlesex debut/cap 2007. **Tests** (I): 8 (1999-00 to 2006-07); HS 43 v B (Dhaka) 2000-01; BB 4-44 v A (Bombay) 2004-05. **LOI** (I): 37 (2001-02 to 2007-08); HS 32* v A (Perth) 2003-04; BB 6-27 v A (Bombay) 2007-08. F-c Tours (Ind A): E 2003; A 2003-04 (Ind); SA 2001-02; WI 1999-00, 2002-03; P 1997-98; SL 2002; B 2000-01 (Ind). HS 96 Railways v Rest of India (Delhi) 2005-06. CC HS 40 La v Hants (Southampton) 2006. M HS 35* v Glos (Lord's) 2007. 50 wkts (1): 51 (2007). BB 9-70 Rest of India v Bombay (Bombay) 2000-01. CC BB 6-21 v Glamorgan (Lord's) 2007. LO HS 37* Central Zone v South Zone (Poona) 2004-05. LO BB 6-27 (*see LOI*). IT20 HS – . IT20 BB – . T20 HS 1*. T20 BB 5-13.

‡MALAN, Dawid Johannes (Paarl HS), b Roehampton, Surrey 3 Sep 1987. Son of D.J.Malan (WP B and Transvaal B 1978-79 to 1981-82). LHB, LB. Boland 2005-06. MCC YC 2006-07. Awaiting Middlesex f-c and List A debuts. HS 64 Boland v Border (Paarl) 2005-06 – on debut. BB 1-22 Boland v EP (Port Elizabeth) 2005-06. LO HS 42 Boland v EP (Port Elizabeth) 2005-06. LO BB – . T20 HS 11.

NQMORGAN, Eoin Joseph Gerard, b Dublin, Ireland 10 Sep 1986. 6'0". LHB, RM. British passport. Ireland 2004 to date. Middlesex debut 2006. **LOI** (Ire): 18 (2006 to 2007); HS 115 v Canada (Nairobi) 2006-07. F-c Tours (Ire): Namibia 2005-06; UAE 2006-07. HS 209* Ire v UAE (Abu Dhabi) 2006-07. UK HS 84 Ireland v Canada (Leicester) 2007. M HS 76 v Glos (Bristol) 2007. BB 2-24 v Notts (Lord's) 2007. LO HS 115 (*see LOI*). T20 HS 66.

MURTAGH, Timothy James (John Fisher S; St Mary's C), b Lambeth, London 2 Aug 1981. Elder brother of C.P.Murtagh (*see SURREY*); nephew of A.J.Murtagh (Hampshire and E Province 1973-77). 6'0". LHB, RFM. British U 2000-03. Surrey 2001-06. Middlesex debut 2007. HS 74* Sy v Middlesex (Oval) 2004 and 74* Sy v Warwks (Croydon) 2005. M HS 40 v Northants (Lord's) 2007. BB 6-86 Brit U v P (Nottingham) 2001. M BB 6-87 v Notts (Nottingham) 2007. LO HS 31* Sy v Durham (Oval) 2005 (NL). LO BB 4-14 Sy v Derbys (Derby) 2005 (NL). T20 HS 40*. T20 BB 6-24.

NASH, David Charles (Sunbury Manor S; Malvern C), b Chertsey, Surrey 19 Jan 1978. 5'8". RHB, occ LB, WK. Debut (Middlesex) 1997; cap 2000; benefit 2007. F-c Tour (Eng A): SL 1997-98. HS 114 v Somerset (Lord's) 1998. BB 1-8 v Essex (Chelmsford) 1997. LO HS 67 v Sussex (Lord's) 2002 (BHC).

NQNOFFKE, Ashley Allan (Immanuel Lutheran C; Sunshine Coast U), b Nambour, Queensland, Australia 30 Apr 1977. 6'3". RHB, RFM. Debut (Aus Academy in Zim) 1998-99. Queensland 1999-00 to date. Middlesex 2002-03; cap 2003. Durham 2005. Gloucestershire debut/cap 2007 – taking 6-68 (9-113 match) v Notts (Bristol). F-c Tours (A): E 2001 (*part*); WI 2002-03; P 2007-08 (Aus A); Z 1998-99 (Aus Acad). HS 114* Q v S Aus (Brisbane) 2003-04. UK HS 76 M v Worcs (Worcester) 2002. Gs HS 61 v Glamorgan (Bristol) 2007. BB 8-24 (12-108 match) M v Derbys (Derby) 2002. Gs BB 6-68 (*see above*). LO HS 58 M v Sussex (Lord's) 2002 (BHC). LO BB 4-32 Q v Tasmania (Hobart) 2001-02. IT20 HS 0. IT20 BB 3-18. T20 HS 19. T20 BB 3-18.

PEPLOE, Christopher Thomas (Twyford C of E HS; Surrey U, Roehampton), b Hammersmith, London 26 Apr 1981. 6'4". LHB, SLA. MCC YC 2002-03. Debut (Middlesex) 2003. HS 46 v Lancs (Lord's) 2006. BB 4-31 v Yorks (Southgate) 2006. LO HS 14* v Hants (Southampton) 2005 (NL). LO BB 4-38 v Glamorgan (Cardiff) 2005 (NL). T20 HS 7. T20 BB 3-35.

RICHARDSON, Alan (Alleyne's HS; Stafford CFE; Durham U), b Newcastle-under-Lyme, Staffs 6 May 1975. 6'2". RHB, RMF. Derbyshire 1995 (one match). Warwickshire 1999-2004, cap 2002. Middlesex debut/cap 2005, taking 7-113 v Notts (Lord's) on debut. Staffordshire 1996-98. Minor Counties 1998. HS 91 Wa v Hants (Birmingham) 2002 – adding 214 for 10th wicket with N.V.Knight. M HS 25 v Notts (Nottingham) 2005. 50 wkts (1): 57 (2005). BB 8-46 Wa v Sussex (Birmingham) 2002. M BB 7-113 (*see above*). LO HS 21* v Lancs (Lord's) 2005 (NL). LO BB 5-35 Wa v Staffs (Stone) 2002 (CGT). T20 HS 6*. T20 BB 3-13.

SCOTT, Ben James Matthew (Whitton S, Richmond; Richmond C), b Isleworth, Middlesex 4 Aug 1981. 5'8". RHB, WK. Surrey 2003. Middlesex debut 2004; cap 2007. MCC YC 2000. HS 112 v Glos (Bristol) 2007. LO HS 73* v Surrey (Southgate) 2006 (CGT). T20 HS 32*.

SHAH, Owais Alam (Isleworth & Syon S), b Karachi, Pakistan 22 Oct 1978. 6'0". RHB, OB. Debut (Middlesex) 1996; cap 2000; captain 2004 (*part*); benefit 2008. MCC 2002-07. YC 2001. Tests: 2 (2005-06 to 2007); HS 88 v I (Bombay) 2005-06. **LOI:** 36 (2001 to 2007-08); HS 107* v India (Oval) 2007; BB 1-18 v SL (Colombo) 2007-08. F-c Tours (Eng A): A 1996-97; WI 2005-06 (*part*); I 2005-06 (Eng – *part*). SL 1997-98, 2004-05, 2007-08. 1000 runs (7); most 1728 (2005). HS 203 v Derbys (Southgate) 2001. BB 3-33 v Glos (Bristol) 1999. LO HS 134 v Sussex (Arundel) 1999 (NL). LO BB 2-2 v Glamorgan (Cardiff) 1998 (BHC). IT20 HS 55*. T20 HS 79. T20 BB 1-10.

SILVERWOOD, Christopher Eric Wilfred (Garforth CS), b Pontefract, Yorks 5 Mar 1975. 6'1". RHB, RFM. Yorkshire 1993-2005; cap 1996; benefit 2004. MCC 1996. Middlesex debut/cap 2006. YC 1996. **Tests:** 6 (1996-97 to 2002-03); HS 10 v A (Perth) 2002-03; BB 5-91 v SA (Cape Town) 1999-00. **LOI:** 7 (1996-97 to 2001-02); HS 12 v NZ (Auckland) 1996-97; BB 3-43 v Z (Bulawayo) 2001-02. F-c Tours: A 2002-03 (*part*); SA 1999-00 (*part*); WI 1997-98, 2000-01 (Eng A); NZ 1996-97; Z 1995-96 (Y), 1996-97. M 80 Y v Durham (Chester-le-St) 2005. M HS 50 v Sussex (Horsham) 2006. 50 wkts (3); most – 63 (2006). BB 7-93 (12-148 match) Y v Kent (Leeds) 1997. M BB 6-49 v Somerset (Lord's) 2007. LO HS 61 Y v Northants (Northampton) 2002 (CGT). LO BB 5-28 Y v Scot (Leeds) 1996 (BHC). T20 HS 13*. T20 BB 2-22.

SMITH, Edward Thomas (Tonbridge S; Peterhouse, Cambridge), b Pembury, Kent 19 Jul 1977. 6'2". RHB, RM. Cambridge U 1996-98, scoring 101 v Glamorgan (Cambridge) on debut; blue 1996-97 (*injured 1998*). Kent 1996-2004; cap 2001. Middlesex debut/cap 2005; captain 2007 to date. British U 1998. **Tests:** 3 (2003); HS 64 v SA (Nottingham) 2003 on debut. F-c Tour (Eng A): I 2003-04. 1000 runs (8): most – 1534 (2003). Scored 135, 0, 149, 113, 203 and 108 in successive f-c innings 2003. M HS 213 K v Warwks (Canterbury) 2003. M HS 166 v Warwks (Lord's) 2006. BB 1-60 (off 5 overs) v Sussex (Southgate) 2006. LO HS 122 K v Glamorgan (Maidstone) 2003 (NL). T20 HS 85.

STRAUSS, Andrew John (Radley C; Durham U), b Johannesburg, South Africa 2 Mar 1977. 5'11". LHB, LM. Debut (Middlesex) 1998; cap 2001; captain 2002 (*part*) to 2004 (*part*). MCC 2002. Northern Districts 2004-05. Oxfordshire 1996. British U (List A) 1997-98. *Wisden* 2004. MBE 2005. **ECB central contract 2007-08. Tests:** 43 (2004 to 2007, 5 as captain); HS 147 v SA (Johannesburg) 2004-05. Scored 112 & 83 (run out) v NZ (Lord's) on debut and 126 & 94* v SA (Pt Elizabeth) 2004-05 on his debut overseas. **LOI:** 78 (2003-04 to 2006-07, 13 as captain); HS 152 v B (Nottingham) 2005. F-c Tours: A 2006-07; SA 2004-05; I 2005-06; P 2005-06. 1000 runs (3); most – 1529 (2003). HS 176 v Durham (Lord's) 2001. BB 1-16 v Notts (Lord's) 2007. LO HS 152 (*see LOI*). IT20 HS 33. T20 HS 60.

‡**UDAL, Shaun** David (Cove CS), b Cove, Farnborough, Hants 18 Mar 1969. Grandson of G.F.U.Udal (Middlesex and RAF 1932; Leics 1946); great great grandson of J.S.Udal (MCC 1871-75; Fiji 1894-95). 6'2". RHB, OB. Hampshire 1989-2007; cap 1992; benefit 2002. **Tests**: 4 (2005-06); HS 33* v P (Faisalabad) 2005-06; BB 4-14 v I (Bombay) 2005-06. **LOI**: 11 (1994 to 2005-06); HS 11* v Z (Brisbane) 1994-95; BB 2-37 v A (Sydney) 1994-95. F-c Tours: A 1994-95; I 2005-06; P 1995-96 (Eng A); 2005-06. HS 117* H v Warwks (Southampton) 1997. 50 wkts (7); most – 74 (1993). BB 8-50 H v Sussex (Southampton) 1992. LO HS 78 H v Surrey (Guildford) 1997 (SL). LO BB 5-43 H v Surrey (Oval) 1998 (SL). T20 HS 37. T20 BB 3-21.

WILLIAMS, Robert Edward Morgan (Marlborough C; St Mary's C, Durham U); b Pembury, Kent 19 Jan 1987. 6'0". RHB, RMF. Durham UCCE 2007. MCC 2007. Middlesex debut 2007. HS 15 and M BB 5-112 v Essex (Chelmsford) 2007 – on Middlesex debut. BB 5-70 DU v Lancs (Durham) 2007. LO HS – and BB – v Derbys (Lord's) 2007 (P40).

RELEASED/RETIRED
(Having made a County 1st XI appearance in 2007)

DALRYMPLE, J.W.M. – *see GLAMORGAN*.

NQ**HENDERSON, Tyron** (Durban HS), b Durban, South Africa 1 Aug 1974. Grandson of J.K.Henderson (N E Transvaal 1950-51); great-nephew of W.A.Henderson (N E Transvaal 1937-38 to 1946-47). 6'2". RHB, RFM. Border 1998-99 to 2003-04. Warriors 2004-05 to 2005-06. Kent 2006. Lions 2006-07. Middlesex 2007 (T20 only). Cape Cobras 2007-08. Boland 2007-08. Berkshire 2002-03. F-c Tours (SA A): Ireland/Scotland 1999 (SA Acad); SL 2005-06. HS 81 Border v Gauteng (Johannesburg) 1999-00. UK HS 59 K v Hants (Canterbury) 2006. BB 7-67 Boland v WP (Paarl) 2007-08. UK BB 5-44 SA Acad v Scotland (Linlithgow) 1999. CC BB 4-29 K v Lancs (Canterbury) 2006. LO HS 126* Border v GW (Kimberley) 2003-04. LO BB 5-5 Border v WP (E London) 1998-99. IT20 HS 0. IT20 BB – . T20 HS 85. T20 BB 3-11.

HUTTON, Benjamin Leonard (Radley C; Durham U), b Johannesburg, South Africa 29 Jan 1977. Elder son of R.A.Hutton (Yorkshire, CU, Transvaal & England 1962 to 1975-76); grandson of Sir Leonard (Yorkshire and England 1934-60); elder brother of O.R.Hutton (OU 2004); nephew of J.L.Hutton (MCC 1973-74). 6'2". LHB, RMF. British U 1998-99. Middlesex 1999-2007; cap 2002; captain 2005-06. 1000 runs (2); most – 1129 (2004). HS 152 v Kent (Lord's) 2005. BB 4-37 v SL (Shenley) 2002. CC BB 3-14 v Northants (Lord's) 2004. LO HS 77 v Durham (Chester-le-St) 2001 (NL). LO BB 5-45 v Derbys (Southgate) 2001 (NL). T20 HS 27*. T20 BB 2-21.

JOHNSON, Richard Leonard (Sunbury Manor S; S Pelthorne C), b Chertsey, Surrey 29 Dec 1974. 6'2". RHB, RFM. Middlesex 1992-2000, 2007; cap 1995. MCC 1999-00. Somerset 2001-06; cap 2001; benefit 2006. Registered by Berkshire 2008. **Tests**: 3 (2003 to 2003-04); HS 26 v SL (Galle) 2003-04; BB 6-33 v Z (Chester-le-St) 2003 on debut, including wickets with his third and fourth balls. Hit first ball in Test cricket for four. **LOI**: 10 (2003 to 2003-04); HS 10 v SA (Manchester) 2003; BB 3-22 v B (Dhaka) 2003-04. Took wicket with his second ball in LOI. F-c Tours: I 1994-95 (Eng A – *part*), 2001-02; SL 2003-04, B 1999-00 (MCC); 2003-04. HS 118 Sm v Glos (Bristol) 2003 (100 off 75 balls). Won Walter Lawrence Trophy 2004 for 63-ball hundred Sm v Durham (Chester-le-St). M HS 69 v Essex (Chelmsford) 2000. 50 wkts (4); most – 62 (2001). BB 10-45 v Derbys (Derby) 1994 (second youngest to take all ten wickets in any f-c match). LO HS 53 Sm v Derbys (Derby) 2003 (NL). LO BB 5-50 v Kent (Lord's) 1997 (NWT). T20 HS 10. T20 BB 3-21.

KEEGAN, Chad Blake (Durban HS), b Sandton, near Johannesburg, South Africa 30 Jul 1979. 6'1". RHB, RFM. Middlesex 2001-06; cap 2003. MCC YC 2000. Qualified for England March 2005. No f-c appearances 2007. HS 44 v Surrey (Oval) 2004. 50 wkts (1): 63 (2003). BB 6-114 v Leics (Southgate) 2003. LO HS 50 v Notts (Lord's) 2003 (NL). LO BB 6-33 v Notts (Nottingham) 2005 (NL). T20 HS 42. T20 BB 3-14.

RELEASED/RETIRED continued on p 90

MIDDLESEX 2007

RESULTS SUMMARY

	Place	Won	Lost	Tied	Drew	No Result
LV County Championship (2nd Division)	3rd	6	2		8	
All First-Class Matches		6	2		9	
Friends Provident Trophy (South Conference)	7th	3	5			1
NatWest Pro40 League (2nd Division)	3rd	5	3			
Twenty/20 Cup (South Division)	5th	2	3			3

LV COUNTY CHAMPIONSHIP AVERAGES

BATTING AND FIELDING

Cap		M	I	NO	HS	Runs	Avge	100	50	Ct/St
2000	O.A.Shah	10	16	4	193	870	72.50	3	1	6
2007	W.P.U.C.J.Vaas	7	8	3	79	277	55.40	–	2	2
2005	E.T.Smith	16	24	3	134	1070	50.95	4	4	9
2000	D.C.Nash	6	8	2	103*	279	46.50	2	–	17/2
2002	E.C.Joyce	14	20	2	106	704	39.11	1	4	5
2007	B.J.M.Scott	10	13	3	112	374	37.40	1	2	23/5
–	B.A.Godleman	14	22	2	113*	732	36.60	1	4	20
2001	A.J.Strauss	7	12	–	120	426	35.50	1	2	7
–	E.J.G.Morgan	5	7	–	76	227	32.42	–	3	4
2006	N.R.D.Compton	10	16	–	67	385	24.06	–	3	6
2003	B.L.Hutton	3	6	1	37	112	22.40	–	–	4
2004	J.W.M.Dalrymple	12	17	2	57	305	20.33	–	1	3
2007	M.Kartik	12	15	4	35*	209	19.00	–	–	12
–	T.J.Murtagh	13	15	1	40	241	17.21	–	–	2
2005	A.Richardson	13	12	4	24*	99	12.37	–	–	2
2006	C.E.W.Silverwood	10	10	1	30	110	12.22	–	–	2
–	D.Evans	4	5	1	7	7	1.75	–	–	4
–	S.T.Finn	3	5	2	3	4	1.33	–	–	–

Also batted: R.L.Johnson (3 matches – cap 1995) 0, 9, 0 (1 ct); C.T.Peploe (1) 13 (1 ct); R.E.M.Williams (1) 15, 6; C.J.C.Wright (2) 3, 12.

BOWLING

	O	M	R	W	Avge	Best	5wI	10wM
S.T.Finn	72.5	13	239	11	21.72	4- 51	–	–
A.Richardson	340.1	87	972	41	23.70	5- 50	1	–
M.Kartik	464.3	109	1273	51	24.96	6- 21	3	–
T.J.Murtagh	278.2	75	985	37	26.62	6- 87	1	–
W.P.U.C.J.Vaas	162	30	552	20	27.60	5-126	1	–
C.E.W.Silverwood	241.4	50	809	29	27.89	6- 49	1	–
J.W.M.Dalrymple	198.3	23	689	12	57.41	3- 86	–	–

Also bowled:

C.T.Peploe	25.0	5	65	5	13.00	3- 58		
R.E.M.Williams	34.4	7	126	5	25.20	5-112	1	–
D.Evans	54	14	169	5	33.80	3- 31	–	–

N.R.D.Compton 4-0-20-0; B.A.Godleman 5-1-35-0; B.L.Hutton 8-2-28-0; R.L.Johnson 76.1-5-338-4; E.C.Joyce 20-1-103-0; E.J.G.Morgan 11.1-2-32-2; O.A.Shah 30.1-3-137-0; E.T.Smith 1-1-0-0; A.J.Strauss 6-0-16-1; C.J.C.Wright 28-5-107-3.

The First-Class Averages (pp 140–158) give the records of Middlesex players in all first-class county matches (Middlesex's other opponents being Oxford UCCE), with the exception of N.R.D.Compton, E.J.G.Morgan, O.A.Shah, A.J.Strauss and R.E.M.Williams, whose full county figures are as above.

MIDDLESEX RECORDS

FIRST-CLASS CRICKET

Highest Total	For 642-3d		v	Hampshire	Southampton	1923
	V 850-7d		by	Somerset	Taunton	2007
Lowest Total	For 20		v	MCC	Lord's	1864
	V 31		by	Glos	Bristol	1924
Highest Innings	For 331*	J.D.B.Robertson	v	Worcs	Worcester	1949
	V 341	C.M.Spearman	for	Glos	Gloucester	2004

Highest Partnership for each Wicket

1st	372	M.W.Gatting/J.L.Langer	v	Essex	Southgate	1998
2nd	380	F.A.Tarrant/J.W.Hearne	v	Lancashire	Lord's	1914
3rd	424*	W.J.Edrich/D.C.S.Compton	v	Somerset	Lord's	1948
4th	325	J.W.Hearne/E.H.Hendren	v	Hampshire	Lord's	1919
5th	338	R.S.Lucas/T.C.O'Brien	v	Sussex	Hove	1895
6th	270	J.D.Carr/P.N.Weekes	v	Glos	Lord's	1994
7th	271*	E.H.Hendren/F.T.Mann	v	Notts	Nottingham	1925
8th	182*	M.H.C.Doll/H.R.Murrell	v	Notts	Lord's	1913
9th	160*	E.H.Hendren/T.J.Durston	v	Essex	Leyton	1927
10th	230	R.W.Nicholls/W.Roche	v	Kent	Lord's	1899

Best Bowling	For 10- 40	G.O.B.Allen	v	Lancashire	Lord's	1929
(Innings)	V 9- 38	R.C.R.Glasgow†	for	Somerset	Lord's	1924
Best Bowling	For 16-114	G.Burton	v	Yorkshire	Sheffield	1888
(Match)	16-114	J.T.Hearne	v	Lancashire	Manchester	1898
	V 16-100	J.E.B.B.P.Q.C.Dwyer	for	Sussex	Hove	1906

Most Runs – Season	2669	E.H.Hendren	(av 83.41)		1923
Most Runs – Career	40302	E.H.Hendren	(av 48.81)		1907-37
Most 100s – Season	13	D.C.S.Compton			1947
Most 100s – Career	119	E.H.Hendren			1907-37
Most Wkts – Season	158	F.J.Titmus	(av 14.63)		1955
Most Wkts – Career	2361	F.J.Titmus	(av 21.27)		1949-82
Most Career W-K Dismissals	1223	J.T.Murray	(1024 ct/199 st)		1952-75
Most Career Catches in the Field	561	E.H.Hendren			1907-37

LIMITED-OVERS CRICKET

Highest Total	FPT	304-7		v	Surrey	The Oval	1995
		304-8		v	Cornwall	St Austell	1995
	P40	337-5		v	Somerset	Southgate	2003
	T20	210-6		v	Hampshire	Southampton	2005
Lowest Total	FPT	41		v	Essex	Westcliff	1972
	P40	23		v	Yorkshire	Leeds	1974
	T20	108		v	Sussex	Richmond	2006
Highest Innings	FPT	158	G.D.Barlow	v	Lancashire	Lord's	1984
	P40	147*	M.R.Ramprakash	v	Worcs	Lord's	1990
	T20	85	E.T.Smith	v	Kent	Beckenham	2005
Best Bowling	FPT	6-15	W.W.Daniel	v	Sussex	Hove	1980
	P40	6- 6	R.W.Hooker	v	Surrey	Lord's	1969
	T20	5-13	M.Kartik	v	Essex	Lord's	2007

† R.C.Robertson-Glasgow

NORTHAMPTONSHIRE

Formation of Present Club: 31 July 1878
Inaugural First-Class Match: 1905
Colours: Maroon
Badge: Tudor Rose
County Champions: (0); best – 2nd 1912, 1957, 1965, 1976
Gillette/NatWest/C&G/FP Trophy Winners: (2) 1976, 1992
Benson and Hedges Cup Winners: (1) 1980
Pro 40/National League (Div 1) Winners: (0); best – 2nd 2006, 2007
Sunday League Winners: (0); best – 3rd 1991
Twenty20 Cup Winners: (0); best – Quarter-Finalist 2005, 2006, 2007

Chief Executive: Mark J.Tagg, County Ground, Wantage Road, Northampton, NN1 4TJ • Tel: 01604 514455 • Fax: 01604 609288 • Email: post@nccc.co.uk • Web: www.nccc.co.uk

First XI Coach: David J.Capel. **Captain**: N.Boje. **Vice-Captain**: none. **Overseas Player**: none. **2008 Beneficiary**: J.F.Brown. **Head Groundsman**: Paul Marshall. **Scorer**: A.C. (Tony) Kingston. ‡ New registration. NQ Not qualified for England.

NQBOJE, Nico (*'Nicky'*) (Grey C, Bloemfontein), b Bloemfontein, SA 20 Mar 1973. Brother of E.H.L.Boje (OFS 1989-1990 to 1990-91). LHB, SLA. (Orange) Free State 1990-91 to 2001-02. Nottinghamshire 2002. Eagles 2004-05 to 2006-07. Northamptonshire debut 2007 (Kolpak registration; captain 2008). **Tests** (SA): 43 (1999-00 to 2006); HS 85 v I (Bangalore) 1999-00; BB 5-62 v SL (Colombo) 2000-01. **LOI** (SA): 113 (1995-96 to 2005-06); HS 129 v NZ (Pretoria) 2000-01; BB 5-21 v A (Cape Town) 2001-02. Tours (SA): E 1996 (SA A); A 2001-02, 2002-03 (SA A), 2005-06; WI 2000-01, 2004-05; NZ 1998-99, 2003-04; I 1996-97, 1999-00; SL 1995 (SA U-24), 1998 (SA A), 2000, 2004, 2006; Z 1994-95. HS 125 and Nh BB 6-110 v Leics (Leicester) 2007. BB 8-93 Eagles v Dolphins (Durban) 2005-06. LO HS 129 (*see LOI*). LO BB 5-21 (*see LOI*). IT20 HS – . IT20 BB 1-27. T20 HS 52*. T20 BB 3-31.

BROWN, Jason Fred (St Margaret Ward HS & SFC), b Newcastle-under-Lyme, Staffs 10 Oct 1974. 6'0". RHB, OB. Debut (Northamptonshire) 1996; cap 2000; benefit 2008. Staffordshire 1994-95. F-c Tours: WI 2000-01 (*part*) (Eng A); SL 2000-01 (*no f-c*). HS 38 v Hants (Northampton) 2003. 50 wkts (3): most – 66 (2003). BB 7-69 v Durham (Chester-le-St) 2003. LO HS 16 v Lancs (Manchester) 2002 (NL). LO BB 5-19 v Cambs (Northampton) 2004 (CGT). T20 HS 6*. T20 BB 5-27.

BROWNING, Richard James (Wolverhampton GS; Leeds/Bradford U), b Wolverhampton, Staffs 9 Oct 1987. 6'3". RHB, RMF. Derbyshire (l-o only) 2006. Northamptonshire 2nd XI 2007. Summer contract. Awaiting County 1st XI and f-c debut. LO HS 2 De v Worcs (Worcester) 2006 (P40).

CROOK, Andrew Richard (Rostrevor C), b Modbury, S Australia 14 Oct 1980. 6'4". Elder brother of S.P.Crook. RHB, OB. British passport. S Australia 1998-99 (one match). Aus Academy 1999-2000. Lancashire 2004-05. Northamptonshire debut 2007. HS 88 La v OU (Oxford) 2005. Nh HS 72 v Leics (Leicester) 2007. BB 3-71 La v Essex (Manchester) 2005. Nh BB – . LO HS 162* La v Bucks (Wormsley) 2005 (Lancs CGT record). LO BB 3-32 La v Hants (Manchester) 2005. T20 HS 15. T20 BB 2-25.

CROOK, Steven Paul (Rostrevor C; Magill U), b Modbury, S Australia 28 May 1983. Younger brother of A.R.Crook. 5'11". RHB, RFM. British passport. Lancashire 2003-05. Northamptonshire debut 2005 (whilst on loan from Lancashire). Aus Academy 2001-02. HS 97 v Yorks (Northampton) 2005. BB 4-56 v Essex (Northampton) 2007. LO HS 23 v Glamorgan (Cardiff) 2006 (P40). LO BB 4-20 v Sussex (Northampton) 2006 (P40). T20 HS 27. T20 BB 2-24.

‡^{NQ}**HALL, Andrew** James (Alberton HS), b Alberton, Johannesburg, South Africa 31 Jul 1975. 6'0". RHB, RFM. Transvaal/Gauteng 1995-96 to 2000-01. Easterns 2001-02 to 2003-04. Worcestershire 2003-04. Lions 2004-05 to 2005-06. Kent 2005-07; cap 2005. Joins Northamptonshire 2008 as Kolpak registration. Durham CB 1999. Suffolk 2002. **Tests** (SA): 21 (2001-02 to 2006-07); HS 163 v I (Kanpur) 2004-05; BB 3-1 v SL (Johannesburg) 2002-03. **LOI** (SA): 88 (1998-99 to 2007); HS 81 v SL (Galle) 2000-01; BB 5-18 v E (Bridgetown) 2006-07. F-c Tours (SA): E 2003; WI 2004-05; SL 2006; Z 1995-96 (Transvaal B), 2007-08 (SA A). HS 163 (see Tests). UK HS 133 K v Glamorgan (Canterbury) 2005. BB 6-77 (11-99 match) Easterns v WP (Port Elizabeth) 2002-03. UK BB 5-59 K v Surrey (Croydon) 2007. LO HS 129* Gauteng v Border (E London) 1999-00. LO BB 5-18 (see LOI). IT20 HS 11. IT20 BB 3-22. T20 HS 59. T20 BB 3-15.

^{NQ}**KLUSENER, Lance** (Durban HS), b Durban, South Africa 4 Sep 1971. 5'10". LHB, RM/OB. Natal/KwaZulu-Natal 1993-94 to 2003-04. Nottinghamshire 2002. Middlesex 2004. Dolphins 2004-05 to 2006-07. Northamptonshire debut/cap 2006 (Kolpak registration). Wisden 2000. **Tests** (SA): 49 (1996-97 to 2004); HS 174 v E (Pt Elizabeth) 1999-00; BB 8-64 v I (Calcutta) 1996-97 – on debut. **LOI** (SA): 171 (1995-96 to 2004); HS 103* v NZ (Auckland) 1998-99; BB 6-49 v SL (Lahore) 1997-98. F-c Tours (SA): E 1996 (SA A), 1998; A 1997-98, 2001-02; WI 2000-01; NZ 1998-99; I 1996-97, 1999-00; P 1997-98; SL 1995 (SA U-24), 2000, 2004; Z 1999-00, 2001-02. 1000 runs (2); most – 1251 (2006 – inc 6 hundreds). HS 174 (see Tests). CC HS 147* v Somerset (Northampton) 2006. BB 8-34 Natal v WP (Durban) 1995-96. CC BB 6-69 v Leics (Oakham) 2006. LO HS 142* SA v Northants (Northampton) 1998. LO BB 6-49 (see LOI). T20 HS 111*. T20 BB 2-13.

LOGAN, Richard James (Wolverhampton GS), b Stone, Staffs 28 Jan 1980. 6'1". RHB, RMF. Northamptonshire 1999-2000, 2007. Nottinghamshire 2001-04. Hampshire 2005-06. HS 37* Nt v Hants (Nottingham) 2001. Nh HS 24 v Essex (Ilford) 2000. BB 6-93 Nt v Derbys (Nottingham) 2001. Nh BB 5-61 v Middlesex (Northampton) 2000. LO HS 28* H v Northants (Northampton) 2005 (NL). LO BB 5-24 Nt v Suffolk (Mildenhall) 2001 (CGT). T20 HS 11*. T20 BB 5-26.

LUCAS, David Scott (Djanogly CTC, Nottingham), b Nottingham 19 Aug 1978. 6'2". RHB, LMF. Nottinghamshire 1999-2002. Yorkshire 2005. Northamptonshire debut 2007. Lincolnshire 2006. HS 49 Nt v DU (Nottingham) 2002. CC HS 46* Nt v Middlesex (Nottingham) 2000. Nh HS 37 v Derbys (Derby) 2007. BB 5-49 Y v Bangladesh A (Leeds) 2005 and 5-49 v Leics (Leicester) 2007. LO HS 32 v Derbys (Derby) 2005 (NL). LO BB 4-27 Nt v Derbys (Derby) 2000 (NL). T20 HS 5*. T20 BB 2-37.

NELSON, Mark Anthony George (Lord Grey S, Milton Keynes; Stowe S), b Milton Keynes, Bucks 24 Sep 1986. 5'11". LHB, RM. Debut (Northamptonshire) 2007. HS 13 and BB 2-62 v Middlesex (Northampton) 2007 – in his only f-c match. LO HS 26 v Durham (Northampton) 2007 (FPT). LO BB 1-37 v Worcs (Northampton) 2007 (FPT).

O'BRIEN, Niall John (Marian C, Dublin), b Dublin, Ireland 8 Nov 1981. 5'6". Son of B.A.O'Brien (Ireland 1966-81); elder brother of K.J.O'Brien (Ireland 2006 to 2007). LHB, WK. Kent 2004-06. Ireland debut 2005-06 to 2007. Northamptonshire debut 2007. **LOI** (Ire): 21 (2006 to 2007); HS 72 v Scotland (Belfast) 2007. HS 176 Ireland v UAE (Windhoek) 2005. Nh HS 109 v Leics (Leicester) 2007. BB 1-4 K v CU (Cambridge) 2006 – his only f-c spell. LO HS 72 (*see LOI*). T20 HS 12.

PANESAR, Mudhsuden Singh (*'Monty'*) (Stopsley HS; Bedford Modern S; Loughborough U), b Luton, Beds 25 Apr 1982. 6'0". LHB, SLA. Debut (Northamptonshire) 2001; cap 2006. British U 2002-05. Loughborough UCCE 2004. MCC 2006. Bedfordshire 1998-99. *Wisden* 2007. **ECB central contract 2007-08. Tests:** 23 (2005-06 to 2007-08); HS 26 v SL (Nottingham) 2006; BB 6-129 v WI (Lord's) 2007. **LOI:** 26 (2006-07 to 2007-08); HS 13 v WI (Nottingham) 2007; BB 3-25 v B (Bridgetown) 2006-07. F-c Tours: A 2006-07; I 2005-06; SL 2002-03 (ECB Acad), 2007-08. HS 39* v Worcs (Northampton) 2005. 50 wkts (3); most – 71 (2006). BB 7-181 v Essex (Chelmsford) 2005. LO HS 16* v Essex (Colchester) 2002 (NL). LO BB 5-20 ECB Acad v SL Acad XI (Colombo) 2002-03. IT20 HS 1. IT20 BB 2-40. T20 HS 2. T20 BB 2-22.

PETERS, Stephen David (Coopers Coborn & Co S), b Harold Wood, Essex 10 Dec 1978. 5'11". RHB, occ LB. Essex 1996-2001, scoring 110 and 12* v CU (Cambridge) on debut. Worcestershire 2002-05. Northamptonshire debut 2006; cap 2007. 1000 runs (2); most – 1177 (2003). HS 178 v Essex (Northampton) 2006. BB 1-19 Ex v OU (Chelmsford) 1999. LO HS 107 v Yorks (Leeds) 2007 (FPT). T20 HS 26*.

SALES, David John Grimwood (Caterham S; Cumnor House S), b Carshalton, Surrey 3 Dec 1977. 6'0". RHB, RM. Debut (Northamptonshire) 1996 v Worcs (Kidderminster) scoring 0 and 210* – record Championship score on f-c debut; youngest (18 years 237 days) to score 200 in a Championship match; cap 1999; captain 2004-07; benefit 2007. Wellington 2001-02. F-c Tours (Eng A): NZ 1999-00; SL 1997-98; K 1997-98; B 1999-00. Sustained severe knee injury prior to start of England A tour of WI 2000-01 – no f-c appearances 2001. 1000 runs (5); most – 1384 (2007). HS 303* v Essex (Northampton) 1999 – youngest Englishman (21 years 240 days) to score a f-c 300. BB 4-25 v SL A (Northampton) 1999. CC BB 2-7 v Yorks (Scarborough) 1999. LO HS 161 v Yorks (Northampton) 2006 (CGT). T20 HS 78*. T20 BB 1-10.

NQ**VAN DER WATH, Johannes** Jacobus (Ermelo HS), b Newcastle, Natal, South Africa 10 Jan 1978. RHB, RFM. Easterns 1996-97. Free State 1997-98 to 2003-04. Eagles 2004-05 to 2006-07. Sussex 2005. Northamptonshire debut 2007. Kolpak registration 2008. **LOI** (SA): 10 (2005-06 to 2007-08); HS 37* v A (Sydney) 2005-06; BB 2-21 v SA (Melbourne) 2005-06 – on debut. F-c Tour (SA A): SL 2005-06. UK HS 113* FS v KZ-Natal (Bloemfontein) 2001-02. UK HS 94 v Essex (Northampton) 2007. BB 6-27 Eagles v Dolphins (Durban) 2006-07. UK BB 6-49 v Middlesex (Lord's) 2007. LO HS 91 FS v GW (Bloemfontein) 2000-01. LO BB 4-31 SA A v NZ (Potchefstroom) 2005-06. IT20 HS 21. IT20 BB 2-31. T20 HS 48*. T20 BB 2-8.

WAKELY, Alexander George (Bedford S), b Hammersmith, London 3 Nov 1988. RHB, OB. Debut (Northamptonshire) 2007. Bedfordshire 2004-05. Northamptonshire 2nd XI debut when aged 15 years 295 days. HS 66 and BB 2-62 v Somerset (Taunton) 2007 – on debut. LO HS 14 and BB 2-14 v Lancs (Northampton) 2007 (P40).

NQWESSELS, Mattheus Hendrik ('Riki') (Woodridge C, Pt Elizabeth; Northampton U), b Marogudoore, Queensland, Australia 12 Nov 1985. Left Australia when 2 months old. Son of K.C.Wessels (OFS, Sussex, WP, NT, Q, EP, GW, Australia and South Africa 1973-74 to 1999-00). 5'11". RHB, WK. MCC 2004. Northamptonshire debut 2005 (Kolpak registration). Nondescripts (Sri Lanka) 2007-08. HS 107 v Durham (Chester-le-St) 2005. LO HS 83 Nondescripts v Tamil Union (Colombo) 2007-08. T20 HS 49*.

WHITE, Graeme Geoffrey (Stowe S), b Milton Keynes, Bucks 18 Apr 1987. 5'11". RHB, SLA. Debut (Northamptonshire) 2006. HS 65 and CC BB 1-18 v Glamorgan (Colwyn Bay) 2007. 37 v Derbys (Northampton) 2006 – on debut. BB 2-35 v CU (Cambridge) 2007. LO HS 14 v Middlesex (Southgate) 2007 (P40). LO BB 2-44 v Worcs (Kidderminster) 2007 (P40). T20 HS – . T20 BB 1-10.

WHITE, Robert Allan (Stowe S; Durham U; Loughborough U), b Chelmsford, Essex 15 Oct 1979. 5'11". RHB, LB. Debut (Northamptonshire) 2000. Loughborough UCCE 2003. British U 2003. HS 277 and BB 2-30 v Glos (Northampton) 2002 – highest maiden f-c hundred in UK; included 107 before lunch on first day. LO HS 101 v Glamorgan (Northampton) 2004 (NL). LO BB 2-18 v Sussex (Northampton) 2002 (NL). T20 HS 66.

WIGLEY, David Harry (St Mary's RCS, Menstom, Ilkley; Loughborough U), b Bradford, Yorks 26 Oct 1981. 6'4". RHB, RFM. Yorkshire 2002 (one match). Loughborough UCCE 2003-04. British U 2004. Worcestershire 2003, 2005. Northamptonshire debut 2006. HS 70 v Middlesex (Northampton) 2007. BB 5-77 v P (Northampton) 2006. CC BB 4-68 Wo v Derbys (Derby) 2005. LO HS 10 v Middlesex (Southgate) 2007 (P40). LO BB 4-37 Wo v Leics (Worcester) 2004 (NL). T20 HS 1. T20 BB 1-8.

RELEASED/RETIRED
(Having made a County 1st XI appearance in 2007)

AFZAAL, U. – *to SURREY.*

COVERDALE, Paul Stephen (Wellingborough S; Loughborough U), b Harrogate, Yorks 24 Jul 1983. Son of S.P.Coverdale (Yorkshire, Cambridge U and Northamptonshire 1973-80, 1987; Northants Secretary-Manager/Chief Executive 1985-2004). 5'10". RHB, RM. Northamptonshire 2007. HS 11 and BB 1-36 v CU (Cambridge) 2007 in his only f-c match. LO HS 19 Northants CB v Leics CB (Barwell) 2001 (CGT). LO BB 1-21 Northants CB v Yorks CB (Northampton) 2001 (CGT) – on List A debut.

DAWSON, Richard Kevin James (Batley GS; Exeter U), b Doncaster, Yorks 4 Aug 1980. 6'3". RHB, OB. British U 2000. Yorkshire 2001-06; cap 2004. MCC 2002. Northamptonshire 2007. Devon 1999-2000. **Tests**: 7 (2001-02 to 2002-03); HS 19* v A (Perth) 2002-03; BB 4-134 v I (Chandigarh) 2001-02 – on debut. F-c Tours: A 2002-03; NZ 2001-02; I 2001-02; SL 2002-03 (ECB Acad), 2004-05 (Eng A). HS 87 Y v Kent (Canterbury) 2002. Nh HS 26 v Essex (Chelmsford) 2007. BB 6-82 Y v Glamorgan (Scarborough) 2001. Nh BB 3-25 v CU (Cambridge) 2007. LO HS 41 Y v Leics (Scarborough) 2002 (NL). LO BB 4-13 Y v Derbys (Derby) 2002 (BHC). T20 HS 22. T20 BB 3-24.

NQJACOBS, David Johan (Hoer Volkskool, Potchefstroom), b Klerksdorp, Transvaal, South Africa 4 Nov 1982. RHB, RM, WK. North West 2001-02 to 2003-04. Eagles 2004-05 to 2006-07. Northamptonshire 2007. Warriors 2007-08. HS 218 Eagles v Dolphins (Bloemfontein) 2004-05. LO HS 101* Eagles v Warriors (Port Elizabeth) 2004-05. T20 HS 53*.

NQROGERS, C.J.L. – *see DERBYSHIRE.*

P.J.Foster left the staff without making a County 1st XI appearance in 2007.

NORTHAMPTONSHIRE 2007

RESULTS SUMMARY

	Place	Won	Lost	Tied	Drew	No Result
LV County Championship (2nd Division)	5th	5	5		6	
All First-Class Matches		6	5		6	
Friends Provident Trophy (North Conference)	9th	1	6			2
NatWest Pro40 League (1st Division)	7th	2	5			1
Twenty/20 Cup (Midlands/West Wales Division)	4th	2	3			3

LV COUNTY CHAMPIONSHIP AVERAGES

BATTING AND FIELDING

Cap		M	I	NO	HS	Runs	Avge	100	50	Ct/St
1999	D.J.G.Sales	16	29	4	219	1384	55.36	3	7	23
2006	L.Klusener	16	26	5	122	1013	48.23	2	5	6
–	N.Boje	4	7	1	125	251	41.83	1	1	1
–	A.R.Crook	4	8	1	72	269	38.42		2	1
2005	U.Afzaal	8	16	–	73	570	35.62		5	3
–	R.A.White	12	21	3	75	601	33.38		3	8
2007	S.D.Peters	15	29	2	107	854	31.62	2	4	13
–	M.H.Wessels	10	17	1	58	436	27.25		2	26/2
–	J.J.van der Wath	9	14	2	94	321	26.75		3	2
–	S.P.Crook	9	15	2	60	315	24.23		2	3
–	D.S.Lucas	9	13	4	37	215	23.88			2
–	N.J.O'Brien	8	13	2	109	249	22.63	1		23/2
–	D.H.Wigley	9	13	3	70	223	22.30		2	5
–	C.J.L.Rogers	7	13	1	69	264	22.00		3	10
–	A.G.Wakely	4	8	–	66	169	21.12		2	1
–	D.J.Jacobs	4	8	–	56	143	17.87		1	2
–	R.K.J.Dawson	2	4	1	26	45	15.00			–
2006	M.S.Panesar	5	6	–	33	83	13.83			2
2000	J.F.Brown	14	17	6	25	108	9.81			3
–	R.J.Logan	7	8	3	10	32	6.40			1

Also batted: M.A.G.Nelson (1 match) 13 (1 ct); I.J.Sutcliffe (1) 9; G.G.White (2) 65, 6 (1 ct).

BOWLING

	O	M	R	W	Avge	Best	5wI	10wM
N.Boje	136.1	29	382	16	23.87	6-110	1	–
M.S.Panesar	189.3	38	580	22	26.36	6- 65	1	–
J.J.van der Wath	227.3	52	785	29	27.06	6- 49	1	–
D.H.Wigley	214	32	879	30	29.30	3- 10	–	–
S.P.Crook	216.4	40	778	21	37.04	4- 56	–	–
L.Klusener	432.3	107	1280	33	38.78	5- 40	2	–
D.S.Lucas	202	29	751	19	39.52	5- 49	1	–
J.F.Brown	453.5	113	1235	30	41.16	5- 47	1	–
R.J.Logan	189	36	656	15	43.73	3- 38	–	–

Also bowled: U.Afzaal 3-0-10-1; A.R.Crook 17-5-60-0; R.K.J.Dawson 32-1-129-1; M.A.G.Nelson 8-1-62-2; D.J.G.Sales 1-0-3-0; A.G.Wakely 29-1-127-3; G.G.White 48-15-107-1; R.A.White 39-1-188-2.

The First-Class Averages (pp 140–158) give the records of Northamptonshire players in all first-class county matches (Northamptonshire's other opponents being Cambridge UCCE), with the exception of M.S.Panesar and I.J.Sutcliffe, whose full first-class figures for Northamptonshire are as above.

NORTHAMPTONSHIRE RECORDS

FIRST-CLASS CRICKET

Highest Total	For 781-7d		v	Notts	Northampton	1995
	V 673-8d		by	Yorkshire	Leeds	2003
Lowest Total	For 12		v	Glos	Gloucester	1907
	V 33		by	Lancashire	Northampton	1977
Highest Innings	For 331*	M.E.K.Hussey	v	Somerset	Taunton	2003
	V 333	K.S.Duleepsinhji	for	Sussex	Hove	1930

Highest Partnership for each Wicket

1st	375	R.A.White/M.J.Powell	v	Glos	Northampton	2002
2nd	344	G.Cook/R.J.Boyd-Moss	v	Lancashire	Northampton	1986
3rd	393	A.Fordham/A.J.Lamb	v	Yorkshire	Leeds	1990
4th	370	R.T.Virgin/P.Willey	v	Somerset	Northampton	1976
5th	401	M.B.Loye/D.Ripley	v	Glamorgan	Northampton	1998
6th	376	R.Subba Row/A.Lightfoot	v	Surrey	The Oval	1958
7th	293	D.J.G.Sales/D.Ripley	v	Essex	Northampton	1999
8th	164	D.Ripley/N.G.B.Cook	v	Lancashire	Manchester	1987
9th	156	R.Subba Row/S.Starkie	v	Lancashire	Northampton	1955
10th	148	B.W.Bellamy/J.V.Murdin	v	Glamorgan	Northampton	1925

Best Bowling	For	10-127	V.W.C.Jupp	v	Kent	Tunbridge W	1932
(Innings)	V	10- 30	C.Blythe	for	Kent	Northampton	1907
Best Bowling	For	15- 31	G.E.Tribe	v	Yorkshire	Northampton	1958
(Match)	V	17- 48	C.Blythe	for	Kent	Northampton	1907

Most Runs – Season	2198	D.Brookes	(av 51.11)		1952
Most Runs – Career	28980	D.Brookes	(av 36.13)		1934-59
Most 100s – Season	8	R.A.Haywood			1921
Most 100s – Career	67	D.Brookes			1934-59
Most Wkts – Season	175	G.E.Tribe	(av 18.70)		1955
Most Wkts – Career	1102	E.W.Clark	(av 21.26)		1922-47
Most Career W-K Dismissals	810	K.V.Andrew	(653 ct/157 st)		1953-66
Most Career Catches in the Field	469	D.S.Steele			1963-84

LIMITED-OVERS CRICKET

Highest Total	FPT	360-2		v	Staffs	Northampton	1990
	P40	319-7		v	Scotland	Northampton	2003
	T20	224-5		v	Glos	Milton Keynes	2005
Lowest Total	FPT	62		v	Leics	Leicester	1974
	P40	41		v	Middlesex	Northampton	1972
	T20	128-5		v	Glos	Bristol	2003
Highest Innings	FPT	161	D.J.G.Sales	v	Yorkshire	Northampton	2006
	P40	172*	W.Larkins	v	Warwicks	Luton	1983
	T20	111*	L.Klusener	v	Worcs	Kidderminster	2007
Best Bowling	FPT	7-10	C.Pietersen	v	Denmark	Brondby	2005
	P40	7-39	A.Hodgson	v	Somerset	Northampton	1976
	T20	5-27	J.F.Brown	v	Somerset	Northampton	2003

NOTTINGHAMSHIRE

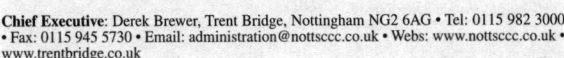

Formation of Present Club: March/April 1841
Substantial Reorganisation: 11 December 1866
Inaugural First-Class Match: 1864
Colours: Green and Gold
Badge: Badge of City of Nottingham
County Champions (since 1890): (5) 1907, 1929, 1981, 1987, 2005
Gillette/NatWest/C&G/FP Trophy Winners: (1) 1987
Benson and Hedges Cup Winners: (1) 1989
Pro 40/National League (Div 1) Winners: (0); best – 2nd 2007
Sunday League Winners: (1) 1991
Twenty20 Cup Winners: (0); best – Finalist 2006

Chief Executive: Derek Brewer, Trent Bridge, Nottingham NG2 6AG • Tel: 0115 982 3000 • Fax: 0115 945 5730 • Email: administration@nottsccc.co.uk • Webs: www.nottsccc.co.uk • www.trentbridge.co.uk

Director of Cricket: Mick Newell. **Club Coach**: Paul Johnson. **Captain**: C.M.W.Read. **Vice-Captain**: none. **Overseas Player**: D.J.Hussey. **2008 Beneficiary**: A.J.Harris. **Head Groundsman**: Steve Birks. **Scorer**: L. Brian Hewes. ‡ New registration. NQ Not qualified for England.

ALLEYNE, David (Enfield GS; Hertford Regional C; City & Islington C), b York 17 Apr 1976. 5'11". RHB, WK. Middlesex 2001-02. Nottinghamshire debut 2004. No 1st XI appearances 2007. HS 109* v Warwks (Nottingham) 2006. LO HS 58 M v Notts (Nottingham) 2000 (NL). T20 HS 24*.

‡BROAD, Stuart Christopher John (Oakham S), b Nottingham 24 Jun 1986. 6'6". LHB, RFM. Son of B.C.Broad (Glos, Notts, OFS and England 1979-94). Debut (Leicestershire) 2005; cap 2007. YC 2006. **Tests**: 1 (2007-08); HS 2 and BB 1-95 v SL (Colombo) 2007-08. **LOI**: 26 (2006 to 2007-08); HS 45* and BB 4-51 v I (Manchester) 2007. F-c Tours (Eng A): WI 2005-06; SL 2007-08; B 2006-07. HS 91* and BB 5-67 Le v Derbys (Leicester) 2007. LO HS 45* (*see LOI*). LO BB 4-51 (*see LOI*). IT20 HS 3*. IT20 BB 3-37. T20 HS 3*. T20 BB 3-13.

CLOUGH, Gareth David (Pudsey Grangefield S), b Leeds, Yorks 23 May 1978. 6'0". RHB, RM. Yorkshire 1998. Nottinghamshire debut 2003. HS 55 v Ind A (Nottingham) 2003. CC HS 33 Y v Glamorgan (Cardiff) 1998 – on debut. BB 3-69 v Glos (Nottingham) 2001. LO HS 42* v Durham (Nottingham) 2003 (NL). LO BB 6-25 v Sussex (Nottingham) 2006 (P40). T20 HS 40*. T20 BB 4-24.

EALHAM, Mark Alan (Stour Valley SS, Chartham), b Willesborough, Ashford, Kent 27 Aug 1969. Son of A.G.E.Ealham (Kent 1966-82). 5'9". RHB, RMF. Kent 1989-2003; cap 1992; benefit 2003. Nottinghamshire debut/cap 2004. Lawrence Trophy (fastest f-c hundred of 2006 – 45 balls v MCC at Lord's). **Tests**: 8 (1996 to 1998); HS 53* v A (Birmingham) 1997; BB 4-21 v I (Nottingham) 1996. **LOI**: 64 (1996 to 2001); HS 45 v WI (Bridgetown) 1997-98; BB 5-15 v Z (Kimberley) 1999-00 – Eng record (then). F-c Tours: A 1996-97 (Eng A); SA 1999-00 (*part*); SL 1997-98; Z 1992-93 (K); K 1997-98. 1000 runs (1): 1055 (1997). HS 153* K v Northants (Canterbury) 2001. Nt HS 139 v Leics (Leicester) 2004. BB 8-36 (10-74 match) K v Warwks (Birmingham) 1996. 50 wkts (1): 56 (2005). Nt BB 5-31 v Glos (Nottingham) 2005. LO HS 112 K v Derbys (Maidstone) 1995 (off 44 balls – SL record). LO BB 6-53 K v Hants (Basingstoke) 1993 (SL). T20 HS 91. T20 BB 3-26.

FERLEY, Robert Steven (King Edward VII HS; Sutton Valence S; Grey C, Durham U), b Norwich, Norfolk 4 Feb 1982. 5'8". RHB, SLA. Durham UCCE 2001-03. British U 2001-03. Kent 2003-06. Nottinghamshire debut 2007. Norfolk 1998. HS 78* DU v Durham (Chester-le-St) 2003. CC/Nt HS 43* and Nt BB 1-151 v Essex (Chelmsford) 2007 – on Notts debut. BB 6-136 K v Middlesex (Canterbury) 2006. LO HS 42 K v Lancs (Manchester) 2004 (NL). LO BB 4-33 K v Yorks (Scarborough) 2006 (P40). T20 HS 16*. T20 BB 2-29.

FOOTITT, Mark Harold Alan (Carlton le Willows S; West Notts C), b Nottingham 25 Nov 1985. 6'2". RHB, LFM. Debut (Nottinghamshire) 2005. MCC 2006. HS 19* v Hants (Southampton) 2005. BB 5-45 v West Indies A (Nottingham) 2006. CC BB 5-59 v Essex (Nottingham) 2007. LO HS – Nt CB v Oxon (Oxford) 2001 (CGT). T20 HS – .

FRANKS, Paul John (Southwell Minster CS), b Mansfield 3 Feb 1979. 6'2". LHB, RMF. Debut (Nottinghamshire) 1996; cap 1999; benefit 2007. Canterbury 2002-03. YC 2000. **LOI**: 1 (2000); HS 4 v WI (Nottingham) 2000. F-c Tours (Eng A): SA 1998-99; WI 2000-01; NZ 1999-2000; SL 2004-05; B 1999-00. HS 123* v Lics (Leicester) 2003. 50 wkts (2); most – 63 (1999). BB 7-56 v Middlesex (Lord's) 2000. Hat-trick 1997. LO HS 84* v Lincs (Lincoln) 2003 (CGT). LO BB 6-27 v Durham (Chester-le-St) 2000 (NL). T20 HS 29*. T20 BB 2-19.

‡**HALES, Alexander** Daniel (Chesham S), b Hillingdon, Middlesex 3 Jan 1989. RHB, RM, occ WK. Buckinghamshire 2006-07. MCC YC 2006-07. Awaiting f-c and List A debuts.

HARRIS, Andrew James (Hadfield CS; Glossopdale Community C), b Ashton-under-Lyne, Lancs 26 Jun 1973. 6'1". RHB, RM. Derbyshire 1994-99; cap 1996. Nottinghamshire debut/cap 2000; benefit 2008. F-c Tour (Eng A): A 1996-97. HS 41* v Northants (Northampton) 2002. Dismissed 'Timed Out' v DU (Nottingham) 2003 – third instance in f-c cricket. 50 wkts (2); most – 67 (2002). BB 7-54 (11-122 match) v Northants (Nottingham) 2002. LO HS 34 v Durham (Nottingham) 2006 (CGT). LO BB 5-35 v Hants (Nottingham) 2000 (NL). T20 HS 6. T20 BB 2-13.

[NO]**HUSSEY, David** John (Prendiville Catholic C; Edith Cowan U), b Morley, Perth, Australia 15 Jul 1977. Younger brother of M.E.K.Hussey (WA, Northants, Glos, Durham and Australia 1994-95 to date). 5'11". RHB, OB. Victoria 2002-03 to date. Nottinghamshire debut/cap 2004, scoring 107* v Oxford UCCE (Oxford) – UK debut. Sussex CB (List A) 2001. F-c Tour (Aus A): P 2007-08. 1000 runs (4); most – 1315 (2004). HS 275 v Essex (Nottingham) 2007. Scored 170, 116 and 140 in successive innings 2004. BB 4-105 v Hants (Nottingham) 2005. LO HS 130 Vic v Q (Brisbane) 2005-06. LO BB 3-26 v Northants (Northampton) 2007 (P40). T20 HS 86. T20 BB 2-10.

JEFFERSON, William Ingleby (Beeston Hall S, Norfolk; Oundle S; St Hild & St Bede C, Durham U), b Derby 25 Oct 1979. Son of R.I.Jefferson (Cambridge U and Surrey 1961-66); grandson of J.Jefferson (Army 1919, Comb Services 1922). 6'10½". RHB, RMF. British U 2000-02. Essex 2000-06; cap 2002. Durham UCCE 2001-02. Nottinghamshire debut 2007. Scored 50 and 65 in first two 1-o innings. F-c Tour (Eng A): B 2006-07. 1000 runs (1): 1555 (2004). HS 222 Ex v Hants (Southampton) 2004. Nt HS 73 v Middlesex (Lord's) 2007. BB 1-16 Ex v Yorks (Leeds) 2005. LO HS 132 Ex v Essex CB (Chelmsford) 2003 (CGT). LO BB 2-9 Ex v Worcs (Worcester) 2005 (NL). T20 HS 51.

MIERKALNS, Joshua Aleck (Arnold Hill S), b Nottingham 11 Sep 1985. 6'0". RHB, RM. Debut (Nottinghamshire) 2006. No 1st XI appearances 2007. HS 18 v West Indies A (Nottingham) 2006. Awaiting CC debut. LO HS 4 v Durham (Chester-le-St) 2006 (P40). T20 HS 4.

PATEL, Samit Rohit (Worksop C), b Leicester 30 Nov 1984. 5'8". Elder brother of A.Patel (*see DERBYSHIRE*). RHB, SLA. Debut (Nottinghamshire) 2002. Notts 2nd XI debut 1999 when aged 14 years 274 days. HS 176 v Glos (Nottingham) 2007. BB 4-68 v DU (Durham) 2007. CC BB 3-39 v Derbys (Chesterfield) 2007. LO HS 93* v Scot (Nottingham) 2006 (CGT). LO BB 3-40 v Durham (Chester-le-St) 2006 (P40). T20 HS 84*. T20 BB 3-11.

READ, Christopher Mark Wells (Torquay GS; Bath U), b Paignton, Devon 10 Aug 1978. 5'8". RHB, WK. Gloucestershire (l-o only) 1997. Debut 1997-98 for England A in Kenya. Nottinghamshire debut 1998; cap 1999; captain 2008. MCC 2002. Devon 1995-97. **Tests**: 15 (1999 to 2006-07); HS 55 v P (Leeds) 2006. Made six dismissals twice in successive innings 2006-07 to establish an Ashes record. **LOI**: 36 (1999-00 to 2006-07); HS 30* v SA (Manchester) 2003. F-c Tours: A 2006-07; SA 1998-99 (Eng A), 1999-00; WI 2000-01 (Eng A), 2003-04, 2005-06 (Eng A); SL 1997-98 (Eng A), 2002-03 (ECB Acad), 2003-04; Z 1998-99 (Eng A); B 2003-04; K 1997-98 (Eng A). 1000 runs (1): 1001 (2007). HS 240 v Essex (Chelmsford) 2007. LO HS 135 v Durham (Nottingham) 2006 (CGT). IT20 HS 13. T20 HS 48*.

SHAFAYAT, Bilal Mustapha (Greenwood Dale; Nottingham Bluecoat SFC), b Nottingham 10 Jul 1984. 5'7". RHB, RMF. Nottinghamshire 2001-04, 2007. National Bank of Pakistan 2004-05. Northamptonshire 2005-06. Pakistan Customs 2007-08. Captained Eng U-19 tour of Australia 2002-03. F-c Tour (Eng A): I 2003-04. 1000 runs (1): 1058 (2005). HS 161 Nh v Derbys (Derby) 2005. Nt HS 105 and BB 1-22 v DU (Nottingham) 2003. BB 2-25 Nh v P (Northampton) 2006. CC-BB 1-24 v Essex (Chelmsford) 2007. LO HS 104 v Northants (Northampton) 2007 (FPT). LO BB 4-33 Nh v Worcs (Worcester) 2005 (NL). T20 HS 40. T20 BB 2-13.

SHRECK, Charles Edward (Truro S), b Truro, Cornwall 6 Jan 1978. 6'7". RHB, RFM. Debut (Nottinghamshire) 2003; cap 2006. Wellington 2005-06 to date. Cornwall 1997-2002. HS 19 v Essex (Chelmsford) 2003. 50 wkts (1): 61 (2006). BB 8-31 (12-129 match) v Middlesex (Nottingham) 2006. Hat-trick v Middlesex (Lord's) 2006. LO HS 9* Wellington v CD (Palmerston N) 2005-06. LO BB 5-19 Cornwall v Worcs (Truro) 2002 (CGT). Took 5-35 v Worcs (Nottingham) 2002 (NL) – on 1st XI debut. T20 HS 6*. T20 BB 3-33.

SIDEBOTTOM, Ryan Jay (King James's GS, Almondbury), b Huddersfield, Yorks 15 Jan 1978. Son of A.Sidebottom (Yorks, OFS and England 1973-91). 6'3". LHB, LFM. Yorkshire 1997-2003; cap 2000. Nottinghamshire debut/cap 2004. **ECB central contract 2007-08**. **Tests**: 10 (2001 to 2007-08); HS 31 v SL (Kandy) 2007-08; BB 5-88 v WI (Chester-le-St) 2007. **LOI**: 13 (2001-02 to 2007-08); HS 15 v WI (Birmingham) 2007; BB 3-19 v SL (Dambulla) 2007-08. F-c Tours: WI 2000-01 (Eng A); SL 2007-08. HS 54 Y v Glamorgan (Cardiff) 1998. Nt HS 33 v Durham (Chester-le-St) 2006. 50 wkts (2); most – 50 (2005, 2006). BB 7-97 Y v Derbys (Leeds) 2003. Nt BB 5-22 v Kent (Nottingham) 2006. LO HS 32 v Middlesex (Nottingham) 2005 (NL). LO BB 6-40 Y v Glamorgan (Cardiff) 1998 (SL). IT20 HS – . IT20 BB 2-25. T20 HS 12*. T20 BB 3-20.

SWANN, Graeme Peter (Sponne SS, Towcester), b Northampton 24 Mar 1979. Son of R.Swann (Northumberland 1969-72; Bedfordshire 1988-95); younger brother of A.J.Swann (Northamptonshire and Lancashire 1996-2004). 6'0". RHB, OB. Northamptonshire 1998-2004; cap 1999. Nottinghamshire debut 2005. MCC 2005. Bedfordshire 1996. **LOI**: 7 (1999-00 to 2007-08); HS 34 v SL (Dambulla) 2007-08; BB 4-34 v SL (Dambulla) 2007-08. F-c Tours (Eng A): SA 1999-00, 1999-00 (Eng); WI 2000-01 (*part*); SL 2004-05, 2007-08 Eng – no f-c matches); Z 1998-99. HS 183 Nh v Glos (Bristol) 2002 – including 114 before lunch on third day. Nt HS 97 v Essex (Chelmsford) 2007. 50 wkts (1): 57 (1999). BB 7-33 Nh v Derbys (Northampton) 2003. Nt BB 7-100 v Glamorgan (Swansea) 2005. LO HS 83 Nh v Leics (Northampton) 2001 (NL). LO BB 5-17 v Glos (Nottingham) 2007 (P40). T20 HS 62. T20 BB 3-16.

WAGH, Mark Anant (King Edward's S, Birmingham; Keble C, Oxford), b Birmingham, Warwks 20 Oct 1976. 6'2". RHB, OB. Oxford U 1996-98; blue 1996-97-98; captain 1997. Warwickshire 1997-2006; cap 2000. British U 1996-1998. Mashonaland A 1998-99. Nottinghamshire debut/cap 2007. Zimbabwe CA (List A) 1998-99. 1000 runs (5); most – 1310 (2007). HS 315 Wa v Middlesex (Lord's) 2001. Nt HS 152 v Northants (Northampton) 2007. BB 7-222 Wa v Lancs (Birmingham) 2003. Nt BB 2-6 v Somerset (Taunton) 2007. LO HS 102* Wa v Kent (Birmingham) 2004 (NL). LO BB 4-35 Wa v Glamorgan (Birmingham) 2004 (NL). T20 HS 56. T20 BB 2-16.

‡**WOOD, Matthew** James (Exmouth Community C; Exeter U), b Exeter, Devon 30 Sep 1980. 5'11". RHB, OB. Somerset 2001-07; cap 2005. MCC 2007. Devon 1998-2004. 1000 (1): 1058 (2005). HS 297 Sm v Yorks (Taunton) 2005. LO HS 129 Sm v Yorks (Taunton) 2005 (NL). T20 HS 94.

RELEASED/RETIRED
(Having made a County 1st XI appearance in 2007)

NQ**ADAMS, Andre** Ryan (Westlake BHS, Auckland), b Mangere, Auckland, New Zealand 17 Jul 1975. 5'9". RHB, RMF. Auckland 1997-98 to date. Essex 2004-06, scoring 124 on debut (*see below*); cap 2004. Nottinghamshire 2007; cap 2007. Herefordshire 2001. **Tests** (NZ): 1 (2001-02); HS 11 and BB 3-44 v E (Auckland) 2001-02 – on debut. **LOI** (NZ): 41 (2000-01 to 2006-07); HS 45 v P (Rawalpindi) 2001-02; BB 5-22 v I (Queenstown) 2002-03. HS 124 Ex v Leics (Leics) 2004 (91 balls, 7 sixes, 13 fours; 100 off 80 balls) on UK debut. Nt HS 33 v Middlesex (Lord's) 2007. BB 6-25 Auckland v Wellington (Auckland) 2004-05. UK BB 5-60 Ex v Durham (Southend) 2005. LO HS 90* N is Selection XI v SL (New Plymouth) 2000-01. LO BB 5-7 Auckland v ND (Auckland) 1999-00. IT20 HS 7. IT20 BB 2-20. T20 HS 54*. T20 BB 3-35.

NQ**FLEMING, Stephen** Paul (Cashmere HS, Canterbury; Christchurch C of Ed), b Christchurch, New Zealand 1 Apr 1973. 6'3". LHB, RSM. Canterbury 1991-92 to 1999-00. Middlesex 2001; cap 2001. Wellington 2001-02 to 2006-07. Yorkshire 2003. Nottinghamshire 2005-07; cap 2005; captain 2005-07. **Tests** (NZ): 108 (1993-94 to 2007-08, 80 as captain); HS 274* v SL (Colombo) 2002-03. **LOI** (NZ): 277 (1993-94 to 2006-07, 216 as captain); HS 134* v SA (Johannesburg) 2002-03; BB 1-8 v Holland (Baroda) 1995-96. F-c Tours (NZ) (C=captain): E 1994, 1999C, 2004C; A 1997-98C, 2001-02C, 2004-05C; SA 1993-94 (Cant), 1994-95, 2000-01C, 2005-06C, 2007-08; WI 1995-96, 2002C; I 1995-96, 1999-00C, 2003-04C; P 1996-97, 2002C; SL 1998C, 2003C; Z 1997-98C, 2000-01C, 2005C; B 2004-05C. 1000 runs (1): 1091 (2001). HS 274* (*see Tests*). UK HS 243 v Derbys (Chesterfield) 2007. LO HS 139* Y v Warwks (Leeds) 2003 (NL). LO BB 1-3 NZ v Gauteng (Soweto) 2000-01. IT20 HS 38. T20 HS 64*.

FRANCIS, Simon Richard George (Yardley Court, Tonbridge; King Edward VI S, Southampton; Durham U), b Bromley, Kent 15 Aug 1978. Elder brother of J.D.Francis (*see SOMERSET*). 6'2". RHB, RMF. Hampshire 1997-2000. British U 1998-99. Somerset 2002-06. Nottinghamshire 2007. F-c Tour (Eng A): I 2003-04. HS 44 Sm v Yorks (Taunton) 2003. Nt HS – . BB 5-42 Sm v Glamorgan (Taunton) 2004. Nt BB 1-43 v Derbys (Nottingham) 2007 – on Notts debut. Hat-trick 2003. LO HS 33* Sm v Derbys (Taunton) 2003 (NL). LO BB 8-66 Sm v Derbys (Derby) 2004 (CGT) – record l-o Somerset analysis. T20 HS 9*. T20 BB 2-22.

GALLIAN, J.E.R. – *see ESSEX*.

NOTTINGHAMSHIRE 2007

RESULTS SUMMARY

	Place	Won	Lost	Tied	Drew	No Result
LV County Championship (2nd Division)	2nd	6	3		7	
All First-Class Matches		6	3		8	
Friends Provident Trophy (North Conference)	3rd	6	2			1
NatWest Pro40 League (1st Division)	2nd	4	2			2
Twenty/20 Cup (North Division)	Quarter-Finalist	4	2			3

LV COUNTY CHAMPIONSHIP AVERAGES

BATTING AND FIELDING

Cap		M	I	NO	HS	Runs	Avge	100	50	Ct/St
2004	D.J.Hussey	12	15	2	275	1219	93.76	4	5	16
2005	S.P.Fleming	11	17	1	243	930	58.12	4	2	21
2007	M.A.Wagh	16	24	2	152	1253	56.95	3	10	2
1999	C.M.W.Read	16	21	4	240	921	54.17	2	3	39/6
–	S.R.Patel	13	18	1	176	887	52.17	4	4	7
1998	J.E.R.Gallian	16	24	–	178	867	36.12	2	3	8
–	W.I.Jefferson	5	9	–	73	316	35.11	–	1	3
2005	G.P.Swann	15	18	3	97	467	31.13	–	3	11
–	B.M.Shafayat	11	17	1	79	488	30.50	–	4	14
2004	M.A.Ealham	12	14	3	74*	261	23.72	–	2	14
1999	P.J.Franks	11	13	1	92	275	22.91	–	1	5
2007	A.R.Adams	4	6	1	33	104	20.80	–	–	1
2004	R.J.Sidebottom	8	7	1	18	55	9.16	–	–	1
2000	A.J.Harris	5	8	1	10	24	3.42	–	–	2
2006	C.E.Shreck	10	10	8	3	4	2.00	–	–	6

Also batted: G.D.Clough (1 match) 2, 7; A.M.Davies (1) 35*; R.S.Ferley (3) 43*, 2*, 40; K.W.Hogg (2) 10*, 26; M.N.Malik (1) 12*, 1. M.H.A.Footitt (3) and S.R.G.Francis (2) did not bat.

BOWLING

	O	M	R	W	Avge	Best	5wI	10wM
S.R.Patel	81	14	261	10	26.10	3- 39	–	–
M.A.Ealham	318.4	101	862	31	27.80	4- 37	–	–
C.E.Shreck	372.5	84	1213	43	28.20	7- 35	4	–
P.J.Franks	263.4	40	1090	32	34.06	3- 28	–	–
G.P.Swann	463.2	82	1472	43	34.23	7-100	1	1
A.R.Adams	137.1	29	501	14	35.78	4- 74	–	–
R.J.Sidebottom	189.4	44	507	13	39.00	3- 49	–	–
A.J.Harris	184.3	30	693	15	46.20	3- 39	–	–
Also bowled:								
A.M.Davies	33	8	90	8	11.25	7- 59	1	–
M.H.A.Footitt	45.4	6	191	7	27.28	5- 59	1	–

G.D.Clough 26.5-5-82-4; R.S.Ferley 63-8-283-1; S.R.G.Francis 12-1-74-1; J.E.R.Gallian 2-0-17-0; K.W.Hogg 26-7-79-0; D.J.Hussey 4.5-0-23-0; M.N.Malik 35-5-140-2; C.M.W.Read 2-0-6-0; B.M.Shafayat 10.5-1-55-1; M.A.Wagh 4-1-13-2.

The First-Class Averages (pp 140–158) give the records of Nottinghamshire players in all first-class county matches (Nottinghamshire's other opponents being Durham UCCE), with the exception of A.M.Davies, K.W.Hogg and M.N.Malik, whose full first-class figures for Nottinghamshire are as above, and:
  R.J.Sidebottom 7-8-1-18-62-8.85-0-0-1ct. 212.4-53-548-15-36.53-4/92-0-0.

NOTTINGHAMSHIRE RECORDS

FIRST-CLASS CRICKET

Highest Total	For 791		v	Essex	Chelmsford	2007
	V 781-7d		by	Northants	Northampton	1995
Lowest Total	For 13		v	Yorkshire	Nottingham	1901
	V 16		by	Derbyshire	Nottingham	1879
	16		by	Surrey	The Oval	1880
Highest Innings	For 312*	W.W.Keeton	v	Middlesex	The Oval	1939
	V 345	C.G.Macartney	for	Australians	Nottingham	1921

Highest Partnership for each Wicket

1st	406*	D.J.Bicknell/G.E.Welton	v	Warwicks	Birmingham	2000
2nd	398	A.Shrewsbury/W.Gunn	v	Sussex	Nottingham	1890
3rd	367	W.Gunn/J.R.Gunn	v	Leics	Nottingham	1903
4th	361	A.O.Jones/J.R.Gunn	v	Essex	Leyton	1905
5th	359	D.J.Hussey/C.M.W.Read	v	Essex	Nottingham	2007
6th	372*	K.P.Pietersen/J.E.Morris	v	Derbyshire	Derby	2001
7th	301	C.C.Lewis/B.N.French	v	Durham	Chester-le-St	1993
8th	220	G.F.H.Heane/R.Winrow	v	Somerset	Nottingham	1935
9th	170	J.C.Adams/K.P.Evans	v	Somerset	Taunton	1994
10th	152	E.B.Alletson/W.Riley	v	Sussex	Hove	1911
	152	U.Afzaal/A.J.Harris	v	Worcs	Nottingham	2000

Best Bowling	For 10-66	K.Smales	v	Glos	Stroud	1956
(Innings)	V 10-10	H.Verity	for	Yorkshire	Leeds	1932
Best Bowling	For 17-89	F.C.L.Matthews	v	Northants	Nottingham	1923
(Match)	V 17-89	W.G.Grace	for	Glos	Cheltenham	1877

Most Runs – Season	2620	W.W.Whysall	(av 53.46)	1929
Most Runs – Career	31592	G.Gunn	(av 35.69)	1902-32
Most 100s – Season	9	W.W.Whysall		1928
	9	M.J.Harris		1971
	9	B.C.Broad		1990
Most 100s – Career	65	J.Hardstaff jr		1930-55
Most Wkts – Season	181	B.Dooland	(av 14.96)	1954
Most Wkts – Career	1653	T.G.Wass	(av 20.34)	1896-1920
Most Career W-K Dismissals	957	T.W.Oates	(733 ct/224 st)	1897-1925
Most Career Catches in the Field	466	A.O.Jones		1892-1914

LIMITED-OVERS CRICKET

Highest Total	FPT	344-6	v	Northumb	Jesmond	1994
	P40	329-6	v	Derbyshire	Nottingham	1993
	T20	213-6	v	Northants	Nottingham	2006
Lowest Total	FPT	123	v	Yorkshire	Scarborough	1969
	P40	66	v	Yorkshire	Bradford	1969
	T20	91	v	Lancashire	Manchester	2006
Highest Innings	FPT	149* D.W.Randall	v	Devon	Torquay	1988
	P40	167* P.Johnson	v	Kent	Nottingham	1993
	T20	91 M.A.Ealham	v	Yorkshire	Nottingham	2004
Best Bowling	FPT	6-10 K.P.Evans	v	Northumb	Jesmond	1994
	P40	6-12 R.J.Hadlee	v	Lancashire	Nottingham	1980
	T20	5-26 R.J.Logan	v	Lancashire	Nottingham	2003

SOMERSET

Formation of Present Club: 18 August 1875
Inaugural First-Class Match: 1882
Colours: Black, White and Maroon
Badge: Somerset Dragon
County Champions: (0); best – 2nd (Div 1) 2001
Gillette/NatWest/C&G/FP Trophy Winners: (3) 1979, 1983, 2001
Benson and Hedges Cup Winners: (2) 1981, 1982
Pro 40/National League (Div 1) Winners: (0); best – 4th 2001
Sunday League Winners: (1) 1979
Twenty20 Cup Winners: (1) 2005

Chief Executive: Richard A.Gould, County Ground, Taunton TA1 1JT • Tel: 0845 337 1875 • Fax: 01823 332395 • Email: enquiries@somersetcountycc.co.uk • Web: www.somerset countycc.co.uk

Director of Cricket: Brian C.Rose. **Captain**: J.L.Langer. **Vice-Captain**: A.R.Caddick. **Overseas Player**: J.L.Langer. **2008 Beneficiary**: M.E.Trescothick. **Head Groundsman**: Phil Frost. **Scorer**: Gerald A.Stickley. ‡ New registration. NQ Not qualified for England.

‡NQ**BANKS, Omari** Ahmed Clemente, b Road Bay, Antigua 17 Jul 1982. RHB, OB. Leeward Islands 2000-01 to date. Leicestershire 2001 (1 match – v Pakistanis). Carib Beer XI 2002-03 to 2003-04. **Tests** (WI): 10 (2002-03 to 2005): HS 50* v SL (Gros Islet, St Lucia) 2003; BB 4-87 v B (Kingston) 2004. **LOI** (WI): 5 (2002-03 to 2005): HS 33 and BB 2-24 v SL (Colombo) 2005. F-c Tours (WI): E 2004, 2006 (WI A); SL 2005; Z 2003-04. HS 100 Leeward Is v Jamaica (Cayon, St Kitts) 2006-07. BB 7-70 Leeward Is v Jamaica (Molyneaux, St Kitts) 2000-01. LO HS 77* Rest of Leeward Is v Canada (Kingston) 2003-04. LO BB 4-23 Rest of Leeward Is v N Windward Is (Kingston) 2001-02.

BLACKWELL, Ian David (Brookfield Community S), b Chesterfield, Derbys 10 Jun 1978. 6'2". LHB, SLA. Derbyshire 1997-99. Somerset debut 2000; cap 2001; captain 2006 (part). **Tests**: 1 (2005-06): HS 4 v I (Nagpur) 2005-06. **LOI**: 34 (2002-03 to 2005-06); HS 82 v I (Colombo) 2002-03; BB 3-26 v A (Adelaide) 2002-03. F-c Tour: I 2005-06. 1000 runs (2); most – 1256 (2005). HS 247* v Derbys (Taunton) 2003 – off 156 balls and including 204 off 98 balls in reduced post-lunch session. Won Walter Lawrence Trophy 2005 for 67-ball hundred v Derbys (Taunton). BB 7-90 v Glamorgan (Taunton) 2004 and 7-90 v Notts (Nottingham) 2004. LO HS 134* v Sussex (Taunton) 2005 (NL). LO BB 5-26 v Derbys (Taunton) 2005 (NL). T20 HS 82. T20 BB 4-26.

CADDICK, Andrew Richard (Papanui HS), b Christchurch, NZ 21 Nov 1968. Son of English emigrants – qualified for England 1992. 6'5". RHB, RFM. Debut (Somerset) 1991; cap 1992; benefit 1999. Represented NZ in 1987-88 Youth World Cup. **Tests**: 62 (1993 to 2002-03); HS 49* v A (Birmingham) 2001; BB 7-46 v SA (Durban) 1999-00. **LOI**: 54 (1993 to 2002-03); HS 36 v A (Oval) 2001; BB 4-19 v SA (Johannesburg) 1999-00. F-c Tours: A 1992-93 (Eng A), SA 1999-00; WI 1993-94, 1997-98; NZ 1996-97, 2001-02; P 2000-01; SL 2000-01; Z 1996-97. HS 92 v Worcs (Worcester) 1995. 50 wkts (12) inc 100 (1): 105 (1998). BB 9-32 (12-120 match) v Lancs (Taunton) 1993. LO HS 39 v Hants (Taunton) 1996 (SL). LO BB 6-30 v Glos (Taunton) 1992 (NWT). T20 HS 0. T20 BB 2-12.

DURSTON, Wesley John (Millfield S; University C, Worcester), b Taunton 6 Oct 1980. 5'10". RHB, OB. Debut (Somerset) 2002. HS 146* v Derbys (Derby) 2005. BB 3-23 v SL A (Taunton) 2004. CC BB 2-31 v Surrey (Bath) 2006. LO HS 62* v Yorks (Taunton) 2006 (P40). LO BB 3-44 v Surrey (Taunton) 2006 (P40). T20 HS 34. T20 BB 3-25.

EDWARDS, Neil James (Cape Cornwall CS; Richard Huish C), b Treliske, Truro, Cornwall 14 Oct 1983. 6'3". LHB, RM. Debut (Somerset) 2002. Cornwall 2000-06. 1000 runs (1): 1251 (2007). HS 212 v LU (Taunton) 2007. CC HS 160 v Hants (Taunton) 2003. BB 1-16 V Derbys (Taunton) 2004. LO HS 65 v Yorks (Taunton) 2006 (P40). T20 HS 1.

FRANCIS, John Daniel (King Edward VI S, Southampton; Durham U; Loughborough U), b Bromley, Kent 13 Nov 1980. Younger brother of S.R.G.Francis (see *NOTTINGHAMSHIRE*). 5'11". LHB, SLA. Hampshire 2001-03. British U 2002-03. Loughborough UCCE 2003. Somerset debut 2004. 1000 (1): 1062 (2005). HS 125* v Yorks (Leeds) 2005 – carrying bat. BB 1-1 H v Leics (Leicester) 2002. Sm BB 1-4 v Durham (Chester-le-St) 2004. LO HS 103* H v Northants (Southampton) 2002 (NL). T20 HS 49.

GAZZARD, Carl Matthew (Mounts Bay CS, Penzance; Richard Huish C), b Penzance, Cornwall 15 Apr 1982. 6'0". RHB, WK. Debut (Somerset) 2002. Cornwall 1998-2007. HS 74 v Worcs (Worcester) 2005. LO HS 157 v Derbys (Derby) 2004 (NL). T20 HS 39.

HILDRETH James Charles (Millfield S), b Milton Keynes, Bucks 9 Sep 1984. 5'10", RHB, RMF. Debut (Somerset) 2003; cap 2007. 1000 runs (1): 1270 (2007). HS 227* v Northants (Taunton) 2006. BB 2-39 v Hants (Taunton) 2004. LO HS 122 v Derbys (Derby) 2006 (P40). LO BB 1-8 v Glamorgan (Taunton) 2007 (FPT). T20 HS 71. T20 BB 3-24.

JONES, Philip Steffan (Stradey CS, Llanelli; Neath TC; Loughborough U; Homerton C, Cambridge), b Llanelli, Carms, Wales 9 Feb 1974. 6'2". RHB, RMF. Cambridge U 1997; blue 1997. Somerset 1997-2003, 2007; cap 2001. Northamptonshire 2004-05. Derbyshire 2006. Wales MC 1994-97. HS 114 v Leics (Leicester) 2007. 50 wkts (2): 59 (2001, 2006). BB 6-25 De v Glamorgan (Cardiff) 2006. Sm BB 6-61 v Leics (Taunton) 2007. LO HS 27 v Northants (Northampton) 2000 (NL). LO BB 6-56 Nh v Ire (Clontarf) 2004 (CGT). T20 HS 24*. T20 BB 3-26.

KIESWETTER, Craig (Diocesan C; Millfield S), b Johannesburg, South Africa 18 Nov 1987. 6'1". RHB, WK. Debut (Somerset) 2007. Represented South Africa in U-19 World Cup 2006. HS 93 v Glamorgan (Taunton) 2007. LO HS 69* v Glamorgan (Taunton) 2007 (FPT). T20 HS 48.

NQLANGER, Justin Lee (Aquinas C; U of WA), b Perth, Australia 21 Nov 1970. Nephew of R.S.Langer (W Australia 1973-74 to 1981-82). 5'8". LHB, RM. W Australia 1991-92 to date. Middlesex 1998-2000; cap 1998; captain 2000. Somerset debut 2006; cap 2007; captain 2007 to date. *Wisden* 2000. **Tests** (A): 104 (1992-93 to 2006-07); blue 2005. HS 250 v E (Melbourne) 2002-03. **LOI**: 8 (1993-94 to 1997); HS 36 v I (Sharjah) 1993-94. F-c Tours (A): E 1995 (Young A), 1997, 2001, 2005; SA 1996-97, 2001-02, 2005-06; WI 1994-95, 1998-99, 2002-03; NZ 1992-93, 1999-00, 2004-05; I 2000-01, 2004-05; P 1994-95, 1998-99, 2002-03 (*in UAE*); SL 1999, 2002-03 (*v P*), 2003-04; Z 1999-00. 1000 runs (4+6); most – 1472 (2000). HS 342 v Surrey (Guildford) 2006 – Somerset record f-c score. Scored 315 v Middlesex (Taunton) 2007 in his next CC innings. BB 2-17 Aus A v SA A (Brisbane) 1997-98. UK BB 1-10 M v Northants (Northampton) 1998. LO HS 146 WA v S Aus (Perth) 1999-00 (MM). LO BB 3-51 v Surrey (Guildford) 1998 (SL). T20 HS 97.

LETT, Robin Jonathan Hugh (Millfield S; Oxford Brookes U), b Westminster, London 23 Dec 1986. 6'2". RHB, RM. Debut (Somerset) 2006 – summer contract. Oxford UCCE 2007. HS 57 OU v Glamorgan (Oxford) 2007. Sm HS 50 v Glamorgan (Taunton) 2006 – on debut.

MUNDAY, Michael Kenneth (Truro S, Cornwall; Corpus Christi C, Oxford), b Nottingham 22 Oct 1984. 5'7½". RHB, LB. Oxford U 2003-06; blue 2003-04-05-06. Somerset debut 2005. Cornwall 2001-07. HS 17* and OU BB 6-77 (11-143 match) v CU (Oxford) 2006. BB 8-55 (10-65 match) and Sm HS 9 v Notts (Taunton) 2007. LO HS – and BB 1-39 Cornwall v Sussex (Truro) 2001 (CGT).

PARSONS, Keith Alan (The Castle S, Taunton; Richard Huish C), b Taunton 2 May 1973. Identical twin brother of K.J.Parsons (Somerset staff 1992-94). 6'1". RHB, RM. Debut (Somerset) 1992; cap 1999; benefit 2004. No f-c appearances 2007. HS 193* v WI (Taunton) 2000. CC HS 153 v Essex (Taunton) 2006. BB 5-13 v Lancs (Taunton) 2000. LO HS 121 v Worcs (Taunton) 2002 (CGT). LO BB 5-39 v Derbys (Derby) 2004 (NL). T20 HS 57*. T20 BB 3-12.

PHILLIPS, Ben James (Langley Park S and SFC, Beckenham), b Lewisham, London 30 Sep 1974. 6'6". RHB, RFM. Kent 1996-98. Northamptonshire 2002-06; cap 2005. Joined Somerset staff 2007 but injury prevented his appearing for 1st XI. HS 100* K v Lancs (Manchester) 1997. BB 6-29 Nh v CU (Cambridge) 2006. CC BB 5-47 K v Sussex (Horsham) 1997. LO HS 44* Nh v Kent (Canterbury) 2004 (NL). LO BB 4-25 K v Northants (Canterbury) 2000 (NL). T20 HS 41*. T20 BB 4-18.

SUPPIAH, Arul Vivasvan (Exeter U), b Kuala Lumpur, Malaysia 30 Aug 1983. Son of R.Suppiah (Kuala Lumpur). Brother of R.V.Suppiah (Malaysia 1997-98 to 2006; f-c 2004). 6'0". RHB, SLA. Somerset debut (Somerset) 2002. Malaysia 2000-01 to 2005 (not f-c). Devon 2003-05. HS 123 v Derbys (Derby) 2005. BB 3-46 v WI A (Taunton) 2002. CC BB 2-36 v Leics (Leicester) 2004. LO HS 79 v Derbys (Derby) 2005 (NL). LO BB 4-39 v Surrey (Oval) 2006 (CGT). T20 HS 18*. T20 BB 2-14.

‡**SUTTON, Andrew** Peter, b Worcester 29 Nov 1985. Herefordshire 2004-05. MCC YC 2005-07. Awaiting f-c and List A debuts.

THOMAS, Alfonso Clive (Ravensmead SS; Parow HS), b Cape Town, South Africa 9 Feb 1977. RHB, RFM. W Province 1998-99. North West 2000-01 to 2002-03. Northerns 2003-04 to 2005-06. Titans 2004-05 to date. Warwickshire 2007. F-c Tour (SA A): Z 2004. HS 119* North West v Northerns (Pretoria) 2002-03. Wa HS 42 and BB 4-109 v Yorks (Scarborough) 2007. BB 7-54 Titans v Cape Cobras (Cape Town) 2005-06. LO HS 27* Titans v WP Boland (Cape Town) 2004-05. LO BB 4-31 Northerns v Gauteng (Pretoria) 2003-04. IT20 HS – . IT20 BB 3-25. T20 HS 27. T20 BB 3-29.

TREGO, Peter David (Wyvern CS, W-s-M), b Weston-super-Mare 12 Jun 1981. 6'0". RHB, RMF. Somerset 2000-02, 2006 to date; cap 2007; 2nd XI debut 1997 when aged 16 years 20 days. Kent 2003. Middlesex 2005. Herefordshire 2005. HS 140 v West Indies A (Taunton) 2002. CC HS 135 v Derbys (Taunton) 2006. BB 6-59 M v Notts (Nottingham) 2007. Sm BB 4-49 v Leics (Leicester) 2007. LO HS 78 v Middlesex (Lord's) 2007 (FPT). BB 5-44 v Kent (Canterbury) 2007 (P40). T20 HS 47. T20 BB 2-17.

TRESCOTHICK, Marcus Edward (Sir Bernard Lovell S), b Keynsham 25 Dec 1975. 6'2". LHB, RM, occ WK. Debut (Somerset) 1993; cap 1999; joint captain 2002; Benefit 2008. PCA 2000. *Wisden* 2004. MBE 2005. **Tests**: 76 (2000 to 2006, 2 as captain); HS 219 v SA (Oval) 2003; BB 1-34 v P (Karachi) 2000-01. **LOI**: 123 (2000 to 2006, 10 as captain); HS 137 v P (Lord's) 2001; BB 2-7 v Z (Manchester) 2000. F-c Tours: A 2002-03; SA 2004-05; WI 2003-04; NZ 1999-00 (Eng A), 2001-02; I 2001-02, 2005-06 (*part*); P 2000-01, 2005-06; SL 2000-01, 2003-04; B 1999-00 (Eng A), 2003-04. 1000 runs (1): 1343 (2007). HS 284 v Northants (Northampton) 2007. BB 4-36 (inc hat-trick) v Young A (Taunton) 1995. CC BB 4-82 v Yorks (Leeds) 1998. Hat-trick 1995. LO HS 158 v Kent (Canterbury) 2006 (CGT). LO BB 4-50 v Northants (Northampton) 2000 (NL). T20 HS 76.

TURNER, Mark Leif (Thornhill CS), b Sunderland, Co Durham 23 Oct 1984. 5'11". RHB, RMF. Durham 2005-06. Somerset debut 2007. HS 57 v Derbys (Taunton) 2007. BB 4-30 v LU (Taunton) 2007. CC BB 1-30 v Glos (Taunton) 2007. LO BB 11* v Essex (Chelmsford) 2007 (FPT). LO HS 2-40 v Surrey (Bath) 2007 (FPT). T20 HS 2. T20 BB 1-31.

‡**WALLER, Max**imilian Thomas Charles (Millfield S), b Salisbury, Wiltshire 3 March 1988. RHB, LB. Somerset 2nd XI 2006-07. Dorset 2007. Awaiting 1st XI debut.

NQ**WILLOUGHBY, Charl** Myles (Wynberg BHS; Stellenbosch U), b Cape Town, South Africa 3 Dec 1974. 6'2". LHB, LMF. Boland 1994-95 to 1999-00. W Province 2000-01 to 2003-04. MCC 2001, 2004. WP-Boland 2004-05. Leicestershire 2005 (Kolpak registration). Cape Cobras 2005-06 to 2006-07. Somerset debut 2006 (Kolpak); cap 2007. Berkshire 2000. **Tests** (SA): 2 (2003); HS – ; BB 1-47 v B (Chittagong) 2002-03 – on debut. **LOI** (SA): 3 (1999-00 to 2003); HS 0; BB 2-39 v P (Sharjah) 1999-00 – on debut. F-c Tours (SA): E 2003; WI 2000 (SA A); Z 1998-99 (SA Acad), 2004 (SA A); B 2003. HS 47 v Worcs (Taunton) 2006. 50 wkts (2+2); most – 66 (2006). BB 7-44 v Glos (Taunton) 2006. LO HS 12* v Middlesex (Bath) 2006 (CGT). LO BB 6-16 Le v Somerset (Leicester) 2005 (NL). T20 HS 11. T20 BB 4-9.

NQ**WOODMAN, Robert** James (Castle School; Taunton; Richard Huish S), b Taunton 12 Oct 1986. 5'11". LHB, LMF. Debut (Somerset) 2005. No 1st XI appearances 2006-07. Devon 2006-07. HS 46* v Worcs (Worcester) 2005 – on debut. BB 1-78 v Essex (Colchester) 2005 – dismissing A.N.Cook first ball. LO HS – . LO BB 1-38 v Durham (Taunton) 2005 (NL). T20 HS 1*. T20 BB 2-37.

RELEASED/RETIRED
(Having made a County 1st XI appearance in 2007)

ANDREW, G.M. – *see WORCESTERSHIRE.*

NQ**McKENZIE, N.D.** – *see DURHAM.*

SPURWAY, Samuel Harold Patrick (Richard Huish C), b Taunton 13 Mar 1987. 6'0". LHB, WK. Somerset 2006-07. MCC YC 2007. HS 83 v Northants (Taunton) 2006. LO HS 31 v Leics (Leicester) 2006 (P40). T20 HS 15*.

NQ**WHITE, Cameron** Leon, b Bairnsdale, Victoria, Australia 18 Aug 1983. 6'1½". RHB, LBG. Victoria 2000-01 to date. Somerset 2006-07; captain 2006 (*part*); cap 2007. **LOI** (A): 16 (2005-06 to 2006-07); HS 45 v NZ (Hobart) 2006-07; BB 1-5 v E (Brisbane) 2006-07. F-c Tours (Aus A): P 2005-06, 2007-08. 1000 runs (2); most – 1190 (2006). HS 260* v Derbys (Derby) 2006 – world record score in the fourth innings of a f-c match. BB 6-66 Vic v WA (Perth) 2002-03. Sm BB 5-148 v Surrey (Guildford) 2006. LO HS 126* Vic v NSW (Canberra) 2006-07. LO BB 4-15 Vic v Tas (Melbourne) 2004-05. IT20 HS 40*. IT20 BB 1-11. T20 HS 141*. T20 BB 3-8.

WOOD, M.J. – *see NOTTINGHAMSHIRE.*

MIDDLESEX RELEASED/RETIRED (continued from p 72)

NQ**VAAS, Warnakulasuriya Patabendige Ushantha Chaminda** Joseph, b Mattumagala 27 Jan 1974. LHB, LFM. Colts 1990-91 to 2006-07. Hampshire 2003. Worcestershire 2005. Middlesex 2007; cap 2007. **Tests:** 102 (1994-95 to 2007-08); HS 100* v B (Colombo) 2007; BB 7-71 (14-191 match) v WI (Colombo) 2001-02. **LOI:** 303 (1993-94 to 2007-08, 1 as captain); HS 50* v P (Sharjah) 2000-01; BB 8-19 v Z (Colombo) 2001-02, including the first of two LOI hat-tricks. F-c Tours (SL): E 2002, 2006; A 1995-96, 2004, 2007-08; SA 1994-95, 1997-98, 2000-01, 2002-03; WI 2003; NZ 1994-95, 1996-97, 2004-05, 2006-07; I 1993-94, 1997-98, 2005-06; P 1995-96, 1999-00, 2001-02, 2004-05; Z 1994-95, 1999-00, 2004; B 1998-99 (v P). HS 134 Colts v Burgher (Colombo) 2004-05. UK HS 79 M v Glamorgan (Lord's) 2007. 50 wkts (0+2); most 62 (2001-02). BB 7-54 W Province v S Province (Colombo) 2004-05. UK BB 5-126 M v Notts (Lord's) 2007. LO HS 62* Colts v Sinhalese (Colombo) 1999-00. LO BB 8-19 (*see LOI*). IT20 HS 21. IT20 BB 2-14. T20 HS 21. T20 BB 2-14.

WHELAN, C.D. – *see WORCESTERSHIRE.*

WRIGHT, C.J. – *see ESSEX.*

SOMERSET 2007

RESULTS SUMMARY

	Place	Won	Lost	Tied	Drew	No Result
LV County Championship (2nd Division)	**1st**	10	1		5	
All First-Class Matches		11	1		5	
Friends Provident Trophy (South Conference)	6th	4	3	1		1
NatWest Pro40 League (2nd Division)	2nd	5	2			1
Twenty/20 Cup (Midlands/West Wales Division)	5th	3	5			

LV COUNTY CHAMPIONSHIP AVERAGES

BATTING AND FIELDING

Cap		M	I	NO	HS	Runs	Avge	100	50	Ct/St
2007	C.L.White	12	19	4	241	1083	72.20	5	3	7
–	N.D.McKenzie	3	5	1	84	271	67.75	–	3	2
1999	M.E.Trescothick	15	23	2	284	1315	62.61	4	5	33
2007	J.L.Langer	16	23	1	315	1231	55.95	3	3	14
2007	P.D.Trego	16	20	5	130	814	54.26	2	5	4
2007	J.C.Hildreth	16	24	2	163	1147	52.13	4	5	13
–	W.J.Durston	3	4	1	58	140	46.66	–	2	–
–	N.J.Edwards	16	25	–	133	1039	41.56	1	8	9
2001	I.D.Blackwell	14	17	1	141	590	36.87	1	4	2
2001	P.S.Jones	12	11	4	114	254	36.28	1	1	3
–	C.Kieswetter	14	16	3	93	377	29.00	–	3	46
1992	A.R.Caddick	15	13	2	51	147	13.36	–	1	2
2007	C.M.Willoughby	16	12	7	23*	58	11.60	–	–	2

Also batted: M.K.Munday (3 matches) 0, 4*, 9 (2 ct); S.H.P.Spurway (2) 44*, 0, 1 (4 ct); M.L.Turner (2) 57, 5 (1 ct); M.J.Wood (1 – cap 2005) 20.

BOWLED

	O	M	R	W	Avge	Best	5wI	10wM
M.K.Munday	44	2	192	14	13.71	8-55	1	1
A.R.Caddick	522.5	109	1690	70	24.14	7-30	3	–
C.M.Willoughby	462.4	105	1530	62	24.67	5-33	5	–
I.D.Blackwell	298.3	68	808	26	31.07	3- 8	–	–
C.L.White	178.4	17	655	20	32.75	4-28	–	–
P.D.Trego	267.2	40	1080	31	34.83	4-49	–	–
P.S.Jones	238.3	33	1011	23	43.95	6-61	1	–

Also bowled: W.J.Durston 24-1-117-0; J.C.Hildreth 16-2-89-1; M.L.Turner 56.1-5-240-2.

The First-Class Averages (pp 140–158) give the records of Somerset players in all first-class county matches (Somerset's other opponents being Loughborough UCCE), with the exception of M.J.Wood, whose full county figures are as above.

SOMERSET RECORDS

FIRST-CLASS CRICKET

Highest Total	For 850-7d		v	Middlesex	Taunton	2007
	V 811		by	Surrey	The Oval	1899
Lowest Total	For 25		v	Glos	Bristol	1947
	V 22		by	Glos	Bristol	1920
Highest Innings	For 342	J.L.Langer	v	Surrey	Guildford	2006
	V 424	A.C.MacLaren	for	Lancashire	Taunton	1895

Highest Partnership for each Wicket

1st	346	L.C.H.Palairet/H.T.Hewett	v	Yorkshire	Taunton	1892
2nd	290	J.C.W.MacBryan/M.D.Lyon	v	Derbyshire	Burton upon T	1924
3rd	319	P.M.Roebuck/M.D.Crowe	v	Leics	Taunton	1984
4th	310	P.W.Denning/I.T.Botham	v	Glos	Taunton	1980
5th	320	J.D.Francis/I.D.Blackwell	v	Durham UCCE	Taunton	2005
6th	265	W.E.Alley/K.E.Palmer	v	Northants	Northampton	1961
7th	279	R.J.Harden/G.D.Rose	v	Sussex	Taunton	1997
8th	172	I.V.A.Richards/I.T.Botham	v	Leics	Leicester	1983
	172	A.R.K.Pierson/P.S.Jones	v	N Zealanders	Taunton	1999
9th	183	C.H.M.Greetham/H.W.Stephenson	v	Leics	Weston-s-Mare	1963
	183	C.J.Tavaré/N.A.Mallender	v	Sussex	Hove	1990
10th	163	I.D.Blackwell/N.A.M.McLean	v	Derbyshire	Taunton	2003

Best Bowling	For 10- 49	E.J.Tyler	v	Surrey	Taunton	1895
(Innings)	V 10- 35	A.Drake	for	Yorkshire	Weston-s-Mare	1914
Best Bowling	For 16- 83	J.C.White	v	Worcs	Bath	1919
(Match)	V 17-137	W.Brearley	for	Lancashire	Manchester	1905

Most Runs – Season	2761	W.E.Alley	(av 58.74)	1961
Most Runs – Career	21142	H.Gimblett	(av 36.96)	1935-54
Most 100s – Season	11	S.J.Cook		1991
Most 100s – Career	49	H.Gimblett		1935-54
Most Wkts – Season	169	A.W.Wellard	(av 19.24)	1938
Most Wkts – Career	2165	J.C.White	(av 18.03)	1909-37
Most Career W-K Dismissals	1007	H.W.Stephenson	(698 ct/309 st)	1948-64
Most Career Catches in the Field	381	J.C.White		1909-37

LIMITED-OVERS CRICKET

Highest Total	FPT	413-4	v	Devon	Torquay	1990
	P40	377-9	v	Sussex	Hove	2003
	T20	250-3	v	Glos	Taunton	2006
Lowest Total	FPT	58	v	Middlesex	Southgate	2000
	P40	58	v	Essex	Chelmsford	1977
	T20	119-9	v	Glos	Taunton	2003
Highest Innings	FPT	162* C.J.Tavaré	v	Devon	Torquay	1990
	P40	175* I.T.Botham	v	Northants	Wellingborough	1986
	T20	141* C.L.White	v	Worcs	Worcester	2006
Best Bowling	FPT	8-66 S.R.G.Francis	v	Derbyshire	Derby	2004
	P40	6-24 I.V.A.Richards	v	Lancashire	Manchester	1983
	T20	4-15 A.W.Laraman	v	Worcs	Taunton	2004

SURREY

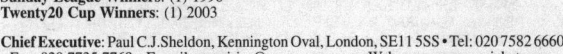

Formation of Present Club: 22 August 1845
Inaugural First-Class Match: 1864
Colours: Chocolate
Badge: Prince of Wales' Feathers
County Champions (since 1890): (18) 1890, 1891, 1892, 1894, 1895, 1899, 1914, 1952, 1953, 1954, 1955, 1956, 1957, 1958, 1971, 1999, 2000, 2002
Joint Champions: (1) 1950
Gillette/NatWest/C&G/FP Trophy Winners: (1) 1982
Benson and Hedges Cup Winners: (3) 1974, 1997, 2001
Pro 40/National League (Div 1) Winners: (1) 2003
Sunday League Winners: (1) 1996
Twenty20 Cup Winners: (1) 2003

Chief Executive: Paul C.J.Sheldon, Kennington Oval, London, SE11 5SS • Tel: 020 7582 6660 • Fax: 020 7735 7769 • E-mail: enquiries@surreyccc.com • Web: www.surreycricket.com

First XI Coach: Alan R.Butcher. **Captain:** M.A.Butcher. **Vice-Captain:** tba. **Overseas Players:** Mohammad (*tbc*) and M.J.Nicholson. **2008 Joint Testimonial:** M.R.Ramprakash and W.H.Gordon. **Head Groundsman:** W.H. (Bill) Gordon. **Scorer:** Keith R.Booth. ‡ New registration. ^NQ Not qualified for England.

‡**AFZAAL, Usman** (Manvers Pierrepont CS; S Notts C), b Rawalpindi, Pakistan 9 Jun 1977. 6'0". LHB, SLA. Nottinghamshire 1995-2003; cap 2000. MCC 2002. Northamptonshire 2004-07; cap 2005. **Tests:** 3 (2001); HS 54 and BB 1-49 v A (Oval) 2001. F-c Tours: SA 1996-97 (Nt); WI 2000-01 (Eng A); NZ 2001-02. 1000 runs (6): most – 1365 (2004). HS 168* Nt v Essex (Northampton) 2005. BB 4-101 Nt v Glos (Nottingham) 1998. LO HS 132 Nh v Yorks (Leeds) 2007 (FPT). LO BB 3-4 Nh v Cambs (Northampton) 2004 (CGT). T20 HS 64*. T20 BB 2-15.

BATTY, Jonathan Neil (Wheatley Park S, Oxon; Repton S; Durham U; Keble C, Oxford), b Chesterfield, Derbys 18 Apr 1974. 5'10". RHB, WK. Comb U 1994-95. Oxford U 1996; blue 1996. Surrey debut 1997; cap 2001; captain 2004. Oxfordshire 1993-96. Minor C 1996. 1000 runs (1): 1025 (2006). HS 168* v Essex (Chelmsford) 2003. BB 1-21 v Lancs (Manchester) 2000. LO HS 158* v Hants (Oval) 2005 (CGT). T20 HS 59.

BENNING, James Graham Edward (Beacon S; Chesham S; Caterham S), b Mill Hill, N London 4 May 1983. 6'0". RHB, RM. Debut (Surrey) 2003. Buckinghamshire 2000-01. HS 128 v OU (Oxford) 2004. CC HS 112 v Glos (Oval) 2006. BB 3-57 v Kent (Tunbridge Wells) 2005. LO HS 189* v Glos (Bristol) 2006 (CGT). LO BB 4-43 v Leics (Oval) 2003 (NL). T20 HS 88. T20 BB 1-7.

BROWN, Alistair Duncan (Caterham S), b Beckenham, Kent 11 Feb 1970. 5'10". RHB, OB, occ WK. Debut (Surrey) 1992; cap 1994; benefit 2002. TCCB XI 1996. Walter Lawrence Trophy for fastest f-c hundred 1998. **LOI:** 16 (1996 to 2001); HS 118 v I (Manchester) 1996. 1000 runs (8); most – 1382 (1993). HS 295* v Leics (Oakham) 2000 – record score (all levels) in Rutland. BB 3-25 v Somerset (Guildford) 2006. LO HS 268 v Glamorgan (Oval) 2002 (CGT) – world record l-o score (160 balls, 12 sixes, 30 fours). LO BB 3-39 v Notts (Nottingham) 2000 (NL). T20 HS 83.

BUTCHER, Mark Alan (Trinity S; Archbishop Tenison's S, Croydon), b Croydon 23 Aug 1972. Son of A.R.Butcher (Surrey, Glamorgan and England 1972-92, 1998); brother of G.P.Butcher (Glamorgan and; Surrey 1994-2001); nephew of I.P.Butcher (Leics and Glos 1980-90) and M.S.Butcher (Surrey 1982). 5'11". LHB, RM/OB. Debut (Surrey) 1992; cap 1996; captain 2005 to date; benefit 2005. TCCB XI 1995-96. **Tests**: 71 (1997 to 2004-05, 1 as captain); HS 173* v A (Leeds) 2001; BB 4-42 v A (Birmingham) 2001. F-c Tours: A 1996-97 (Eng A), 1998-99, 2002-03; SA 1999-00, 2004-05; WI 1997-98, 2003-04; NZ 2001-02; I 2001-02; SL 2003-04; B 2003-04. 1000 runs (8); most – 1604 (1996). HS 259 v Leics (Leicester) 1999. BB 5-86 v Lancs (Manchester) 2000. LO HS 104 v Yorks (Oval) 2003 (NL). LO BB 3-23 v Sussex (Oval) 1992 (SL). T20 HS 60.

CLINTON, Richard Selvey (Colfes S), b Sidcup, Kent 1 Sep 1981. Son of G.S.Clinton (Kent and Surrey 1974-90); cousin of P.J.S.Clinton (OU 2004-06). 6'3". LHB, RM. Kent staff 1999-2000 – no f-c appearances. Essex 2001-02. Loughborough UCCE 2004-06. Surrey 2004-07. British U 2006. HS 108* LU v Essex (Chelmsford) 2006. Sy HS 105 v Kent (Tunbridge Wells) 2005. BB 2-30 Ex v A (Chelmsford) 2001. CC/Sy BB – . LO HS 56 Ex v Durham (Ilford) 2001 (NL). LO BB 2-16 v Staffs (Leek) 2005 (CGT).

‡[NQ]**COLLINS, Pedro** Tyrone (St James S), b Boscobelle, Barbados 12 Aug 1976. Half-brother of F.H.Edwards (Barbados & West Indies 2001-02 to date). 6'2". RHB, LFM. Barbados 1996-97 to date. Busta Cup XI 2001-02. Joins Surrey 2008 (Kolpak registration). **Tests** (WI): 32 (1998-99 to 2006); HS 24 v I (Kingston) 2001-02; BB 6-53 v B (Kingston) 2004. **LOI** (WI): 30 (1999-00 to 2004-05); HS 10* v NZ (Wellington) 1999-00; BB 5-43 v A (Adelaide) 2004-05. F-c Tours (WI): E 2004; SA 1997-98 (WI A), 2007-08; NZ 1999-00; I 1998-99 (WI A), 2002-03; P (Sharjah) 2001-02; SL 2001-02; Z 2001; B 1998-99 (WI A), 1999-00, 2002-03; Kenya 2001. HS 25 Barbados v Trinidad (Pointe-a-Pierre) 2003-04. UK HS 19* WI v E (Manchester) 2004. 50 wkts (0+1): 54 (2003-04). BB 6-24 Barbados v Windward Is (Portsmouth, Dominica) 2006-07. UK BB 4-113 WI v E (Lord's) 2004. LO HS 55* Barbados v Guyana (Georgetown) 2001-02. LO BB 7-11 Barbados v WI U-19 (Blairmont, Berbice) 2007-08. T20 HS 1. T20 BB 3-13.

[NQ]**DERNBACH, Jade** Winston (St John the Baptist S), b Johannesburg, South Africa 3 Mar 1986. 6'1½". RHB, RMF. Italian passport. UK resident since 1998. Debut (Surrey) 2003, when aged 17. HS 10 v Warwks (Birmingham) 2007. BB 3-67 v Glos Bristol) 2006. LO HS 21 v Warwks (Birmingham) 2005 (NL). LO BB 5-44 v Somerset (Oval) 2007 (P40). T20 HS 1. T20 BB 1-19.

‡**EVANS, Laurie** John (Whitgift S; The John Fisher S; St Mary's C, Durham U), b Lambeth, London 12 Oct 1987. 6'0". RHB, RFM. Durham UCCE 2007. MCC 2007. Surrey 2nd XI 2005-07. Joins Surrey staff 2008. HS 133* DU v Lancs (Durham) 2007.

‡**HARINATH, Arun** (Whitgift S; Loughborough U), b Sutton 26 Mar 1987. LHB, OB. Loughborough UCCE 2007. Surrey 2nd XI debut 2003. Summer contract. Buckinghamshire 2007. HS 69 LU v Worcs (Worcester) 2007.

JORDAN, Christopher James (Comber Mere S, Barbados; Dulwich C), b Christ Church, Barbados 4 Oct 1988. 6'0". RHB, RFM. Debut (Surrey) 2007. HS 34 v Lancs (Oval) 2007. BB 3-42 v Durham (Chester-le-St) 2007. LO HS 8 v Kent (Canterbury) 2007 (P40). LO BB 3-28 v Yorks (Scarborough) 2007 (P40).

‡**KING, Simon** James (Warlingham S; John Fisher S), b Warlingham 4 Sep 1987. RHB, OB. Surrey 2nd XI debut 2005. Awaiting 1st XI debut.

‡**MEAKER, Stuart** Christopher (Cranleigh S), b Durban, South Africa 21 Jan 1989. Surrey 2nd XI debut 2007. England U-19 2007. Awaiting 1st XI debut.

‡**NQMOHAMMAD ASIF**, b Sheikhupura, Pakistan 20 Dec 1982. LHB, RFM. Sheikhupura 2000-01 to 2001-02. Khan Research Labs 2001-02 to 2003-04. Quetta 2003-04. Sialkot 2004-05 to 2006-07. National Bank 2004-05 to 2005-06. Leicestershire 2006. **Tests** (P): 11 (2004-05 to 2007-08); HS 12* v A (Sydney) 2004-05 – on debut; BB 6-44 (11-71 match) v SL (Kandy) 2005-06. **LOI** (P): 26 (2005-06 to 2007-08); HS 6 v I (Multan) 2005-06; BB 3-28 v E (Cardiff) 2006. F-c Tours (P): E 2006; A 2004-05; SA 2006-07; I 2006-07 (Sialkot); SL 2004-05 (Pak A), 2005-06; Z 2004-05 (Pak A). HS 42 KRL v Allied Bank (Karachi) 2002-03. 50 wkts (0+1): 54 (2005-06). BB 7-35 Sialkot v Multan (Multan) 2004-05. LO HS 12* Pakistan A v Sri Lanka A (Colombo) 2004-05. LO BB 4-30 KRL v Rawalpindi (Rawalpindi) 2001-02. IT20 HS 4*. IT20 BB 4-8. T20 HS 4*. T20 BB 5-11.

‡**MURTAGH, Christopher** Paul (John Fisher S; Loughborough U), b Lambeth, S London 14 Oct 1984. Younger brother of T.J.Murtagh (*see MIDDLESEX*); nephew of A.J.Murtagh (Hampshire and E Province 1973-77). 5'10". RHB, LB. Loughborough UCCE 2005-07. Surrey List A debut 2005. Surrey 2nd XI debut 2002. HS 107 LU v Yorks (Leeds) 2007. LO HS 30* v Warwks (Birmingham) 2005 (NL).

NQMURTAZA HUSSAIN (Abbasia HS), b Bahawalpur, Pakistan 20 Dec 1974. British passport. 5'11". RHB, OB. Bahawalpur 1990-91 to 2001-02. Pakistan Automobiles Corp 1992-93 to 1993-94. United Bank 1994-95. PNSC 1995-96 to 1996-97. KRL 1997-98 to 1999-00. Islamabad 1998-99. Pakistan Customs 2004-05 to date. Surrey 2007. HS 117 Pakistan Customs v Attock Group (Karachi) 2006-07. 50 wkts (0+5), inc 100 wkts (1): 105 (1995-96). BB 9-54 Bahawalpur v Islamabad (Bahawalpur) 1995-96. LO HS 85 KRL v Rawalpindi (Rawalpindi) 1998-99. LO BB 5-18 Bahawalpur v Lahore City (Bahawalpur) 1992-93.

NEWMAN, Scott Alexander (Trinity S, Croydon; Coulsdon C; Brighton U), b Epsom 3 Nov 1979. 6'2". LHB, RM. Debut (Surrey) 2002 – scoring 99 v Hants (Oval) 2002; cap 2005. F-c Tour (Eng A): I 2003-04. 1000 runs (3); most – 1404 (2006). HS 219 and 117) v Glamorgan (Oval) 2005. LO HS 106 v Essex (Oval) 2004 (NL). T20 HS 59.

NQNICHOLSON, Matthew James (Knox GS; Edith Cowan U, Perth), b St Leonards, Sydney, Australia 2 Oct 1974. 6'6". RHB, RFM. W Australia.1996-97 to 2002-03. NSW 2003-04 to date. Missed entire 1997-98 season (salmonella poisoning, glandular fever, Ross River fever, chronic fatigue syndrome). Registered as an overseas player by Sussex for 2005 but was unable to take up his contract because of injury. Northamptonshire 2006. Surrey debut/cap 2007. **Tests** (A): 1 (1998-99); HS 9 and BB 3-56 v E (Melbourne) 1998-99. F-c Tour (A): Z 1999-00. HS 106* Nh v Derbys (Northampton) 2006. Sy HS 48* v Kent (Croydon) 2007. BB 7-62 Nh v Glos (Northampton) 2006. Sy BB 5-89 v Sussex (Hove) 2007. LO HS 57* v Leics (Leicester) 2007 (P40). LO BB 3-23 Nh v Middlesex (Northampton) 2006 (P40). T20 HS 20*. T20 BB 3-12.

ORMOND, James (St Thomas More S, Nuneaton), b Walsgrave, Coventry, Warwks 20 Aug 1977. 6'3". RHB, RFM. Leicestershire 1995-2001; cap 1999. Surrey debut 2002; cap 2003. **Tests**: 2 (2001 to 2001-02); HS 18 v A (Oval) 2001; BB 1-70. F-c Tours: NZ 2001-02; I 2001-02; SL 1997-98 (Eng A); K 1997-98 (Eng A). HS 57 v Glos (Bristol) 2004. 50 wkts (4); most – 52 (1999, 2004). BB 7-63 v Glamorgan (Cardiff) 2005. Hat-trick (4 wkts in 6 balls) 2003. LO HS 32 v Somerset (Taunton) 2005 (NL). LO BB 4-12 Le v Middlesex (Leicester) 1998 (SL). T20 HS 6. T20 BB 5-26.

RAMPRAKASH, Mark Ravin (Gayton HS; Harrow Weald SFC), b Bushey, Herts 5 Sep 1969. 5'9". RHB, OB. Middlesex 1987-2000; cap 1990; captain 1997-99. Surrey debut 2001 – scoring 146 v Kent (Oval); cap 2002; joint Testimonial 2008. YC 1991. *Wisden* 2006. PCA 2006. **Tests**: 52 (1991 to 2001-02); HS 154 v WI (Bridgetown) 1997-98; BB 1-2 v WI (Georgetown) 1997-98. **LOI**: 18 (1991 to 2001-02); HS 51 v WI (Port-of-Spain) 1997-98; BB 3-28 v Z (Harare) 2001-02. F-c Tours: A 1994-95 (*part*), 1998-99; SA 1995-96; WI 1991-92 (Eng A), 1993-94, 1997-98; NZ 1991-92, 2001-02; I 1994-95 (Eng A), 2001-02; P 1990-91 (Eng A); SL 1990-91 (Eng A). 1000 runs (17, inc 2000 (3): 2258 (1995), 2278 (2006), 2026 (2207). Averaged 103.54 in f-c matches 2006, the second-highest average by any batsman scoring 1000 runs in a season (105.28 in CC), setting world records by scoring 2000 runs in only 20 innings, posting scores of at least 150 in five successive matches and reaching double figures in each of his 24 innings. In 2007 he became the first to score 2000 f-c runs in a season and average over 100 (101.30) twice. Ten hundreds in a season (2): 1995, 2007. HS 301* v Northants (Oval) 2006. BB 3-32 M v Glamorgan (Lord's) 1998. Sy BB 2-35 v Northants (Northampton) 2004. LO HS 147* M v Worcs (Lord's) 1990 (SL). LO BB 5-38 M v Leics (Lord's) 1993 (SL). T20 HS 85*.

SAKER, Neil Clifford (Raynes Park HS; Nescot C), b Tooting, London 20 Sep 1984. 6'4". RHB, RFM. Debut (Surrey) 2003. HS 58* Sy v Essex (Colchester) 2006. BB 5-76 Sy v Lancs (Manchester) 2007. LO HS 22 Sy v Glos (Bristol) 2006 (CGT). LO BB 4-43 Sy v Kent (Canterbury) 2005 (NL). T20 HS 0. T20 BB 1-28.

SAQLAIN MUSHTAQ (Govt Muslim League HS, M.A.O. College, Lahore), b Lahore, Pakistan 29 Dec 1976. British passport (English wife); qualified for England from April 2008. Brother of Sibtain Mushtaq (Lahore 1988-89). 5'11". RHB, OB. Islamabad 1994-95 to 1997-98. PIA 1994-95 to 2003-04. Surrey 1997-2005; cap 1998. Lahore 2003-04. Sussex 2007. Ireland (not f-c) 2006. *Wisden* 1999. **Tests** (P): 49 (1995-96 to 2003-04); HS 101* v NZ (Christchurch) 2000-01; BB 8-164 v E (Lahore) 2000-01 (all eight wickets to fall). **LOI** (P): 169 (1995-96 to 2003-04); HS 37* v A (Brisbane) 1999-00; BB 5-20 v E (Rawalpindi) 2000-01, 2 hat-tricks. F-c Tours (P): E 1996, 2001; A 1995-96, 1996-97, 1999-00; SA 1997-98, 2002-03; WI 1999-00; NZ 2000-01; I 1998-99, SL 1996-97, 2002-03; Z 1997-98, 2002-03; B 1998-99, 2001-02. HS 101* (*see Tests*). UK HS 78 P v Northants (Northampton) 1996 – on UK debut. CC HS 69 Sy v Middlesex (Lord's) 2003. 50 wkts (5+1); most – 66 (2000). BB 8-65 (11-107 match) Sy v Derbys (Oval) 1988. Took 7-11 (including 7-5 in 34 balls) Sy v Derbys (Oval) 2000. Three hat-tricks, all for Surrey, 1997 and 1999 (2). LO HS 38* v Yorks (Leeds) 2001 (NL). LO BB 5-20 (*see LOI*). T20 HS 5. T20 BB 2-22.

SCHOFIELD, Christopher Paul (Wardle HS), b Birch Hill, Rochdale 6 Oct 1978. 6'2". LHB, LBG. Lancashire 1998-2004; cap 2002. Surrey debut 2006. **Tests**: 2 (2000); HS 57 v Z (Nottingham) 2000. F-c Tours (Eng A): WI 2000-01; NZ 1999-00; B 1999-00. HS 99 La v Warwks (Manchester) 2004. Sy HS 95 v Glos (Bristol) 2006. BB 6-120 Eng A v Bangladesh (Chittagong) 1999-00. Sy BB 5-52 v Hants (Southampton) 2007. LO HS 75* v Hants (Southampton) 2007 (FPT). LO BB 5-31 La v Derbys (Manchester) 2001 (NL). IT20 HS 9*. IT20 BB 2-15. T20 HS 27. T20 BB 4-12.

‡**SPRIEGEL, Matthew** Neil William (Whitgift S; Loughborough U), b Epsom 4 Mar 1987. 6'3". LHB, OB. Loughborough UCCE 2007; captain 2007. Surrey 2nd XI debut 2004. Summer contract. HS 30 and BB 1-12 v Somerset (Taunton) 2007 – on debut.

NQ**WALTERS, Stewart** Jonathan (Guildford GS, Perth, WA), b Mornington, Victoria, Australia 25 Jun 1983. 6'1". RHB, RM. Debut (Surrey) 2006. W Australia U-19 2001-02. HS 70 v Durham (Oval) 2007. BB 1-4 v Durham (Chester-le-St) 2007. LO HS 32* v Sussex (Hove) 2005 (NL). LO BB 1-12 v Yorks (Scarborough) 2007 (P40). T20 HS 18. T20 BB – .

‡**WILSON, Gary** Craig (Methodist C, Belfast; Manchester Met), b Dundonald, N Ireland 5 Feb 1986. RHB, WK. Ireland 2005 to 2007. Ireland U-19 2003-04 to 2005-06. MCC YC 2005. Surrey 2nd XI debut 2006. **LOI** (Ire): 1 (2007); HS 13 v India (Belfast) 2007. HS 11 Ireland v Scotland (Aberdeen) 2005 – on f-c debut. LO HS 58 Ireland A v UAE (Abu Dhabi) 2006 – on List A debut.

RELEASED/RETIRED
(Having made a County 1st XI appearance in 2007)

NQ**AZHAR MAHMOOD** – *see KENT.*

CLARKE, R. – *see DERBYSHIRE.*

DOSHI, N.D. – *see DERBYSHIRE.*

HAMILTON-BROWN, R.J. – *see SUSSEX.*

NQ**HARBHAJAN SINGH** PLAHA, b Jullundur City, India 3 Jul 1980. 6'0". RHB, OB. Punjab 1997-98 to 2006-07. Surrey 2005, 2007. **Tests** (I): 63 (1997-98 to 2007-08); HS 66 v Z (Bulawayo) 2001; BB 8-84 (15-217 match) v A (Madras) 2000-01. Took 28 wickets, including a hat-trick, in 2 Tests v Australia 2000-01. **LOI** (I): 159 (1997-98 to 2007-08); HS 46 v A (Vishakapatnam) 2000-01; BB 5-31 v E (Delhi) 2005-06. F-c Tours (I): E 2002; A 1999-00, 2003-04, 2007-08; SA 2001-02, 2006-07; WI 2001-02, 2006; NZ 1998-99, 2002-03; P 2005-06; SL 1998-99, 2001; Z 1998-99, 2001, 2005-06 ; B 2004-05. HS 84 Punjab v Haryana (Amritsar) 2000-01 and 84 v Glos (Bristol) 2005. 50 wkts (0+2); most – 70 (2000-01). BB 8-84 (15-217 match) (*see Tests*). Hat-trick (India 2000-01). UK BB 7-83 I v Essex (Chelmsford) 2002. Sy BB 6-36 v Hants (Southampton) 2005. LO HS 46 (*see LOI*). LO BB 5-31 (*see LOI*). IT20 HS 7. IT20 BB 2-24. T20 HS 31*. T20 BB 2-22.

NQ**MAGOFFIN, Stephen** James (Indooroopilly HS and Curtin U, Perth), b Corinda, Queensland, Australia, 17 Dec 1979. 6'2". LHB, RFM. Western Australia 2004-05 to date. Surrey 2007. HS 45 WA v Tas (Hobart) 2007-08. BB 8-47 WA v S Australia (Perth) 2005-06. LO HS 23* WA v S Australia (Perth) 2007-08. LO BB 4-58 v Kent (Oval) 2007 (FPT). T20 HS –. T20 BB 2-15.

NQ**MOHAMMAD AKRAM** AWAN (Modern SS; Gordon C, Rawalpindi), b Islamabad, Pakistan 10 Sep 1972. 6'2". RHB, RFM. Rawalpindi 1992-93 to 1998-99, 2001-02 to 2002-03. Allied Bank 1996-97 to 2000-01. Northamptonshire 1997. Essex 2003. Sussex 2004; cap 2004. Surrey 2005-07; cap 2006. **Tests** (P): 9 (1995-96 to 2000-01); HS 10* and BB 5-138 v A (Perth) 1999-00. **LOI** (P): 23 (1995-96 to 2000; HS 7* v WI (Sharjah) 1995-96; BB 2-28 v I (Toronto) 1997. F-c Tours (P): E 1996; A 1995-96; 1999-00; SA 1997-98; WI 1999-00; NZ 2000-01. HS 35* Sx v Warwks (Birmingham) 2004. Sy HS 27* v Notts (Oval) 2005. BB 8-49 (10-142 match) Ex v Surrey (Oval) 2003. Sy BB 6-34 v Glos (Oval) 2006. LO HS 33 Allied Bank v Faisalabad (Faisalabad) 1998-99. LO BB 4-19 Nh v Surrey (Northampton) 1997 (SL). T20 HS 7*. T20 BB 2-22.

SALISBURY, I.D.K. – *see WARWICKSHIRE.*

D.J.Miller left the staff without making a County 1st XI appearance in 2007.

SURREY 2007

RESULTS SUMMARY

	Place	Won	Lost	Tied	Drew	No Result
LV County Championship (1st Division)	4th	5	4		6	1
All First-Class Matches		5	4		6	1
Friends Provident Trophy (South Conference)	5th	4	3			2
NatWest Pro40 League (2nd Division)	4th	5	3			
Twenty/20 Cup (South Division)	3rd	4	4			

LV COUNTY CHAMPIONSHIP AVERAGES

BATTING AND FIELDING

Cap		M	I	NO	HS	Runs	Avge	100	50	Ct/St
2002	M.R.Ramprakash	15	25	5	266*	2026	101.30	10	4	13
2001	J.N.Batty	15	25	3	154*	965	43.86	4	3	42/5
1996	M.A.Butcher	14	21	2	179	752	39.57	2	2	14
2005	S.A.Newman	15	25	–	124	812	32.48	1	5	17
2007	M.J.Nicholson	12	12	4	48*	240	30.00	–	–	6
2004	Azhar Mahmood	3	6	–	69	168	28.00	–	1	2
–	J.G.E.Benning	8	11	1	51	277	27.70	–	1	5
–	C.J.Jordan	5	6	2	34	97	24.25	–	–	1
2005	R.Clarke	10	14	1	68*	301	23.15	–	2	10
1994	A.D.Brown	9	14	2	69	277	23.08	–	3	7
–	S.J.Walters	8	12	1	70	228	20.72	–	1	9
1998	I.D.K.Salisbury	6	9	–	103	174	19.33	1	–	4
–	C.P.Schofield	6	7	1	28	86	14.33	–	–	3
–	Harbhajan Singh	6	7	1	29	82	13.66	–	–	3
–	N.C.Saker	8	9	3	19	74	12.33	–	–	1
2003	J.Ormond	7	10	2	25*	83	10.37	–	–	1
2006	N.D.Doshi	5	6	1	15	42	8.40	–	–	1
–	J.W.Dernbach	4	4	1	10	16	5.33	–	–	1
2006	Mohammad Akram	3	6	2	8*	17	4.25	–	–	–

Also batted: R.S.Clinton (3 matches) 0, 0 (1 ct); S.J.Magoffin (1) 6, 9*; Murtaza Hussain (2) 6, 9* (1 ct).

BOWLING

	O	M	R	W	Avge	Best	5wI	10wM
Harbhajan Singh	284.1	83	686	37	18.54	6- 57	3	1
C.J.Jordan	139.1	22	490	20	24.50	3- 42	–	–
Murtaza Hussain	94.4	25	282	11	25.63	4-126	–	–
M.J.Nicholson	378.0	75	1289	44	29.29	5- 89	1	–
C.P.Schofield	186.5	29	650	16	40.62	5- 52	1	–
R.Clarke	154.5	19	633	15	42.20	3- 57	–	–
N.C.Saker	156.0	33	649	15	43.26	5- 76	1	–
J.Ormond	189.0	48	640	12	53.33	2- 42	–	–
N.D.Doshi	174.2	26	697	13	53.61	6-111	1	–
I.D.K.Salisbury	188.5	15	745	11	67.72	4-121	–	–
Also bowled:								
J.W.Dernbach	78.1	14	335	9	37.22	3- 85	–	–
Mohammad Akram	73.0	20	236	6	39.33	2- 22	–	–

Azhar Mahmood 87-16-278-3; J.G.E.Benning 17-0-91-0; A.D.Brown 8-0-38-0; M.A.Butcher 6.3-1-28-0; R.S.Clinton 17-3-55-0; S.J.Magoffin 30-9-94-2; M.R.Ramprakash 1-0-18-0; S.J.Walters 8-1-28-1.

Surrey played no fixtures outside the County Championship in 2007. The First-Class Averages (pp 140–158) give the records of their players in all first-class county matches.

SURREY RECORDS

FIRST-CLASS CRICKET

Highest Total	For 811		v	Somerset	The Oval	1899
	V 863		by	Lancashire	The Oval	1990
Lowest Total	For 14		v	Essex	Chelmsford	1983
	V 16		by	MCC	Lord's	1872
Highest Innings	For 357*	R.Abel	v	Somerset	The Oval	1899
	V 366	N.H.Fairbrother	for	Lancashire	The Oval	1990

Highest Partnership for each Wicket

1st	428	J.B.Hobbs/A.Sandham	v	Oxford U	The Oval	1926
2nd	371	J.B.Hobbs/E.G.Hayes	v	Hampshire	The Oval	1909
3rd	413	D.J.Bicknell/D.M.Ward	v	Kent	Canterbury	1990
4th	448	R.Abel/T.W.Hayward	v	Yorkshire	The Oval	1899
5th	318	M.R.Ramprakash/Azhar Mahmood	v	Middlesex	The Oval	2005
6th	298	A.Sandham/H.S.Harrison	v	Sussex	The Oval	1913
7th	262	C.J.Richards/K.T.Medlycott	v	Kent	The Oval	1987
8th	205	I.A.Greig/M.P.Bicknell	v	Lancashire	The Oval	1990
9th	168	E.R.T.Holmes/E.W.J.Brooks	v	Hampshire	The Oval	1936
10th	173	A.Ducat/A.Sandham	v	Essex	Leyton	1921

Best Bowling	For	10-43	T.Rushby	v	Somerset	Taunton	1921
(Innings)	V	10-28	W.P.Howell	for	Australians	The Oval	1899
Best Bowling	For	16-83	G.A.R.Lock	v	Kent	Blackheath	1956
(Match)	V	15-57	W.P.Howell	for	Australians	The Oval	1899

Most Runs – Season	3246	T.W.Hayward	(av 72.13)	1906
Most Runs – Career	43554	J.B.Hobbs	(av 49.72)	1905-34
Most 100s – Season	13	T.W.Hayward		1906
	13	J.B.Hobbs		1925
Most 100s – Career	144	J.B.Hobbs		1905-34
Most Wkts – Season	252	T.Richardson	(av 13.94)	1895
Most Wkts – Career	1775	T.Richardson	(av 17.87)	1892-1904
Most Career W-K Dismissals	1221	H.Strudwick	(1035 ct/186 st)	1902-27
Most Career Catches in the Field	605	M.J.Stewart		1954-72

LIMITED-OVERS CRICKET

Highest Total	FPT	496-4		v	Glos	The Oval	2007
	P40	375-4		v	Yorkshire	Scarborough	1994
	T20	224-5		v	Glos	Bristol	2006
Lowest Total	FPT	74		v	Kent	The Oval	1967
	P40	64		v	Worcs	Worcester	1978
	T20	118		v	Hampshire	The Oval	2005
Highest Innings	FPT	268	A.D.Brown	v	Glamorgan	The Oval	2002
	P40	203	A.D.Brown	v	Hampshire	Guildford	1997
	T20	88	J.G.E.Benning	v	Kent	The Oval	2006
Best Bowling	FPT	7-33	R.D.Jackman	v	Yorkshire	Harrogate	1970
	P40	7-30	M.P.Bicknell	v	Glamorgan	The Oval	1999
	T20	6-24	T.J.Murtagh	v	Middlesex	Lord's	2005

SUSSEX

Formation of Present Club: 1 March 1839
Substantial Reorganisation: August 1857
Inaugural First-Class Match: 1864
Colours: Dark Blue, Light Blue and Gold
Badge: County Arms of Six Martlets
County Champions: (3) 2003, 2006, 2007
Gillette/NatWest/C&G/FP Trophy Winners: (5) 1963,
1964, 1978, 1986, 2006
Benson and Hedges Cup Winners: (0); best –
Semi-Finalist 1982, 1999
Pro 40/National League (Div 1) Winners: (0); best – 3rd
2006
Sunday League Winners: (1) 1982
Twenty20 Cup Winners: (0); best – Semi-Finalist 2007

Chief Executive: Gus Mackay, County Ground, Eaton Road, Hove BN3 3AN • Tel: 01273
827100 • Fax: 01273 771549 • Email: info@sussexcricket.co.uk • Web: www.sussexcricket
.co.uk

Professional Cricket Manager: Mark A.Robinson. **Club Coach**: Mark J.G.Davis. **Captain**:
C.J.Adams. **Vice-Captain**: None. **Overseas Player**: Mushtaq Ahmed. **2008 Beneficiary**:
R.S.C.Martin-Jenkins. **Head Groundsman**: Lawrence Gosling. **Scorer**: M.J. (Mike)
Charman. ‡ New registration. NQ Not qualified for England.

ADAMS, Christopher John (Repton S), b Whitwell, Derbyshire 6 May 1970. 6'0". RHB,
RM/OB. Derbyshire 1988-97; cap 1992. Sussex debut/cap 1998; captain 1998 to date;
benefit 2003. ACT (l-o) 1998-99. *Wisden* 2003. **Tests**: 5 (1999-00); HS 31 v SA (Cape
Town) 1999-00; BB 1-42 v SA (Durban) 1999-00. **LOI**: 5 (1998 to 1999-00); HS 42 v SA
(Cape Town) 1999-00. F-c Tour: SA 1999-00. 1000 runs (9); most – 1742 (1996). HS 239
De v Hants (Southampton) 1996. Sx HS 217 v Lancs (Manchester) 2002. BB 4-28 v
Durham (Chester-le-St) 2001. LO HS 163 v Middlesex (Arundel) 1999 (NL). LO BB 5-16 v
Middlesex (Hove) 1998 (SL). T20 HS 63.

‡AGA, Ragheb Gul (Hillcrest S; Brighton U), b Nairobi, Kenya 10 Jul 1984. RHB, RMF.
Kenya 2003-04 to 2005-06. Joins Sussex staff 2008. List A (P40) debut 2007. **LOI** (Kenya):
2 (2004); HS 1 and BB 2-17 K v P (Birmingham) 2004. F-c Tours (K): WI 2003-04; Z
2005-06; UAE 2004-05. HS 43 K v Namibia (Nairobi) 2004-05. BB 4-71 K v Guyana
(Georgetown) 2003-04. LO HS 16 K v India A (Nairobi) 2004. LO BB 4-14 K v Zimbabwe
A (Harare) 2005-06.

‡BEER, William Andrew Thomas (Reigate GS; Collyer's C, Horsham), b Crawley 8 Oct
1988. RHB, LB. Awaiting f-c debut. Sussex 2nd XI 2006-07.

‡BROWN, Ben Christopher (Ardingly C), b Crawley 23 Nov 1988. RHB, WK. Debut
(Sussex) 2007 – awaiting CC debut. HS 46 v Sri Lanka A (Hove) 2007 – on debut. LO HS
4 v Notts (Hove) 2007 (P40).

NQGOODWIN, Murray William (Newton Moore HS, Bunbury, WA), b Salisbury, Rhodesia 11 Dec 1972. Younger brother of D.G.Goodwin (Zimbabwe 1986-97 to 1989-90). 5'9".
Migrated to Australia in Nov 1986 and gained Australian citizenship in Sep 1997. Kolpak
registration 2005 to date. RHB, LB. W Australia 1994-95 to 1996-97, 2000-01 to 2005-06.
Mashonaland 1997-98 to 1998-99. Sussex debut/cap 2001. Warriors 2006-07. Holland 1997.
Tests (Z): 19 (1997-98 to 2000); HS 166* v P (Bulawayo) 1997-98. **LOI** (Z): 71 (1997-98
to 2000); HS 112* v WI (Chester-le-St) 2000; BB 1-12 v SL (Sharjah) 1998-99. F-c Tours
(Z): E 2000, SA 1999-00; WI 1999-00; NZ 1997-98; P 1998-99; SL 1997-98. 1000 runs
(6+1); most – 1654 (2001). HS 335* (Sussex record) v Leics (Hove) 2003. BB 2-23 Z v
Lahore City (Lahore) 1998-99. Sx BB – . LO HS 167 WA v NSW (Perth) 2000-01 (MC).
LO BB 1-9 Mashonaland v Eng A (Harare) 1998-99. T20 HS 102*.

GREEN, Jeremy Arthur Graham (Lancing C), b Cuckfield 17 Sep 1984. 6'2". RHB, RMF. Debut (Sussex) 2007 – awaiting CC debut. HS 28 and BB – v Sri Lanka A (Hove) 2007. LO HS 7 v West Indies A (Hove) 2002.

‡HAMILTON-BROWN, Rory James (Millfield S), b St John's Wood, London 3 Sep 1987. 6'0". RHB, OB. Surrey 2005. Awaiting CC debut. No f-c appearances 2006-07. HS 9 Sy v Bangladesh A (Oval) 2005. LO HS 20 Sy v Sussex (Guildford) 2005 (NL). LO BB 3-28 Sy v Leics (Leicester) 2007 (P40).

‡ᴺᵠHARRIS, Ryan James, b Nowra, NSW, Australia 11 Oct 1979. British passport. RHB, RFM. South Australia 2001-02 to date. HS 74 S Aus v Vic (Melbourne) 2006-07. BB 7-108 S Aus v Tas (Adelaide) 2007-08. LO HS 39 S Aus v Vic (Traralgon) 2007-08. LO BB 5-58 S Aus v Vic (Adelaide) 2007-08. IT20 HS 31. IT20 BB 2-18.

HODD, Andrew John (Bexhill C), b Chichester, Sussex 12 Jan 1984. RHB, WK. Sussex 2003 (1 match), 2006-07. Surrey 2005 (one match). HS 123 v Yorks (Hove) 2007. LO HS 42 v Notts (Hove) 2007 (P40). T20 HS 14.

HOPKINSON, Carl Daniel (Brighton C), b Brighton 14 Sep 1981. 5'11". RHB, RM. Debut (Sussex) 2002. HS 83 v Worcs (Worcester) 2007. BB 1-20. CC BB 1-35. LO HS 123* v Notts (Hove) 2007 (P40). LO BB 3-19 v Scot (Edinburgh) 2003 (NL). T20 HS 26*.

KIRTLEY, Robert James (Clifton C), b Eastbourne 10 Jan 1975. 6'0". RHB, RFM. Debut (Sussex) 1995; cap 1998; benefit 2006. TCCB XI 1996. Mashonaland 1996-97. MCC 2002. **Tests**: 4 (2003 to 2003-04); HS 12 v SL (Colombo) 2003-04; BB 6-34 v SA (Nottingham) 2003 – on debut. **LOI**: 11 (2001-02 to 2003-04); HS 1 (*twice*); BB 2-33 v Z (Harare) 2001-02 on debut, and 2-33 v B (Dhaka) 2003-04. F-c Tours (Eng A): NZ 1999-00; SL 2003-04 (Eng); B 1999-00. HS 59 v Durham (Eastbourne) 1998. 50 wkts (7); most – 75 (2001). BB 7-21 v Hants (Southampton) 1999. Took 5-53 (7-88 match) for Mashonaland v Eng XI (Harare) 1996-97. LO HS 30* v Middlesex (Lord's) 2003 (CGT). LO BB 5-27 v Lancs (Lord's) 2006 (CGT Final). IT20 HS 2*. IT20 BB – . T20 HS 2*. T20 BB 4-22.

LEWRY, Jason David (Durrington HS, Worthing), b Worthing 2 Apr 1971. 6'2". LHB, LFM. Debut (Sussex) 1994; cap 1996; benefit 2002. F-c Tour: Z 1998-99 (Eng A). HS 72 v Surrey (Oval) 2004. 50 wkts (5); most – 62 (1998). BB 8-106 v Leics (Hove) 2003. 2 hat-tricks (1998, 2001). LO HS 16* v Yorks (Arundel) 2004 (NL). LO BB 4-29 v Somerset (Bath) 1995 (SL). T20 HS 8*. T20 BB 3-34.

LIDDLE, Christopher John (Nunthorpe CS), b Middlesbrough, Yorks 1 Feb 1984. 6'5". RHB, LFM. Leicestershire 2005-06. Sussex debut 2007. HS 53 v Worcs (Hove) 2007. BB 3-42 Le v Somerset (Leicester) 2006. Sx BB 2-43 v Sri Lanka A (Hove) 2007. LO HS 11 v Essex (Arundel) 2007 (FPT). LO BB 3-60 v Notts (Hove) 2007 (P40).

MARTIN-JENKINS, Robin Simon Christopher (Radley C; Durham U), b Guildford, Surrey 28 Oct 1975. Son of C.D.A.Martin-Jenkins (Cricket Broadcaster and Writer). 6'5". RHB, RFM. Debut (Sussex) 1995; cap 2000; benefit 2008. British U 1996. 1000 runs (1): 1008 (2002). HS 205* v Somerset (Taunton) 2002. BB 7-51 v Leics (Horsham) 2002. LO HS 68* v Northants (Hove) 2003 (NL). LO BB 4-22 v Kent (Canterbury) 2002 (BHC). T20 HS 56*. T20 BB 4-20.

NQMUSHTAQ AHMED (Mahmoodia HS, Sahiwal), b Sahiwal, Pakistan 28 Jun 1970. 5'5". RHB, LBG. Multan 1986-87, 1988-89, 1990-91. United Bank 1987-88 to 1995-96. Somerset 1993-95, 1997-98; cap 1993. Islamabad 1994-95. Lahore 1996-97 (City), 2000-01 (Blues). Peshawar 1998-99. National Bank 2001-02 to 2004-05. Surrey 2002 (2 matches). Sussex début/cap 2003. WAPDA 2005-06 to 2006-07. *Wisden* 1996. PCA 2003. **Tests** (P): 52 (1989-90 to 2003-04); HS 59 v SA (Rawalpindi) 1997-98; BB 7-56 (10-171 match) v NZ (Christchurch) 1995-96. **LOI** (P): 144 (1988-89 to 2003-04); HS 34* v SA (Colombo) 2000-01; BB 5-36 v I (Toronto) 1996-97. F-c Tours (P): E 1992, 1996; A 1989-90, 1991-92, 1992-93, 1995-96, 1996-97, 1999-00; SA 1997-98; WI 1992-93, 1999-00; NZ 1992-93, 1993-94, 1995-96, 2000-01; I 1998-99; SL 1994-95, 1996-97, 2000-01; Z 1997-98. HS 90* v Kent (Hove) 2005. 50 wkts (9+2) inc 100 (2): 103 (2003), 102 (2006). Took 1000th f-c wicket during 2004 season. BB 9-48 (13-132 match) v Notts (Nottingham) 2006. LO HS 41 Sm v Durham (Taunton) 1998 (SL). LO BB 7-24 Sm v Ireland (Taunton) 1997 (BHC). T20 HS 20*. T20 BB 5-11.

NASH, Christopher David (Collyer's SFC; Loughborough U), b Cuckfield 19 May 1983. 5'11". RHB, OB. Début (Sussex) 2002 – no f-c appearances 2003-04. Loughborough UCCE 2003-04. British U 2004. HS 89 v Worcs (Hove) 2007. BB 2-1 v Lancs (Hove) 2007. LO HS 82 v Warwks (Hove) 2006 (P40). LO BB 1-26 v Hants (Southampton) 2007 (FPT). T20 HS 37.

PRIOR, Matthew James (Brighton C), b Johannesburg, South Africa 26 Feb 82. 5'11". RHB, WK. Début (Sussex) 2001; cap 2003. MCC 2005. **Tests**: (2007 to 2007-08); HS 126* v WI (Lord's) 2007 – on début (first instance while keeping wicket for England). **LOI**: 22 (2004-05 to 2007); HS 52 v WI (Birmingham) 2007. F-c Tours (Eng A): I 2003-04; SL 2004-05, 2007-08; B 2006-07. 1000 runs (2); most – 1158 (2004). HS 201* v LU (Hove) 2004. CC HS 153* v Essex (Colchester) 2003. LO HS 144 v Warwks (Hove) 2005 (NL). T20 HS 73.

RAYNER, Oliver Philip (St Bede's S, Sussex), b Fallingbostel, W Germany, 1 Nov 1985. 6'5". RHB, OB. Début (Sussex) 2006, scoring 101 v SL (Hove) – first hundred on début for Sussex since 1920. HS 101 (*see above*). BB 5-68 (8-96 match) v Sri Lanka A (Hove) 2007. CC HS 23 and BB 3-89 v Kent (Hove) 2006. LO HS 61 v Lancs (Hove) 2006 (P40). LO BB 1-25 v Warwks (Hove) 2006 (P40). T20 HS 11. T20 BB 1-20.

SMITH, Thomas Michael John (Sussex Downs C), b Eastbourne 22 Aug 1987. RHB, SLA. Début (Sussex) 2007. Awaiting CC début. HS 2 and BB 1-52 v Sri Lanka A (Hove) 2007 – on début. LO HS – and BB 2-45 v Durham (Chester-le-St) 2006 (P40). T20 HS – .

THORNELY, Michael Alistair (Brighton C), b Camden, London 19 Oct 1987. RHB, RM. Début (Sussex) 2007. Awaiting CC début. HS 11 v Indians (Hove) 2007 – on début. LO HS – 2007 (P40).

WRIGHT, Luke James (Belvoir HS; Ratcliffe C; Loughborough U), b Grantham, Lincs 7 Mar 1985. 5'11". Younger brother of A.S.Wright (Leicestershire 2001-02). RHB, RM. Leicestershire 2003 (one f-c match). Sussex début 2004; cap 2007. **LOI**: 5 (2007 to 2007-08); HS 50 (off 39 balls) v I (Oval) 2007. LO 100 v LU (Hove) 2004 – on Sx début. CC HS 61 v Warwks (Hove) 2007. BB 3-33 v Surrey (Hove) 2005. LO HS 125 v Glos (Hove) 2007 (P40). LO BB 4-12 v Middlesex (Hove) 2004 (NL). IT20 HS 24. T20 HS 103*. T20 BB 3-17.

YARDY, Michael Howard (William Parker S, Hastings), b Pembury, Kent 27 Nov 1980. 6'0". LHB, LM/SLA. Début (Sussex) 2000; cap 2005. **LOI**: 6 (2006 to 2007); HS 19 v WI (Birmingham) 2007. F-c Tour (Eng A): WI 2005-06; B 2006-07 (captain). 1000 (1): 1520 (2005). HS 257 (record Sussex score v touring team) and BB 5-83 v B (Hove) 2005. CC HS 179 v Middlesex (Lord's) 2005. CC BB 2-62 v Glamorgan (Swansea) 2005. LO HS 98* v Surrey (Oval) 2006 (CGT). LO BB 6-27 v Warwks (Birmingham) 2005 (NL). IT20 HS 24*. IT20 BB 1-20. T20 HS 68*. T20 BB 2-15.

MONTGOMERIE, Richard Robert (Rugby S; Worcester C, Oxford), b Rugby, Warwks 3 Jul 1971. 5'10½". RHB, OB. Oxford U 1991-94; blue 1991-92-93-94; captain 1994; half blues for rackets and real tennis. Northamptonshire 1991-98; cap 1995. Combined U 1992-94. TCCB XI 1996. Sussex 1999-2007; cap 1999; benefit 2007. F-c Tour: Z 1994-95 (Nh). 1000 runs (6); most – 1704 (2001). HS 196 v Hants (Hove) 2002. BB 1-0 v Middlesex (Lord's) 2001. LO HS 132* v Somerset (Hove) 2005 (NL). T20 HS 20.

[NQ]**NAVED-UL-HASAN, Rana** – *see YORKSHIRE.*

SAQLAIN MUSHTAQ – *see SURREY.*

COUNTY CAPS AWARDED IN 2007

Derbyshire	S.M.Katich, T.Lungley, D.J.Pipe, G.G.Wagg
Durham	–
Essex	A.J.Bichel
Glamorgan	A.P.Davies
Gloucestershire	B.M.Edmondson, A.J.Ireland, A.A.Noffke, M.J.North, T.P.Stayt, J.G.Thompson
Hampshire	M.J.Brown, S.R.Clark
Kent	S.J.Cook, R.McLaren, J.C.Tredwell, Yasir Arafat
Lancashire	P.J.Horton, S.I.Mahmood, L.D.Sutton
Leicestershire	S.C.J.Broad, D.D.Masters, D.D.J.Robinson, R.P.Singh
Middlesex	M.Kartik, B.J.M.Scott, W.P.U.C.J.Vaas
Northamptonshire	S.D.Peters
Nottinghamshire	A.R.Adams, M.A.Wagh
Somerset	J.C.Hildreth, J.L.Langer, P.D.Trego, C.L.White, C.M.Willoughby
Surrey	M.J.Nicholson
Sussex	L.J.Wright
Warwickshire	T.R.Ambrose, D.L.Maddy, K.C.Sangakkara, D.W.Steyn
Worcestershire	Abdul Razzaq, M.M.Ali, D.E.Bollinger, K.W.Hogg, R.A.Jones, J.P.T.Knappett, J.D.Nel
Yorkshire	J.N.Gillespie, J.A.Rudolph, J.J.Sayers, Younus Khan

Durham abolished their capping system after 2005. Gloucestershire award caps on first-class debut. Worcestershire award club colours on Championship debut.

SUSSEX 2007

RESULTS SUMMARY

	Place	Won	Lost	Tied	Drew	No Result
LV County Championship (1st Division)	**1st**	7	3		5	1
All First-Class Matches		7	3		8	1
Friends Provident Trophy (South Conference)	8th	2	5			2
NatWest Pro40 League (1st Division)	5th	3	3			2
Twenty/20 Cup (South Division)	Semi-Finalist 6	3				1

LV COUNTY CHAMPIONSHIP AVERAGES
BATTING AND FIELDING

Cap		M	I	NO	HS	Runs	Avge	100	50	Ct/St
2001	M.W.Goodwin	14	25	5	205*	1078	53.90	3	5	10
2007	L.J.Wright	9	11	5	61	303	50.50	–	3	3
1998	C.J.Adams	15	24	2	193	1030	46.81	3	3	27
1999	R.R.Montgomerie	15	26	1	195	1000	40.00	2	5	27
–	A.J.Hodd	12	17	3	123	475	33.92	1	2	18/6
2000	R.S.C.Martin-Jenkins	13	18	4	99	428	30.57	–	2	6
–	C.D.Nash	15	26	–	89	785	30.19	–	7	8
2005	M.H.Yardy	10	17	1	119	450	28.12	1	3	6
–	Saqlain Mushtaq	3	4	1	57*	81	27.00	–	1	1
–	C.D.Hopkinson	7	12	–	83	296	24.66	–	2	8
1998	R.J.Kirtley	4	6	2	51	70	17.50	–	1	4
2003	M.J.Prior	3	5	–	35	74	14.80	–	–	7/2
2005	Naved-ul-Hasan	14	18	1	75	251	14.76	–	1	5
2003	Mushtaq Ahmed	15	17	3	54	170	12.14	–	1	3
1996	J.D.Lewry	13	13	5	13*	65	8.12	–	–	4

Also batted: C.J.Liddle (2 matches) 4, 15, 53; O.P.Rayner (1) 4.

BOWLED

	O	M	R	W	Avge	Best	5wI	10wM
Saqlain Mushtaq	84.3	16	235	14	16.78	5- 96	1	–
R.S.C.Martin-Jenkins	234	69	624	30	20.80	5- 67	1	–
Mushtaq Ahmed	668.5	91	2310	90	25.66	7- 72	8	3
Naved-ul-Hasan	377.3	59	1454	50	29.08	5-106	2	–
J.D.Lewry	319.1	78	933	31	30.09	4- 81	–	–
L.J.Wright	122.3	15	435	11	39.54	2- 30	–	–

Also bowled: C.J.Adams 4-0-9-0; M.W.Goodwin 1-0-6-0; C.D.Hopkinson 2-0-16-0; R.J.Kirtley 88-19-303-1; C.J.Liddle 34-10-93-0; C.D.Nash 9.1-1-36-3; O.P.Rayner 21-4-61-2; M.H.Yardy 18.3-2-66-0.

The First-Class Averages (pp 140–158) give the records of Sussex players in all first-class county matches (Sussex's other opponents being MCC, the Indians and Sri Lanka A), with the exception of:
    M.J.Prior 4-7-0-47-158-22.57-0-0-11ct-2st. Did not bowl.

SUSSEX RECORDS

FIRST-CLASS CRICKET

Highest Total	For 705-8d		v	Surrey	Hastings	1902
	V 726		by	Notts	Nottingham	1895
Lowest Total	For 19		v	Surrey	Godalming	1830
	19		v	Notts	Hove	1873
	V 18		by	Kent	Gravesend	1867
Highest Innings	For 335*	M.W.Goodwin	v	Leics	Hove	2003
	V 322	E.Paynter	for	Lancashire	Hove	1937

Highest Partnership for each Wicket

1st	490	E.H.Bowley/J.G.Langridge	v	Middlesex	Hove	1933
2nd	385	E.H.Bowley/M.W.Tate	v	Northants	Hove	1921
3rd	385*	M.H.Yardy/M.W.Goodwin	v	Warwicks	Hove	2006
4th	326*	J.Langridge/G.Cox	v	Yorkshire	Leeds	1949
5th	297	J.H.Parks/H.W.Parks	v	Hampshire	Portsmouth	1937
6th	255	K.S.Duleepsinhji/M.W.Tate	v	Northants	Hove	1930
7th	344	K.S.Ranjitsinhji/W.Newham	v	Essex	Leyton	1902
8th	291	R.S.C.Martin-Jenkins/M.J.G.Davis	v	Somerset	Taunton	2002
9th	178	H.W.Parks/A.F.Wensley	v	Derbyshire	Horsham	1930
10th	156	G.R.Cox/H.R.Butt	v	Cambridge U	Cambridge	1908

Best Bowling	For 10- 48	C.H.G.Bland	v	Kent	Tonbridge	1899
(Innings)	V 9- 11	A.P.Freeman	for	Kent	Hove	1922
Best Bowling	For 17-106	G.R.Cox	v	Warwicks	Horsham	1926
(Match)	V 17- 67	A.P.Freeman	for	Kent	Hove	1922

Most Runs – Season	2850	J.G.Langridge	(av 64.77)	1949
Most Runs – Career	34150	J.G.Langridge	(av 37.69)	1928-55
Most 100s – Season	12	J.G.Langridge		1949
Most 100s – Career	76	J.G.Langridge		1928-55
Most Wkts – Season	198	M.W.Tate	(av 13.47)	1925
Most Wkts – Career	2211	M.W.Tate	(av 17.41)	1912-37
Most Career W-K Dismissals	1176	H.R.Butt	(911 ct/265 st)	1890-1912
Most Career Catches in the Field	779	J.G.Langridge		1928-55

LIMITED-OVERS CRICKET

Highest Total	FPT	384-9	v	Ireland	Belfast	1996
	P40	323-5	v	Leics	Horsham	2004
	T20	205-5	v	Hampshire	Hove	2007
Lowest Total	FPT	49	v	Derbyshire	Chesterfield	1969
	P40	59	v	Glamorgan	Hove	1996
	T20	67	v	Hampshire	Hove	2004
Highest Innings	FPT	158*	M.W.Goodwin	v	Essex	Chelmsford	2006
	P40	163	C.J.Adams	v	Middlesex	Arundel	1999
	T20	103	L.J.Wright	v	Kent	Canterbury	2007
Best Bowling	FPT	6- 9	A.I.C.Dodemaide	v	Ireland	Downpatrick	1990
	P40	7-41	A.N.Jones	v	Notts	Nottingham	1986
	T20	5-11	Mushtaq Ahmed	v	Essex	Hove	2005

WARWICKSHIRE

Formation of Present Club: 8 April 1882
Substantial Reorganisation: 19 January 1884
Inaugural First-Class Match: 1894
Colours: Dark Blue, Gold and Silver
Badge: Bear and Ragged Staff
County Champions: (6) 1911, 1951, 1972, 1994, 1995, 2004
Gillette/NatWest/C&G/FP Trophy Winners: (5) 1966, 1968, 1989, 1993, 1995
Benson and Hedges Cup Winners: (2) 1994, 2002
Pro 40/National League (Div 1) Winners: (0); best – 3rd 2001, 2002
Sunday League Winners: (3) 1980, 1994, 1997
Twenty20 Cup Winners: (0); best – Finalist 2003

Chief Executive: Colin Povey, County Ground, Edgbaston, Birmingham, B5 7QU • Tel: 0121 446 4422 • Fax: 0121 446 4544 • Email: info@edgbaston.com • Web: www.edgbaston.com

Director of Coaching/First XI Coach: Ashley F.Giles. **Captain**: D.L.Maddy. **Vice-Captain**: tba. **Overseas Players**: M.Zondeki and S.T.Jayasuriya (T20). **2008 Beneficiary**: M.J.Powell. **Head Groundsman**: Steve Rouse. **Scorer**: David E.Wainwright. ‡ New registration. [NQ] Not qualified for England.

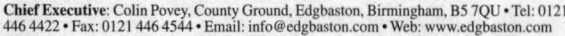

AMBROSE, Timothy Raymond (Merewether HS, NSW; TAFE C), b Newcastle, NSW, Australia 1 Dec 1982. ECB qualified – British/EU passport. 5'7". RHB, WK. Sussex 2001-05; cap 2003. Warwickshire debut 2006; cap 2007. NSW U-17 1999-00. HS 251* v Worcs (Worcester) 2007. LO HS 135 v Durham (Birmingham) 2007 (FPT). T20 HS 77.

ANYON, James Edward (Garstang HS; Preston C; Loughborough U), b Lancaster, Lancs 5 May 1983. 6'1". LHB, RFM. Loughborough U 2003-04. Warwickshire debut 2005. Cumberland 2003. HS 37* v Durham (Chester-le-St) 2007. BB 5-83 v Notts (Birmingham) 2006. LO HS 12 v Worcs (Birmingham) 2006 (CGT). LO BB 3-41 v Scot (Birmingham) 2006 (CGT). T20 HS 8*. T20 BB 3-6.

BELL, Ian Ronald (Princethorpe C), b Walsgrave-on-Sowe 11 Apr 1982. 5'9". RHB, RM. Debut (Warwickshire) 1999; cap 2001. MCC 2004. YC 2004. MBE 2005. **ECB central contract 2007-08. Tests**: 33 (2004 to 2007-08); HS 162* (inc 105* before lunch 2nd day) v B (Chester-le-St) 2005; BB 1-33 v P (Faisalabad) 2005-06. **LOI**: 64 (2004-05 to 2007-08; HS 126 v I (Southampton) 2007; BB 3-9 v Z (Bulawayo) 2004-05 – taking a wicket with his third ball in LOI. F-c Tours: A 2006-07; WI 2000-01 (Eng A – part); I 2005-06; P 2005-06; SL 2002-03 (ECB Acad), 2004-05, 2007-08. 1000 runs (2): most – 1714 (2004). Scored 480 runs (avge 80.00) in April 2005 – record f-c UK aggregate before May. HS 262* v Sussex (Horsham) 2004. BB 4-4 v Middlesex (Lord's) 2004. LO HS 137 v Yorks (Birmingham) 2005 (NL). LO BB 5-41 v Essex (Chelmsford) 2003 (NL). IT20 HS 22. T20 HS 66*. T20 BB 1-12.

[NQ]**BOTHA, Anthony** Greyvensteyn (Maritzburg C; Maritzburg Technikon), b Pretoria, South Africa 17 Nov 1976. 6'0". LHB, SLA. Natal/KwaZulu Natal 1995-96 to 1998-99. EP/Easterns 1999-00 to 2002-03. Derbyshire 2004-07 (cap 2004). Moved to Warwickshire in mid-season – debut 2007. HS 156* De v Yorks (Derby) 2005. Wa HS 27 and BB 2-37 v Lancs (Manchester) 2007. 50 wkts (1): 55 (2007). BB 8-53 Natal B v Northerns B (Pretoria) 1997-98. CC BB 6-101 De v Somerset (Derby) 2007. LO HS 60* Easterns v EP (Benoni) 2001-02. LO BB 5-60 De v West Indies A (Derby) 2006. T20 HS 26. T20 BB 4-14.

CARTER, Neil Miller (Hottentots Holland HS; Cape Technicon), b Cape Town, South Africa 29 Jan 1975. British passport. 6'2". LHB, LFM. Boland 1999-00 to 2000-01. Warwickshire debut 2001; cap 2005. HS 103 v Sussex (Hove) 2002 – completed maiden hundred off 67 balls. BB 6-63 Boland v GW (Kimberley) 2000-01 and 6-63 v Sussex (Birmingham) 2006. LO HS 135 v Scot (Birmingham) 2006 (CGT). LO BB 5-31 v Durham (Birmingham) 2002 (NL). T20 HS 58. T20 BB 5-19.

DAGGETT, Lee Martin (Woodhey HS, and Holy Cross C, Bury; John Snow C, Durham) b Bury, Lancs 1 Oct 1982. 6'0". RHB, RFM. Durham UCCE 2003-05. British U 2004. Warwickshire debut 2006. HS 33 v Durham (Chester-le-St) 2007. BB 8-94 DU v Durham (Chester-le-St) 2004. Wa BB 6-30 v Durham (Birmingham) 2006. LO HS 5* (twice – CGT, P40). LO BB 2-33 v Essex (Birmingham) 2006 (P40). T20 HS – . T20 BB 1-13.

FROST, Tony (James Brinkley HS; Stoke-on-Trent C), b Stoke-on-Trent, Staffs 17 Nov 1975. 5'11". RHB, WK. Warwickshire 1997-2006; cap 1999. Recalled for 2008. HS 135* v Sussex (Horsham) 2004. LO HS 47 v Beds (Luton) (CGT). T20 HS 33*.

NQGROENEWALD, Timothy Duncan (Maritzburg C; South Africa U), b Pietermaritzburg, South Africa 10 Jan 1984. 6'0". RHB, RFM. Debut (Warwickshire) 2006. HS 76 v Durham (Chester-le-St) 2006. BB 3-26 v Hants (Birmingham) 2007. LO HS 36 v Lancs (Manchester) 2007 (FPT). LO BB 3-25 v Worcs (Birmingham) 2007 (P40). T20 HS 41. T20 BB 2-10.

HOLE, Stuart Mark (Bartholomew S), b Oxford 17 Jul 1985. RHB, RM. Debut (Warwickshire) 2007. Oxfordshire 2005-07. HS 24 v and BB – v Yorks (Scarborough) 2007 – on debut. LO HS – and BB 1-16 v Essex (Southend) 2007 (P40).

JAMES, Nicholas Alexander (King Edward VI S, Aston), b Sandwell, Birmingham 17 Sep 1986. 5'9". LHB, SLA. Staffordshire 2006-07. Awaiting f-c debut. LO HS 30 v Worcs (Birmingham) 2006 (CGT) on Wa debut. LO BB 2-34 v Notts (Birmingham) 2006 (CGT). T20 HS 12*.

‡NQJAYASURIYA, Sanath Teran (St Servatius C, Matara), b Matara, Ceylon 30 Jun 1969. 5'6". LHB, SLA. Colombo 1988-89 to 1992-93. Southern Districts/Province 1989-90 to 2004-05. Bloomfield 1994-95 to date. Somerset 2005. MCC 2007. Lancashire 2007. *Wisden* 1996. **Tests** (SL): 110 (1990-91 to 2007-08, 38 as captain); HS 340 v I (Colombo) 1997-98; BB 5-34 v SA (Colombo) 2004. **LOI** (SL): 398 (1989-90 to 2007-08, 118 as captain); HS 189 v I (Sharjah) 2000-01. Scored fastest LOI hundred (48 balls) v P (Singapore) 1995-96; BB 6-29 v E (Moratuwa) 1992-93. F-c Tours (SL) (C=captain): E 1991, 1998, 2002C, 2006 (part), 2007 (MCC); A 1995-96, 2004, 2007; SA 1992-93 (SL U-24), 1994-95, 1997-98, 2000-01C, 2002-03C; WI 1996-97, 2003; NZ 1990-91, 1994-95, 1996-97, 2004-05, 2006-07; I 1993-94, 1997-98; P 1988-89 (SL B), 1991-92, 1995-96, 1999-00C, 2001-02C, 2004-05; Z 1994-95, 1999-00C, 2003-04. 1000 (0+1): 1229 (2003-04). HS 340 (*see Tests*). La HS 38 and BB 1-10 v Yorks (Manchester) 2007 (only f-c appearance). BB 5-34 (*see Tests*). LO HS 189 (*see LOI*). LO BB 6-29 (*see LOI*). IT20 HS 88. IT20 BB 3-21. T20 HS 88. T20 BB 4-24.

‡JOHNSON, Richard Matthew, b Solihull 1 Sep 1988. RHB, WK. Herefordshire 2006. Warwickshire Academy/2nd XI 2007. Joins staff 2008 – awaiting 1st XI debut.

‡MacLEOD, Calum Scott (Hillpark S), b Glasgow, Scotland 15 Nov 1988. RHB, RMF. Scotland 2007. Warwickshire 2nd XI 2006-07. Awaiting county 1st XI debut. HS – and BB – Scotland v UAE (Ayr) 2007 – on debut (only f-c match).

MADDY, Darren Lee (Wreake Valley C), b Leicester 23 May 1974. 5'9". RHB, RM/OB. Leicestershire 1994-2006; cap 1996; benefit 2006. Warwickshire debut/cap 2007; captain 2007 (after first week) to date. **Tests**: 3 (1999 to 1999-00); HS 24 v SA (Durban) 1999-00. **LOI**: 8 (1998 to 1999-00); HS 53 v Z (Harare) 1999-00. F-c Tours (Eng A): SA 1996-97 (Le), 1998-99, 1999-00 (Eng); SL 1997-98; Z 1998-99; KV 1997-98. 1000 runs (4); most – 1187 (2002). HS 229* Le v LU (Leicester) 2003. Scored 202 Eng A v Kenya (Nairobi) 1997-98. CC HS 162 Le v Durham (Darlington) 1998. Wa HS 148* v Kent (Canterbury) 2007. BB 5-37 Le v Hants (Southampton) 2002. Wa BB 5-63 v Durham (Chester-le-St) 2007. LO HS 167* Le v Scot (Edinburgh) 2006 (CGT). LO BB 4-16 Le v Somerset (Taunton) 2000 (NL). IT20 HS 50. IT20 BB 2-6. T20 HS 111. T20 BB 2-6.

PARKER, Luke Charles (Finham Park S; Oxford Brookes U), b Coventry 27 Sep 1983. 6'0". RHB, RM. Oxford UCCE 2004-06. British U 2005-06. Warwickshire debut 2005. MCC 2006. HS 140 OU v Durham (Oxford) 2006. Wa HS 73 v Notts (Birmingham) 2006. BB 2-37 v Glos (Oxford) 2005. LO HS 17 Warwks CB v Cumb (Millom) 2001. T20 HS 3*.

NQPOLLOCK, Shaun Maclean (Northwood HS; Durban U), b Port Elizabeth, SA 16 Jul 1973. Son of P.M.Pollock (EP and SA 1958-59 to 1971-72); nephew of R.G.Pollock (EP, Transvaal and SA 1960-61 to 1986-87). 6'3". RHB, RFM. Natal/KZ-Natal 1991-92 to 2003-04. Warwickshire 1996, 2002; cap 1996. Dolphins 2004-05 to date. **Tests** (SA): 108 (1995-96 to 2007-08, 26 as captain); HS 111 v SL (Pretoria) 2000-01; BB 7-87 v A (Adelaide) 1997-98. **LOI** (SA): 290 (1995-96 to 2007-08, 92 as captain; HS (90 v P (Multan) 2007-08; BB 6-35 v WI (E London) 1998-99. Tours (SA) (C=captain): E 1998, 2003; A 1997-98, 2001-02C, 2005-06; WI 2000-01C, 2004-05 (part); NZ 1998-99, 2003-04; I 1999-00, 2004-05; P 1997-98, 2003-04; SL 1995 (SA U-24), 2000C, 2004, 2006; Z 1999-00, 2001-02C; B 2003. HS 150* v Glam (Birmingham) 1996. 50 wkts (1): 51 (1995-96). BB 7-33 Natal v Border (E London) 1995-96. Wa BB 6-56 v Middlesex (Lord's) 1996. LO HS 134* KZ-Natal v EP (Durban) 2003-04. LO BB 6-21 v Leics (Birmingham) 1996 (BHC) – inc 4 wkts in 4 balls on Wa debut. IT20 HS 36*. IT20 BB 3-28. T20 HS 59. T20 BB 3-28.

POONIA, Navdeep Singh (Moseley Park S; Wolverhampton U), b Govan, Glasgow, Scotland 11 May 1986. 6'3". RHB, RM. Debut (Warwickshire) 2006 (only match) – awaiting CC debut. Scotland 2006 to date (no f-c appearances). **LOI** (Scot): 14 (2006 to 2007); HS 67 v Canada (Mombasa) 2006-07. HS 35 v West Indies A (Birmingham) 2006. LO HS 67 (see LOI). IT20 HS 4. T20 HS 19.

POWELL, Michael James (Lawrence Sheriff S, Rugby), b Bolton, Lancs 5 Apr 1975. 5'11". RHB, RM. Debut (Warwickshire) 1996; cap 1999; captain 2001-03; benefit 2008. Griqualand West 2001-02. MCC 2004. Otago 2005-06. F-c Tour (Eng A): WI 2000-01. 1000 runs (1): 1046 (2000). HS 236 v OU (Oxford) 2001. CC HS 146 v Glamorgan (Birmingham) 2005. BB 2-16 v OU (Oxford) 1998. CC BB 2-29 v Somerset (Taunton) 2002. LO HS 101* v Northants (Birmingham) 2002 (BHC). LO BB 5-40 v Kent (Canterbury) 2002 (CGT). T20 HS 44*.

‡NQRANKIN, William Boyd (Strabane GS; Harper Adams UC), b Londonderry, Co Derry, N Ireland 5 Jul 1984. 6'8". LHB, RMF. Brother of R.J.Rankin (Ireland U-19 – 2003-04). Debut (Ireland) 2006-07. Middlesex summer contract 2004-05. Derbyshire 2007. Joins Warwickshire 2008. **LOI** (Ireland): 10 (2006-07) HS 7* v SL (St George's) 2006-07; BB 3-32 v P (Kingston) 2006-07. HS 3 and BB 4-41 De v Middlesex (Derby) 2007. LO HS 7* (see LOI). LO BB 3-32 (see LOI).

‡**SALISBURY, Ian** David Kenneth (Moulton CS), b Northampton 21 Jan 1970. 5'11". RHB, LBG. Sussex 1989-96; cap 1991. TCCB XI 1996. Surrey 1997-2007; cap 1998; benefit 2007. MCC YC 1988. YC 1992. *Wisden* 1992. Tests: 15 (1992 to 2000-01); HS 50 v P (Manchester) 1992; BB 4-163 v WI (Georgetown) 1993-94. LOI: 4 (1992-93 to 1993-94); HS 5 and BB 3-41 v WI (Port-of-Spain) 1993-94. F-c Tours: WI 1991-92 (Eng A), 1993-94; I 1992-93; 1994-95 (Eng A); P 1990-91 (Eng A), 1995-96 (Eng A), 2000-01; SL 1990-91 (Eng A). HS 103 Sy v Hants (Oval) 2007. 50 wkts (7); most – 87 (1992). BB 8-60 (12-91 match) Sy v Somerset (Oval) 2000. LO HS 59* Sy v Glamorgan (Oval) 2004 (NL). LO BB 5-30 Sx v Leics (Leicester) 1992 (SL). T20 HS 20. T20 BB 2-6.

TAHIR, Naqaash (Moseley S; Spring Hill C), b Birmingham 14 Nov 1983. 5'10", RHB, RFM. Debut (Warwickshire) 2004. HS 49 v Worcs (Worcester) 2004. BB 7-107 v Lancs (Blackpool) 2006. LO HS 1* (NL). LO BB 1-19 v Glos (Bristol) 2007 (P40).

TROTT, Ian Jonathan Leonard (Rondebosch BHC; Stellenbosch U), b Cape Town, South Africa 22 Apr 1981. 6'0". Stepbrother of K.C.Jackson (WP and Boland 1988-89 to 2001-02). RHB, RM. Boland 2000-01. W Province 2001-02. EU/British passport. Warwick-shire debut 2003 scoring 134 v Sussex (Birmingham); cap 2005. Otago 2005-06. 1000 runs (3); most – 1170 (2004). HS 210 v Sussex (Birmingham) 2005. BB 7-39 v Kent (Canterbury) 2003. LO HS 125* v Northants (Birmingham) 2007 (FPT). LO BB 4-55 v Hants (Lord's) 2005 (CGT). IT20 HS 9. T20 HS 75*. T20 BB 2-19.

TROUGHTON, Jamie Oliver ('Jim') (Trinity S; Leamington Spa; Birmingham U), b Camden, London 2 Mar 1979. Great-grandson of H.T.Crichton (Warwicks 1908). 5'11". LHB, SLA. Debut (Warwickshire) 2001; cap 2002. LOI: 6 (2003); HS 20 v P (Lord's) 2003. F-c Tour (ECB Acad): SL 2002-03. 1000 runs (1): 1067 (2002). HS 162 v Worcs (Worcester) 2007. BB 3-1 v CU (Cambridge) 2004. CC BB 2-26 v Lancs (Birmingham) 2006. LO HS 115* and BB 4-23 Warwks CB v Cumb (Millom) 2001 (CGT). T20 HS 51. T20 BB 2-10.

WESTWOOD, Ian James (Wheelers Lane S; Solihull SFC), b Birmingham 13 Jul 1982. 5'7½". LHB, OB. Debut (Warwickshire) 2003. HS 178 v West Indies A (Birmingham) 2006. CC HS 116 v Durham (Chester-le-St) 2007. BB 2-46 v Kent (Birmingham) 2006. LO HS 55 and BB 1-28 Warwks CB v Cambs (March) 2001 (CGT). T20 HS 19*. BB 3-29.

WOAKES, Christopher Roger (Barr Beacon Language C), b Birmingham 2 March 1989. RHB, RM. Debut (Warwickshire) 2006. Herefordshire 2006-07. HS 14* and CC BB 1-42 v Surrey (Birmingham) 2007. BB 2-64 v West Indies A (Birmingham) 2006. LO HS – 2007 (P40).

‡**ZONDEKI, Monde** (Dale C), b King William's Town, Cape Province, South Africa 25 Jul 1982. 6'1". RHB, RF. Border 2001-02 to 2004-05. Warriors 2004-05. Cape Cobras 2005-06 to date. Tests (SA): 5 (2003 to 2004-05); HS 59 v E (Leeds) 2003 – on debut; BB 6-39 v Z (Pretoria) 2004-05. LOI (SA): 9 (2002-03 to 2005-06); HS 3* v P (Cape Town) 2002-03. BB 2-46 v Z (Port Elizabeth) 2004-05. F-c Tours (SA): E 2003; A 2005-06; WI 2004-05; SL 2005-06 (SA A). HS 59 (*see* Tests). BB 6-39 (*see* Tests). LO HS 23 SA A v SL (Potchefstroom) 2002-03 and 23 SA A v SL A (Benoni) 2003-04. LO BB 6-37 SA A v SL A (Pretoria) 2003-04. IT20 HS 0. IT20 BB 1-41. T20 HS 1*. T20 BB 2-19.

RELEASED/RETIRED
(Having made a County 1st XI appearance in 2007)

BARNES, Michael William (Bohunt S; South Downs C), b Frimley, Surrey 3 Apr 1985. RHB, WK. Warwickshire 2007. HS – v Yorks (Birmingham) 2007. LO HS 1* v Lancs (Manchester) 2007 (FPT).

BROWN, Douglas Robert (Alloa Academy; W London IHE), b Stirling, Scotland 29 Oct 1969. 6'2". RHB, RFM. Scotland 1989, 2006 to 2006-07. Warwickshire 1991-92 (SA tour) to 2006; cap 1995; benefit 2005. Wellington 1995-96. **LOI** (E): 9 (1997-98); HS 21 v WI (Bridgetown) 1997-98; BB 2-28 v WI (Sharjah) 1997-98. **LOI** (Scot): 16 (2006 to 2006-07); HS 50*v Canada (Nairobi) 2006-07; BB 3-37 v K (Mombasa) 2006-07. F-c Tours (Wa): SA 1991-92, 1994-95; SL 1997-98 (Eng A); UAE 2006-07. 1000 runs (1): 1028 (2003). HS 203 v Sussex (Hove) 2000. 50 wkts (4); most – 81 (1997). BB 8-89 (11-154 match) F-C Counties XI v Pak A (Chelmsford) 1997. Wa BB 7-66 v Durham (Chester-le-St) 1999. LO HS 108 v Essex (Birmingham) 2003 (CGT). LO BB 5-31 v Worcs (Worcester) 1997 (BHC). IT20 HS 1. IT20 BB – . T20 HS 37. T20 BB 3-21.

ᴺᑫ**HARRIS, Paul** Lee (Fish Hoek HS; Cape Town CFE), b Salisbury, Rhodesia 2 Nov 1978. RHB, SLA. W Province 1998-99 to 2001-02. Northerns 2002-03 to 2005-06. Titans 2004-05 to date. Warwickshire 2006-07. **Tests** (SA): 10 (2006-07 to 2007-08); HS 46 v P (Lahore) 2007-08; BB 5-73 v P (Karachi) 2007-08. F-c Tours (SA): P 2007-08; Z 2007-08 (SA A). HS 55 v Durham (Chester-le-St) 2007. 50 wkts (0+1): 50 (2005-06). BB 6-54 Titans v Cobras (Benoni) 2005-06. Wa BB 6-80 v Hants (Southampton) 2006. LO HS 10 Northerns v GW (Pretoria) 2003-04. LO BB 3-33 v Essex (Birmingham) 2006 (P40). T20 HS 3. T20 BB 3-18.

LOUDON, Alexander Guy Rushworth (Wellesley House; Eton C; Collingwood C, Durham U), b Westminster, London 6 Sep 1980. Younger brother of H.J.H.Loudon (Durham UCCE 2001). 6'3". RHB, OB. Durham UCCE 2001-03; captain 2003. Kent 2003-04. Warwickshire 2005-07; cap 2006. MCC 2006-07. **LOI**: 1 (2006); HS 0 v SL (Chester-le-St) 2006. F-c Tours (Eng A): WI 2005-06; B 2006-07. HS 172 DU (record) v Durham (Chester-le-St) 2003. Wa HS 105 v Durham (Birmingham) 2007. BB 6-47 K v Middlesex (Canterbury) 2004. Wa BB 6-66 v Glos (Birmingham) 2005. LO HS 73* v Kent (Canterbury) 2005 (NL). LO BB 4-48 K v Essex (Colchester) 2004 (NL). T20 HS 27. T20 BB 5-33.

ᴺᑫ**SANGAKKARA, Kumar** Chokshanada (Trinity C, Kandy; Colombo U), b Matale, Sri Lanka 27 Oct 1977. 5'11". LHB, OB, WK. Nondescripts 1997-98 to 2006-07. Central Province 2003-04 to 2004-05. Warwickshire 2007; cap 2007. **Tests** (SL): 71 (2000 to 2007-08); HS 287 v SA (Colombo SSC) 2006-07 – sharing in world record f-c partnership for any wicket of 624 with D.P.M.D.Jayawardena. **LOI** (SL): 200 (2000 to 2007-08); HS 138* v I (Jaipur) 2005-06. F-c Tours (SL): E 2002, 2006; A 2004, 2007-08; SA 1999-00 (SL A), 2000-01, 2002-03; WI 2003; NZ 2004-05, 2006-07; I 2005-06; P 2001-02, 2004-05; Z 2004; B 2005-06. 1000 runs (0+1): 1191 (2003-04). HS 287 (see Tests). BB 1-13 SL v Zim A (Harare) 2004. LO HS 156* SL A v Zim A (Moratuwa) 1999-00. IT20 HS 30. T20 HS 93.

SHANTRY, A.J. – see GLAMORGAN.

ᴺᑫ**STEYN, Dale** Willem (Hans Merensky HS, Phalaborwa), b Phalaborwa, N Province, South Africa 27 Jun 1983. RHB, RF. Northerns 2003-04 to 2005-06. Titans 2004-05 to date. Essex 2005. Warwickshire 2007; cap 2007. **Tests** (SA): 18 (2004-05 to 2007-08); HS 33* v WI (Port Elizabeth) 2007-08; BB 6-49 (10-91 match) v NZ (Pretoria) 2007-08. **LOI** (SA): 6 (2005-06 to 2007-08); HS – ; BB 3-65 v Z (Harare) 2007-08. F-c Tours (SA): I 2007-08; P 2007-08; SL 2005-06 (SA A), 2006. HS 82 Ex v Durham (Chester-le-St) 2005. Wa HS 51 v Surrey (Oval) 2007. 50 wkts (0+2); most – 69 (2005-06). BB 8-41 Titans v Eagles (Bloemfontein) 2007-08. UK/Wa BB 5-49 v Worcs (Worcester) 2007. LO HS 14 v Hants (Southampton) 2007 (FPT). LO BB 5-20 SA A v SL A (Colombo) 2005-06. IT20 HS 1*. IT20 BB 4-9. T20 HS 4*. T20 BB 4-9.

RELEASED/RETIRED continued on p 117

WARWICKSHIRE 2007

RESULTS SUMMARY

	Place	Won	Lost	Tied	Drew	No Result
LV County Championship (1st Division)	8th	2	5		9	
All First-Class Matches		2	5		9	1
Friends Provident Trophy (North Conference)	Semi-Finalist	6	2			2
NatWest Pro40 League (1st Division)	8th	2	5			1
Twenty/20 Cup (Midlands/West Wales Division)	Quarter-Finalist	5	3			1

LV COUNTY CHAMPIONSHIP AVERAGES

BATTING AND FIELDING

Cap		M	I	NO	HS	Runs	Avge	100	50	Ct/St
2007	K.C.Sangakkara	7	11	1	149	496	49.60	2	2	4
2007	D.L.Maddy	14	20	3	148*	796	46.82	4	2	14
2007	T.R.Ambrose	15	22	3	251*	858	45.15	1	4	36
2002	J.O.Troughton	14	19	1	162	771	42.83	3	1	1
–	I.J.Westwood	14	22	2	116	771	38.55	2	5	8
2006	A.G.R.Loudon	15	22	1	105	712	33.90	3	1	8
–	D.W.Steyn	7	7	2	51	145	29.00	–	1	–
1999	M.J.Powell	4	6	–	82	165	27.50	–	1	2
2005	H.H.Streak	11	15	3	66	278	23.16	–	2	–
–	A.C.Thomas	4	7	1	42	130	21.66	–	–	2
–	L.M.Daggett	3	4	2	33	42	21.00	–	–	–
2005	I.J.L.Trott	14	20	–	84	396	19.80	–	2	16
–	T.D.Groenewald	8	9	2	41*	133	19.00	–	–	8
2005	N.M.Carter	3	5	2	27	56	18.66	–	–	1
–	J.E.Anyon	14	16	5	37*	199	18.09	–	–	3
–	L.C.Parker	5	6	–	49	81	13.50	–	–	3
–	A.G.Botha	4	4	–	27	37	9.25	–	1	–
–	N.Tahir	11	11	1	32	87	8.70	–	–	–

Also batted: I.R.Bell (2 matches – cap 2001) 9, 65 (1 ct); P.L.Harris (4) 4, 55, 0; S.M.Hole (1) 0*, 24; A.J.Shantry (2) 5, 5, 0 (1 ct); C.R.Woakes (1) 9, 14* (1 ct). M.W.Barnes (1) (5ct) did not bat.

BOWLING

	O	M	R	W	Avge	Best	5wI	10wM
D.W.Steyn	203.3	45	595	23	25.86	5- 49	1	–
D.L.Maddy	166	50	409	15	27.26	5- 63	1	–
N.Tahir	238.4	57	694	25	27.76	4- 47	–	–
N.M.Carter	85.4	14	283	10	28.30	5- 62	1	–
A.C.Thomas	129.2	37	367	10	36.70	4-109	–	–
J.E.Anyon	374.1	67	1424	32	44.50	4- 55	–	–
H.H.Streak	255.2	54	789	13	60.69	3-105	–	–

Also bowled:

T.D.Groenewald	132.3	37	430	9	47.77	3- 26	–	–
A.G.R.Loudon	208.3	24	667	8	83.37	4-123	–	–

A.G.Botha 73.3-22-155-4; L.M.Daggett 45-9-154-1; P.L.Harris 120.5-20-341-4; S.M.Hole 15-4-65-0; L.C.Parker 2-0-16-0; A.J.Shantry 33-11-111-4; I.J.L.Trott 74-19-214-2; J.O.Troughton 85-12-276-2; I.J.Westwood 6.5-1-26-1; C.R.Woakes 19.4-3-90-1.

The First-Class Averages (pp 140–158) give the records of Warwickshire's players in all first-class county matches (Warwickshire's other opponents being Sri Lanka A), with the exception of T.R.Ambrose, I.R.Bell, A.G.Botha, A.G.R.Loudon and I.J.L.Trott, whose full first-class figures for Warwickshire are as above.

WARWICKSHIRE RECORDS

FIRST-CLASS CRICKET

Highest Total	For 810-4d		v	Durham	Birmingham	1994
	V 887		by	Yorkshire	Birmingham	1896
Lowest Total	For 16		v	Kent	Tonbridge	1913
	V 15		by	Hampshire	Birmingham	1922
Highest Innings	For 501*	B.C.Lara	v	Durham	Birmingham	1994
	V 322	I.V.A.Richards	for	Somerset	Taunton	1985

Highest Partnership for each Wicket

1st	377*	N.F.Horner/K.Ibadulla	v	Surrey	The Oval	1960
2nd	465*	J.A.Jameson/R.B.Kanhai	v	Glos	Birmingham	1974
3rd	327	S.P.Kinneir/W.G.Quaife	v	Lancashire	Birmingham	1901
4th	470	A.I.Kallicharran/G.W.Humpage	v	Lancashire	Southport	1982
5th	322*	B.C.Lara/K.J.Piper	v	Durham	Birmingham	1994
6th	226	T.R.Ambrose/H.H.Streak	v	Worcs	Worcester	2007
7th	289*	I.R.Bell/T.Frost	v	Sussex	Horsham	2004
8th	228	A.J.W.Croom/R.E.S.Wyatt	v	Worcs	Dudley	1925
9th	154	G.W.Stephens/A.J.W.Croom	v	Derbyshire	Birmingham	1925
10th	214	N.V.Knight/A.Richardson	v	Hampshire	Birmingham	2002

Best Bowling	For 10-41	J.D.Bannister	v	Comb Servs	Birmingham	1959
(Innings)	V 10-36	H.Verity	for	Yorkshire	Leeds	1931
Best Bowling	For 15-76	S.Hargreave	v	Surrey	The Oval	1903
(Match)	V 17-92	A.P.Freeman	for	Kent	Folkestone	1932

Most Runs – Season	2417	M.J.K.Smith	(av 60.42)	1959
Most Runs – Career	35146	D.L.Amiss	(av 41.64)	1960-87
Most 100s – Season	9	A.I.Kallicharran		1984
	9	B.C.Lara		1994
Most 100s – Career	78	D.L.Amiss		1960-87
Most Wkts – Season	180	W.E.Hollies	(av 15.13)	1946
Most Wkts – Career	2201	W.E.Hollies	(av 20.45)	1932-57
Most Career W-K Dismissals	800	E.J.Smith	(662 ct/138 st)	1904-30
Most Career Catches in the Field	422	M.J.K.Smith		1956-75

LIMITED-OVERS CRICKET

Highest Total	FPT	392-5	v	Oxfordshire	Birmingham	1984
	P40	310-5	v	Lancs	Birmingham	2004
	T20	205-7	v	Glamorgan	Swansea	2005
		205-2	v	Northants	Birmingham	2005
Lowest Total	FPT	98	v	Leics	Leicester	1998
	P40	59	v	Yorks	Leeds	2001
	T20	115	v	Surrey	Nottingham	2003
Highest Innings	FPT	206	A.I.Kallicharran	v	Oxfordshire	Birmingham	1984
	P40	137	I.R.Bell	v	Yorkshire	Birmingham	2005
	T20	89	N.V.Knight	v	Worcestershire	Worcester	2003
Best Bowling	FPT	6-32	K.Ibadulla	v	Hampshire	Birmingham	1965
		6-32	A.I.Kallicharran	v	Oxfordshire	Birmingham	1984
	P40	6-15	A.A.Donald	v	Yorkshire	Birmingham	1995
	T20	5-19	N.M.Carter	v	Worcestershire	Birmingham	2005

WORCESTERSHIRE

Formation of Present Club: 11 March 1865
Inaugural First-Class Match: 1899
Colours: Dark Green and Black
Badge: Shield Argent a Fess between three Pears Sable
County Championships: (5) 1964, 1965, 1974, 1988, 1989
Gillette/NatWest/C&G/FP Trophy Winners: (1) 1994
Benson and Hedges Cup Winners: (1) 1991
Pro 40/National League (Div 1) Winners: (1) 2007
Sunday League Winners: (3) 1971, 1987, 1988
Twenty20 Cup Winners: (0); best – Quarter-Finalist 2004, 2007

Chief Executive: Mark S.Newton, County Ground, New Road, Worcester, WR2 4QQ • Tel: 01905 748474 • Fax: 01905 748005 • Email: admin@wccc.co.uk • Web: www.wccc.co.uk

Director of Cricket/First XI Coach: Steve J.Rhodes. **Captain**: V.S.Solanki. **Vice-Captain**: G.J.Batty. **Overseas Player**: tba. **2008 Beneficiary**: none. **Head Groundsman**: Tim Packwood. **Scorer**: Neil D.Smith. ‡ New registration. [NQ] Not qualified for England.

Worcestershire revised their capping policy in 2002 and now award players with their County Colours when they make their Championship debut.

‡**AHMED, Mehraj**, b Birmingham, Warwks 5 Jan 1989. RHB, RFM. Worcestershire 2nd XI 2006-07. Awaiting 1st XI debut.

ALI, Kabir (Moseley CS and SFC), b Moseley, Birmingham, Warwks 24 Nov 1980. 6'0". Cousin of Kadeer Ali (*see GLOUCESTERSHIRE*) and M.M.Ali (*see below*). RHB, RMF. Debut (Worcestershire) 1999. Rajasthan 2006-07. **Tests**: 1 (2003); HS 9 and BB 3-80 v SA (Leeds) 2003 – on debut. **LOI**: 14 (2003 to 2006); HS 39* v P (Rawalpindi) 2005-06; BB 4-45 v I (Delhi) 2005-06. F-c Tours (Eng A): WI 2005-06; SL 2002-03 (ECB Acad). HS 84* v Durham (Stockton) 2003. 50 wkts (4); most – 71 (2002). BB 8-50 v Lancs (Manchester) 2007. Took 8-53 before lunch first day v Yorks (Scarborough) 2003. LO HS 92 v Essex (Worcester) 2003 (NL). LO BB 5-36 v Yorks (Leeds) 2002 (NL). T20 HS 49. T20 BB 3-18.

ALI, Moeen Munir (Moseley S), b Birmingham, Warwks 18 Jun 1987. Brother of Kadeer Ali (*see GLOUCESTERSHIRE*) and cousin of Kabir Ali (*see above*). 6'0". LHB, OB. Warwickshire 2005-06 having joined staff when aged 15. Worcestershire debut 2007. HS 85 v Sussex (Hove) 2007. BB 2-50 Wa v Lancs (Birmingham) 2006. Wo BB – . LO HS 100 v Northants (Kidderminster) 2006 (P40). LO BB 2-45 v Northants (Northampton) 2007 (FPT). T20 HS 12.

‡**ANDREW, Gareth** Mark (Ansford Community S; Richard Huish C), b Yeovil 27 Dec 1983. 6'0". LHB, RMF. Somerset 2003-05; 2nd XI debut 1999 when aged 15 years 247 days. HS 44 and BB 4-63 Sm v SL A (Taunton) 2004. CC HS 32 Sm v Lancs (Taunton) 2005. CC BB 4-134 Sm v Derbys (Taunton) 2005. LO HS 33 Sm v Leics (Leicester) 2006 (P40). LO BB 4-48 Sm v Scot (Taunton) 2004 (NL). T20 HS 12*. T20 BB 4-22.

BATTY, Gareth Jon (Bingley GS), b Bradford, Yorks 13 Oct 1977. Younger brother of J.D.Batty (Yorkshire and Somerset 1989-96). 5'11". RHB, OB. Yorkshire 1997. Surrey 1999-2001. Worcestershire debut 2002. **Tests**: 7 (2003-04 to 2005); HS 38 v SL (Kandy) 2003-04; BB 3-55 v SL (Galle) 2003-04. Took wicket with his third ball in Test cricket. **LOI**: 7 (2002-03 to 2005-06); HS 3 v A (Melbourne) 2002-03; BB 2-40 v WI (Gros Islet, St Lucia) 2003-04. F-c Tours: WI 2003-04, 2005-06; SL 2002-03 (ECB Acad); SL 2003-04; B 2003-04. HS 133 v Surrey (Oval) 2004. 50 wkts (2); most – 60 (2003). BB 7-52 (10-113 match) v Northants (Northampton) 2004. LO HS 83* Sy v Yorks (Oval) 2001 (NL). LO BB 4-27 v Leics (Leicester) 2006 (CGT). T20 HS 87. T20 BB 3-38.

DAVIES, Steven Michael (King Charles I S, Kidderminster), b Bromsgrove 17 Jun 1986. 5'10". LHB, WK. Debut (Worcestershire) 2005. 2nd XI debut 2001 when 15 years 8 days. MCC 2006-07. F-c Tour (Eng A): B 2006-07. 1000 runs (1): 1052 (2006). HS 192 v Glos (Bristol) 2006. LO HS 84 v Glos (Bristol) 2007 (P40). T20 HS 30.

HICK, Graeme Ashley (Prince Edward HS, Salisbury), b Salisbury, Rhodesia 23 May 1966. 6'3". RHB, OB. Zimbabwe 1983-84 to 1985-86. Worcestershire debut 1984; cap 1986; benefit 1999; captain 2000-02; Testimonial 2006. N Districts 1987-88 to 1988-89. MCC 1988-1991. Queensland 1990-91. *Wisden* 1986. PCA 1988. Lawrence Trophy 1988. **Tests**: 65 (1991 to 2000-01); HS 178 v I (Bombay) 1992-93; BB 4-126 v NZ (Wellington) 1991-92. Took wicket with his third ball in Test cricket. **LOI**: 120 (1991 to 2000-01); HS 126* v SL (Adelaide) 1998-99; BB 5-33 v Z (Harare) 1999-00. F-c Tours: E 1985 (Z); A 1994-95, 1998-99 (*part*); SA 1995-96, 1999-00 (*part*); WI 1993-94; NZ 1991-92; I 1992-93; P 2000-01; SL 1983-84 (Z), 1992-93, 2000-01; Z 1990-91 (Wo), 1996-97 (Wo). 1000 runs (19+1), inc 2000 (3): 2004 (1986), 2713 (1988), 2347 (1990); youngest to score 2000 (1986). Scored 1019 runs before June 1988, including a record 410 runs in April. Fewest innings for 10,000 runs in county cricket (179). Youngest (24) to score 50 f-c hundreds. Second-youngest (32) to score 100 f-c hundreds. Scored 645 runs without being dismissed (UK record) in 1990. 100th f-c hundred for Worcestershire 1998. HS 405* (Worcs record and then second highest in UK f-c matches) v Somerset (Taunton) 1988. BB 5-18 v Leics (Worcester) 1995. LO HS 172* v Devon (Worcester) 1987 (NWT). LO BB 5-19 Eng v Pak A (Lahore) 1998-99. T20 HS 116*.

JONES, Richard Alan (Grange HS and King Edward VI C, Stourbridge; Loughborough U), b Wordsley, Stourbridge 6 Nov 1986. 6'2". RHB, RMF. Worcestershire debut 2007. HS 24 and BB 3-37 v Loughborough U (Worcester) 2007. CC HS 11* v Warwks (Worcester) 2007. CC BB 2-125 v Sussex (Hove) 2007.

‡**JONES, Simon** Philip (Coedcae CS; Millfield S), b Morriston, Swansea 25 Dec 1978. Son of I.J.Jones (Glamorgan and England 1960-68). 6'3½". LHB, RF. Glamorgan 1998-2007; cap 2002. MCC 2002-04. MBE 2005. *Wisden* 2005. **Tests**: 18 (2002 to 2005); HS 44 v I (Lord's) 2002 – on debut; BB 6-53 v A (Manchester) 2005. **LOI**: 8 (2004-05 to 2005); HS 1; BB 2-43 v Z (Bulawayo) 2004-05 – on debut. F-c Tours: A 2002-03 (*part*); SA 2004-05; WI 2003-04; I 2003-04 (Eng A – *part*). HS 46 Gm v Hants (Scarborough) 2001. BB 6-45 Gm v Derbys (Cardiff) 2002. LO HS 26 Gm v Hants (Swansea) 2007 (FPT). LO BB 3-19 Gm v Lancs (Manchester) 2005 (NL).

NQ**KERVEZEE, Alexei** Nicolaas, b Walvis Bay, Namibia 11 Sep 1989. RHB, OB. Holland 2005-07. Worcestershire 2nd XI 2007 – awaiting 1st XI debut. **LOI** (H): 18 (2006 to 2007); HS 62 v Bermuda (Rotterdam) 2007. HS 98 Holland v Canada (King City, Ontario) 2007. BB 1-33 Holland v Scotland (Aberdeen) 2007. LO HS 62 (*see LOI*).

KNAPPETT, Joshua Philip Thomas, East Barnet S; Oxford Brookes U), b Westminster, London 15 Apr 1985. 6'0". RHB, occ RM, WK. Oxford UCCE 2004-06. British U 2005-06. Worcestershire debut 2007. HS 100* OU v Durham (Oxford) 2006. Wo HS 18 v Sussex (Hove) 2007 – on Wo debut.

MASON, Matthew Sean (Mazenod C, Lesmurdie, WA), b Claremont, Perth, Australia 20 Mar 1974. British passport. 6'5". RHB, RFM. W Australia 1996-97 to 1997-98. Worcestershire debut 2002. HS 63 v Warwks (Worcester) 2004. 50 wkts (3); most – 53 (2003, 2005). BB 8-45 (10-117) v Glos (Worcester) 2006. LO HS 25 v Durham (Worcester) 2004 (NL). LO BB 4-34 v Surrey (Guildford) 2003 (NL). T20 HS 8*. T20 BB 3-42.

MITCHELL, Daryl Keith Henry (Prince Henry's HS; University C, Worcester), b Badsey, near Evesham 25 Nov 1983. 5'10". RHB, RM. Debut (Worcestershire) 2005. HS 134* v Glamorgan (Colwyn Bay) 2006. BB 3-50 v Sussex (Hove) 2007. LO HS 53 v Warwks (Birmingham) 2007 (P40). LO BB 4-42 v Lancs (Worcester) 2006 (CGT). T20 HS 4. T20 BB 3-18.

MOORE, Stephen Colin (St Stithian's C, Johannesburg; Exeter U), b Johannesburg, South Africa 4 Nov 1980. 6'1". RHB, RM. Debut (Worcestershire) 2003. 1000 runs (2); most – 1399 (2005). HS 246 v Derbys (Worcester) 2005. BB 1-13 v Lancs (Worcester) 2004. LO HS 105* v Leics (Leicester) 2006 (P40). LO BB 1-1 v Scotland (Worcester) 2004 (NL). T20 HS 53.

SMITH, Benjamin Francis (Kibworth HS), b Corby, Northants 3 Apr 1972. 5'9". RHB, RM. Leicestershire 1990-2001; cap 1995. MCC 1999-00. Central Districts 2000-01 to 2001-02. Worcestershire debut 2002; captain 2003 to 2004 (*part*). F-c Tours (Le): SA 1996-97; B 1999-00 (MCC). 1000 runs (7); most – 1546 (2005). HS 204 Le v Surrey (Oval) 1998. Wo HS 203 v Somerset (Taunton) 2006. BB 1-5 Le v Essex (Ilford) 1991. Wo BB 1-39 v Surrey (Oval) 2006. LO HS 115 Le v Somerset (Weston-s-M) 1995 (SL). LO BB 1-2 v Worcs CB (Worcester) 2003 (CGT). T20 HS 105.

SOLANKI, Vikram Singh (Regis S, Wolverhampton), b Udaipur, India 1 Apr 1976. 6'0". RHB, OB, occ WK. Debut (Worcestershire) 1995; cap 1998; captain 2005 to date; benefit 2007. Rajasthan 2006-07. F-c Tours (Eng A): SA 1998-99, 1999-00 (Eng – *part*); WI 2000-01, 2005-06 (Captain); NZ 1999-00; SL 2004-05; Z 1996-97 (Wo), 1998-99; B 1999-00. **LOI:** 51 (1999-00 to 2006); HS 106 v SA (Oval) 2003; BB 1-17 v SL (Leeds) 2006. 1000 runs (3); most – 1339 (1999). HS 232 v Surrey (Worcester) 2007. BB 5-40 v Middlesex (Lord's) 2004. LO HS 164* v Worcs CB (Worcester) 2003 (CGT). LO BB 4-14 v Somerset (Taunton) 2006 (P40). IT20 HS 43. T20 HS 92. T20 BB 1-25.

‡**WHELAN, Christopher** David (St Margaret's HS), b Liverpool, Lancs 8 May 1986. 6'2". RHB, RMF. Middlesex 2005-07. HS 9* and CC 2-54 M v Hants (Southampton) 2005. BB 2-13 M v OU (Oxford) 2007. LO HS 6 M v Sussex (Hove) 2004 (NL). LO BB 1-43 M v Notts (Lord's) 2006 (P40).

^{NQ}**ABDUL RAZZAQ** (Furqan Model HS, Shahdara, Lahore), b Lahore, Pakistan 2 Dec 1979. 5'11". RHB, RFM. Lahore City 1996-97 to 1998-99. KRL 1997-98 to 1998-99. Lahore Blues 2000-01. PIA 2002-02. Middlesex 2002-03; cap 2002. Zarai Taraqiati Bank 2003-04 to date. Lahore 2003-04. Lahore Ravi 2006-07. Worcestershire 2007. **Tests** (P): 46 (1999-00 to 2006-07); HS 134 v B (Dhaka) 2001-02; BB 5-35 v SL (Karachi) 2004-05. Hat-trick v SL (Galle) 1999-00. **LOI** (P): 227 (1996-97 to 2007); HS 112 v SA (Pt Elizabeth) 2002-03; BB 6-35 v B (Dhaka) 2001-02. F-c Tours: E 1997 (Pak A), 2001, 2006; A 1999-00, 2004-05; SA 2002-03; WI 1999-00, 2004-05; NZ 1998-99 (Pak A), 2003-04; I 2004-05; SL 2000, 2005-06; B 2001-02; UAE 2001-02, 2002-03. HS 203* M v Glam (Cardiff) 2002. BB 7-51 Lahore City v Karachi Whites (Thatta) 1996-97 – on debut. UK BB 7-133 M v Essex (Southgate) 2002. LO HS 112 (*see LOI*). LO BB 6-35 (*see LOI*). IT20 HS 17*. IT20 BB 3-30. T20 HS 63. T20 BB 3-30.

^{NQ}**BOLLINGER, Douglas** Erwin (Newman C, WA; Greystanes, NSW), b Baulkham Hills, Sydney, Australia 24 Jul 1981. 6'4". LHB, LFM. New South Wales 2002-03 to date. Worcestershire 2007. Tour (Aus A): P 2007-08. HS 31* NSW v Q (Brisbane) 2006-07. Wo HS 21 v Durham (Worcester) 2007 – on debut. BB 6-63 NSW v Vic (Sydney) 2007-08. Wo BB 4-82 v Yorks (Kidderminster) 2007. LO HS 7* Aus A v Pak A (Sheikhupura) 2007-08. LO BB 4-24 NSW v S Aus (Canberra) 2004-05. T20 HS 5. T20 BB 2-26.

^{NQ}**JAQUES, Philip** Anthony (Fig Tree HS, Wollongong; Australian C of PE, Homebush), b Wollongong, NSW, Australia 3 May 1979. 6'1". LHB, SLC. British passport (English parents). Northamptonshire 2003; cap 2003. Yorkshire 2004-05; cap 2005. Worcestershire 2006-07. **Tests** (A): 8 (2005-06 to 2007-08); HS 150 v SL (Hobart) 2007-08. **LOI** (A): 6 (2005-06 to 2006-07); HS 94 v SA (Melbourne) 2005-06. Tours (A): P 2005-06 (Aus A), 2007-08 (Aus A); B 2005-06. 1000 runs (4+1); most – 1409 (2003). HS 244 v Essex (Chelmsford) 2006. First to score 200s for (243 v Hants 2004) and against Yorkshire (222 for Northants 2003). LO HS 158* NSW v S Aus (Adelaide) 2005-06. T20 HS 92.

MALIK, M.N. – *see LEICESTERSHIRE.*

NEL, Johann **Dewald**, b Klerksdorp, Transvaal, South Africa 6 Jun 1980. 6'0". RHB, RMF. Scotland 2004-07. Worcestershire 2007. **LOI** (Scotland): 8 (2006 to 2007); HS 3* v P (Edinburgh) 2006 – on debut; BB 1-34 v Canada (Mombasa) 2006-07. HS 25 Scotland v Namibia (Aberdeen) 2006. BB 4-74 Wo v Yorks (Leeds) 2007. LO HS 36* Scotland v Durham (Edinburgh) 2006 (CGT). LO BB 3-22 Scotland v Oman (Belfast) 2005. IT20 HS 13*. IT20 BB 2-25. T20 HS 13*. T20 BB 2-25.

^{NQ}**PRICE, Raymond** William (Watershed C), b Salisbury, Rhodesia 12 Jun 1976. 6'2". RHB, SLA. Mashonaland CD 1995-96. Zimbabwe Academy 1998-99 to 1999-00. Midlands 1999-00 to 2003-04. Worcestershire 2004-07 (Kolpak registration 2005-07). Tests (Z): 18 (1999-00 to 2003-04); HS 36 v A (Perth) 2003-04; BB 6-73 (10-161 match) v WI (Harare) 2003-04. LOI (Z): 30 (2002-03 to 2007-08); HS 20* v B (Harare) 2003-04; BB 2-16 v WI (Bulawayo) 2003-04. F-c Tours (Z): E 2003; A 2003-04; SA 2007-08; I 2001-02; P 2007-08; SL 1999-00 (Zim A); K 2001-02 (Zim A). HS 117* Midlands v Manicaland (Mutare) 2003-04. Wo HS 76 * v Lancs (Worcester) 2004. BB 8-35 Midlands v CFX Academy (Kwekwe) 2001-02. Wo BB 4-38 v Northants (Northampton) 2006. LO HS 49 v Sri Lanka A (Worcester) 2007. LO BB 4-21 v Notts (Worcester) 2005 (NL). T20 HS 10. T20 BB 2-13.

SILLENCE, Roger John (Highbury SS; Salisbury Art C), b Salisbury, Wilts 29 Jun 1977. 6'3". RHB, RMF. Gloucestershire 2001-05, taking 5-97 v Sussex (Hove) on debut; cap 2004. Worcestershire 2006-7. Wiltshire 1996-2000. HS 101 Gs v Derbys (Bristol) 2002. Wo HS 64 v Northants (Northampton) 2006. BB 7-96 v Somerset (Taunton) 2006. LO HS 94 v West Indies A (Worcester) 2006. LO BB 4-35 Gs v West Indies A (Cheltenham) 2002. T20 HS 22*. T20 BB 2-27.

E.J.Foster, W.M.Gifford, S.A.Khalid and S.A.Wedge left the staff without making a County 1st XI appearance in 2007.

WARWICKSHIRE RELEASED/RETIRED (continued from p 110)

[NQ]**STREAK, Heath** Hilton (Falcon C), b Bulawayo, Rhodesia 16 Mar 1974. 6'1". Son of D.H.Streak (Rhodesia 1976-77 to 1978-79, Matabeleland 1995-96). RHB, RFM. Debut for Zimbabwe B v Kent (Harare) 1992-93. Matabeleland 1993-94 to 2003-04. Hampshire 1995. Warwickshire 2004-07; cap 2005; captain 2006-07 (first week). **Tests** (Z): 65 (1993-94 to 2005-06, 21 as captain); HS 127* v WI (Harare) 2003-04; BB 6-73 v I (Harare) 2005-06. **LOI** (Z): 187 (1993-94 to 2005, 68 as captain); HS 79* v NZ (Auckland) 2000-01; BB 5-32 v I (Bulawayo) 1996-97. F-c Tours (Z) (C=captain): E 1993, 2000, 2003C; A 1994-95, 2003-04C; SA 2004-05; WI 1999-00; NZ 1995-96, 1997-98, 2000-01C; I 2000-01C, 2001-02; P 1993-94, 1998-99; SL 1996, 1997-98, 2001-02; B 2001-02C. HS 131 Matabeleland – v Mashonaland CD (Bulawayo) 1995-96 and 131 v Midlands (Bulawayo) 2003-04. Wa HS 68* v Yorks (Scarborough) 2006. 50 wkts (1): 53 (1995). BB 7-55 Matabeleland – v Mashonaland (Bulawayo) 2003-04. Wa BB 7-80 (13-158 match) v Northants (Birmingham) 2004 – on Wa debut. LO HS 90* Matabeleland v Manicaland (Bulawayo) 2003-04. LO BB 5-32 (see LOI). T20 HS 59. T20 BB 3-18.

[NQ]**THOMAS, A.C.** – see SOMERSET.

Van JAARSVELD, Vaughn Bernard (King Edward VII S), b Johannesburg, South Africa 2 Feb 1985. LHB, RM. Gauteng 2003-04 to 2004-05. Lions 2004-05 to 2006-07. Warwickshire (one P40 game) 2007. HS 159 Lions v Dolphins (Pietermaritzburg) 2006-07. LO HS 81 Lions v Dolphins (Durban) 2006-07. T20 HS 64.

A.F.Giles left the playing staff without making a county 1st XI appearance in 2007 – subsequently appointed Warwickshire's Director of Coaching and an ECB Selector.

WORCESTERSHIRE 2007

RESULTS SUMMARY

	Place	Won	Lost	Tied	Drew	No Result
LV County Championship (1st Division)	9th	1	8		5	2
All First-Class Matches		2	8		5	2
Friends Provident Trophy (North Conference)	4th	4	3			2
NatWest Pro40 League (1st Division)	**1st**	6	1			1
Twenty/20 Cup (Midlands/West Wales Division)	Quarter-Finalist	3	3			3

LV COUNTY CHAMPIONSHIP AVERAGES

BATTING AND FIELDING

Cap		M	I	NO	HS	Runs	Avge	100	50	Ct/St
2007c	Abdul Razzaq	3	5	1	78	172	43.00	–	1	1
1986	G.A.Hick	14	23	1	110	938	42.63	2	6	15
2007c	M.M.Ali	2	4	–	85	168	42.00	–	2	–
2003c	S.C.Moore	14	23	–	143	785	34.13	2	2	7
1998	V.S.Solanki	12	20	–	232	649	32.45	1	2	4
2006c	P.A.Jaques	10	17	–	124	541	31.82	2	1	6
2005c	S.M.Davies	14	24	2	87	690	31.36	–	4	43/4
2002c	B.F.Smith	13	21	2	98*	530	27.89	–	6	8
2005c	D.K.H.Mitchell	4	6	1	70*	136	27.20	–	1	5
2002c	G.J.Batty	14	22	3	84	487	25.63	–	3	7
2007c	J.D.Nel	5	8	6	8	30	15.00	–	–	–
2006c	R.J.Sillence	9	12	1	36	151	13.72	–	–	3
2002c	Kabir Ali	13	18	–	39	211	11.72	–	1	3
2004c	M.N.Malik	12	16	7	24*	89	9.88	–	–	3
2004c	R.W.Price	2	4	1	15*	24	8.00	–	–	–
2007c	D.E.Bollinger	7	8	2	21	38	6.33	–	–	–

Also batted: K.W.Hogg (2 matches – 2007c) 2*, 13; R.A.Jones (2 – 2007c) 1, 11*, 0, 2 (1 ct); J.P.T.Knappett (1 – 2007c) 7, 4; M.S.Mason (1 – 2002c) 0, 15.

BOWLING

	O	M	R	W	Avge	Best	5wI	10wM
Kabir Ali	378.1	69	1314	45	29.20	8- 50	1	1
G.J.Batty	489.3	104	1523	38	40.07	6-106	3	–
D.E.Bollinger	191	40	713	16	44.56	4- 82	–	–
R.J.Sillence	214.5	32	863	14	61.64	2- 48	–	–
M.N.Malik	306.4	44	1272	20	63.60	3- 94	–	–

Also bowled:

D.K.H.Mitchell	37.3	9	109	5	21.80	3- 50		
K.W.Hogg	46	14	136	6	22.66	3- 44		
Abdul Razzaq	67.3	15	219	6	36.50	2- 35		
J.D.Nel	96.1	17	345	7	49.28	4- 74		

M.M.Ali 5-1-14-0; R.A.Jones 39-7-207-3; M.S.Mason 24-8-62-1; S.C.Moore 9-1-42-0; R.W.Price 58.5-6-256-4; B.F.Smith 7-1-49-0; V.S.Solanki 40-3-136-1.

The First-Class Averages (pp 140–158) give the records of Worcestershire's players in all first-class county matches (Worcestershire's other opponents being Loughborough UCCE), with the exception of K.W.Hogg, whose full first-class figures for Worcestershire are as above, and:

S.M.Davies 15-25-2-87-690-30.00-0-4-43ct-4st. Did not bowl.
M.N.Malik 13-17-7-24*-91-9.10-0-0-5ct. 340.4-62-1330-23-57.82-3/94-0-0.
2007c denotes the award of county colours on Championship debut in 2007, a system that replaced capping in 2002.

WORCESTERSHIRE RECORDS

FIRST-CLASS CRICKET

Highest Total	For	701-6d		v	Surrey	Worcester	2007
	V	701-4d		by	Leics	Worcester	1906
Lowest Total	For	24		v	Yorkshire	Huddersfield	1903
	V	30		by	Hampshire	Worcester	1903
Highest Innings	For	405*	G.A.Hick	v	Somerset	Taunton	1988
	V	331*	J.D.B.Robertson	for	Middlesex	Worcester	1949

Highest Partnership for each Wicket

1st	309	H.K.Foster/F.L.Bowley	v	Derbyshire	Derby	1901
2nd	300	W.P.C.Weston/G.A.Hick	v	Indians	Worcester	1996
3rd	438*	G.A.Hick/T.M.Moody	v	Hampshire	Southampton	1997
4th	330	B.F.Smith/G.A.Hick	v	Somerset	Taunton	2006
5th	393	E.G.Arnold/W.B.Burns	v	Warwicks	Birmingham	1909
6th	265	G.A.Hick/S.J.Rhodes	v	Somerset	Taunton	1988
7th	256	D.A.Leatherdale/S.J.Rhodes	v	Notts	Nottingham	2002
8th	184	S.J.Rhodes/S.R.Lampitt	v	Derbyshire	Kidderminster	1991
9th	181	J.A.Cuffe/R.D.Burrows	v	Glos	Worcester	1907
10th	119	W.B.Burns/G.A.Wilson	v	Somerset	Worcester	1906

Best Bowling	For	9- 23	C.F.Root	v	Lancashire	Worcester	1931
(Innings)	V	10- 51	J.Mercer	for	Glamorgan	Worcester	1936
Best Bowling	For	15- 87	A.J.Conway	v	Glos	Moreton-in-M	1914
(Match)	V	17-212	J.C.Clay	for	Glamorgan	Swansea	1937

Most Runs – Season	2654	H.H.I.H.Gibbons (av 52.03)		1934
Most Runs – Career	34490	D.Kenyon (av 34.18)		1946-67
Most 100s – Season	10	G.M.Turner		1970
	10	G.A.Hick		1988
Most 100s – Career	104	G.A.Hick		1984-2007
Most Wkts – Season	207	C.F.Root (av 17.52)		1925
Most Wkts – Career	2143	R.T.D.Perks (av 23.73)		1930-55
Most Career W-K Dismissals	1095	S.J.Rhodes (991 ct/104 st)		1985-2004
Most Career Catches in the Field	503	G.A.Hick		1984-2007

LIMITED-OVERS CRICKET

Highest Total	FPT	404-3		v	Devon	Worcester	1987
	P40	307-4		v	Derbyshire	Worcester	1975
	T20	227-6		v	Northants	Kidderminster	2007
Lowest Total	FPT	98		v	Durham	Chester-le-St	1968
	P40	86		v	Yorkshire	Leeds	1969
	T20	86		v	Northants	Worcester	2006
Highest Innings	FPT	180*	T.M.Moody	v	Surrey	The Oval	1994
	P40	160	T.M.Moody	v	Kent	Worcester	1991
	T20	116*	G.A.Hick	v	Northants	Luton	2004
Best Bowling	FPT	7-19	N.V.Radford	v	Beds	Bedford	1991
	P40	6-16	Shoaib Akhtar	v	Glos	Worcester	2005
	T20	3-18	Kabir Ali	v	Somerset	Taunton	2007
		3-18	D.K.H.Mitchell	v	Warwicks	Birmingham	2007

YORKSHIRE

Formation of Present Club: 8 January 1863
Substantial Reorganisation: 10 December 1891
Inaugural First-Class Match: 1864
Colours: Dark Blue, Light Blue and Gold
Badge: White Rose
County Championships (since 1890): (30) 1893, 1896, 1898, 1900, 1901, 1902, 1905, 1908, 1912, 1919, 1922, 1923, 1924, 1925, 1931, 1932, 1933, 1935, 1937, 1938, 1939, 1946, 1959, 1960, 1962, 1963, 1966, 1967, 1968, 2001
Joint Champions: (1) 1949
Gillette/NatWest/C&G/FP Trophy Winners: (3) 1965, 1969, 2002
Benson and Hedges Cup Winners: (1) 1987
Pro 40/National League (Div 1) Winners: (0); best – 2nd 2000
Sunday League Winners: (1) 1983
Twenty20 Cup Winners: (0); best – Quarter-Finalist 2007

Chief Executive: Stewart M.Regan, Headingley Cricket Ground, Leeds, LS6 3BU • Tel: 0113 278 7394 • Fax: 0113 278 4099 • Email: cricket@yorkshireccc.org.uk • Web: www.yorkshireccc.org.uk

Director of Cricket: Martyn D.Moxon. **Captain**: D.Gough. **Vice-Captain**: A.McGrath. **Overseas Players**: M.Morkel and Naved-ul-Hasan. **2008 Beneficiary**: M.J.Hoggard. **Head Groundsman**: Andy Fogarty. **Scorer**: John T.Potter. ‡ New registration. NQ Not qualified for England.

‡**BALLANCE, Gary** Simon (Peterhouse S, Marondera, Zimbabwe; Harrow S), b Harare, Zimbabwe 22 Nov 1989. Nephew of G.S.Ballance (Rhodesia B 1978-79) and D.L.Houghton (Rhodesia/Zimbabwe 1978-79 to 1997-98). 5'10". LHB, LB. Awaiting f-c debut. Derbyshire (List A) 2006-07. LO HS 73 De v Hants (Southampton) 2006 (P40).

BRESNAN, Timothy Thomas (Castleford HS and TC; Pontefract New C), b Pontefract 28 Feb 1985. 6'0". RHB, RMF. Debut (Yorkshire) 2003; cap 2006. MCC 2006. **LOI**: 4 (2006); HS 20 v SL (Manchester) 2006; BB 1-38 v SL (Oval) 2006. F-c Tour (Eng A): B 2006-07. HS 126* Eng A v Indians (Chelmsford) 2007. Y HS 116 v Surrey (Oval) 2007, sharing in Yorkshire record 9th wicket partnership of 246 with J.N.Gillespie. BB 5-42 v Worcs (Worcester) 2005. LO HS 61 v Leics (Leeds) 2003 (NL). BB 4-25 v Somerset (Leeds) 2005 (NL). IT20 6*. IT20 BB – . T20 HS 42. T20 BB 3-21.

BROPHY, Gerard Louis (Christian Brothers C, Boksburg; Witwatersrand TC), b Welkom, Orange Free State, South Africa 26 Nov 1975. 5'11". British/EU passport. Qualified for England 2006. RHB, WK. Transvaal/Gauteng 1996-97 to 1998-99. Free State 1999-00 to 2000-01. Northamptonshire 2002-05. Yorkshire debut 2006. F-c Tour (SA Acad): Z 1998. HS 185 SA Academy v Zim President's XI (Harare) 1998-99. UK HS 181 Nh v Sussex (Hove) 2004. Y HS 100* v Hants (Southampton) 2007. LO HS 66 v Glamorgan (Cardiff) 2007 (P40). T20 HS 57.

GALE, Andrew William (Whitcliffe Mount S; Heckmondwike GS), b Dewsbury 28 Nov 1983. 6'2". LHB, LB. Debut (Yorkshire) 2004, 2006 to date. HS 149 v Warwks (Scarborough) 2006. BB 1-33 v LU (Leeds) 2007 (only f-c spell – 2 overs). LO HS 81 v Sri Lanka A (Leeds) 2007. T20 HS 56.

GOUGH, Darren (Priory CS, Lundwood), b Monk Bretton, Barnsley 18 Sep 1970. 5'11". RHB, RFM. Yorkshire 1989-2003, 2007 to date; cap 1993; benefit 2001; captain 2007 to date. Essex 2004-06; cap 2004. *Wisden* 1998. **Tests**: 58 (1994 to 2003); HS 65 v NZ (Manchester) 1994 – on debut; BB 6-42 v SA (Leeds) 1998; hat-trick v A (Sydney) 1998-99 – first for E v A since 1899. **LOI**: 158 (1994 to 2006); HS 46* v A (Chester-le-St) 2005; BB 5-44 v Z (Sydney) 1994-95 and 5-44 v A (Lord's) 1997. Took wickets with his sixth balls in both Tests and LOI. F-c Tours: A 1994-95, 1998-99; SA 1991-92 (Y), 1992-93 (Y), 1993-94 (Eng A), 1995-96, 1999-00; NZ 1996-97; P 2000-01; SL 2000-01; Z 1996-97. HS 121 Y v Warwks (Leeds) 1996. 50 wkts (5); most – 67 (1996). BB 7-28 (10-80 match) v Lancs (Leeds) 1995 (not CC). CC BB 7-42 (10-96 match) v Somerset (Taunton) 1993. 2 hat-tricks (1995, 1998-99); took 4 wkts in 5 balls v Kent (Leeds) 1995. LO HS 72* v Leics (Leicester) 1991 (SL). LO BB 7-27 v Ireland (Leeds) 1997 (NWT). IT20 HS – . IT20 BB 3-16. T20 HS 37. T20 BB 3-16.

GUY, Simon Mark (Wickersley CS), b Rotherham 17 Nov 1978. 5'7". RHB, WK. Debut (Yorkshire) 2000. HS 52* v Durham (Leeds) 2006. LO HS 40 v Leics (Leeds) 2005 (NL).

HOGGARD, Matthew James (Grangefield S, Pudsey), b Leeds 31 Dec 1976. 6'2". RHB, RFM. Debut (Yorkshire) 1996; cap 2000; benefit 2008. Free State 1998-99 to 1999-00. MCC 2004-07. MBE 2005. *Wisden* 2005. **ECB central contract 2007-08. Tests**: 66 (2000 to 2007-08); HS 38 v WI (Oval) 2004; BB 7-61 (12-205 match) v SA (Johannesburg) 2004-05; hat-trick v WI (Bridgetown) 2003-04. **LOI**: 26 (2001-02 to 2005-06); HS 7 v I (Cochin) 2005-06; BB 5-49 v Z (Harare) 2001-02. F-c Tours: A 2002-03, 2006-07; SA 2004-05; WI 2003-04; NZ 2001-02; I 2001-02, 2005-06; P 2000-01, 2005-06; SL 2000-01, 2003-04, 2007-08; B 2003-04. HS 89* v Glamorgan (Leeds) 2004. 50 wkts (2); most – 50 (2000, 2005). BB 7-49 v Somerset (Leeds) 2003. Hat-trick 2003-04. LO HS 7* (*twice*). LO BB 5-28 v Leics (Leicester) 2000 (NL). T20 HS 18. T20 BB 3-23.

NQKRUIS, Gideon (*'Deon'*) Jacobus (St Albans C, Pretoria; Pretoria U), b Pretoria, South Africa 9 May 1974. 6'3". RHB, RFM. N Transvaal 1993-94 to 1996-97. Griqualand West 1997-98 to 2003-04. MCC 2000-01. Eagles 2005-06. Yorkshire debut 2005; cap 2006. Kolpak registration. HS 59 GW v B (Kimberley) 2000-01. Y HS 37* v Durham (Chester-le-St) 2006. 50 wkts (1): 64 (2005). BB 7-58 GW v Northerns (Pretoria) 1997-98. Y BB 5-59 v Northants (Leeds) 2005. LO HS 31* v Surrey (Oval) 2006 (P40). LO BB 4-17 v Derbys (Leeds) 2007 (P40). T20 HS 5*. T20 BB 2-15.

LAWSON, Mark Anthony Kenneth (Castle Hall Language C, Mirfield), b Leeds 24 Oct 1985. 5'8". RHB, LB. Debut (Yorkshire) 2004. HS 44 v Hants (Southampton) 2006. BB 6-88 v Middlesex (Scarborough) 2006. LO HS 20 v Warwks (Birmingham) 2005 (NL). LO BB 2-50 v Hants (Leeds) 2006 (P40). T20 HS 4*. T20 BB 2-34.

LEE, James Edward (Immanuel Community C), b Sheffield 23 Dec 1988. 6'1". LHB, RMF. Debut (Yorkshire) 2006. HS 21* and BB – v Yorks (Manchester) 2006 – in only f-c match. No 1-o appearances.

LYTH, Adam (Caedmon S, Whitby; Whitby Community C), b Whitby 25 Sep 1987. 5'8". LHB, RM. Debut (Yorkshire) 2007. Awaiting CC debut. HS 31 and BB 1-12 v LU (Leeds) 2007 – only f-c match. LO HS 23 v Hants (Leeds) 2006 (P40).

McGRATH, Anthony (Yorkshire Martyrs Collegiate S), b Bradford 6 Oct 1975. 6'2". RHB, RM. Debut (Yorkshire) 1995; cap 1999; captain 2003. MCC 1999-00. **Tests**: 4 (2003); HS 81 v Z (Chester-le-St) 2003; BB 3-16 v Z (Lord's) 2003 – on debut. **LOI**: 14 (2003 to 2004); HS 52 v SA (Manchester) 2003; BB 1-13 v WI (Nottingham) 2004. F-c Tours (Eng A): A 1996-97; P 1995-96; Z 1995-96 (Y); B 1999-00 (MCC). 1000 runs (2); most – 1425 (2005). HS 188* v Warwks (Birmingham) 2007. BB 5-39 v Derbys (Derby) 2004. LO HS 148 v Somerset (Taunton) 2006 (P40). LO BB 4-41 v Surrey (Leeds) 2003 (NL). T20 HS 58*. T20 BB 3-27.

MORKEL, Morne (Hoerskool, Vereeniging, b Vereeniging, South Africa 6 Oct 1984. Younger brother of J.A.Morkel (Easterns and Titans 1999-00 to date). LHB, RFM. Easterns 2003-04 to 2006-07. Titans 2004-05 to 2006-07. Kent (T20 only) 2007. **Tests** (SA): 1 (2006-07); HS 31* and BB 3-86 v I (Durban) 2006-07 – on debut. **LOI** (SA): 3 (2007 to 2007-08); HS 23* and BB 2-39 v Z (Harare) 2007. HS 57 Titans v Eagles (Pretoria) 2006-07. BB 6-66 Easterns/Northerns v Z (Benoni) 2004-05. LO HS 35 Easterns v Northerns (Pretoria) 2005-06. LO BB 4-41 Titans v Cape Cobras (Paarl) 2005-06. IT20 HS 1*. IT20 BB 4-17. T20 HS 6*. T20 BB 4-17.

‡**NQNAVED-UL-HASAN**, Rana, b Sheikhupura, Pakistan 28 Feb 1978. RHB, RMF. Debut Pakistan A v England A (Multan) 1995-96. Lahore 1999-00. Pakistan Customs 2000-01. Sheikhupura 2000-01 to 2001-02. Allied Bank 2001-02. WAPDA 2002-03 to 2006-07. Sialkot 2003-04 to 2005-06. Sussex 2005-07; cap 2005. Herefordshire 2002. **Tests** (P): 9 (2004-05 to 2006-07); HS 42* v E (Lahore) 2005-06; BB 3-30 v E (Faisalabad) 2005-06. **LOI** (P): 62 (2002-03 to 2006-07); HS 29 v A (Melbourne) 2004-05; BB 6-27 v I (Jamshedpur) 2004-05. F-c Tours (P): A 2004-05; SA 2006-07; WI 2004-05; I 2004-05. HS 139 Sx v Middlesex (Lord's) 2005. 50 wkts (2+3); most – 91 (2000-01). BB 7-49 Sheikhupura v Sialkot (Muridke) 2001-02. CC BB 7-62 (11-148 match) Sx v Yorks (Leeds) 2006. LO HS 70* Lahore v Habib Bank (Sheikhupura) 1999-00. LO BB 6-27 (see LOI). IT20 HS 17*. IT20 BB 1-26. T20 HS 40*. T20 BB 3-9.

PATTERSON, Steven Andrew (Malet Lambert CS; St Mary's SFC, Hull; Leeds U), b Hull 3 Oct 1983. RHB, RMF. Debut (Yorkshire) 2005. Bradford/Leeds UCCE 2003 (not f-c). HS 46 v Lancs (Manchester) 2006. BB 2-30 v LU (Leeds) 2007. CC BB 1-25 v Warwks (Scarborough) 2006 – on CC debut. LO HS 25* v Worcs (Leeds) 2006 (P40). LO BB 3-11 Yorks CB v Northants CB (Northampton) 2002.

PYRAH, Richard Michael (Ossett S; Wakefield C), b Dewsbury 1 Nov 1982. 6'0". RHB, RM. Debut (Yorkshire) 2004. HS 106 and 1-3 v LU (Leeds) 2007. CC HS 78 v Worcs (Worcester) 2005. CC BB 1-9 v Worcs (Worcester) 2005. LO HS 42 v Durham (Scarborough) 2004 (NL). LO BB 5-50 Yorks CB v Somerset (Scarborough) 2002 (CGT). T20 HS 33*. T20 BB 2-8.

RASHID, Adil Usman (Belle Vue S, Bradford), b Bradford 17 Feb 1988. 5'8". RHB, LBG. Debut (Yorkshire) 2006. MCC 2007. YC 2007. F-c Tour (Eng A): B 2006-07. Match double (114, 48, 8-157 and 2-45) for Eng U-19 v Ind U-19 (Taunton) 2006. HS 108 v Worcs (Kidderminster) 2007. BB 6-67 v Warwks (Scarborough) 2006 – on debut. LO HS 28 and BB 2-63 v Surrey (Oval) 2006 (P40) – on l-o debut.

NQRUDOLPH, Jacobus Andries ('Jacques') (Afrikaanse Hoer Seunskool), b Springs, Transvaal, South Africa 4 May 1981. Elder brother of G.J.Rudolph (Limpopo and Namibia 2006-07 to date). 5'11". LHB, LBG. Northerns 1999-00 to 2003-04. Titans 2004-05. Eagles 2005-06 to date. Yorkshire debut 2007 (Kolpak registration) scoring 122 v Surrey (Oval); cap 2007. **Tests** (SA): 35 (2003 to 2006); HS 222* v B (Chittagong) 2003 – on debut; BB 1-1 v E (Leeds) 2003. **LOI** (SA): 43 (2003 to 2005-06); HS 81 v B (Dhaka) 2003. F-c Tours (SA): E 2003; A 2001-02, 2005-06; WI 2004-05; NZ 2003-04; I 2004-05; SL 2004, 2005-06, 2006; B 2003. 1000 runs (1): 1078 (2007). HS 222* (see Tests). UK HS 220 v Warwks (Scarborough) 2007. BB 5-80 Eagles v Cape Cobras (Cape Town) 2007-08. UK BB 1-1 (see Tests). LO HS 134* South Africa A v Kenya (Laudium) 2001-02. LO BB 4-40 South Africa A v New Zealand A (Colombo) 2005-06. IT 20 HS 6*. T20 HS 71. T20 BB 3-16.

SAYERS, Joseph John (St Mary's RC CS, Menston; Worcester C, Oxford) b Leeds 5 Nov 1983. 6'0". LHB, OB. Oxford U 2002-04; blue 2002-03-04. Yorkshire debut 2004; cap 2007. HS 187 v Kent (Tunbridge Wells) 2007. BB – . LO HS 62 v Glos (Leeds) 2003 (NL). LO BB 1-31 v Warwks (Birmingham) 2005 (NL). T20 HS 12.

SHAHZAD, Ajmal (Woodhouse Grove S; Bradford U), b Huddersfield 27 Jul 1985. 6'0". RHB, RMF. Debut (Yorkshire) 2006 (first British-born Asian to play for Yorkshire). HS 32* and BB 4-22 v Sussex (Leeds) 2007. LO HS 11* v Leics (Leicester) 2006 (CGT). LO BB 5-51 v Sri Lanka A (Leeds) 2007. 3-30 v Kent (Scarborough) 2006 (P40). T20 HS 2*. T20 BB 2-22.

TAYLOR, Christopher Robert (Benton Park HS, Rawdon), b Leeds 21 Feb 1981. 6'4". RHB, RMF. Yorkshire 2001-05. Derbyshire 2006-07. HS 121 De v Glamorgan (Cardiff) 2006. LO HS 111* De v Durham (Derby) 2006 (CGT). T20 HS 28*.

VAUGHAN, Michael Paul (Silverdale CS, Sheffield), b Salford, Lancs 29 Oct 1974. 6'2". RHB, OB. Yorkshire 1993; cap 1995; benefit 2005. *Wisden* 2002. PCA 2002. OBE 2005. **ECB central contract 2007-08. Tests**: 73 (1999-00 to 2007-08, 42 as captain); HS 197 and BB 2-71 v I (Nottingham) 2002. Scored Eng record 1,481 runs (avge 61.70) with six hundreds in 2002. **LOI**: 86 (2000-01 to 2006-07, 60 as captain); HS 90* v Z (Bulawayo) 2004-05; BB 4-22 v SL (Manchester) 2002. F-c Tours (C=captain): A 1996-97 (Eng A), 2002-03; SA 1998-99C (Eng A), 1999-00, 2004-05C; WI 2003-04C; NZ 2001-02; I 1994-95 (Eng A), 2001-02; P 2000-01, 2005-06C; SL 2000-01, 2003-04C, 2007-08C; Z 1995-96 (Y), 1998-99C (Eng A); B 2003-04C. 1000 runs (4); most – 1244 (1995). HS 197 (see *Tests*). Y HS 183 v Glamorgan (Cardiff) 1996. BB 4-39 v OU (Oxford) 1994. CC BB 4-47 v Somerset (Leeds) 2001. LO HS 125* v Somerset (Taunton) 2001 (BHC). LO BB 4-22 (see *LOI*). IT20 HS 27. T20 HS 27.

WAINWRIGHT, David John (Hemsworth HS and SFC; Loughborough U); b Pontefract 21 Mar 1985. LHB, SLA. Debut (Yorkshire) 2004. Loughborough UCCE 2005-06. British U 2006. HS 62 v Bangladesh A (Leeds) 2005. CC HS 5 v Somerset (Taunton) 2004 – on f-c debut. BB 4-48 LU v Worcs (Worcester) 2005. Y BB 3-22 v Bangladesh A (Leeds) 2005. CC HS 1-86 v Northants (Northampton) 2005. LO HS 26 and BB 2-30 v Surrey (Scarborough) 2007 (P40). T20 HS 2. T20 BB 3-6.

WHITE, Craig (Flora Hill HS, Bendigo, Australia; Bendigo HS), b Morley 16 Dec 1969. Brother-in-law of D.S.Lehmann (S Australia, Victoria, Yorkshire and Australia 1987-88 to 2007-08). 6'0". RHB, RFM/OB. Debut (Yorkshire) 1990; cap 1993; benefit 2002; captain 2004-06. Victoria 1990-91 (2 matches). **Tests**: 30 (1994-5 to 2002-03); HS 121 v I (Ahmedabad) 2001-02; BB 5-32 v WI (Oval) 2000. **LOI**: 51 (1994-95 to 2002 03); HS 57* v A (Melbourne) 2002-03; BB 5-21 v Z (Bulawayo) 1999-00. F-c Tours: A 1994-95, 1996-97 (Eng A), 2002-03; SA 1991-92 (Y), 1992-93 (Y); NZ 1996-97, 2001-02; I 2001-02; P 1995-96 (Eng A), 2000-01; SL 2000-01; Z 1996-97 (*part*). HS 186 v Lancs (Manchester) 2001. BB 8-55 v Glos (Gloucester) 1998 – inc hat-trick. Hat-trick 1998. LO HS 148 v Leics (Leicester) 1997 (SL). LO BB 5-19 v Somerset (Scarborough) 2002 (NL). T20 HS 55. T20 BB 1-22.

WOOD, Gregory Luke (Queen Elizabeth GS, Wakefield, b Dewsbury 2 Dec 1988. 5'11". LHB, WK. Debut (Yorkshire) 2007 – one List A game – awaiting f-c debut. HS 26 v Sri Lanka A (Leeds) 2007.

RELEASED/RETIRED
(Having made a County 1st XI appearance in 2007)

GILBERT, Chris Robert (Scarborough C), b Scarborough 16 Apr 1984. 5'10". RHB, RM. Yorkshire 2007. HS 64 v LU (Leeds) 2007 – his only f-c match. LO HS 37 v Sri Lanka A (Leeds) 2007. LO BB 3-33 v Leics (Leicester) 2006 (CGT). T20 HS 36*.

^{NQ}**GILLESPIE, J.N.** – *see GLAMORGAN.*

^{NQ}**IMRAN TAHIR,** Mohammad (Government Pakistan Angels HS and MAO College, Lahore), b Lahore, Pakistan 4 Jun 1979. 5'11". RHB, LB. Lahore City 1996-97 to 1997-98. WAPDA 1998-99. REDCO 1999-00. Lahore Whites 2000-01. Sui Northern Gas Pipelines 2001-02 to 2003-04. Sialkot 2002-03. Middlesex 2003. Lahore Blues 2004-05. PIA 2004-05 to 2006-07. Lahore Ravi 2005-06. Yorkshire 2007. (1 match). Titans 2007-08. Staffordshire 2004-05. F-c Tour (Pak A): SL 2004-05. HS 48 REDCO v KRL (Rawalpindi) 1999-00. UK HS 29 M v Kent (Canterbury) 2003. Y HS 5 and BB – v Sussex (Hove) 2007. 50 wkts (0+1): 74 (2004-05). BB 8-76 REDCO v Karachi Blues (Lahore) 1999-00. UK BB 1-128 M v Lancs (Lord's) 2003. Y BB – . LO HS 41* Staffs v Lancs (Stone) 2004 (CGT). LO BB 5-30 Pak A v Sri Lanka A (Colombo) 2004-05. T20 HS 13. T20 BB 3-25.

^{NQ}**INZAMAM-UL-HAQ** (Government C, Multan), Multan 3 Mar 1970. 6'2". RHB, SLA. Multan 1985-86 to 2003-04. United Bank 1988-89 to 1996-97. Faisalabad 1996-97 to 2000-01. Rawalpindi 1998-99. National Bank 2001-02. WAPDA 2006-07. Yorkshire 2007. **Tests** (P): 119 (1992 to 2007-08, 31 as captain); HS 329 v NZ (Lahore) 2001-02. **LOI** (P): 375 (1991-92 to 2006-07, 86 as captain): HS 137* v NZ (Sharjah) 1993-94; BB 1-0 v B (Chittagong) 2001-02. F-c Tours (P) (C=Captain): E 1992; 1996, 2001, 2006C; A 1991-92, 1992-93, 1995-96, 1996-97, 1999-00, 2004-05C (*part*); SA 1994-95, 1997-98, 2002-03, 2006-07C; WI 1992-93; 1999-00, 2004-05C (*part*); NZ 1992-93, 1993-94, 1995-96, 2000-01, 2003-04C; I 1998-99, 2004-05C; SL 1991 (Pak A), 1994, 1996-97, 2000, 2005-06C; Z 1994-95, 1997-98, 2002-03; B 1998-99 (v SL), 2001-02; UAE 2001-02 (v WI). HS 329 (*see Tests*). 1000 runs 0+2; most – 1645 (1989-90). BB 5-80 Multan v Bahawalpur (Sahiwal) 1989-90. LO HS 157* P v Sussex (Hove) 1992. LO BB 3-18 United Bank v National Bank (Bahawalpur) 1989-90. IT20 HS 11*. T20 HS 21.

THORNICROFT, Nicholas David (Easingwold S), b York 23 Jan 1985. 5'11". LHB, RMF. Yorkshire 2002-07. Essex 2005 (on loan). HS 30 v Notts (Leeds) 2004. BB 6-60 v LU (Leeds) 2007. CC BB 2-27 v Durham (Chester-le-St) 2004. LO HS 20 v Surrey (Oval) 2006 (P40). LO BB 5-42 v Glos (Leeds) 2003 (NL). T20 HS 0*. T20 BB – .

WOOD, M.J. – *see GLAMORGAN.*

^{NQ}**YOUNUS KHAN,** Mohammad (Shah Latif SS, Karachi; All Hadeed GHS, Karachi), b Mardan, North-West Frontier Province, Pakistan 29 Nov 1977. 5'11½". RHB, RM/LB. Peshawar 1998-99 to 2004-05. Habib Bank 1999-00 to date. Nottinghamshire 2005. Yorkshire 2007; cap 2007. **Tests** (P): 58 (1999-00 to 2007-08, 2 as captain); HS 267 v I (Bangalore) 2004-05; BB 1-24 v I (Chandigarh) 2004-05. **LOI** (P): 163 (1999-00 to 2007-08, 6 as captain); HS 144 v Hong Kong (Colombo) 2004; BB 1-24 v Z (Harare) 2002-03. F-c Tours (P): E 2001, 2006; A 2004-05; SA 2002-03, 2006-07; WI 1999-00, 2004-05; NZ 2000-01; I 2004-05, 2007-08; SL 2000, 2002-03 (v A), 2005-06; Z 2002-03; B 2001-02; UAE 2001-02 (v WI), 2002-03 (v A). 1000 runs (0+1): 1315 (1999-00). HS 267 (*see Tests*). UK HS 217* Y v K (Scarborough) 2007. BB 4-52 v Hants (Southampton) 2007. HS LO: 144 (*see LOI*). LO BB 3-5 v Glos (Cheltenham) 2005 (NL). IT20 HS 51. IT20 BB 3-18. T20 HS 51. T20 BB 3-18.

₁₂₄

YORKSHIRE 2007

RESULTS SUMMARY

	Place	Won	Lost	Tied	Drew	No Result
LV County Championship (1st Division)	6th	4	4		8	
All First-Class Matches		5	4		8	
Friends Provident Trophy (North Conference)	5th	4	3			2
NatWest Pro40 League (2nd Division)	6th	4	3			1
Twenty/20 Cup (North Division)	Quarter-Finalist	4	4			1

LV COUNTY CHAMPIONSHIP AVERAGES

BATTING AND FIELDING

Cap		M	I	NO	HS	Runs	Ave	100	50	Ct/St
2007	J.A.Rudolph	15	22	3	220	1078	56.73	4	3	19
2007	Younus Khan	13	19	2	217*	824	48.47	3	–	11
1999	A.McGrath	14	22	1	188*	931	46.55	3	6	11
–	A.U.Rashid	15	21	4	108	790	46.47	1	7	8
2006	T.T.Bresnan	15	20	6	116	553	39.50	2	2	6
2007	J.J.Sayers	14	22	3	187	644	33.89	3	1	5
2007	J.N.Gillespie	12	13	5	123*	270	33.75	1	–	3
–	G.L.Brophy	13	19	1	100*	593	32.94	1	2	35/3
1995	M.P.Vaughan	6	8	1	74	212	30.28	–	2	–
1993	C.White	11	18	–	117	446	24.77	1	2	4
–	Inzamam-ul-Haq	3	4	–	51	89	22.25	–	1	5
–	A.W.Gale	5	7	–	51	155	22.14	–	1	3
–	S.M.Guy	3	4	–	28	78	19.50	–	–	11
2000	M.J.Hoggard	10	9	2	61	121	17.28	–	1	2
–	A.Shahzad	5	7	3	32*	65	16.25	–	–	–
1993	D.Gough	14	15	1	50	219	15.64	–	1	2
2006	G.J.Kruis	6	6	3	20	44	14.66	–	–	1

Also batted (1 match each): Imran Tahir 0, 5; M.A.K.Lawson 5.

BOWLED

	O	M	R	W	Avge	Best	5wI	10wM
M.J.Hoggard	205.4	47	644	32	20.12	5-32	2	–
D.Gough	287.4	74	876	37	23.67	6-47	3	–
T.T.Bresnan	332	71	1090	34	32.05	4-10	–	–
J.N.Gillespie	238.3	53	803	23	34.91	3-40	–	–
A.U.Rashid	412.2	46	1578	40	39.45	5-88	3	–
Also bowled:								
A.Shahzad	80.4	10	313	9	34.77	4-22	–	–
Younus Khan	85.5	10	342	8	42.75	4-52	–	–
A.McGrath	76	16	223	5	44.60	2-12	–	–
G.J.Kruis	110.2	21	409	8	51.12	2-39	–	–

Imran Tahir 37-2-141-0; M.A.K.Lawson 9-0-65-0; J.A.Rudolph 16-4-55-0; M.P.Vaughan 8-0-29-0; C.White 6-0-11-0.

The First-Class Averages (pp 140–158) give the records of Yorkshire players in all first-class county matches (Yorkshire's other opponents being Loughborough UCCE), with the exception of T.T.Bresnan, M.J.Hoggard, A.U.Rashid and M.P.Vaughan, whose full county figures are as above.

YORKSHIRE RECORDS

FIRST-CLASS CRICKET

Highest Total	For 887		v	Warwicks	Birmingham	1896
	V 681-7d		by	Leics	Bradford	1996
Lowest Total	For 23		v	Hampshire	Middlesbrough	1965
	V 13		by	Notts	Nottingham	1901
Highest Innings	For 341	G.H.Hirst	v	Leics	Leicester	1905
	V 318*	W.G.Grace	for	Glos	Cheltenham	1876

Highest Partnership for each Wicket

1st	555	P.Holmes/H.Sutcliffe	v	Essex	Leyton	1932
2nd	346	W.Barber/M.Leyland	v	Middlesex	Sheffield	1932
3rd	323*	H.Sutcliffe/M.Leyland	v	Glamorgan	Huddersfield	1928
4th	358	D.S.Lehmann/M.J.Lumb	v	Durham	Leeds	2006
5th	340	E.Wainwright/G.H.Hirst	v	Surrey	The Oval	1899
6th	276	M.Leyland/E.Robinson	v	Glamorgan	Swansea	1926
7th	254	W.Rhodes/D.C.F.Burton	v	Hampshire	Dewsbury	1919
8th	292	R.Peel/Lord Hawke	v	Warwicks	Birmingham	1896
9th	246	T.T.Bresnan/J.N.Gillespie	v	Surrey	The Oval	2007
10th	149	G.Boycott/G.B.Stevenson	v	Warwicks	Birmingham	1982

Best Bowling	For 10-10	H.Verity	v	Notts	Leeds	1932
(Innings)	V 10-37	C.V.Grimmett	for	Australians	Sheffield	1930
Best Bowling	For 17-91	H.Verity	v	Essex	Leyton	1933
(Match)	V 17-91	H.Dean	for	Lancashire	Liverpool	1913

Most Runs – Season	2883	H.Sutcliffe	(av 80.08)	1932
Most Runs – Career	38558	H.Sutcliffe	(av 50.20)	1919-45
Most 100s – Season	12	H.Sutcliffe		1932
Most 100s – Career	112	H.Sutcliffe		1919-45
Most Wkts – Season	240	W.Rhodes	(av 12.72)	1900
Most Wkts – Career	3597	W.Rhodes	(av 16.02)	1898-1930
Most Career W-K Dismissals	1186	D.Hunter	(863 ct/323 st)	1888-1909
Most Career Catches in the Field	665	J.Tunnicliffe		1891-1907

LIMITED-OVERS CRICKET

Highest Total	FPT	411-6		v	Devon	Exmouth	2004
	P40	352-6		v	Notts	Scarborough	2001
	T20	211-6		v	Leics	Leeds	2004
Lowest Total	FPT	76		v	Surrey	Harrogate	1970
	P40	54		v	Essex	Leeds	2003
	T20	97		v	Lancashire	Manchester	2005
Highest Innings	FPT	160	M.J.Wood	v	Devon	Exmouth	2004
	P40	191	D.S.Lehmann	v	Notts	Scarborough	2001
	T20	109	I.J.Harvey	v	Derbyshire	Leeds	2005
Best Bowling	FPT	7-27	D.Gough	v	Ireland	Leeds	1997
	P40	7-15	R.A.Hutton	v	Worcs	Leeds	1969
	T20	3- 6	D.J.Wainwright	v	Durham	Leeds	2007

WHAT IS A KOLPAK REGISTRATION?

The Kolpak ruling was made by the European Court of Justice on 8 May 2003 in favour of Maros Kolpak, a Slovak handball player. The Court's decision was based upon the dictum that no resident of the European Union should be prevented from working in another part of the EU.

Specifically the case meant that, in professional sports, if a sporting club chose a player who resided in the EU, then there could be no law preventing this. For example, a German basketball team could not be prevented from hiring a Greek player since both nations are members of the EU. Moreover, since Kolpak was not from the EU at the time the case was decided, but from a country that had an associate trading relationship, the decision meant that any player from any nation which had such a relationship with the EU, provided that they held a valid UK work permit, must be treated for the purposes of employment as if they were a citizen of an EU country.

Counties could already employ any number of EU residents under the Bosman ruling. However, there are no other strong cricketing countries within the EU, and so Kolpak, not Bosman, has had the significant impact on county cricket. The largest group of countries with an associate agreement with the EU is the ACP countries, which include South Africa, Zimbabwe, and many of the islands which supply the West Indies cricket team.

There is no residential requirement. The ECB had originally stated that a player must not have represented their own country for over twelve months in order to qualify for Kolpak status but after Jacques Rudolph signed for Yorkshire, they admitted that they were powerless to enforce this rule.

In an effort to combat the influx of Kolpak players, the ECB has linked the central payments made to counties, to the amount of English qualified players who represent the county.

Kolpak players are not qualified for England; the main requirement for that qualification is that the player must be a British or an Irish citizen and, if born outside England or Wales, he must complete a four-year residence period.

2008 COUNTY KOLPAK REGISTRATIONS

Derbyshire: Greg Smith, Wavell Hinds.
Durham: Neil McKenzie.
Essex: Grant Flower.
Gloucestershire: Anthony Ireland.
Hampshire: Sean Ervine.
Kent: Martin van Jaarsveld, Ryan McLaren, Justin Kemp.
Lancashire: Francois du Plessis.
Leicestershire: Hylton Ackerman, Claude Henderson, Garnett Kruger.
Middlesex: Gareth Berg, Friedel de Wet.
Northamptonshire: Nicky Boje, Andrew Hall, Lance Klusener, Johannes van der Ewath, Riki Wessels.
Somerset: Charl Willoughby.
Surrey: Pedro Collins.
Sussex: Murray Goodwin.
Yorkshire: Deon Kruis, Jacques Rudolph.

FIRST-CLASS UMPIRES 2008

† New appointment. See page 11 for key to abbreviations.

BAILEY, Robert John (Biddulph HS), b Biddulph, Staffs 28 Oct 1963. RHB, OB. Northamptonshire 1982-99; cap 1985; benefit 1993; captain 1996-97. Derbyshire 2000-01; cap 2000. Staffordshire 1980. YC 1984. **Tests:** 4 (1988 to 1989-90); HS 43 v WI (Oval) 1988. **LOI:** 4 (1984-85 to 1989-90); HS 43* v SL (Oval) 1988. Tours: SA 1991-92 (Nh); WI 1989-90; Z 1994-95 (Nh). 1000 runs (13); most – 1987 (1990). HS 224* Nh v Glamorgan (Swansea) 1986. BB 5-54 Nh v Notts (Northampton) 1993. F-c career: 374 matches; 21844 runs @ 40.52, 47 hundreds; 121 wickets @ 42.51; 272 ct. Appointed 2006.

BAINTON, Neil Laurence, b Romford, Essex 2 October 1970. No f-c appearances. Appointed 2006.

BENSON, Mark Richard (Sutton Valence S), b Shoreham, Sussex 6 Jul 1958. LHB, OB. Kent 1980-95; cap 1981; captain 1991-96 (did not play in 1996); benefit 1991. **Tests:** 1 (1986); HS 30 v I (Birmingham) 1986. **LOI:** 1 (1986; HS 24). 1000 runs (11); most – 1725 (1987). HS 257 K v Hants (Southampton) 1991. BB 2-55 K v Surrey (Dartford) 1986. F-c career: 292 matches; 18387 runs @ 40.23, 48 hundreds; 5 wickets @ 98.60; 140 ct. Appointed 2000. Umpired 21 Tests (2004-05 to 2007-08) and 61 LOI (2004 to 2007-08). ICC International Panel 2004-06. **ICC Elite panel 2006 to date.** Occasionally available for ECB matches.

BURGESS, Graham Iefvion (Millfield S), b Glastonbury, Somerset 5 May 1943. RHB, RM. Somerset 1966-79; cap 1968; testimonial 1977. HS 129 Sm v Glos (Taunton) 1973. BB 7-43 (13-75 match) Sm v OU (Oxford) 1975. F-c career: 252 matches; 7129 runs @ 18.90, 2 hundreds; 474 wickets @ 28.57. Appointed 1991.

COWLEY, Nigel Geoffrey (Dutchy Manor SS, Mere), b Shaftesbury, Dorset 1 Mar 1953. RHB, OB. Dorset 1972. Hampshire 1974-89; cap 1978; benefit 1988. Glamorgan 1990. 1000 runs (1): 1042 (1984). HS 109* H v Somerset (Taunton) 1977. BB 6-48 H v Leics (Southampton) 1982. F-c career: 271 matches; 7309 runs @ 23.35, 2 hundreds; 437 wickets @ 34.04. Appointed 2000.

DUDLESTON, Barry (Stockport S), b Bebington, Cheshire 16 Jul 1945. RHB, SLA. Leicestershire 1966-80; cap 1969; benefit 1980. Gloucestershire 1981-83. Rhodesia 1976-77 to 1979-80. 1000 runs (8); most – 1374 (1970). HS 202 Le v Derbys (Leicester) 1979. BB 4-6 Le v Surrey (Leicester) 1972. F-c career: 295 matches; 14747 runs @ 32.48, 32 hundreds; 47 wickets @ 29.04. Appointed 1984. Umpired 2 Tests (1991 to 1992) and 4 LOI (1992 to 2001).

EVANS, Jeffery Howard, b Llanelli, Carms 7 Aug 1954. No f-c appearances. Appointed 2001. Umpired in Indian Cricket League 2007-08.

GARRETT, Stephen Arthur, b Nottingham 5 Jul 1953. No f-c appearances. Reserve List 2003-07 standing in 20 f-c matches. Appointed 2008.

GOULD, Ian James (Westgate SS, Slough), b Taplow, Bucks 19 Aug 1957. LHB, WK. Middlesex 1975 to 1980-81, 1996; cap 1977. Auckland 1979-80. Sussex 1981-90; cap 1981; captain 1987; benefit 1990. MCC YC. **LOI:** 18 (1982-83 to 1983; HS 42). Tours: A 1982-83; P 1980-81 (Int); Z 1980-81 (M). HS 128 M v Worcs (Worcester) 1990. HS 201* Nt v Glamorgan (Nottingham) 1973. Middlesex coach 1991-2000. Reappeared in one match (v OU) 1996. F-c career: 298 matches; 8756 runs @ 26.05, 4 hundreds; 7 wickets @ 52.14; 603 dismissals (536 ct, 67 st). Appointed 2002. Umpired 18 LOI (2006 to 2007-08).

HARRIS, Michael John ('*Pasty*') (Gerrans S, nr Truro), b St Just-in-Roseland, Cornwall 25 May 1944. RHB, LB, WK. Middlesex 1964-68; cap 1967. Nottinghamshire 1969-82; cap 1970; benefit 1977. E Province 1971-72. Wellington 1975-76. 1000 runs (11); most – 2238 (1971). Equalled Notts record with 9 hundreds in 1971. HS 201* Nt v Glamorgan (Nottingham) 1973. BB 4-16 Nt v Warwks (Nottingham) 1969. F-c career: 344 matches; 19196 runs @ 36.70, 41 hundreds; 79 wickets @ 43.78; 302 dismissals (288 ct, 14 st). Appointed 1998.

HARTLEY, Peter John (Greenhead GS; Bradford C), b Keighley, Yorks 18 Apr 1960. RHB, RMF. Warwickshire 1982. Yorkshire 1985-97; cap 1987; benefit 1996. Hampshire 1998-2000; cap 1998. Tours (Y): SA 1991-92; WI 1986-87; Z 1995-96. HS 127* Y v Lancs (Manchester) 1988. 50 wkts (7); most – 81 (1995). BB 9-41 (inc hat-trick, 4 wkts in 5 balls and 5 in 9; 11-68 match) Y v Derbys (Chesterfield) 1995. Hat-trick 1995. F-c career: 232 matches; 4321 runs @ 19.91, 2 hundreds; 683 wickets @ 30.21. Appointed 2003. Umpired 1 LOI (2007). **ICC International Panel (Third Umpire) 2006 to date.**

HOLDER, John Wakefield (Combermere S), b St George, Barbados 19 Mar 1945. RHB, RFM. Hampshire 1968-72. HS 33 H v Sussex (Hove) 1971. BB 7-79 H v Glos (Gloucester) 1972. Hat-trick 1972. F-c career: 47 matches; 374 runs @ 10.68; 139 wickets @ 24.56. Appointed 1983. Umpired 11 Tests (1988 to 2001) and 19 LOI (1988 to 2001).

HOLDER, Vanburn Alonza (Richmond SM), b Deans Village, St Michael, Barbados 8 Oct 1945. RHB, RFM. Barbados 1966-67 to 1977-78. Worcestershire 1968-80; cap 1970; benefit 1979. Shropshire 1981. **Tests** (WI): 40 (1969 to 1978-79); 682 runs @ 14.20, HS 42 v NZ (P-o-S) 1971-72; 109 wkts @ 33.27, BB 6-28 v A (P-o-S) 1977-78. **LOI** (WI): 12. Tours (WI): E 1969, 1973, 1976; A 1975-76; I 1974-75, 1978-79; P 1973-74 (RW), 1974-75; SL 1974-75, 1978-79. HS 122 Barbados v Trinidad (Bridgetown) 1973-74. BB 7-40 Wo v Glamorgan (Cardiff) 1974. F-c career: 311 matches; 3559 runs @ 13.03, 1 hundred; 947 wickets @ 24.48. Appointed 1992.

ILLINGWORTH, Richard Keith (Salts GS), b Bradford, Yorks 23 Aug 1963. RHB, SLA. Worcestershire 1982-2000; cap 1986; benefit 1997. Natal 1988-89. Derbyshire 2001. Wiltshire 2005. **Tests:** 9 (1991 to 1995-96); HS 28 v SA (Pt Elizabeth) 1995-96; BB 4-96 v WI (Nottingham) 1995. Took wicket of P.V.Simmons with his first ball in Tests – v WI (Nottingham) 1991. **LOI:** 25 (1991 to 1995-96); HS 14 v P (Melbourne) 1991-92; BB 3-33 v Z (Albury) 1991-92. Tours: SA 1995-96; NZ 1991-92; P 1990-91 (Eng A); SL 1990-91 (Eng A); Z 1989-90 (Eng A), 1990-91 (Wo), 1993-94 (Wo), 1996-97 (Wo). HS 120* Wo v Warwks (Worcester) 1987 – as night-watchman. Scored 106 for England A v Z (Harare) 1989-90 – also as night-watchman. 50 wkts (5); most – 75 (1990). BB 7-50 Wo v OU (Oxford) 1985. F-c career: 376 matches; 7027 runs @ 22.45, 4 hundreds; 831 wickets @ 31.54; 161 ct. Appointed 2006.

JESTY, Trevor Edward (Privet County SS, Gosport), b Gosport, Hants 2 Jun 1948. RHB, RM. Hampshire 1966-84; cap 1971; benefit 1982. Surrey 1985-87; cap 1985; captain 1985. Lancashire 1987-88 to 1991; cap 1989. Border 1973-74. GW 1974-75 to 1980-81. Canterbury 1979-80. *Wisden* 1982. **LOI:** 10. Tours: WI 1987-88 (La), 1982-83 (Int); Z 1988-89 (La). 1000 runs (10); most – 1645 (1982). HS 248 H v CU (Cambridge) 1984. Scored 122* La v OU (Oxford) 1991 in his final f-c innings. 50 wkts (2); most – 52 (1981). BB 7-75 H v Worcs (Southampton) 1976. F-c career: 490 matches; 21916 runs @ 32.71, 35 hundreds; 585 wickets @ 27.47. Appointed 1994. Umpired in Indian Cricket League 2007-08.

JONES, Allan Arthur (St John's C, Horsham), b Horley, Surrey 9 Dec 1947. RHB, RFM. Sussex 1966-69. Somerset 1970-75; cap 1972. Middlesex 1976-79; cap 1976. Glamorgan 1980-81. Northern Transvaal 1972-73. Orange Free State 1976-77. HS 33 M v Kent (Canterbury) 1978. BB 9-51 Sm v Sussex (Hove) 1972. F-c career: 214 matches; 799 runs @ 5.39; 549 wickets @ 28.07. Appointed 1985. Umpired 1 LOI (1996).

KETTLEBOROUGH, Richard Allan (Worksop C), b Sheffield, Yorks 15 Mar 1973. LHB, RM. Yorkshire 1994-97. Middlesex 1998-99. Tour: Z 1995-96 (Y). HS 108 Y v Essex (Leeds) 1996. BB 2-26 Y v Notts (Scarborough) 1996. F-c career: 33 matches; 1258 runs @ 25.16, 1 hundred; 3 wickets @ 81.00; 20 ct. Appointed 2006.

LEADBEATER, Barrie (Harehills SS), b Harehills, Leeds, Yorks 14 Aug 1943. RHB, RM. Yorkshire 1966-79; cap 1969; joint benefit with G.A.Cope 1980. Tour: WI 1969-70 (DN). HS 140* Y v Hants (Portsmouth) 1976. BB 1-1. F-c career: 147 matches; 5373 runs @ 25.34, 1 hundred; 1 wicket @ 5.00. Appointed 1981. Umpired 5 LOI (1983 to 2000).

LLONG, Nigel James (Ashford North S), b Ashford, Kent 11 Feb 1969. LHB, OB. Kent 1990-98; cap 1993. Tour: Z 1992-93 (K). HS 130 K v Hants (Canterbury) 1996. BB 5-21 K v Middx (Canterbury) 1996. F-c career: 68 matches; 3024 runs @ 31.17, 6 hundreds; 35 wickets @ 35.97. Appointed 2002. Umpired 2 Tests (2007-08) and 13 LOI (2006 to 2007-08). **ICC International Panel 2004 to date.**

LLOYDS, Jeremy William (Blundell's S), b Penang, Malaya 17 Nov 1954. LHB, OB. Somerset 1979-84; cap 1982. Gloucestershire 1985-91; cap 1985. Orange Free State 1983-84 to 1987-88, Tour (Glos): SL 1986-87. 1000 runs (3); most – 1295 (1986). HS 132* Sm v Northants (Northampton) 1982. BB 7-88 Sm v Essex (Chelmsford) 1982. F-c career: 267 matches; 10679 runs @ 31.04, 10 hundreds; 333 wickets @ 38.86; 229 ct. Appointed 1998. Umpired 5 Tests (2003-04 to 2004-05) and 18 LOI (2000 to 2005-06). **ICC International Panel 2003-06.**

MALLENDER, Neil Alan (Beverley GS), b Kirk Sandall, Yorks 13 Aug 1961. RHB, RFM. Northamptonshire 1980-86 and 1995-96; cap 1984. Somerset 1987-94; cap 1987; benefit 1994. Otago 1983-84 to 1992-93; captain 1990-91 to 1992-93. **Tests:** 2 (1992); 8 runs @ 2.66, HS 4; 10 wkts @ 21.50, BB 5-50 v P (Leeds) 1992 – on debut. Tour: Z 1994-95 (Nh). HS 100* Otago v CD (Palmerston N) 1991-92. UK HS 87* Sm v Sussex (Hove) 1990. 50 wkts (6); most – 56 (1983). BB 7-27 Otago v Auckland (Auckland) 1984-85. UK BB 7-41 Nh v Derbys (Northampton) 1982. F-c career: 345 matches; 4709 runs @ 17.18, 1 hundred; 937 wickets @ 26.31; 111 ct. Appointed 1999. Umpired 3 Tests (2003-04) and 22 LOI (2001 to 2003-04), including 2002-03 World Cup. **ICC Elite Panel 2004**.

ROBINSON, Robert Timothy (Dunstable GS; High Pavement SFC; Sheffield U), b Sutton in Ashfield 21 Nov 1958. RHB, RM. Nottinghamshire 1978-99; cap 1983; captain 1988-95; benefit 1992. *Wisden* 1985. **Tests:** 29 (1984-85 to 1989); HS 175 v A (Leeds) 1985. **LOI:** 26 (1984-85 to 1988); HS 83 v P (Sharjah) 1986-87. Tours: A 1987-88; SA 1989-90 (Eng XI), 1996-97 (Nt); NZ 1987-88; WI 1985-86; I/SL 1984-85; P 1987-88. 1000 runs (14) inc 2000 (1): 2032 (1984). HS 220* v Yorks (Nottingham) 1990. BB 1-22. F-c career: 425 matches; 27571 runs @ 42.15, 63 hundreds; 4 wickets @ 72.25; 257 ct. Appointed 2007.

SHARP, George (Elwick Road SS, Hartlepool), b West Hartlepool, Co Durham 12 Mar 1950. RHB, WK, occ LM. Northamptonshire 1968-85; cap 1973; benefit 1982. HS 98 Nh v Yorks (Northampton) 1983. BB 1-47. F-c career: 306 matches; 6254 runs @ 19.85; 1 wicket @ 70.00; 565 dismissals (565 ct, 90 st). Appointed 1992. Umpired 15 Tests (1996 to 2001-02) and 31 LOI (1995-96 to 2001-02). **ICC International Panel 1996 to 2001-02.**

STEELE, John Frederick (Endon SS), b Brown Edge, Staffs 23 Jul 1946. RHB, SLA. Brother of D.S. (Northants, Derbys and England 1963-84). Leicestershire 1970-83; cap 1971; benefit 1983. Glamorgan 1984-86; cap 1984. Natal 1973-74 to 1977-78. Staffordshire 1965-69. Tour: SA 1974-75 (DHR). 1000 runs (6); most – 1347 (1972). HS 195 Le v Derbys (Leicester) 1971. BB 7-29 Natal B v GW (Umzinto) 1973-74 and 7-29 Le v Glos (Leicester) 1980. F-c career: 379 matches; 15054 runs @ 28.95, 21 hundreds; 584 wickets @ 27.04; 413 ct. Appointed 1997.

WILLEY, Peter (Seaham SS), b Sedgefield, Co Durham 6 Dec 1949. RHB, OB. Northamptonshire 1966-83; cap 1971; benefit 1981. Leicestershire 1984-91; cap 1984; captain 1987. E Province 1982-83 to 1984-85. Northumberland 1992. **Tests:** 26 (1976 to 1986); 1184 runs @ 26.90, HS 102* v WI (St John's) 1980-81; 7 wkts @ 65.14, BB 2-73 v WI (Lord's) 1980. **LOI:** 26. Tours: A 1979-80; SA 1972-73 (DHR), 1981-82 (SAB); WI 1980-81, 1985-86; I 1979-80; SL 1977-78 (DHR). 1000 runs (10); most – 1783 (1982). HS 227 Nh v Somerset (Northampton) 1976. 50 wkts (3); most – 52 (1979). BB 7-37 Nh v OU (Oxford) 1975. F-c career: 559 matches; 24361 runs @ 30.56, 44 hundreds; 756 wickets @ 30.95. Appointed 1993. Umpired 25 Tests (1995-96 to 2003-04) and 34 LOI (1996 to 2003), including 1999 and 2002-03 World Cups. **ICC International Panel 1996 to 2001-02 and 2003-04.**

RESERVE FIRST-CLASS LIST: Martin J.Bodenham, Keith Coburn, Nicholas G.B.Cook, Stephen C.Gale, Michael A.Gough, Andrew Hicks, Steven J.Malone, David J.Millns, Terence J.Urben.

Test Match and LOI statistics to 23 February 2008 (inclusive).

INTERNATIONAL UMPIRES AND REFEREES 2008

ELITE PANEL OF UMPIRES 2008

The Elite Panel of ICC Umpires and Referees was introduced in April 2002 to raise standards and guarantee impartial adjudication. Two umpires from this panel stand in Test matches while one officiates with a home umpire from the Supplementary International Panel in limited-overs internationals.

Full Names	Birthdate	Birthplace	Tests	Debut	LOI	Debut
ALIM Sarwar DAR	06.06.68	Jhang, Pakistan	43	2003-04	101	1999-00
ASAD RAUF	12.05.56	Lahore, Pakistan	17	2004-05	51	1999-00
BENSON, Mark Richard	06.07.58	Shoreham, England	21	2004-05	61	2004
BOWDEN, Brent Fraser	11.04.63	Auckland, New Zealand	44	1999-00	122	1994-95
BUCKNOR, Stephen Anthony	31.05.46	Montego Bay, Jamaica	120	1988-89	167	1988-89
DOCTROVE, Billy Raymond	03.07.55	Marigot, Dominica	15	1997-98	70	1997-98
HAIR, Darrell Bruce	30.09.52	Mudgee, Australia	76	1991-92	133	1991-92
HARPER, Daryl John	23.10.61	Adelaide, Australia	69	1998-99	147	1993-94
KOERTZEN, Rudolf Eric ('Rudi')	26.03.49	Knysna, South Africa	87	1992-93	186	1992-93
TAUFEL, Simon James Arthur	21.01.71	Sydney, Australia	48	2000-01	118	1998-99

ELITE PANEL OF REFEREES 2008

Full Names	Birthdate	Birthplace	Tests	Debut	LOI	Debut
BROAD, Brian Christopher	29.09.57	Bristol, England	25	2003-04	118	2003-04
CROWE, Jeffrey John	14.09.58	Auckland, New Zealand	23	2004-05	90	2003-04
HURST. Alan George	15.07.50	Melbourne, Australia	17	2004-05	52	2004-05
MADUGALLE, Ranjan Senerath	22.04.59	Kandy, Sri Lanka	99	1993-94	206	1993-94
MAHANAMA, Roshan Siriwardena	31.05.66	Colombo, Sri Lanka	18	2004	83	2004
PROCTER, Michael John	15.09.46	Durban, South Africa	47	2001-02	142	2001-02
SRINATH, Javagal	31.08.69	Mysore, India	6	2006	31	2006-07

INTERNATIONAL UMPIRES PANEL 2008

Nominated by their respective cricket boards, members from this panel officiate in home LOI and supplement the Elite panel for Test matches. Specialist third umpires have been selected to undertake adjudication involving television replays. The number of Test matches/LOI in which they have stood is shown in brackets.

			Third Umpire
Australia	S.J.Davis (9/67)	P.D.Parker (10/60)	B.N.J.Oxenford (-/1)
Bangladesh	Nadir Shah (-/13)	Enamal Haque (-/4)	Aktaruddin Sahin (2/16)
England	I.J.Gould (-/18)	N.J.Llong (2/13)	P.J.Hartley (-/1)
India	A.M.Saheba (-/18)	S.L.Shastri (2/19)	G.A.Pratapkumar (-/2)
New Zealand	G.A.Baxter (-/16)	A.L.Hill (5/46)	E.A.Watkin (2/21)
Pakistan	Zamir Haider (-/3)	Nadeem Ghauri (5/35)	Riazuddin (12/12)
South Africa	I.L.Howell (9/63)	B.G.Jerling (4/61)	K.H.Hurter (-/5), M.Erasmus (-/3)
Sri Lanka	E.A.R.de Silva (33/76)	T.H.Wijewardene (4/37)	M.G.Silva (3/15)
West Indies	C.R.Duncan (2/10)	N.Malcolm (-/-)	C.E.Mack (-/1), G.E.Greaves (-/-)
Zimbabwe	K.C.Barbour (4/41)	R.B.Tiffin (40/100)	I.D.Robinson (28/90)

Test Match and LOI statistics to 23 February 2008 (inclusive).

UNIVERSITY FIRST-CLASS REGISTER 2007

CAMBRIDGE († Blue 2007)

Full Names	Birthdate	Birthplace	College	Bat/Bowl	F-C Debut
†AUSTIN, Matthew Lorenzo	31.01.85	Colchester	Emmanuel	RHB	2006
†BAKER, Fergus Braan	18.05.87	Leicester	Downing	LHB/SLA	2007
BOTT, Mark Daniel	13.05.86	Nottingham	(Anglia RU)	RHB/LB	2006
FRIEDLANDER, Matthew James	01.08.79	Durban, S Africa	(Anglia RU)	RHB/RM	2003-04
†HEMINGWAY, Thomas Lewis	19.05.86	Stevenage, Herts	Trinity Hall	RHB/OB	2007
†HEYWOOD, James John Neville	24.09.82	Eastbourne	Homerton	RHB/WK	2003
HUNTINGTON, Christopher James	29.03.87	Cambridge	(Anglia RU)	LHB/RSM	2006
†JACKLIN, Benjamin David	26.04.84	Leeds	Magdalene	RHB/RM	2005
JAMES, Gareth David	01.12.84	Walthamstow	(Anglia RU)	RHB/LB	2004
JOGIA, Kunal Ashokkumar	18.09.84	Leicester	(Anglia RU)	RHB/RSM	2006
†KEMP, Robin Andrew	29.09.84	Luton	St John's	RHB/RM	2005
MacLENNAN, Scott Keith	30.11.87	Glasgow, Scotland	St John's	RHB/RM	2007
†MASSEY, Ian Robert	10.09.85	Hereford	Queens	RHB/OB	2007
MODHA, Bhargav Ramesh	20.10.85	Jamnagar, India	(Anglia RU)	RHB/LB	2007
MOHAMMAD AMIN	19.10.84	Gujranwala, Pakistan	(Anglia RU)	RHB/RMF	2007
†O'DRISCOLL, William John Finian	16.07.87	Gloucester	Gonville & Caius	RHB/RM	2007
†OWEN, Frederick Gerard	25.09.85	Chester	Corpus Christi	RHB	2006
RIST, William Henry	22.03.87	Guildford	(Anglia RU)	RHB/WK	2007
SHARIF, Zoheb Khalid	22.02.83	Leytonstone	(Anglia RU)	LHB/LB	2001
†SMITH, Benjamin David	11.10.84	Shrewsbury	St John's	RHB	2007
SMITH, Brendan Mitchell	24.09.85	Basildon	(Anglia RU)	LHB/LFM	2006
TAVARASA, Banutheeban	17.01.87	Jaffna, Sri Lanka	(Anglia RU)	RHB/OB	2007
†WARD, Glen Bernard	22.01.79	Melbourne, Australia	Corpus Christi	RHB	2007

DURHAM

Full Names	Birthdate	Birthplace	College	Bat/Bowl	F-C Debut
BALCOMBE, David John	24.12.84	City of London	St Hild & St Bede	RHB/RFM	2005
BUTTLEMAN, Joseph Edward Lewis	23.08.87	Basildon, Essex	St Hild & St Bede	RHB/WK	2007
DIXEY, Paul Garrod	02.11.87	Canterbury	Hatfield	RHB/WK	2005
DOBSON, William Thomas	11.03.86	Oxford	St Aidan's	RHB/RMF	2006
EVANS, Laurie John	12.10.87	Lambeth, London	St Mary's	RHB/RFM	2005
FOSTER, Patrick John	20.03.87	Nairobi, Kenya	St Hild & St Bede	RHB/RMF	2007
LAMB, Nicholas John	09.11.85	St Albans	Collingwood	RHB/RMF	2005
MORRIS, James Calum	17.01.85	Welwyn Gdn City	University	RHB/LB	2005
PAGET, Christopher David	02.11.87	Stafford	Van Mildert	RHB/OB	2004
PHYTHIAN, Mark John	26.04.85	Peterborough	University	RHB/WK	2005
PROWTING, Nicholas Roger	26.10.85	Chelmsford	Van Mildert	RHB	2005
THOMPSON, Greg James	17.09.87	Lisburn, N.Ireland	St Mary's	RHB/LB	2004
WILLIAMS, Robert Edward Morgan	19.01.87	Pembury, Kent	St Mary's	RHB/RMF	2007
WOOD, James Robert	08.09.85	Cape Town, SA	Van Mildert	RHB	2005

LOUGHBOROUGH

Full Names	Birthdate	Birthplace	Bat/Bowl	F-C Debut
BRATHWAITE, Ruel Marlon Ricardo	06.09.85	Bridgetown, Barbados	RHB/RFM	2006
FOSTER, Edward John	21.01.85	Shrewsbury	LHB/RM	2005
GIFFORD, William McLean	10.10.85	Sutton Coldfield	RHB/RM	2005
HARINATH, Arun	26.03.87	Sutton, Surrey	LHB/OB	2007
HUGHES, Jonathan Adam	12.09.85	Slough	RHB/RMF	2007
KING, Richard Eric	03.01.84	Hitchin, Herts	RHB/LMF	2003
LEWIS, Liam James	23.10.86	Exeter	RHB, SRA	2007
MALCOLM-HANSEN, Richard Johan Anders	22.04.86	Farnborough, Kent	RHB/OB	2007
MURTAGH, Christopher Paul	14.10.84	Lambeth, London	RHB/LB	2005
NAIK, Jigar Kumar Hakumatrai	10.08.84	Leicester	RHB/OB	2005
PARSONS, Thomas William	02.05.87	Melbourne, Australia	RHB/RFM	2007
SPRIEGEL, Matthew Neil William	04.03.87	Epsom, Surrey	LHB/OB	2006
WHEELER, Stephen James	16.10.86	Frimley, Surrey	RHB/RFM	2007

Full Names	Birthdate	Birthplace	College	Bat/Bowl	F-C Debut
†BALL, Alexander Henry	03.10.86	Westminster, London	St Catherine's	RHB/OB	2007
BRADSHAW, Duncan Phillip	19.02.86	Harare, Zimbabwe	(Brookes U)	RHB/RFM	2006
†DINGLE, Lewis Allen	16.09.88	Blackpool	Christ Church	RHB/RMF	2007
DUFFELL, Charlie Basil Royson	20.10.86	Hanover, Germany	(Brookes U)	RHB/WK	
†DUNBAR, Peter Raymond	18.09.84	Harrow	Balliol	RHB/RM	2006
†FROGGETT, Thomas Joseph	05.05.88	Wakefield	St John's	RHB/WK	2007
†HILL, Charles Michael McLean	27.11.85	Wimbledon	Trinity	LHB/SLC	2007
†HOBBISS, Michael Holland	17.08.85	Manchester	Worcester	RHB/RM	2006
HOOPER, John Harry Patrick	14.01.86	Tooting Bec	(Brookes U)	LHB/LM	2006
†HOWELL, Thomas Henry	14.09.87	Derby	New	RHB/LB	2007
KALAM, Tarique	20.03.87	Cape Town, SA	(Brookes U)	RHB/RMF	2006
LETT, Robin Jonathan Hugh	23.12.86	Westminster	(Brookes U)	RHB/RM	2006
†MACADAM, James Chalmers	29.06.88	Paddington, London	Keble	RHB/RMF	2007
MENDIS, Balapuwaduge Gerald Anthony Shamilal	13.06.83	Colombo, Sri Lanka	(Brookes U)	RHB/OB	2007
†MORSE, Edward James	30.01.86	Stevenage	St Edmund Hall	RHB/RM	2005
MOTTRAM, William James	20.09.86	Edgbaston, Birmingham	(Brookes U)	LHB/RM	2007
RICHARDS, Mali Alexander	02.09.83	Taunton	(Brookes U)	LHB/RM	2004
RYAN, Luke Charles	05.08.88	Welwyn Garden City	(Brookes U)	RHB/SLA	2007
†SADLER, Oliver James	02.04.87	Newcastle-u-Lyme	Oriel	RHB/SLA	
SANDBACH, Christopher James Lister	17.11.85	Oxford	(Brookes U)	RHB/LB	2007
WILSHAW, Peter James	15.07.87	Newcastle-u-Lyme	(Brookes U)	RHB/RM	2006
†WOODS, Nicholas James	02.01.86	Bolton	Queens	RHB/LB	2005
YOUNG, Peter James William	14.09.86	Hammersmith	(Brookes U)	LHB/RM	2006

2007 TOURING TEAMS FIRST-CLASS REGISTER

INDIA

Full Names	Birthdate	Birthplace	Team	Type	F-C Debut
BOSE, Ranadeb Ranjit	27.02.79	Calcutta	Bengal	RHB/RMF	1998-99
DHONI, Mahendra Singh	07.07.81	Ranchi	Jharkhand	RHB/WK	1999-00
DRAVID, Rahul	11.01.73	Indore	Karnataka	RHB/OB/WK	1990-91
GAMBHIR, Gautam	14.10.81	Delhi	Delhi	LHB/LB	1999-00
GANGULY, Sourav Chandidas	08.07.72	Calcutta	Bengal	LHB/RM	1989-90
JAFFER, Wasim	16.02.78	Bombay	Bombay	RHB/OB	1996-97
KARTHIK, Krishankumar Dinesh	01.06.85	Madras	Tamil Nadu	RHB/WK	2002-03
KHAN, Zaheer	07.10.78	Shrirampur	Baroda	RHB/LFM	1999-00
KUMBLE, Anil	17.10.70	Bangalore	Karnataka	RHB/LBG	1989-90
LAXMAN, Vangipurappu Venkata Sai	01.11.74	Hyderabad	Hyderabad	RHB/OB	1992-93
POWAR, Ramesh Rajaram	20.05.78	Bombay	Bombay	RHB/.OB	1999-00
SHARMA, Ishant	02.09.88	Delhi	Delhi	RHB/RM	2006-07
SINGH, Rudra Pratap	06.12.85	Rae Bareli	Uttar Pradesh	RHB/LMF	2003-04
SREESANTH, Shanthakumaran	06.02.83	Kothamangalam	Kerala	RHB/RFM	2002-03
TENDULKAR, Sachin Ramesh	24.04.73	Bombay	Bombay	RHB/RM/LB/OB	1988-89
YUVRAJ SINGH	12.12.81	Chandigarh	Punjab	LHB/LM/SLA	1996-97

SRI LANKA 'A'

Full Names	Birthdate	Birthplace	Team	Type	F-C Debut
AMERASINGHE, Merenna Koralage Don Ishara	05.03.78	Colombo	Colts	RHB/RFM	1997-98
FERNANDO, Charith Sylvester	30.12.82	Badulla	Chilaw Marians	LHB	2001
GANEGAMA, Withanaarchchige Chamara Akalanka	29.03.81	Colombo	Nondescripts	RHB/RFM	2000-01
GUNAWARDENA, Kanchana Deshsapriya	09.10.84	Colombo	Nondescripts	LHB/OB	2000-01
HERATH, Mudiyanselage Rangana Keerthi Bandara	19.03.78	Kurunegala	Moors	LHB/SLA	1996-97
KANDAMBY, Sahan Hewa Thilina	04.06.82	Colombo	Bloomfield	LHB/LB	2000-01
KAPUGEDARA, Chamara Kantha	24.02.87	Kandy	Colombo	RHB/RM	2005-06
LOKUARACHCHI, Kaushal Samaraweera	20.05.82	Colombo	Sinhalese	RHB/LB	2000-01
MUBARAK, Jehan	10.01.81	Washington, USA	Colombo	LHB/OB	1999-00
PERERA, Mahawaduge Dilruwan Kamalaneth	22.07.82	Panadura	Panadura	RHB/OB	2000-01
PRASAD, Kariyawasam Tirana Gamage Dammika	30.05.83	Ragama	Sinhalese	RHB/RFM	2001-02
RAMYAKUMARA, Wijekoon Mudiyanselage Gayan	21.12.76	Gampaha	Chilaw Marians	LHB/LM	1996-97
SAMARAWEERA, Thilan T.	22.09.76	Colombo	Sinhalese	RHB/OB	1995-96
SILVA, Jayan Kaushal	27.05.86	Colombo	Sinhalese	RHB	2002-03
UDAWATTE, Mahela Lakmal	19.07.86	Colombo	Chilaw Marians	LHB/OB	2005-06
VANDORT, Michael G.	19.01.80	Colombo	Colombo	LHB/RM	1998-99
WARNAPURA, Basnayake Shalith Malinda	26.05.79	Colombo	Colts	LHB/OB	1998
WELEGEDARA, Uda Walawwe Mahim Bandaralage Chanaka Asanka	20.03.81	Matale	Moors	RHB/LFM	2002-03

WEST INDIES

Full Names	Birthdate	Birthplace	Team	Type	F-C Debut
BRAVO, Dwayne John	07.10.83	Santa Cruz	Trinidad	RHB/RFM	2001-02
CHANDERPAUL, Shivnarine	16.08.74	Unity Village	Guyana	LHB/LB	1991-92
COLLYMORE, Corey Dalanelo	21.12.77	Boscobelle	Barbados	RHB/RFM	1998-99
EDWARDS, Fidel Henderson	06.02.82	St Peter	Barbados	RHB/RF	2001-02
GANGA, Daren	14.01.79	Barrackpore	Trinidad	RHB/OB	1996-97
GAYLE, Christopher Henry	21.09.79	Kingston	Jamaica	LHB/OB	1998-99
JOSEPH, Sylvester Cleofoster	05.09.78	New Winthorpes, Antigua	Leeward Is	RHB/OB	1996-97
MORTON, Runako Shakur	22.07.78	Rawlins, Nevis	Leeward Is	RHB/OB	1996-97
POWELL, Daren Brentlyle	15.04.78	Malvenn	Jamaica	RHB/RFM	2000-01
RAMDIN, Denesh	13.03.85	Freeport, Couva	Trinidad	RHB/WK	2003-04
RAMPAUL, Ravindranath	15.10.84	Preysal, Trinidad	Trinidad	LHB/RFM	2001-02
SAMMY, Darren Julius Garvey	20.12.83	Micoud, St Lucia	Windward Is	RHB/RM	2002-03
SAMUELS, Marlon Nathaniel	05.01.81	Kingston	Jamaica	RHB/OB	1996-97
SARWAN, Ramnaresh Ronnie	23.06.80	Wakenaam Island	Guyana	RHB/LB	1995-96
SMITH, Devon Sheldon	21.10.81	Sauters, Grenada	Windward Is	LHB/OB	1998-99
TAYLOR, Jerome Everton	22.06.84	St Elizabeth	Jamaica	RHB/RF	2002-03

THE 2007 FIRST-CLASS SEASON
STATISTICAL HIGHLIGHTS

FIRST TO INDIVIDUAL TARGETS

1000 RUNS	D.J.Hussey	Nottinghamshire	14 July
2000 RUNS	M.R.Ramprakash	Surrey	21 September
100 WICKETS	–	Most 90 – Mushtaq Ahmed (Sussex)	

TEAM HIGHLIGHTS

HIGHEST INNINGS TOTALS († *County record*)

850-7d†	Somerset v Middlesex	Taunton
801-8d†	Derbyshire v Somerset	Taunton
791†	Nottinghamshire v Essex	Chelmsford
701-6d†	Worcestershire v Surrey	Worcester
700-9d	Essex v Nottinghamshire	Chelmsford
675-5d	Somerset v Leicestershire	Taunton
664-7d	Nottinghamshire v Essex	Nottingham
664	India v England (3rd Test)	The Oval
650-8d	Gloucestershire v Leicestershire	Leicester
649-5d	Essex v Northamptonshire	Chelmsford
641-6d	Somerset v Northamptonshire	Northampton
626-3d	Surrey v Sussex	Hove
610-6d	Warwickshire v Worcestershire	Worcester
600-4d	Middlesex v Somerset	Taunton

HIGHEST FOURTH INNINGS TOTALS

467	Surrey (set 503) v Hampshire	The Oval
464	Lancashire (set 489) v Surrey	The Oval
411	Northamptonshire (set 416) v Gloucestershire	Gloucester
405-5	Sussex (set 504) v Warwickshire	Hove

LOWEST INNINGS TOTALS

52	Derbyshire v Somerset	Derby
60	Glamorgan v Middlesex	Swansea
77	Loughborough UCCE v Somerset	Taunton
79	Cambridge UCCE v Northamptonshire	Cambridge
86	Worcestershire v Hampshire	Southampton
88	Essex v Gloucestershire	Southend
89	Yorkshire v Sussex	Hove
92	Canada v Ireland	Leicester

MATCH AGGREGATES OF 1500 RUNS

1659-13	Middlesex (600-4d, 209-2) v Somerset (850-7d)	Taunton
1640-22	Derbyshire (801-8d) v Somerset (530, 309-4)	Taunton
1558-32	India (664, 180-6d) v England (345, 369-6) (3rd Test)	The Oval
1554-20	Essex (700-9d, 63-1) v Nottinghamshire (791)	Chelmsford

BATSMEN'S MATCH (Qualification: 1200 runs, average 70 per wicket)

127.61 (1659-13)	Middlesex (600-4d, 209-2) v Somerset (850-7d)	Taunton
77.70 (1554-20)	Essex (700-9d, 63-1) v Nottinghamshire (791)	Chelmsford
74.54 (1640-22)	Derbyshire (801-8d) v Somerset (530, 309-4)	Taunton

LARGE MARGINS OF VICTORY

Inns & 329 runs	Northamptonshire (577-6d) beat Cambridge UCCE (79, 169)	Cambridge
346 runs	Yorkshire (594-9d, 266-7d) beat Surrey (344, 170)	The Oval

NARROW MARGIN OF VICTORY

1 run   Yorkshire (383-6d, forfeit) beat Loughborough UCCE (93-3d, 289)   Leeds

FOUR HUNDREDS IN AN INNINGS

Somerset (850-7d) v Middlesex	Taunton
Derbyshire (801-8d) v Somerset	Taunton
England (553-5d) v West Indies (1st Test)	Lord's
Somerset (675-5d) v Leicestershire	Taunton

EIGHT HUNDREDS IN A MATCH

Somerset (850-7d) v Middlesex (600-4d, 209-2)   Taunton

SIX FIFTIES IN AN INNINGS

Derbyshire (801-8d) v Somerset	Taunton
India (664) v England (3rd Test)	The Oval
Gloucestershire (650-8d) v Leicestershire	Leicester
Sussex (532) v Worcestershire	Hove

SIXTY EXTRAS IN AN INNINGS

	B	LB	W	NB		
62	11	12	13	26	Sussex (510) v Kent	Hove
62	13	15	16	18	Leicestershire (344) v Derbyshire	Leicester
61	15	12	6	28	Nottinghamshire (399) v Gloucestershire	Bristol

Under ECB regulations, Test matches excluded, two penalty extras were scored for each no-ball.

BATTING HIGHLIGHTS

TRIPLE HUNDREDS

J.L.Langer   315   Somerset v Middlesex   Taunton

DOUBLE HUNDREDS

T.R.Ambrose	251*	Warwickshire v Worcestershire	Worcester
R.S.Bopara	229	Essex v Northamptonshire	Chelmsford
M.J. Di Venuto	204*	Durham v Kent	Chester-le-St
N.J.Edwards	212	Somerset v Loughborough UCCE	Taunton
S.P.Fleming	243	Nottinghamshire v Derbyshire	Chesterfield
G.W.Flower	203	Essex v Northamptonshire	Chelmsford
J.S.Foster	204	Essex v Nottinghamshire	Chelmsford
M.W.Goodwin	205*	Sussex v Surrey	Hove
D.J.Hussey	275	Nottinghamshire v Essex	Nottingham
R.C.Irani	218	Essex v Glamorgan	Chelmsford
S.M.Katich	221	Derbyshire v Somerset	Taunton
S.G.Law	206	Lancashire v Yorkshire	Leeds
R.S.Morton	201	West Indians v MCC	Durham
K.P.Pietersen	226	England v West Indies (2nd Test)	Leeds
M.R.Ramprakash	266*	Surrey v Sussex	Hove

C.M.W.Read		240	Nottinghamshire v Essex	Chelmsford
J.A.Rudolph		220	Yorkshire v Warwickshire	Scarborough
D.J.G.Sales		219	Northamptonshire v Glamorgan	Colwyn Bay
V.S.Solanki		232	Worcestershire v Surrey	Worcester
M.E.Trescothick		284	Somerset v Northamptonshire	Northampton
C.L.White		241	Somerset v Gloucestershire	Taunton
Younus Khan	(2)	202*	Yorkshire v Hampshire	Southampton
		217*	Yorkshire v Kent	Scarborough

HUNDREDS IN THREE CONSECUTIVE INNINGS

| M.W.Goodwin (Sussex) | 119 and 205* | v Surrey | Hove |
| | 112 | v Worcestershire | Worcester |

HUNDRED IN EACH INNINGS OF A MATCH

T.R.Birt	140	162	Derbyshire v Gloucestershire	Bristol
M.A.Carberry	127	120	Hampshire v Worcestershire	Kidderminster
A.P.R.Gidman	130	105*	Gloucestershire v Northamptonshire	Gloucester
M.W.Goodwin	119	205*	Sussex v Surrey	Hove
M.R.Ramprakash	196	130*	Surrey v Lancashire	The Oval
M.J.Walker	142	157	Kent v Lancashire	Canterbury
Younus Khan	106	202*	Yorkshire v Hampshire	Southampton

FASTEST HUNDRED (WALTER LAWRENCE TROPHY)

| M.J.North (106) | 73 balls | Gloucestershire v Leicestershire | Bristol |

HUNDRED BEFORE LUNCH

| | | *Day* | | |
| D.J.Birch | 0*-122* | 1 | Derbyshire v Cambridge UCCE | Cambridge |

TEN OR MORE SIXES IN AN INNINGS

| 14 | D.J.Hussey (275) | Nottinghamshire v Essex | Nottingham |
| 10 | S.J.Mullaney (165*) | Lancashire v Durham UCCE | Durham |

HUNDRED ON FIRST-CLASS DEBUT

| D.J.Birch | 130 | Derbyshire v Cambridge UCCE | Cambridge |

HUNDRED ON FIRST-CLASS DEBUT IN ENGLAND AND WALES

J.P.Bray	146	Ireland v Canada	Leicester
A.S.Chopra	106	MCC v Sri Lanka A	Arundel
J.K.Silva	118*	Sri Lanka A v MCC	Arundel

CARRYING BAT THROUGH COMPLETED INNINGS

M.J.Brown		56*	Hampshire (115) v Durham	Chester-le-St
J.L.Denly		115*	Kent (199) v Hampshire	Canterbury
M.J.Di Venuto	(2)	155*	Durham (313) v Worcestershire	Worcester
		204*	Durham (407) v Kent	Chester-le-St
R.W.T.Key		75*	Kent (150) v Surrey	Canterbury
D.K.H.Mitchell		70*	Worcestershire (213) v Sussex	Hove
J.J.Sayers		149*	Yorkshire (414) v Durham	Leeds

FIRST-WICKET PARTNERSHIP OF 100 IN EACH INNINGS

111/199   M.A.Carberry/M.J.Brown   Hampshire v Worcestershire   Kidderminster

OTHER NOTABLE PARTNERSHIPS († *County record*)

Second Wicket

283* J.N.Batty/M.R.Ramprakash   Surrey v Warwickshire   The Oval

Third Wicket

403	M.R.Ramprakash/M.A.Butcher	Surrey v Sussex	Hove
320	R.S.Bopara/G.W.Flower	Essex v Northamptonshire	Chelmsford
288	R.W.T.Key/M.J.Walker	Kent v Lancashire	Canterbury
265	T.R.Birt/S.M.Katich	Derbyshire v Gloucestershire	Bristol
258	P.J.Horton/S.G.Law	Lancashire v Yorkshire	Leeds

Fourth Wicket

253* M.W.Goodwin/C.J.Adams   Sussex v Surrey   Hove

Fifth Wicket

359†	D.J.Hussey/C.M.W.Read	Nottinghamshire v Essex	Nottingham
313	R.C.Irani/R.N.ten Doeschate	Essex v Glamorgan	Chelmsford
252	S.M.Katich/I.J.Harvey	Derbyshire v Somerset	Taunton
229	K.C.Sangakkara/A.G.R.Loudon	Warwickshire v Durham	Birmingham

Sixth Wicket

226† T.R.Ambrose/ H.H.Streak   Warwickshire v Worcestershire   Worcester

Seventh Wicket

| 254 | J.S.Foster/A.J.Bichel | Essex v Nottinghamshire | Chelmsford |
| 200 | A.G.Botha/D.J.Pipe | Derbyshire v Somerset | Taunton |

Eighth Wicket

216	C.M.W.Read/G.P.Swann	Nottinghamshire v Essex	Chelmsford
195	J.S.Foster/G.R.Napier	Essex v Nottinghamshire	Chelmsford
177	Azhar Mahmood/I.D.K.Salisbury	Surrey v Hampshire	The Oval
177†	G.O.Jones/Yasir Arafat	Kent v Warwickshire	Canterbury

Ninth Wicket

| 246† | T.T.Bresnan/J.N.Gillespie | Yorkshire v Surrey | The Oval |
| 185 | R.D.B.Croft/J.A.R.Harris | Glamorgan v Nottinghamshire | Swansea |

BOWLING HIGHLIGHTS

EIGHT OR MORE WICKETS IN AN INNINGS († *County record*)

Kabir Ali		8-50	Worcestershire v Lancashire	Manchester
O.D.Gibson	(2)	10-47†	Durham v Hampshire	Chester-le-St
		8-68	Durham v Lancashire	Blackpool
M.K.Munday		8-55	Somerset v Nottinghamshire	Taunton
G.Onions		8-101	Durham v Warwickshire	Birmingham

TEN OR MORE WICKETS IN A MATCH

Kabir Ali	(2)	11-55	Worcestershire v Loughborough UCCE	Worcester
		10-102	Worcestershire v Lancashire	Manchester
A.J.Bichel		11-132	Essex v Derbyshire	Derby
A.R.Caddick		12-71	Somerset v Gloucestershire	Bristol
G.Chapple		10-86	Lancashire v Durham	Blackpool
R.D.B.Croft		11-150	Glamorgan v Derbyshire	Cardiff
Danish Kaneria		13-181	Essex v Glamorgan	Chelmsford
O.D.Gibson	(3)	10-144	Durham v Yorkshire	Chester-le-St
		12-100	Durham v Hampshire	Chester-le-St
		11-150	Durham v Worcestershire	Chester-le-St
Harbhajan Singh		11-91	Surrey v Kent	Canterbury
J.A.R.Harris		12-118	Glamorgan v Gloucestershire	Bristol

Harris became the youngest to take seven wickets in an innings (17y 2d) and ten in a match (17y 3d) in the county championship

S.P.Kirby		10-116	Gloucestershire v Essex	Southend
M.K.Munday		10-65	Somerset v Nottinghamshire	Taunton
Mushtaq Ahmed	(3)	10-219	Sussex v Kent	Hove
		11-281	Sussex v Warwickshire	Hove
		13-225	Sussex v Worcestershire	Hove
M.S.Panesar		10-187	England v West Indies (3rd Test)	Manchester
G.P.Swann		10-243	Nottinghamshire v Glamorgan	Swansea
S.K.Warne		11-133	Hampshire v Durham	Southampton

OUTSTANDING INNINGS ANALYSIS

O.D.Gibson	17.3-1-47-10	Durham v Hampshire	Chester-le-St

FOUR WICKETS WITH FIVE BALLS

Umar Bhatti	Canada v Ireland *(all lbw)*	Leicester

HAT-TRICKS

Umar Bhatti	Canada v Ireland *(all lbw)*	Leicester

NINE OR MORE WICKET-KEEPING DISMISSALS IN A MATCH

J.N.Batty	8 ct, 1 st	Surrey v Lancashire	The Oval

NO BYES CONCEDED IN TOTAL OF 600 OR MORE

700-9d	C.M.W.Read	Nottinghamshire v Essex	Chelmsford
675-5d	P.A.Nixon	Leicestershire v Somerset	Taunton

FIVE OR MORE CATCHES IN AN INNINGS IN THE FIELD

T.R.Birt	5 ct	Derbyshire v Northamptonshire	Northampton
M.E.Trescothick	5 ct	Somerset v Gloucestershire	Bristol
M.van Jaarsveld	5 ct	Kent v Warwickshire	Birmingham

2007 FIRST-CLASS AVERAGES

These averages involve the 546 cricketers who appeared in the 169 first-class matches played (excluding five abandoned without play) by 34 teams in England and Wales during the 2007 season.

'Cap' denotes the season in which the player was awarded a 1st XI cap by the county he represented in 2007. If he played for more than one county in 2007, the county who awarded him his cap is underlined. Durham abolished their capping and 'awards' systems after the 2005 season. Gloucestershire now cap players on first-class debut. For Worcestershire players, 2007[c] denotes the award of county colours in 2007.

Team abbreviations: Can – Canada; CU – Cambridge University/Cambridge UCCE; De – Derbyshire; Du – Durham; DU – Durham UCCE; E – England; EA – England A; Ex – Essex; Gm – Glamorgan; Gs – Gloucestershire; H – Hampshire; Ind – India/Indians; Ire – Ireland; K – Kent; La – Lancashire; Le – Leicestershire; LU – Loughborough UCCE; M – Middlesex; MCC – Marylebone Cricket Club; Nh – Northamptonshire; Nt – Nottinghamshire; OU – Oxford University/Oxford UCCE; SLA – Sri Lanka A; Sm – Somerset; Sy – Surrey; Sx – Sussex; Wa – Warwickshire; WI – West Indies/Indians; Wo – Worcestershire; Y – Yorkshire.

† Left-handed batsman.

BATTING AND FIELDING

	Cap	M	I	NO	HS	Runs	Avge	100	50	Ct/St
Abdul Razzaq (Wo)	2007[c]	3	5	1	78	172	43.00	–	1	1
H.D.Ackerman (Le)	2005	15	26	–	153	723	27.80	3	1	15
A.R.Adams (Nt)	2007	4	1	33		104	20.80	–	–	1
C.J.Adams (Sx)	1998	15	24	2	193	1030	46.81	3	3	27
† J.H.K.Adams (H)	2006	11	20	1	110	773	40.68	1	5	10
M.Hassan Adnan (De)	2004	11	21	2	63	399	21.00	–	2	5
S.J.Adshead (Gs)	2004	13	18	1	99	447	26.29	–	3	28/2
† U.Afzaal (Nh)	2005	8	16	–	73	570	35.62	–	5	3
J.S.Ahmed (Ex)	–	3	3	2	7*	14	14.00	–	–	2
Kabir Ali (Wo)	2002[c]	14	19	–	39	211	11.10	–	–	1
Kadeer Ali (Gs)	2005	16	28	1	140	903	33.44	2	4	8
† M.M.Ali (Wo)	2007[c]	3	5	–	85	180	36.00	–	2	–
J.Allenby (Le)	–	16	26	4	93	755	34.31	–	5	15
T.R.Ambrose (Wa/EA)	2007	16	23	3	251*	862	43.10	1	4	39
M.K.D.I.Amerasinghe (SLA)	–	1	–			–	–	–	–	–
† J.M.Anderson (E/La)	2003	9	8	2	16	23	3.83	–	–	4
† J.E.Anyon (Wa)	–	14	16	5	37*	199	18.09	–	–	3
M.L.Austin (CU)	–	1	1	–	25	25	25.00	–	–	–
Azhar Mahmood (Sy)	2004	3	6	–	69	168	28.00	–	1	2
A.Bagai (Can)	–	1	2	–	13	17	8.50	–	–	2
† F.B.Baker (CU)	–	2	3	–	18	35	11.66	–	–	–
D.J.Balcombe (DU/H)	–	5	8	2	29	144	24.00	–	–	3
A.H.Ball (OU)	–	2	1	1	44*	50	50.00	–	–	–
† V.Banerjee (Gs)	2006	11	15	10	11*	46	9.20	–	–	3
M.W.Barnes (Wa)	–	1	–			–	–	–	–	5
† G.E.F.Barnett (Can)	–	1	2	–	4	5	2.50	–	–	–
T.C.Bastiampillai (Can)	–	1	2	–	20	25	12.50	–	–	–
G.J.Batty (Wo)	2002[c]	14	22	3	84	487	25.63	–	3	7
J.N.Batty (Sy)	2001	15	25	3	154*	965	43.86	4	3	42/5
I.R.Bell (E/Wa)	2001	9	14	1	109*	491	37.76	1	4	6
C.C.Benham (H)	–	9	14	–	76	312	22.28	–	1	10

140

F-C	Cap	M	I	NO	HS	Runs	Avge	100	50	Ct/St
D.M.Benkenstein (Du)	2005	16	28	5	117	1278	55.56	3	8	5
J.G.E.Benning (Sy)	–	8	11	1	51	277	27.70	–	1	5
A.J.Bichel (Ex)	2007	8	12	4	148	482	60.25	2	2	7
† D.J.Birch (De)	–	4	7	–	130	236	33.71	1	1	1
† T.R.Birt (De)	–	13	24	1	162	884	38.43	2	5	22
† I.D.Blackwell (Sm)	2001	15	19	2	141	667	39.23	1	5	2
N.Boje (Nh)	–	4	7	1	125	251	41.83	1	1	1
† D.E.Bollinger (Wo)	2007[c]	7	8	2	21	38	6.33	–	–	–
R.S.Bopara (Ex/EA)	2005	12	18	2	229	960	60.00	3	4	5
P.M.Borrington (De)	–	1	2	–	50	64	32.00	–	1	2
R.R.Bose (Ind)	–	2	–	–	–	–	–	–	–	1
† A.G.Botha (De/Wa)	2004	16	23	1	101	447	20.31	1	2	12
M.D.Bott (CU)	–	3	5	1	12*	21	5.25	–	–	2
† M.A.G.Boyce (Le)	–	1	1	–	5	5	5.00	–	–	–
D.P.Bradshaw (OU)	–	3	6	2	96	182	45.50	–	1	–
† W.D.Bragg (Gm)	–	2	4	–	24	51	12.75	–	–	–
R.M.R.Brathwaite (LU/MCC)	–	4	7	1	76*	99	16.50	–	1	–
D.J.Bravo (WI)	–	4	7	–	56	291	41.57	–	2	7
† J.P.Bray (Ire)	–	1	1	–	146	146	146.00	1	–	–
G.R.Breese (Du)	–	5	10	1	53	145	16.11	–	1	6
T.T.Bresnan (Y/EA)	2006	16	21	7	126*	679	48.50	3	2	6
† S.C.J.Broad (Le/EA)	2007	6	7	2	91*	247	49.40	–	2	–
G.L.Brophy (Y)	–	13	19	1	100*	593	32.94	1	2	35/3
A.D.Brown (Sy)	1994	9	14	2	69	277	23.08	–	3	7
B.C.Brown (Sx)	–	1	1	–	46	46	46.00	–	–	4
D.O.Brown (Gs)	2006	3	6	–	43	92	15.33	–	–	–
J.F.Brown (Nh)	2000	14	17	6	25	108	9.81	–	–	3
† K.R.Brown (La)	–	1	2	–	27	27	13.50	–	–	1
M.J.Brown (H)	2007	16	29	4	126*	1078	43.12	3	5	14
J.T.A.Bruce (H)	2006	14	18	7	32	84	7.63	–	–	4
T.G.Burrows (H)	–	1	1	–	35	35	35.00	–	–	4
† M.A.Butcher (Sy)	1996	14	21	2	179	752	39.57	2	2	14
S.M.Butler (MCC)	–	2	4	2	21*	36	18.00	–	–	–
J.E.L.Buttleman (DU)	–	1	2	–	12	16	8.00	–	–	–
A.R.Caddick (Sm)	1992	16	13	2	51	147	13.36	–	1	2
† M.A.Carberry (H)	2006	13	24	3	192*	1067	50.80	5	3	2
† N.M.Carter (Wa)	2005	3	5	2	27	56	18.66	–	–	1
† S.Chanderpaul (WI/Du)	–	7	12	3	136*	670	74.44	2	5	4
G.Chapple (La)	1994	12	16	1	88	338	22.53	–	2	4
S.P.Cheetham (La)	–	1	–	–	–	–	–	–	–	–
† D.D.Cherry (Gm)	–	7	12	–	48	198	16.50	–	–	3
M.J.Chilton (La)	2002	14	24	2	115	616	28.00	1	2	7
A.S.Chopra (MCC)	–	1	2	–	106	113	56.50	1	–	1
V.Chopra (Ex)	–	16	26	3	86	649	28.21	–	5	15
S.H.Choudhry (MCC)	–	1	2	–	54*	61	–	–	1	–
J.L.Clare (De)	–	2	3	–	22	42	14.00	–	–	–
S.R.Clark (H)	2007	6	9	2	17	71	10.14	–	–	3
R.Clarke (Sy)	2005	10	14	1	68*	301	23.15	–	2	10
† M.E.Claydon (Du)	–	2	1	1	14*	14	–	–	–	–
S.J.Cliff (Le)	–	2	3	2	11	21	21.00	–	–	–
† R.S.Clinton (Sy)	–	3	2	–	0	0	0.00	–	–	1
G.D.Clough (Nt)	–	1	2	–	7	9	4.50	–	–	–

F-C	Cap	M	I	NO	HS	Runs	Avge	100	50	Ct/St
J.J.Cobb (Le)	–	1	2	–	21	23	11.50	–	–	–
A.Codrington (Can)	–	1	2	–	4	4	2.00	–	–	–
† K.J.Coetzer (Du)	–	14	26	3	153*	880	38.26	2	2	14
P.D.Collingwood (E/Du)	1998	8	15	1	128	614	43.85	2	3	11
C.D.Collymore (WI)	–	4	7	2	16*	37	7.40	–	–	–
N.R.D.Compton (MCC/M)	2006	11	18	–	67	399	22.16	–	3	6
† A.N.Cook (E/Ex/MCC)	2005	11	20	–	142	1094	54.70	5	3	12
S.J.Cook (K)	2007	12	14	5	50*	151	16.77	–	1	4
D.G.Cork (La)	2004	13	17	4	48*	329	25.30	–	–	4
D.A.Cosker (Gm)	2000	11	16	2	30	137	9.78	–	–	2
P.S.Coverdale (Nh)	–	1	1	–	11	11	11.00	–	–	–
J.P.Crawley (H)	2002	15	27	5	113*	866	39.36	1	6	4
R.D.B.Croft (Gm)	1992	16	24	2	115	595	24.79	1	1	10
S.J.Croft (La)	–	11	19	2	65	328	19.29	–	2	12
A.R.Crook (Nh)	–	5	9	1	72	269	33.62	–	2	4
S.P.Crook (Nh)	–	10	16	3	60	344	26.46	–	2	3
G.D.Cross (La)	–	1	2	1	61*	71	71.00	–	1	4/2
R.A.G.Cummins (Le)	–	5	9	3	34*	104	17.33	–	–	2
S.M.J.Cusden (De)	–	1	1	–	14	14	14.00	–	–	–
L.M.Daggett (Wa)	–	3	4	2	33	42	21.00	–	–	–
J.W.M.Dalrymple (M)	2004	12	17	2	57	305	20.33	–	1	3
Danish Kaneria (Ex)	2004	13	16	1	65	216	14.40	–	1	1
A.M.Davies (Du/Nt)	2005	11	13	5	35*	102	12.75	–	–	5
† A.P.Davies (Gm)	2007	7	12	6	54	220	36.66	–	1	3
† S.M.Davies (MCC/Wo)	2005c	16	27	3	87	753	31.37	–	4	47/4
J.M.Davison (Can)	–	1	2	–	28	28	14.00	–	–	–
L.A.Dawson (H)	–	1								
R.K.J.Dawson (Nh)	–	3	4	1	26	45	15.00	–	–	2
† K.J.Dean (De)	1998	10	12	6	16	46	7.66	–	–	2
J.L.Denly (K/EA)	–	16	27	3	115*	1003	41.79	2	6	9
J.W.Dernbach (Sy)	–	4	4	1	10	16	5.33	–	–	1
N.J.Dexter (K)	–	8	10	2	86	350	43.75	–	3	6
M.S.Dhoni (Ind)	–	6	10	1	92	302	33.55	–	3	7/2
M.G.Dighton (De)	–	7	14	1	68	418	32.15	–	2	10
L.A.Dingle (OU)	–	1	1	–	0	0	0.00	–	–	–
† M.J.Di Venuto (Du)	–	13	25	5	204*	1329	66.45	3	9	21
P.G.Dixey (DU/MCC)	–	4	8	–	25	84	10.50	–	–	9/1
W.T.Dobson (DU)	–	1	2	1	13*	14	14.00	–	–	–
N.D.Doshi (Sy)	2006	5	6	1	15	42	8.40	–	–	1
R.Dravid (Ind)	–	5	10	4	67*	295	49.16	–	3	4
C.B.R.Duffell (OU)	–	3	5	1	6	15	3.75	–	–	5
P.R.Dunbar (OU)	–	1	1	–	2	2	2.00	–	–	–
W.J.Durston (Sm)	–	3	4	1	58	140	46.66	–	2	–
M.A.Ealham (Nt)	2004	13	16	4	74*	300	25.00	–	2	16
† B.M.Edmondson (Gs)	2007	6	2	18	28	28	7.00	–	–	2
F.H.Edwards (WI)	–	3	5	2	7*	12	4.00	–	–	–
† N.J.Edwards (Sm)	–	17	26	–	212	1251	48.11	2	8	10
† M.T.G.Elliott (Gm)	2000	4	6	–	95	251	41.83	–	2	6
† S.M.Ervine (H)	2005	7	10	2	103*	276	34.50	1	1	5
D.Evans (M)	–	4	5	1	7	7	1.75	–	–	1
L.Evans (Du)	–	1	2	1	1	1	1.00	–	–	–
L.J.Evans (DU/MCC)	–	4	8	1	133*	365	52.14	1	2	4

142

F-C	Cap	M	I	NO	HS	Runs	Avge	100	50	Ct/St
R.S.Ferley (Nt)	–	3	3	2	43*	85	85.00	–	–	–
† C.S.Fernando (SLA)	–	1	2	–	4	5	2.50	–	–	1
S.T.Finn (M)	–	3	5	2	3	4	1.33	–	–	–
† I.D.Fisher (Gs)	2004	3	6	–	41	67	11.16	–	–	1
† S.P.Fleming (Nt)	2005	11	17	1	243	930	58.12	4	2	21
A.Flintoff (La)	1998	3	4	–	61	128	32.00	–	1	4
G.W.Flower (Ex)	2005	11	16	1	203	611	40.73	2	1	17
M.H.A.Footitt (Nt)	–	3								–
† E.J.Foster (LU)	–	3	6	–	34	81	13.50	–	–	4/1
J.S.Foster (Ex)	2001	15	23	1	204	827	37.59	1	5	31/5
P.J.Foster (DU)	–	5	5	–	19	46	9.20	–	–	1
M.J.Fourie (Ire)	–	1	1	–	0	0	0.00	–	–	–
† J.D.Francis (Sm)	–	1	2	–	30	40	20.00	–	–	–
S.R.G.Francis (Nt)	–	2								1
† P.J.Franks (Nt)	1999	11	13	1	92	275	22.91	–	1	5
M.J.Friedlander (CU)	–	3	3	–	36	55	18.33	–	–	2
T.J.Froggett (OU)	–	1	1	1	21*	21	–	–	–	1
† A.W.Gale (Y)	–	6	8	–	68	223	27.87	–	2	5
J.E.R.Gallian (Nt)	1998	17	25	–	178	940	37.60	2	4	9
† G.Gambhir (Ind)	–	2	4	1	81	208	69.33	–	3	2
W.C.A.Ganegama (SLA)	–	4	6	2	20	39	9.75	–	–	2
D.Ganga (WI)	–	5	9	1	49	152	19.00	–	–	4
† S.C.Ganguly (Ind)	–	4	7	1	79	263	43.83	–	2	1
† C.H.Gayle (WI)	–	5	8	1	52	220	31.42	–	1	3
O.D.Gibson (Du)	–	15	23	2	71	578	27.52	–	4	6
A.P.R.Gidman (Gs/MCC)	2004	17	29	4	130	1003	40.12	3	5	10
† W.R.S.Gidman (Du)	–	1	2	–	8	8	4.00	–	–	–
W.M.Gifford (LU)	–	3	6	1	71	174	34.80	–	2	1
C.R.Gilbert (Y)	–	1	1	–	64	64	64.00	–	1	1
J.N.Gillespie (Y)	2007	12	13	5	123*	270	33.75	1	–	3
P.G.Gillespie (Ire)	–	1	1	–	18	18	18.00	–	–	1
L.J.Goddard (Du)	–	1	2	–	52	59	29.50	–	1	5
† B.A.Godleman (M)	–	15	24	2	113*	842	38.27	1	6	22
M.W.Goodwin (Sx)	2001	15	27	5	205*	1214	55.18	4	5	10
D.Gough (Y)	1993	14	15	1	50	219	15.64	–	1	2
R.N.Grant (Gm)	–	8	13	–	79	350	26.92	–	2	1
J.A.G.Green (Sx)	–	1	1	–	28	28	28.00	–	–	–
C.G.Greenidge (Gs)	2005	8	11	1	27	95	9.50	–	–	3
† D.A.Griffiths (H)	–	5	8	3	31*	42	8.40	–	–	1
T.D.Groenewald (Wa)	–	8	9	2	41*	133	19.00	–	–	8
† K.D.Gunawardene (SLA)	–	1	2	–	25	44	22.00	–	–	1
H.F.Gurney (Le)	–	1	2	1	1	1	1.00	–	–	–
S.M.Guy (Y)	–	4	5	–	37	115	23.00	–	–	11
A.J.Hall (K)	2005	7	10	1	77	264	29.33	–	2	6
Harbhajan Singh (Sy)	–	6	7	1	29	82	13.66	–	–	3
M.A.Hardinges (Gs)	2004	9	15	1	104	335	23.92	1	1	6
† A.Harinath (LU)	–	3	5	–	69	128	25.60	–	2	3
† B.W.Harmison (Du)	–	9	16	2	101	358	25.57	1	2	7
S.J.Harmison (E/Du/MCC)	1999	12	16	5	30	162	14.72	–	–	1
A.J.Harris (Nt)	2000	6	9	2	15*	39	5.57	–	–	2
J.A.R.Harris (Gm)	–	9	14	2	87*	196	16.33	–	1	4
P.L.Harris (Wa)	–	4	3	–	55	59	19.66	–	1	–

143

F-C	Cap	M	I	NO	HS	Runs	Avge	100	50	Ct/St
P.W.Harrison (Le)	–	1	1	–	1	1	1.00	–	–	1
I.J.Harvey (De)	–	2	3	1	153	289	144.50	2	–	4
T.L.Hemingway (CU)	–	1	1	–	4	4	4.00	–	–	1
† D.L.Hemp (Gm)	1994	15	25	1	152*	827	34.45	1	5	8
C.W.Henderson (Le)	–	10	13	–	81	326	25.07	–	1	3
† M.R.K.B.Herath (SLA)	–	4	6	2	40	76	19.00	–	–	3
J.J.N.Heywood (CU)	–	1	1	–	0	0	0.00	–	–	2
G.A.Hick (Wo)	1986	15	24	1	110	963	41.86	2	6	16
J.C.Hildreth (Sm)	2007	17	26	2	163	1270	52.91	4	6	15
† C.M.M.Hill (OU)	–	1	1	–	0	0	0.00	–	–	1
M.H.Hobbiss (OU)	–	1	1	–	15	15	15.00	–	–	–
A.J.Hodd (Sx)	–	14	21	5	123	628	39.25	2	2	21/7
B.J.Hodge (La)	2006	8	13	2	156*	354	32.18	1	–	4
R.Hodgkinson (De)	–	1	1	–	6	6	6.00	–	–	–
G.P.Hodnett (Gs)	2005	15	25	1	168	886	36.91	2	6	8
† K.W.Hogg (La/Nt/Wo)	2007c	6	6	2	30	110	27.50	–	–	1
M.J.Hoggard (E/MCC/Y)	2000	13	11	2	61	121	13.44	–	1	2
S.M.Hole (Wa)	–	1	2	1	24	24	24.00	–	–	–
† J.H.P.Hooper (OU)	–	3	6	–	79	151	25.16	–	1	1
C.D.Hopkinson (Sx)	–	10	17	–	83	347	20.41	–	2	10
P.J.Horton (La)	2007	14	25	2	152	1116	48.52	3	5	17
T.H.Howell (OU)	–	1	2	–	82	82	41.00	–	1	–
J.A.Hughes (LU)	–	3	5	1	45	105	26.25	–	–	–
I.D.Hunter (De)	–	1	1	1	1*	1	–	–	–	–
† C.J.Huntington (CU)	–	3	5	–	40	74	14.80	–	–	1
D.J.Hussey (Nt)	2004	13	17	2	275	1259	83.93	4	5	16
† B.L.Hutton (M)	2003	4	7	1	118	230	38.33	1	–	4
Imran Tahir (Y)	–	1	2	–	5	5	2.50	–	–	–
Inzamam-ul-Haq (Y)	–	3	4	–	51	89	22.25	–	1	5
R.C.Irani (Ex)	1994	4	6	2	218	465	116.25	2	–	4
A.J.Ireland (Gs)	2007	3	5	3	10*	21	10.50	–	–	2
B.D.Jacklin (CU)	–	1	1	–	7	7	7.00	–	–	1
† A.Jacobs (Le)	–	6	9	2	55	184	26.28	–	1	5
D.J.Jacobs (Nh)	–	4	8	–	56	143	17.87	–	1	2
W.Jaffer (Ind)	–	6	12	1	62	327	29.72	–	3	1
G.D.James (CU)	–	2	3	–	51	71	23.66	–	1	–
† P.A.Jaques (Wo)	2006c	10	17	–	124	541	31.82	2	1	6
† S.T.Jayasuriya (La/MCC)	–	2	2	–	38	56	28.00	–	–	–
W.I.Jefferson (Nt)	–	5	9	–	73	316	35.11	–	1	3
K.A.Jogia (CU)	–	3	5	1	74	161	40.25	–	1	4
R.L.Johnson (M)	1995	4	4	–	39	48	12.00	–	–	1
D.T.Johnston (Ire)	–	1	1	–	9	9	9.00	–	–	–
G.O.Jones (K)	2003	15	21	3	106*	623	34.61	2	3	42/4
P.S.Jones (Sm)	2001	13	12	4	114	255	31.87	1	1	3
R.A.Jones (Wo)	2007c	3	5	1	24	38	9.50	–	–	1
† S.P.Jones (Gm)	2002	4	7	1	39	86	14.33	–	–	–
C.J.Jordan (Sy)	–	5	6	2	34	97	24.25	–	–	1
R.H.Joseph (K)	–	3	5	4	36*	60	60.00	–	–	2
S.C.Joseph (WI)	–	2	3	–	41	55	18.33	–	–	1
† E.C.Joyce (M)	2002	14	20	2	106	704	39.11	1	4	5
S.Jyoti (Can)	–	1	2	–	2	2	1.00	–	–	–
T.Kalam (OU)	–	3	5	2	64	111	37.00	–	1	2

144

F-C	Cap	M	I	NO	HS	Runs	Avge	100	50	Ct/St
† S.H.T.Kandamby (SLA)	–	1	2	–	45	63	31.50	–	–	–
C.K.Kapugedara (SLA)	–	1	1	–	9	9	9.00	–	–	3
KD Karthik (Ind)	–	6	12	–	91	448	37.33	–	5	12
† M.Kartik (M)	2007	12	15	4	35*	209	19.00	–	–	12
† S.M.Katich (De)	2007	13	23	6	221	1284	75.52	3	8	9
† G.Keedy (La)	2000	10	9	5	9	34	8.50	–	–	3
R.A.Kemp (CU)	–	2	2	1	7	7	7.00	–	–	1
R.W.T.Key (K)	2001	15	25	3	182	1250	56.81	5	4	4
Z.Khan (Ind)	–	4	5	1	28	56	14.00	–	–	2
C.Kieswetter (Sm)	–	14	16	3	93	377	29.00	–	3	46
N.Killeen (Du)	1999	2	–	–	–	–	–	–	–	–
R.E.King (LU/MCC)	–	4	7	–	22	67	9.57	–	–	–
S.P.Kirby (Gs)	2005	11	13	1	37	119	9.91	–	–	1
R.J.Kirtley (Sx)	1998	7	8	2	51	98	16.33	–	1	6
† F.A.Klokker (De)	–	2	3	1	100*	171	85.50	1	–	3
† L.Klusener (Nh)	2006	16	26	5	122	1013	48.23	2	5	6
J.P.T.Knappett (Wo)	2007[c]	1	2	–	7	11	5.50	–	–	–
G.J-P.Kruger (Le)	–	4	4	–	15	28	7.00	–	–	1
G.J.Kruis (Y)	2006	6	6	3	20	44	14.66	–	–	1
A.Kumble (Ind)	–	5	7	2	110*	177	35.40	1	–	2
N.J.Lamb (DU)	–	3	6	–	32	84	14.00	–	–	2
† J.L.Langer (Sm)	2007	16	23	1	315	1231	55.95	3	3	14
C.K.Langeveldt (Le)	–	3	4	3	10*	25	25.00	–	–	–
D.Langford-Smith (Ire)	–	1	1	–	1*	1	–	–	–	–
S.G.Law (La)	2002	14	22	2	206	1277	63.85	3	9	17
M.A.K.Lawson (Y)	–	2	2	1	5	9	9.00	–	–	1
V.V.S.Laxman (Ind/La)	–	11	18	2	103	713	44.56	2	5	15
R.J.H.Lett (OU)	–	3	6	1	57	143	28.60	–	2	2
J.Lewis (Gs)	1998	8	8	1	42*	91	13.00	–	–	2
L.J.Lewis (LU)	–	2	4	–	21	26	6.50	–	–	1
† J.D.Lewry (Sx)	1996	14	14	6	13*	73	9.12	–	–	4
C.J.Liddle (Sx)	–	5	5	1	53	99	24.75	–	1	3
R.J.Logan (Nh)	–	7	8	3	10	32	6.40	–	–	1
K.S.Lokuarachchi (SLA)	–	3	6	–	45	166	27.66	–	–	–
A.G.R.Loudon (MCC/Wa)	2006	16	24	1	105	782	34.00	3	2	9
M.B.Loye (La)	2003	8	14	2	105*	427	35.58	1	1	5
D.S.Lucas (Nh)	–	9	13	4	37	215	23.88	–	–	2
† M.J.Lumb (H)	2003	16	25	–	89	775	31.00	–	8	13
† T.Lungley (De)	2007	15	21	6	30*	169	11.26	–	–	5
† A.Lyth (Y)	–	1	1	–	31	31	31.00	–	–	–
J.C.Macadam (OU)	–	1	1	–	7	7	7.00	–	–	–
W.K.McCallan (Ire)	–	1	1	–	2	2	2.00	–	–	1
A.C.McGarry (Ex)	–	4	2	1	10	15	15.00	–	–	1
A.McGrath (Y)	1999	14	22	2	188*	931	46.55	3	6	11
N.D.McKenzie (Sm)	–	3	5	1	84	271	67.75	–	3	2
† R.McLaren (K)	2007	15	18	5	54*	272	20.92	–	1	7
S.K.MacLennan (CU)	–	1	2	1	5	9	9.00	–	–	–
C.D.McMillan (MCC)	–	1	2	–	2	2	1.00	–	–	–
D.L.Maddy (Wa)	2007	14	20	3	148*	796	46.82	4	2	14
† S.J.Magoffin (Sy)	–	1	2	1	9*	15	15.00	–	–	–
† J.P.Maher (Gm)	2001	8	15	–	55	252	16.80	–	1	9
S.I.Mahmood (La)	2007	10	14	3	41	148	13.45	–	–	3

145

F-C	Cap	M	I	NO	HS	Runs	Avge	100	50	Ct/St
R.J.A.Malcolm-Hansen (LU)	–	1	2	–	30	35	17.50	–	–	–
M.N.Malik (Nt/Wo)	2004c	14	19	8	24*	104	9.45	–	–	5
S.L.Malinga (K)	–	4	3	1	12	13	6.50	–	–	–
Mansoor Amjad (Le)	–	9	13	2	105*	319	29.00	1	1	6
H.J.H.Marshall (Gs)	2006	13	21	1	123	817	40.85	3	3	9
S.J.Marshall (La)	–	1	1	–	7	7	7.00	–	–	1
R.S.C.Martin-Jenkins (Sx)	2000	15	22	6	99	521	32.56	–	2	8
A.D.Mascarenhas (H)	1998	10	16	2	90	489	34.92	–	3	2
M.S.Mason (Wo)	2002c	1	2	–	15	15	7.50	–	–	–
I.R.Massey (CU)	–	3	5	–	65	143	28.60	–	1	–
D.D.Masters (Le)	2007	11	16	2	46	242	17.28	–	–	1
† J.K.Maunders (Le)	–	13	22	–	97	575	26.13	–	4	12
T.L.Maynard (Gm)	–	2	3	–	18	35	11.66	–	–	–
† B.G.A.S.Mendis (OU)	–	1	1	–	0	0	0.00	–	–	–
J.D.Middlebrook (Ex)	2003	17	24	6	127	583	32.38	1	3	15
D.K.H.Mitchell (Wo)	2005c	5	8	2	112	260	43.33	1	1	7
B.R.Modha (CU)	–	3	3	–	27	41	13.66	–	–	2
Mohammad Akram (Sy)	2006	3	6	2	8*	17	4.25	–	–	–
Mohammad Amin (CU)	–	3	3	–	1	1	0.33	–	–	–
Mohammad Nabi (MCC)	–	1	2	–	43	61	30.50	–	–	–
R.R.Montgomerie (Sx)	1999	17	29	1	195	1129	40.32	2	7	31
S.C.Moore (Wo)	2003c	15	25	1	143	882	36.75	2	3	7
† E.J.G.Morgan (Ire/M)	–	6	8	–	84	311	38.87	–	4	5
J.C.Morris (DU/MCC)	–	5	10	–	67	259	25.90	–	2	6
E.J.Morse (OU)	–	3	4	–	4	5	1.25	–	–	1
R.S.Morton (WI)	–	5	8	–	201	347	43.37	1	1	8
† W.J.Mottram (OU)	–	1	2	–	9	11	5.50	–	–	–
† J.Mubarak (SLA)	–	1	1	–	62	62	62.00	–	1	–
G.J.Muchall (Du)	2005	12	22	1	66	520	24.76	–	4	9
A.A.Mulla (Can)	–	1	2	–	48	51	25.50	–	–	1
S.J.Mullaney (La)	–	1	1	1	165*	165	–	1	–	2
M.K.Munday (Sm)	–	3	3	1	9	13	6.50	–	–	2
M.Muralitharan (La)	1999	8	7	5	28	58	29.00	–	–	1
C.P.Murtagh (LU)	–	3	6	–	107	161	26.83	1	–	3
† T.J.Murtagh (M)	–	14	16	1	40	267	17.80	–	–	2
Murtaza Hussain (Sy)	–	2	2	1	9*	15	15.00	–	–	1
Mushtaq Ahmed (Sx)	2003	15	17	3	54	170	12.14	–	1	3
† P.Mustard (Du)	–	17	31	2	76	743	25.62	–	4	70/3
J.K.H.Naik (Le/LU)	–	3	5	3	15	46	23.00	–	–	2
G.R.Napier (Ex)	2003	10	10	3	125	317	45.28	1	1	4
C.D.Nash (Sx)	–	17	30	–	89	835	27.83	–	7	10
D.C.Nash (M)	2000	7	10	3	103*	426	60.85	3	–	20/2
Naved-ul-Hasan (Sx)	2005	14	18	1	75	251	14.76	–	1	5
J.Needham (De)	–	4	6	2	48	125	31.25	–	–	2
A.Nel (Ex)	–	4	5	1	10	19	4.75	–	–	–
J.D.Nel (Wo)	2007c	5	8	6	8	30	15.00	–	–	1
† M.A.G.Nelson (Nh)	–	1	1	–	13	13	13.00	–	–	1
† T.J.New (Le)	–	16	29	3	125	957	36.80	1	8	20/1
O.J.Newby (La)	–	9	8	1	26	48	6.85	–	–	2
† S.A.Newman (Sy)	2005	15	25	–	124	812	32.48	1	5	17
M.J.Nicholson (Sy)	2007	12	12	4	48*	240	30.00	–	–	6
† P.A.Nixon (Le)	1994	13	21	3	126	879	48.83	2	5	36/1

146

F-C	Cap	M	I	NO	HS	Runs	Avge	100	50	Ct/St
A.A.Noffke (Gs)	2007	3	5	–	61	109	21.80	–	1	1
† M.J.North (Gs)	2007	5	10	–	109	565	56.50	3	2	4
S.A.Northeast (K)	–	1	2	–	5	5	2.50	–	–	–
K.J.O'Brien (Ire)	–	1	1	–	35	35	35.00	–	–	1
† N.J.O'Brien (Nh)	–	8	13	2	109	249	22.63	1	–	23/2
W.J.F.O'Driscoll (CU)	–	2	1	–	28	28	28.00	–	–	1
G.Onions (Du/MCC/EA)	–	14	17	5	41	213	17.75	–	–	3
J.Ormond (Sy)	2003	7	10	2	25*	83	10.37	–	–	1
M.P.O'Shea (Gm)	–	2	2	–	10	10	5.00	–	–	–
H.Osinde (Can)	–	1	2	–	8	12	6.00	–	–	–
F.G.Owen (CU)	–	1	1	–	41	41	41.00	–	–	–
W.T.Owen (Gm)	–	1	–	–	–	–	–	–	–	–
C.D.Paget (DU)	–	2	4	–	46	66	16.50	–	–	3
A.P.Palladino (Ex)	–	7	8	2	18	51	8.50	–	–	1
† M.S.Panesar (E/Nh)	2006	12	15	2	33	121	9.30	–	–	3
G.T.Park (Du)	–	4	7	–	61	177	25.28	–	2	1
L.C.Parker (Wa)	–	5	6	–	49	81	13.50	–	–	3
S.D.Parry (La)	–	1	–	–	–	–	–	–	–	–
T.W.Parsons (LU)	–	2	3	–	10	10	3.33	–	–	–
† A.Patel (De)	–	1	2	1	31	43	43.00	–	–	–
M.M.Patel (K)	1994	1	2	–	52	67	33.50	–	1	1
S.R.Patel (Nt)	–	14	20	1	176	963	50.68	4	5	8
S.A.Patterson (Y)	–	1	–	–	–	–	–	–	–	–
N.Peng (Gm)	–	3	6	–	65	111	18.50	–	1	2
† C.T.Peploe (M)	–	2	2	–	13	20	10.00	–	–	2
M.D.K.Perera (SLA)	–	4	8	2	57	229	38.16	–	1	–
S.D.Peters (Nh)	2007	16	30	2	112	966	34.50	3	4	14
M.L.Pettini (Ex)	2006	17	27	1	86*	64	23.23	–	6	17
† T.J.Phillips (Ex)	2006	10	14	–	68	193	13.78	–	1	4
M.J.Phythian (DU)	–	2	3	–	41	66	22.00	–	–	1
K.P.Pietersen (E (H))	2005	7	13	–	226	811	62.38	4	1	5
D.J.Pipe (De)	2007	14	21	5	133*	577	36.06	2	1	42/4
L.E.Plunkett (E/Du)	–	15	23	5	59*	367	20.38	–	2	10
† W.T.S.Porterfield (Ire/MCC)	–	2	3	–	54	75	25.00	–	1	2
N.Pothas (H)	2003	15	23	7	126*	750	46.87	1	5	36/6
R.R.Powar (Ind)	–	2	2	1	14*	18	18.00	–	–	2
D.B.L.Powell (WI/H)	–	8	12	1	36*	130	11.81	–	–	1
M.J.Powell (Gm)	2000	6	10	2	114	407	50.87	1	4	4
M.J.Powell (Wa)	1999	4	6	–	82	165	27.50	–	1	2
T.Poynton (De)	–	2	3	–	2	2	0.66	–	–	3
K.T.G.D.Prasad (SLA)	–	2	4	1	89	164	54.66	–	1	1
R.W.Price (Wo)	2004c	2	4	1	15*	24	8.00	–	–	–
M.J.Prior (E/Sx)	2003	11	19	2	126*	555	32.64	1	2	31/2
C.G.Prowting (MCC)	–	1	2	–	48	50	25.00	–	–	–
N.R.Prowting (DU)	–	3	6	–	78	167	27.83	–	1	2
R.M.Pyrah (Y)	–	1	1	–	106	106	106.00	1	–	–
Qaiser Ali (Can)	–	1	2	–	9	15	7.50	–	–	–
D.Ramdin (WI)	–	5	8	–	131	258	32.25	1	1	14/1
† R.Rampaul (WI)	–	1	–	–	–	–	–	–	–	–
M.R.Ramprakash (Sy)	2002	15	25	5	266*	2026	101.30	10	4	13
† W.M.G.Ramyakumara (SLA)	–	2	3	–	68	80	26.66	–	1	–
† W.B.Rankin (De)	–	3	4	1	3	5	1.66	–	–	3

147

F-C	Cap	M	I	NO	HS	Runs	Avge	100	50	Ct/St
A.U.Rashid (MCC/Y/EA)	–	17	23	4	108	837	44.05	1	7	9
O.P.Rayner (Sx)	–	4	5	1	39	61	15.25	–	–	3
C.M.W.Read (Nt)	1999	17	23	4	240	1001	52.68	2	4	42/6
† D.J.Redfern (De)	–	5	7	1	51	180	30.00	–	1	5
† G.P.Rees (Gm)	–	10	18	–	109	429	23.83	2	2	8
† M.A.Richards (MCC/OU)	–	4	6	–	26	72	12.00	–	–	2
A.Richardson (M)	2005	14	13	5	24*	104	13.00	–	–	5
W.H.Rist (CU)	–	2	2	–	10	13	6.50	–	–	–
D.D.J.Robinson (Le)	2007	8	14	1	122	407	31.30	1	1	4
† C.J.L.Rogers (Nh)	–	8	14	1	138	402	30.92	1	3	13
M.C.Rosenberg (Le)	–	7	8	1	64*	130	18.57	–	1	2
D.T.Rowe (Le)	–	5	6	1	85	137	27.40	–	1	–
W.D.Rudge (Gs)	2005	1	2	1	3*	3	3.00	–	–	–
† J.A.Rudolph (Y)	2007	15	22	3	220	1078	56.73	4	3	19
L.C.Ryan (OU)	–	1	2	–	4	5	2.50	–	–	–
† J.L.Sadler (Le)	–	10	17	–	45	304	17.88	–	–	7
O.J.Sadler (OU)	–	1	2	1	62*	70	70.00	–	1	1
O.H.J.Saffell (De)	–	1	1	1	35*	35	–	–	–	–
M.J.Saggers (Ex/K)	2001	9	8	2	16	49	8.16	–	–	–
N.C.Saker (Sy)	–	8	9	3	19	74	12.33	–	–	1
D.J.G.Sales (Nh)	1999	16	29	4	219	1384	55.36	3	7	23
I.D.K.Salisbury (Sy)	1998	6	9	–	103	174	19.33	1	–	4
A.M.Samad (Can)	–	1	2	–	29	36	18.00	–	–	1
T.T.Samaraweera (SLA)	–	4	7	–	79	277	39.57	–	2	1
D.J.G.Sammy (WI)	–	2	3	–	25	44	14.66	–	–	2
M.N.Samuels (WI)	–	1	2	–	19	21	10.50	–	–	1
C.J.L.Sandbach (OU)	–	2	4	–	8	14	3.50	–	–	2
† K.C.Sangakkara (Wa)	2007	7	11	1	149	496	49.60	2	2	4
Saqlain Mushtaq (Sx)	–	4	5	1	57*	90	22.50	–	1	1
R.R.Sarwan (WI)	–	2	1	–	35	35	35.00	–	–	–
† J.J.Sayers (Y)	2007	14	22	3	187	644	33.89	3	1	5
† C.P.Schofield (Sy)	–	6	7	1	28	86	14.33	–	–	3
B.J.M.Scott (M)	2007	11	14	3	112	389	35.36	1	2	23/5
B.M.Shafayat (Nt)	–	12	19	1	79	560	31.11	–	4	15/1
O.A.Shah (E/MCC/M/EA)	2000	13	22	6	193	1135	70.93	4	2	10
A.Shahzad (Y)	–	6	7	3	32*	65	16.25	–	–	1
† A.J.Shantry (Wa)	–	2	3	–	5	10	3.33	–	–	1
† Z.K.Sharif (CU/MCC)	–	3	6	1	55*	157	31.40	–	1	1
I.Sharma (Ind)	–	2	1	1	0*	0	–	–	–	–
C.E.Shreck (Nt)	2006	11	11	8	3	4	1.33	–	–	6
† R.J.Sidebottom (E/Nt)	2004	13	17	6	26*	169	15.36	–	–	3
R.J.Sillence (Wo)	2006c	10	13	2	51*	202	18.36	–	1	4
J.K.Silva (SLA)	–	3	5	3	118*	208	104.00	1	–	7/1
C.E.W.Silverwood (M)	2006	11	10	1	30	110	12.22	–	–	2
R.P.Singh (Ind/Le)	2007	6	9	1	41*	99	12.37	–	–	4
B.D.Smith (CU)	–	1	1	–	13	13	13.00	–	–	1
B.F.Smith (Wo)	2002c	14	22	2	98*	559	27.95	–	6	11
† B.M.Smith (CU)	–	3	3	1	11*	13	–	–	–	–
† D.S.Smith (WI)	–	5	8	–	42	165	20.62	–	–	4
E.T.Smith (M)	2005	17	25	4	149*	1219	58.04	5	4	4
G.M.Smith (De)	–	12	20	2	74	407	22.61	–	3	4
† T.C.Smith (La)	–	6	6	2	44	119	29.75	–	–	4

F-C	Cap	M	I	NO	HS	Runs	Avge	100	50	Ct/St
T.M.J.Smith (Sx)	–	1	1	–	2	2	2.00	–	–	–
W.R.Smith (Du)	–	12	23	–	105	551	23.95	1	–	7
S.D.Snell (Gs)	2005	4	8	–	12	57	7.12	–	–	8
V.S.Solanki (Wo)	1998	13	21	–	232	660	31.42	1	2	4
C.M.Spearman (Gs)	2002	11	17	–	110	688	40.47	2	3	15
M.N.W.Spriegel (LU)	–	3	6	1	30	100	20.00	–	–	4
† S.H.P.Spurway (Sm)	–	3	4	1	44*	46	15.33	–	–	9
S.Sreesanth (Ind)	–	5	7	3	35	48	12.00	–	–	1
T.P.Stayt (Gs)	2007	3	3	1	6	9	4.50	–	–	2
D.I.Stevens (K)	2005	11	17	–	174	628	36.94	2	2	7
D.W.Steyn (Wa)	2007	7	7	2	51	145	29.00	–	1	–
† M.D.Stoneman (Du)	–	8	15	–	101	369	24.60	1	1	5
† A.J.Strauss (E/M/EA)	2001	15	27	–	120	886	32.81	1	6	17
H.H.Streak (Wa)	2005	11	15	3	66	278	23.16	–	2	–
† S.D.Stubbings (De)	2001	16	31	3	128	876	31.28	2	2	7
S.B.Styris (Du)	–	5	10	–	48	210	21.00	–	–	–
A.V.Suppiah (Sm)	–	1	2	1	51	92	92.00	–	1	2
† I.J.Sutcliffe (La/Nh)	2003	5	9	2	104*	203	29.00	1	1	5
L.D.Sutton (La)	2007	15	19	3	111	587	36.68	2	1	42/2
G.P.Swann (Nt)	2005	16	20	4	97	516	32.25	–	3	15
N.Tahir (Wa)	–	11	11	1	32	87	8.70	–	–	–
B.Tavarasa (CU)	–	1	–	–	–	–	–	–	–	–
C.G.Taylor (Gs)	2001	15	23	4	112*	733	38.57	3	2	13
C.R.Taylor (De)	–	4	6	–	96	168	28.00	–	2	4
J.E.Taylor (WI/Le)	–	7	11	2	40	176	19.55	–	–	1
R.N.ten Doeschate (Ex)	2006	16	23	2	148	849	40.42	3	3	10
S.R.Tendulkar (Ind)	–	4	7	–	171	399	57.00	1	2	4
A.C.Thomas (Wa)	–	4	7	1	42	130	21.66	–	–	2
G.J.Thompson (DU)	–	1	2	–	38	38	19.00	–	–	–
† J.G.Thompson (Gs)	2007	1	2	–	21	32	16.00	–	–	–
M.A.Thornely (Sx)	–	2	3	–	11	15	5.00	–	–	4
N.D.Thornicroft (Y)	–	1	–	–	–	–	–	–	–	–
C.D.Thorp (Du)	–	2	4	1	30*	40	13.33	–	–	–
† J.A.Tomlinson (H)	–	5	4	2	9	19	9.50	–	–	1
† J.C.Tredwell (K)	2007	14	19	2	116*	454	26.70	1	2	11
P.D.Trego (Sm)	2007	17	22	6	130	836	52.25	2	5	4
C.T.Tremlett (E/H/EA)	2004	10	14	6	62*	232	29.00	–	1	3
† M.E.Trescothick (Sm)	1999	16	24	2	284	1343	61.04	4	5	34
I.J.L.Trott (Wa/EA)	2005	15	22	1	84	473	22.52	–	2	16
J.O.Troughton (Wa)	2002	14	19	1	162	771	42.83	3	1	1
A.J.Tudor (Ex)	–	10	13	3	35	112	11.20	–	–	3
M.L.Turner (Sm)	–	3	3	1	57	63	31.50	–	1	1
S.D.Udal (H)	1992	5	8	1	17*	34	4.85	–	–	–
† M.L.Udawatte (SLA)	–	3	6	1	57	171	34.20	–	2	1
† Umar Bhatti (Can)	–	1	2	2	22*	32	–	–	–	–
† W.P.U.C.J.Vaas (M)	2007	7	8	3	79	277	55.40	–	2	2
J.J.van der Wath (Nh)	–	10	15	3	94	346	28.83	–	3	3
† M.G.Vandort (SLA)	–	2	4	–	117	179	44.75	1	1	–
M.van Jaarsveld (SLA)	2005	15	23	1	166	1011	45.95	5	3	17
M.P.Vaughan (E/Y)	1995	12	19	2	124	758	44.58	2	3	2
G.G.Wagg (De)	2007	15	21	4	82	530	31.17	–	4	7
M.A.Wagh (Nt)	2007	17	26	2	152	1310	54.58	3	11	2

F-C	Cap	M	I	NO	HS	Runs	Avge	100	50	Ct/St
† D.J.Wainwright (Y)	–	1	1	1	46*	46	–	–	–	1
A.G.Wakely (Nh)	–	4	8	–	66	169	21.12	–	2	1
† M.J.Walker (K)	2000	12	18	–	157	733	40.72	3	2	6
N.G.E.Walker (Le)	–	8	11	5	31	143	23.83	–	–	4
† M.A.Wallace (Gm)	2003	16	27	–	128	669	24.77	2	1	40/6
S.J.Walters (Sy)	–	8	12	1	70	228	20.72	–	1	9
G.B.Ward (CU)	–	1	1	–	33	33	33.00	–	–	3
† B.S.M.Warnapura (SLA)	–	3	6	–	44	86	14.33	–	–	5
S.K.Warne (H)	2000	15	19	–	50	364	19.15	–	1	17
H.T.Waters (Gm)	–	10	16	8	33	87	10.87	–	–	4
† R.E.Watkins (Gm)	–	8	13	–	30	172	13.23	–	–	3
U.W.M.B.C.A.Welagedara (SLA)	–	4	3	1	1*	3	1.50	–	–	1
M.H.Wessels (Nh)	–	11	18	1	97	533	31.35	–	3	28/2
M.S.Westfield (Ex)	–	1	1	1	4*	4	–	–	–	–
T.Westley (Ex/MCC)	–	6	9	2	72	223	31.85	–	1	3
† W.P.C.Weston (De)	–	9	15	–	38	198	13.20	–	–	5
† I.J.Westwood (Wa)	–	14	22	2	116	771	38.55	2	5	8
A.G.Wharf (Gm)	2000	15	26	4	128*	726	33.00	3	1	7
S.J.Wheeler (LU)	–	3	5	1	13	33	8.25	–	–	1
C.D.Whelan (M)	–	1	1	–	0	0	0.00	–	–	–
A.R.White (Ire)	–	1	1	–	0	0	0.00	–	–	2
C.White (Y)	1993	11	18	–	117	446	24.77	1	2	4
C.L.White (Sm)	2007	12	19	4	241	1083	72.20	5	3	7
G.G.White (Nh)	–	3	2	–	65	71	35.50	–	1	1
R.A.White (Nh)	–	13	22	3	108	709	37.31	1	3	9
W.A.White (De)	–	4	6	–	19	61	10.16	–	–	3
D.H.Wigley (Nh)	–	10	13	3	70	223	22.30	–	2	6
R.E.M.Williams (DU/MCC/M)	–	5	8	4	15	30	7.50	–	–	2
† C.M.Willoughby (Sm)	2007	16	12	7	23*	58	11.60	–	–	2
P.J.Wilshaw (OU)	–	3	6	–	38	124	20.66	–	–	1
G.C.Wilson (Ire)	–	1	1	–	0	0	0.00	–	–	2
P.J.Wiseman (Du)	–	13	19	5	44	288	20.57	–	–	6
C.R.Woakes (Wa)	–	1	2	1	14*	23	23.00	–	–	1
J.R.Wood (DU)	–	2	4	–	31	76	19.00	–	–	2
M.J.Wood (MCC/Sm)	2005	2	3	–	35	55	18.33	–	–	1
M.J.Wood (Y)	2001	1	1	–	23	23	23.00	–	–	–
M.J.Wood (MCC)	–	1	2	1	6*	6	6.00	–	–	–
N.J.Woods (OU)	–	3	5	1	27	100	25.00	–	–	2
B.J.Wright (Gm)	–	11	18	2	108	329	20.56	1	1	13
C.J.C.Wright (M)	–	2	2	–	12	15	7.50	–	–	1
D.G.Wright (Gm)	–	1	2	–	1	1	0.50	–	–	1
L.J.Wright (Sx)	2007	11	13	6	61	347	49.57	–	3	3
† M.H.Yardy (Sx)	2005	13	21	2	125	732	38.52	2	5	11
Yasir Arafat (K)	2007	10	13	-1	122	369	30.75	2	–	2
† P.J.W.Young (OU)	–	3	6	–	54	132	22.00	–	1	1
Younus Khan (Y)	2007	13	19	2	217*	824	48.47	3	–	11
† Yuvraj Singh (Ind)	–	3	6	2	59	162	40.50	–	1	1

BOWLING

See BATTING and FIELDING section for details of matches, caps and teams

	Cat	O	M	R	W	Avge	Best	5wI	10wM
Abdul Razzaq (Wo)	RFM	67.3	15	219	6	36.50	2- 35	–	–
A.R.Adams (Nt)	RMF	137.1	29	501	14	35.78	4- 74	–	–
C.J.Adams (Sx)	RM/OB	4	0	9	0				
J.H.K.Adams (La)	LM	40	8	137	3	45.66	2- 37	–	–
U.Afzaal (Nh)	SLA	3	0	10	1	10.00	1- 5	–	–
J.S.Ahmed (Ex)	RMF	28.3	5	143	3	47.66	2- 41	–	–
Kabir Ali (Wo)	RMF	398.5	75	1369	56	24.44	8- 50	3	2
M.M.Ali (Wo)	OB	21	2	106	0				
J.Allenby (Le)	RM	210.2	43	662	15	44.13	5-125	1	–
M.K.D.I.Amerasinghe (SLA)	RFM	22	4	84	6	14.00	3- 28	–	–
J.M.Anderson (E/La)	RFM	317.3	71	1067	32	33.34	5- 42	2	–
J.E.Anyon (Wa)	RFM	374.1	67	1424	32	44.50	4- 55	–	–
Azhar Mahmood (Sy)	RFM	87	16	278	3	92.66	3- 73	–	–
F.B.Baker (CU)	SLA	38	5	128	2	64.00	1- 18	–	–
D.J.Balcombe (DU/H)	RMF	125.5	23	479	10	47.90	3- 58	–	–
V.Banerjee (Gs)	SLA	348.5	57	1178	26	45.30	4- 38	–	–
G.J.Batty (Wo)	OB	489.3	104	1523	38	40.07	6-106	3	–
D.M.Benkenstein (Du)	RM/OB	59	11	202	2	101.00	1- 24	–	–
J.G.E.Benning (Sy)	RM	17	0	91	0				
A.J.Bichel (Ex)	RFM	217.4	43	842	41	20.53	7- 36	3	1
T.R.Birt (De)	RM	3.3	0	26	0				
I.D.Blackwell (Sm)	SLA	324.3	77	860	29	29.65	3- 8	–	–
N.Boje (Nh)	SLA	136.1	29	382	16	23.87	6-110	1	–
D.E.Bollinger (Wo)	LFM	191	40	713	16	44.56	4- 82	–	–
R.S.Bopara (Ex/EA)	RMF	140.2	24	533	12	44.41	3- 60	–	–
R.R.Bose (Ind)	RMF	57.2	13	193	8	24.12	5- 51	1	–
A.G.Botha (De/Wa)	SLA	553	139	1619	55	29.43	6-101	3	–
D.P.Bradshaw (OU)	RMF	8	0	40	0				
R.M.R.Brathwaite (LU/MCC)	RFM	99.4	18	379	7	54.14	3- 77	–	–
D.J.Bravo (WI)	RMF	107.3	19	412	6	68.66	2- 91	–	–
J.P.Bray (Ire)	(WK)	0.1	0	0	0				
G.R.Breese (Du)	OB	84	8	368	5	73.60	3-102	–	–
T.T.Bresnan (Y/EA)	RMF	354	73	1157	34	34.02	4- 10	–	–
S.C.J.Broad (Le/EA)	RFM	160.4	21	602	24	25.08	5- 67	2	–
A.D.Brown (Sy)	LB	8	0	38	0				
D.O.Brown (Gs)	RM	38	8	140	2	70.00	2- 25	–	–
J.F.Brown (Nh)	OB	453.5	113	1235	30	41.16	5- 47	1	–
K.R.Brown (La)	RMF	3	0	7	0				
J.T.A.Bruce (H)	RMF	352.5	71	1199	39	30.74	5- 64	2	–
M.A.Butcher (Sy)	RM/OB	6.3	1	28	0				
S.M.Butler (MCC)	RMF	39.2	7	168	5	33.60	3-121	–	–
J.E.L.Buttleman (DU)	RFM	8	0	30	0				
A.R.Caddick (Sm)	RFM	541.5	114	1733	75	23.10	7- 30	4	1
M.A.Carberry (H)	OB	30	3	125	2	62.50	1- 13	0	–
N.M.Carter (Wa)	LFM	85.4	14	283	10	28.30	5- 62	1	–
S.Chanderpaul (WI/Du)	LB	19	4	66	0				
G.Chapple (La)	RFM	365.1	79	1027	47	21.85	7- 53	1	1
S.P.Cheetham (La)	RFM	24	1	127	1	127.00	1- 44	–	–
D.D.Cherry (Gm)	RM	2	0	5	0				

F-C	Cat	O	M	R	W	Avge	Best	5wI	10wM
M.J.Chilton (La)	RM	4	0	13	0			–	–
A.S.Chopra (MCC)	RM	2	0	9	0			–	–
V.Chopra (Ex)	LB	5	0	25	0			–	–
S.H.Choudhry (MCC)	LB	12	0	43	0			–	–
J.L.Clare (De)	RMF	49.2	10	203	10	20.30	5- 90	1	–
S.R.Clark (H)	RFM	175.2	32	602	24	25.08	7- 82	1	–
R.Clarke (Sy)	RFM	154.5	19	633	15	42.20	3- 57	–	–
M.E.Claydon (Du)	RMF	53	9	219	6	36.50	3- 26	–	–
S.J.Cliff (Le)	RM	28	0	126	1	126.00	1- 28	–	–
R.S.Clinton (Sy)	RM	17	3	55	0			–	–
G.D.Clough (Nt)	RM	26	5	82	4	20.50	3- 72	–	–
J.J.Cobb (Le)	LB	9	0	44	0			–	–
A.Codrington (Can)	RM	13	4	38	0			–	–
P.D.Collingwood (E/Du)	RMF	70.5	13	199	5	39.80	2- 24	–	–
C.D.Collymore (WI)	RFM	137	19	478	11	43.45	3- 58	–	–
N.R.D.Compton (MCC/M)	OB	4	0	20	0			–	–
A.N.Cook (E/Ex/MCC)	OB	1	0	6	0			–	–
S.J.Cook (K)	RM	241.4	58	740	22	33.63	6- 35	1	–
D.G.Cork (La)	RFM	360.5	83	1011	30	33.70	3- 39	–	–
D.A.Cosker (Gm)	SLA	305	56	939	29	32.37	5- 69	1	–
P.S.Coverdale (Nh)	RM	13.1	6	39	1	39.00	1- 36	–	–
J.P.Crawley (H)	RM	2	0	22	0			–	–
R.D.B.Croft (Gm)	OB	600.1	87	1877	56	33.51	6- 44	5	1
S.J.Croft (La)	RMF	79	11	286	6	47.66	3- 40	–	–
A.R.Crook (Nh)	OB	17	5	60	0			–	–
S.P.Crook (Nh)	RFM	231.4	44	831	23	36.13	4- 56	–	–
R.A.G.Cummins (Le)	RM	148.2	34	512	13	39.38	5- 60	1	–
S.M.J.Cusden (De)	RFM	24	2	98	2	49.00	2- 61	–	–
L.M.Daggett (Wa)	RFM	45	9	154	1	154.00	1- 61	–	–
J.W.M.Dalrymple (M)	OB	198.3	23	689	12	57.41	3- 86	–	–
Danish Kaneria (Ex)	LBG	560.5	124	1643	74	22.20	7- 95	7	1
A.M.Davies (Du/Nt)	RMF	292.4	81	824	34	24.23	7- 59	1	–
A.P.Davies (Gm)	RMF	134	22	542	11	49.27	4- 46	–	–
J.M.Davison (Can)	OB	12	4	48	1	48.00	1- 48	–	–
R.K.J.Dawson (Nh)	OB	47	6	168	5	33.60	3- 25	–	–
K.J.Dean (De)	LMF	267	80	659	23	28.65	5- 24	1	–
J.L.Denly (K/EA)	LB	67.1	15	203	6	33.83	2- 13	–	–
J.W.Dernbach (Sy)	RMF	78.1	14	335	9	37.22	3- 85	–	–
N.J.Dexter (K)	RM	13	0	72	1	72.00	1- 35	–	–
M.S.Dhoni (Ind)	(WK)	3	0	13	0			–	–
M.G.Dighton (De)	RMF	41	4	133	4	33.25	2- 47	–	–
L.A.Dingle (OU)	RMF	5	1	15	0			–	–
W.T.Dobson (DU)	RMF	3	0	18	0			–	–
N.D.Doshi (Sy)	SLA	174.2	26	697	13	53.61	6-111	–	–
W.J.Durston (Sm)	OB	24	1	117	0			–	–
M.A.Ealham (Nt)	RMF	325.4	101	886	32	27.68	4- 37	–	–
B.M.Edmondson (Gs)	RFM	103	12	446	9	49.55	4- 50	–	–
F.H.Edwards (WI)	RM	89.4	7	392	12	32.66	5-112	1	–
S.M.Ervine (H)	RM	149.5	23	549	8	68.62	3- 48	–	–
D.Evans (M)	RFM	54	14	169	5	33.80	3- 31	–	–
L.Evans (Du)	RMF	20.1	1	115	4	28.75	2- 39	–	–
R.S.Ferley (Nt)	SLA	63	8	283	1	283.00	1-151	–	–

F-C	Cat	O	M	R	W	Avge	Best	5wI	10wM
S.T.Finn (M)	RFM	72.5	13	239	11	21.72	4-51	–	–
I.D.Fisher (Gs)	SLA	55	13	153	2	76.50	1-58	–	–
A.Flintoff (La)	RF	34.5	10	120	5	24.00	3-38	–	–
G.W.Flower (Ex)	SLA	16	5	54	1	54.00	1-50	–	–
M.H.A.Footitt (Nt)	LFM	45.4	6	191	7	27.28	5-59	1	–
P.J.Foster (DU)	RFM	79	15	318	11	28.90	4-26	–	–
M.J.Fourie (Ire)	RM	12	2	40	3	13.33	3-31	–	–
S.R.G.Francis (Nt)	RMF	12	1	74	1	74.00	1-43	–	–
P.J.Franks (Nt)	RMF	263.4	40	1090	32	34.06	3-28	–	–
M.J.Friedlander (CU)	RFM	68.2	8	283	9	31.44	6-78	1	–
A.W.Gale (Y)	LB	2	0	33	1	33.00	1-33	–	–
J.E.R.Gallian (Nt)	RM	10	2	53	1	53.00	1-36	–	–
G.Gambhir (Ind)	LB	4	0	30	1	30.00	1-22	–	–
W.C.A.Ganegama (SLA)	RFM	77	12	314	6	52.33	2-45	–	–
D.Ganga (WI)	OB	2.2	0	6	0				
S.C.Ganguly (Ind)	RM	42	11	101	2	50.50	1-11	–	–
C.H.Gayle (WI)	OB	77.1	9	292	6	48.66	3-66	–	–
O.D.Gibson (Du)	RFM	479.5	103	1660	80	20.75	10-47	4	3
A.P.R.Gidman (Gs/MCC)	RM	163	27	581	9	64.55	1- 4	–	–
W.R.S.Gidman (Du)	RM	23	4	86	4	21.50	3-37	–	–
C.R.Gilbert (Y)	MF	3	0	11	0				
J.N.Gillespie (Y)	RFM	238.3	53	803	23	34.91	3-40	–	–
B.A.Godleman (M)	LB	5	1	35	0				
M.W.Goodwin (Sx)	LB	1	0	4	0				
D.Gough (Y)	RFM	287.4	74	876	37	23.67	6-47	3	–
R.N.Grant (Gm)	RM	11.4	0	78	2	39.00	1- 7	–	–
J.A.G.Green (Sx)	RMF	8	1	32	0				
C.G.Greenidge (Gs)	RMF	183	28	752	28	26.85	5-54	1	–
D.A.Griffiths (H)	RFM	100.3	9	411	12	34.25	4-46	–	–
T.D.Groenewald (Wa)	RFM	132.3	37	430	9	47.77	3-26	–	–
H.F.Gurney (Le)	LMF	36	5	173	2	86.50	1-84	–	–
A.J.Hall (K)	RMF	163	27	610	15	40.66	5-59	1	–
Harbhajan Singh (Sy)	OB	284.1	83	686	37	18.54	6-57	3	1
M.A.Hardinges (Gs)	RMF	215	45	822	16	51.37	3-59	–	–
B.W.Harmison (Du)	RMF	53.2	6	286	3	95.33	2-29	–	–
S.J.Harmison (E/Du/MCC)	RF	363.2	72	1184	53	22.33	6-87	3	–
A.J.Harris (Nt)	RM	197	32	762	19	40.10	4-69	–	–
J.A.R.Harris (Gm)	RFM	247.5	53	811	33	24.57	7-66	2	1
P.L.Harris (Wa)	SLA	120.5	20	341	4	85.25	2-50	–	–
I.J.Harvey (De)	RMF	30	5	116	2	58.00	1-14	–	–
T.L.Hemingway (CU)	OB	47	17	103	4	25.75	4-58	–	–
D.L.Hemp (Gm)	RM	4	1	8	0				
C.W.Henderson (Le)	SLA	352.3	79	1035	26	39.80	5-56	2	–
M.R.K.B.Herath (SLA)	SLA	97.3	16	319	11	29.00	3-39	–	–
J.C.Hildreth (Sm)	RMF	21	4	102	2	51.00	1-13	–	–
C.M.M.Hill (OU)	SLC	10	0	32	0				
B.J.Hodge (La)	OB	2	0	5	0				
R.Hodgkinson (De)	RFM	10	0	75	0				
G.P.Hodnett (Gs)	LB	2.3	0	10	0				
K.W.Hogg (La/Nt/Wo)	RFM	125	38	346	7	49.42	3-44	–	–
M.J.Hoggard (E/MCC/Y)	RFM	277.5	66	856	40	21.40	5-32	2	–
S.M.Hole (Wa)	RM	15	4	65	0				

153

F-C	Cat	O	M	R	W	Avge	Best	5wI	10wM
C.D.Hopkinson (Sx)	RM	14	0	79	0				
J.A.Hughes (LU)	RMF	43.2	10	155	6	25.83	3- 33	–	–
I.D.Hunter (De)	RMF	46	9	130	3	43.33	2- 63	–	–
D.J.Hussey (Nt)	OB	4.5	0	23	0				
B.L.Hutton (M)	RMF	8	2	28	0				
Imran Tahir (Y)	LBG	37	2	141	0				
A.J.Ireland (Gs)	RMF	90	15	332	7	47.42	3- 39	–	–
B.D.Jacklin (CU)	RM	48	18	84	2	42.00	2- 69	–	–
A.Jacobs (Le)	OB	2	0	13	0				
S.T.Jayasuriya (La/MCC)	SLA	10	3	15	1	15.00	1- 10	–	–
R.L.Johnson (M)	RFM	96.1	10	384	6	64.00	2- 69	–	–
D.T.Johnston (Ire)	RFM	21.4	5	59	7	8.42	4- 12	–	–
G.O.Jones (K)	(WK)	2	0	14	0				
P.S.Jones (Sm)	RMF	254.3	38	1055	26	40.57	6- 61	1	–
R.A.Jones (Wo)	RMF	63	10	295	7	42.14	3- 37	–	–
S.P.Jones (Gm)	RF	89	13	290	1	290.00	1- 39	–	–
C.J.Jordan (Sy)	RFM	139.1	22	490	20	24.50	3- 42	–	–
R.H.Joseph (K)	RFM	57	11	233	3	77.66	3- 78	–	–
E.C.Joyce (M)	RM	20	1	103	0				
T.Kalam (OU)	RMF	68	18	221	6	36.83	3- 54	–	–
K.D.Karthik (Ind)	(WK)	5	0	28	0				
M.Kartik (M)	SLA	464.3	109	1273	51	24.96	6- 21	3	–
S.M.Katich (De)	SLC	38	4	144	2	72.00	1- 17	–	–
G.Keedy (La)	SLA	272.3	55	813	24	33.87	5-159	1	–
R.A.Kemp (CU)	RM	44.1	12	118	6	19.66	3- 23	–	–
R.W.T.Key (K)	RM/OB	7	0	33	0				
Z.Khan (Ind)	LFM	166.2	47	521	22	23.68	5- 75	1	–
N.Killeen (Du)	RMF	42.3	9	117	6	19.50	4- 22	–	–
R.E.King (LU/MCC)	LMF	69	8	321	6	53.50	4- 34	–	–
S.P.Kirby (Gs)	RFM	312.4	73	961	41	23.43	5- 41	3	1
R.J.Kirtley (Sx)	RFM	185	44	567	12	47.25	4- 44	–	–
L.Klusener (Nh)	RM/OB	432.3	107	1280	33	38.78	5- 40	2	–
G.J-P.Kruger (Le)	RMF	85	16	324	13	24.92	5- 62	1	–
G.J.Kruis (Y)	RFM	110.2	21	409	8	51.12	2- 39	–	–
A.Kumble (Ind)	LBG	205.4	34	690	20	34.50	3- 32	–	–
N.J.Lamb (DU)	RMF	66	12	220	8	27.50	3- 52	–	–
C.K.Langeveldt (Le)	RFM	101.4	27	295	8	36.87	4- 41	–	–
D.Langford-Smith (Ire)	RFM	15.5	2	72	2	36.00	1- 33	–	–
S.G.Law (La)	RM/LB	4	0	21	0				
M.A.K.Lawson (Y)	LB	24	1	122	0				
V.V.S.Laxman (Ind/La)	OB	9	2	36	1	36.00	1- 16	–	–
J.Lewis (Gs)	RMF	150.1	33	472	12	39.33	5- 41	1	–
J.D.Lewry (Sx)	LFM	348.1	85	1017	33	30.81	4- 81	–	–
C.J.Liddle (Sx)	LFM	111.4	20	365	5	73.00	2- 43	–	–
R.J.Logan (Nh)	RMF	189	36	656	15	43.73	3- 38	–	–
K.S.Lokuarachchi (SLA)	LB	39.2	4	107	5	21.40	5- 48	1	–
A.G.R.Loudon (MCC/Wa)	OB	223.3	27	726	8	90.75	4-123	–	–
D.S.Lucas (Nh)	LMF	202	29	751	19	39.52	5- 49	1	–
M.J.Lumb (H)	RM	4	0	30	0				
T.Lungley (De)	RM	435.5	106	1555	59	26.35	5- 20	3	–
A.Lyth (Y)	RM	1	0	12	1	12.00	1- 12	–	–
J.C.Macadam (OU)	RMF	8	0	35	0				

154

F-C	Cat	O	M	R	W	Avge	Best	5wI	10wM
W.K.McCallan (Ire)	OB	9.5	3	34	5	6.80	5- 34	1	–
A.C.McGarry (Ex)	RFM	45.1	10	160	2	80.00	2- 62	–	–
A.McGrath (Y)	RM	76	16	223	5	44.60	2- 12	–	–
R.McLaren (K)	RMF	316	58	1079	44	24.52	5- 24	1	–
C.D.McMillan (MCC)	RM	9	1	19	0				
D.L.Maddy (Wa)	RM/OB	166	50	409	15	27.26	5- 63	1	–
S.J.Magoffin (Sy)	RFM	30	9	94	2	47.00	2- 73	–	–
S.I.Mahmood (La)	RF	270.3	43	955	30	31.83	4- 21	–	–
R.J.A.Malcolm-Hansen (LU)	OB	4	0	28	0				
M.N.Malik (Nt/Wo)	RFM	375.4	75	1470	25	58.80	3- 94	–	–
S.L.Malinga (K)	RF	40	2	197	2	98.50	1- 40	–	–
Mansoor Amjad (Le)	LBG	161.2	17	645	12	53.75	3- 16	–	–
H.J.H.Marshall (Gs)	RM	19	1	81	2	40.50	1- 9	–	–
S.J.Marshall (La)	LB	28	6	84	2	42.00	1- 32	–	–
R.S.C.Martin-Jenkins (Sx)	RFM	299	90	771	36	21.41	5- 67	1	–
A.D.Mascarenhas (H)	RMF	190	56	481	15	32.06	4- 33	–	–
M.S.Mason (Wo)	RFM	24	8	62	1	62.00	1- 51	–	–
D.D.Masters (Le)	RMF	327.4	89	924	41	22.53	6- 60	3	–
J.K.Maunders (Le)	LB	49.5	4	203	2	101.50	1- 8	–	–
T.L.Maynard (Gm)	OB	2	0	18	0				
B.G.A.S.Mendis (OU)	OB	20.5	2	111	1	111.00	1- 11	–	–
J.D.Middlebrook (Ex)	OB	341.5	62	1020	24	42.50	4- 53	–	–
D.K.H.Mitchell (Wo)	RM	41.3	9	116	6	19.33	3- 50	–	–
B.R.Modha (CU)	LB	72	6	312	7	44.57	3-101	–	–
Mohammad Akram (Sy)	RFM	73	20	236	6	39.33	2- 22	–	–
Mohammad Amin (CU)	RMF	58	8	312	2	156.00	1-109	–	–
Mohammad Nabi (MCC)	OB	15	4	47	1	47.00	1- 47	–	–
S.C.Moore (Wo)	RM	9	1	42	0				
E.J.G.Morgan (Ire/M)	RM	11.1	2	32	2	16.00	2- 24	–	–
J.C.Morris (DU/MCC)	LB	68.1	5	316	6	52.66	2- 68	–	–
E.J.Morse (OU)	RM	77	10	314	6	52.33	3-148	–	–
R.S.Morton (WI)	OB	1	0	4	0				
W.J.Mottram (OU)	RM	19	6	46	2	23.00	2- 46	–	–
S.J.Mullaney (La)	RM	7	2	13	0				
M.K.Munday (Sm)	LB	44	2	192	14	13.71	8- 55	1	1
M.Muralitharan (La)	OB	392.3	90	952	51	18.66	6- 72	5	–
C.P.Murtagh (LU)	LB	1	0	8	0				
T.J.Murtagh (M)	RFM	296.2	79	1044	42	24.85	6- 87	1	–
Murtaza Hussain (Sy)	OB	94.4	25	282	11	25.63	4-126	–	–
Mushtaq Ahmed (Sx)	LBG	668.5	91	2310	90	25.66	7- 72	8	3
J.K.H.Naik (Le/LU)	OB	58	7	263	3	87.66	1- 58	–	–
G.R.Napier (Ex)	RM	150.1	32	589	10	58.90	3- 55	–	–
C.D.Nash (Sx)	OB	10.1	1	40	3	13.33	2- 1	–	–
Naved-ul-Hasan (Sx)	RMF	377.3	59	1454	50	29.08	5-106	2	–
J.Needham (De)	OB	83.2	15	256	7	36.57	3- 92	–	–
A.Nel (Ex)	RFM	122.2	31	391	10	39.10	3- 62	–	–
J.D.Nel (Wo)	RMF	96.1	17	345	7	49.28	4- 74	–	–
M.A.G.Nelson (Nh)	RFM	8	1	62	2	31.00	2- 62	–	–
T.J.New (Le)	RM	28.1	4	168	4	42.00	2- 18	–	–
O.J.Newby (La)	RMF	177.4	28	670	22	30.45	3- 44	–	–
M.J.Nicholson (Sy)	RFM	378	75	1289	44	29.29	5- 89	1	–
P.A.Nixon (Le)	RM	2	0	9	0				

155

F-C	Cat	O	M	R	W	Avge	Best	5wI	10wM
A.A.Noffke (Gs)	RFM	124.4	34	335	15	22.33	6- 68	1	–
M.J.North (Gs)	OB	130	16	359	9	39.88	3- 53	–	–
K.J.O'Brien (Ire)	RMF	9	3	24	3	8.00	2- 4	–	–
W.J.F.O'Driscoll (CU)	RM	14	1	55	0				
G.Onions (Du/MCC/EA)	RMF	396.1	77	1490	45	33.11	8-101	2	–
J.Ormond (Sy)	RFM	189	48	640	12	53.33	2- 42	–	–
H.Osinde (Can)	RMF	24	5	81	2	40.50	2- 81	–	–
W.T.Owen (Gm)	RMF	8	0	37	0				
C.D.Paget (DU)	OB	29	4	131	1	131.00	1- 19	–	–
A.P.Palladino (Ex)	RMF	106.5	30	350	12	29.16	4- 44	–	–
M.S.Panesar (E/Nh)	SLA	464.1	88	1413	53	26.66	6- 65	4	1
G.T.Park (Du)	RM	7	1	39	0				
L.C.Parker (Wa)	RM	2	0	16	0				
S.D.Parry (La)	SLA	19.1	4	46	5	9.20	5- 23	1	–
T.W.Parsons (LU)	RFM	41	6	116	4	29.00	3- 70	–	–
A.Patel (De)	SLC	9	2	30	0				
M.M.Patel (K)	SLA	31	4	107	1	107.00	1- 17	–	–
S.R.Patel (Nt)	SLA	104	20	329	14	23.50	4- 68	–	–
S.A.Patterson (Y)	RMF	13	2	39	2	19.50	2- 30	–	–
C.T.Peploe (M)	SLA	33	8	95	5	19.00	3- 58	–	–
M.D.K.Perera (SLA)	OB	60.1	7	203	6	33.83	3- 33	–	–
T.J.Phillips (Ex)	SLA	71	11	246	6	41.00	3- 28	–	–
K.P.Pietersen (E)	OB	13	2	61	1	61.00	1- 41	–	–
L.E.Plunkett (E/Du)	RFM	443.5	92	1530	50	30.60	5-105	1	–
R.R.Powar (Ind)	OB	74	9	267	9	29.66	4- 85	–	–
D.B.L.Powell (WI/H)	RMF	246.3	51	834	25	33.36	4- 8	–	–
K.T.G.D.Prasad (SLA)	RFM	43	3	171	5	34.20	2- 34	–	–
R.W.Price (Wo)	SLA	58.5	6	256	4	64.00	2- 89	–	–
R.M.Pyrah (Y)	RM	12	2	41	1	41.00	1- 3	–	–
Qaiser Ali (Can)	OB	5	0	28	0				
R.Rampaul (WI)	RFM	3	2	3	0				
M.R.Ramprakash (Sy)	OB	1	0	18	0				
W.M.G.Ramyakumara (SLA)	LM	28	9	74	3	24.66	2- 59	–	–
W.B.Rankin (De)	RMF	76.3	11	292	10	29.20	4- 41	–	–
A.U.Rashid (MCC/Y/EA)	LB	457	48	1813	43	42.16	5- 88	3	–
O.P.Rayner (Sx)	RMF	117.2	16	414	14	29.57	5- 68	1	–
C.M.W.Read (Nt)	(WK)	5	0	35	0				
D.J.Redfern (De)	OB	19	3	70	2	35.00	1- 7	–	–
M.A.Richards (MCC/OU)	RM	76	12	218	4	54.50	1- 21	–	–
A.Richardson (M)	RMF	357.1	89	1017	42	24.21	5- 50	1	–
D.D.J.Robinson (Le)	RMF	8	0	50	1	50.00	1- 48	–	–
M.C.Rosenberg (Le)	RM	9.2	1	45	0				
D.T.Rowe (Le)	RM	89	16	427	13	32.84	5- 61	1	–
W.D.Rudge (Gs)	RM	12	2	40	0				
J.A.Rudolph (Y)	LBG	16	4	55	0				
L.C.Ryan (OU)	SLA	24	5	82	1	82.00	1- 82	–	–
J.L.Sadler (Le)	LBG	14	2	95	1	95.00	1- 5	–	–
O.J.Sadler (OU)	SLA	20.2	5	41	3	13.66	3- 41	–	–
O.H.J.Saffell (De)	RMF	16.1	2	59	5	11.80	3- 37	–	–
M.J.Saggers (Ex/K)	RMF	237.4	56	707	29	24.37	5- 39	2	–
N.C.Saker (Sy)	RFM	156	33	649	15	43.26	5- 76	1	–
D.J.G.Sales (Nh)	RM	1	0	3	0				

F-C	Cat	O	M	R	W	Avge	Best	5wI	10wM
I.D.K.Salisbury (Sy)	LBG	188.5	15	745	11	67.72	4-121	–	–
A.M.Samad (Can)	OB	18	0	71	2	35.50	2- 71	–	–
D.J.G.Sammy (WI)	RM	72.3	16	178	12	14.83	7- 66	1	–
M.N.Samuels (WI)	OB	9	0	47	0			–	–
C.J.L.Sandbach (OU)	LB	12.2	1	81	1	81.00	1- 37	–	–
Saqlain Mushtaq (Sx)	OB	118.2	21	316	18	17.55	5- 96	1	–
R.R.Sarwan (WI)	LB	6	0	33	0			–	–
C.P.Schofield (Sy)	LBG	186.5	29	650	16	40.62	5- 52	1	–
B.M.Shafayat (Nt)	RMF	25.5	3	100	1	100.00	1- 24	–	–
O.A.Shah (E/MCC/M/EA)	OB	30.1	3	137	0			–	–
A.Shahzad (Y)	RMF	92.4	12	343	9	38.11	4- 22	–	–
A.J.Shantry (Wa)	LFM	33	11	111	4	27.75	4- 31	–	–
Z.K.Sharif (CU/MCC)	LB	43	2	147	1	147.00	1- 16	–	–
I.Sharma (Ind)	RM	52	9	198	2	99.00	1- 36	–	–
C.E.Shreck (Nt)	RFM	400.5	94	1274	47	27.10	7- 35	4	–
R.J.Sidebottom (E/Nt)	LFM	439.4	112	1166	39	29.89	5- 88	1	–
R.J.Sillence (Wo)	RMF	234.5	36	932	15	62.13	2- 48	–	–
C.E.W.Silverwood (M)	RFM	260.4	52	875	31	28.22	6- 49	1	–
R.P.Singh (Ind/Le)	LMF	182.1	42	691	23	30.04	5- 59	1	–
B.F.Smith (Wo)	RM	7	1	49	0			–	–
B.M.Smith (CU)	LFM	42	2	264	2	132.00	2- 48	–	–
D.S.Smith (WI)	OB	5	0	12	0			–	–
E.T.Smith (M)	RM	1	1	0	0			–	–
G.M.Smith (De)	OB/RM	214.1	51	689	20	34.45	3- 31	–	–
T.C.Smith (La)	RMF	95.5	20	351	8	43.87	2- 47	–	–
T.M.J.Smith (Sx)	SLA	13	1	79	1	79.00	1- 52	–	–
W.R.Smith (Du)	OB	12	2	46	2	23.00	1- 5	–	–
V.S.Solanki (Wo)	OB	45	5	149	1	149.00	1- 54	–	–
M.N.W.Spriegel (LU)	OB	33	4	106	3	35.33	1- 12	–	–
S.Sreesanth (Ind)	RFM	177.1	39	550	14	39.28	3- 53	–	–
T.P.Stayt (Gs)	RMF	59	9	218	4	54.50	3- 51	–	–
D.I.Stevens (K)	RM	112.5	24	305	12	25.41	3- 91	–	–
D.W.Steyn (Wa)	RF	203.3	45	595	23	25.86	5- 49	1	–
A.J.Strauss (E/M/EA)	LM	6	0	16	1	16.00	1- 16	–	–
H.H.Streak (Wa)	RFM	255.2	54	789	13	60.69	3-105	–	–
S.B.Styris (Du)	RMF	51	7	217	4	54.25	2- 56	–	–
A.V.Suppiah (Sm)	SLA	3	1	5	0			–	–
G.P.Swann (Nt)	OB	487.2	93	1503	45	33.40	7-100	1	1
N.Tahir (Wa)	RFM	238.4	57	694	25	27.76	4- 47	–	–
B.Tavarasa (CU)	OB	13	0	65	0			–	–
C.G.Taylor (Gs)	OB	91	13	331	10	33.10	4- 52	–	–
J.E.Taylor (WI/Le)	RF	174	33	702	22	31.90	6- 35	3	–
R.N.ten Doeschate (Ex)	RMF	119.3	18	552	7	78.85	1- 13	–	–
S.R.Tendulkar (Ind)	RM/LB/OB	47	0	176	2	88.00	1- 24	–	–
A.C.Thomas (Wa)	RMF	129.2	37	367	10	36.70	4-109	–	–
N.D.Thornicroft (Y)	RMF	21	4	72	6	12.00	6- 60	1	–
C.D.Thorp (Du)	RMF	47.4	10	163	6	27.16	3- 51	–	–
J.A.Tomlinson (H)	LMF	154.4	31	528	13	40.61	5- 78	1	–
J.C.Tredwell (K)	OB	415.3	76	1285	36	35.69	6- 47	1	–
P.D.Trego (Sm)	RMF	286.3	49	1131	33	34.27	4- 49	–	–
C.T.Tremlett (E/H/EA)	RMF	317.5	69	985	29	33.96	4- 47	–	–
I.J.L.Trott (Wa/EA)	RM	74	19	214	2	107.00	2- 33	–	–

F-C	Cat	O	M	R	W	Avge	Best	5wI	10wM
J.O.Troughton (Wa)	SLA	85	12	276	2	138.00	1- 34	–	–
A.J.Tudor (Ex)	RFM	174.2	42	602	17	35.41	3- 29	–	–
M.L.Turner (Sm)	RMF	77.3	7	312	8	39.00	4- 30	–	–
S.D.Udal (H)	OB	150.1	25	469	14	33.50	4-138	–	–
Umar Bhatti (Can)	LM	22.4	4	85	5	17.00	5- 85	1	–
W.P.U.C.J.Vaas (M)	LFM	162	30	552	20	27.60	5-126	1	–
J.J.van der Wath (Nh)	RFM	240.1	54	805	34	23.67	6- 49	2	–
M.van Jaarsveld (K)	OB	20.2	4	68	5	13.60	2- 17	–	–
M.P.Vaughan (E/Y)	OB	12	0	47	0			–	–
G.G.Wagg (De)	LM	492	94	1785	53	33.67	5-119	2	–
M.A.Wagh (Nt)	OB	12	4	33	2	16.50	2- 6	–	–
D.J.Wainwright (Y)	SLA	19	1	74	2	37.00	2- 72	–	–
A.G.Wakely (Nh)	OB	29	1	127	3	42.33	2- 62	–	–
M.J.Walker (K)	RM	2	0	10	1	10.00	1- 10	–	–
N.G.E.Walker (Le)	RFM	171	27	777	18	43.16	4- 70	–	–
S.J.Walters (Sy)	RM	8	1	28	1	28.00	1- 4	–	–
B.S.M.Warnapura (SLA)	OB	1	0	5	0				
S.K.Warne (H)	LBG	438.1	56	1479	50	29.58	6- 83	5	1
H.T.Waters (Gm)	RMF	201.3	31	741	15	49.40	4- 76	–	–
R.E.Watkins (Gm)	RM	99.3	15	411	10	41.10	4- 89	–	–
U.W.M.B.C.A.Welagedara (SLA)	LFM	97.4	19	338	13	26.00	5- 45	1	–
M.S.Westfield (Ex)	RFM	13	1	64	0				
T.Westley (Ex/MCC)	OB	5	0	24	1	24.00	1- 24	–	–
W.P.C.Weston (De)	LM	2	1	12	0				
I.J.Westwood (Wa)	OB	6.5	1	26	1	26.00	1- 9	–	–
A.G.Wharf (Gm)	RMF	309.2	31	1262	36	35.05	4- 16	–	–
S.J.Wheeler (LU)	RFM	68.4	7	312	1	312.00	1- 72	–	–
C.D.Whelan (M)	RMF	9.1	1	31	4	7.75	2- 13	–	–
C.White (Y)	RFM/OB	6	0	11	0				
C.L.White (Sm)	LBG	178.4	17	655	20	32.75	4- 28	–	–
G.G.White (Nh)	SLA	62	18	142	3	47.33	2- 35	–	–
R.A.White (Nh)	LB	39	1	188	2	94.00	1- 35	–	–
W.A.White (De)	RMF	113	21	463	12	38.58	5- 87	1	–
D.H.Wigley (Nh)	RFM	229	33	936	34	27.52	3- 10	–	–
R.E.M.Williams (DU/MCC/M)	RMF	132.4	22	524	13	40.30	5- 70	2	–
C.M.Willoughby (Sm)	LMF	462.4	105	1530	62	24.67	5- 33	5	–
P.J.Wilshaw (OU)	RM	23	2	68	2	34.00	1- 20	–	–
P.J.Wiseman (Du)	OB	288.3	56	955	32	29.84	5- 65	1	–
C.R.Woakes (Wa)	RM	19.4	3	90	1	90.00	1- 42	–	–
M.J.Wood (MCC)	LMF	21	3	77	2	38.50	2- 77	–	–
M.J.Wood (Y)	OB	1	0	4	0				
N.J.Woods (OU)	SLA	111	14	352	5	70.40	3- 61	–	–
B.J.Wright (Gm)	RM	22	0	89	2	44.50	1- 14	–	–
C.J.C.Wright (M)	RFM	28	5	107	3	35.66	2- 21	–	–
D.G.Wright (Gm)	RFM	16	4	60	3	20.00	3- 60	–	–
L.J.Wright (Sx)	RM	168.3	21	619	14	44.21	3-117	–	–
M.H.Yardy (Sx)	LM/SLA	51.3	8	181	4	45.25	2- 32	–	–
Yasir Arafat (K)	RM	238.5	44	882	27	32.66	5- 63	1	–
P.J.W.Young (OU)	RM	45	4	187	1	187.00	1- 26	–	–
Younus Khan (Y)	RM/LB	85.5	10	342	8	42.75	4- 52	–	–
Yuvraj Singh (Ind)	SLA	30	3	118	0				

COUNTY CHAMPIONSHIP 2007
LV FINAL TABLES

DIVISION 1

		P	W	L	D	A	Bonus Points Bat	Bonus Points Bowl	Deduct Points	Total Points
1	**SUSSEX** (1)	16	7	3	5	1	37	43	–	202
2	Durham (7)	16	7	5	4	–	38	47	1.5	197.5
3	Lancashire (2)	16	5	2	8	1	40	44	–	190
4	Surrey (-)	16	5	4	6	1	41	40	1.0	178
5	Hampshire (3)	16	5	3	8	–	32	43	–	177
6	Yorkshire (6)	16	4	4	8	–	49	38	–	175
7	Kent (5)	16	3	5	7	1	43	36	–	153
8	Warwickshire (4)	16	2	5	9	–	40	35	–	139
9	Worcestershire (-)	16	1	8	5	2	18	35	–	95

DIVISION 2

		P	W	L	D	A	Bonus Points Bat	Bonus Points Bowl	Deduct Points	Total Points
1	**SOMERSET** (9)	16	10	1	5	–	65	41	–	266
2	Nottinghamshire (-)	16	6	3	7	–	60	43	0.5	214.5
3	Middlesex (-)	16	6	2	8	–	35	43	1.5	192.5
4	Essex (3)	16	6	4	6	–	40	36	2.0	182
5	Northamptonshire (6)	16	5	5	6	–	44	38	–	176
6	Derbyshire (5)	16	3	5	8	–	30	44	1.0	147
7	Gloucestershire (7)	16	3	5	8	–	32	37	3.5	139.5
8	Leicestershire (4)	16	2	8	5	1	32	35	4.0	115
9	Glamorgan (8)	16	1	9	5	1	26	35	8.5	92.5

2006 final positions for that division are shown in brackets.

SCORING OF CHAMPIONSHIP POINTS 2007

(a) For a win, 14 points, plus any points scored in the first innings.

(b) In a tie, each side to score seven points, plus any points scored in the first innings.

(c) In a drawn match, each side to score four points, plus any points scored in the first innings (see also paragraph (f) below).

(d) If the scores are equal in a drawn match, the side batting in the fourth innings to score seven points plus any points scored in the first innings, and the opposing side to score four points plus any points scored in the first innings.

(e) **First Innings Points** (awarded only for performances **in the first 130 overs** of each first innings and retained whatever the result of the match).
- A maximum of five batting points to be available as under:-
  200 to 249 runs – 1 point; 250 to 299 runs – 2 points; 300 to 349 runs – 3 points;
  350 to 399 runs – 4 points; 400 runs or over – 5 points.
- A maximum of three bowling points to be available as under:-
  3 to 5 wickets taken – 1 point; 6 to 8 wickets taken – 2 points; 9 to 10 wickets taken – 3 points.

(f) If play starts when fewer than eight hours' playing time remains (in which event a one innings match shall be played as provided for in First-Class Playing Condition 18), no first innings points shall be scored. The side winning on the one innings to score 14 points. In a tie, each side to score seven points. In a drawn match, each side to score four points. If the scores are equal in a drawn match, the side batting in the second innings to score seven points and the opposing side to score four points.

(g) If a match is abandoned without a ball being bowled, each side to score four points.

(h) The side which has the highest aggregate of points gained at the end of the season shall be the Champion County of their respective Division. Should any sides in the Championship table be equal on points, the following tie-breakers will be applied in the order stated: most wins, least losses, team achieving most points in contests between teams level on points, most wickets taken, most runs scored. At the end of the season, the top two teams from the Second Division will be promoted and the bottom two teams from the First Division will be relegated.

COUNTY CHAMPIONS

The English County Championship was not officially constituted until December 1889. Prior to that date there was no generally accepted method of awarding the title; although the 'least matches lost' method existed, it was not consistently applied. Rules governing playing qualifications were agreed in 1873 and the first unofficial points system 15 years later.

Research has produced a list of champions dating back to 1826, but at least seven different versions exist for the period from 1864 to 1889 (see *The Wisden Book of Cricket Records*). Only from 1890 can any authorised list of county champions commence.

That first official Championship was contested between eight counties: Gloucestershire, Kent, Lancashire, Middlesex, Nottinghamshire, Surrey, Sussex and Yorkshire. The remaining counties were admitted in the following seasons: 1891 – Somerset, 1895 – Derbyshire, Essex, Hampshire, Leicestershire and Warwickshire, 1899 – Worcestershire, 1905 – Northamptonshire, 1921 – Glamorgan, and 1992 – Durham.

The Championship pennant was introduced by the 1951 champions, Warwickshire, and the Lord's Taverners' Trophy was first presented in 1973. The first sponsors, Schweppes (1977 to 1983), were succeeded by Britannic Assurance (1984 to 1998), PPP Healthcare (1999-2000), CricInfo (2001), Frizzell (2002 to 2005) and Liverpool Victoria (2006 to 2007). Based on their previous season's positions, the 18 counties were separated into two divisions in 2001. From 2001 to 2005 the bottom three Division 1 teams were relegated and the top three Division 2 sides promoted. This was reduced to two teams from the end of the 2006 season.

1890	Surrey	1931	Yorkshire	1972	Warwickshire
1891	Surrey	1932	Yorkshire	1973	Hampshire
1892	Surrey	1933	Yorkshire	1974	Worcestershire
1893	Yorkshire	1934	Lancashire	1975	Leicestershire
1894	Surrey	1935	Yorkshire	1976	Middlesex
1895	Surrey	1936	Derbyshire	1977	{ Kent
1896	Yorkshire	1937	Yorkshire		{ Middlesex
1897	Lancashire	1938	Yorkshire	1978	Kent
1898	Yorkshire	1939	Yorkshire	1979	Essex
1899	Surrey	1946	Yorkshire	1980	Middlesex
1900	Yorkshire	1947	Middlesex	1981	Nottinghamshire
1901	Yorkshire	1948	Glamorgan	1982	Middlesex
1902	Yorkshire	1949	{ Middlesex	1983	Essex
1903	Middlesex		{ Yorkshire	1984	Essex
1904	Lancashire	1950	{ Lancashire	1985	Middlesex
1905	Yorkshire		{ Surrey	1986	Essex
1906	Kent	1951	Warwickshire	1987	Nottinghamshire
1907	Nottinghamshire	1952	Surrey	1988	Worcestershire
1908	Yorkshire	1953	Surrey	1989	Worcestershire
1909	Kent	1954	Surrey	1990	Middlesex
1910	Kent	1955	Surrey	1991	Essex
1911	Warwickshire	1956	Surrey	1992	Essex
1912	Yorkshire	1957	Surrey	1993	Middlesex
1913	Kent	1958	Surrey	1994	Warwickshire
1914	Surrey	1959	Yorkshire	1995	Warwickshire
1919	Yorkshire	1960	Yorkshire	1996	Leicestershire
1920	Middlesex	1961	Hampshire	1997	Glamorgan
1921	Middlesex	1962	Yorkshire	1998	Leicestershire
1922	Yorkshire	1963	Yorkshire	1999	Surrey
1923	Yorkshire	1964	Worcestershire	2000	Surrey
1924	Yorkshire	1965	Worcestershire	2001	Yorkshire
1925	Yorkshire	1966	Yorkshire	2002	Surrey
1926	Lancashire	1967	Yorkshire	2003	Sussex
1927	Lancashire	1968	Yorkshire	2004	Warwickshire
1928	Lancashire	1969	Glamorgan	2005	Nottinghamshire
1929	Nottinghamshire	1970	Kent	2006	Sussex
1930	Lancashire	1971	Surrey	2007	Sussex

COUNTY CHAMPIONSHIP RESULTS 2007

DIVISION 1

	DURHAM	HANTS	KENT	LANCS	SURREY	SUSSEX	WARWKS	WORCS	YORKS
DURHAM	–	C-le-St Drawn	C-le-St Du 157	C-le-St Drawn	C-le-St Drawn	C-le-St Du 9w	C-le-St Du 9w	C-le-St Du 5w	C-le-St Du 6w
HANTS	So'ton H 50	–	So'ton K 10w	So'ton Drawn	So'ton Sy I/37	So'ton Drawn	So'ton H 5w	So'ton Drawn	So'ton H 285
KENT	Cant Du 8w	Cant Drawn	–	Cant Drawn	Cant Sy 4w	Cant K I/106	Cant Drawn	Cant Drawn	Tun W Drawn
LANCS	B'pool La 7w	Man Drawn	Man La 8w	–	Man La 7w	L'pool Sx 108	Man La 9w	Man Drawn	Man Drawn
SURREY	Oval Sy 6w	Oval H 35	Croydon K I/79	Oval Sy 24	–	Oval Aban'd	Oval Drawn	Guildford Drawn	Oval Y 346
SUSSEX	Horsham Sx I/102	Arundel Sx 166	Hove Sx 8w	Hove Drawn	Hove Drawn	–	Hove Drawn	Hove Sx I/14	Hove Sx I/261
WARWKS	B'ham Drawn	B'ham Drawn	B'ham Drawn	B'ham Drawn	B'ham Sy 9w	B'ham Wa I/34	–	B'ham Drawn	B'ham Drawn
WORCS	Worcs Du 241	Kidd'ster H 294	Worcs Aban'd	Worcs Aban'd	Worcs Drawn	Worcs Sx I/109	Worcs Wa I/113	–	Kidd'ster Wo 6w
YORKS	Leeds Y 9w	Leeds Drawn	Scar Drawn	Leeds La I/126	Leeds Drawn	Leeds Drawn	Scar Y I/210	Leeds Y I/260	–

DIVISION 2

	DERBYS	ESSEX	GLAM	GLOS	LEICS	MIDDX	N'HANTS	NOTTS	SOM'T
DERBYS	–	Derby Ex 227	Derby Drawn	Derby Drawn	Derby De 7w	Derby Drawn	Derby Drawn	Ch'field Nt I/6	Derby Sm 278
ESSEX	Chelms Drawn	–	Chelms Ex I/7	Southend Gs 70	Colchester Ex 114	Chelms Ex 10w	Chelms Ex I/41	Chelms Drawn	Chelms Sm 6w
GLAM	Cardiff De 42	Swansea Ex 4w	–	Cardiff Drawn	Aberg'ny Aban'd	Swansea M I/2	Col Bay Drawn	Swansea Gm 55	Cardiff Drawn
GLOS	Bristol Drawn	Bristol Drawn	Bristol Drawn	–	Bristol Drawn	Bristol M I/89	Glos Gs 4	Bristol Nt 51	Bristol Sm I/151
LEICS	Leics Le 28	Leics Drawn	Leics Le 10w	Leics Gs I/151	–	Leics Drawn	Leics Nh 177	Oakham Drawn	Leics Sm 198
MIDDX	Southgate De 15	Lord's Drawn	Lord's M I/71	Lord's Drawn	Southgate M 38	–	Lord's M 154	Lord's Drawn	Lord's M 7w
N'HANTS	No'ton Nh 6w	No'ton Nh 6w	No'ton Nh 10w	No'ton Nh 138	No'ton Drawn	No'ton Drawn	–	No'ton Drawn	No'ton Drawn
NOTTS	N'ham Drawn	N'ham Nt I/112	N'ham Nt I/8	N'ham Drawn	N'ham Nt 9w	N'ham Drawn	N'ham Nt 2w	–	N'ham Sm 6w
SOM'T	Taunton Drawn	Taunton Drawn	Taunton Sm 299	Taunton Sm 8w	Taunton Sm I/259	Taunton Drawn	Taunton Sm 9w	Taunton Sm I/121	–

COUNTY CHAMPIONSHIP RESULTS 2008

KEEP YOUR OWN RECORD (see page 161)

DIVISION 1

	DURHAM	HANTS	KENT	LANCS	NOTTS	SOM'T	SURREY	SUSSEX	YORKS
DURHAM	–	C-le-St	C-le-St	C-le-St	C-le-St	C-le-St	C-le-St	C-le-St	C-le-St
HANTS	So'ton	–	So'ton	So'ton	So'ton	So'ton	So'ton	So'ton	So'ton
KENT	Cant	Cant	–	Cant	Cant	Tun W	Cant	Cant	Cant
LANCS	Man	Man	L'pool	–	Man	Man	B'pool	Man	Man
NOTTS	N'ham	N'ham	N'ham	N'ham	–	N'ham	N'ham	N'ham	N'ham
SOM'T	Taunton	Taunton	Taunton	Taunton	Taunton	–	Taunton	Taunton	Taunton
SURREY	Guildford	Oval	Oval	Oval	Oval	Croydon	–	Oval	Oval
SUSSEX	Hove	Arundel	Hove	Hove	Hove	Horsham	Hove	–	Hove
YORKS	Leeds	Leeds	Scar	Leeds	Leeds	Leeds	Leeds	Scar	–

DIVISION 2

	DERBYS	ESSEX	GLAM	GLOS	LEICS	MIDDX	N'HANTS	WARWKS	WORCS
DERBYS	–	Derby	Derby	Derby	Derby	Derby	Ch'field	Derby	Ch'field
ESSEX	Chelms	–	Southend	Chelms	Chelms	Chelms	Chelms	Chelms	Colchester
GLAM	Cardiff	Cardiff	–	Cardiff	Cardiff	Colwyn Bay	tba	Cardiff	Cardiff
GLOS	Bristol	Bristol	Bristol	–	Chelt'm	Bristol	Bristol	Glos	Chelt'm
LEICS	Leics	Leics	Leics	Leics	–	Leics	Leics	Leics	Leics
MIDDX	Lord's	Lord's	Lord's	Lord's	Lord's	–	Uxbridge	Uxbridge	Lord's
N'HANTS	No'ton	No'ton	No'ton	No'ton	No'ton	No'ton	–	No'ton	No'ton
WARWKS	B'ham	B'ham	B'ham	B'ham	B'ham	B'ham	B'ham	–	B'ham
WORCS	Worcs	Worcs	Worcs	Worcs	Worcs	Worcs	Worcs	Worcs	–

NATWEST LIMITED-OVERS INTERNATIONALS 2007

ENGLAND v WEST INDIES

TWENTY20 INTERNATIONALS

Kennington Oval, London, 28 June. Toss: West Indies. **WEST INDIES** won by 15 runs. West Indies 208-8 (20; D.S.Smith 61, M.N.Samuels 51, S.Chanderpaul 41). England 193-7 (20; P.D.Collingwood 79; D.R.Smith 3-24). Award: P.D.Collingwood.

Kennington Oval, London, 29 June. Toss: West Indies. **ENGLAND** won by five wickets. West Indies 169-7 (20; C.H.Gayle 61, M.N.Samuels 42). England 173-5 (19.3; O.A.Shah 55). Award: O.A.Shah.

LIMITED-OVERS INTERNATIONALS

Lord's, London, 1 July. Toss: West Indies. **ENGLAND** won by 79 runs. England 225 (49.5; I.R.Bell 56; F.H.Edwards 5-45). West Indies 146 (39.5; S.Chanderpaul 53*; S.C.J.Broad 3-20). Award: F.H.Edwards.

Edgbaston, Birmingham, 4 July. Toss: England. **WEST INDIES** won by 61 runs. West Indies 278-5 (50; S.Chanderpaul 116*, M.N.Samuels 77). England 217 (46; M.J.Prior 52; R.Rampaul 4-41). Award: S.Chanderpaul.

Trent Bridge, Nottingham, 7 July. Toss: West Indies. **WEST INDIES** won by 93 runs. West Indies 289-5 (50; R.S.Morton 82*, C.H.Gayle 82; L.E.Plunkett 3-59). England 196 (44.2; O.A.Shah 51; D.B.L.Powell 4-40, F.H.Edwards 3-30). Award: D.B.L.Powell. Series award: S.Chanderpaul.

ENGLAND v INDIA

LIMITED-OVERS INTERNATIONALS

Rose Bowl, Southampton, 21 August (floodlit). Toss: India. **ENGLAND** won by 104 runs. England 288-2 (50; I.R.Bell 126*, A.N.Cook 102). India 184 (50; J.M.Anderson 4-23). Award: I.R.Bell.

County Ground, Bristol, 24 August (floodlit). Toss: India. **INDIA** won by nine runs. India 329-7 (50; S.R.Tendulkar 99, R.Dravid 92*; A.Flintoff 5-56). England 320-8 (50; I.R.Bell 64, A.D.Mascarenhas 52; P.Chawla 3-60, M.M.Patel 3-70). Award: R.Dravid.

Edgbaston, Birmingham, 27 August. Toss: India. **ENGLAND** won by 42 runs. England 281-8 (50; I.R.Bell 79; R.P.Singh 3-55). India 239 (48.1; S.C.Ganguly 72, R.Dravid 56; J.M.Anderson 3-32). Award: I.R.Bell.

Old Trafford, Manchester 30 August (floodlit). Toss: India. **ENGLAND** won by three wickets. India 212 (49.4; Yuvraj Singh 71, S.R.Tendulkar 55; S.C.J.Broad 4-51, J.M.Anderson 3-38). England 213-7 (48; R.S.Bopara 43* and S.C.J.Broad 45* added 99 in an unbroken eighth-wicket partnership; A.B.Agarkar 4-60) Award: S.C.J.Broad.

Headingley, Leeds 2 September. Toss: England. **INDIA** won by 38 runs (D/L Method). India 324-6 (50; Yuvraj Singh 72, S.R.Tendulkar 71, S.C.Ganguly 59, G.Gambhir 51). England (set 281 from 39 overs) 242-8 (39; P.D.Collingwood 91*). Award: S.C.Ganguly.

Kennington Oval, London 5 September. Toss: England. **INDIA** won by two wickets. England 316-6 (50; O.A.Shah 107*, K.P.Pietersen 53, L.J.Wright 50 – on debut, A.D.Mascarenhas 36* off 15 balls, including 5 sixes off last five balls of innings). India 317-8 (49.4; S.R.Tendulkar 94, S.C.Ganguly 53). Award: S.R.Tendulkar.

Lord's, London, 8 September. Toss: India. **ENGLAND** won by seven wickets. India 187 (47.3; M.S.Dhoni 50; A.D.Mascarenhas 3-23, A.Flintoff 3-45). England 188-3 (36.2; K.P.Pietersen 71*, P.D.Collingwood 64*). Award: K.P.Pietersen. Series award: I.R.Bell.

2007 FRIENDS PROVIDENT TROPHY FINAL

DURHAM v HAMPSHIRE

At Lord's, London on 18, 19 August.
Result: **DURHAM** won by 125 runs.
Toss: Lancashire. Award: O.D.Gibson

DURHAM		Runs	Balls	4/6	Fall
M.J.Di Venuto	c Carberry b Powell	12	25	1	1- 44
† P.Mustard	lbw b Bruce	49	38	6/1	2- 69
K.J.Coetzer	c Warne b Ervine	61	74	7/1	3-180
S.Chanderpaul	run out	78	79	8/2	4-220
P.D.Collingwood	c Mascarenhas b Powell	22	35	–	5-278
* D.M.Benkenstein	not out	61	43	5/3	
O.D.Gibson	not out	15	7	1/1	
G.R.Breese					
L.E.Plunkett					
N.Killeen					
G.Onions					
Extras	(LB 4, W 8, NB 2)	14			
Total	(50 overs; 5 wickets; 213 minutes)	**312**			

HAMPSHIRE		Runs	Balls	4/6	Fall
M.J.Lumb	c Di Venuto b Gibson	0	1	–	1- 0
J.P.Crawley	b Collingwood	68	93	7	5-142
S.M.Ervine	c Di Venuto b Gibson	0	1	–	2- 0
K.P.Pietersen	lbw b Gibson	12	26	–	3- 17
M.A.Carberry	b Onions	23	26	2	4- 75
† N.Pothas	c Onions b Collingwood	47	52	3	6-174
A.D.Mascarenhas	b Plunkett	12	18	1	7-177
* S.K.Warne	b Plunkett	5	9	–	10-187
C.T.Tremlett	c Di Venuto b Collingwood	0	8	–	8-178
D.B.L.Powell	c Collingwood b Plunkett	1	3	–	9-182
J.T.A.Bruce	not out	4	10	–	
Extras	(LB 10, W 3, NB 2)	15			
Total	(41 overs; 178 minutes)	**187**			

HAMPSHIRE	O	M	R	W	DURHAM	O	M	R	W
Powell	10	0	80	2	Gibson	8	1	24	3
Bruce	9	0	43	1	Killeen	8	0	29	0
Mascarenhas	6	0	45	0	Onions	6	0	28	1
Ervine	6	0	34	1	Plunkett	9	1	42	3
Tremlett	9	0	60	0	Breese	3	0	21	0
Warne	10	1	46	0	Collingwood	7	0	33	3

Scores after 15 overs: Durham 77-2; Hampshire 50-3.

Umpires: I.J.Gould and P.J.Hartley.

FRIENDS PROVIDENT TROPHY

PRINCIPAL RECORDS 1963-2007
(Including Gillette Cup, NatWest Trophy and C&G Trophy Matches)

Highest Total		496-4	Surrey v Glos	The Oval	2007
Highest Total in a Final		322-5	Warwicks v Sussex	Lord's	1993
Highest Total Batting Second		429	Glamorgan v Surrey	The Oval	2002
Highest Total to Win Batting Second		359-8	Hampshire v Surrey	The Oval	2005
Lowest Total		39	Ireland v Sussex	Hove	1985
Lowest Total in a Final		57	Essex v Lancashire	Lord's	1996
Lowest Total to Win Batting First		98	Worcs v Durham	Chester-le-St	1968
Highest Score	268	A.D.Brown	Surrey v Glamorgan	The Oval	2002
Fastest Hundred	36 balls	G.D.Rose	Somerset v Devon	Torquay	1990
Most Hundreds	8	R.A.Smith	Hampshire		1985-03
	8	N.V.Knight	Essex/Warwickshire		1992-06
	8	G.A.Hick	Worcestershire		1986-07
Most Runs	3016	(av 52.91)	G.A.Hick	Worcestershire	1986-07

Highest Partnership for each Wicket

1st	311	A.J.Wright/N.J.Trainor	Glos v Scotland	Bristol	1997
2nd	286	I.S.Anderson/A.Hill	Derbys v Cornwall	Derby	1986
3rd	309*	T.S.Curtis/T.M.Moody	Worcs v Surrey	The Oval	1994
4th	234*	D.Lloyd/C.H.Lloyd	Lancashire v Glos	Manchester	1978
5th	202*	I.J.L.Trott/T.R.Ambrose	Warwicks v Northants	Birmingham	2007
6th	226	N.J.Llong/M.V.Fleming	Kent v Cheshire	Bowdon	1999
7th	170	D.R.Brown/A.F.Giles	Warwicks v Essex	Birmingham	2003
8th	174	R.W.T.Key/J.C.Tredwell	Kent v Surrey	The Oval	2007
9th	155	C.M.W.Read/A.J.Harris	Notts v Durham	Nottingham	2006
10th	81	S.Turner/R.E.East	Essex v Yorkshire	Leeds	1982
Best Bowling	8-21	M.A.Holding	Derbys v Sussex	Hove	1988
Most Wickets	88	(av 14.35)	A.A.Donald	Warwks/Worcs	1987-02

Most Wicket-Keeping Dismissals in an Innings

	8 (8ct)	D.J.Pipe	Worcs v Herts	Hertford	2001

Most Match Wins: 101 – Lancashire.   **Most Cup/Trophy Wins:** 7 – Lancashire.

GILLETTE CUP WINNERS

1963	Sussex	1970	Lancashire	1977	Middlesex
1964	Sussex	1971	Lancashire	1978	Sussex
1965	Yorkshire	1972	Lancashire	1979	Somerset
1966	Warwickshire	1973	Gloucestershire	1980	Middlesex
1967	Kent	1974	Kent		
1968	Warwickshire	1975	Lancashire		
1969	Yorkshire	1976	Northamptonshire		

NATWEST TROPHY WINNERS

1981	Derbyshire	1988	Middlesex	1995	Warwickshire
1982	Surrey	1989	Warwickshire	1996	Lancashire
1983	Somerset	1990	Lancashire	1997	Essex
1984	Middlesex	1991	Hampshire	1998	Lancashire
1985	Essex	1992	Northamptonshire	1999	Gloucestershire
1986	Sussex	1993	Warwickshire	2000	Gloucestershire
1987	Nottinghamshire	1994	Worcestershire		

CHELTENHAM & GLOUCESTER TROPHY WINNERS

2001	Somerset	2004	Gloucestershire	2007	Durham
2002	Yorkshire	2005	Hampshire		
2003	Gloucestershire	2006	Sussex		

FRIENDS PROVIDENT TROPHY 2007

After following virtually the same knock-out format since its inauguration as the Gillette Cup in 1963, this competition was drastically revamped for the 2006 season. The Minor Counties were omitted and the 18 first-class counties, joined by Ireland and Scotland, were divided into two leagues or conferences. The winner of each league contested the final at Lord's. A semi-final stage was added for the 2007 competition when Friends Provident took over the sponsorship. Quarter-finals will be restored in 2008.

NORTH CONFERENCE

	P	W	L	T	NR	Pts	Net RR
1 DURHAM (2)	9	7	2	–	–	14	0.86
2 Warwickshire (9)	9	6	1	–	2	14	0.71
3 Nottinghamshire (4)	9	6	2	–	1	13	0.80
4 Worcestershire (3)	9	4	3	–	2	10	0.20
5 Yorkshire (7)	9	4	3	–	2	10	0.08
6 Leicestershire (6)	9	4	3	–	2	10	–0.31
7 Lancashire (1)	9	3	5	–	1	7	–0.62
8 Derbyshire (5)	9	2	6	–	1	5	–0.24
9 Northamptonshire (10)	9	1	6	–	2	4	–0.72
10 Scotland (8)	9	1	7	–	1	3	–1.05

SOUTH CONFERENCE

	P	W	L	T	NR	Pts	Net RR
1 HAMPSHIRE (4)	9	6	1	1	1	14	0.31
2 Essex (3)	9	6	2	–	1	13	1.05
3 Gloucestershire (5)	9	6	2	–	1	13	0.12
4 Kent (7)	9	5	3	–	1	11	0.88
5 Surrey (8)	9	4	3	–	2	10	0.77
6 Somerset (6)	9	4	3	1	1	10	0.19
7 Middlesex (2)	9	3	5	–	1	7	–0.37
8 Sussex (1)	9	2	5	–	2	6	–0.68
9 Glamorgan (9)	9	–	6	–	3	3	–1.41
10 Ireland (10)	9	–	6	–	3	3	–1.79

2006 final positions for that conference are shown in brackets.

SEMI-FINALS

At Riverside, Chester-le-Street, on 20 June. Toss: Durham. DURHAM beat Essex by three wickets. Essex 71 (22.1 overs; A.J.Bichel 24; L.E.Plunkett 4-15, N.Killeen 3-9, O.D.Gibson 3-21). Durham 72-7 (19 overs; L.E.Plunkett 30*; A.J.Bichel 4-22). Award: L.E.Plunkett.

At Rose Bowl, Southampton, on 20 June. Toss: Hampshire. HAMPSHIRE beat Warwickshire by 40 runs. Hampshire 206-7 (50 overs; J.P.Crawley 65, N.Pothas 40*). Warwickshire 166 (43.3 overs; K.C.Sangakkara 44, T.R.Ambrose 41; S.R.Clark 3-38). Award: J.P.Crawley.

BENSON AND HEDGES CUP

PRINCIPAL RECORDS 1972-2002

Highest Total		388-7	Essex v Scotland	Chelmsford	1992
Highest Total Batting Second		318-5	Lancashire v Leics	Manchester	1995
Lowest Total		50	Hampshire v Yorks	Leeds	1991
Largest Victory (Runs)		172	Essex v Scotland	Chelmsford	1992
Highest Score	198*	G.A.Gooch	Essex v Sussex	Hove	1982
Fastest Hundred	62 min	M.A.Nash	Glamorgan v Hants	Swansea	1976

Highest Partnership for each Wicket

1st	252	V.P.Terry/C.L.Smith	Hants v Combined U	Southampton	1990
2nd	285*	C.G.Greenidge/D.R.Turner	Hants v Minor C (S)	Amersham	1973
3rd	271	C.J.Adams/M.G.Bevan	Sussex v Essex	Chelmsford	2000
4th	207	R.C.Russell/A.J.Wright	Glos v British U	Bristol	1998
5th	160	A.J.Lamb/D.J.Capel	Northants v Leics	Northampton	1986
6th	167*	M.G.Bevan/R.J.Blakey	Yorkshire v Lancs	Manchester	1996
7th	149*	J.D.Love/C.M.Old	Yorks v Scotland	Bradford	1981
8th	112	D.C.Nash/A.A.Noffke	Middlesex v Sussex	Lord's	2002
9th	83	P.G.Newman/M.A.Holding	Derbyshire v Notts	Nottingham	1985
10th	80*	D.L.Bairstow/M.Johnson	Yorkshire v Derbys	Derby	1981
Best Bowling	7-12	W.W.Daniel	Middx v Minor C (E)	Ipswich	1978
	7-22	J.R.Thomson	Middx v Hampshire	Lord's	1981
	7-24	Mushtaq Ahmed	Somerset v Ireland	Taunton	1997
	7-32	R.G.D.Willis	Warwicks v Yorks	Birmingham	1981

Four Wickets in Four Balls S.M.Pollock Warwicks v Leics Birmingham 1996

Most Wicket-Keeping Dismissals in an Innings

8 (8ct)	D.J.S.Taylor	Somerset v Combined U	Taunton	1982

Most Catches in an Innings

5	V.J.Marks	Combined U v Kent	Oxford	1976

BENSON AND HEDGES CUP WINNERS

1972	Leicestershire	1983	Middlesex	1994	Warwickshire
1973	Kent	1984	Lancashire	1995	Lancashire
1974	Surrey	1985	Leicestershire	1996	Lancashire
1975	Leicestershire	1986	Middlesex	1997	Surrey
1976	Kent	1987	Yorkshire	1998	Essex
1977	Gloucestershire	1988	Hampshire	1999	Gloucestershire
1978	Kent	1989	Nottinghamshire	2000	Gloucestershire
1979	Essex	1990	Lancashire	2001	Surrey
1980	Northamptonshire	1991	Worcestershire	2002	Warwickshire
1981	Somerset	1992	Hampshire		
1982	Somerset	1993	Derbyshire		

IRELAND

FRIENDS PROVIDENT TROPHY REGISTER 2007

Full Names	Birthdate	Birthplace	Bat/Bowl	F-C Debut
BOTHA, Andre Cornelius	12.09.75	Johannesburg, S Africa	LHB/RM	1998-99
BRAY, Jeremy Paul	30.11.73	Sydney, Australia	LHB	2004
CARROLL, Kenneth Edward Desmond	22.03.83	Dublin	RHB/SLA	–
CUSACK, Alex Richard	29.10.80	Brisbane, Australia	RHB/RM	2007
FOURIE, Marthinus Jacobus	23.07.79	Cape Town, S Africa	RHB/RM	2007
GILLESPIE, Peter Gerard	11.05.74	Strabane	RHB/RM	1996
HAYWARD, Mornantau	06.03.77	Uitenhage, S Africa	RHB/RF	1995-96
JOHNSTON, David Trent	29.04.74	Wollongong, Australia	RHB/RFM	1998-99
JOYCE, Dominick Ignatius	14.06.81	Dublin	RHB	2004
LANGFORD-SMITH, David	07.12.76	Sydney, Australia	RHB/RFM	2006
McCALLAN, William Kyle	27.08.75	Carrickfergus	RHB/OB	1996
MOONEY, John Francis	10.02.82	Dublin	LHB/RM	2004
O'BRIEN, Kevin Joseph	04.03.84	Dublin	RHB/RMF	2006
O'BRIEN, Niall John	08.11.81	Dublin	LHB	2004
PORTERFIELD, William Thomas Stuart	06.09.84	Londonderry	LHB	2006
RYDER, Jesse Daniel	06.08.84	Masterton, New Zealand	LHB/RM	2002-03
WHELAN, Roger Kyran	27.07.80	Dublin	RHB/RFM	–
WILSON, Gary Craig	05.02.86	Dundonald	RHB	2005
WHITE, Andrew Roland	03.07.80	Newtownards, Co Down	RHB/OB	2004

SCOTLAND

FRIENDS PROVIDENT TROPHY REGISTER 2007

Full Names	Birthdate	Birthplace	Bat/Bowl	F-C Debut
BAILEY, George John	07.09.82	Launceston, Australia	RHB/RM	2004-05
BERRINGTON, Richard Douglas	03.04.87	Pretoria, S Africa	RHB/RMF	2007
BLAIN, John Angus Rae	04.01.79	Edinburgh	RHB/RFM	1996
DRUMMOND, Gordon David	21.04.80	Meigle	RHB/RM	2007
HAQ, Rana Majid	11.02.83	Paisley	LHB/OB	2004
HOFFMAN, Paul Jacob Christopher	14.01.70	Rockhampton, Australia	RHB/RMF	2004
HUSSAIN, Rana Omer	03.12.84	Paisley	LHB	2007
JACOBS, Arno	13.03.77	Potchefstroom, S Africa	LHB/OB	1997-98
LYONS, Ross Thomas	08.12.84	Greenock	LHB/SLA	2006
McCALLUM, Neil Francis Ian	22.11.77	Edinburgh	RHB	2006
MORAN, Ian Anthony	16.08.79	Sydney, Australia	RHB, RFM	–
NEL, Johann Dewald	06.06.80	Klerksdorp, S Africa	RHB/RMF	2004
ROGERS, Glenn Alan	12.04.77	Sydney, Australia	RHB/SLA	2006
SHEIKH, Mohammad Qasim	30.10.84	Glasgow	LHB/LM	2005
SMITH, Colin John Ogilvie	27.09.72	Aberdeen	RHB/WK	1999
SMITH, Simon James Stevenson	08.12.79	Ashington, Northumb.	RHB	2004
WATSON, Ryan Robert	12.11.76	Salisbury, Rhodesia	RHB/RM	2004
WATTS, David Fraser	05.06.79	King's Lynn, Norfolk	RHB/RM	1999
WRIGHT, Craig McIntyre	28.04.74	Paisley	RHB/RMF	1997

NATWEST PRO 40 LEAGUE 2007

This competition was drastically revamped in 2006, with each county playing its divisional opponents once instead of twice and with Scotland omitted. The bottom two First Division teams were relegated and replaced by the top two from the Second Division. A play-off for a First Division place was introduced between the team finishing third in the Second Division (given a home tie) and the one finishing seventh in the First Division.

FIRST DIVISION	P	W	L	T	NR	Pts	Net RR
1 Worcestershire (–)	8	6	1	–	1	13	0.75
2 Nottinghamshire (4)	8	4	2	–	2	10	0.95
3 Lancashire (6)	8	3	1	–	4	10	0.18
4 Hampshire (–)	8	4	3	–	1	9	0.17
5 Sussex (3)	8	3	3	–	2	8	0.09
6 Gloucestershire (–)	8	2	4	–	2	6	–0.33
7 Northamptonshire (2)	8	2	4	1	1	6	–0.94
8 Warwickshire (5)	8	2	5	–	1	5	–0.26
9 Essex (1)	8	1	4	1	2	5	–0.53

SECOND DIVISION	P	W	L	T	NR	Pts	Net RR
1 Durham (–)	8	6	2	–	–	12	1.31
2 Somerset (7)	8	5	2	–	1	11	0.55
3 Middlesex (–)	8	5	3	–	–	10	0.48
4 Surrey (4)	8	5	3	–	–	10	0.37
5 Kent (5)	8	5	3	–	–	10	0.26
6 Yorkshire (9)	8	4	3	–	1	9	0.04
7 Leicestershire (6)	8	3	4	–	1	7	–0.26
8 Derbyshire (8)	8	1	7	–	–	2	–0.92
9 Glamorgan (–)	8	–	7	1	1	2	–2.35

Horizontal rules segregate the counties relegated and promoted for the 2008 competition. 2006 final positions for that division are shown in brackets. Win = 2 points. Tie (T)/No Result (NR) = 1 point.

Positions of counties finishing equal on points are decided by most wins or, if equal, the side with higher net run-rate will take precedence (overall run-rate in all matches, i.e. total runs scored times 100 divided by balls received, minus the run-rate of its opponents in those same matches). If still equal, the team with the higher number of wickets taken per balls bowled in matches in which results were achieved will take precedence. If still equal, lots will be drawn.

PLAY-OFF MATCH

At John Walker's Ground, Southgate, on 23 September. Toss: Middlesex. MIDDLESEX beat Northamptonshire by six wickets. Northamptonshire 148 (35.3 overs; D.J.G.Sales 70; C.J.C.Wright 3-29, S.T.Finn 3-30). Middlesex 151-4 (36.2 overs; E.C.Joyce 42). Award: S.T.Finn.

HIGHEST BATTING AGGREGATE – Div 1	373	(av 53.28)	M.J.Lumb	Hampshire
– Div 2	409	(av 58.42)	P.Mustard	Durham
HIGHEST BOWLING AGGREGATE – Div 1	18	(av 15.00)	Kabir Ali	Worcestershire
– Div 2	21	(av 12.04)	T.J.Murtagh	Middlesex

PRO 40/NATIONAL/SUNDAY LEAGUE CHAMPIONS

1969	Lancashire	1982	Sussex	1995	Kent
1970	Lancashire	1983	Yorkshire	1996	Surrey
1971	Worcestershire	1984	Essex	1997	Warwickshire
1972	Kent	1985	Essex	1998	Lancashire
1973	Kent	1986	Hampshire	1999	Lancashire
1974	Leicestershire	1987	Worcestershire	2000	Gloucestershire
1975	Hampshire	1988	Worcestershire	2001	Kent
1976	Kent	1989	Lancashire	2002	Glamorgan
1977	Leicestershire	1990	Derbyshire	2003	Surrey
1978	Hampshire	1991	Nottinghamshire	2004	Glamorgan
1979	Somerset	1992	Middlesex	2005	Essex
1980	Warwickshire	1993	Glamorgan	2006	Essex
1981	Essex	1994	Warwickshire	2007	Worcestershire

PRINCIPAL PRO 40 RECORDS 1969-2007

Highest Total		377-9	Somerset v Sussex	Hove	2003
Highest Total Batting Second		323-5	Sussex v Leics	Horsham	2004
Lowest Total		23	Middlesex v Yorks	Leeds	1974
Largest Victory (Runs)		220	Somerset v Glamorgan	Neath	1990
Highest Scores	203	A.D.Brown	Surrey v Hampshire	Guildford	1997
	191	D.S.Lehmann	Yorks v Notts	Scarborough	2001
	176	G.A.Gooch	Essex v Glamorgan	Southend	1983
	175*	I.T.Botham	Somerset v Northants	Wellingborough	1986
Fastest Hundred	44 balls	M.A.Ealham	Kent v Derbyshire	Maidstone	1995
Most Sixes (Inns)	13	I.T.Botham	Somerset v Northants	Wellingborough	1986
Highest Partnership for each Wicket					
1st	239	G.A.Gooch/B.R.Hardie	Essex v Notts	Nottingham	1985
2nd	273	G.A.Gooch/K.S.McEwan	Essex v Notts	Nottingham	1983
3rd	228*	M.W.Goodwin/C.J.Adams	Sussex v Middlesex	Hove	2003
4th	219	C.G.Greenidge/C.L.Smith	Hampshire v Surrey	Southampton	1987
5th	221*	R.R.Sarwan/M.A.Hardinges	Glos v Lancashire	Manchester	2005
6th	167	C.L.Cairns/C.M.W.Read	Notts v Sussex	Nottingham	2003
7th	164	J.N.Snape/M.A.Hardinges	Glos v Notts	Nottingham	2001
8th	116*	N.D.Burns/P.A.J.DeFreitas	Leics v Northants	Leicester	2001
9th	105	D.G.Moir/R.W.Taylor	Derbyshire v Kent	Derby	1984
10th	82	G.Chapple/P.J.Martin	Lancashire v Worcs	Manchester	1996
Best Bowling	8-26	K.D.Boyce	Essex v Lancashire	Manchester	1971
	7-15	R.A.Hutton	Yorkshire v Worcs	Leeds	1969
	7-16	S.D.Thomas	Glamorgan v Surrey	Swansea	1998
	7-30	M.P.Bicknell	Surrey v Glamorgan	The Oval	1999
	7-39	A.Hodgson	Northants v Somerset	Northampton	1976
	7-41	A.N.Jones	Sussex v Notts	Nottingham	1986
Four Wkts in Four Balls		A.Ward	Derbyshire v Sussex	Derby	1970
		V.C.Drakes	Notts v Derbys	Nottingham	1999
Most Economical Analysis					
	8-8-0-0	B.A.Langford	Somerset v Essex	Yeovil	1969
Most Expensive Analysis					
	9-0-99-1	M.R.Strong	Northants v Glos	Cheltenham	2001
Most Wicket-Keeping Dismissals in an Innings					
	7 (6ct, 1st)	R.W.Taylor	Derbyshire v Lancs	Manchester	1975
Most Catches in an Innings by a Fielder					
	5	J.M.Rice	Hampshire v Warwicks	Southampton	1978
	5	D.J.G.Sales	Northants v Essex	Northampton	2007

TWENTY20 CUP 2007

GROUP TABLES

MIDLANDS/WALES/WEST	P	W	L	T	NR	Pts	Net RR
1 WARWICKSHIRE (3)	8	5	2	–	1	11	0.23
2 GLOUCESTERSHIRE (1)	8	4	2	–	2	10	0.98
3 WORCESTERSHIRE (6)	8	3	2	–	3	9	-0.59
4 Northamptonshire (2)	8	2	3	–	3	7	0.05
5 Somerset (5)	8	3	5	–	–	6	-0.21
6 Glamorgan (4)	8	1	4	–	3	5	-0.66

NORTH	P	W	L	T	NR	Pts	Net RR
1 NOTTINGHAMSHIRE (2)	8	4	1	–	3	11	0.87
2 LANCASHIRE (4)	8	3	1	–	4	10	0.85
3 YORKSHIRE (3)	8	4	3	–	1	9	-0.05
4 Leicestershire (1)	8	2	1	–	5	9	-0.14
5 Durham (6)	8	1	4	–	3	5	-0.57
6 Derbyshire (5)	8	–	4	–	4	4	-1.09

SOUTH	P	W	L	T	NR	Pts	Net RR
1 SUSSEX (4)	8	5	2	–	1	11	0.17
2 KENT (3)	8	4	2	1	1	10	0.32
3 Surrey (2)	8	4	4	–	–	8	0.80
4 Essex (1)	8	3	4	–	1	7	-0.36
5 Middlesex (6)	8	2	3	–	3	7	-0.20
6 Hampshire (5)	8	1	4	1	2	5	-1.11

QUARTER-FINALS: GLOUCESTERSHIRE beat Worcestershire by seven wickets at Bristol.
NOTTINGHAMSHIRE beat Kent by nine wickets at Nottingham.
SUSSEX beat Yorkshire by 38 runs at Hove.
WARWICKSHIRE beat Lancashire by six runs at Birmingham.

SEMI-FINALS: GLOUCESTERSHIRE beat Lancashire by eight wickets at Birmingham.
KENT beat Sussex by five wickets at Birmingham.

LEADING AGGREGATES 2007

BATTING (250 runs)		M	I	NO	HS	Runs	Avge	100	50	R/100b
L.J.Wright	Sussex	9	9	1	103	346	43.25	1	1	177.4
M.W.Goodwin	Sussex	9	9	1	102*	302	37.75	1	1	122.7
R.W.T.Key	Kent	6	6	2	68*	282	70.50	–	4	127.0
H.J.H.Marshall	Gloucestershire	7	7	1	100	281	46.83	1	1	152.7
J.L.Denly	Kent	11	10	1	63*	279	31.00	–	1	118.7
M.R.Ramprakash	Surrey	8	8	2	85*	265	44.16	–	2	133.1
T.R.Ambrose	Warwickshire	8	8	1	77	252	36.00	–	1	131.9

BOWLING (12 wickets)		O	M	R	W	Avge	BB	4w	R/Over
C.P.Schofield	Surrey	25	–	150	17	8.82	4-12	1	6.00
S.J.Cook	Kent	39.5	–	275	17	16.17	3-21	–	6.90
Yasir Arafat	Kent	32.3	–	280	14	20.00	3-24	–	8.61
R.J.Kirtley	Sussex	28.5	–	214	13	16.46	4-22	1	7.42
A.J.Ireland	Gloucestershire	20.2	1	157	12	13.08	3-10	–	7.72
B.M.Edmondson	Gloucestershire	31.3	–	211	12	17.58	3-20	–	6.69

TWENTY20 CUP FINAL 2007

GLOUCESTERSHIRE v KENT

At Edgbaston, Birmingham, on 4 August.
Result: **KENT** won by four wickets.
Toss: Kent. Award: R.McLaren.

GLOUCESTERSHIRE		Runs	Balls	4/6	Fall
H.J.H.Marshall	b McLaren	65	49	8	5-111
C.M.Spearman	c Van Jaarsveld b Arafat	2	4	–	1- 16
Kadeer Ali	c Tredwell b Arafat	6	5	1	2- 36
C.G.Taylor	lbw b Cook	1	2	–	3- 42
A.P.R.Gidman	run out	5	12	–	4- 62
M.A.Hardinges	not out	39	35	3/1	
† S.J.Adshead	b McLaren	0	1	–	6-111
I.D.Fisher	lbw b McLaren	0	1	–	7-111
* J.Lewis	lbw b Malinga	17	10	3	8-137
C.G.Greenidge	not out	1	1	–	
B.M.Edmondson					
Extras	(LB 7, W 3)	10			
Total	(20 overs; 8 wickets)	**146**			

KENT		Runs	Balls	4/6	Fall
J.L.Denly	c Marshall b Hardinges	28	26	5	2- 78
* R.W.T.Key	c Marshall b Greenidge	18	11	4	1- 32
M.J.Walker	c Fisher b Lewis	45	35	7	4-109
M.van Jaarsveld	b Hardinges	9	12	–	3- 96
D.I.Stevens	not out	30	21	4	
R.McLaren	b Lewis	5	7	–	5-123
† G.O.Jones	run out	4	4	–	6-127
Yasir Arafat	not out	3	2	–	
J.C.Tredwell					
S.J.Cook					
S.L.Malinga					
Extras	(LB 1, W 2, NB 2)	5			
Total	(19.3 overs; 6 wickets)	**147**			

GLOUCESTERSHIRE	O	M	R	W	KENT	O	M	R	W
Malinga	4	0	44	1	Lewis	4	0	28	2
Yasir Arafat	2	0	13	2	Greenidge	3.3	0	47	1
Cook	4	0	16	1	Edmondson	4	0	26	0
McLaren	4	0	22	3‡	Hardinges	4	0	24	2
Stevens	4	0	22	0	Gidman	4	0	21	0
Tredwell	2	0	22	0					

‡ *Including a hat-trick*

Umpires: N.A.Mallender and P.Willey.

TWENTY20 CUP WINNERS

2003	Surrey	2005	Somerset	2007	Kent
2004	Leicestershire	2006	Leicestershire		

TWENTY20 CUP RECORDS 2003-07

Highest Total	250-3		Somerset v Glos	Taunton	2006
Lowest Total	67		Sussex v Hampshire	Hove	2004

Hundreds	141*	C.L.White	Somerset v Worcs	Worcester	2006
	116*	G.A.Hick	Worcs v Northants	Luton	2004
	116*	I.J.Thomas	Glamorgan v Somerset	Taunton	2004
	116*	C.L.White	Somerset v Glos	Taunton	2006
	112	A.Symonds	Kent v Middlesex	Maidstone	2004
	111*	L.Klusener	Northants v Worcs	Kidderminster	2007
	111	D.L.Maddy	Leics v Yorks	Leeds	2004
	110	G.A.Hick	Worcs v Northants	Kidderminster	2007
	109	I.J.Harvey	Yorkshire v Derbys	Leeds	2005
	108*	I.J.Harvey	Yorkshire v Lancs	Leeds	2004
	105	B.F.Smith	Worcs v Glamorgan	Worcester	2005
	105	G.C.Smith	Somerset v Northants	Taunton	2005
	103	L.J.Wright	Sussex v Kent	Canterbury	2007
	102*	M.W.Goodwin	Sussex v Essex	Chelmsford	2007
	101	S.G.Law	Lancs v Yorkshire	Manchester	2005
	100*	I.J.Harvey	Glos v Warwicks	Birmingham	2003
	100*	R.C.Irani	Essex v Sussex	Hove	2006
	100	M.B.Loye	Lancs v Durham	Manchester	2005
	100	H.J.H.Marshall	Glos v Worcs	Kidderminster	2007

Highest Partnership for each Wicket

1st	175	V.S.Solanki/G.A.Hick	Worcs v Northants	Kidderminster	2007
2nd	186	J.L.Langer/C.L.White	Somerset v Glos	Taunton	2006
3rd	121	S.R.Patel/D.J.Hussey	Notts v Northants	Nottingham	2006
	121	H.D.Ackerman/P.A.Nixon	Leics v Derbys	Derby	2007
4th	139	M.R.Ramprakash/R.Clarke	Surrey v Glos	Bristol	2006
5th	117	M.van Jaarsveld/M.J.Walker	Kent v Leics	Leicester	2006
6th	98*	R.W.T.Key/M.J.Walker	Kent v Middlesex	Beckenham	2006
7th	63	J.S.Foster/A.R.Adams	Essex v Middlesex	Southgate	2004
	63	M.H.Wessels/B.J.Phillips	Northants v Warwicks	Birmingham	2006
8th	68	M.W.Alleyne/J.Lewis	Glos v Glamorgan	Cardiff	2005
9th	59*	G.Chapple/P.J.Martin	Lancs v Leics	Leicester	2003
10th	59	H.H.Streak/J.E.Anyon	Warwicks v Worcs	Birmingham	2005

Five Wickets	6-24	T.J.Murtagh	Surrey v Middlesex	Lord's	2005
	5-11	Mushtaq Ahmed	Sussex v Essex	Hove	2005
	5-13	M.Kartik	Middlesex v Essex	Lord's	2007
	5-14	A.D.Mascarenhas	Hampshire v Sussex	Hove	2004
	5-19	N.M.Carter	Warwicks v Worcs	Birmingham	2005
	5-21	A.J.Hollioake	Surrey v Hampshire	Southampton	2003
	5-24	C.O.Obuya	Warwicks v Glamorgan	Birmingham	2004
	5-26	R.J.Logan	Notts v Lancs	Nottingham	2003
	5-26	J.Ormond	Surrey v Middlesex	The Oval	2003
	5-27	J.F.Brown	Northants v Somerset	Northampton	2003
	5-33	A.G.R.Loudon	Warwicks v Glamorgan	Swansea	2005
	5-34	A.J.Hollioake	Surrey v Hampshire	The Oval	2004

Hat-Tricks

	J.E.Anyon	Warwicks v Somerset	Birmingham	2005
	D.G.Cork	Lancs v Notts	Manchester	2004
	A.D.Mascarenhas	Hampshire v Sussex	Hove	2004
	J.N.Snape	Leics v Yorkshire	Leicester	2007
	R.McLaren	Kent v Glos	Birmingham	2007

Most Economical Innings Analyses

4-1-6-2	J.Louw	Northants v Warwicks	Birmingham	2004
4-0-6-1	M.W.Alleyne	Glos v Worcs	Worcester	2005
4-1-7-1	R.S.C.Martin-Jenkins	Sussex v Hampshire	Hove	2004
4-1-7-4	N.Killeen	Durham v Leics	Leicester	2004
4-0-7-0	R.J.Sidebottom	Notts v Surrey	Nottingham	2006

Most Maiden Overs in an Innings

4-2-9-1	M.Morkel	Kent v Surrey	Beckenham	2007

Most Expensive Innings Analyses

4-0-65-2	M.J.Hoggard	Yorkshire v Lancs	Leeds	2005
4-0-63-1	R.J.Kirtley	Sussex v Surrey	Hove	2004
4-0-61-0	A.P.Davies	Glamorgan v Glos	Bristol	2006
4-0-60-0	S.P.Kirby	Yorks v Lancs	Leeds	2004
4-0-60-1	J.E.Anyon	Warwicks v Glos	Birmingham	2006

SCORING OF EXTRAS 2008

The variable penalties involved in scoring no-balls and wides in our international and county cricket remain unchanged from last season:

COMPETITION	NO-BALL PENALTY	WIDE PENALTY
npower Test Matches NatWest Series L-O Internationals }	1 + other runs scored	1 + other runs scored
LV County Championship Second XI Championship }	2 + other runs scored	1 + other runs scored
Tourist Matches (First-Class) Tourist Matches (Limited-Overs) }	1 + other runs scored	1 + other runs scored
NatWest International Twenty20 }	1 + other runs scored + a free hit for a foot fault	1 + other runs scored
Friends Provident Trophy (50 overs) NatWest Pro 40 League (40 overs) Twenty20 Cup (20 overs) Second XI Trophy }	2 + other runs scored + a free hit for a foot fault	1 + other runs scored

174

MINOR COUNTIES CHAMPIONSHIP
FINAL TABLES 2007
EASTERN DIVISION

	P	W	L	D	Bonus Points Bat	Points Bowl	Total Points	Net Runs/Wkt
NORTHUMBERLAND (8)	6	3	2*	1	11	17	84	−4.25
Norfolk (4)	6	3	2	1†	7	18	79	2.57
Staffordshire (6)	6	2	1	3	12	19	75	2.28
Cambridgeshire (7)	6	2	1	3†	10	18	74	3.46
Suffolk (2)	6	2	1	3	8	20	72	1.26
Hertfordshire (9)	6	1	1	4	19	20	71	8.27
Cumberland (10)	6	2	2	2	5	18	63	−0.64
Bedfordshire (5)	6	1	2	3†	11	15	56	−1.06
Buckinghamshire (1)	6	1*	3	2	7	15	42	−5.18
Lincolnshire (3)	6	–	2	4†	7	10	35	−9.75

WESTERN DIVISION

	P	W	L	D	Bonus Points Bat	Points Bowl	Total Points	Net Runs/Wkt
CHESHIRE (6)	6	4*	–	2	13	18	99	9.70
Shropshire (4)	6	3	1*	2*	9	16	89	5.63
Berkshire (9)	6	3*	2*	1†	8	12	74	5.11
Wales Minor Counties (7)	6	3*	1	2†	6	12	72	0.77
Oxfordshire (8)	6	2	1	3	8	16	68	−1.74
Devon (1)	6	2*	1	3†	9	15	66	5.04
Cornwall (5)	6	2*	3*	1	12	13	61	−1.25
Dorset (2)	6	1	3	2**	7	16	55	−0.27
Wiltshire (3)	6	1	5**	–	6	14	44	−6.27
Herefordshire (10)	6	–	4	2†*	9	10	33	−23.86

Win = 16 points. Draw/Tie = 4 points. 2006 final positions are shown in brackets.
* Includes match [** 2 matches] reduced to a single innings (points: win 12; draw 8; loss 4).
† Includes a match abandoned without a ball bowled (6 points).

2007 CHAMPIONSHIP FINAL
At Osborne Avenue, Jesmond, on 9, 10, 11 September. Toss: Northumberland. **CHESHIRE beat NORTHUMBERLAND by an innings and 4 runs.** Northumberland 176 (M.A.P.Dale 37; N.R.C.Dumelow 6-74) and 292 (G.D.Bridge 58, D.G.Shurben 40; D.A.Woods 3-86, N.R.C.Dumelow 3-94). Cheshire 472-6 closed (90 overs; D.N.Leech 202 and W.M.Goodwin 154 scored 317 for the first wicket, Extras 60).

2007 MCCA KNOCK-OUT TROPHY FINAL
At Lord's, London, on 27 August. Toss: Suffolk. **SUFFOLK beat CHESHIRE by 35 runs.** Suffolk 219 (49.2 overs; A.P.Grayson 87, C.A.Swallow 38; C.C.Finegan 3-38). Cheshire 184 (47.4 overs; M.R.Dawson 51, B.L.Spendlove 49; B.J.France 4-36).

MINOR COUNTIES RECORDS

Highest Total	621		Surrey II v Devon	The Oval	1928
Lowest Total	14		Cheshire v Staffs	Stoke	1909
Highest Score	282	E.Garnett	Berkshire v Wiltshire	Reading	1908
Most Runs – Season	1212	A.F.Brazier	Surrey II		1949
Record Partnership:					
2nd wkt	388*	T.H.Clark/A.F.Brazier	Surrey II v Sussex II	The Oval	1949
Best Bowling – Innings	10- 11	S.Turner	Cambs v Cumberland	Penrith	1987
– Match	18-100	N.W.Harding	Kent II v Wiltshire	Swindon	1937
Most Wickets – Season	119	S.F.Barnes	Staffordshire		1906

MINOR COUNTIES CHAMPIONS

1895	{ Norfolk	1933	*Undecided*	1976	Durham
	Durham	1934	Lancashire II	1977	Suffolk
	Worcestershire	1935	Middlesex II	1978	Devon
1896	Worcestershire	1936	Hertfordshire	1979	Suffolk
1897	Worcestershire	1937	Lancashire II	1980	Durham
1898	Worcestershire	1938	Buckinghamshire	1981	Durham
1899	{ Northamptonshire	1939	Surrey II	1982	Oxfordshire
	Buckinghamshire	1946	Suffolk	1983	Hertfordshire
	{ Glamorgan	1947	Yorkshire II	1984	Durham
1900	Durham	1948	Lancashire II	1985	Cheshire
	Northamptonshire	1949	Lancashire II	1986	Cumberland
1901	Durham	1950	Surrey II	1987	Buckinghamshire
1902	Wiltshire	1951	Kent II	1988	Cheshire
1903	Northamptonshire	1952	Buckinghamshire	1989	Oxfordshire
1904	Northamptonshire	1953	Berkshire	1990	Hertfordshire
1905	Norfolk	1954	Surrey II	1991	Staffordshire
1906	Staffordshire	1955	Surrey II	1992	Staffordshire
1907	Lancashire II	1956	Kent II	1993	Staffordshire
1908	Staffordshire	1957	Yorkshire II	1994	Devon
1909	Wiltshire	1958	Yorkshire II	1995	Devon
1910	Norfolk	1959	Warwickshire II	1996	Devon
1911	Staffordshire	1960	Lancashire II	1997	Devon
1912	*In abeyance*	1961	Somerset II	1998	Staffordshire
1913	Norfolk	1962	Warwickshire II	1999	Cumberland
1920	Staffordshire	1963	Cambridgeshire	2000	Dorset
1921	Staffordshire	1964	Lancashire II	2001	{ Cheshire
1922	Buckinghamshire	1965	Somerset II		Lincolnshire
1923	Buckinghamshire	1966	Lincolnshire	2002	{ Herefordshire
1924	Berkshire	1967	Cheshire		Norfolk
1925	Buckinghamshire	1968	Yorkshire II	2003	Lincolnshire
1926	Durham	1969	Buckinghamshire	2004	{ Bedfordshire
1927	Staffordshire	1970	Bedfordshire		Devon
1928	Berkshire	1971	Yorkshire II	2005	{ Cheshire
1929	Oxfordshire	1972	Bedfordshire		Suffolk
1930	Durham	1973	Shropshire	2006	Devon
1931	Leicestershire II	1974	Oxfordshire	2007	Cheshire
1932	Buckinghamshire	1975	Hertfordshire		

LEADING CHAMPIONSHIP AGGREGATES 2007

BATTING

		M	I	NO	HS	Runs	Avge	100	50
D.N.Leech	(Cheshire)	7	11	2	202	640	71.11	2	4
A.S.Lewis	(Hertfordshire)	6	10	2	147	607	75.87	2	2
S.Seadon	(Staffordshire)	6	12	1	106*	523	47.54	1	3
A.W.Laraman	(Hertfordshire)	6	10	1	109*	512	56.88	2	3
R.J.Williams	(Oxfordshire)	5	8	3	197*	484	96.80	2	1
I.Pattison	(Northumberland)	7	12	—	100	468	39.00	1	3
A.Worthy	(Northumberland)	6	11	—	119	464	42.18	2	1
G.R.Brown	(Hertfordshire)	6	10	—	83	409	40.90	—	4
M.C.Dobson	(Lincolnshire)	5	8	—	201	408	51.00	1	1
W.M.Goodwin	(Cheshire)	5	8	—	154	397	49.62	1	2
R.J.Foster	(Shropshire)	6	10	1	103*	392	43.55	1	3
P.B.Muchall	(Northumberland)	5	9	—	141	391	43.44	2	1
C.R.Borrett	(Norfolk)	5	10	—	95	390	39.00	—	2
D.M.Ward	(Hertfordshire)	6	10	—	92	390	39.00	—	3
T.R.Ward	(Norfolk)	5	10	2	107	386	48.25	1	3
G.D.Bridge	(Northumberland)	6	10	1	120	382	42.44	1	3
D.J.R.Exall	(Herefordshire)	5	9	1	94	362	45.25	—	4

		M	I	NO	HS	Runs	Avge	100	50
B.Parker	(Northumberland)	7	12	–	116	361	30.08	1	1
N.T.Lee	(Suffolk)	6	11	2	105	357	39.66	1	1
B.J.France	(Suffolk)	6	12	2	77	348	34.80	–	4
S.A.Kellett	(Cambridgeshire)	4	7	1	105	348	58.00	1	2
B.H.D.Mordt	(Berkshire)	5	8	–	80	345	43.12	–	3
A.J.Hall	(Cheshire)	5	8	1	162*	339	48.42	1	2
D.G.Shurben	(Northumberland)	5	9	–	114	324	36.00	1	1
S.P.Naylor	(Berkshire)	5	8	–	80	319	39.87	–	3
Atiq-ur-Rehman	(Shropshire)	6	10	1	109*	318	35.33	1	1
N.G.Park	(Dorset)	6	10	1	122	310	34.44	1	-
G.J.Pratt	(Cumberland)	6	9	1	74	308	38.50	–	3
T.B.Huggins	(Suffolk)	6	12	1	139	304	27.63	1	1
M.A.Sheikh	(Staffordshire)	6	11	3	71	302	37.75	–	3

BOWLING

		O	M	R	W	Avge	BB	5w	10w
N.R.C.Dumelow	(Cheshire)	217.3	47	771	39	19.76	9- 37	2	1
C.Brown	(Norfolk)	204.1	42	639	29	22.03	6- 35	2	1
A.R.Roberts	(Bedfordshire)	173.4	47	421	28	15.03	6- 50	3	–
C.D.Crowe	(Berkshire)	160.1	36	480	28	17.14	5- 30	2	–
R.J.Harrison	(Cornwall)	183.1	58	485	28	17.32	7- 90	2	1
S.A.Taylor	(Shropshire)	138	43	377	25	15.08	6- 23	2	1
A.J.Syddall	(Cheshire)	172.3	41	612	25	24.48	6- 39	1	–
A.K.D.Gray	(Shropshire)	199.1	45	480	23	20.86	4- 49	–	–
I.E.Bishop	(Devon)	174.3	44	535	23	23.26	6- 23	1	–
S.J.Airey	(Lincolnshire)	136.5	22	381	22	17.31	6- 41	2	1
M.J.Metcalfe	(Dorset)	182	52	513	22	23.31	6- 55	2	1
M.A.Sheikh	(Staffordshire)	179.2	45	475	21	22.61	5- 46	1	–
G.R.Willott	(Staffordshire)	107.2	36	328	19	17.26	4- 48	–	–
P.J.Bradshaw	(Norfolk)	113	22	367	19	19.31	5- 46	1	–
P.D.Edwards	(Suffolk)	153.5	39	477	19	25.10	5- 56	1	–
C.A.Swallow	(Suffolk)	132	33	425	18	23.61	5- 52	1	–
S.F.Stanway	(Buckinghamshire)	171.5	45	448	18	24.88	5- 25	1	–
J.E.Bishop	(Suffolk)	139	29	463	18	25.72	4- 87	–	–
S.M.Coleman	(Hertfordshire)	194.3	48	589	18	32.72	4- 95	–	–
J.N.Snape	(Staffordshire)	111	18	351	17	20.64	4- 42	–	–
G.D.Morris	(Staffordshire)	145.4	39	363	17	21.35	3- 25	–	–
D.A.Woods	(Cheshire)	135	23	429	17	25.23	4- 26	–	–
T.C.Hicks	(Dorset)	156.5	33	453	17	26.64	5- 84	1	–
J.D.Shantry	(Shropshire)	107.3	36	246	16	15.37	3- 22	–	–
J.J.Newell	(Buckinghamshire)	134.1	37	286	16	17.87	5- 23	2	–
P.J.McMahon	(Oxfordshire)	106.1	23	380	16	23.75	6-114	2	1
L.C.Ryan	(Oxfordshire)	161.4	31	505	16	31.56	5-103	2	–
A.Roberts	(Cumberland)	89.5	21	226	15	15.06	5- 62	1	–
P.W.Turk	(Wiltshire)	88.5	10	366	15	24.40	7- 53	2	–
P.R.Sawyer	(Buckinghamshire)	130.1	20	462	15	30.80	5- 50	1	–

SECOND XI CHAMPIONSHIP 2007
FINAL TABLE

	P	W	L	D	Deduct	Bat	Bowl	Total Points	Avge
1 SUSSEX (2)	11	6	–	5	0.5	28	34	165.5	15.04
2 Somerset (10)	10	5	1	4	–	28	27	141	14.10
3 Hampshire (12)	12	5	2	5	–	29	44	163	13.58
4 Lancashire (7)	13	7	3	3	–	29	36	175	13.46
5 Durham (5)	14	6	3	5	2	44	40	186	13.28
6 Middlesex (14)	11	4	2	5	2	38	30	142	12.90
7 Leicestershire (11)	11	4	3	4	1.5	28	39	137.5	12.50
8 Warwickshire (6)	12	5	4	3	–	27	34	143	11.91
9 Derbyshire (9)	12	3	1	8	–	31	32	137	11.41
10 Yorkshire (3)	12	4	5	3	–	35	34	137	11.41
11 Surrey (4)	15	3	4	6	–	39	37	170	11.33
12 Nottinghamshire (15)	9	3	3	3	–	18	30	102	11.33
13 Northamptonshire (18)	10	3	4	2	1.5	20	30	102.5	10.25
14 MCC Young Cricketers (17)	13	2	6	5	0.5	32	41	120.5	9.26
15 Scotland A (-)	6	1	4	1	–	9	20	47	7.83
16 Gloucestershire (8)	8	1	5	2	–	15	21	58	7.25
17 Essex (16)	10	1	6	3	1.5	19	28	71.5	7.15
18 Worcestershire (19)	11	1	4	6	–	16	19	73	6.63
19 Glamorgan (13)	7	–	3	4	–	11	19	46	6.57
20 Kent (1)	7	–	3	4	–	9	11	36	5.14

Win = 14 points, plus any first-innings points. Draw = 4 points, plus any first-innings points.
Tie-breakers for teams finishing with equal average points are (i) highest season ratio of runs scored per wickets lost and (ii) the lowest season ratio of runs conceded per wickets taken.
2006 final positions are shown in brackets.

SECOND XI CHAMPIONS

1959	Gloucestershire	1976	Kent	1993	Middlesex
1960	Northamptonshire	1977	Yorkshire	1994	Somerset
1961	Kent	1978	Sussex	1995	Hampshire
1962	Worcestershire	1979	Warwickshire	1996	Warwickshire
1963	Worcestershire	1980	Glamorgan	1997	Lancashire
1964	Lancashire	1981	Hampshire	1998	Northamptonshire
1965	Glamorgan	1982	Worcestershire	1999	Middlesex
1966	Surrey	1983	Leicestershire	2000	Middlesex
1967	Hampshire	1984	Yorkshire	2001	Hampshire
1968	Surrey	1985	Nottinghamshire	2002	Kent
1969	Kent	1986	Lancashire	2003	Yorkshire
1970	Kent	1987	Kent/Yorkshire	2004	Somerset
1971	Hampshire	1988	Surrey	2005	Kent
1972	Nottinghamshire	1989	Middlesex	2006	Kent
1973	Essex	1990	Sussex	2007	Sussex
1974	Middlesex	1991	Yorkshire		
1975	Surrey	1992	Surrey		

SECOND XI TROPHY 2007

Final: MIDDLESEX 198 (45.2 overs; B.A.Godleman 69 and E.J.G.Morgan 85 shared a second-wicket partnership of 142; A.V.Suppiah 5-40) beat SOMERSET 197 (49.1 overs; J.D.Francis 57; R.E.M.Williams 3-20) by one run at Taunton.

YOUNG CRICKETER OF THE YEAR

This annual award, made by The Cricket Writers' Club, which celebrated its 60th anniversary in 2006, is currently restricted to players qualified for England, Andrew Symonds meeting that requirement at the time of his award, and under the age of 23 on 1st May. In 1986 their ballot resulted in a dead heat. Up to 4 March 2008 their selections have gained a tally of 1,944 international Test match caps (shown in brackets).

1950	R.Tattersall (16)	1980	G.R.Dilley (41)
1951	P.B.H.May (66)	1981	M.W.Gatting (79)
1952	F.S.Trueman (67)	1982	N.G.Cowans (19)
1953	M.C.Cowdrey (114)	1983	N.A.Foster (29)
1954	P.J.Loader (13)	1984	R.J.Bailey (4)
1955	K.F.Barrington (82)	1985	D.V.Lawrence (5)
1956	B.Taylor	1986 {	A.A.Metcalfe
1957	M.J.Stewart (8)		J.J.Whitaker (1)
1958	A.C.D.Ingleby-Mackenzie	1987	R.J.Blakey (2)
1959	G.Pullar (28)	1988	M.P.Maynard (4)
1960	D.A.Allen (39)	1989	N.Hussain (96)
1961	P.H.Parfitt (37)	1990	M.A.Atherton (115)
1962	P.J.Sharpe (12)	1991	M.R.Ramprakash (52)
1963	G.Boycott (108)	1992	I.D.K.Salisbury (15)
1964	J.M.Brearley (39)	1993	M.N.Lathwell (2)
1965	A.P.E.Knott (95)	1994	J.P.Crawley (37)
1966	D.L.Underwood (86)	1995	A.Symonds (19-Australia)
1967	A.W.Greig (58)	1996	C.E.W.Silverwood (6)
1968	R.M.H.Cottam (4)	1997	B.C.Hollioake (2)
1969	A.Ward (5)	1998	A.Flintoff (66)
1970	C.M.Old (46)	1999	A.J.Tudor (10)
1971	J.Whitehouse	2000	P.J.Franks
1972	D.R.Owen-Thomas	2001	O.A.Shah (2)
1973	M.Hendrick (30)	2002	R.Clarke (2)
1974	P.H.Edmonds (51)	2003	J.M.Anderson (20)
1975	A.Kennedy	2004	I.R.Bell (33)
1976	G.Miller (34)	2005	A.N.Cook (24)
1977	I.T.Botham (102)	2006	S.C.J.Broad (1)
1978	D.I.Gower (117)	2007	A.U.Rashid
1979	P.W.G.Parker (1)		

THE PROFESSIONAL CRICKETERS' ASSOCIATION
PLAYER OF THE YEAR

Founded in 1967, the Professional Cricketers' Association introduced this award, decided by their membership, in 1970. Since 1998 it has been presented at their Annual Awards Dinner at the Royal Albert Hall. Only John Lever and Andrew Flintoff have won the award in successive years.

1970 {	M.J.Procter	1982	M.D.Marshall	1995	D.G.Cork
	J.D.Bond	1983	K.S.McEwan	1996	P.V.Simmons
1971	L.R.Gibbs	1984	R.J.Hadlee	1997	S.P.James
1972	A.M.E.Roberts	1985	N.V.Radford	1998	M.B.Loye
1973	P.G.Lee	1986	C.A.Walsh	1999	S.G.Law
1974	B.Stead	1987	R.J.Hadlee	2000	M.E.Trescothick
1975	Zaheer Abbas	1988	G.A.Hick	2001	D.P.Fulton
1976	P.G.Lee	1989	S.J.Cook	2002	M.P.Vaughan
1977	M.J.Procter	1990	G.A.Gooch	2003	Mushtaq Ahmed
1978	J.K.Lever	1991	Waqar Younis	2004	A.Flintoff
1979	J.K.Lever	1992	C.A.Walsh	2005	A.Flintoff
1980	R.D.Jackman	1993	S.L.Watkin	2006	M.R.Ramprakash
1981	R.J.Hadlee	1994	B.C.Lara	2007	O.D.Gibson

FIRST-CLASS CAREER RECORDS

Compiled by **Philip Bailey**

The following career records are for all players who appeared in first-class or List A limited-overs cricket during the 2007 season, and are complete to the end of that season. Some players who did not appear in 2007 but may do so in 2008 are also included.

BATTING AND FIELDING

'1000' denotes instances of scoring 1000 runs in a season. Where these have been achieved outside the British Isles they are shown after a plus sign.

	M	I	NO	HS	Runs	Avge	100	50	1000	Ct/St
Abdul Razzaq	108	168	26	203*	4792	33.74	8	23	–	28
Ackerman, H.D.	178	298	27	309*	11729	43.28	31	64	2+1	144
Adams, A.R.	78	104	9	124	2380	25.05	3	10	–	49
Adams, C.J.	321	523	38	239	19061	39.30	48	91	9	391
Adams, J.H.K.	64	115	11	262*	3516	33.80	4	17	1	47
Adnan, M.Hasan	127	213	24	191	7211	38.15	10	48	1	67
Adshead, S.J.	65	107	17	148*	2765	30.72	1	17	–	161/14
Afzaal, U.	190	330	34	168*	11129	37.59	26	56	6	90
Aga, R.G.	8	16	2	43	138	9.85	–	–	–	6
Ahmed, J.S.	5	4	3	14*	28	28.00	–	–	–	3
Ali, Kabir	97	133	19	84*	2002	17.56	–	7	–	24
Ali, Kadeer	65	118	5	145	3041	26.91	3	18	–	32
Ali, M.M.	10	15	–	85	414	27.60	–	5	–	4
Allenby, J.	18	30	6	103*	994	41.41	1	6	–	17
Alleyne, D.	22	33	4	109*	849	29.27	1	4	–	57/5
Ambrose, T.R.	72	113	9	251*	3627	34.87	4	22	–	145/14
Amerasinghe, M.K.D.I.	83	85	42	46	283	6.58	–	–	–	25
Anderson, J.M.	66	76	36	37*	362	9.05	–	–	–	25
Andrew, G.M.	11	14	1	44	163	12.53	–	–	–	5
Anyon, J.E.	36	48	19	37*	311	10.72	–	–	–	11
Austin, M.L.	2	3	–	25	60	20.00	–	–	–	–
Azhar Mahmood	145	226	27	204*	6251	31.41	8	32	–	122
Bagai, A.	9	17	–	76	514	30.23	–	4	–	23/3
Baker, F.B.	2	3	–	18	35	11.66	–	–	–	–
Balcombe, D.J.	12	17	3	73	271	19.35	–	1	–	5
Ball, A.H.	1	2	1	44*	50	50.00	–	–	–	–
Banerjee, V.	20	30	13	29	185	10.88	–	–	–	5
Banks, O.A.C.	56	87	14	100	1754	24.02	1	9	–	32
Barnes, M.W.	1	–	–	–	–	–	–	–	–	5
Barnett, G.E.F.	20	37	2	136	963	27.51	2	5	–	19
Bastiampillai, T.C.	5	9	–	71	281	31.22	–	3	–	–
Batty, G.J.	107	166	30	133	3639	26.75	2	18	–	75
Batty, J.N.	159	243	30	168*	7235	33.96	16	34	1	420/56
Bell, I.R.	115	197	18	262*	7710	43.07	19	43	2	72
Benham, C.C.	27	45	1	95	1135	25.79	–	6	–	24
Benkenstein, D.M.	175	266	33	259	10897	46.76	27	56	3	123
Benning, J.G.E.	28	45	4	128	1442	35.17	4	6	–	13
Bichel, A.J.	183	242	25	148	5694	26.23	8	23	–	89
Birch, D.J.	4	7	–	130	236	33.71	1	1	–	1
Birt, T.R.	58	107	6	181	4002	39.62	9	24	1	40
Blackwell, I.D.	130	196	15	247*	7039	38.88	17	34	2	47

F-C	M	I	NO	HS	Runs	Avge	100	50	1000	Ct/St
Boje, N.	175	261	48	125	7059	33.14	6	42	–	104
Bollinger, D.E.	34	43	20	31*	170	7.39	–	–	–	11
Bond, S.E.	51	57	20	100	694	18.75	1	2	–	22
Bopara, R.S.	60	97	15	229	3206	39.09	6	12	–	40
Borrington, P.M.	4	6	–	50	152	25.33	–	1	–	2
Bose, R.R.	56	61	13	21	204	4.25	–	–	–	12
Botha, A.G.	100	160	22	156*	3336	24.17	4	14	–	74
Bott, M.D.	4	7	1	20	47	7.83	–	–	–	3
Boyce, M.A.G.	2	3	–	6	15	5.00	–	–	–	–
Bradshaw, D.P.	4	8	2	96	208	34.66	–	1	–	–
Bragg, W.D.	2	4	–	24	51	12.75	–	–	–	–
Brathwaite, R.M.R.	7	10	3	76*	140	20.00	–	1	–	–
Bravo, D.J.	76	139	6	197	4110	30.90	7	22	–	62
Bray, J.P.	10	15	–	190	833	55.53	3	3	–	7
Breese, G.R.	110	178	19	165*	4086	25.69	3	26	–	91
Bresnan, T.T.	59	79	14	126*	1671	25.70	3	8	–	22
Broad, S.C.J.	33	40	11	91*	643	22.17	–	4	–	8
Brophy, G.L.	76	121	15	185	3352	31.62	6	15	–	186/13
Brown, A.D.	240	379	41	295*	14705	43.50	44	60	8	242/1
Brown, B.C.	1	1	–	46	46	46.00	–	–	–	–
Brown, D.O.	14	24	–	77	590	24.58	–	4	–	7
Brown, D.R.	209	319	41	203	8511	30.61	10	44	1	130
Brown, J.F.	119	140	57	38	616	7.42	–	–	–	24
Brown, K.R.	2	4	–	32	61	15.25	–	–	–	1
Brown, M.J.	62	110	12	133	3199	32.64	6	18	1	54
Bruce, J.T.A.	49	57	23	32	243	7.14	–	–	–	14
Burrows, T.G.	4	6	–	42	139	23.16	–	–	–	14
Butcher, M.A.	269	460	36	259	17098	40.32	36	92	8	249
Butler, S.M.	2	4	2	21*	36	18.00	–	–	–	–
Buttleman, J.E.L.	1	2	–	12	16	8.00	–	–	–	–
Caddick, A.R.	260	341	65	92	4104	14.86	–	9	–	85
Carberry, M.A.	65	114	11	192*	4152	40.31	11	20	1	28
Carter, N.M.	74	101	21	103	1507	18.83	1	3	–	21
Chambers, M.A.	1	1	1	2*	2	–	–	–	–	–
Chanderpaul, S.	208	340	56	303*	14757	51.96	41	73	1+1	128
Chapple, G.	216	297	55	155	6023	24.88	6	27	–	72
Cheetham, S.P.	1	–	–	–	–	–	–	–	–	1
Cherry, D.D.	40	71	1	226	1824	26.05	3	4	–	12
Chilton, M.J.	143	233	16	131	6965	32.09	17	25	1	110
Chopra, A.S.	103	172	18	222	6880	44.67	17	38	–	125
Chopra, V.	25	42	4	106	1218	32.05	1	9	–	22
Choudhry, S.H.	1	2	1	54*	61	–	–	1	–	–
Clare, J.L.	2	3	–	22	42	14.00	–	–	–	–
Clark, S.R.	79	106	29	62	1092	14.18	–	1	–	23
Clarke, R.	76	122	13	214	4201	38.54	10	17	1	87
Claydon, M.E.	5	3	1	38	52	26.00	–	–	–	–
Cliff, S.J.	2	3	2	11	21	21.00	–	–	–	–
Clinton, R.S.	42	70	5	108*	1837	28.26	4	9	–	24
Clough, G.D.	12	17	2	55	156	10.40	–	1	–	4
Cobb, J.J.	1	2	–	21	23	11.50	–	–	–	–
Codrington, A.	4	6	–	48	96	16.00	–	–	–	1
Coetzer, K.J.	23	41	6	153*	1336	38.17	3	4	–	14
Collingwood, P.D.	146	257	19	206	8573	36.02	19	40	2	157
Collins, P.T.	99	124	30	25	607	6.45	–	–	–	26

F-C	M	I	NO	HS	Runs	Avge	100	50	1000	Ct/St
Collymore, C.D.	84	123	59	20	499	7.79	–	–	–	28
Compton, N.R.D.	35	61	7	190	2060	38.14	6	9	1	18
Cook, A.N.	69	123	11	195	5297	47.29	17	25	3	71
Cook, S.J.	103	133	18	93*	1887	16.40	–	5	–	31
Cork, D.G.	278	407	54	200*	8965	25.39	8	50	–	200
Cosker, D.A.	145	182	56	52	1624	12.88	–	1	–	94
Coverdale, P.S.	1	1	–	11	11	11.00	–	–	–	–
Crawley, J.P.	334	554	56	311*	23637	47.46	53	129	10	211/1
Croft, R.D.B.	350	521	92	143	11317	26.37	7	49	–	169
Croft, S.J.	13	21	2	65	351	18.47	–	2	–	13
Crook, A.R.	10	16	1	88	469	31.26	–	3	–	8
Crook, S.P.	29	38	7	97	954	30.77	–	6	–	10
Cross, G.D.	7	11	1	72	271	27.10	–	3	–	26/8
Cummins, R.A.G.	20	25	11	34*	177	12.64	–	–	–	5
Cusden, S.M.J.	7	8	5	14	42	14.00	–	–	–	2
Daggett, L.M.	17	24	12	33	100	8.33	–	–	–	1
Dalrymple, J.W.M.	75	122	12	244	3727	33.88	5	19	–	38
Danish Kaneria	121	149	65	65	819	9.75	–	1	–	39
Davies, A.M.	54	78	28	62	590	11.80	–	1	–	14
Davies, A.P.	41	58	17	54	707	17.24	–	1	–	11
Davies, S.M.	46	78	6	192	2510	34.86	4	9	1	125/12
Davison, J.M.	51	74	7	165	1177	16.57	1	4	–	25
Dawson, L.A.	1	–	–	–	–	–	–	–	–	–
Dawson, R.K.J.	91	136	16	87	2541	21.17	–	11	–	48
Dean, K.J.	115	153	50	54*	1176	11.41	–	2	–	22
Denly, J.L.	21	35	4	115*	1404	45.29	4	8	1	10
Dernbach, J.W.	10	11	5	10	34	5.66	–	–	–	2
De Wet, F.	23	32	8	43*	391	16.29	–	–	–	10
Dexter, N.J.	19	28	7	131*	989	47.09	2	6	–	13
Dhoni, M.S.	58	95	7	148	3098	35.20	4	19	–	155/28
Dighton, M.G.	62	112	6	182*	3917	36.95	8	19	–	49
Dingle, L.A.	1	1	–	0	0	0.00	–	–	–	–
Dippenaar, H.H.	121	202	18	250*	7781	42.28	24	31	0+1	98
Di Venuto, M.J.	255	454	27	230	19035	44.57	42	115	7	302
Dixey, P.G.	6	11	1	25	124	12.40	–	–	–	15/1
Dobson, W.T.	3	5	3	13*	29	14.50	–	–	–	1
Doshi, N.D.	53	68	16	37	505	9.71	–	–	–	8
Dravid, R.S.	228	374	54	270	18240	57.00	49	95	1+3	268/1
Duffell, C.B.R.	3	5	1	6	15	3.75	–	–	–	5
Dunbar, P.R.	2	3	–	46	52	17.33	–	–	–	1
Du Plessis, F.	18	33	4	156	1152	39.72	2	8	–	14
Durston, W.J.	28	47	7	146*	1443	36.07	1	10	–	33
Ealham, M.A.	253	385	59	153*	10527	32.29	12	65	1	143
Edmondson, B.M.	38	40	20	18	102	5.10	–	–	–	11
Edwards, F.H.	43	66	22	20	190	4.31	–	–	–	7
Edwards, N.J.	41	67	–	212	2557	38.16	3	13	1	27
Elliott, M.T.G.	206	379	27	203	16822	47.78	50	81	3+5	223
Ervine, S.M.	70	110	12	126	3075	31.37	5	17	–	63
Evans, D.	4	5	1	7	7	1.75	–	–	–	1
Evans, L.	1	2	1	1	1	1.00	–	–	–	–
Evans, L.J.	4	8	1	133*	365	52.14	1	2	–	4
Ferley, R.S.	29	37	9	78*	587	20.96	–	2	–	8
Fernando, C.S.	65	107	15	109	2763	30.03	2	13	–	150/25
Finn, S.T.	4	5	2	3	4	1.33	–	–	–	–

F-C	M	I	NO	HS	Runs	Avge	100	50	1000	Ct/St
Fisher, I.D.	78	118	19	103*	2197	22.19	1	7	–	27
Fleming, S.P.	239	392	32	274*	15819	43.94	35	88	1	327
Flintoff, A.	163	257	18	167	8343	34.90	15	49	–	168
Flower, G.W.	179	305	23	243*	10679	37.86	23	58	–	168
Footitt, M.H.A.	8	6	4	19*	40	20.00	–	–	–	1
Foster, E.J.	6	10	1	105	291	32.33	1	1	–	5/1
Foster, J.S.	121	177	22	212	5415	34.93	9	27	1	307/33
Foster, P.J.	3	5	–	19	46	9.20	–	–	–	1
Fourie, M.J.	2	2	1	6*	6	6.00	–	–	–	2
Francis, J.D.	55	98	8	125*	2678	29.75	6	14	1	32
Francis, S.R.G.	60	77	33	44	509	11.56	–	–	–	19
Franks, P.J.	146	210	41	123*	4432	26.22	3	21	–	49
Friedlander, M.J.	12	17	–	81	256	15.05	–	1	–	5
Froggett, T.J.	1	1	1	21*	21	–	–	–	–	1
Frost, T.	92	134	21	135*	3178	28.12	3	16	–	225/16
Gale, A.W.	15	24	–	149	520	21.66	1	2	–	9
Gallian, J.E.R.	235	399	35	312	14173	38.93	36	67	6	200
Gambhir, G.	88	144	15	233*	6766	52.44	20	28	–	58
Ganegama, W.C.A.	69	87	17	75	1044	14.91	–	2	–	30
Ganga, D.	137	238	20	265	8072	37.02	20	37	0+1	85
Ganguly, S.C.	222	346	40	200*	13385	43.74	28	77	–	159
Gayle, C.H.	139	248	17	317	10046	43.48	22	52	0+1	126
Gazzard, C.M.	27	42	6	74	732	20.33	–	1	–	58/1
Gibson, O.D.	177	267	36	155	5604	24.25	2	29	–	68
Gidman, A.P.R.	85	150	17	142	5114	38.45	11	31	3	52
Gidman, W.R.S.	1	2	–	8	8	4.00	–	–	–	–
Gifford, W.M.	8	13	2	71	252	22.90	–	2	–	4
Gilbert, C.R.	1	1	–	64	64	64.00	–	1	–	1
Gillespie, J.N.	166	219	54	201*	3010	18.24	2	7	–	62
Gillespie, P.G.	13	18	3	53	322	21.46	–	2	–	7
Goddard, L.J.	10	14	4	91	324	32.40	–	2	–	22
Godleman, B.A.	16	25	3	113*	911	41.40	1	7	–	22
Goodwin, M.W.	218	383	30	335*	17037	48.26	52	72	6+1	130
Gough, D.	240	315	59	121	4459	17.41	1	20	–	47
Grant, R.N.	19	31	1	79	649	21.63	–	2	–	5
Green, J.A.G.	1	1	–	28	28	28.00	–	–	–	–
Greenidge, C.G.	49	60	8	46	443	8.51	–	–	–	18
Griffiths, D.A.	6	9	4	31*	58	11.60	–	–	–	1
Groenewald, T.D.	14	18	4	76	290	20.71	–	1	–	9
Gunawardene, K.D.	31	48	2	127*	1519	33.02	2	8	–	26
Gurney, H.F.	1	2	1	1	1	1.00	–	–	–	–
Guy, S.M.	36	50	6	52*	727	16.52	–	1	–	97/12
Hall, A.J.	124	182	24	163	5288	33.46	5	36	–	90
Hamilton-Brown, R.J.	1	2	–	9	14	7.00	–	–	–	1
Harbhajan Singh	120	158	34	84	2367	19.08	–	6	–	63
Hardinges, M.A.	44	67	7	172	1510	25.16	4	4	–	22
Harinath, A.	3	5	–	69	128	25.60	–	2	–	1
Harmison, B.W.	18	33	4	110	921	31.75	3	5	–	12
Harmison, S.J.	147	204	55	42	1493	10.02	–	–	–	24
Harris, A.J.	123	167	41	41*	1069	8.48	–	–	–	36
Harris, J.A.R.	9	14	2	87*	196	16.33	–	1	–	4
Harris, P.L.	55	67	10	55	794	13.92	–	1	–	21
Harris, R.J.	16	28	2	74	377	14.50	–	1	–	10
Harrison, A.J.	3	3	1	34*	37	18.50	–	–	–	–

F-C	M	I	NO	HS	Runs	Avge	100	50	1000	Ct/St
Harrison, D.S.	68	98	14	88	1341	15.96	–	4	–	24
Harrison, P.W.	11	17	4	54	298	22.92	–	1	–	16
Harvey, I.J.	165	272	29	209*	8409	34.60	15	46	–	114
Hemingway, T.L.	1	1	–	4	4	4.00	–	–	–	1
Hemp, D.L.	253	431	40	247*	14487	37.05	28	78	6	171
Henderson, C.W.	180	245	55	81	3590	18.89	–	10	–	68
Henderson, T.	81	129	17	81	1867	16.66	–	6	–	29
Herath, M.R.K.B.	141	198	47	71*	2282	15.11	–	7	–	60
Heywood, J.J.N.	9	13	2	27	65	5.90	–	–	–	14
Hick, G.A.	515	853	81	405*	40423	52.36	134	156	19+1	684
Hildreth, J.C.	61	101	9	227*	3774	41.02	9	20	1	53
Hill, C.M.M.	1	1	–	0	0	0.00	–	–	–	1
Hinds, W.W.	124	214	8	213	7119	34.55	18	32	–	62
Hobbiss, M.H.	2	2	1	78*	93	93.00	–	1	–	–
Hodd, A.J.	19	27	7	123	769	38.45	2	4	–	32/7
Hodge, B.J.	198	348	35	302*	15089	48.20	46	55	2+3	113
Hodgkinson, R.	1	1	–	6	6	6.00	–	–	–	–
Hodnett, G.P.	16	27	1	168	945	36.34	2	6	–	9
Hogg, K.W.	39	48	5	71	982	22.83	–	7	–	11
Hoggard, M.J.	160	203	61	89*	1273	8.96	–	3	–	45
Hole, S.M.	1	2	1	24	24	24.00	–	–	–	–
Holioake, A.J.	173	263	21	208	9376	38.74	18	55	2	157
Hooper, J.H.P.	4	7	1	79	154	25.66	–	1	–	1
Hopkinson, C.D.	38	63	1	83	1473	23.75	–	11	–	25
Horton, P.J.	26	43	5	152	1717	45.18	3	9	1	23/1
Howell, T.H.	1	2	–	82	82	41.00	–	1	–	–
Hughes, J.A.	3	5	1	45	105	26.25	–	–	–	–
Hunter, I.D.	50	68	17	65	898	17.60	–	2	–	15
Huntington, C.J.	5	8	–	40	111	13.87	–	–	–	1
Hussey, D.J.	106	161	18	275	7811	54.62	28	31	4	120
Hutton, B.L.	110	189	16	275	5746	33.21	18	18	2	136
Iles, J.A.	1	–	–	–	–	–	–	–	–	–
Imran Tahir	60	73	13	48	614	10.23	–	–	–	31
Inzamam-ul-Haq	244	391	58	329	16768	50.35	45	87	0+2	172
Irani, R.C.	232	373	49	218	13472	41.58	28	72	7	79
Ireland, A.J.	12	21	6	15	63	4.20	–	–	–	3
Jacklin, B.D.	3	5	2	19*	34	11.33	–	–	–	1
Jacobs, A.	76	133	19	197	4295	37.67	9	22	–	89
Jacobs, D.J.	48	90	4	218	3372	39.20	11	13	–	48/1
Jaffer, W.	142	238	25	314*	10596	49.74	30	50	0+3	156
James, G.D.	13	23	1	51	378	17.18	–	1	–	4
Jaques, P.A.	107	189	8	244	9885	54.61	29	46	4+1	85
Jayasuriya, S.T.	252	397	33	340	14295	39.27	29	67	0+1	158
Jayawardena, D.P.M.D.	166	260	19	374	12219	50.70	35	56	0+2	209
Jefferson, W.I.	74	132	11	222	4669	38.58	11	18	1	62
Jogia, K.A.	5	8	1	74	185	26.42	–	1	–	6
Johnson, R.L.	166	227	28	118	3545	17.81	2	8	–	63
Johnston, D.T.	15	19	4	71	343	22.86	–	3	–	4
Jones, G.O.	92	135	16	108*	3683	30.94	6	21	–	277/19
Jones, P.S.	113	132	34	114	1804	18.40	2	5	–	24
Jones, R.A.	3	5	1	24	38	9.50	–	–	–	1
Jones, S.P.	79	97	31	46	802	12.15	–	–	–	17
Jordan, C.J.	5	6	2	34	97	24.25	–	–	–	1
Joseph, R.H.	22	30	13	36*	212	12.47	–	–	–	7

F-C	M	I	NO	HS	Runs	Avge	100	50	1000	Ct/St
Joseph, S.C.	87	152	9	211*	4517	31.58	9	20	–	83
Joyce, E.C.	108	178	16	211	7519	46.41	18	41	5	84
Jyoti, S.	2	4	–	17	20	5.00	–	–	–	2
Kalam, T.	6	8	2	64	125	20.83	–	1	–	3
Kandamby, S.H.T.	74	117	3	144	3302	28.96	3	17	–	41
Kapugedara, C.K.	20	35	5	134*	983	32.76	1	7	–	13
Karthik, K.D.	52	82	5	134	2514	32.64	4	16	–	142/15
Kartik, M.	115	136	19	96	2182	18.64	–	11	–	75
Katich, S.M.	168	288	41	228*	12841	51.98	34	68	3+3	153
Keedy, G.	157	176	93	57	895	10.78	–	1	–	44
Keegan, C.B.	47	57	6	44	607	11.90	–	–	–	14
Kemp, J.M.	91	147	18	188	4799	37.20	11	23	–	106
Kemp, R.A.	4	6	1	7	14	2.80	–	–	–	1
Kervezee, A.N.	8	11	2	98	304	33.77	–	2	–	2
Key, R.W.T.	175	303	18	221	11900	41.75	35	46	5	104
Khan, A.	57	65	23	78	824	19.61	–	3	–	9
Khan, Z.	109	143	31	75	1589	14.18	–	2	–	35
Kieswetter, C.	14	16	3	93	377	29.00	–	3	–	46
Killeen, N.	100	143	30	48	1297	11.47	–	–	–	25
King, R.E.	10	14	–	30	116	8.28	–	–	–	–
Kirby, S.P.	87	119	37	57	672	8.19	–	1	–	17
Kirtley, R.J.	165	226	75	59	1976	13.08	–	4	–	58
Klokker, F.A.	3	4	1	100*	211	70.33	1	–	–	6
Klusener, L.	183	263	55	174	8426	40.50	19	39	2	96
Knappett, J.P.T.	11	18	2	100*	518	32.37	1	3	–	21/3
Kruger, G.J.P.	73	89	26	58	795	12.61	–	2	–	18
Kruis, G.J.	111	157	48	59	1535	14.08	–	2	–	42
Kumble, A.	227	293	59	154*	5259	22.47	7	16	–	112
Lamb, G.A.	29	44	5	100*	903	23.15	1	5	–	24
Lamb, N.J.	9	16	1	62	220	14.66	–	1	–	2
Langer, J.L.	320	556	52	342	25698	50.98	78	97	4+6	277
Langeveldt, C.K.	67	84	32	56	780	15.00	–	1	–	17
Langford-Smith, D.	6	3	2	6*	7	7.00	–	–	–	4
Latouf, K.J.	1	1	–	29	29	29.00	–	–	–	–
Law, S.G.	352	576	63	263	26337	51.33	78	124	9+2	395
Lawson, M.A.K.	15	21	5	44	197	12.31	–	–	–	7
Laxman, V.V.S.	193	312	33	353	14450	51.79	42	65	0+4	210/1
Lee, J.E.	1	2	1	21*	22	22.00	–	–	–	–
Lett, R.J.H.	6	10	1	57	208	23.11	–	3	–	2
Lewis, J.	166	230	48	62	2604	14.30	–	5	–	40
Lewis, L.J.	2	4	–	21	26	6.50	–	–	–	1
Lewry, J.D.	166	219	59	72	1682	10.51	–	5	–	45
Liddle, C.J.	12	11	4	53	105	15.00	–	1	–	5
Logan, R.J.	53	72	16	37*	526	9.39	–	–	–	16
Lokuarachchi, K.S.	71	99	10	101*	2479	27.85	2	9	–	35
Loudon, A.G.R.	76	122	7	172	3594	31.25	5	20	–	52
Loye, M.B.	222	354	32	322*	13317	41.35	39	53	6	109
Lucas, D.S.	32	41	12	49	651	22.44	–	–	–	5
Lumb, M.J.	97	166	12	144	5061	32.86	8	33	1	61
Lungley, T.	38	57	12	47	593	13.17	–	–	–	13
Lyth, A.	1	1	–	31	31	31.00	–	–	–	–
Macadam, J.C.	1	1	–	7	7	7.00	–	–	–	–
MacLennan, S.K.	1	2	1	5	9	9.00	–	–	–	–
MacLeod, C.S.	1	–	–	–	–	–	–	–	–	–

F-C	M	I	NO	HS	Runs	Avge	100	50	1000	Ct/St
McCallan, W.K.	17	21	2	65	397	20.89	–	2	–	11
McGarry, A.C.	19	20	14	11*	43	7.16	–	–	–	4
McGrath, A.	184	312	25	188*	10747	37.44	25	52	2	133
McKenzie, N.D.	145	244	29	175	9201	42.79	23	50	–	110
McLaren, R.	48	69	13	140	1613	28.80	1	9	–	28
McMillan, C.D.	138	226	27	168*	7817	39.28	16	42	–	58
Maddy, D.L.	228	370	24	229*	11469	33.14	23	55	4	242
Magoffin, S.J.	30	41	13	30	348	12.42	–	–	–	11
Maher, J.P.	196	352	31	223	12803	39.88	26	61	1+2	199/3
Mahmood, S.I.	54	71	10	94	862	14.13	–	2	–	10/3
Malan, D.J.	4	7	0	64	158	22.57	–	1	–	2
Malcolm-Hansen, R.J.A.	1	2	–	30	35	17.50	–	–	–	–
Malik, M.N.	51	67	25	39*	380	9.04	–	–	–	8
Malinga, S.L.	75	90	38	30	426	8.19	–	–	–	22
Mansoor Amjad	48	72	7	122*	1805	27.76	3	8	–	26
Marshall, H.J.H.	97	163	12	168	5496	36.39	13	25	1	49
Marshall, S.J.	19	30	6	126*	780	32.50	1	3	–	5
Martin-Jenkins, R.S.C.	145	223	31	205*	5878	30.61	3	29	1	42
Mascarenhas, A.D.	156	236	26	131	5258	25.03	7	19	–	60
Mason, M.S.	69	89	23	63	939	14.22	–	3	–	13
Massey, I.R.	5	9	–	65	253	28.11	–	1	–	–
Masters, D.D.	89	110	22	119	1195	13.57	1	2	–	27
Maunders, J.K.	69	124	3	180	3544	29.28	5	18	–	38
Maynard, T.L.	2	3	–	18	35	11.66	–	–	–	–
Mendis, B.G.A.S.	1	1	–	0	0	0.00	–	–	–	–
Middlebrook, J.D.	121	172	22	127	3795	25.30	4	15	–	62
Mierkalns, J.A.	1	1	–	18	18	18.00	–	–	–	–
Mitchell, D.K.H.	15	26	6	134*	738	36.90	2	5	–	16
Modha, B.R.	3	3	–	27	41	13.66	–	–	–	2
Mohammad Akram	125	155	45	35*	944	8.58	–	–	–	30
Mohammad Amin	7	7	2	25*	43	8.60	–	–	–	1
Mohammad Asif	68	91	37	42	448	8.29	–	–	–	26
Mohammad Nabi	1	2	–	43	61	30.50	–	–	–	–
Montgomerie, R.R.	251	433	33	196	14337	35.84	29	80	6	248
Moore, S.C.	68	121	11	246	4342	39.47	7	22	2	33
Morgan, E.J.G.	18	29	1	209*	959	34.25	2	5	–	9/1
Morkel, M.	19	26	6	57	379	18.95	–	1	–	13
Morris, J.C.	10	19	–	81	444	23.36	–	3	–	9
Morse, E.J.	8	8	3	7*	12	2.40	–	–	–	4
Morton, R.S.	68	112	6	201	3818	36.01	8	24	–	81
Mottram, W.J.	1	2	–	9	11	5.50	–	–	–	–
Mubarak, J.	89	157	14	169	4306	30.11	4	24	–	81
Muchall, G.J.	91	165	7	219	4529	28.66	7	23	–	60
Mulla, A.A.	7	13	–	87	204	15.69	–	1	–	19/3
Mullaney, S.J.	2	2	1	165*	209	209.00	1	–	–	3
Munday, M.K.	22	19	9	17*	71	7.10	–	–	–	10
Muralitharan, M.	212	256	76	67	2048	11.37	–	1	–	115
Murtagh, C.P.	8	13	2	107	259	23.54	1	–	–	5
Murtagh, T.J.	52	69	23	74*	1200	26.08	–	6	–	19
Murtaza Hussain	131	187	37	117	3231	21.54	1	10	–	66
Mushtaq Ahmed	303	379	56	90*	5059	15.66	–	20	–	118
Mustard, P.	67	110	6	130	2846	27.36	2	13	–	221/10
Naik, J.K.H.	6	7	3	15	60	15.00	–	–	–	4
Napier, G.R.	78	108	21	125	2746	31.56	3	17	–	34

F-C	M	I	NO	HS	Runs	Avge	100	50	1000	Ct/St
Nash, C.D.	30	49	2	89	1382	29.40	–	12	–	15
Nash, D.C.	131	188	40	114	5181	35.00	10	24	–	272/23
Naved-ul-Hasan	101	143	15	139	2944	23.00	3	9	–	51
Needham, J.	6	10	3	48	161	23.00	–	–	–	2
Nel, A.	91	104	34	44	928	13.25	–	–	–	33
Nel, J.D.	11	15	9	25	82	13.66	–	–	–	2
Nelson, M.A.G.	1	1	–	13	13	13.00	–	–	–	1
New, T.J.	34	59	7	125	1794	34.50	1	16	–	40/3
Newby, O.J.	20	19	5	38*	148	10.57	–	–	–	3
Newman, S.A.	73	126	3	219	5261	42.77	11	30	3	62
Nicholson, M.J.	107	150	29	106*	2504	20.69	2	4	–	59
Nixon, P.A.	310	458	102	144*	12001	33.71	18	57	1	822/66
Noffke, A.A.	87	114	20	114*	2275	24.20	1	9	–	36
North, M.J.	100	177	17	239*	7045	44.03	19	37	0+1	70
Northeast, S.A.	1	2	–	5	5	2.50	–	–	–	–
O'Brien, K.J.	4	4	–	50	99	24.75	–	1	–	2
O'Brien, N.J.	51	74	12	176	1833	29.56	3	8	–	138/21
O'Driscoll, W.J.F.	2	1	–	28	28	28.00	–	–	–	1
Onions, G.	44	60	19	41	544	13.26	–	–	–	9
Ormond, J.	130	158	38	57	1827	15.22	–	2	–	27
O'Shea, M.P.	5	7	–	24	62	8.85	–	–	–	1
Osinde, H.	10	16	5	60*	161	14.63	–	1	–	3
Owen, F.G.	2	3	–	41	42	14.00	–	–	–	–
Owen, W.T.	1	–	–	–	–	–	–	–	–	–
Paget, C.D.	6	8	2	46	73	12.16	–	–	–	3
Palladino, A.P.	30	32	12	41	229	11.45	–	–	–	11
Panesar, M.S.	65	84	30	39*	460	8.51	–	–	–	16
Park, G.T.	17	28	6	100*	824	37.45	1	4	–	20
Parker, L.C.	25	39	3	140	984	27.33	1	4	–	13
Parry, S.D.	1	–	–	–	–	–	–	–	–	–
Parsons, K.A.	130	209	23	193*	5324	28.62	6	28	–	115
Parsons, T.W.	2	3	–	10	10	3.33	–	–	–	–
Patel, A.	1	2	1	31	43	43.00	–	–	–	–
Patel, M.M.	208	278	51	87	3945	17.37	–	17	–	102
Patel, S.R.	27	39	3	176	1701	47.25	6	8	–	12
Patterson, S.A.	7	7	1	46	85	14.16	–	–	–	2
Peng, N.	79	137	2	158	3200	23.70	4	15	–	47
Peploe, C.T.	29	40	6	46	524	15.41	–	–	–	11
Perera, M.D.K.	73	126	4	134	2917	23.90	3	9	–	68
Peters, S.D.	148	253	21	178	7366	31.75	15	36	2	111
Pettini, M.L.	45	75	6	208*	2338	33.88	3	14	1	41
Phillips, B.J.	80	114	17	100*	2009	20.71	1	11	–	19
Phillips, T.J.	44	60	7	89	1033	19.49	–	3	–	27
Phythian, M.J.	7	9	2	62*	158	22.57	–	1	–	15/1
Pietersen, K.P.	111	185	14	254*	8917	52.14	31	35	3	99
Pipe, D.J.	59	88	14	133*	1873	25.31	3	6	–	166/18
Plunkett, L.E.	55	83	19	74*	1254	19.59	–	4	–	23
Pollock, S.M.	183	265	55	150*	6950	33.09	6	34	–	129
Poonia, N.S.	1	1	–	35	35	35.00	–	–	–	–
Porterfield, W.T.S.	7	9	–	166	371	41.22	1	1	–	4
Pothas, N.	176	272	50	165	8825	39.75	20	45	–	490/44
Powar, R.R.	81	102	14	131	2778	31.56	4	15	–	36
Powell, D.B.L.	75	106	15	62	1133	12.45	–	3	–	22
Powell, M.J. (Gm)	160	272	25	299	9852	39.88	22	48	5	98

F-C	M	I	NO	HS	Runs	Avge	100	50	1000	Ct/St
Powell, M.J. (Wa)	138	230	11	236	7022	32.06	12	38	1	99
Poynton, T.	2	3	–	2	2	0.66	–	–	–	3
Prasad, K.T.G.D.	33	37	6	89	461	14.87	–	2	–	8
Price, R.W.	81	128	24	117*	1632	15.69	1	7	–	28
Prior, M.J.	115	182	17	201*	6321	38.30	15	32	2	262/21
Prowting, C.G.	1	2	–	48	50	25.00	–	–	–	–
Prowting, N.R.	6	11	–	78	227	20.63	–	1	–	3
Pyrah, R.M.	7	11	1	106	342	34.20	1	1	–	1
Qaiser Ali	10	18	2	174	672	42.00	1	4	–	6
Ramdin, D.	45	75	8	131	1761	26.28	3	9	–	113/15
Rampaul, R.	21	27	3	64*	314	13.08	–	1	–	8
Ramprakash, M.R.	401	661	84	301*	30659	53.13	97	134	17	235
Ramyakumara, W.M.G.	119	187	23	150*	5935	36.18	11	31	–	50
Rankin, W.B.	4	4	1	3	5	1.66	–	–	–	3
Rashid, A.U.	23	30	5	108	961	38.44	1	8	–	11
Rayner, O.P.	9	11	2	101	194	21.55	1	–	–	9
Read, C.M.W.	190	285	45	240	7826	32.60	11	41	1	548/30
Redfern, D.J.	5	7	1	51	180	30.00	–	1	–	5
Rees, G.P.	13	23	1	109	513	23.31	2	3	–	9
Richards, M.A.	12	18	2	43	226	14.12	–	–	–	9
Richardson, A.	92	93	36	91	642	11.26	–	1	–	25
Rist, W.H.	2	2	–	10	13	6.50	–	–	–	2
Robinson, D.D.J.	189	334	16	200	10489	32.98	22	50	3	156
Rogers, C.J.L.	97	174	10	319	7964	48.56	21	40	1+1	99
Rosenberg, M.C.	13	18	2	86	385	24.06	–	2	–	3
Rowe, D.T.	6	7	1	85	137	22.83	–	1	–	1
Rudge, W.D.	10	12	3	15	47	5.22	–	–	–	4
Rudolph, J.A.	117	204	13	222*	8063	42.21	23	35	1	93
Ryan, L.C.	1	2	–	4	5	2.50	–	–	–	–
Sadler, J.L.	52	89	12	145	2630	34.15	3	15	1	38
Sadler, O.J.	2	4	2	62*	109	54.50	–	1	–	1
Saffell, O.H.J.	1	1	1	35*	35	–	–	–	–	–
Saggers, M.J.	104	127	34	64	1059	11.38	–	2	–	26
Saker, N.C.	18	23	4	58*	272	14.31	–	1	–	5
Sales, D.J.G.	171	272	24	303*	10321	41.61	20	53	5	153
Salisbury, I.D.K.	311	400	79	103	6619	20.61	3	23	–	199
Samad, A.M.	2	3	–	119	155	51.66	1	–	–	–
Samaraweera, T.T.	182	244	46	206	8474	42.79	17	49	0+1	152
Sammy, D.J.G.	36	60	5	87	1318	23.96	–	10	–	50
Samuels, M.N.	59	100	7	257	3272	35.18	5	20	–	32
Sandbach, C.J.L.	2	4	–	8	14	3.50	–	–	–	2
Sangakkara, K.C.	150	237	19	287	9417	43.19	20	46	0+1	302/33
Saqlain Mushtaq	180	247	55	101*	3201	16.67	1	13	–	65
Sarwan, R.R.	161	272	20	261*	9358	37.13	21	52	–	119
Sayers, J.J.	53	87	8	187	2739	34.67	8	12	–	26
Schofield, C.P.	76	105	15	99	2623	29.14	–	21	–	45
Scott, B.J.M.	45	68	15	112	1394	26.30	2	6	–	109/16
Shafayat, B.M.	73	125	4	161	3837	31.71	6	22	1	66/5
Shah, O.A.	181	306	29	203	11913	43.00	32	60	7	139
Shahzad, A.	7	8	3	32*	67	13.40	–	–	–	–
Shantry, A.J.	8	10	5	38*	76	15.20	–	–	–	3
Sharif, Z.K.	15	25	6	140*	771	40.57	2	4	–	4
Sharma, I.	9	7	6	7*	11	11.00	–	–	–	1
Shreck, C.E.	45	51	29	19	82	3.72	–	–	–	14

F-C	M	I	NO	HS	Runs	Avge	100	50	1000	Ct/St
Sidebottom, R.J.	113	143	42	54	1193	11.81	–	1	–	42
Sillence, R.J.	36	50	3	101	1068	22.72	1	5	–	12
Silva, J.K.	35	58	9	155	1845	37.65	4	6	–	100/11
Silverwood, C.E.W.	175	231	45*	80	2892	15.54	–	9	–	40
Singh, R.P.	32	41	10.	41*	279	9.00	–	–	–	13
Smith, B.D.	1	1	–	13	13	13.00	–	–	–	1
Smith, B.F.	296	463	52	204	16794	40.86	40	83	7	184
Smith, B.M.	5	4	3	11*	13	13.00	–	–	–	1
Smith, D.S.	96	173	6	181	6069	36.34	13	30	0+1	83
Smith, E.T.	185	315	19	213	12392	41.86	34	50	8	82
Smith, G.M.	26	47	4	86	945	21.97	–	6	–	9
Smith, T.C.	23	26	7	49	365	19.21	–	–	–	22
Smith, T.M.J.	1	1	–	2	2	2.00	–	–	–	–
Smith, W.R.	41	67	3	156	1674	26.15	3	3	–	25
Snape, J.N.	121	180	31	131	4194	28.14	3	23	–	74
Snell, S.D.	6	12	1	83*	198	18.00	–	1	–	12
Solanki, V.S.	220	362	23	232	12179	35.92	21	66	3	237
Spearman, C.M.	190	342	15	341	12642	38.66	30	54	3	186
Spriegel, M.N.W.	3	6	1	30	100	20.00	–	–	–	4
Spurway, S.H.P.	6	8	1	83	210	30.00	–	1	–	16
Sreesanth, S.	39	53	18	35	338	9.65	–	–	–	8
Stayt, T.P.	3	3	1	6	9	4.50	–	–	–	2
Stevens, D.I.	124	205	13	208	6344	33.04	12	37	1	102
Steyn, D.W.	48	59	17	82	514	12.23	–	2	–	7
Stoneman, M.D.	8	15	–	101	369	24.60	1	1	–	5
Strauss, A.J.	142	253	12	176	9677	40.15	23	44	3	109
Streak, H.H.	175	264	48	131	5684	26.31	6	27	–	58
Stubbings, S.D.	122	222	11	151	6755	32.01	12	35	3	55
Styris, S.B.	114	189	18	212*	5391	31.52	9	26	–	88
Suppiah, A.V.	25	42	1	123	1161	28.31	1	7	–	11
Sutcliffe, I.J.	184	294	28	203	9300	34.96	16	50	3	107
Sutton, L.D.	115	189	26	151*	5351	32.82	9	17	–	261/12
Swann, G.P.	157	222	15	183	5448	26.31	4	26	–	109
Tahir, N.	31	33	10	49	368	16.00	–	–	–	2
Tavarasa, B.	1	–	–	–	–	–	–	–	–	–
Taylor, B.V.	53	68	26	40	431	10.26	–	–	–	6
Taylor, C.G.	97	171	11	196	5335	33.34	14	18	1	68
Taylor, C.R.	35	59	3	121	1492	26.64	3	8	–	22
Taylor, J.E.	43	65	14	40	557	10.92	–	–	–	10
Ten Doeschate, R.N.	36	47	6	259*	2175	3.04	9	6	–	19
Tendulkar, S.R.	239	373	38	248*	19894	59.38	63	91	1+3	160
Thomas, A.C.	66	99	23	119*	2151	28.30	2	8	–	24
Thompson, G.J.	8	7	3	38	97	24.25	–	–	–	7
Thompson, J.G.	1	2	–	21	32	16.00	–	–	–	–
Thornely, M.A.	2	3	–	11	15	5.00	–	–	–	4
Thornicroft, N.D.	8	12	5	30	54	7.71	–	–	–	2
Thorp, C.D.	25	39	3	75	481	13.36	–	2	–	9
Tomlinson, J.A.	22	30	13	23	95	5.58	–	–	–	6
Tredwell, J.C.	53	74	9	116*	1407	21.64	1	5	–	52
Trego, P.D.	51	74	10	140	2200	34.37	6	10	–	17
Tremlett, C.T.	71	94	28	64	1247	18.89	–	3	–	19
Trescothick, M.E.	223	384	20	284	13570	37.28	28	68	1	274
Trott, I.J.L.	98	167	15	210	5770	37.96	11	31	3	100
Troughton, J.O.	79	123	9	162	4338	38.05	13	21	1	30

F-C	M	I	NO	HS	Runs	Avge	100	50	1000	Ct/St
Tudge, K.D.	1	2	1	4	7	7.00	–	–	–	–
Tudor, A.J.	116	148	31	144	2601	22.23	2	8	–	34
Turner, M.L.	6	5	2	57	82	27.33	–	1	–	1
Udal, S.D.	260	367	68	117*	6761	22.61	1	28	–	116
Udawatte, M.L.	29	54	4	100	1604	32.08	1	14	–	14
Umar Bhatti	12	20	7	83*	350	26.92	–	3	–	3
Vaas, W.P.U.J.C.	175	235	49	134	4661	25.05	4	20	–	53
Van der Wath, J.J.	70	110	19	113*	2228	24.48	2	13	–	25
Vandort, M.G.	109	182	13	226	5872	34.74	14	26	–	85
Van Jaarsveld, M.	177	300	28	262*	12291	45.18	36	56	3+1	241
Van Jaarsveld, V.B.	30	51	4	159	1814	38.59	4	15	–	32
Vaughan, M.P.	242	426	27	197	15307	38.36	41	64	4	108
Voges, A.C.	29	49	8	178	1724	42.04	6	5	–	35
Wagg, G.G.	34	50	7	94	1131	26.30	–	7	–	12
Wagh, M.A.	157	260	22	315	9387	39.44	23	45	5	73
Wainwright, D.J.	10	12	3	62	274	30.44	–	1	–	7
Wakely, A.G.	4	8	–	66	169	21.12	–	2	–	1
Walker, M.J.	177	291	31	275*	9674	37.20	25	40	3	121
Walker, N.G.E.	31	40	11	80	558	19.24	–	3	–	13
Wallace, M.A.	118	195	16	128	4909	27.42	6	24	–	313/22
Walters, S.J.	11	18	1	70	394	23.17	–	2	–	12
Ward, G.B.	1	1	–	33	33	33.00	–	–	–	3
Warnapura, B.S.M.	112	163	18	242	5265	36.31	12	24	–	74
Warne, S.K.	301	404	48	107*	6919	19.43	2	26	–	264
Waters, H.T.	22	36	17	34	135	7.10	–	–	–	5
Watkins, R.E.	27	47	2	87	857	19.04	–	2	–	15
Watson, S.R.	55	94	14	203*	3938	49.22	11	19	–	37
Welagedara, U.W.M.B.C.A.	41	50	20	30	302	10.06	–	–	–	9
Wessels, M.H.	36	60	6	107	1534	28.40	3	7	–	82/8
Westfield, M.S.	5	7	3	32	45	11.25	–	–	–	1
Westley, T.	6	9	2	72	223	31.85	–	1	–	3
Weston, W.P.C.	237	417	34	205	12789	33.39	24	64	4	133
Westwood, I.J.	40	70	9	178	2305	37.78	5	12	–	19
Wharf, A.G.	111	170	26	128*	3333	23.14	6	13	–	60
Wheeler, S.J.	3	5	1	13	33	8.25	–	–	–	1
Whelan, C.D.	3	3	1	9*	10	5.00	–	–	–	–
White, A.R.	12	13	3	152*	350	35.00	1	1	–	11
White, C.	276	438	57	186	12395	32.53	21	62	–	167
White, C.L.	81	133	16	260*	4769	40.76	12	19	2	76
White, G.G.	5	5	–	65	108	21.60	–	1	–	1
White, R.A.	55	94	7	277	2653	30.49	3	11	–	33
White, W.A.	7	10	2	19*	106	13.25	–	–	–	3
Wigley, D.H.	29	36	10	70	398	15.30	–	2	–	15
Williams, R.E.M.	5	8	4	15	30	7.50	–	–	–	2
Willoughby, C.M.	160	185	81	47	606	5.82	–	–	–	36
Wilshaw, P.J.	6	11	–	63	341	31.00	–	3	–	4
Wilson, G.C.	4	5	1	11	24	6.00	–	–	–	6
Wiseman, P.J.	170	232	49	130	3775	20.62	2	13	–	78
Woakes, C.R.	2	3	1	14*	27	13.50	–	–	–	4
Wood, J.R.	6	11	–	31	170	15.45	–	–	–	2/1
Wood, M.J. (Sm)	76	132	9	297	4375	34.72	9	27	1	26
Wood, M.J. (Y)	129	224	20	207	6820	33.43	16	30	4	113
Wood, M.J. (MCC)	1	2	1	6*	6	6.00	–	–	–	–
Woodman, R.J.	3	4	1	46*	54	18.00	–	–	–	–

F-C	M	I	NO	HS	Runs	Avge	100	50	1000	Ct/St
Woods, N.J.	9	13	3	27	231	23.10	–	–		5
Wright, B.J.	12	19	2	108	401	23.58	1	2	–	15
Wright, C.J.C.	18	25	3	76	444	20.18	–	2	–	5
Wright, D.G.	86	133	21	111	2689	24.00	1	13	–	40
Wright, L.J.	32	43	9	100	915	26.91	1	6	–	16
Yardy, M.H.	85	144	15	257	4978	38.58	11	23	1	66
Yasir Arafat	120	183	23	122	4234	26.46	3	23	–	41
Young, P.J.W.	6	10	1	54	227	25.22	–	1	–	2
Younus Khan	121	196	21	267	8713	49.78	27	35	0+1	133
Yuvraj Singh	72	115	14	209	4410	43.66	14	20	–	78
Zondeki, M.	55	80	23	59	508	8.91	–	1		18

BOWLING

'50wS' denotes instances of taking 50 or more wickets in a season. Where these have been achieved outside the British Isles they are shown after a plus sign.

	Runs	Wkts	Avge	Best	5wI	10wM	50wS
Abdul Razzaq	10071	307	32.80	7- 51	10	2	–
Ackerman, H.D.	57	0					
Adams, A.R.	7524	292	25.76	6- 25	10	1	–
Adams, C.J.	1922	41	46.87	4- 28	–	–	–
Adams, J.H.K.	527	10	52.70	2- 16	–	–	–
Adnan, M.Hasan	318	4	79.50	1- 4	–	–	–
Afzaal, U.	4118	79	52.12	4-101	–	–	–
Aga, R.G.	436	13	33.53	4- 71	–	–	–
Ahmed, J.S.	360	6	60.00	2- 41	–	–	–
Ali, Kabir	9929	359	27.65	8- 50	16	4	4
Ali, Kadeer	289	3	96.33	1- 4	–	–	–
Ali, M.M.	439	3	146.33	2- 50	–	–	–
Allenby, J.	685	15	45.66	5-125	1	–	–
Ambrose, T.R.	1	0					
Amerasinghe, M.K.D.I.	4878	228	21.39	5- 12	7	1	0+1
Anderson, J.M.	6741	228	29.56	6- 23	10	1	2
Andrew, G.M.	989	28	35.32	4- 63	–	–	–
Anyon, J.E.	3354	82	40.90	5- 83	1	–	–
Azhar Mahmood	12644	494	25.59	8- 61	19	3	0+1
Bagai, A.	28	0					
Baker, F.B.	128	2	64.00	1- 18	–	–	–
Balcombe, D.J.	1320	27	48.88	5-112	1	–	–
Banerjee, V.	2267	42	53.97	4- 38	–	–	–
Banks, O.A.C.	5908	159	37.15	7- 70	6	1	–
Barnett, G.E.F.	102	1	102.00	1- 10	–	–	–
Bastiampillai, T.C.	49	0					
Batty, G.J.	10410	318	32.73	7- 52	13	1	2
Batty, J.N.	61	1	61.00	1- 21	–	–	–
Bell, I.R.	1490	47	31.70	4- 4	–	–	–
Benham, C.C.	37	0					
Benkenstein, D.M.	2999	84	35.70	4- 16	–	–	–
Benning, J.G.E.	794	11	72.18	3- 57	–	–	–
Bichel, A.J.	19791	766	25.83	9- 93	36	7	1+3
Birt, T.R.	145	2	72.50	1- 24	–	–	–
Blackwell, I.D.	9098	217	41.92	7- 90	7	–	–
Boje, N.	15874	499	31.81	8- 93	22	2	–
Bollinger, D.E.	3409	79	43.15	5- 73	1	–	–

191

F-C	Runs	Wkts	Avge	Best	5wI	10wM	50wS
Bond, S.E.	4486	181	24.78	6- 51	9	1	–
Bopara, R.S.	2831	58	48.81	5- 75	1	–	–
Bose, R.R.	4898	202	24.24	7- 24	17	4	0+1
Botha, A.G.	8703	260	33.47	8- 53	8	1	1
Bradshaw, D.P.	85	0					
Brathwaite, R.M.R.	730	13	56.15	3- 61	–	–	–
Bravo, D.J.	4057	120	33.80	6- 11	6	–	–
Bray, J.P.	32	0					
Breese, G.R.	8266	273	30.27	7- 60	12	3	–
Bresnan, T.T.	4730	145	32.62	5- 42	2	–	–
Broad, S.C.J.	3181	112	28.40	5- 67	6	–	–
Brophy, G.L.	1	0					
Brown, A.D.	630	5	126.00	3- 25	–	–	–
Brown, D.O.	819	12	68.25	2- 25	–	–	–
Brown, D.R.	16177	567	28.53	8- 89	21	4	4
Brown, J.F.	13210	404	32.69	7- 69	22	5	3
Brown, K.R.	7	0					
Bruce, J.T.A.	4225	124	34.07	5- 43	3	–	–
Butcher, M.A.	4237	125	33.89	5- 86	1	–	–
Butler, S.M.	168	5	33.60	3-121	–	–	–
Buttleman, J.E.L.	30	0					
Caddick, A.R.	29815	1145	26.03	9- 32	77	17	12
Carberry, M.A.	490	7	70.00	2- 85	–	–	–
Carter, N.M.	7147	189	37.81	6- 63	6	–	–
Chambers, M.A.	84	1	84.00	1- 73	–	–	–
Chanderpaul, S.	2434	56	43.46	4- 48	–	–	–
Chapple, G.	18352	651	28.19	7- 53	25	2	4
Cheetham, S.P.	127	1	127.00	1- 44	–	–	–
Cherry, D.D.	18	0					
Chilton, M.J.	664	10	66.40	1- 1	–	–	–
Chopra, A.S.	193	5	38.60	2- 5	–	–	–
Chopra, V.	25	0					
Choudhry, S.H.	43	0					
Clare, J.L.	203	10	20.30	5- 90	1	–	–
Clark, S.R.	7926	294	26.95	8- 58	12	1	–
Clarke, R.	4585	110	41.68	4- 21	–	–	–
Claydon, M.E.	482	9	53.55	3- 26	–	–	–
Cliff, S.J.	126	1	126.00	1- 28	–	–	–
Clinton, R.S.	207	2	103.50	2- 30	–	–	–
Clough, G.D.	766	16	47.87	3- 69	–	–	–
Cobb, J.J.	44	0					
Codrington, A.	203	5	40.60	2- 56	–	–	–
Coetzer, K.J.	22	0					
Collingwood, P.D.	4241	105	40.39	5- 52	1	–	–
Collins, P.T.	8691	335	25.94	6- 24	7	–	0+1
Collymore, C.D.	6954	262	26.54	7- 57	10	2	–
Compton, N.R.D.	123	1	123.00	1- 94	–	–	–
Cook, A.N.	117	3	39.00	3- 13	–	–	–
Cook, S.J.	8322	259	32.13	8- 63	9	–	–
Cork, D.G.	23277	875	26.60	9- 43	32	5	7
Cosker, D.A.	13241	347	38.15	6-140	3	–	–
Coverdale, P.S.	39	1	39.00	1- 36	–	–	–
Crawley, J.P.	283	2	141.50	1- 7	–	–	–
Croft, R.D.B.	36201	1004	36.05	8- 66	46	9	9

F-C	Runs	Wkts	Avge	Best	5wI	10wM	50wS
Croft, S.J.	335	6	55.83	3- 40	–	–	–
Crook, A.R.	569	7	81.28	3- 71	–	–	–
Crook, S.P.	2363	52	45.44	4- 56	–	–	–
Cummins, R.A.G.	1916	42	45.61	5- 60	1	–	–
Cusden, S.M.J.	692	20	34.60	4- 68	–	–	–
Daggett, L.M.	1366	34	40.17	8- 94	2	–	–
Dalrymple, J.W.M.	5370	120	44.75	5- 49	1	–	–
Danish Kaneria	15410	581	26.52	7- 39	42	6	2+1
Davies, A.M.	4122	182	22.64	7- 59	8	–	1
Davies, A.P.	3400	77	44.15	5- 79	1	–	–
Davison, J.M.	5063	111	45.61	9- 76	5	1	–
Dawson, R.K.J.	7814	186	42.01	6- 82	5	–	–
Dean, K.J.	10208	387	26.37	8- 52	16	4	2
Denly, J.L.	307	10	30.70	2- 13	–	–	–
Dernbach, J.W.	835	18	46.38	3- 67	–	–	–
De Wet, F.	2418	116	20.84	7- 61	9	2	0+1
Dexter, N.J.	514	9	57.11	2- 40	–	–	–
Dhoni, M.S.	33	0					
Dighton, M.G.	242	5	48.40	2- 47	–	–	–
Dingle, L.A.	15	0					
Dippenaar, H.H.	13	0					
Di Venuto, M.J.	484	5	96.80	1- 0	–	–	–
Dobson, W.T.	144	1	144.00	1- 67	–	–	–
Doshi, N.D.	5026	136	36.95	7-110	6	3	1
Dravid, R.S.	273	5	54.60	2- 16	–	–	–
Du Plessis, F.	317	15	21.13	4- 39	–	–	–
Durston, W.J.	1287	24	53.62	3- 23	–	–	–
Ealham, M.A.	16092	585	27.50	8- 36	22	1	1
Edmondson, B.M.	4624	141	32.79	6- 28	2	1	–
Edwards, F.H.	4526	125	36.20	5- 22	7	1	–
Edwards, N.J.	193	2	96.50	1- 16	–	–	–
Elliott, M.T.G.	754	13	58.00	3- 68	–	–	–
Ervine, S.M.	5271	135	39.04	6- 82	5	–	–
Evans, D.	169	5	33.80	3- 31	–	–	–
Evans, L.	115	4	28.75	2- 39	–	–	–
Ferley, R.S.	2551	55	46.38	6-136	1	–	–
Finn, S.T.	292	13	22.46	4- 51	–	–	–
Fisher, I.D.	6706	157	42.71	5- 30	7	1	–
Fleming, S.P.	129	0					
Flintoff, A.	9452	297	31.82	5- 24	3	–	–
Flower, G.W.	5504	163	33.76	7- 31	3	–	–
Footitt, M.H.A.	671	20	33.55	5- 45	2	–	–
Foster, J.S.	6	0					
Foster, P.J.	318	11	28.90	4- 26	–	–	–
Fourie, M.J.	126	4	31.50	3- 31	–	–	–
Francis, J.D.	164	4	41.00	1- 1	–	–	–
Francis, S.R.G.	5595	136	41.13	5- 42	3	–	–
Franks, P.J.	12496	395	31.63	7- 56	11	–	2
Friedlander, M.J.	996	24	41.50	6- 78	1	–	–
Frost, T.	15	0					
Gale, A.W.	33	1	33.00	1- 33	–	–	–
Gallian, J.E.R.	4152	96	43.25	6-115	1	–	–
Gambhir, G.	277	7	39.57	3- 12	–	–	–
Ganegama, W.C.A.	4612	189	24.40	7- 25	10	–	–

F-C	Runs	Wkts	Avge	Best	5wI	10wM	50wS
Ganga, D.	328	4	82.00	1- 7	–	–	–
Ganguly, S.C.	5829	160	36.43	6- 46	4	–	–
Gayle, C.H.	4197	107	39.22	5- 34	2	–	–
Gibson, O.D.	18319	659	27.79	10- 47	28	8	3
Gidman, A.P.R.	3606	74	48.72	4- 47	–	–	–
Gidman, W.R.S.	86	4	21.50	3- 37	–	–	–
Gilbert, C.R.	11	0					
Gillespie, J.N.	14630	563	25.98	8- 50	21	2	0+1
Gillespie, P.G.	153	5	30.60	3- 93	–	–	–
Godleman, B.A.	35	0					
Goodwin, M.W.	363	7	51.85	2- 23	–	–	–
Gough, D.	22689	846	26.81	7- 28	33	3	5
Grant, R.N.	224	5	44.80	1- 7	–	–	–
Green, J.A.G.	32	0					
Greenidge, C.G.	4972	140	35.51	6- 40	5	–	1
Griffiths, D.A.	440	12	36.66	4- 46	–	–	–
Groenewald, T.D.	826	15	55.06	3- 26	–	–	–
Gunawardene, K.D.	181	7	25.85	4- 28	–	–	–
Gurney, H.F.	173	2	86.50	1- 84	–	–	–
Guy, S.M.	8	0					
Hall, A.J.	9902	373	26.54	6- 77	13	1	–
Harbhajan Singh	13566	509	26.65	8- 84	33	6	0+2
Hardinges, M.A.	3485	85	41.00	5- 51	1	–	–
Harmison, B.W.	286	3	95.33	2- 29	–	–	–
Harmison, S.J.	14960	516	28.99	7- 12	18	1	4
Harris, A.J.	12717	406	31.32	7- 54	16	3	2
Harris, J.A.R.	811	33	24.57	7- 66	2	1	–
Harris, P.L.	5464	184	29.69	6- 54	10	–	0+1
Harris, R.J.	1374	30	45.80	5- 92	1	–	–
Harrison, A.J.	243	5	48.60	2- 65	–	–	–
Harrison, D.S.	6200	170	36.47	5- 48	6	–	1
Harvey, I.J.	11693	425	27.51	8-101	15	2	–
Hemingway, T.L.	103	4	25.75	4- 58	–	–	–
Hemp, D.L.	821	17	48.29	3- 23	–	–	–
Henderson, C.W.	19352	616	31.41	7- 57	22	1	–
Henderson, T.	6627	242	27.38	6- 56	9	–	–
Herath, M.R.K.B.	11755	505	23.27	8- 43	26	5	0+2
Hick, G.A.	10308	232	44.43	5- 18	5	1	–
Hildreth, J.C.	278	4	69.50	2- 39	–	–	–
Hill, C.M.M.	32	0					
Hinds, W.W.	1127	29	38.86	3- 9	–	–	–
Hobbiss, M.H.	31	0					
Hodge, B.J.	2751	68	40.45	4- 17	–	–	–
Hodgkinson, R.	75	0					
Hodnett, G.P.	10	0					
Hogg, K.W.	2696	66	40.84	5- 48	1	–	–
Hoggard, M.J.	15217	560	27.17	7- 49	18	1	2
Hole, S.M.	65	0					
Hollioake, A.J.	4927	120	41.05	5- 62	1	–	–
Hopkinson, C.D.	246	2	123.00	1- 20	–	–	–
Hughes, J.A.	155	6	25.83	3- 33	–	–	–
Hunter, I.D.	4910	121	40.57	5- 63	1	–	–
Hussey, D.J.	1101	19	57.94	4-105	–	–	–
Hutton, B.L.	2239	35	63.97	4- 37	–	–	–

194

F-C	Runs	Wkts	Avge	Best	5wI	10wM	50wS
Iles, J.A.	37	1	37.00	1- 27	–	–	–
Imran Tahir	5573	209	26.66	8- 76	11	2	0+1
Inzamam-ul-Haq	1295	39	33.20	5- 80	2	–	–
Irani, R.C.	10007	339	29.51	6- 71	9	–	1
Ireland, A.J.	977	33	29.60	7- 36	1	1	–
Jacklin, B.D.	269	2	134.50	2- 69	–	–	–
Jacobs, A.	375	3	125.00	1- 2	–	–	–
Jacobs, D.J.	20	0					
Jaffer, W.	74	2	37.00	2- 18	–	–	–
James, G.D.	7	0					
Jaques, P.A.	87	0					
Jayasuriya, S.T.	6352	192	33.08	5- 34	2	–	–
Jayawardena, D.P.M.D.	1531	50	30.62	5- 72	1	–	–
Jefferson, W.I.	60	1	60.00	1- 16	–	–	–
Jogia, K.A.	0	0					
Johnson, R.L.	15094	528	28.58	10- 45	20	3	4
Johnston, D.T.	1027	54	19.01	6- 23	2	–	–
Jones, G.O.	18	0					
Jones, P.S.	11105	292	38.03	6- 25	7	1	2
Jones, R.A.	295	7	42.14	3- 37	–	–	–
Jones, S.P.	7190	218	32.98	6- 45	11	1	–
Jordan, C.J.	490	20	24.50	3- 42	–	–	–
Joseph, R.H.	2013	56	35.94	5- 19	2	–	–
Joseph, S.C.	203	4	50.75	2- 13	–	–	–
Joyce, E.C.	1016	10	101.60	2- 34	–	–	–
Jyoti, S.	101	4	25.25	2- 46	–	–	–
Kalam, T.	476	8	59.50	3- 54	–	–	–
Kandamby, S.H.T.	924	18	51.33	3- 16	–	–	–
Kapugedara, C.K.	72	0					
Karthik, K.D.	28	0					
Kartik, M.	10110	399	25.33	9- 70	23	3	1
Katich, S.M.	3130	80	39.12	7-130	3	–	–
Keedy, G.	15113	481	31.41	7- 95	23	5	3
Keegan, C.B.	4887	140	34.90	6-114	6	–	1
Kemp, J.M.	4747	176	26.97	6- 56	5	–	–
Kemp, R.A.	284	9	31.55	3- 23	–	–	–
Kervezee, A.N.	44	1	44.00	1- 33	–	–	–
Key, R.W.T.	92	0					
Khan, A.	6192	190	32.58	6- 52	6	–	2
Khan, Z.	12344	454	27.18	9-138	26	7	1
Killeen, N.	8150	254	32.08	7- 70	8	–	1
King, R.E.	819	14	58.50	4- 34	–	–	–
Kirby, S.P.	9306	319	29.17	8- 80	13	4	1
Kirtley, R.J.	16292	606	26.88	7- 21	29	4	7
Klusener, L.	14809	502	29.50	8- 34	20	4	–
Kruger, G.J.P.	7204	238	30.26	8-112	10	2	–
Kruis, G.J.	11085	362	30.62	7- 58	18	1	1
Kumble, A.	26990	1071	25.20	10- 74	70	19	1+2
Lamb, G.A.	854	31	27.54	7- 73	1	–	–
Lamb, N.J.	708	17	41.64	4- 92	–	–	–
Langer, J.L.	204	5	40.80	2- 17	–	–	–
Langeveldt, C.K.	5986	207	28.91	6- 48	6	1	–
Langford-Smith, D.	383	20	19.15	5- 45	2	–	–
Law, S.G.	4236	83	51.03	5- 39	1	–	–

F-C	Runs	Wkts	Avge	Best	5wI	10wM	50wS
Lawson, M.A.K.	1699	42	40.45	6- 88	4	–	–
Laxman, V.V.S.	707	20	35.35	3- 11	–	–	–
Lee, J.E.	36	0					
Lewis, J.	15672	586	26.74	8- 95	31	5	6
Lewry, J.D.	15065	570	26.42	8-106	31	4	5
Liddle, C.J.	888	16	55.50	3- 42	–	–	–
Logan, R.J.	5129	132	38.85	6- 93	4	–	–
Lokuarachchi, K.S.	4848	208	23.30	7- 17	7	1	0+1
Loudon, A.G.R.	4611	116	39.75	6- 47	7	–	–
Loye, M.B.	61	1	61.00	1- 8	–	–	–
Lucas, D.S.	2744	79	34.73	5- 49	3	–	–
Lumb, M.J.	242	6	40.33	2- 10	–	–	–
Lungley, T.	3297	108	30.52	5- 20	3	–	1
Lyth, A.	12	1	12.00	1- 12	–	–	–
Macadam, J.C.	35	0					
MacLeod, C.S.	30	0					
McCallan, W.K.	1076	37	29.08	5- 34	1	–	–
McGarry, A.C.	1546	29	53.31	5- 27	1	–	–
McGrath, A.	3446	100	34.46	5- 39	1	–	–
McKenzie, N.D.	322	5	64.40	1- 6	–	–	–
McLaren, R.	3876	158	24.53	8- 38	7	1	0+1
McMillan, C.D.	3167	88	35.98	6- 71	1	–	–
Maddy, D.L.	6143	188	32.67	5- 37	5	–	–
Magoffin, S.J.	2813	95	29.61	8- 47	2	–	–
Maher, J.P.	504	10	50.40	3- 11	–	–	–
Mahmood, S.I.	4755	150	31.70	5- 37	3	–	–
Malan, D.J.	152	3	50.66	1- 22	–	–	–
Malcolm-Hansen, R.J.A.	28	0					
Malik, M.N.	4992	137	36.43	5- 57	4	–	–
Malinga, S.L.	6792	230	29.53	6- 17	6	–	–
Mansoor Amjad	4005	127	31.53	6- 19	6	–	–
Marshall, H.J.H.	493	10	49.30	1- 6	–	–	–
Marshall, S.J.	1976	30	65.86	6-128	1	–	–
Martin-Jenkins, R.S.C.	9815	299	32.82	7- 51	6	–	–
Mascarenhas, A.D.	10223	364	28.08	6- 25	14	–	1
Mason, M.S.	6046	226	26.75	8- 45	8	1	3
Masters, D.D.	7477	236	31.68	6- 27	8	–	–
Maunders, J.K.	928	24	38.66	4- 15	–	–	–
Maynard, T.L.	18	0					
Mendis, B.G.A.S.	111	1	111.00	1- 11	–	–	–
Middlebrook, J.D.	10775	274	39.32	6- 82	7	1	1
Mitchell, D.K.H.	215	7	30.71	3- 50	–	–	–
Modha, B.R.	312	7	44.57	3-101	–	–	–
Mohammad Akram	11963	416	28.75	8- 49	18	1	–
Mohammad Amin	801	11	72.81	3- 66	–	–	–
Mohammad Asif	6713	280	23.97	7- 35	17	5	0+1
Mohammad Nabi	47	1	47.00	1- 47	–	–	–
Montgomerie, R.R.	147	2	73.50	1- 0	–	–	–
Moore, S.C.	321	5	64.20	1- 13	–	–	–
Morgan, E.J.G.	46	2	23.00	2- 24	–	–	–
Morkel, M.	1948	66	29.51	6- 66	3	–	–
Morris, J.C.	671	13	51.61	2- 29	–	–	–
Morse, E.J.	740	16	46.25	4- 78	–	–	–
Morton, R.S.	289	8	36.12	3- 17	–	–	–

F-C	Runs	Wkts	Avge	Best	5wI	10wM	50wS
Mottram, W.J.	46	2	23.00	2- 46	–	–	–
Mubarak, J.	1283	28	45.82	4- 59	–	–	–
Muchall, G.J.	615	15	41.00	3- 26	–	–	–
Mullaney, S.J.	49	0					
Munday, M.K.	1772	66	26.84	8- 55	4	2	–
Muralitharan, M.	23748	1274	18.64	9- 51	112	32	3+3
Murtagh, C.P.	8	0					
Murtagh, T.J.	3862	118	32.72	6- 86	4	–	–
Murtaza Hussain	12580	535	23.51	9- 54	36	7	0+5
Mushtaq Ahmed	35350	1388	25.46	9- 48	103	32	9+2
Naik, J.K.H.	444	4	111.00	1- 55	–	–	–
Napier, G.R.	5988	142	42.16	5- 56	2	–	–
Nash, C.D.	584	9	64.88	2- 1	–	–	–
Nash, D.C.	105	2	52.50	1- 8	–	–	–
Naved-ul-Hasan	10751	454	23.68	7- 49	26	4	2+3
Needham, J.	412	9	45.77	3- 92	–	–	–
Nel, A.	8493	318	26.70	6- 25	12	1	–
Nel, J.D.	765	18	42.50	4- 74	–	–	–
Nelson, M.A.G.	62	2	31.00	2- 62	–	–	–
New, T.J.	168	4	42.00	2- 18	–	–	–
Newby, O.J.	1605	49	32.75	4- 58	–	–	–
Newman, S.A.	22	0					
Nicholson, M.J.	10992	377	29.15	7- 62	11	–	–
Nixon, P.A.	100	0					
Noffke, A.A.	8721	292	29.86	8- 24	12	1	–
North, M.J.	2850	60	47.50	4- 16	–	–	–
O'Brien, K.J.	104	8	13.00	4- 38	–	–	–
O'Brien, N.J.	4	1	4.00	1- 4	–	–	–
O'Driscoll, W.J.F.	55	0					
Onions, G.	4284	120	35.70	8-101	3	–	1
Ormond, J.	12918	435	29.69	7- 63	20	1	4
Osinde, H.	1068	40	26.70	7- 53	1	–	–
Owen, W.T.	37	0					
Paget, C.D.	337	4	84.25	3- 63	–	–	–
Palladino, A.P.	2342	52	45.03	6- 41	2	–	–
Panesar, M.S.	7308	250	29.23	7-181	16	3	3
Park, G.T.	300	0					
Parker, L.C.	274	6	45.66	2- 37	–	–	–
Parry, S.D.	46	5	9.20	5- 23	1	–	–
Parsons, K.A.	4646	106	43.83	5- 13	2	–	–
Parsons, T.W.	116	4	29.00	3- 70	–	–	–
Patel, A.	30	0					
Patel, M.M.	19309	630	30.64	8- 96	30	9	4
Patel, S.R.	715	22	32.50	4- 68	–	–	–
Patterson, S.A.	295	4	73.75	2- 30	–	–	–
Peng, N.	2	0					
Peploe, C.T.	2824	54	52.29	4- 31	–	–	–
Perera, M.D.K.	5444	207	26.29	7- 71	8	–	–
Peters, S.D.	31	1	31.00	1- 19	–	–	–
Phillips, B.J.	5339	176	30.33	6- 29	4	–	–
Phillips, T.J.	3887	81	47.98	5- 41	1	–	–
Pietersen, K.P.	2904	58	50.06	4- 31	–	–	–
Plunkett, L.E.	5447	173	31.48	6- 74	5	–	2
Pollock, S.M.	15318	656	23.35	7- 33	22	2	0+1

F-C	Runs	Wkts	Avge	Best	5wI	10wM	50wS
Pothas, N.	63	1	63.00	1- 16	–	–	–
Powar, R.R.	7787	287	27.13	7- 44	15	2	0+2
Powell, D.B.L.	6677	219	30.48	6- 49	6	–	–
Powell, M.J. (Gm)	132	2	66.00	2- 39	–	–	–
Powell, M.J. (Wa)	744	11	67.63	2- 16	–	–	–
Prasad, K.T.G.D.	2619	105	24.94	6- 25	2	1	–
Price, R.W.	9239	274	33.71	8- 35	15	3	–
Prowting, N.R.	39	0					
Pyrah, R.M.	77	4	19.25	1- 3	–	–	–
Qaiser Ali	197	7	28.14	4- 61	–	–	–
Rampaul, R.	1702	57	29.85	7- 51	3	–	–
Ramprakash, M.R.	2196	34	64.58	3- 32	–	–	–
Ramyakumara, W.M.G.	5110	189	27.03	7- 25	2	1	–
Rankin, W.B.	382	15	25.46	4- 41	–	–	–
Rashid, A.U.	2514	69	36.43	6- 67	4	–	–
Rayner, O.P.	762	20	38.10	5- 68	1	–	–
Read, C.M.W.	68	0					
Redfern, D.J.	70	2	35.00	1- 7	–	–	–
Richards, M.A.	847	15	56.46	3- 62	–	–	–
Richardson, A.	7995	269	29.72	8- 46	8	1	1
Robinson, D.D.J.	449	2	224.50	1- 7	–	–	–
Rogers, C.J.L.	106	1	106.00	1- 16	–	–	–
Rosenberg, M.C.	114	2	57.00	1- 27	–	–	–
Rowe, D.T.	449	14	32.07	5- 61	1	–	–
Rudge, W.D.	856	16	53.50	3- 46	–	–	–
Rudolph, J.A.	1911	45	42.46	5- 87	2	–	–
Ryan, L.C.	82	1	82.00	1- 82	–	–	–
Sadler, J.L.	193	2	96.50	1- 5	–	–	–
Sadler, O.J.	41	3	13.66	3- 41	–	–	–
Saffell, O.H.J.	59	5	11.80	3- 37	–	–	–
Saggers, M.J.	9376	381	24.60	7- 79	18	–	4
Saker, N.C.	1578	31	50.90	5- 76	1	–	–
Sales, D.J.G.	174	9	19.33	4- 25	–	–	–
Salisbury, I.D.K.	28000	853	32.82	8- 60	35	6	7
Samad, A.M.	110	2	55.00	2- 71	–	–	–
Samaraweera, T.T.	8121	347	23.40	6- 55	15	2	0+1
Sammy, D.J.G.	1924	89	21.61	7- 66	6	–	–
Samuels, M.N.	2091	35	59.74	5- 87	1	–	–
Sandbach, C.J.L.	81	1	81.00	1- 37	–	–	–
Sangakkara, K.C.	74	1	74.00	1- 13	–	–	–
Saqlain Mushtaq	18342	793	23.12	8- 65	57	15	5+1
Sarwan, R.R.	2034	51	39.88	6- 62	1	–	–
Sayers, J.J.	54	0					
Schofield, C.P.	6293	195	32.27	6-120	5	–	–
Shafayat, B.M.	439	4	109.75	2- 25	–	–	–
Shah, O.A.	1235	21	58.80	3- 33	–	–	–
Shahzad, A.	388	9	43.11	4- 22	–	–	–
Shantry, A.J.	439	21	20.90	5- 49	1	–	–
Sharif, Z.K.	943	15	62.86	4- 98	–	–	–
Sharma, I.	830	32	25.93	5- 35	1	–	–
Shreck, C.E.	4931	177	27.85	8- 31	14	2	1
Sidebottom, R.J.	8893	348	25.55	7- 97	12	1	2
Sillence, R.J.	2960	72	41.11	7- 96	3	–	–
Silverwood, C.E.W.	15234	564	27.01	7- 93	25	1	3

F-C	Runs	Wkts	Avge	Best	5wI	10wM	50wS
Singh, R.P.	3167	127	24.93	5- 33	7	1	–
Smith, B.F.	488	4	122.00	1- 5	–	–	–
Smith, B.M.	486	7	69.42	4-102	–	–	–
Smith, D.S.	200	2	100.00	1- 2	–	–	–
Smith, E.T.	119	1	119.00	1- 60	–	–	–
Smith, G.M.	1122	28	40.07	3- 31	–	–	–
Smith, T.C.	1509	45	33.53	4- 57	–	–	–
Smith, T.M.J.	79	1	79.00	1- 52	–	–	–
Smith, W.R.	494	8	61.75	3- 34	–	–	–
Snape, J.N.	5583	113	49.40	5- 65	1	–	–
Solanki, V.S.	3945	84	46.96	5- 40	4	1	–
Spearman, C.M.	55	1	55.00	1- 37	–	–	–
Spriegel, M.N.W.	106	3	35.33	1- 12	–	–	–
Sreesanth, S.	3891	124	31.37	5- 40	3	–	–
Stayt, T.P.	218	4	54.50	3- 51	–	–	–
Stevens, D.I.	2061	54	38.16	4- 36	–	–	–
Steyn, D.W.	5072	178	28.49	5- 27	8	1	0+1
Strauss, A.J.	74	2	37.00	1- 16	–	–	–
Streak, H.H.	14352	499	28.76	7- 55	17	2	1
Stubbings, S.D.	79	0					
Styris, S.B.	6215	203	30.61	6- 32	9	1	–
Suppiah, A.V.	785	12	65.41	3- 46	–	–	–
Sutcliffe, I.J.	330	9	36.66	2- 21	–	–	–
Swann, G.P.	13254	400	33.13	7- 33	15	3	1
Tahir, N.	2173	77	28.22	7-107	1	–	–
Tavarasa, B.	65	0					
Taylor, B.V.	4483	135	33.20	6- 32	4	–	–
Taylor, C.G.	863	16	53.93	4- 52	–	–	–
Taylor, J.E.	3523	140	25.16	8- 59	10	2	–
Ten Doeschate, R.N.	2406	59	40.77	6- 20	2	–	–
Tendulkar, S.R.	4024	67	60.05	3- 10	–	–	–
Thomas, A.C.	5780	228	25.35	7- 54	11	1	–
Thompson, G.J.	429	13	33.00	3- 76	–	–	–
Thornicroft, N.D.	615	17	36.17	6- 60	1	–	–
Thorp, C.D.	1889	59	32.01	6- 55	2	1	–
Tomlinson, J.A.	2259	47	48.06	6- 63	2	–	–
Tredwell, J.C.	5037	127	39.66	6- 47	3	1	–
Trego, P.D.	3944	97	40.65	6- 59	1	–	–
Tremlett, C.T.	6586	243	27.10	6- 44	6	–	–
Trescothick, M.E.	1541	36	42.80	4- 36	–	–	–
Trott, I.J.L.	1387	34	40.79	7- 39	1	–	–
Troughton, J.O.	1391	22	63.22	3- 1	–	–	–
Tudge, K.D.	58	0					
Tudor, A.J.	9870	333	29.63	7- 48	14	–	–
Turner, M.L.	564	12	47.00	4- 30	–	–	–
Udal, S.D.	23649	724	32.66	8- 50	33	4	7
Udawatte, M.L.	3	0					
Umar Bhatti	1115	59	18.89	8- 40	6	2	–
Vaas, W.P.U.J.C.	15216	618	24.62	7- 54	26	3	0+2
Van der Wath, J.J.	5831	217	26.87	6- 27	11	–	–
Vandort, M.G.	53	1	53.00	1- 46	–	–	–
Van Jaarsveld, M.	873	23	37.95	2- 17	–	–	–
Van Jaarsveld, V.B.	11	0					
Vaughan, M.P.	5189	114	45.51	4- 39	–	–	–

F-C	Runs	Wkts	Avge	Best	5wI	10wM	50wS
Voges, A.C.	672	15	44.80	4- 92	–	–	–
Wagg, G.G.	3415	100	34.15	6- 38	3	–	1
Wagh, M.A.	4600	100	46.00	7-222	2	–	–
Wainwright, D.J.	766	22	34.81	4- 48	–	–	–
Wakely, A.G.	127	3	42.33	2- 62	–	–	–
Walker, M.J.	1081	21	51.47	2- 21	–	–	–
Walker, N.G.E.	2834	67	42.29	5- 59	2	–	–
Walters, S.J.	97	3	32.33	1- 4	–	–	–
Warnapura, B.S.M.	3042	114	26.68	6- 22	4	–	–
Warne, S.K.	34449	1319	26.11	8- 71	69	12	7+2
Waters, H.T.	1453	38	38.23	5- 86	1	–	–
Watkins, R.E.	1458	32	45.56	4- 40	–	–	–
Watson, S.R.	3106	103	30.15	6- 32	2	1	–
Welagedara, U.W.M.B.C.A.	2813	111	25.34	5- 37	4	–	–
Westfield, M.S.	334	7	47.71	4- 72	–	–	–
Westley, T.	24	1	24.00	1- 24	–	–	–
Weston, W.P.C.	670	5	134.00	2- 39	–	–	–
Westwood, I.J.	171	4	42.75	2- 46	–	–	–
Wharf, A.G.	10045	272	36.93	6- 59	5	1	1
Wheeler, S.J.	312	1	312.00	1- 72	–	–	–
Whelan, C.D.	213	11	19.36	2- 13	–	–	–
White, A.R.	400	14	28.57	3- 7	–	–	–
White, C.	11260	395	28.50	8- 55	11	–	–
White, C.L.	5786	153	37.81	6- 66	2	1	–
White, G.G.	221	3	73.66	2- 35	–	–	–
White, R.A.	800	14	57.14	2- 30	–	–	–
White, W.A.	826	23	35.91	5- 87	1	–	–
Wigley, D.H.	2858	80	35.72	5- 77	1	–	–
Williams, R.E.M.	524	13	40.30	5- 70	2	–	–
Willoughby, C.M.	15044	608	24.74	7- 44	27	3	2+2
Wilshaw, P.J.	68	2	34.00	1- 20	–	–	–
Wiseman, P.J.	15113	449	33.65	9- 13	18	4	–
Woakes, C.R.	192	4	48.00	2- 64	–	–	–
Wood, M.J. (Sm)	68	0					
Wood, M.J. (Y)	43	2	21.50	1- 4	–	–	–
Wood, M.J. (MCC)	77	2	38.50	2- 77	–	–	–
Woodman, R.J.	268	2	134.00	1- 78	–	–	–
Woods, N.J.	718	11	65.27	3- 46	–	–	–
Wright, B.J.	89	2	44.50	1- 14	–	–	–
Wright, C.J.C.	1624	23	70.60	2- 21	–	–	–
Wright, D.G.	8249	271	30.43	8- 60	8	–	1
Wright, L.J.	1729	43	40.20	3- 33	–	–	–
Yardy, M.H.	1304	20	65.20	5- 83	1	–	–
Yasir Arafat	11238	492	22.84	7-102	28	3	0+4
Young, P.J.W.	334	2	167.00	1- 26	–	–	–
Younus Khan	1011	20	50.55	4- 52	–	–	–
Yuvraj Singh	591	10	59.10	3- 25	–	–	–
Zondeki, M.	4767	149	31.99	6- 39	3	–	–

LIMITED-OVERS INTERNATIONALS
CAREER RECORDS

These records, complete to 23 February 2008 (the conclusion of the New Zealand v England series), include all players registered for county cricket in 2008 at the time of going to press, plus those who have appeared in LOI matches for ICC full member countries since 1 September 2006. They exclude all matches involving multinational teams, as well as any abandoned without a ball bowled, regardless of the toss having been made.

ENGLAND – BATTING AND FIELDING

	M	I	NO	HS	Runs	Avge	100	50	Ct/St
C.J.Adams	5	4	–	42	71	17.75	–	–	3
Kabir Ali	14	9	3	39*	93	15.50	–	–	1
J.M.Anderson	86	35	17	15	111	6.17	–	–	22
G.J.Batty	7	5	1	3	6	1.50	–	–	4
I.R.Bell	64	62	4	126*	2105	36.29	1	14	16
I.D.Blackwell	34	29	2	82	403	14.92	–	1	8
R.S.Bopara	21	19	7	52	330	27.50	–	1	7
T.T.Bresnan	4	4	1	20	51	17.00	–	–	1
S.C.J.Broad	26	18	11	45*	208	29.71	–	–	7
A.D.Brown	16	16	–	118	354	22.12	1	1	6
A.R.Caddick	54	38	18	36	249	12.45	–	–	9
G.Chapple	1	1	–	14	14	14.00	–	–	–
R.Clarke	20	13	–	39	144	11.07	–	–	11
P.D.Collingwood	141	129	29	120*	3526	35.26	4	19	85
A.N.Cook	21	21	–	102	667	31.76	1	3	7
D.G.Cork	32	21	3	31*	180	10.00	–	–	6
J.P.Crawley	13	12	1	73	235	21.36	–	2	1/1
R.D.B.Croft	50	36	12	32	345	14.37	–	–	11
J.W.M.Dalrymple	27	26	1	67	487	19.48	–	2	12
M.A.Ealham	64	45	4	45	716	17.46	–	–	9
A.Flintoff	124	109	14	123	2989	31.46	3	16	40
J.S.Foster	11	6	3	13	41	13.66	–	–	13/7
P.J.Franks	1	1	–	4	4	4.00	–	–	1
D.Gough	158	87	38	46*	609	12.42	–	–	24
S.J.Harmison	46	22	13	13*	67	7.44	–	–	8
G.A.Hick	120	118	15	126*	3846	37.33	5	27	64
M.J.Hoggard	26	6	2	7	17	4.25	–	–	5
G.O.Jones	49	41	8	80	815	24.69	–	4	68/4
S.P.Jones	8	1	–	1	1	1.00	–	–	–
E.C.Joyce	17	17	–	107	471	27.70	1	3	6
R.W.T.Key	5	5	–	19	54	10.80	–	–	–
R.J.Kirtley	11	2	–	1	2	1.00	–	–	5
J.Lewis	13	8	2	17	50	8.33	–	–	–
M.B.Loye	7	7	–	45	142	20.28	–	–	–
A.McGrath	14	12	2	52	166	16.60	–	1	4
D.L.Maddy	8	6	–	53	113	18.83	–	1	1
S.I.Mahmood	25	15	4	22*	85	7.72	–	–	1
A.D.Mascarenhas	10	6	2	52	127	31.75	–	1	3
P.Mustard	10	10	–	83	233	23.30	–	1	9/2
P.A.Nixon	19	18	4	49	297	21.21	–	–	20/3
M.S.Panesar	26	8	3	13	26	5.20	–	–	3
K.P.Pietersen	69	63	12	116	2536	49.72	5	18	28
L.E.Plunkett	27	24	10	56	295	21.07	–	1	7
M.J.Prior	22	22	–	52	469	21.31	–	1	23/2
M.R.Ramprakash	18	18	4	51	376	26.85	–	1	8
C.M.W.Read	36	24	7	30*	300	17.64	–	–	41/2

	M	I	NO	HS	Runs	Avge	100	50	Ct/St
I.D.K.Salisbury	4	2	1	5	7	7.00	–	–	1
O.A.Shah	36	35	4	107*	774	24.96	1	4	9
R.J.Sidebottom	13	8	3	15	33	6.60	–	–	2
C.E.W.Silverwood	7	4	–	12	17	4.25	–	–	–
J.N.Snape	10	7	3	38	118	29.50	–	–	5
V.S.Solanki	51	46	5	106	1097	26.75	2	5	16
A.J.Strauss	78	77	7	152	2239	31.98	2	14	28
G.P.Swann	7	5	–	34	91	18.20	–	–	4
C.T.Tremlett	8	5	2	19*	35	11.66	–	–	1
M.E.Trescothick	123	122	6	137	4335	37.37	12	21	49
J.O.Troughton	6	5	1	20	36	9.00	–	–	1
A.J.Tudor	3	2	1	6	9	9.00	–	–	1
S.D.Udal	11	7	4	11*	35	11.66	–	–	1
M.P.Vaughan	86	83	10	90*	1982	27.15	–	16	25
A.G.Wharf	13	5	3	9	19	9.50	–	–	1
C.White	51	41	5	57*	568	15.77	–	1	12
L.J.Wright	5	4	–	50	121	30.25	–	1	1
M.H.Yardy	6	5	1	19	49	12.25	–	–	1

ENGLAND – BOWLING

	O	M	R	W	Avge	Best	4wI	R/Over
Kabir Ali	112.1	4	682	20	34.10	4-45	1	6.08
J.M.Anderson	717.3	71	3540	121	29.25	4-23	7	4.93
G.J.Batty	60.2	1	294	4	73.50	2-40	–	4.87
I.R.Bell	14.4	0	88	6	14.66	3-9	–	6.00
I.D.Blackwell	205	8	877	24	36.54	3-26	–	4.27
R.S.Bopara	35.1	1	172	4	43.00	2-43	–	4.89
T.T.Bresnan	25	1	169	2	84.50	1-38	–	6.76
S.C.J.Broad	219	14	1115	38	29.34	4-51	–	5.09
A.D.Brown	1	0	5	0	–	–	–	5.00
P.D.Collingwood	609.3	11	3063	76	40.30	6-31	3	5.02
D.G.Cork	295.2	17	1368	41	33.36	3-27	–	4.63
R.D.B.Croft	411	25	1743	45	38.73	3-51	–	4.24
J.W.M.Dalrymple	140	2	666	14	47.57	2-5	–	4.75
M.A.Ealham	537.5	32	2197	67	32.79	5-15	3	4.08
A.Flintoff	816.2	66	3512	145	24.22	5-56	7	4.30
P.J.Franks	9	0	48	0	–	–	–	5.33
D.Gough	1403.3	120	6154	234	26.29	5-44	12	4.38
S.J.Harmison	407.1	25	2057	67	30.70	5-33	3	5.05
G.A.Hick	206	6	1026	30	34.20	5-33	1	4.98
M.J.Hoggard	217.4	13	1152	32	36.00	5-49	1	5.29
S.P.Jones	58	9	275	7	39.28	2-43	–	4.74
R.J.Kirtley	91.3	4	481	9	53.44	2-33	–	5.25
J.Lewis	119.2	13	500	18	27.77	4-36	1	4.19
A.McGrath	38	2	175	4	43.75	1-13	–	4.60
S.I.Mahmood	192.3	7	1128	29	38.89	4-50	–	5.85
A.D.Mascarenhas	70	5	307	6	51.16	3-23	–	4.38
M.S.Panesar	218	10	980	24	40.83	3-25	–	4.49
K.P.Pietersen	16.5	0	106	2	53.00	1-4	–	6.29
L.E.Plunkett	215.1	7	1260	37	34.05	3-24	–	5.85
M.R.Ramprakash	22	0	108	4	27.00	3-28	–	4.90
I.D.K.Salisbury	31	1	177	5	35.40	3-41	–	5.70
O.A.Shah	16	0	96	3	32.00	1-18	–	6.00
R.J.Sidebottom	116.1	10	511	22	23.22	3-19	–	4.39
C.E.W.Silverwood	51	0	244	6	40.66	3-43	–	4.78

ENGLAND – BOWLING (continued)

	O	M	R	W	Avge	Best	4wI	R/Over
J.N.Snape	88.1	2	403	13	31.00	3-43	–	4.57
V.S.Solanki	18.3	0	105	1	105.00	1-17	–	5.66
A.J.Strauss	1	0	3	0	–	–	–	3.00
G.P.Swann	50	5	224	7	32.00	4-34	1	4.48
C.T.Tremlett	69.5	1	395	8	49.37	4-32	1	5.65
M.E.Trescothick	38.4	0	219	4	54.75	2-7	–	5.66
A.J.Tudor	21.1	1	136	4	34.00	2-30	–	6.42
S.D.Udal	102	4	400	9	44.44	2-37	–	3.92
M.P.Vaughan	132.4	2	649	16	40.56	4-22	1	4.89
A.G.Wharf	97.2	10	428	18	23.77	4-24	1	4.39
C.White	394	25	1725	65	26.53	5-21	2	4.37
L.J.Wright	7	0	39	0	–	–	–	5.57
M.H.Yardy	42	3	135	4	33.75	3-24	–	3.21

AUSTRALIA – BATTING AND FIELDING

	M	I	NO	HS	Runs	Avge	100	50	Ct/St
N.W.Bracken	77	22	10	21*	147	12.25	–	–	16
S.R.Clark	30	10	6	16*	67	16.75	–	–	8
M.J.Clarke	125	109	26	130	3842	44.28	3	29	47
M.J.Cosgrove	3	3	–	74	112	37.33	–	1	–
D.J.Cullen	5	1	1	2*	2	–	–	–	2
M.J.Di Venuto	9	9	–	89	241	26.77	–	2	1
B.R.Dorey	4	1	–	2	2	2.00	–	–	–
A.C.Gilchrist	279	271	11	172	9307	35.79	15	54	408/53
J.N.Gillespie	97	39	16	44*	289	12.56	–	–	10
B.J.Haddin	28	25	2	87*	698	30.34	–	3	31/4
M.L.Hayden	157	151	15	181*	5940	43.67	10	33	67
B.W.Hilfenhaus	1	–	–	–	–	–	–	–	–
B.J.Hodge	25	21	2	123	575	30.26	1	3	16
G.B.Hogg	120	63	25	71*	746	19.63	–	2	37
J.R.Hopes	24	15	1	43	323	23.07	–	–	6
M.E.K.Hussey	78	58	24	109*	1897	55.79	2	11	43
P.A.Jaques	6	6	–	94	125	20.83	–	1	2
M.G.Johnson	31	12	5	24*	72	10.28	–	–	4
S.M.Katich	42	40	5	107*	1219	34.82	1	8	13
J.L.Langer	8	7	2	36	160	32.00	–	–	2/1
S.G.Law	54	51	5	110	1237	26.89	1	7	12
B.Lee	161	77	32	57	749	16.64	–	2	39
M.L.Lewis	7	1	1	4	4*	–	–	–	1
G.D.McGrath	247	67	38	11	115	3.96	–	–	34
D.R.Martyn	205	179	51	144*	5259	41.08	5	36	67
A.A.Noffke	1	–	–	–	–	–	–	–	–
R.T.Ponting	290	281	35	164	10627	43.19	24	61	127
A.Symonds	183	147	31	156	4645	40.04	6	26	75
S.W.Tait	18	1	–	11	11	11.00	–	–	2
A.C.Voges	1	1	1	16*	16	–	–	–	1
S.K.Warne	193	106	28	55	1016	13.02	–	1	80
S.R.Watson	62	45	17	79	927	33.10	–	6	13
C.L.White	13	10	3	45	157	22.42	–	–	3

AUSTRALIA – BOWLING

	O	M	R	W	Avge	Best	4wI	R/Over
N.W.Bracken	633.3	66	2752	126	21.84	5-47	5	4.34
S.R.Clark	239.4	14	1204	40	30.10	4-54	2	5.02
M.J.Clarke	249.2	3	1290	35	36.85	5-35	2	5.17
M.J.Cosgrove	5	0	13	1	13.00	1-1	–	2.60
D.J.Cullen	35.3	4	147	2	73.50	2-25	–	4.14
B.R.Dorey	27	2	146	2	73.00	1-12	–	5.40
J.N.Gillespie	857.2	79	3611	142	25.42	5-22	6	4.21
M.L.Hayden	1	0	18	0	–	–	–	18.00
B.W.Hilfenhaus	7	1	26	1	26.00	1-26	–	3.71
B.J.Hodge	11	0	51	1	51.00	1-17	–	4.63
G.B.Hogg	901.2	36	4055	153	26.50	5-32	2	4.49
J.R.Hopes	143	13	598	17	35.17	2-16	–	4.18
M.E.K.Hussey	32	2	167	2	83.50	1-22	–	5.21
M.G.Johnson	244	18	1139	50	22.78	5-26	3	4.66
S.G.Law	134.3	3	635	12	52.91	2-22	–	4.72
B.Lee	1368.5	103	6439	281	22.91	5-22	17	4.70
M.L.Lewis	56.5	1	391	7	55.85	3-56	–	6.87
G.D.McGrath	2141.4	276	8315	377	22.05	7-15	16	3.88
D.R.Martyn	132.2	2	704	12	58.66	2-21	–	5.31
A.A.Noffke	9	0	46	1	46.00	1-46	–	5.11
R.T.Ponting	25	0	104	3	34.66	1-12	–	4.16
A.Symonds	937.1	29	4682	122	38.37	5-18	3	4.99
S.W.Tait	141.4	3	774	33	23.45	4-39	1	5.46
A.C.Voges	3	0	33	0	–	–	–	11.00
S.K.Warne	1766.4	110	7514	291	25.82	5-33	13	4.25
S.R.Watson	404.2	13	1977	54	36.61	4-43	1	4.88
C.L.White	26	2	179	4	44.75	1-5	–	6.88

SOUTH AFRICA – BATTING AND FIELDING

	M	I	NO	HS	Runs	Avge	100	50	Ct/St
D.M.Benkenstein	23	20	3	69	305	17.94	–	1	3
G.H.Bodi	2	2	–	51	83	41.50	–	1	1
N.Boje	113	69	18	129	1410	27.64	2	4	33
I.L.Bosman	11	9	–	88	202	22.44	–	1	3
J.Botha	22	12	4	46	131	16.37	–	–	11
M.V.Boucher	258	188	48	147*	4040	28.85	1	24	360/17
A.B.de Villiers	59	57	6	146	1888	37.01	3	11	28
H.H.Dippenaar	101	89	14	125*	3300	44.00	4	25	33
J.P.Duminy	25	22	5	79*	569	33.47	–	3	8
H.H.Gibbs	224	217	16	175	7383	36.73	20	33	96
A.J.Hall	88	56	13	81	905	21.04	–	3	29
C.W.Henderson	4	–	–	–	–	–	–	–	–
J.H.Kallis	269	255	49	139	9512	46.17	16	65	101
J.M.Kemp	79	60	18	100*	1371	32.64	1	9	31
L.Klusener	171	137	50	103*	3576	41.10	2	19	35
G.J.P.Kruger	3	2	1	0*	0	0.00	–	–	1
C.K.Langeveldt	57	14	5	12	41	4.55	–	–	9
J.A.Morkel	19	12	1	97	214	19.45	–	1	2
M.Morkel	6	2	1	23*	23	23.00	–	–	1
A.Nel	73	20	12	30*	104	13.00	–	–	21
M.Ntini	164	41	20	42*	186	8.85	–	–	30
J.L.Ontong	21	12	1	32	121	11.00	–	–	10
A.N.Peterson	2	2	–	80	100	50.00	–	1	–

	M	I	NO	HS	Runs	Avge	100	50	Ct/St
R.J.Peterson	35	15	4	36	147	13.36	–	–	7
V.D.Philander	5	3	2	17*	40	40.00	–	–	1
S.M.Pollock	294	196	70	90	3193	25.34	–	13	104
N.Pothas	3	1	–	24	24	24.00	–	–	4/1
A.G.Prince	49	38	11	89*	940	34.81	–	2	26
J.A.Rudolph	43	37	6	81	1157	37.32	–	7	11
G.C.Smith	129	127	7	134*	4817	40.14	6	35	68
D.W.Steyn	101	1	1	1*	1	–	–	–	2
R.Telemachus	37	15	3	29	73	6.08	–	–	4
T.Tshabalala	4	1	1	2*	2	–	–	–	–
J.J.van der Wath	10	8	2	37*	89	14.83	–	–	3
M.van Jaarsveld	11	7	1	45	124	20.66	–	–	4
J.J.van der Wyk	6	6	–	82	195	32.50	–	2	1
C.M.Willoughby	3	2	–	0	0	0.00	–	–	–
M.Zondeki	9	2	2	3*	4	–	–	–	3

SOUTH AFRICA – BOWLING

	O	M	R	W	Avge	Best	4wI	R/Over
D.M.Benkenstein	10.5	1	44	4	11.00	3-5	–	4.06
G.H.Bodi	1	0	8	0	–	–	–	8.00
N.Boje	742.5	21	3352	95	35.28	5-21	3	4.51
J.Botha	165.1	2	780	14	55.71	2-29	–	4.72
J.P.Duminy	34	1	184	3	61.33	1-6	–	5.41
A.J.Hall	554.1	29	2509	95	26.41	5-18	4	4.52
C.W.Henderson	36.1	2	132	7	18.85	4-17	1	3.64
J.H.Kallis	1546	70	7424	235	31.59	5-30	4	4.80
J.M.Kemp	195.1	10	916	29	31.58	3-20	–	4.69
L.Klusener	1222.4	48	5751	192	29.95	6-49	7	4.70
G.J.P.Kruger	23	1	139	2	69.50	1-43	–	6.04
C.K.Langeveldt	449.4	23	2271	77	29.49	5-39	3	5.05
J.A.Morkel	125.4	4	649	20	32.45	4-44	1	5.16
M.Morkel	57.2	2	261	11	23.72	4-36	1	4.55
A.Nel	598.4	53	2806	99	28.34	5-45	3	4.68
M.Ntini	1374.5	119	6119	255	23.99	6-22	12	4.45
J.L.Ontong	89.4	3	396	9	44.00	3-30	–	4.41
R.J.Peterson	208.4	4	992	17	58.35	2-26	–	4.75
V.D.Philander	32.5	5	129	6	21.50	4-12	1	3.92
S.M.Pollock	2571.4	307	9410	387	24.31	6-35	17	3.65
A.G.Prince	2	0	3	0	–	–	–	1.50
J.A.Rudolph	4	0	26	0	–	–	–	6.50
G.C.Smith	171	0	951	18	52.83	3-30	–	5.56
D.W.Steyn	77.5	1	469	13	36.07	3-65	–	6.02
R.Telemachus	319.4	23	1565	56	27.94	4-43	1	4.89
T.Tshabalala	24	2	143	3	47.66	1-22	–	5.95
J.J.van der Wath	87.4	2	551	13	42.38	2-21	–	6.28
M.van Jaarsveld	5.1	1	18	2	9.00	1-0	–	3.48
C.M.Willoughby	28	2	148	2	74.00	2-39	–	5.28
M.Zondeki	67	4	350	8	43.75	2-46	–	5.22

WEST INDIES – BATTING AND FIELDING

† Excluding match abandoned without a ball bowled after toss

	M	I	NO	HS	Runs	Avge	100	50	Ct/St
O.A.C.Banks	5	5	–	33	83	16.60	–	–	–
C.S.Baugh	25	19	7	29	186	15.50	–	–	12/1
I.D.R.Bradshaw	62	34	11	37	287	12.47	–	–	6
D.J.Bravo†	79	64	16	112*	1166	24.29	1	2	33
P.A.Browne	3	3	1	49*	118	59.00	–	–	–
S.Chanderpaul†	228	215	31	150	7291	39.62	8	49	64
S.Chattergoon	6	6	1	54*	197	39.40	–	2	1
P.T.Collins	30	12	5	10*	30	4.28	–	–	8
C.D.Collymore	84	35	17	13*	103	5.72	–	–	12
N.Deonarine	5	5	–	41	99	19.80	–	–	2
F.H.Edwards	33	12	8	12*	40	10.00	–	–	3
R.R.Emrit	2	2	1	13	13	13.00	–	–	1
D.Ganga	35	34	1	71	843	25.54	–	9	11
C.H.Gayle†	172	169	12	153*	6189	39.42	15	33	80
W.W.Hinds	114	107	9	127*	2835	28.92	5	14	28
B.C.Lara†	294	285	32	169	10348	40.90	19	62	117
R.N.Lewis	26	19	5	49	248	17.71	–	–	6
D.Mohammed	5	1	1	0*	0	–	–	–	1
R.S.Morton	48	43	4	110*	1313	33.66	2	9	17
B.A.Parchment	7	7	–	48	122	17.42	–	–	–
K.A.Pollard	1	1	–	10	10	10.00	–	–	–
D.B.L.Powell	38	17	3	48*	74	5.28	–	–	5
D.Ramdin	45	35	10	74*	494	19.76	–	2	65/3
R.Rampaul	30	9	2	26*	88	12.57	–	–	3
A.C.L.Richards	1	1	–	2	2	2.00	–	–	–
D.J.G.Sammy	9	6	1	51	105	21.00	–	–	5
M.N.Samuels	104	96	14	108*	2456	29.95	2	17	29
R.R.Sarwan†	123	116	24	115*	4099	44.55	3	26	34
L.M.P.Simmons	8	8	1	70	126	18.00	–	1	3
D.R.Smith†	72	58	3	68	798	14.50	–	2	24
D.S.Smith†	22	21	2	91	491	25.84	–	2	10
J.E.Taylor	42	17	7	43*	113	11.30	–	–	13

WEST INDIES – BOWLING

	O	M	R	W	Avge	Best	4wI	R/Over
O.A.C.Banks	45	1	189	7	27.00	2-24	–	4.20
I.D.R.Bradshaw	528.4	38	2299	78	29.47	3-15	–	4.34
D.J.Bravo	496.1	21	2631	86	30.59	4-39	1	5.30
S.Chanderpaul	123.2	0	636	14	45.42	3-18	–	5.15
S.Chattergoon	9	0	36	0	–	–	–	4.00
P.T.Collins	262.5	18	1212	39	31.07	5-43	–	4.61
C.D.Collymore	679	45	2924	83	35.22	5-51	2	4.30
N.Deonarine	24	0	158	5	31.60	2-18	–	6.58
F.H.Edwards	254.5	21	1177	44	26.75	6-22	2	4.61
R.R.Emrit	14	0	99	0	–	–	–	7.07
D.Ganga	0.1	0	4	0	–	–	–	24.00
C.H.Gayle	982.4	35	4558	142	32.09	5-46	4	4.63
W.W.Hinds	157.3	3	837	28	29.89	3-24	–	5.31
B.C.Lara	8.1	0	61	4	15.25	2-5	–	7.46
R.N.Lewis	173.4	2	895	20	44.75	3-43	–	5.15
D.Mohammed	38.5	3	170	8	21.25	3-37	–	4.37
R.S.Morton	1	0	2	0	–	–	–	2.00
K.A.Pollard	3	0	20	0	–	–	–	6.66

	O	M	R	W	Avge	Best	4wI	R/Over
D.B.Powell	333	30	1528	51	29.96	4-27	2	4.58
R.Rampaul	184.5	13	919	25	36.76	4-41	1	4.97
D.J.G.Sammy	53.2	1	297	5	59.40	2-2	–	5.56
M.N.Samuels	513.1	11	2465	57	43.24	3-25	–	4.80
R.R.Sarwan	80.5	2	472	12	39.33	3-31	–	5.83
L.M.P.Simmons	1	0	9	0	–	–	–	9.00
D.R.Smith	377.2	18	1813	49	37.00	5-45	4	4.80
J.E.Taylor	365.5	18	1739	64	27.17	5-48	4	4.75

NEW ZEALAND – BATTING AND FIELDING

† Excluding matches abandoned without a ball bowled after toss

	M	I	NO	HS	Runs	Avge	100	50	Ct/St
A.R.Adams†	41	34	10	45	419	17.45	–	–	8
N.J.Astle††	221	217	14	145*	7090	34.92	16	41	83
S.E.Bond†	66	28	14	31*	200	14.28	–	–	15
S.P.Fleming††	277	268	21	134*	8007	32.41	8	49	132
D.R.Flynn	1	1	–	0	0	0.00	–	–	1
J.E.C.Franklin†	64	44	15	45*	508	17.51	–	–	19
P.G.Fulton†	42	40	5	112	1235	35.29	1	8	15
M.R.Gillespie†	23	11	5	28	87	14.50	–	–	6
P.A.Hitchcock	14	7	3	11*	41	10.25	–	–	4
G.J.Hopkins	8	3	–	9	9	3.00	–	–	8
J.M.How	20	18	1	139	718	42.23	1	6	5
B.B.McCullum†	127	104	21	96	2280	27.47	–	12	142/13
C.D.McMillan††	195	183	16	117	4707	28.19	3	28	44
H.J.H.Marshall†	65	62	9	101*	1454	27.43	1	12	19
J.A.H.Marshall	8	8	–	50	85	10.62	–	1	–
C.S.Martin	20	7	2	3	8	1.60	–	–	7
M.J.Mason†	20	5	2	13*	22	7.33	–	–	4
K.D.Mills	79	43	21	44*	303	13.77	–	–	26
I.E.O'Brien	1	–	–	–	–	–	–	–	–
J.D.P.Oram	115	85	11	101*	1764	23.83	1	8	33
J.S.Patel	29	8	3	34	57	11.40	–	–	10
J.S.Ryder	5	5	1	79*	196	49.00	–	1	2
M.S.Sinclair	53	49	4	118*	1302	28.93	2	8	17
C.M.Spearman	51	50	–	86	936	18.72	–	5	15
S.B.Styris†	146	126	18	141	3488	32.29	4	21	55
L.R.P.L.Taylor†	37	34	6	128*	996	35.57	2	4	22
D.R.Tuffey†	79	41	20	20*	154	7.33	–	–	19
D.L.Vettori††	209	129	40	83	1322	14.85	–	3	53
L.Vincent	102	99	0	172	2413	27.11	3	11	36

NEW ZEALAND – BOWLING

	O	M	R	W	Avge	Best	4wI	R/Over
A.R.Adams	314.1	15	1643	53	31.00	5-22	3	5.22
N.J.Astle	808.2	28	3809	99	38.47	4-43	1	4.71
S.E.Bond	574.2	70	2415	125	19.32	6-19	10	4.20
S.P.Fleming	4.5	0	28	1	28.00	1-8	–	5.79
J.E.C.Franklin	467.2	32	2392	64	37.37	5-42	1	5.11
M.R.Gillespie	189.3	19	1105	25	44.20	3-27	–	5.83
P.A.Hitchcock	92	5	468	12	39.00	3-30	–	5.08
C.D.McMillan	313.1	7	1715	49	35.00	3-20	–	5.47

NEW ZEALAND – BOWLING (continued)

	O	M	R	W	Avge	Best	4wI	R/Over
C.S.Martin	158	14	804	18	44.66	3-62	–	5.08
M.S.Mason	163.3	15	817	25	32.68	4-24	1	4.99
K.D.Mills	658.4	58	3067	115	26.66	5-25	6	4.65
I.E.O'Brien	6	0	59	1	59.00	1-59	–	9.83
J.D.P.Oram	829.1	71	3718	119	31.24	5-26	4	4.48
J.S.Patel	241	4	1207	36	33.52	3-11	–	5.00
J.S.Ryder	8	0	64	2	32.00	2-14	–	8.00
C.M.Spearman	0.3	0	6	0	–	–	–	12.00
S.B.Styris	856.3	38	4041	119	33.95	6-25	5	4.71
L.R.P.L.Taylor	3	0	18	0	–	–	–	6.00
D.R.Tuffey	612.2	63	2910	91	31.97	4-24	2	4.75
D.L.Vettori	1658	67	6932	215	32.24	5-7	7	4.18
L.Vincent	3.2	1	25	1	25.00	1-0	–	7.50

INDIA – BATTING AND FIELDING

	M	I	NO	HS	Runs	Avge	100	50	Ct/St
A.B.Agarkar	191	113	26	95	1268	14.57	–	3	52
P.Chawla	13	7	3	13*	20	5.00	–	–	5
M.S.Dhoni	99	89	23	183*	2924	44.30	2	19	94/28
R.Dravid	329	304	39	153	10464	39.48	12	80	193/14
G.Gambhir	43	43	4	103	1289	33.05	3	6	12
S.C.Ganguly	308	297	23	183	11221	40.95	22	71	100
Harbhajan Singh	165	87	26	46	839	13.75	–	–	46
W.Jaffer	2	2	–	10	10	5.00	–	–	–
M.Kaif	125	110	24	111*	2753	32.01	2	17	55
K.D.Karthik	26	20	5	63	330	22.00	–	2	23/2
M.Kartik	38	14	5	32*	126	14.00	–	–	10
Z.Khan	138	75	30	34*	621	13.80	–	–	28
P.Kumar	2	2	–	12	18	9.00	–	–	1
A.Kumble	269	134	47	26	903	10.37	–	–	85
V.V.S.Laxman	86	83	7	131	2338	30.76	6	10	39
D.Mongia	57	51	7	159*	1230	27.95	1	4	21
A.Nehra	69	25	14	24	86	7.81	–	–	9
M.M.Patel	27	11	5	15	32	5.33	–	–	2
I.K.Pathan	91	68	17	83	1221	23.94	–	5	16
R.R.Powar	31	19	5	54	163	11.64	–	1	3
S.K.Raina	36	28	5	81*	612	26.60	–	3	15
V.Sehwag	172	167	7	130	5017	31.35	8	24	69
I.Sharma	7	3	3	2*	3	–	–	–	2
J.Sharma	4	3	2	29*	35	35.00	–	–	3
R.G.Sharma	10	9	2	70*	224	32.00	–	2	5
R.P.Singh	38	14	9	12*	52	10.40	–	–	9
S.Sreesanth	39	14	6	10*	30	3.75	–	–	6
S.R.Tendulkar	413	403	37	186*	16088	43.95	41	87	122
M.K.Tiwari	1	1	–	2	2	2.00	–	–	–
R.V.Uthappa	31	27	4	86	640	27.82	–	4	14
Yuvraj Singh	197	179	25	139	5594	36.32	8	35	61

INDIA – BOWLING

	O	M	R	W	Avge	Best	4wI	R/Over
A.B.Agarkar	1580.4	100	8021	288	27.85	6-42	12	5.07
P.Chawla	111	4	538	17	31.64	3-29	–	4.84
R.Dravid	31	1	170	4	42.50	2-43	–	5.48
G.Gambhir	1	0	13	0	–	–	–	13.00
S.C.Ganguly	757.1	29	3835	100	38.35	5-16	3	5.06

INDIA – BOWLING (continued)

	O	M	R	W	Avge	Best	4wI	R/Over
Harbhajan Singh	1461.1	69	6085	181	33.61	5-31	4	4.16
M.Kartik	317.5	19	1612	37	43.56	6-27	1	5.07
Z.Khan	1155.1	76	5711	188	30.37	5-42	7	4.94
P.Kumar	20	1	99	0	–	–	–	4.95
A.Kumble	2396	109	10300	334	30.83	6-12	10	4.29
V.V.S.Laxman	7	0	40	0	–	–	–	5.71
D.Mongia	106.4	1	571	14	40.78	3-31	–	5.35
A.Nehra	577	38	2777	90	30.85	6-23	4	4.81
M.M.Patel	216.1	22	1013	34	29.79	4-49	1	4.68
I.K.Pathan	728.2	45	3696	134	27.58	5-27	5	5.07
R.R.Powar	256	6	1191	34	35.02	3-24	–	4.65
S.K.Raina	5.2	0	37	1	37.00	1-23	–	6.93
V.Sehwag	578.2	12	3019	74	40.79	3-25	–	5.22
I.Sharma	41.1	2	185	8	23.12	4-38	1	4.49
J.Sharma	25	3	115	1	115.00	1-28	–	4.60
R.P.Singh	290.3	22	1522	48	31.70	4-35	2	5.23
S.Sreesanth	303.5	14	1755	55	31.90	6-55	2	5.77
S.R.Tendulkar	1334.5	25	6795	154	44.12	5-32	6	5.09
Yuvraj Singh	410.4	13	2108	53	39.77	4-6	1	5.13

PAKISTAN – BATTING AND FIELDING

	M	I	NO	HS	Runs	Avge	100	50	Ct/St
Abdur Razzaq	227	195	49	112	4417	30.25	2	22	31
Abdur Rauf	1	–	–	–	–	–	–	–	–
Abdur Rehman	11	8	1	31	59	8.42	–	–	2
Azhar Mahmood	143	110	26	67	1521	18.10	–	3	37
Danish Kaneria	18	10	8	6*	12	6.00	–	–	2
Faisal Iqbal	18	16	2	100*	314	22.42	1	–	3
Fawad Alam	4	4	3	32	58	58.00	–	–	1
Iftikhar Anjum	41	23	15	32	169	21.12	–	–	8
Imran Farhat	33	33	1	107	974	30.43	1	6	11
Imran Nazir	74	74	2	160	1784	24.77	2	9	24
Inzamam-ul-Haq	375	348	52	137*	11701	39.53	10	83	113
Kamran Akmal	80	68	10	124	1397	24.08	3	2	71/13
Kamran Hussain	2	1	1	28*	28	–	–	–	–
Khalid Latif	1	1	–	19	19	19.00	–	–	–
Khurram Manzoor	1	1	–	50	50	50.00	–	1	1
Misbah-ul-Haq	27	25	5	55*	727	36.35	–	3	11
Mohammad Asif	26	10	4	6	28	4.66	–	–	2
Mohammad Hafeez	48	48	1	92	874	18.59	–	4	20
Mohammad Sami	83	46	19	46	314	11.62	–	–	18
Mohd Yousuf Youhana	249	237	37	141*	8673	43.53	14	59	50
Mushtaq Ahmed	144	76	34	34*	399	9.50	–	–	30
Najaf Shah	1	1	–	0	0	0.00	–	–	–
Nasir Jamshed	5	5	–	74	197	39.40	–	2	1
Naved-ul-Hasan	62	41	14	29	359	13.29	–	–	13
Rizwan Ahmed	1	–	–	–	–	–	–	–	1
Salman Butt	44	44	1	129	1368	31.81	4	5	11
Samiullah Khan	2	–	–	–	–	–	–	–	–
Saqlain Mushtaq	169	98	39	37*	709	12.01	–	–	40
Sarfaz Ahmed	3	–	–	–	–	–	–	–	2
Shahid Afridi	248	235	14	109	5332	24.12	4	29	89
Shoaib Akhtar	133	63	30	43	312	9.45	–	–	17
Shoaib Malik	155	138	17	143	4142	34.23	5	26	56
Sohail Khan	1	–	–	–	–	–	–	–	–
Sohail Tanvir	13	8	3	26	55	11.00	–	–	5

	M	I	NO	HS	Runs	Avge	100	50	Ct/St
Umar Gul	39	12	5	17*	57	8.14	–	–	5
Wahab Riaz	1	–	–	–	–	–	–	–	–
Yasir Arafat	8	6	2	27	48	12.00	–	–	1
Yasir Hamid	56	56	1	127*	2028	36.87	3	12	14
Younus Khan	164	159	18	144	4600	32.62	3	31	86

PAKISTAN – BOWLING

	O	M	R	W	Avge	Best	4wI	R/Over
Abdul Razzaq	1617.5	91	7546	245	30.80	6-35	11	4.66
Abdur Rauf	8.4	–	45	3	15.00	3-45	–	5.19
Abdur Rehman	99	6	437	12	36.41	2-20	–	4.41
Azhar Mahmood	1040.2	58	4813	123	39.13	6-18	5	4.62
Danish Kaneria	142.2	11	683	15	45.53	3-31	–	4.79
Faisal Iqbal	3	0	33	0	–	–	–	11.00
Fawad Alam	28	0	129	2	64.50	1-28	–	4.60
Iftikhar Anjum	320.3	26	1540	45	34.22	3-33	–	4.80
Imran Farhat	14.2	2	89	5	17.80	3-10	–	6.20
Imran Nazir	8.1	0	48	1	48.00	1-3	–	5.87
Inzamam-ul-Haq	9.4	1	64	3	21.33	1-0	–	6.61
Kamran Hussain	17	0	67	3	22.33	2-32	–	3.94
Misbah-ul-Haq	4	0	30	0	–	–	–	7.50
Mohammad Asif	208.4	25	927	26	35.65	3-28	–	4.44
Mohammad Hafeez	286.5	9	1278	38	33.63	3-17	–	4.45
Mohammad Sami	682.2	38	3357	118	28.44	5-10	4	4.91
Mohd Yousuf Youhana	0.2	0	1	1	1.00	1-0	–	3.00
Mushtaq Ahmed	1257.1	51	5361	161	33.29	5-36	4	4.26
Najaf Shah	10	1	59	0	–	–	–	5.90
Naved-ul-Hasan	475.4	23	2630	95	27.68	6-27	6	5.52
Rizwan Ahmed	4	0	26	0	–	–	–	6.50
Salman Butt	7.3	0	58	0	–	–	–	7.73
Samiullah Khan	20	0	115	0	–	–	–	5.75
Saqlain Mushtaq	1461.4	66	6275	288	21.78	5-20	17	4.29
Shahid Afridi	1676.4	48	7759	215	36.08	5-11	4	4.62
Shoaib Akhtar	1050.3	83	4864	213	22.83	6-16	10	4.63
Shoaib Malik	894.3	25	4046	120	33.71	4-19	1	4.52
Sohail Khan	7	0	38	1	38.00	1-38	–	5.42
Sohail Tanvir	110.5	8	493	18	27.38	4-34	2	4.44
Umar Gul	304.5	22	1487	49	30.34	5-17	1	4.87
Wahab Riaz	8	3	19	2	9.50	2-19	–	2.37
Yasir Arafat	49	0	274	4	68.50	1-28	–	5.59
Yasir Hamid	3	0	26	0	–	–	–	8.66
Younus Khan	24.1	0	151	1	151.00	1-24	–	6.24

SRI LANKA – BATTING AND FIELDING

† Excluding match abandoned without a ball bowled after toss

	M	I	NO	HS	Runs	Avge	100	50	Ct/St
M.K.D.I.Amerasinghe	5	2	1	1*	1	–	–	–	–
R.P.Arnold	180	155	43	103	3950	35.26	1	28	48
M.S.Atapattu†	267	259	32	132*	8529	37.57	11	59	70
C.M.Bandara	28	15	4	28*	129	11.72	–	–	8
U.D.U.Chandana	147	111	17	89	1627	17.30	–	5	78
T.M.Dilshan	137	116	26	117*	2680	29.77	1	11	62/1
C.R.D.Fernando†	121	47	28	20	189	9.94	–	–	21
S.T.Jayasuriya†	404	393	18	189	12187	32.49	25	64	116
D.P.M.D.Jayawardena†	261	244	26	128	7124	32.67	9	41	132

	M	I	NO	HS	Runs	Avge	100	50	Ct/St
H.A.P.W.Jayawardena	6	5	–	20	27	5.40	–	–	4/1
C.K.Kapugedara†	26	21	1	50	300	15.00	–	1	7
M.D.N.Kulasekara	22	13	7	11	34	5.66	–	–	5
K.S.Lokuarachchi	21	18	3	69	210	14.00	–	1	5
M.F.Maharoof†	78	52	13	69*	761	19.51	–	2	17
S.L.Malinga†	50	23	11	15	80	6.66	–	–	10
J.Mubarak	28	27	3	72	486	20.25	–	3	10
M.Muralitharan†	295	136	51	27	502	5.90	–	–	116
M.D.K.Perera	2	2	–	30	31	15.50	–	–	–
P.D.R.L.Perera	19	7	2	4*	8	1.60	–	–	2
K.C.Sangakkara†	206	190	22	138*	6040	35.95	7	39	191/51
L.P.C.Silva	41	35	4	107*	1087	35.06	1	9	13
W.U.Tharanga†	65	62	–	120	1995	32.17	6	9	10
W.P.U.C.J.Vaas†	309	210	69	50*	1946	13.80	–	1	58
B.S.M.Warnapura	1	1	–	5	5	5.00	–	–	–
D.N.T.Zoysa	95	47	21	49*	343	13.19	–	–	13

SRI LANKA – BOWLING

	O	M	R	W	Avge	Best	4wI	R/Over
M.K.D.I.Amerasinghe	47	4	223	6	37.16	3-49	–	4.74
R.P.Arnold	360.3	8	1745	40	43.62	3-47	–	4.84
M.S.Atapattu	8.3	0	41	0	–	–	–	4.82
C.M.Bandara	219	3	1105	34	32.50	4-31	2	5.04
U.D.U.Chandana	1022.4	20	4809	151	31.84	5-61	5	4.70
T.M.Dilshan	407.3	11	1927	44	43.79	4-29	2	4.72
C.R.D.Fernando	874	46	4536	154	29.45	6-37	3	5.18
S.T.Jayasuriya	2330.5	39	11065	304	36.39	6-29	12	4.74
D.P.M.D.Jayawardena	94.4	1	539	7	77.00	2-56	–	5.69
C.K.Kapugedara	16	0	77	1	77.00	1-54	–	4.81
M.D.N.Kulasekara	157.2	13	693	15	46.20	2-17	–	4.40
K.S.Lokuarachchi	169.3	7	731	31	22.58	4-44	1	4.31
M.F.Maharoof	544.4	42	2537	104	24.39	6-14	5	4.65
S.L.Malinga	405.5	33	1937	77	25.15	4-44	4	4.77
J.Mubarak	8.3	0	50	1	50.00	1-10	–	5.88
M.Muralitharan	2674.2	180	10318	450	22.92	7-30	21	3.85
P.D.R.L.Perera	148	11	820	19	43.15	3-23	–	5.54
W.P.U.C.J.Vaas	2535.1	268	10596	391	27.09	8-19	13	4.17
D.N.T.Zoysa	709.5	60	3213	108	29.75	5-26	3	4.52

ZIMBABWE – BATTING AND FIELDING

	M	I	NO	HS	Runs	Avge	100	50	Ct/St
G.B.Brent	70	54	20	59*	408	12.00	–	–	20
C.J.Chibhabha	34	34	–	73	820	24.11	–	6	15
E.Chigumbura	68	62	7	77*	1358	24.69	–	7	24
K.M.Dabengwa	20	17	6	45	260	23.63	–	–	5
T.Duffin	23	23	–	88	546	23.73	–	3	6
S.M.Ervine	42	34	7	100	698	25.85	1	2	5
G.W.Flower	219	212	18	142*	6536	33.69	6	40	86
M.W.Goodwin	71	70	3	112*	1818	27.13	2	8	20
R.S.Higgins	11	8	2	7*	15	2.50	–	–	5
A.J.Ireland	26	13	5	8*	30	3.75	–	–	2
T.Kamungozi	4	3	2	0*	0	0.00	–	–	2
F.Kasteni	3	3	–	9	18	6.00	–	–	–
N.B.Mahwire	23	19	8	22*	117	10.63	–	–	6
T.Maruma	2	1	–	7	7	7.00	–	–	–

	M	I	NO	HS	Runs	Avge	100	50	Ct/St
H.Masakadza	51	51	2	87	1038	21.18	–	7	19
S.Matsikenyeri	72	70	5	89	1339	20.60	–	7	22
T.M.K.Mawayo	2	2	–	14	24	12.00	–	–	–
C.B.Mpofu	26	16	7	4	19	2.11	–	–	3
T.V.Mufambisi	6	6	–	21	55	9.16	–	–	1
T.Mupariwa	23	18	6	33	149	12.41	–	–	7
M.L.Nkala	50	35	5	47	324	10.80	–	–	6
R.W.Price	35	17	7	20*	107	10.70	–	–	2
E.C.Rainsford	24	14	6	9*	38	4.75	–	–	4
H.P.Rinke	18	18	–	72	317	17.61	–	3	–
V.Sibanda	61	60	2	116	1360	23.44	1	10	23
G.M.Strydom	12	10	–	58	147	14.70	–	1	4
T.Taibu	95	82	16	107*	1781	26.98	1	9	84/10
B.R.M.Taylor	75	74	6	98	1929	28.36	–	12	43/12
P.Utseya	71	57	20	31	400	10.81	–	–	21
S.C.Williams	24	24	4	71	606	30.30	–	7	10

ZIMBABWE – BOWLING

	O	M	R	W	Avge	Best	4wI	R/Over
G.B.Brent	565	40	2776	75	37.01	4-22	3	4.91
C.J.Chibhabha	79	1	581	11	52.81	2-36	–	7.35
E.Chigumbura	241.1	16	1444	35	41.25	3-25	–	5.98
K.M.Dabengwa	90.3	0	527	9	58.55	3-19	–	5.82
S.M.Ervine	274.5	10	1561	41	38.07	3-29	–	5.67
G.W.Flower	903.1	11	4187	104	40.25	4-32	2	4.63
M.W.Goodwin	41.2	1	210	4	52.50	1-12	–	5.08
R.S.Higgins	90.4	6	380	13	29.23	4-21	1	4.19
A.J.Ireland	221	13	1116	38	29.36	3-41	–	5.04
T.Kamungozi	30	–	163	5	32.60	2-55	–	5.43
N.B.Mahwire	147.3	12	775	21	36.90	3-29	–	5.25
H.Maruma	12.5	0	74	0	–	–	–	5.76
H.Masakadza	88.1	2	495	14	35.35	3-39	–	5.61
S.Matsikenyeri	126.2	2	663	13	51.00	2-33	–	5.24
C.B.Mpofu	206.1	11	1086	27	40.22	4-42	1	5.26
T.Mupariwa	207.3	17	1053	40	26.32	4-46	2	5.07
M.L.Nkala	263.4	8	1570	22	71.36	3-12	–	5.95
R.W.Price	308.2	12	1281	21	61.00	2-16	–	4.15
E.C.Rainsford	203	24	923	24	38.45	3-16	–	4.54
H.P.Rinke	46.1	2	273	8	34.12	2-11	–	5.90
V.Sibanda	15	0	87	2	43.50	1-12	–	5.80
G.M.Strydom	11	0	61	1	61.00	1-28	–	5.54
T.Taibu	14	1	61	2	30.50	2-42	–	4.35
B.R.M.Taylor	35	0	224	8	28.00	3-54	–	6.40
P.Utseya	601.1	31	2482	46	53.95	3-35	–	4.12
S.C.Williams	100.4	1	518	9	57.55	3-23	–	5.14

BANGLADESH – BATTING AND FIELDING

	M	I	NO	HS	Runs	Avge	100	50	Ct/St
Abdur Razzaq	55	34	16	28	242	13.44	–	–	13
Aftab Ahmed	72	72	6	92	1745	26.43	–	13	24
Farhad Reza	18	16	3	50	295	22.69	–	1	6
Habibul Bashar	111	105	5	78	2168	21.68	–	14	26
Javed Omar	59	59	4	85*	1312	23.85	–	10	12
Junaid Siddique	3	3	–	15	29	9.66	–	–	–
Khaled Masud	126	110	27	71*	1818	21.90	–	7	91/35

	M	I	NO	HS	Runs	Avge	100	50	Ct/St
Mahmudullah	1	1	–	36	36	36.00	–	–	–
Mashrafe Mortaza	70	54	10	51*	732	16.63	–	1	21
Mehrab Hossain II	11	10	–	54	203	20.30	–	1	3
Mohammed Ashraful	105	99	9	100	2016	22.40	1	12	17
Mohammed Rafique	123	104	16	77	1190	13.52	–	2	28
Mohammad Sharif	9	9	5	13*	53	13.25	–	–	1
Mushfiqur Rahim	26	21	5	57	332	20.75	–	2	17/4
Mushfiqur Rahman	30	26	4	49	378	17.18	–	–	8
Rajin Saleh	43	43	1	108*	1005	23.92	1	6	10
Shahadat Hossain	27	13	8	9*	30	6.00	–	–	1
Shahriar Nafiz	49	49	4	123*	1566	34.80	4	7	7
Shakib Al Hasan	37	36	9	134*	968	35.85	1	5	7
Syed Rasel	31	16	5	15	56	5.09	–	–	4
Tamim Iqbal	21	21	–	54	455	21.66	–	3	9
Tapash Baisya	56	41	13	35*	336	12.00	–	–	8
Tushar Imran	41	40	–	65	574	14.35	–	2	6

BANGLADESH – BOWLING

	O	M	R	W	Avge	Best	4wI	R/Over
Abdur Razzaq	479.1	33	1964	82	23.95	5-33	3	4.09
Aftab Ahmed	119.1	0	629	12	52.42	5-31	1	5.28
Farhad Reza	94	5	492	6	82.00	1-19	–	5.23
Habibul Bashar	29.1	0	142	1	142.00	1-31	–	4.86
Mahmudullah	5	0	28	2	14.00	2-28	2	5.60
Mashrafe Mortaza	597.1	55	2748	92	29.86	6-26	4	4.60
Mehrab Hossain II	23.1	0	108	3	36.00	2-30	–	4.66
Mohammed Ashraful	60	1	364	11	33.09	3-26	–	6.06
Mohammed Rafique	1049	63	4613	119	38.76	5-47	3	4.39
Mohammad Sharif	83.1	5	424	10	42.40	3-40	–	5.09
Mushfiqur Rahman	222	18	983	19	51.73	2-21	–	4.42
Rajin Saleh	89.5	1	459	15	30.60	4-16	1	5.10
Shahadat Hossain	195.4	14	1002	27	37.11	3-34	–	5.12
Shakib Al Hasan	280	12	1189	35	33.97	3-18	–	4.24
Syed Rasel	274.3	35	1139	44	25.88	4-22	1	4.14
Tapash Baisya	434.4	18	2452	59	41.55	4-16	2	5.64
Tushar Imran	21	0	103	1	103.00	1-24	–	4.90

ASSOCIATES – BATTING AND FIELDING

	M	I	NO	HS	Runs	Avge	100	50	Ct/St
D.L.Hemp (Bermuda)	20	20	2	76*	458	25.44	–	3	5
E.J.G.Morgan (Ireland)	18	18	1	115	549	32.29	1	3	8
K.J.O'Brien (Ireland)	20	20	1	142	573	30.15	1	2	9
N.J.O'Brien (Ireland)	21	21	–	72	503	23.95	–	5	14/3
N.S.Poonia (Scotland)	14	14	–	67	184	13.14	–	1	4
W.T.S.Porterfield (Ireland)	20	20	2	112*	614	34.11	2	2	6
W.B.Rankin (Ireland)	10	4	3	7*	15	15.00	–	–	2
R.N.ten Doeschate (Holland)	17	16	5	109*	615	55.90	1	4	7

ASSOCIATES – BOWLING

	O	M	R	W	Avge	Best	4wI	R/Over
D.L.Hemp	19	0	119	1	119.00	1-25	–	6.26
K.J.O'Brien	79	3	424	10	42.40	2-38	–	5.36
W.B.Rankin	63.2	4	349	12	29.08	3-32	–	5.51
R.N.ten Doeschate	129.3	7	654	30	21.80	4-31	2	5.05

TEST MATCH CAREER RECORDS

These records, complete to 23 February 2008, contain all players registered for county cricket in 2008 at the time of going to press, plus those who have played Test cricket since 1 September 2006 (Test No. 1813). They do not include matches, erroneously entitled Tests, that involve multi-national teams.

ENGLAND – BATTING AND FIELDING

	M	I	NO	HS	Runs	Avge	100	50	Ct/St
C.J.Adams	5	8	–	31	104	13.00	–	–	6
U.Afzaal	3	6	1	54	83	16.60	–	1	–
K.Ali	1	2	–	9	10	5.00	–	–	–
J.M.Anderson	20	30	17	21*	143	11.00	–	–	7
I.R.Bell	33	60	6	162*	2296	42.51	6	17	32
R.S.Bopara	3	5	–	34	42	8.40	–	–	1
S.C.J.Broad	1	1	–	2	2	2.00	–	–	–
M.A.Butcher	71	131	7	173*	4288	34.58	8	23	61
A.R.Caddick	62	95	12	49*	861	10.37	–	–	21
R.Clarke	2	3	–	55	96	32.00	–	1	1
P.D.Collingwood	30	57	6	206	2181	42.76	5	7	39
A.N.Cook	24	45	2	127	1936	45.02	7	8	20
D.G.Cork	37	56	8	59	864	18.00	–	3	18
J.P.Crawley	37	61	9	156*	1800	34.61	4	9	29
R.D.B.Croft	21	34	8	37*	421	16.19	–	–	10
R.K.J.Dawson	7	13	3	19*	114	11.40	–	–	3
M.A.Ealham	8	13	3	53*	210	21.00	–	2	4
A.Flintoff	66	108	6	167	3331	32.65	5	24	44
J.S.Foster	7	12	3	48	226	25.11	–	–	17/1
J.E.R.Gallian	3	6	–	28	74	12.33	–	–	1
A.F.Giles	54	81	13	59	1421	20.89	–	4	33
D.Gough	58	86	18	65	855	12.57	–	2	13
S.J.Harmison	55	73	19	42	640	11.85	–	–	7
G.A.Hick	65	114	6	178	3383	31.32	6	18	90
M.J.Hoggard	66	90	27	38	467	7.41	–	–	23
R.L.Johnson	3	4	–	26	59	14.75	–	–	–
G.O.Jones	34	53	4	100	1172	23.91	1	6	128/5
S.P.Jones	18	18	5	44	205	15.76	–	–	4
R.W.T.Key	15	26	1	221	775	31.00	1	3	11
R.J.Kirtley	4	7	1	12	32	5.33	–	–	3
J.Lewis	1	2	–	20	27	13.50	–	–	–
A.McGrath	4	5	–	81	201	40.20	–	2	3
D.L.Maddy	3	4	–	24	46	11.50	–	–	4
S.I.Mahmood	8	11	1	34	81	8.10	–	–	–
M.S.Panesar	23	32	14	26	128	7.11	–	–	4
K.P.Pietersen	33	63	3	226	3024	50.40	10	10	20
L.E.Plunkett	9	13	2	44*	126	11.45	–	–	3
M.J.Prior	10	17	3	126*	562	40.14	1	4	28
M.R.Ramprakash	52	92	6	154	2350	27.32	2	12	39
C.M.W.Read	15	23	4	55	360	18.94	–	1	48/6
M.J.Saggers	3	3	–	1	1	0.33	–	–	1
I.D.K.Salisbury	15	25	3	50	368	16.72	–	1	5
C.P.Schofield	2	3	–	57	67	22.33	–	1	1
O.A.Shah	3	4	–	88	136	34.00	–	1	1
R.J.Sidebottom	10	15	6	31	171	19.00	–	–	2
C.E.W.Silverwood	6	7	3	10	29	7.25	–	–	2
E.T.Smith	3	5	–	64	87	17.40	–	1	5
A.J.Strauss	43	81	2	147	3223	40.79	10	11	51
C.T.Tremlett	3	5	1	25*	50	12.50	–	–	1
M.E.Trescothick	76	143	10	219	5825	43.79	14	29	95
A.J.Tudor	10	16	4	99*	229	19.08	–	1	3
M.P.Vaughan	73	132	9	197	5356	43.54	17	17	43
C.White	30	50	7	121	1052	24.46	1	5	14

	O	M	R	W	Avge	Best	5wI	10wM
C.J.Adams	20	5	59	1	59.00	1- 42	–	–
U.Afzaal	9	0	49	1	49.00	1- 49	–	–
K.Ali	36	5	136	5	27.20	3- 80	–	–
J.M.Anderson	648.3	136	2431	62	39.20	5- 42	3	–
I.R.Bell	18	3	76	1	76.00	1- 33	–	–
R.S.Bopara	26	6	81	1	81.00	1- 39	–	–
S.C.J.Broad	36	5	95	1	95.00	1- 95	–	–
M.A.Butcher	150.1	27	541	15	36.06	4- 42	–	–
A.R.Caddick	2259.4	501	6999	234	29.91	7- 46	13	1
R.Clarke	29	11	60	4	15.00	2- 7	–	–
P.D.Collingwood	147.4	23	488	9	54.22	2- 24	–	–
D.G.Cork	1279.4	264	3906	131	29.81	7- 43	5	–
R.D.B.Croft	769.5	195	1825	49	37.24	5- 95	1	–
R.K.J.Dawson	186	20	677	11	61.54	4-134	–	–
M.A.Ealham	176.4	43	488	17	28.70	4- 21	–	–
A.Flintoff	2059.4	420	6201	190	32.63	5- 58	2	–
J.E.R.Gallian	14	1	62	0			–	–
A.F.Giles	2030	397	5806	143	40.60	5- 57	5	–
D.Gough	1970.1	369	6503	229	28.39	6- 42	9	–
S.J.Harmison	2010	390	6433	207	31.07	7- 12	8	1
G.A.Hick	509.3	128	1306	23	56.78	4-126	–	–
M.J.Hoggard	2280.1	488	7413	247	30.01	7- 61	7	1
R.L.Johnson	91.1	25	275	16	17.18	6- 33	2	–
S.P.Jones	470.1	78	1666	59	28.23	6- 53	3	–
R.J.Kirtley	179.5	50	561	19	29.52	6- 34	1	–
J.Lewis	41	9	122	3	40.66	3- 68	–	–
A.McGrath	17	1	56	4	14.00	3- 16	–	–
D.L.Maddy	14	1	40	0			–	–
S.I.Mahmood	188.2	25	762	20	38.10	4- 22	–	–
M.S.Panesar	900.3	181	2654	81	32.76	6-129	6	1
K.P.Pietersen	74	5	330	2	165.00	1- 11	–	–
L.E.Plunkett	256.2	39	916	23	39.82	3- 17	–	–
M.R.Ramprakash	149.1	16	477	4	119.25	1- 2	–	–
M.J.Saggers	82.1	20	247	7	35.28	2- 29	–	–
I.D.K.Salisbury	415.2	50	1539	20	76.95	4-163	–	–
C.P.Schofield	18	2	73	0			–	–
R.J.Sidebottom	357	79	1000	29	34.48	5- 88	1	–
C.E.W.Silverwood	138	27	444	11	40.36	5- 91	1	–
C.T.Tremlett	143.1	36	386	13	29.69	3- 12	–	–
M.E.Trescothick	50	6	155	1	155.00	1- 34	–	–
A.J.Tudor	252	51	963	28	34.39	5- 44	1	–
M.P.Vaughan	163	21	561	6	93.50	2- 71	–	–
C.White	659.5	119	2220	59	37.62	5- 32	3	–

TEST　　　　**AUSTRALIA – BATTING AND FIELDING**

	M	I	NO	HS	Runs	Avge	100	50	Ct/St
S.R.Clark	15	15	2	39	172	13.23	–	–	2
M.J.Clarke	32	48	6	151	2000	47.61	6	8	28
M.T.G.Elliott	21	36	1	199	1172	33.48	3	4	14
A.C.Gilchrist	95	135	20	204*	5475	47.60	17	25	374/35
J.N.Gillespie	71	93	28	201*	1218	18.73	1	2	27
M.L.Hayden	93	165	13	380	8054	52.98	29	26	118
G.B.Hogg	7	10	3	79	186	26.57	–	1	1
M.E.K.Hussey	22	36	8	182	2188	78.14	8	8	20
P.A.Jaques	8	13	–	150	657	50.53	2	5	3
M.G.Johnson	6	5	3	50*	112	56.00	–	1	2
J.L.Langer	104	180	12	250	7674	45.67	23	30	72
B.Lee	64	70	15	64	1180	21.45	–	4	18
S.C.G.MacGill	41	43	9	43	347	10.20	–	–	16
G.D.McGrath	123	136	51	61	639	7.51	–	1	38
D.R.Martyn	67	109	14	165	4406	46.37	13	23	36
M.J.Nicholson	1	2	–	9	14	7.00	–	–	–
R.T.Ponting	115	191	26	257	9676	58.64	34	38	132
C.J.L.Rogers	1	2	–	15	19	9.50	–	–	1
A.Symonds	19	28	3	162*	1031	41.24	2	6	14
S.W.Tait	3	5	2	8	20	6.66	–	–	1
S.K.Warne	144	197	17	99	3142	17.45	–	12	125
S.R.Watson	2	2	–	31	47	23.50	–	–	–

AUSTRALIA – BOWLING

	O	M	R	W	Avge	Best	5wI	10wM
S.R.Clark	565.4	146	1488	68	21.88	5- 55	1	–
M.J.Clarke	88.1	10	264	12	22.00	6- 9	1	–
M.T.G.Elliott	2	1	4	0				
J.N.Gillespie	2372.2	630	6770	259	26.13	7- 37	8	–
M.L.Hayden	9	0	40	0				
G.B.Hogg	254	40	933	17	54.88	2- 40	–	–
M.E.K.Hussey	5	0	23	0				
M.G.Johnson	250.1	45	771	24	32.12	4- 86	–	–
J.L.Langer	1	0	3	0				
B.Lee	2310	463	8027	269	29.84	5- 30	8	–
S.C.G.MacGill	1772.4	355	5631	194	29.02	8-108	11	2
G.D.McGrath	4856.4	1464	12144	560	21.68	8- 24	29	3
D.R.Martyn	58	16	168	2	84.00	1- 0	–	–
M.J.Nicholson	25	4	115	4	28.75	3- 56	–	–
R.T.Ponting	87.5	23	231	5	46.20	1- 0	–	–
A.Symonds	282	64	766	22	34.81	3- 50	–	–
S.W.Tait	69	6	302	5	60.40	3- 97	–	–
S.K.Warne	6753	1754	17924	702	25.53	8- 71	37	10
S.R.Watson	25	5	85	2	42.50	1- 25	–	–

SOUTH AFRICA – BATTING AND FIELDING

	M	I	NO	HS	Runs	Avge	100	50	Ct/St
H.D.Ackerman	4	8	–	57	161	20.12	–	1	1
H.M.Amla	20	37	2	176*	1180	33.71	3	6	21
N.Boje	43	62	10	85	1312	25.23	–	4	18
M.V.Boucher	108	151	18	125	4047	30.42	4	27	392/19
A.B.de Villiers	35	63	4	178	2201	37.30	4	13	48/1
H.H.Dippenaar	38	62	6	177*	1718	30.14	3	7	27
H.H.Gibbs	90	154	7	228	6167	41.95	14	26	94
A.J.Hall	21	33	4	163	760	26.20	1	3	16
P.L.Harris	10	15	2	46	90	6.92	–	–	7
C.W.Henderson	7	7	–	30	65	9.28	–	–	2
J.H.Kallis	113	192	31	189*	9331	57.95	29	47	115
J.M.Kemp	4	6	–	55	80	13.33	–	1	3
L.Klusener	49	69	11	174	1906	32.86	4	8	34
N.D.McKenzie	42	66	4	120	2051	33.08	2	13	38
M.Morkel	1	2	1	31*	58	58.00	–	–	–
A.Nel	34	39	7	34	330	10.31	–	–	16
M.Ntini	82	93	30	32*	623	9.88	–	–	22
R.J.Peterson	5	6	1	61	159	31.80	–	1	4
S.M.Pollock	108	156	39	111	3781	32.31	2	16	72
A.G.Prince	36	59	8	139*	2257	44.25	7	7	20
J.A.Rudolph	35	63	7	222*	2028	36.21	5	8	22
G.C.Smith	60	106	5	277	4830	47.82	13	19	72
D.W.Steyn	18	24	7	33*	177	10.41	–	–	5
M.van Jaarsveld	9	15	2	73	397	30.53	–	3	11
C.M.Willoughby	2	–	–	–	–	–	–	–	–
M.Zondeki	5	4	–	59	82	20.50	–	1	1

SOUTH AFRICA – BOWLING

	O	M	R	W	Avge	Best	5wI	10wM
H.M.Amla	5	0	22	0				
N.Boje	1436.4	292	4265	100	42.65	5- 62	3	–
M.V.Boucher	1.2	0	6	1	6.00	1- 6	–	–
A.B.de Villiers	33	6	99	2	49.50	2- 49	–	–
H.H.Dippenaar	2	1	1	0				
H.H.Gibbs	1	0	4	0				
A.J.Hall	500.1	95	1617	45	35.93	3- 1	–	–
P.L.Harris	326.5	81	761	30	25.36	5- 73	1	–
C.W.Henderson	327	79	928	22	42.18	4-116	–	–
J.H.Kallis	2494.5	650	6979	223	31.29	6- 54	4	–
J.M.Kemp	79.5	20	222	9	24.66	3- 33	–	–
L.Klusener	1147.5	318	3033	80	37.91	8- 64	1	–
N.D.McKenzie	12	0	63	0				
M.Morkel	24	1	111	3	37.00	3- 86	–	–
A.Nel	1210.2	265	3716	119	31.22	6- 32	3	1
M.Ntini	2857.1	628	9214	329	28.00	7- 37	17	4
R.J.Peterson	130.5	37	403	8	50.37	3- 46	–	–
S.M.Pollock	4058.5	1222	9733	421	23.11	7- 87	16	1
A.G.Prince	13	1	31	1	31.00	1- 2	–	–
J.A.Rudolph	110.4	13	432	4	108.00	1- 1	–	–
G.C.Smith	219.5	28	801	8	100.12	2-145	–	–
D.W.Steyn	569.1	106	2113	91	23.21	6- 49	7	2
M.van Jaarsveld	7	0	28	0				
C.M.Willoughby	50	18	125	1	125.00	1- 47	–	–
M.Zondeki	115.2	21	438	16	27.37	6- 39	1	–

TEST **WEST INDIES – BATTING AND FIELDING**

	M	I	NO	HS	Runs	Avge	100	50	Ct/St
O.A.C.Banks	10	16	4	50*	318	26.50	–	1	6
D.J.Bravo	26	48	1	113	1526	32.46	2	9	25
G.R.Breese	1	2	–	5	5	2.50	–	–	1
S.Chanderpaul	107	183	26	203*	7429	47.31	17	45	44
P.T.Collins	32	47	7	24	235	5.87	–	–	7
C.D.Collymore	30	52	27	16*	197	7.88	–	–	6
F.H.Edwards	30	51	13	21	159	4.18	–	–	4
D.Ganga	48	86	2	135	2160	25.71	3	9	30
C.H.Gayle	70	125	4	317	4658	38.49	7	28	73
W.W.Hinds	45	80	1	213	2608	33.01	5	14	32
S.C.Joseph	5	10	–	45	147	14.70	–	–	3
B.C.Lara	130	230	6	400*	11912	53.17	34	48	164
R.N.Lewis	5	10	–	40	89	8.90	–	–	
D.Mohammed	5	8	1	52	225	32.14	–	1	1
R.S.Morton	13	23	1	70*	481	21.86	–	3	17
B.A.Parchment	1	2	–	20	31	15.50	–	–	
D.B.L.Powell	25	40	3	36*	239	6.45	–	–	4
D.Ramdin	22	40	5	71	813	23.22	–	5	58/2
D.J.G.Sammy	3	6	–	38	112	18.66	–	–	1
M.N.Samuels	27	49	4	105	1379	30.64	2	9	11
R.R.Sarwan	67	119	8	261*	4303	38.76	9	26	46
D.S.Smith	20	37	1	108	884	24.55	1	3	18
J.E.Taylor	16	27	5	25	266	12.09	–	–	2

WEST INDIES – BOWLING

	O	M	R	W	Avge	Best	5wI	10wM
O.A.C.Banks	400.1	62	1367	28	48.82	4- 87	–	–
D.J.Bravo	666.1	128	2155	55	39.18	6- 55	2	–
G.R.Breese	31.2	3	135	2	67.50	2-108	–	–
S.Chanderpaul	280	50	845	8	105.62	1- 2	–	–
P.T.Collins	1160.4	221	3671	106	34.63	6- 53	3	–
C.D.Collymore	1056.1	245	3004	93	32.30	7- 57	4	1
F.H.Edwards	820.2	90	3331	75	44.41	5- 36	5	–
D.Ganga	31	2	106	1	106.00	1- 20	–	–
C.H.Gayle	877.5	178	2336	59	39.59	5- 34	2	–
W.W.Hinds	187.1	41	590	16	36.87	3- 79	–	–
S.C.Joseph	2	0	8	0				
B.C.Lara	10	1	28	0				
R.N.Lewis	147.1	27	456	4	114.00	2- 42	–	–
D.Mohammed	177.3	20	668	13	51.38	3- 98	–	–
R.S.Morton	11	0	50	0				
D.B.L.Powell	826.3	150	2856	63	45.33	5- 25	1	–
D.J.G.Sammy	74.3	15	237	10	23.70	7- 66	1	–
M.N.Samuels	266	36	889	7	127.00	2- 49	–	–
R.R.Sarwan	316	33	1075	23	46.73	4- 37	–	–
J.E.Taylor	460.4	79	1675	44	38.06	5- 50	2	–

TEST | NEW ZEALAND – BATTING AND FIELDING

	M	I	NO	HS	Runs	Avge	100	50	Ct/St
N.J.Astle	81	137	10	222	4702	37.02	11	24	70
M.D.Bell	15	26	2	107	612	25.50	2	2	16
S.E.Bond	17	18	7	41*	139	12.63	–	–	6
C.D.Cumming	11	19	2	74	441	25.94	–	1	3
S.P.Fleming	108	183	10	274*	6875	39.73	9	43	166
J.E.C.Franklin	21	28	5	122*	505	21.95	1	1	9
P.G.Fulton	7	10	1	75	236	26.22	–	1	6
M.R.Gillespie	1	2	–	–	–	–	–	–	–
J.M.How	6	10	1	37	131	14.55	–	–	8
B.B.McCullum	29	45	3	143	1273	30.30	2	6	81/6
H.J.H.Marshall	13	19	2	160	652	38.35	2	2	1
C.S.Martin	37	50	24	12*	64	2.46	–	–	9
K.D.Mills	9	14	3	31	124	11.27	–	–	3
I.E.O'Brien	6	9	1	14*	33	4.12	–	–	1
J.D.P.Oram	25	43	8	133	1380	39.42	4	4	14
M.H.W.Papps	8	16	1	86	246	16.40	–	2	11
M.S.Sinclair	29	48	5	214	1524	35.44	3	4	28
C.M.Spearman	19	37	2	112	922	26.34	1	3	21
S.B.Styris	29	48	4	170	1586	36.04	5	6	23
L.R.P.L.Taylor	2	4	–	17	44	11.00	–	–	1
D.L.Vettori	76	109	17	137*	2446	26.58	2	14	36
L.Vincent	23	40	1	224	1332	34.15	3	9	19
P.J.Wiseman	25	34	8	36	366	14.07	–	–	11

NEW ZEALAND – BOWLING

	O	M	R	W	Avge	Best	5wI	10wM
N.J.Astle	948	317	2143	51	42.01	3- 27	–	–
S.E.Bond	513.1	105	1769	79	22.39	6- 51	4	1
J.E.C.Franklin	596.1	111	2143	76	28.19	6-119	3	–
M.R.Gillespie	30	7	136	5	27.20	5-136	1	–
H.J.H.Marshall	1	0	4	0				
C.S.Martin	1157	246	4059	125	32.47	6- 54	8	1
K.D.Mills	212.4	59	665	23	28.91	4- 43	–	–
I.E.O'Brien	145.3	35	505	12	42.08	3- 34	–	–
J.D.P.Oram	630.2	169	1598	49	32.61	4- 41	–	–
M.S.Sinclair	4	0	13	0				
S.B.Styris	326.4	77	1015	20	50.75	3- 28	–	–
L.R.P.L.Taylor	3.2	0	10	0				
D.L.Vettori	3012.2	744	8034	237	33.89	7- 87	13	3
L.Vincent	1	0	2	0				
P.J.Wiseman	943.2	209	2903	61	47.59	5- 82	2	–

TEST   **INDIA – BATTING AND FIELDING**

	M	I	NO	HS	Runs	Avge	100	50	Ct/St
M.S.Dhoni	26	43	5	148	1304	34.31	1	8	65/13
R.Dravid	118	203	25	270	9897	55.60	24	51	165
G.Gambhir	14	23	2	139	692	32.95	1	3	14
S.C.Ganguly	103	169	14	239	6581	42.45	15	32	66
Harbhajan Singh	63	87	18	66	1132	16.40	–	4	33
W.Jaffer	28	53	1	212	1818	34.96	5	10	21
K.D.Karthik	19	30	1	129	931	32.10	1	7	42/5
M.Kartik	8	10	1	43	88	9.77	–	–	2
Z.Khan	53	69	17	75	629	12.09	–	1	13
A.Kumble	125	162	32	110*	2419	18.60	1	5	56
V.V.S.Laxman	90	148	20	281	5658	44.20	12	32	96
M.M.Patel	9	10	3	13	32	4.57	–	–	5
I.K.Pathan	28	38	3	102	1041	29.74	1	6	8
R.R.Powar	2	2	–	7	13	6.50	–	–	–
V.Sehwag	53	89	3	309	4358	50.67	13	12	44
I.Sharma	5	7	5	23	43	21.50	–	–	3
R.P.Singh	11	14	3	30	83	7.54	–	–	4
V.R.Singh	5	6	2	29	47	11.75	–	–	1
S.Sreesanth	11	17	6	35	167	15.18	–	–	2
S.R.Tendulkar	146	237	25	248*	11782	55.57	39	49	98
Yuvraj Singh	22	35	4	169	1018	32.83	3	3	24

INDIA – BOWLING

	O	M	R	W	Avge	Best	5wI	10wM
M.S.Dhoni	1	0	13	0				
R.Dravid	20	4	39	1	39.00	1- 18	–	–
S.C.Ganguly	500.2	106	1617	32	50.53	3- 28	–	–
Harbhajan Singh	2833.5	563	8039	256	31.40	8- 84	20	4
W.Jaffer	11	3	18	2	9.00	2- 18	–	–
M.Kartik	322	74	820	24	34.16	4- 44	–	–
Z.Khan	1735	355	5712	170	33.60	5- 29	5	–
A.Kumble	6477	1526	17428	604	28.85	10- 74	35	8
V.V.S.Laxman	44	10	107	2	53.50	1- 2	–	–
M.M.Patel	315	68	940	28	33.57	4- 25	–	–
I.K.Pathan	959.2	209	3141	100	31.41	7- 59	7	2
R.R.Powar	42	8	118	6	19.66	3- 33	–	–
V.Sehwag	241.2	37	749	18	41.61	3- 33	–	–
I.Sharma	153.1	26	547	12	45.58	5-118	1	–
R.P.Singh	335.2	48	1329	40	33.22	5- 59	1	–
V.R.Singh	111.3	20	427	8	53.37	3- 48	–	–
S.Sreesanth	397.5	99	1299	46	28.23	5- 40	1	–
S.R.Tendulkar	643.4	80	2212	42	52.66	3- 10	–	–
Yuvraj Singh	35	3	121	3	40.33	2- 9	–	–

PAKISTAN – BATTING AND FIELDING

	M	I	NO	HS	Runs	Avge	100	50	Ct/St
Abdul Razzaq	46	77	9	134	1946	28.61	3	7	15
Abdur Rehman	2	3	1	25*	34	17.00	–	–	1
Azhar Mahmood	21	34	4	136	900	30.00	3	1	14
Danish Kaneria	51	69	31	29	260	6.84	–	–	16
Faisal Iqbal	21	37	2	139	897	25.62	1	6	15
Imran Farhat	27	51	1	128	1655	33.10	2	11	30
Inzamam-ul-Haq	119	198	22	329	8829	50.16	25	46	81
Kamran Akmal	38	65	4	154	1944	31.86	5	8	123/19
Misbah-ul-Haq	10	18	2	161*	671	41.93	2	1	8
Mohammad Asif	11	16	6	12*	60	6.00	–	–	2
Mohammad Hafeez	11	21	1	104	677	33.85	2	3	4
Mohammad Sami	33	51	13	49	458	12.05	–	–	7
Mohd Yousuf Youhana	79	134	12	223	6770	55.49	23	28	59
Mushtaq Ahmed	52	72	16	59	656	11.71	–	2	23
Naved-ul-Hasan	9	15	3	42*	239	19.91	–	–	3
Salman Butt	19	36	–	122	1047	29.08	2	6	8
Saqlain Mushtaq	49	78	14	101*	927	1.48	1	2	15
Shahid Nazir	15	19	3	40	194	12.12	–	–	5
Shoaib Akhtar	46	67	13	47	544	10.07	–	–	12
Shoaib Malik	21	35	5	148*	1076	35.86	1	6	9
Sohail Tanvir	2	3	–	13	17	5.66	–	–	2
Umar Gul	16	20	2	26	136	7.55	–	–	4
Yasir Arafat	1	2	–	44	44	22.00	–	–	–
Yasir Hamid	23	45	3	170	1450	34.52	2	8	16
Younus Khan	58	105	7	267	4816	49.14	15	20	66

PAKISTAN – BOWLING

	O	M	R	W	Avge	Best	5wI	10wM
Abdul Razzaq	1168	219	3694	100	36.94	5- 35	1	–
Abdur Rehman	125	21	352	11	32.00	4-105	–	–
Azhar Mahmood	502.3	111	1402	39	35.94	4- 50	–	–
Danish Kaneria	2499	464	7458	220	33.90	7- 77	12	2
Faisal Iqbal	1	0	7	0				
Imran Farhat	49.1	3	218	3	72.66	2- 69	–	–
Inzamam-ul-Haq	1.3	0	8	0				
Mohammad Asif	389	91	1180	51	23.13	6- 44	4	1
Mohammad Hafeez	125	23	319	4	79.75	1- 11	–	–
Mohammad Sami	1164	183	4161	81	51.37	5- 36	2	–
Mohd Yousuf Youhana	1	0	3	0				
Mushtaq Ahmed	2088.4	405	6100	185	32.97	7- 56	10	3
Naved-ul-Hasan	260.5	36	1044	18	58.00	3- 30	–	–
Salman Butt	21.5	1	95	1	95.00	1- 36	–	–
Saqlain Mushtaq	2345	541	6206	208	29.83	8-164	13	3
Shahid Nazir	372.2	71	1272	36	35.33	5- 53	1	–
Shoaib Akhtar	1357.1	237	4574	178	25.69	6- 11	12	2
Shoaib Malik	251.1	37	871	13	67.00	4- 42	–	–
Sohail Tanvir	84	15	316	5	63.20	3- 83	–	–
Umar Gul	602	100	2114	67	31.55	5- 31	3	–
Yasir Arafat	52.3	8	210	7	30.00	5-161	1	–
Yasir Hamid	12	0	72	0				
Younus Khan	50	7	203	2	101.50	1- 24	–	–

TEST

SRI LANKA – BATTING AND FIELDING

	M	I	NO	HS	Runs	Avge	100	50	Ct/St
M.S.Atapattu	90	156	15	249	5502	39.02	16	17	58
W.R.S.de Silva	3	2	1	5*	10	10.00	–	–	1
T.M.Dilshan	43	67	8	168	2236	37.89	4	11	46
C.R.D.Fernando	30	38	12	36*	184	7.07	–	–	10
S.T.Jayasuriya	110	188	14	340	6973	40.07	14	31	78
D.P.M.D.Jayawardena	93	151	11	374	7271	51.93	21	30	129
H.A.P.W.Jayawardena	17	19	1	120*	483	26.83	1	2	34/10
C.K.Kapugedara	6	11	1	63	221	22.10	–	2	3
M.F.Maharoof	20	31	4	72	538	19.92	–	3	6
S.L.Malinga	28	34	13	42*	192	9.14	–	–	7
J.Mubarak	10	17	1	48	254	15.87	–	–	13
M.Muralitharan	117	147	51	67	1142	11.89	–	1	64
T.T.Samaraweera	40	60	8	142	2122	40.80	5	13	30
K.C.Sangakkara	71	116	9	287	6032	56.37	16	24 · 149/20
L.P.C.Silva	10	15	1	152*	448	32.00	1	1	7
W.U.Tharanga	15	26	1	165	713	28.52	1	3	11
W.P.U.C.J.Vaas	102	148	30	100*	2815	23.85	1	12	30
M.G.Vandort	14	22	2	140	948	47.40	4	3	4
B.S.M.Warnapura	2	2	–	82	82	41.00	–	1	3
U.W.M.B.C.A.Welagedara	1	–	–	–	–	–	–	–	1

SRI LANKA – BOWLING

	O	M	R	W	Avge	Best	5wI	10wM
M.S.Atapattu	8	0	24	1	24.00	1- 9	–	–
W.R.S.de Silva	72	18	209	11	19.00	4-35	–	–
T.M.Dilshan	108	26	306	7	43.71	2- 4	–	–
C.R.D.Fernando	783.2	119	2848	84	33.90	5-42	3	–
S.T.Jayasuriya	1364.4	323	3366	98	34.34	5-34	2	–
D.P.M.D.Jayawardena	78.2	17	232	4	58.00	2-32	–	–
M.F.Maharoof	438	99	1458	24	60.75	4-52	–	–
S.L.Malinga	796.1	106	3076	91	33.80	5-68	2	–
J.Mubarak	14	2	50	0				
M.Muralitharan	6479.4	1671	15585	718	21.70	9-51	62	20
T.T.Samaraweera	215.1	36	679	14	48.50	4-49	–	–
K.C.Sangakkara	1	0	4	0				
L.P.C.Silva	15	2	60	1	60.00	1-57	–	–
W.P.U.C.J.Vaas	3631	831	9744	331	29.43	7-71	11	2
U.W.M.B.C.A.Welagedara	22	2	76	4	19.00	2-17	–	–

TEST   **ZIMBABWE – BATTING AND FIELDING**

	M	I	NO	HS	Runs	Avge	100	50	Ct/St
S.M.Ervine	5	8	–	86	261	32.62	–	3	7
G.W.Flower	67	123	6	201*	3457	29.54	6	15	43
M.W.Goodwin	19	37	4	166*	1414	42.84	3	8	10

ZIMBABWE – BOWLING

	O	M	R	W	Avge	Best	5wI	10wM
S.M.Ervine	95	18	388	9	43.11	4-116	–	–
G.W.Flower	563	122	1537	25	61.48	4- 41	–	–
M.W.Goodwin	19.5	3	69	0			–	–

BANGLADESH – BATTING AND FIELDING

	M	I	NO	HS	Runs	Avge	100	50	Ct/St
Abdur Razzak	2	4	–	15	19	6.33	–	–	–
Aftab Ahmed	12	24	2	82*	425	19.31	–	1	6
Enamul Haque	12	21	14	9	36	5.14	–	–	3
Habibul Bashar	49	97	1	113	3013	31.38	3	24	21
Javed Omar	40	80	2	119	1720	22.05	1	8	10
Junaid Siddique	2	4	–	74	90	22.50	–	1	1
Khaled Masud	44	84	10	103*	1409	19.04	1	3	78/9
Mashrafe Mortaza	27	50	4	79	510	11.08	–	2	7
Mehrab Hossain	1	2	–	8	14	7.00	–	–	–
Mohammad Ashraful	40	78	4	158*	1860	25.13	4	7	13
Mohammad Rafique	31	59	6	111	1035	19.52	1	4	7
Mohammad Sharif	10	20	3	24*	122	7.17	–	–	5
Mushfiqur Rahim	6	12	1	80	146	13.27	–	1	7
Rajin Saleh	22	43	2	89	1115	27.19	–	7	13
Sajidul Islam	2	4	–	6	14	3.50	–	–	–
Shahadat Hossain	13	25	5	31	102	5.10	–	–	3
Shahriar Nafees	13	26	–	138	669	25.73	1	3	11
Shakib Al Hasan	4	7	1	41*	142	23.66	–	–	2
Syed Rasel	6	12	4	19	37	4.62	–	–	–
Tamim Iqbal	2	3	–	84	152	50.66	–	2	–
Tushar Imran	5	10	–	28	89	8.90	–	–	1

BANGLADESH – BOWLING

	O	M	R	W	Avge	Best	5wI	10wM
Abdur Razzak	60	7	208	1	208.00	1-109	–	–
Aftab Ahmed	47.2	8	207	5	41.40	2- 31	–	–
Enamul Haque	435.3	84	1320	32	41.25	7- 95	3	1
Habibul Bashar	47	1	217	0			–	–
Javed Omar	1	0	12	0			–	–
Mashrafe Mortaza	786.5	163	2566	66	38.87	4- 60	–	–
Mehrab Hossain	7.5	0	29	2	14.50	2- 29	–	–
Mohammad Ashraful	191.1	8	888	11	80.72	2- 42	–	–
Mohammad Rafique	1360.2	284	3835	94	40.79	6- 77	7	–
Mohammad Sharif	275.1	47	1106	14	79.00	4- 98	–	–
Rajin Saleh	73	5	268	2	134.00	1- 9	–	–
Sajidul Islam	36	4	175	3	58.33	2- 71	–	–
Shahadat Hossain	304.3	33	1337	30	44.56	5- 86	1	–
Shakib Al Hasan	67	10	192	2	96.00	2- 44	–	–
Syed Rasel	146.3	18	573	12	47.75	4-129	–	–
Tushar Imran	10	0	48	0			–	–

LEADING CURRENT FIRST-CLASS PLAYERS

These are the leading career batting/bowling averages and wicket-keeping/fielding aggregates among players currently registered for first-class county cricket at the time of going to press. All figures are to the end of the 2007 English season.

BATTING

(Qualification: 100 innings)

	Runs	Avge		Runs	Avge
D.J.Hussey	7811	54.62	E.T.Smith	12392	41.86
M.R.Ramprakash	30659	53.13	R.W.T.Key	11900	41.75
G.A.Hick	40423	52.36	D.J.G.Sales	10321	41.61
K.P.Pietersen	8917	52.14	M.B.Loye	13317	41.35
S.Chanderpaul	14757	51.96	J.C.Hildreth	3774	41.02
S.G.Law	26337	51.33	B.F.Smith	16794	40.86
J.L.Langer	25698	50.98	L.Klusener	8426	40.50
D.P.M.D.Jayawardena	12219	50.70	M.A.Butcher	17098	40.32
C.J.L.Rogers	7964	48.56	M.A.Carberry	4152	40.31
M.W.Goodwin	17037	48.26	A.J.Strauss	9677	40.15
B.J.Hodge	15089	48.20	M.J.Powell (Gm)	9852	39.88
J.P.Crawley	23637	47.46	S.C.Moore	4342	39.47
A.N.Cook	5297	47.29	M.A.Wagh	9387	39.44
D.M.Benkenstein	10897	46.76	C.J.Adams	19061	39.30
E.C.Joyce	7519	46.41	J.E.R.Gallian	14173	38.93
M.van Jaarsveld	12291	45.18	I.D.Blackwell	7039	38.88
M.J.Di Venuto	19035	44.57	C.M.Spearman	12642	38.66
M.J.North	7045	44.03	W.I.Jefferson	4669	38.58
A.D.Brown	14705	43.50	M.H.Yardy	4978	38.58
H.D.Ackerman	11729	43.28	R.Clarke	4201	38.54
I.R.Bell	7710	43.07	A.P.R.Gidman	5114	38.45
O.A.Shah	11913	43.00	M.P.Vaughan	15307	38.36
S.A.Newman	5261	42.77	M.J.Prior	6321	38.30
J.A.Rudolph	8063	42.21	J.O.Troughton	4338	38.05

WICKET-KEEPING

(Qualification 300 dismissals)

	Total	Ct	St		Total	Ct	St
P.A.Nixon	888	822	66	J.N.Batty	476	420	56
C.M.W.Read	578	548	30	J.S.Foster	340	307	33
N.Pothas	534	490	44	M.A.Wallace	335	313	22

BOWLING

(Qualification: 100 wickets)

	Wkts	Avge		Wkts	Avge
A.M.Davies	182	22.64	R.McLaren	158	24.53
Yasir Arafat	492	22.84	M.J.Saggers	381	24.60
Saqlain Mushtaq	793	23.12	C.M.Willoughby	608	24.74
Murtaza Hussain	535	23.51	M.Kartik	399	25.33
Naved-ul-Hasan	454	23.68	A.C.Thomas	228	25.35
Mohammad Asif	280	23.97	Mushtaq Ahmed	1388	25.46

	Wkts	Avge		Wkts	Avge
R.J.Sidebottom	348	25.55	D.G.Cork	875	26.60
Azhar Mahmood	494	25.59	Imran Tahir	209	26.66
J.N.Gillespie	563	25.98	J.Lewis	586	26.74
A.R.Caddick	1145	26.03	J.D.Lewry	570	26.42
S.K.Warne	1319	26.11	M.S.Mason	226	26.75
K.J.Dean	387	26.37	D.Gough	846	26.81
Danish Kaneria	581	26.52	J.J.van der Wath	217	26.87
A.J.Hall	373	26.54	R.J.Kirtley	606	26.88

FIELDING

(Qualification 250 catches)

G.A.Hick	684		M.J.Di Venuto	302
S.G.Law	395		J.L.Langer	277
C.J.Adams	391		M.E.Trescothick	274

LIMITED-OVERS 'LIST A' CAREER RECORDS

Compiled by **Philip Bailey**

The following career records are for all players who appeared in 'List A' limited-overs county cricket during the 2007 season, and are complete to the end of that season. Some players who did not appear in 2007 but may do so in 2008 are also included.

These records are restricted to performances in limited-overs matches of 'List A' status as defined by the Association of Cricket Statisticians and Historians now incorporated by ICC into their Classification of Cricket. The following matches qualify for 'List A' status and are included in the figures that follow: Limited-Overs Internationals; Other International matches (e.g. Commonwealth Games, 'A' team internationals); Premier domestic limited-overs tournaments in Test status countries; Official tourist matches against the main first-class teams.

The following matches do NOT qualify for inclusion: World Cup warm-up games; Tourist matches against first-class teams outside the major domestic competitions (e.g. Universities, Minor Counties etc.); Festival, pre-season friendly games and Twenty20 Cup matches.

Specialist wicket-keepers' *Ct/St* are shown in the bowlers' *Econ* column.

Editor's note: I have deducted from Philip's match totals New Zealand's internationals scheduled against West Indies at Southampton on 8 July 2004 and Sri Lanka at Hamilton on 9 January 2007, both of which were abandoned without a ball bowled. Although the ICC ruled on 30 June 2004 that henceforth such aborted games should count as played matches because the toss had taken place, Law 16 clearly states that the umpire's call of 'play' heralds the start of a match and not the toss. Daggers indicate players involved in one (†) or both (††) of those games.

	M	Runs	Avge	HS	100	50	Wkts	Avge	Best	Econ
Abdul Razzaq	285	5626	30.24	112	2	30	330	30.08	6-35	4.79
Ackerman, H.D.	185	5095	32.87	114*	1	37	0	–	–	6.50
Adams, A.R.	119	1190	18.03	90*	–	1	153	28.45	5- 7	4.76
†Adams, C.J.	357	11176	39.91	163	20	69	32	38.03	5-16	5.24
Adams, J.H.K.	14	217	18.08	40	–	–	1	61.00	1-34	6.65
Adnan, M.Hasan	73	1875	30.73	113*	2	14	6	27.00	2-13	5.19
Adshead, S.J.	69	1028	20.97	77*	–	4	–	–	–	79/26
Afzaal, U.	155	4541	36.91	132	5	30	39	25.84	3- 4	5.67
Aga, R.G.	10	68	7.55	16	–	–	11	30.54	4-14	5.89

L-O	M	Runs	Avge	HS	100	50	Wkts	Avge	Best	Econ
Ahmed, J.S.	6	1	–	1*	–	–	10	20.20	4-32	5.05
Ali, Kabir	146	975	15.23	92	–	3	216	24.86	5-36	5.14
Ali, Kadeer	41	1231	30.77	114	2	8	1	59.00	1- 4	5.61
Ali, M.M.	20	532	29.55	100	1	4	5	44.40	2-45	5.45
Allenby, J.	38	530	27.89	91*	–	3	21	26.23	5-43	4.64
Alleyne, D.	38	321	11.06	58	–	1	–	–	–	29/7
Ambrose, T.R.	77	1872	30.68	135	2	8	–	–	–	88/11
Anderson, J.M.	121	192	10.10	15	–	–	178	25.94	4-23	4.69
Andrew, G.M.	43	180	9.47	33	–	–	42	35.16	4-48	6.28
Anyon, J.E.	31	16	3.20	12	–	–	31	34.38	3-41	5.59
Azhar Mahmood	254	3341	21.14	101*	2	12	269	31.99	6-18	4.58
Balcombe, D.J.	1	2	2.00	2	–	–	0	–	–	3.80
Ballance, G.S.	4	129	32.25	73	–	1	–	–	–	–
Banks, O.A.C.	45	833	29.75	77*	–	5	56	26.01	4-23	4.20
Barnes, M.W.	1	1	–	1*	–	–	–	–	–	5/-
Batty, G.J.	150	1599	16.83	83*	–	4	129	33.96	4-27	4.48
Batty, J.N.	163	2385	22.28	158*	1	12	–	–	–	166/27
Bell, I.R.	146	4642	36.55	137	3	36	33	34.48	5-41	5.29
Benham, C.C.	24	806	36.63	158	3	4	–	–	–	–
Benkenstein, D.M.	240	5742	35.66	107*	1	33	76	28.90	4-16	4.95
Benning, J.G.E.	61	1960	34.38	189*	2	12	28	33.96	4-43	6.68
Bichel, A.J.	235	2491	20.58	100	1	5	320	26.13	7-20	4.38
Birch, D.J.	8	199	24.87	60	–	1	–	–	–	–
Birt, T.R.	62	1599	27.10	145	2	7	5	17.80	2-15	5.86
Blackwell, I.D.	209	4730	27.18	134*	3	28	159	35.38	5-26	4.80
Blake, A.J.	3	15	–	11*	–	–	1	61.00	1-25	5.08
Boje, N.	247	3379	26.60	129	2	13	232	32.53	5-21	4.28
Bollinger, D.E.	34	29	5.80	7	–	–	43	29.72	4-24	4.71
Bond, S.E.	98	376	15.04	40	–	–	159	22.11	6-19	4.30
Bopara, R.S.	86	1894	32.10	101*	2	11	56	28.12	3-13	5.38
Botha, A.J.	109	1328	22.50	60*	–	4	107	29.69	5-60	4.83
Boyce, M.A.G.	1	36	36.00	36	–	–	–	–	–	–
Bragg, W.D.	1	41	–	41*	–	–	–	–	–	1/-
Breese, G.R.	105	1146	19.10	68*	–	3	112	27.46	5-49	4.48
Bresnan, T.T.	108	971	18.32	61	–	1	95	38.87	4-25	5.08
Broad, S.C.J.	31	155	22.14	45*	–	–	41	32.68	4-51	5.26
Brophy, G.L.	78	1238	23.80	66	–	6	–	–	–	66/16
Brown, A.D.	369	10698	31.74	268	19	49	14	37.42	3-39	6.42
Brown, B.C.	1	4	4.00	4	–	–	–	–	–	–
Brown, D.O.	11	203	29.00	63*	–	1	8	29.00	3-29	5.94
Brown, D.R.	314	4883	22.81	108	1	23	370	26.97	5-31	4.62
Brown, J.F.	142	116	5.80	16	–	–	127	38.89	5-19	4.36
Brown, K.R.	1	1	1.00	1	–	–	–	–	–	–
Brown, M.J.	9	228	25.33	76	–	1	–	–	–	–
Browning, R.J.	1	2	2.00	2	–	–	0	–	–	8.66
Bruce, J.T.A.	31	76	12.66	19*	–	–	44	22.18	4-18	4.75
Burrows, T.G.	3	18	9.00	16	–	–	–	–	–	3/2
Butcher, M.A.	185	4179	30.72	104	1	27	49	45.10	3-23	5.24
Caddick, A.R.	261	810	10.65	39	–	–	341	26.49	6-30	4.24
Carberry, M.A.	80	1730	25.07	88	–	14	1	41.00	1-21	5.85
Carter, N.M.	124	1779	19.54	135	1	5	171	25.59	5-31	4.77
†Chanderpaul, S.	321	10055	40.38	150	8	72	56	24.03	4-22	4.90
Chapple, G.	252	1869	17.80	81*	–	9	278	29.17	6-18	4.50
Cherry, D.D.	22	312	15.60	42	–	–	1	91.00	1-26	8.27

L-O	M	Runs	Avge	HS	100	50	Wkts	Avge	Best	Econ
Chilton, M.J.	158	3885	29.65	115	4	19	41	24.19	5-26	5.50
Chopra, V.	12	283	23.58	102	1	1	–	–	–	–
Clare, J.L.	3	17	5.66	12	–	–	4	29.25	3-44	6.50
Clark, S.R.	119	186	8.45	26*	–	–	165	27.13	6-27	4.35
Clarke, R.	110	2161	25.72	98*	–	11	71	38.42	4-49	5.70
Claydon, M.E.	7	15	7.50	9	–	–	8	36.62	2-41	5.14
Clinton, R.S.	19	191	14.69	56	–	1	2	29.00	2-16	7.25
Clough, G.D.	96	625	17.85	42*	–	–	86	32.73	6-25	5.23
Coetzer, K.J.	26	517	24.61	76	–	3	0	–	–	4.70
Collingwood, P.D.	292	7450	33.11	120*	6	43	172	35.26	6-31	4.81
Collins, P.T.	63	122	7.17	55*	–	1	96	24.45	5-43	4.30
Compton, N.R.D.	43	831	28.65	110*	1	4	0	–	–	5.00
Cook, A.N.	40	1147	32.77	125	2	4	0	–	–	3.33
Cook, S.J.	151	1149	17.14	67*	–	2	193	27.63	6-37	4.72
Cork, D.G.	282	3995	21.36	93	–	19	343	27.55	6-21	4.24
Cosker, D.A.	162	464	9.87	39*	–	–	167	33.17	5-54	4.78
Coverdale, P.S.	4	33	11.00	19	–	–	1	69.00	1-21	3.63
Crawley, J.P.	300	8457	32.15	114	7	54	0	–	–	4.00
Croft, R.D.B.	385	6268	23.83	143	4	31	394	32.36	6-20	4.33
Croft, S.J.	23	474	29.62	63	–	2	11	36.27	4-59	5.78
Crook, A.R.	21	444	27.75	162*	1	–	12	34.33	3-32	5.84
Crook, S.P.	25	152	10.85	23	–	–	18	50.44	4-20	6.17
Cross, G.D.	16	265	22.08	76	–	1	–	–	–	9/5
Cummins, R.A.G.	16	15	5.00	10	–	–	20	25.45	2-14	5.14
Cusden, S.M.J.	6	5	2.50	3	–	–	4	48.25	1-29	6.03
Daggett, L.M.	14	15	–	5*	–	–	15	32.26	2-33	4.71
Dalrymple, J.W.M.	127	2519	27.38	107	2	14	94	35.24	4-14	4.97
Danish Kaneria	106	209	7.46	33*	–	–	167	21.73	5-21	4.06
Davies, A.M.	65	164	7.45	31*	–	–	62	29.54	4-13	4.13
Davies, A.P.	108	330	12.69	27	–	–	147	28.04	5-19	5.24
Davies, S.M.	52	863	24.65	84	–	4	–	–	–	50/14
Dawson, L.A.	3	40	20.00	32	–	–	0	–	–	5.66
Dawson, R.K.J.	106	484	9.49	41	–	–	109	30.15	4-13	4.79
Dean, K.J.	144	261	8.70	16*	–	–	160	30.55	5-32	4.59
Denly, J.L.	26	448	21.33	102*	1	2	0	–	–	6.00
Dernbach, J.W.	23	38	5.42	21	–	–	38	22.97	5-44	6.19
De Wet, F.	36	158	31.60	56*	–	1	38	33.94	5-59	4.86
Dexter, N.J.	25	480	26.66	135*	1	1	14	27.57	3-17	5.21
Dighton, M.G.	55	1524	28.75	113	1	12	4	31.50	2-46	4.84
Dippenaar, H.H.	183	5728	40.62	125*	7	40	0	–	–	2.00
Di Venuto, M.J.	271	8255	33.15	173*	13	42	5	36.20	1-10	5.43
Dixey, P.G.	1	–	–	–	–	–	–	–	–	3/-
Doshi, N.D.	60	197	8.95	38*	–	–	54	43.61	5-30	5.55
Du Plessis, F.	27	805	40.25	114	1	5	14	34.42	4-47	4.94
Durston, W.J.	43	754	29.00	62*	–	5	19	41.73	3-44	6.10
Ealham, M.A.	394	6121	24.48	112	1	26	450	26.61	6-53	4.09
Edmondson, B.M.	19	18	4.50	4	–	–	29	28.55	5-39	5.01
Edwards, N.J.	5	113	22.60	65	–	1	–	–	–	–
Elliott, M.T.G.	153	5690	44.45	156	15	33	0	–	–	6.00
Ervine, S.M.	122	2646	29.40	104	3	13	129	32.38	5-50	5.41
Ferley, R.S.	40	239	17.07	42	–	–	51	28.33	4-33	4.81
Ferraby, N.J.	3	14	7.00	13*	–	–	0	–	–	4.42
Finn, S.T.	5	2	2.00	2	–	–	8	19.00	3-23	4.90
Fisher, I.D.	66	288	10.66	37*	–	–	67	29.80	3-18	4.66

227

L-O	M	Runs	Avge	HS	100	50	Wkts	Avge	Best	Econ
††Fleming, S.P.	455	13667	34.60	139*	22	82	2	15.50	1- 3	5.31
Flintoff, A.	265	6292	29.53	143	6	32	262	23.03	5-56	4.16
Flower, G.W.	324	9516	33.62	148*	11	62	176	35.17	4-32	4.44
Footitt, M.H.A.	1	–	–	–	–	–	–	0	–	6.00
Foster, J.S.	117	1522	23.06	69*	–	5	–	–	–	144/32
Francis, J.D.	65	1745	34.21	103*	1	12	–	–	–	–
Francis, S.R.G.	70	240	12.63	33*	–	–	77	34.33	8-66	5.41
Franks, P.J.	138	1542	21.12	84*	–	4	161	27.27	6-27	4.85
Frost, T.	79	485	17.96	47	–	–	–	–	–	76/19
Gale, A.W.	42	886	30.55	81	–	5	–	–	–	–
Gallian, J.E.R.	213	6070	31.28	134	8	38	55	32.87	5-15	5.29
Gazzard, C.M.	52	924	23.10	157	1	4	–	–	–	48/6
Gibson, O.D.	212	2548	21.05	102*	1	5	310	24.30	5-19	4.59
Gidman, A.P.R.	104	2178	25.92	88*	–	13	44	36.06	5-42	5.26
Gidman, W.R.S.	1	12	12.00	12	–	–	–	–	–	–
Gilbert, C.R.	6	68	13.60	37	–	–	8	29.00	3-33	6.32
Gillespie, J.N.	168	533	12.69	44*	–	–	230	26.99	5-22	4.13
Goddard, L.J.	6	69	23.00	36	–	–	–	–	–	8/-
Godleman, B.A.	2	33	16.50	18	–	–	–	–	–	–
Goodman, J.E.	1	–	–	–	–	–	–	–	–	–
Goodwin, M.W.	299	8961	34.86	167	12	56	7	43.71	1- 9	5.23
Gough, D.	404	2054	13.87	72*	–	2	577	24.17	7-27	4.17
Grant, R.N.	39	662	19.47	45	–	–	7	45.00	2-21	7.65
Green, J.A.G.	1	7	7.00	7	–	–	–	–	–	–
Greenidge, C.G.	65	140	8.23	29	–	–	77	34.05	4-15	5.64
Groenewald, T.D.	18	132	12.00	36	–	–	14	39.50	3-25	5.98
Guy, S.M.	25	254	16.93	40	–	–	–	–	–	23/7
Hall, A.J.	242	4686	30.23	129*	5	25	277	26.80	5-18	4.49
Hamilton-Brown, R.J.	9	71	10.14	20	–	–	6	26.50	3-28	5.67
Harbhajan Singh	197	1026	13.15	46	–	–	233	30.85	5-31	4.14
Hardinges, M.A.	73	1100	19.64	111*	1	6	65	35.81	4-19	5.48
Harmison, B.W.	13	175	17.50	57	–	1	2	39.50	1- 8	5.26
Harmison, S.J.	109	168	7.00	17	–	–	139	31.56	5-33	4.89
Harris, A.J.	140	216	7.20	34	–	–	182	28.78	5-35	5.02
Harris, J.A.R.	3	15	5.00	5	–	–	4	30.00	2-57	6.31
Harris, P.L.	30	30	5.00	10	–	–	30	32.06	3-33	4.55
Harris, R.J.	35	193	14.84	31*	–	–	41	33.17	4-43	5.02
Harrison, A.J.	3	13	4.33	7	–	–	2	70.50	1-45	8.29
Harrison, D.S.	58	357	14.28	37*	–	–	68	27.20	5-26	4.53
Harrison, P.W.	7	139	19.85	61	–	1	–	–	–	5/-
Harvey, I.J.	304	5973	24.88	112	2	28	445	22.35	5-19	4.38
Hemp, D.L.	277	5733	26.41	121	5	30	12	24.75	4-32	5.88
Henderson, C.W.	198	928	16.87	45	–	–	242	25.66	6-29	4.19
Henderson, T.	90	1287	23.40	126*	1	7	107	26.25	5- 5	4.21
Hick, G.A.	641	21881	41.67	172*	40	139	225	29.55	5-19	4.63
Hildreth, J.C.	77	1884	30.38	122	1	7	3	46.00	1- 8	7.26
Hinds, W.W.	186	4551	28.26	127*	6	24	44	26.04	4-35	5.29
Hodd, A.J.	14	192	19.20	42	–	–	–	–	–	8/-
Hodge, B.J.	199	6911	41.63	164	17	34	37	34.16	5-28	5.24
Hodgkinson, R.	2	0	0.00	0	–	–	3	26.00	2-36	4.87
Hodnett, G.P.	4	114	28.50	50	–	1	–	–	–	–
Hogg, K.W.	87	586	15.83	41*	–	–	86	29.15	4-20	4.75
Hoggard, M.J.	125	66	3.66	7*	–	–	174	25.20	5-28	4.45
Hole, S.M.	2	–	–	–	–	–	1	16.00	1-16	5.33

228

L-O	M	Runs	Avge	HS	100	50	Wkts	Avge	Best	Econ
Hollioake, A.J.	284	5984	28.09	117*	2	30	352	23.25	6-17	5.41
Hopkinson, C.D.	78	1225	22.68	123*	1	6	15	35.93	3-19	5.90
Horton, P.J.	18	296	19.73	47	–	–	–	–	–	–
Hunter, I.D.	76	277	7.91	39	–	–	81	33.41	4-29	4.92
Hussey, D.J.	112	3452	40.13	130	5	20	18	35.38	3-26	5.59
Hutton, B.L.	120	1603	20.03	77	–	7	52	31.44	5-45	5.55
Iles, J.A.	1	–	–	–	–	–	1	27.00	1-27	4.50
Imran Tahir	33	147	18.37	41*	–	–	48	23.62	5-30	4.19
Inzamam-ul-Haq	458	13746	38.07	157*	12	97	30	24.66	3-18	4.95
Irani, R.C.	315	7733	30.93	158*	7	46	309	25.22	5-26	4.47
Ireland, A.J.	42	69	6.90	17	–	–	63	26.71	4-16	5.06
Jacobs, A.	102	3018	33.53	118	6	12	8	26.00	2-22	5.67
Jacobs, D.J.	54	1275	27.12	101*	1	7	–	–	–	39/5
James, N.A.	8	99	33.00	30	–	–	6	23.50	2-34	4.02
Jaques, P.A.	116	4488	41.94	158*	12	24	0	–	–	6.33
†Jayasuriya, S.T.	473	13978	32.13	189	28	72	363	35.12	6-29	4.77
†Jayawardena, D.P.M.D.	314	8652	33.79	128	10	52	22	47.36	3-25	5.30
Jefferson, W.I.	74	2487	36.57	132	4	14	2	4.50	2- 9	2.25
Johnson, R.L.	194	1108	11.42	53	–	1	213	32.84	5-50	4.87
Jones, G.O.	120	1996	23.48	80	–	7	–	–	–	140/20
Jones, P.S.	166	574	12.47	27	–	–	221	29.64	6-56	5.24
Jones, S.P.	30	76	15.20	26	–	–	22	49.95	3-19	5.22
Jordan, C.J.	7	13	3.25	8	–	–	13	20.76	3-28	5.19
Joseph, R.H.	16	23	11.50	15	–	–	18	28.66	3-50	4.77
Joyce, E.C.	151	4364	34.63	115*	4	30	6	45.00	2-10	6.75
Kartik, M.	139	444	11.10	37*	–	–	172	30.30	5-29	4.37
Katich, S.M.	202	6483	37.47	136*	7	49	24	31.91	3-21	5.58
Keedy, G.	43	52	8.66	22	–	–	47	29.10	5-30	4.78
Keegan, C.B.	87	610	16.48	50	–	1	133	23.86	6-33	4.75
Kemp, J.M.	218	4656	35.81	107*	3	31	175	29.44	6-20	4.77
Kervezee, A.N.	20	392	26.13	62	–	1	0	–	–	9.40
Key, R.W.T.	156	4333	31.39	114	4	28	–	–	–	–
Khan, A.	51	265	12.04	65*	–	1	56	32.46	4-26	5.17
Kieswetter, C.	15	329	27.41	69*	–	2	–	–	–	18/2
Killeen, N.	214	644	9.33	32	–	–	288	24.27	6-31	4.14
Kirby, S.P.	44	64	4.57	15	–	–	45	38.71	5-36	5.82
Kirtley, R.J.	218	396	9.42	30*	–	–	328	22.53	5-27	4.60
Klokker, F.A.	12	241	26.77	138*	1	1	–	–	–	14/3
Klusener, L.	313	6424	39.90	142*	3	33	328	31.15	6-49	4.67
Kruger, G.J.P.	96	93	8.45	20*	–	–	135	24.85	6-23	4.77
Kruis, G.J.	107	404	12.24	31*	–	–	131	30.03	4-17	4.71
Lamb, G.A.	46	826	23.60	100*	1	4	18	27.05	4-38	5.33
Langer, J.L.	204	6994	39.29	146	11	49	7	30.71	3-51	6.68
Langeveldt, C.K.	139	250	7.14	33*	–	–	203	24.47	5- 7	4.53
Latouf, K.J.	10	76	10.85	25	–	–	–	–	–	–
Law, D.J.	375	11419	34.81	163	20	61	90	35.17	5-26	4.92
Lawson, M.A.K.	4	30	7.50	20	–	–	3	47.00	2-50	7.16
Laxman, V.V.S.	166	4944	34.57	131	9	27	8	68.50	2-42	4.71
Lewis, J.	172	635	10.40	40	–	–	225	26.92	5-19	4.48
Lewry, J.D.	78	217	7.48	16*	–	–	100	27.12	4-29	4.60
Liddle, C.J.	6	12	6.00	11	–	–	5	57.80	3-60	6.28
Logan, R.J.	65	215	11.31	28*	–	–	70	35.20	5-24	5.80
Loudon, A.G.R.	77	1312	23.42	73*	–	8	44	40.43	4-48	4.85
Loye, M.B.	278	8383	34.78	127	10	54	–	–	–	–

L-O	M	Runs	Avge	HS	100	50	Wkts	Avge	Best	Econ
Lucas, D.S.	44	130	10.83	32	–	–	53	32.13	4-27	5.87
Lumb, M.J.	125	3303	29.75	108	1	24	0	–	–	14.00
Lungley, T.	67	366	12.62	45	–	–	74	29.29	4-28	5.14
Lyth, A.	3	34	17.00	23	–	–	–	–	–	–
McGarry, A.C.	16	2	1.00	1	–	–	11	38.18	2-20	5.15
McGrath, A.	245	6271	32.15	148	6	35	65	34.84	4-41	5.02
McKenzie, N.D.	190	5124	36.34	131*	7	34	4	62.00	2-19	5.83
McLaren, R.	49	713	31.00	78*	–	4	42	30.73	4-29	4.84
Maddy, D.L.	310	7929	30.85	167*	11	47	180	29.24	4-16	5.05
Magoffin, S.J.	23	38	9.50	9*	–	–	31	31.32	4-58	4.90
Maher, J.P.	207	7265	39.69	187	15	36	6	28.00	3-29	6.10
Mahmood, S.I.	95	332	8.51	29	–	–	142	25.14	5-16	5.19
Malan, D.J.	5	90	18.00	42	–	–	9	–	–	13.00
Malik, M.N.	58	94	13.42	11	–	–	54	36.50	4-42	5.32
†Malinga, S.L.	65	125	6.94	23*	–	–	101	23.48	4-16	4.79
Mansoor Amjad	71	860	20.00	56	–	5	91	30.17	5-37	4.91
†Marshall, H.J.H.	181	4204	27.65	122	4	28	1	101.00	1-14	7.21
Marshall, S.J.	21	54	5.40	22	–	–	15	44.73	3-36	4.77
Martin-Jenkins, R.S.C.	195	1778	14.69	68*	–	3	206	29.13	4-22	4.20
Mascarenhas, A.D.	199	3316	23.35	79	–	21	237	24.77	5-27	4.20
Mason, M.S.	70	153	7.65	25	–	–	84	27.51	4-34	4.26
Masters, D.D.	91	383	11.96	39	–	–	76	37.38	5-20	4.69
Maunders, J.K.	30	629	23.29	109*	1	1	4	25.75	2-16	4.44
Maynard, T.L.	2	72	36.00	71	–	1	–	–	–	–
Middlebrook, J.D.	123	1109	18.48	47	–	–	101	33.79	4-27	4.58
Mierkalns, J.A.	1	4	4.00	4	–	–	–	–	–	–
Mitchell, D.K.H.	10	114	16.28	53	–	1	6	34.66	4-42	6.30
Mohammad Akram	129	233	7.51	33	–	–	148	30.54	4-19	4.60
Mohammad Asif	55	90	11.25	12*	–	–	63	33.50	4-30	4.71
Montgomerie, R.R.	199	6513	37.43	132*	9	44	0	–	–	0.00
Moore, S.C.	64	1746	30.63	105*	2	10	1	42.00	1- 1	7.20
Morgan, E.J.G.	59	1596	33.25	115	2	10	0	–	–	8.80
Morkel, M.	18	79	19.75	35	–	–	28	23.32	4-41	4.66
Muchall, G.J.	72	1554	29.88	101*	1	7	1	137.00	1-15	5.07
Mullaney, S.J.	5	22	11.00	12	–	–	6	13.16	3-13	4.55
Munday, M.K.	1	–	–	–	–	–	1	39.00	1-39	7.80
†Muralitharan, M.	378	693	6.41	27	–	–	575	21.97	7-30	3.77
Murtagh, T.J.	82	428	12.22	31*	–,	–	119	26.94	4-14	5.14
Murtaza Hussain	104	771	14.54	85	–	1	131	24.83	5-18	4.13
Mushtaq Ahmed	380	1624	11.27	41	–	–	461	28.47	7-24	4.16
Mustard, P.	76	1556	27.78	108	1	9	–	–	–	81/14
Naik, J.K.H.	4	1	1.00	1	–	–	6	25.33	3-24	4.56
Napier, G.R.	139	1469	16.50	79	–	7	130	25.46	6-29	5.12
Nash, C.D.	20	462	24.31	82	–	3	2	75.50	1-26	6.04
Nash, D.C.	120	1480	20.84	67	–	6	–	–	–	91/18
Naved-ul-Hasan	132	1339	19.69	70*	–	5	207	25.86	6-27	5.16
Needham, J.	22	177	17.70	42	–	–	8	72.50	2-36	5.40
Nel, A.	171	298	9.93	22	–	–	243	24.55	6-27	4.21
Nel, J.D.	47	130	10.00	36*	–	–	40	39.10	3-22	5.39
Nelson, M.A.G.	7	70	23.33	26	–	–	1	74.00	1-37	5.69
New, T.J.	24	549	24.95	68	–	3	–	–	–	1/1
Newby, O.J.	12	19	6.33	7*	–	–	9	52.00	2-37	5.89
Newman, S.A.	59	1395	25.36	106	1	8	–	–	–	–
Nicholson, M.J.	63	381	14.65	57*	–	1	65	38.01	3-23	5.31

L-O	M	Runs	Avge	HS	100	50	Wkts	Avge	Best	Econ
Nixon, P.A.	376	6578	25.89	101	1	29	0	–	–	392/92
Noffke, A.A.	88	444	16.44	58	–	1	100	33.30	4-32	4.56
North, M.J.	102	2914	33.49	134*	5	20	48	26.93	4-26	5.08
Northeast, S.A.	1	–	–	–	–	–	–	–	–	–
O'Brien, N.J.	66	831	20.26	72	–	5	–	–	–	50/17
Onions, G.	34	46	5.11	11	–	–	34	34.47	3-39	5.27
Ormond, J.	117	356	9.12	32	–	–	144	27.16	4-12	4.43
O'Shea, M.P.	7	90	15.00	49	–	–	3	64.66	2-37	6.46
Paget, C.D.	2	3	3.00	3	–	–	2	54.50	1-48	6.81
Palladino, A.P.	20	43	4.77	16	–	–	22	29.04	3-32	5.07
Panesar, M.S.	37	73	10.42	16*	–	–	36	36.61	5-20	4.43
Park, G.T.	10	125	17.85	33	–	–	–	–	–	5/-
Parker, L.C.	4	40	13.33	17	–	–	0	–	–	5.50
Parsons, K.A.	247	5225	29.68	121	2	28	146	36.23	5-39	5.01
Parsons, T.W.	1	–	–	–	–	–	2	20.50	2-41	6.83
Patel, M.M.	85	269	9.96	27*	–	–	88	30.69	3-20	4.44
Patel, S.R.	56	1142	31.72	93*	–	5	29	30.58	3-40	5.11
Patterson, S.A.	17	69	69.00	25*	–	–	14	47.85	3-11	5.28
Peng, N.	106	2395	24.19	121	3	12	–	–	–	–
Peploe, C.T.	18	36	5.14	14*	–	–	26	22.92	4-38	4.38
Peters, S.D.	132	2310	20.26	107	1	12	–	–	–	–
Pettini, M.L.	68	1335	24.27	103*	1	10	–	–	–	–
Phillips, B.J.	92	802	18.65	44*	–	–	99	30.38	4-25	4.78
Phillips, T.J.	31	168	15.27	24*	–	–	31	22.74	5-34	4.67
Pietersen, K.P.	167	5627	45.37	147	10	36	36	49.75	3-14	5.29
Pipe, D.J.	58	683	18.45	83	–	3	–	–	–	47/16
Plunkett, L.E.	68	569	21.88	56	–	1	93	29.69	4-15	5.26
Pollock, S.M.	417	5179	26.28	134*	3	22	561	22.41	6-21	3.66
Poonia, N.S.	24	435	18.12	67	–	2	–	–	–	–
Porterfield, W.T.S.	32	965	32.16	112*	2	5	–	–	–	–
Pothas, N.	208	4114	35.77	114*	3	22	–	–	–	194/47
Powell, D.B.L.	66	171	8.14	48*	–	–	101	25.60	5-23	4.76
Powell, M.J. (Gm)	180	4212	28.08	91*	–	24	1	26.00	1-26	6.50
Powell, M.J. (Wa)	112	1967	25.21	101*	1	5	25	29.08	5-40	5.29
Poynton, T.	1	–	–	–	–	–	–	–	–	2/-
Price, R.W.	109	407	10.71	49	–	–	104	33.39	4-21	4.07
Prior, M.J.	147	3261	25.27	144	3	18	–	–	–	118/22
Pyrah, R.M.	36	426	17.04	42	–	–	34	25.05	5-50	5.48
Ramprakash, M.R.	379	12195	39.59	147*	14	79	46	29.43	5-38	4.68
Rankin, W.B.	17	24	8.00	7*	–	–	17	35.47	3-32	5.86
Rashid, A.U.	6	50	10.00	28	–	–	5	51.00	2-63	5.66
Rayner, O.P.	12	120	20.33	61	–	1	6	63.00	1-25	6.40
Read, C.M.W.	222	3702	28.25	135	2	11	–	–	–	224/48
Redfern, D.J.	6	60	12.00	32	–	–	–	–	–	–
Rees, G.P.	6	163	27.16	63	–	1	–	–	–	–
Richardson, A.	61	104	10.40	21*	–	–	57	36.87	5-35	4.70
Robinson, D.D.J.	195	4488	26.09	137*	4	21	1	26.00	1- 7	9.17
Rogers, C.J.L.	72	1952	30.98	117*	1	12	2	13.00	2-22	6.50
Rosenberg, M.C.	6	29	9.66	26	–	–	3	5.66	3-17	5.66
Rowe, D.T.	4	4	4.00	2*	–	–	1	121.00	1-26	7.11
Rudge, D.T.	5	9	3.00	4	–	–	5	29.80	2- 1	5.35
Rudolph, J.A.	126	4385	45.67	134*	6	27	7	35.71	4-40	5.45
Sadler, J.L.	73	1507	26.43	113*	1	6	1	33.00	1-33	4.12
Saggers, M.J.	122	299	9.06	34*	–	–	166	25.02	5-22	4.48

L-O	M	Runs	Avge	HS	100	50	Wkts	Avge	Best	Econ
Saker, N.C.	20	53	10.60	22	–	–	18	43.77	4-43	5.94
Sales, D.J.G.	217	6020	34.01	161	4	41	0	–	–	4.78
Salisbury, I.D.K.	249	1569	13.52	59*	–	1	247	32.80	5-30	4.59
†Sangakkara, K.C.	267	8260	38.06	156*	9	56	–	–	–	242/69
Saqlain Mushtaq	322	1335	11.71	38*	–	–	477	23.47	5-20	4.19
Sayers, J.J.	13	249	22.63	62	–	2	1	71.00	1-31	7.88
Schofield, C.P.	107	1325	22.84	75*	–	5	105	25.91	5-31	5.20
Scott, B.J.M.	65	484	21.04	73*	–	3	–	–	–	57/20
Shafayat, B.M.	88	1726	22.71	104	1	6	24	30.41	4-33	5.54
Shah, O.A.	245	6781	33.40	134	11	40	16	38.18	2- 2	5.79
Shahzad, A.	7	27	6.75	11*	–	–	11	25.36	5-51	5.36
Shantry, A.J.	9	26	8.66	15	–	–	11	20.72	5-37	4.65
Shreck, C.E.	30	28	14.00	9*	–	–	42	29.78	5-19	5.54
Sidebottom, R.J.	140	362	10.96	32	–	–	141	30.79	6-40	4.28
Sillence, R.J.	32	400	22.22	94	–	2	29	30.03	4-35	5.83
Silverwood, C.E.W.	192	1002	13.72	61	–	4	250	24.58	5-28	4.27
Singh, R.P.	67	213	10.14	35	–	–	89	27.88	5-30	4.93
Smith, B.F.	364	9170	30.46	115	2	58	2	60.50	1- 2	5.71
Smith, E.T.	129	3668	31.35	122	2	25	–	–	–	–
Smith, G.M.	30	705	24.31	88	–	4	19	34.73	3-19	5.88
Smith, T.C.	18	86	14.33	30	–	–	16	29.00	3- 8	4.64
Smith, T.M.J.	3	–	–	–	–	–	3	48.33	2-45	7.25
Smith, W.R.	38	854	27.54	103	1	6	–	–	–	–
Snape, J.N.	271	3716	23.22	104*	1	13	222	29.19	5-32	4.64
Snell, S.D.	10	31	3.87	17	–	–	–	–	–	16/-
Solanki, V.S.	318	8236	30.84	164*	13	43	26	33.61	4-14	5.27
Spearman, C.M.	267	7326	28.39	153	7	45	0	–	–	7.81
Spurway, S.H.P.	4	31	15.50	31	–	–	–	–	–	4/2
Stevens, D.I.	177	4381	28.63	133	3	29	39	30.41	5-32	4.82
Steyn, D.W.	46	39	3.90	14	–	–	68	23.08	5-20	4.50
Stokes, M.S.T.	5	53	13.25	36	–	–	0	–	–	6.50
Strauss, A.J.	186	4959	29.87	152	4	33	0	–	–	3.00
Streak, H.H.	309	4088	25.71	90*	–	14	385	28.55	5-32	4.47
Stubbings, S.D.	108	2417	25.17	110	1	13	–	–	–	–
†Styris, S.B.	260	6167	32.28	141	5	40	263	29.02	6-25	4.60
Suppiah, A.V.	35	821	25.65	79	–	5	25	31.20	4-39	5.32
Sutcliffe, I.J.	123	3222	29.29	105*	4	20	–	–	–	–
Sutton, L.D.	132	1741	19.13	83	–	6	–	–	–	145/19
Swann, G.P.	172	2414	20.11	83	–	13	172	28.09	5-17	4.45
Tahir, N.	9	2	2.00	1*	–	–	3	75.66	1-19	4.93
Taylor, B.V.	118	182	6.50	21*	–	–	148	25.47	5-28	4.35
Taylor, C.G.	127	2231	22.31	93	–	11	8	28.37	2- 5	5.23
Taylor, C.R.	20	693	49.50	111*	2	2	–	–	–	–
Taylor, J.E.	48	128	10.66	22	–	–	67	28.68	4-23	4.81
Ten Doeschate, R.N.	70	1571	41.34	109*	1	8	70	19.85	5-50	5.31
Thomas, A.C.	68	344	14.95	27*	–	–	78	32.38	4-31	4.87
Thompson, J.G.	2	8	4.00	7	–	–	–	–	–	–
Thornely, M.A.	1	–	–	–	–	–	–	–	–	–
Thornicroft, N.D.	15	52	17.33	20	–	–	17	35.88	5-42	6.21
Thorp, C.D.	29	233	19.41	52	–	1	37	27.29	6-17	4.53
Tomlinson, J.A.	20	15	2.14	6	–	–	18	36.16	4-47	4.68
Tredwell, J.C.	104	1051	19.83	88	–	4	101	32.38	4-16	4.65
Trego, P.D.	59	564	13.75	78	–	1	57	30.36	5-44	5.73
Tremlett, C.T.	95	373	9.32	38*	–	–	137	24.58	4-25	4.60

L-O	M	Runs	Avge	HS	100	50	Wkts	Avge	Best	Econ
Trescothick, M.E.	288	9373	37.04	158	24	44	57	28.70	4-50	4.89
Trott, I.J.L.	117	3473	40.85	125*	6	21	36	25.94	4-55	5.65
Troughton, J.O.	98	2197	27.81	115*	2	10	25	25.76	4-23	5.25
Tudge, K.D.	1	4	4.00	4	–	–	0	–	–	6.20
Tudor, A.J.	74	442	12.27	56	–	1	105	23.81	4-26	4.70
Turner, M.L.	6	15	7.50	11*	–	–	5	44.00	2-40	5.45
Udal, S.D.	371	2556	15.68	78	–	8	418	29.97	5-43	4.40
†Vaas, W.P.U.J.C.	353	2472	15.74	62*	–	3	453	26.18	8-19	4.17
Van der Wath, J.J.	115	1801	28.14	91	–	11	145	27.38	4-31	4.80
Van Jaarsveld, M.	209	6289	38.34	123	8	41	21	39.38	3-43	5.12
Van Jaarsveld, V.B.	40	903	33.44	81	–	7	0	–	–	5.66
Vaughan, M.P.	274	6920	28.83	125*	3	43	78	32.53	4-22	4.61
Voges, A.C.	30	989	43.00	100*	1	8	9	53.22	2-27	5.50
Wagg, G.G.	50	546	16.05	45	–	–	52	32.73	4-36	5.83
Wagh, M.A.	83	2099	29.15	102*	1	16	25	34.48	4-35	4.71
Wainwright, D.J.	12	33	11.00	26	–	–	9	32.55	2-30	4.96
Wakely, A.G.	3	17	5.66	14	–	–	2	7.00	2-14	4.66
Walker, M.J.	250	5497	28.48	117	3	34	30	24.66	4-24	5.01
Walker, N.G.E.	30	189	9.94	43	–	–	23	32.17	4-26	5.60
Wallace, M.A.	113	1205	17.21	48	–	–	–	–	–	115/26
Walters, S.J.	19	215	16.53	32*	–	1	2	67.50	1-12	6.00
Warne, S.K.	311	1879	11.81	55	–	1	473	24.61	6-42	4.25
Waters, H.T.	11	22	5.50	9	–	–	8	59.62	3-47	6.27
Watkins, R.E.	18	215	17.91	39	–	–	13	43.92	2-25	6.61
Watson, S.R.	124	2677	34.32	132	2	17	100	36.59	4-39	5.06
Wessels, M.H.	38	634	22.64	80	–	2	–	–	–	31/-
Westfield, M.S.	2	6	–	4*	–	–	0	–	–	–
Westley, T.	3	37	18.50	36	–	–	–	–	–	6.33
Weston, W.P.C.	199	4385	25.64	134	4	24	1	2.00	1- 2	2.00
Westwood, I.J.	25	434	24.11	55	–	1	2	74.00	1-28	4.77
Wharf, A.G.	141	1323	16.53	72	–	1	170	30.16	6- 5	5.12
Whelan, C.D.	5	11	2.75	6	–	–	1	172.00	1-43	6.88
White, C.	355	7122	26.18	148	5	28	337	25.10	5-19	4.38
White, C.L.	96	2220	32.64	126*	3	13	69	36.44	4-15	5.41
White, G.G.	5	16	5.33	14	–	–	4	36.25	2-44	5.00
White, R.A.	53	984	20.08	101	1	4	2	27.50	2-18	6.11
White, W.A.	11	61	15.25	25	–	–	7	62.42	1-23	5.76
Wigley, D.H.	21	32	3.20	10	–	–	15	50.13	4-37	6.31
Williams, R.E.M.	1	–	–	–	–	–	0	–	–	8.16
Willoughby, C.M.	178	123	4.92	12*	–	–	223	26.84	6-16	4.14
Wiseman, P.J.	119	967	15.34	65*	–	2	82	41.30	4-45	4.28
Woakes, C.R.	1	–	–	–	–	–	–	–	–	–
Wood, G.L.	1	26	26.00	26	–	–	–	–	–	–
Wood, M.J. (Sm)	75	1948	29.07	129	2	13	–	–	–	–
Wood, M.J. (Y)	146	3271	27.03	160	5	14	3	25.33	3-45	6.90
Woodman, R.J.	4	–	–	–	–	–	1	136.00	1-38	6.18
Wright, B.J.	14	264	20.30	61	–	1	0	–	–	6.62
Wright, C.J.C.	21	69	11.50	21*	–	–	15	50.26	3-21	5.34
Wright, D.G.	90	867	17.34	55	–	4	113	27.96	5-37	4.15
Wright, L.J.	71	814	19.38	125	1	2	52	39.50	4-12	5.22
Yardy, M.H.	118	1747	19.41	98*	–	8	68	34.14	6-27	4.74
Yasir Arafat	154	1856	21.58	87	–	7	240	24.45	6-24	4.77
Younus Khan	190	5009	31.90	144	4	32	18	29.72	3- 5	5.64
Zondeki, M.	64	98	7.00	23	–	–	78	28.67	6-37	4.90

FIRST-CLASS CRICKET RECORDS

To the end of the 2007 season

TEAM RECORDS

HIGHEST INNINGS TOTALS

1107	Victoria v New South Wales	Melbourne	1926-27
1059	Victoria v Tasmania	Melbourne	1922-23
952-6d	Sri Lanka v India	Colombo	1997-98
951-7d	Sind v Baluchistan	Karachi	1973-74
944-6d	Hyderabad v Andhra	Secunderabad	1993-94
918	New South Wales v South Australia	Sydney	1900-01
912-8d	Holkar v Mysore	Indore	1945-46
910-6d	Railways v Dera Ismail Khan	Lahore	1964-65
903-7d	England v Australia	The Oval	1938
900-6d	Queensland v Victoria	Brisbane	2005-06
887	Yorkshire v Warwickshire	Birmingham	1896
863	Lancashire v Surrey	The Oval	1990
860-6d	Tamil Nadu v Goa	Panjim	1988-89
850-7d	Somerset v Middlesex	Taunton	2007

Excluding penalty runs in India, there have been 32 innings totals of 800 runs or more in first-class cricket. Tamil Nadu's total of 860-6d was boosted to 912 by 52 penalty runs.

HIGHEST SECOND INNINGS TOTAL

770	New South Wales v South Australia	Adelaide	1920-21

HIGHEST FOURTH INNINGS TOTAL

654-5	England (set 696 to win) v South Africa	Durban	1938-39

HIGHEST MATCH AGGREGATE

2376-37	Maharashtra v Bombay	Poona	1948-49

RECORD MARGIN OF VICTORY

Innings and 851 runs: Railways v Dera Ismail Khan	Lahore	1964-65

MOST RUNS IN A DAY

721	Australians v Essex	Southend	1948

MOST HUNDREDS IN AN INNINGS

6	Holkar v Mysore	Indore	1945-46

LOWEST INNINGS TOTALS

12	†Oxford University v MCC and Ground	Oxford	1877
12	Northamptonshire v Gloucestershire	Gloucester	1907
13	Auckland v Canterbury	Auckland	1877-78
13	Nottinghamshire v Yorkshire	Nottingham	1901
14	Surrey v Essex	Chelmsford	1983
15	MCC v Surrey	Lord's	1839
15	†Victoria v MCC	Melbourne	1903-04
15	†Northamptonshire v Yorkshire	Northampton	1908
15	Hampshire v Warwickshire	Birmingham	1922

† Batted one man short

There have been 27 instances of a team being dismissed for under 20.

LOWEST MATCH AGGREGATE BY ONE TEAM

34 (16 and 18) Border v Natal   East London   1959-60

LOWEST COMPLETED MATCH AGGREGATE BY BOTH TEAMS

105   MCC v Australians   Lord's   1878

FEWEST RUNS IN AN UNINTERRUPTED DAY'S PLAY

95   Australia (80) v Pakistan (15-2)   Karachi   1956-57

TIED MATCHES

Before 1949 a match was considered to be tied if the scores were level after the fourth innings, even if the side batting last had wickets in hand when play ended. Law 22 was amended in 1948 and since then a match has been tied only when the scores are level after the fourth innings have been completed. There have been 56 tied first-class matches, five of which would not have qualified under the current law. The most recent are:

Warwickshire (446-7d & forfeit) v Essex (66-0d & 380)   Birmingham   2003
Worcestershire (262 & 247) v Zimbabweans (334 & 175)   Worcester   2003

BATTING RECORDS
HIGHEST INDIVIDUAL INNINGS

501*	B.C.Lara	Warwickshire v Durham	Birmingham	1994
499	Hanif Mohammed	Karachi v Bahawalpur	Karachi	1958-59
452*	D.G.Bradman	New South Wales v Queensland	Sydney	1929-30
443*	B.B.Nimbalkar	Maharashtra v Kathiawar	Poona	1948-49
437	W.H.Ponsford	Victoria v Queensland	Melbourne	1927-28
429	W.H.Ponsford	Victoria v Tasmania	Melbourne	1922-23
428	Aftab Baloch	Sind v Baluchistan	Karachi	1973-74
424	A.C.MacLaren	Lancashire v Somerset	Taunton	1895
405*	G.A.Hick	Worcestershire v Somerset	Taunton	1988
400*	B.C.Lara	West Indies v England	St John's	2003-04
394	Naved Latif	Sargodha v Gujranwala	Gujranwala	2000-01
385	B.Sutcliffe	Otago v Canterbury	Christchurch	1952-53
383	C.W.Gregory	New South Wales v Queensland	Brisbane	1906-07
380	M.L.Hayden	Australia v Zimbabwe	Perth	2003-04
377	S.V.Manjrekar	Bombay v Hyderabad	Bombay	1990-91
375	B.C.Lara	West Indies v England	St John's	1993-94
374	D.P.M.D.Jayawardena	Sri Lanka v South Africa	Colombo	2006
369	D.G.Bradman	South Australia v Tasmania	Adelaide	1935-36
366	N.H.Fairbrother	Lancashire v Surrey	The Oval	1990
366	M.V.Sridhar	Hyderabad v Andhra	Secunderabad	1993-94
365*	C.Hill	South Australia v NSW	Adelaide	1900-01
365*	G.St A.Sobers	West Indies v Pakistan	Kingston	1957-58
364	L.Hutton	England v Australia	The Oval	1938
359*	V.M.Merchant	Bombay v Maharashtra	Bombay	1943-44
359	R.B.Simpson	New South Wales v Queensland	Brisbane	1963-64
357*	R.Abel	Surrey v Somerset	The Oval	1899
357	D.G.Bradman	South Australia v Victoria	Melbourne	1935-36
356	B.A.Richards	South Australia v W Australia	Perth	1970-71
355*	G.R.Marsh	W Australia v S Australia	Perth	1989-90
355	B.Sutcliffe	Otago v Auckland	Dunedin	1949-50
353	V.V.S.Laxman	Hyderabad v Karnataka	Bangalore	1999-00
352	W.H.Ponsford	Victoria v New South Wales	Melbourne	1926-27
350	Rashid Israr	Habib Bank v National Bank	Lahore	1976-77

There have been 162 triple hundreds in first-class cricket, W.V.Raman (313) and Arjan Kripal Singh (302*) for Tamil Nadu v Goa at Panjim in 1988-89 providing the only instance of two batsmen scoring 300 in the same innings.

MOST HUNDREDS IN SUCCESSIVE INNINGS

6	C.B.Fry	Sussex and Rest of England		1901
6	D.G.Bradman	South Australia and D.G.Bradman's XI		1938-39
6	M.J.Procter	Rhodesia		1970-71

TWO DOUBLE HUNDREDS IN A MATCH

244	202*	A.E.Fagg	Kent v Essex	Colchester	1938

TRIPLE HUNDRED AND HUNDRED IN A MATCH

333	123	G.A.Gooch	England v India	Lord's	1990

DOUBLE HUNDRED AND HUNDRED IN A MATCH MOST TIMES

4	Zaheer Abbas	Gloucestershire	1976-81

TWO HUNDREDS IN A MATCH MOST TIMES

8	Zaheer Abbas	Gloucestershire and PIA	1976-82
8	R.T.Ponting	Tasmania, Australia and Australians	1992-2006
7	W.R.Hammond	Gloucestershire, England and MCC	1927-45

MOST HUNDREDS IN A SEASON

18	D.C.S.Compton	1947	16	J.B.Hobbs	1925

100 HUNDREDS IN A CAREER

	Total		100th Hundred	
	Hundreds	Inns	Season	Inns
J.B.Hobbs	197	1315	1923	821
E.H.Hendren	170	1300	1928-29	740
W.R.Hammond	167	1005	1935	679
C.P.Mead	153	1340	1927	892
G.Boycott	151	1014	1977	645
H.Sutcliffe	149	1088	1932	700
F.E.Woolley	145	1532	1929	1031
G.A.Hick	134	853	1998	574
L.Hutton	129	814	1951	619
G.A.Gooch	128	990	1992-93	820
W.G.Grace	126	1493	1895	1113
D.C.S.Compton	123	839	1952	552
T.W.Graveney	122	1223	1964	940
D.G.Bradman	117	338	1947-48	295
I.V.A.Richards	114	796	1988-89	658
Zaheer Abbas	108	768	1982-83	658
A.Sandham	107	1000	1935	871
M.C.Cowdrey	107	1130	1973	1035
T.W.Hayward	104	1138	1913	1076
G.M.Turner	103	792	1982	779
J.H.Edrich	103	979	1977	945
L.E.G.Ames	102	951	1950	915
G.E.Tyldesley	102	961	1934	919
D.L.Amiss	102	1139	1986	1081

MOST 400s: 2 – B.C.Lara, W.H.Ponsford

MOST 300s or more: 6 – D.G.Bradman; 4 – W.R.Hammond, W.H.Ponsford

MOST 200s or more: 37 – D.G.Bradman; 36 – W.R.Hammond; 22 – E.H.Hendren

MOST RUNS IN A MONTH

1294 (avge 92.42)   L.Hutton   Yorkshire   June 1949

MOST RUNS IN A SEASON

Runs			I	NO	HS	Avge	100	Season
3816	D.C.S.Compton	Middlesex	50	8	246	90.85	18	1947
3539	W.J.Edrich	Middlesex	52	8	267*	80.43	12	1947
3518	T.W.Hayward	Surrey	61	8	219	66.37	13	1906

The feat of scoring 3000 runs in a season has been achieved 28 times, the most recent instance being by W.E.Alley (3019) in 1961. The highest aggregate in a season since 1969 is 2755 by S.J.Cook in 1991.

1000 RUNS IN A SEASON MOST TIMES

28   W.G.Grace (Gloucestershire), F.E.Woolley (Kent)

HIGHEST BATTING AVERAGE IN A SEASON

(Qualification: 12 innings)

Avge			I	NO	HS	Runs	100	Season
115.66	D.G.Bradman	Australians	26	5	278	2429	13	1938
104.66	D.R.Martyn	Australians	14	5	176*	942	5	2001
103.54	M.R.Ramprakash	Surrey	24	2	301*	2278	8	2006
102.53	G.Boycott	Yorkshire	20	5	175*	1538	6	1979
102.00	W.A.Johnston	Australians	17	16	28*	102	–	1953
101.70	G.A.Gooch	Essex	30	3	333	2746	12	1990
101.30	M.R.Ramprakash	Surrey	25	5	266*	2026	10	2007
100.12	G.Boycott	Yorkshire	30	5	233	2503	13	1971

FASTEST HUNDRED AGAINST AUTHENTIC BOWLING

35 min   P.G.H.Fender   Surrey v Northamptonshire   Northampton   1920

FASTEST DOUBLE HUNDRED

113 min   R.J.Shastri   Bombay v Baroda   Bombay   1984-85

FASTEST TRIPLE HUNDRED

181 min   D.C.S.Compton   MCC v NE Transvaal   Benoni   1948-49

MOST SIXES IN AN INNINGS

16   A.Symonds   Gloucestershire v Glamorgan   Abergavenny   1995

MOST SIXES IN A MATCH

20   A.Symonds   Gloucestershire v Glamorgan   Abergavenny   1995

MOST SIXES IN A SEASON

80   I.T.Botham   Somerset and England   1985

MOST FOURS IN AN INNINGS

72   B.C.Lara   Warwickshire v Durham   Birmingham   1994

MOST RUNS OFF ONE OVER

36	G.St A.Sobers	Nottinghamshire v Glamorgan	Swansea	1968
36	R.J.Shastri	Bombay v Baroda	Bombay	1984-85

Both batsmen hit for six all six balls of overs bowled by M.A.Nash and Tilak Raj respectively.

MOST RUNS IN A DAY

390*   B.C.Lara   Warwickshire v Durham   Birmingham   1994

There have been 19 instances of a batsman scoring 300 or more runs in a day.

LONGEST INNINGS

1015 min R.Nayyar (271)   Himachal Pradesh v Jammu & Kashmir Chamba   1999-00

HIGHEST PARTNERSHIPS FOR EACH WICKET

First Wicket

561	Waheed Mirza/Mansoor Akhtar	Karachi W v Quetta	Karachi	1976-77
555	P.Holmes/H.Sutcliffe	Yorkshire v Essex	Leyton	1932
554	J.T.Brown/J.Tunnicliffe	Yorkshire v Derbys	Chesterfield	1898

Second Wicket

576	S.T.Jayasuriya/R.S.Mahanama	Sri Lanka v India	Colombo (RPS)	1997-98
475	Zahir Alam/L.S.Rajput	Assam v Tripura	Gauhati	1991-92
465*	J.A.Jameson/R.B.Kanhai	Warwickshire v Glos	Birmingham	1974

Third Wicket

624	K.C.Sangakkara/D.P.M.D.Jayawardena	Sri Lanka v South Africa	Colombo	2006
467	A.H.Jones/M.D.Crowe	N Zealand v Sri Lanka	Wellington	1990-91
459	C.J.L.Rogers/M.J.North	W Australia v Victoria	Perth	2006-07
456	Khalid Irtiza/Aslam Ali	United Bank v Multan	Karachi	1975-76
451	Mudassar Nazar/Javed Miandad	Pakistan v India	Hyderabad	1982-83
445	P.E.Whitelaw/W.N.Carson	Auckland v Otago	Dunedin	1936-37
438*	G.A.Hick/T.M.Moody	Worcestershire v Hants	Southampton	1997

Fourth Wicket

577	V.S.Hazare/Gul Mahomed	Baroda v Holkar	Baroda	1946-47
574*	C.L.Walcott/F.M.M.Worrell	Barbados v Trinidad	Port-of-Spain	1945-46
502*	F.M.M.Worrell/J.D.C.Goddard	Barbados v Trinidad	Bridgetown	1943-44
470	A.I.Kallicharran/G.W.Humpage	Warwickshire v Lancs	Southport	1982

Fifth Wicket

464*	M.E.Waugh/S.R.Waugh	NSW v W Australia	Perth	1990-91
420	Mohd. Ashraful/Marshall Ayub	Dhaka v Chittagong	Chittagong	2006-07
405	S.G.Barnes/D.G.Bradman	Australia v England	Sydney	1946-47
401	M.B.Loye/D.Ripley	Northants v Glamorgan	Northampton	1998

Sixth Wicket

487*	G.A.Headley/C.C.Passailaigue	Jamaica v Tennyson's	Kingston	1931-32
428	W.W.Armstrong/M.A.Noble	Australians v Sussex	Hove	1902
411	R.M.Poore/E.G.Wynyard	Hampshire v Somerset	Taunton	1899

Seventh Wicket

460	Bhupinder Singh jr/P.Dharmani	Punjab v Delhi	Delhi	1994-95
347	D.St E.Atkinson/C.C.Depeiza	W Indies v Australia	Bridgetown	1954-55
344	K.S.Ranjitsinhji/W.Newham	Sussex v Essex	Leyton	1902

Eighth Wicket

433	V.T.Trumper/A.Sims	Australians v C'bury	Christchurch	1913-14
313	Wasim Akram/Saqlain Mushtaq	Pakistan v Zimbabwe	Sheikhupura	1996-97
292	R.Peel/Lord Hawke	Yorkshire v Warwicks	Birmingham	1896

Ninth Wicket

283	J.Chapman/A.Warren	Derbys v Warwicks	Blackwell	1910
268	J.B.Commins/N.Boje	SA 'A' v Mashonaland	Harare	1994-95
251	J.W.H.T.Douglas/S.N.Hare	Essex v Derbyshire	Leyton	1921

Tenth Wicket

307	A.F.Kippax/J.E.H.Hooker	NSW v Victoria	Melbourne	1928-29
249	C.T.Sarwate/S.N.Banerjee	Indians v Surrey	The Oval	1946
239	Aqil Arshad/Ali Raza	Lahore Whites v Hyderabad	Lahore	2004-05
235	F.E.Woolley/A.Fielder	Kent v Worcs	Stourbridge	1909

35,000 RUNS IN A CAREER

	Career	I	NO	HS	Runs	Avge	100
J.B.Hobbs	1905-34	1315	106	316*	61237	50.65	197
F.E.Woolley	1906-38	1532	85	305*	58969	40.75	145
E.H.Hendren	1907-38	1300	166	301*	57611	50.80	170
C.P.Mead	1905-36	1340	185	280*	55061	47.67	153
W.G.Grace	1865-1908	1493	105	344	54896	39.55	126
W.R.Hammond	1920-51	1005	104	336*	50551	56.10	167
H.Sutcliffe	1919-45	1088	123	313	50138	51.95	149
G.Boycott	1962-86	1014	162	261*	48426	56.83	151
T.W.Graveney	1948-71/72	1223	159	258	47793	44.91	122
G.A.Gooch	1973-2000	990	75	333	44846	49.01	128
T.W.Hayward	1893-1914	1138	96	315*	43551	41.79	104
D.L.Amiss	1960-87	1139	126	262*	43423	42.86	102
M.C.Cowdrey	1950-76	1130	134	307	42719	42.89	107
A.Sandham	1911-37/38	1000	79	325	41284	44.82	107
G.A.Hick	1983/84-2007	853	81	405*	40423	52.36	134
L.Hutton	1934-60	814	91	364	40140	55.51	129
M.J.K.Smith	1951-75	1091	139	204	39832	41.84	69
W.Rhodes	1898-1930	1528	237	267*	39802	30.83	58
J.H.Edrich	1956-78	979	104	310*	39790	45.47	103
R.E.S.Wyatt	1923-57	1141	157	232	39405	40.04	85
D.C.S.Compton	1936-64	839	88	300	38942	51.85	123
G.E.Tyldesley	1909-36	961	106	256*	38874	45.46	102
J.T.Tyldesley	1895-1923	994	62	295*	37897	40.60	86
K.W.R.Fletcher	1962-88	1167	170	228*	37665	37.77	63
C.G.Greenidge	1970-92	889	75	273*	37354	45.88	92
J.W.Hearne	1909-36	1025	116	285*	37252	40.98	96
L.E.G.Ames	1926-51	951	95	295	37248	43.51	102
D.Kenyon	1946-67	1159	59	259	37002	33.63	74
W.J.Edrich	1934-58	964	92	267*	36965	42.39	86
J.M.Parks	1949-76	1227	172	205*	36673	34.76	51
M.W.Gatting	1975-98	861	123	258	36549	49.52	94
D.Denton	1894-1920	1163	70	221	36479	33.37	69
G.H.Hirst	1891-1929	1215	151	341	36323	34.13	60
I.V.A.Richards	1971/72-93	796	63	322	36212	49.40	114
A.Jones	1957-83	1168	72	204*	36049	32.89	56
W.G.Quaife	1894-1928	1203	185	255*	36012	35.37	72
R.E.Marshall	1945/46-72	1053	59	228*	35725	35.94	68
G.Gunn	1902-32	1061	82	220	35208	35.96	62

BOWLING RECORDS

ALL TEN WICKETS IN AN INNINGS

This feat has been achieved 79 times in first-class matches (excluding 12-a-side fixtures).

Three Times: A.P.Freeman (1929, 1930, 1931)

Twice: V.E.Walker (1859, 1865); H.Verity (1931, 1932); J.C.Laker (1956)

Instances since 1945:

W.E.Hollies	Warwickshire v Notts	Birmingham	1946
J.M.Sims	East v West	Kingston on Thames	1948
J.K.R.Graveney	Gloucestershire v Derbyshire	Chesterfield	1949
T.E.Bailey	Essex v Lancashire	Clacton	1949
R.Berry	Lancashire v Worcestershire	Blackpool	1953
S.P.Gupte	President's XI v Combined XI	Bombay	1954-55
J.C.Laker	Surrey v Australians	The Oval	1956

K.Smales	Nottinghamshire v Glos	Stroud	1956
G.A.R.Lock	Surrey v Kent	Blackheath	1956
J.C.Laker	England v Australia	Manchester	1956
P.M.Chatterjee	Bengal v Assam	Jorhat	1956-57
J.D.Bannister	Warwicks v Combined Services	Birmingham (M & B)	1959
A.J.G.Pearson	Cambridge U v Leicestershire	Loughborough	1961
N.I.Thomson	Sussex v Warwickshire	Worthing	1964
P.J.Allan	Queensland v Victoria	Melbourne	1965-66
I.J.Brayshaw	Western Australia v Victoria	Perth	1967-68
Shahid Mahmood	Karachi Whites v Khairpur	Karachi	1969-70
E.E.Hemmings	International XI v W Indians	Kingston	1982-83
P.Sunderam	Rajasthan v Vidarbha	Jodhpur	1985-86
S.T.Jefferies	Western Province v OFS	Cape Town	1987-88
Imran Adil	Bahawalpur v Faisalabad	Faisalabad	1989-90
G.P.Wickremasinghe	Sinhalese v Kalutara	Colombo	1991-92
R.L.Johnson	Middlesex v Derbyshire	Derby	1994
Naeem Akhtar	Rawalpindi B v Peshawar	Peshawar	1995-96
A.Kumble	India v Pakistan	Delhi	1998-99
D.S.Mohanty	East Zone v South Zone	Agartala	2000-01
O.D.Gibson	Durham v Hampshire	Chester-le-Street	2007

MOST WICKETS IN A MATCH

| 19 | J.C.Laker | England v Australia | Manchester | 1956 |

MOST WICKETS IN A SEASON

Wkts		Season	Matches	Overs	Mdns	Runs	Avge
304	A.P.Freeman	1928	37	1976.1	423	5489	18.05
298	A.P.Freeman	1933	33	2039	651	4549	15.26

The feat of taking 250 wickets in a season has been achieved on 12 occasions, the last instance being by A.P.Freeman in 1933. 200 or more wickets in a season have been taken on 59 occasions, the last being by G.A.R.Lock (212 wickets, average 12.02) in 1957.

The highest aggregates of wickets taken in a season since the reduction of County Championship matches in 1969 are as follows:

Wkts		Season	Matches	Overs	Mdns	Runs	Avge
134	M.D.Marshall	1982	22	822	225	2108	15.73
131	L.R.Gibbs	1971	23	1024.1	295	2475	18.89
125	F.D.Stephenson	1988	22	819.1	196	2289	18.31
121	R.D.Jackman	1980	23	746.2	220	1864	15.40

Since 1969 there have been 50 instances of bowlers taking 100 wickets in a season.

MOST HAT-TRICKS IN A CAREER

7	D.V.P.Wright
6	T.W.J.Goddard, C.W.L.Parker
5	S.Haigh, V.W.C.Jupp, A.E.G.Rhodes, F.A.Tarrant

2000 WICKETS IN A CAREER

	Career	Runs	Wkts	Avge	100w
W.Rhodes	1898-1930	69993	4187	16.71	23
A.P.Freeman	1914-36	69577	3776	18.42	17
C.W.L.Parker	1903-35	63817	3278	19.46	16
J.T.Hearne	1888-1923	54352	3061	17.75	15
T.W.J.Goddard	1922-52	59116	2979	19.84	16
W.G.Grace	1865-1908	51545	2876	17.92	10
A.S.Kennedy	1907-36	61034	2874	21.23	15
D.Shackleton	1948-69	53303	2857	18.65	20
G.A.R.Lock	1946-70/71	54709	2844	19.23	14

	Career	Runs	Wkts	Avge	100w
F.J.Titmus	1949-82	63313	**2830**	22.37	16
M.W.Tate	1912-37	50571	**2784**	18.16	13+1
G.H.Hirst	1891-1929	51282	**2739**	18.72	15
C.Blythe	1899-1914	42136	**2506**	16.81	14
D.L.Underwood	1963-87	49993	**2465**	20.28	10
W.E.Astill	1906-39	57783	**2431**	23.76	9
J.C.White	1909-37	43759	**2356**	18.57	14
W.E.Hollies	1932-57	48656	**2323**	20.94	14
F.S.Trueman	1949-69	42154	**2304**	18.29	12
J.B.Statham	1950-68	36999	**2260**	16.37	13
R.T.D.Perks	1930-55	53771	**2233**	24.07	16
J.Briggs	1879-1900	35431	**2221**	15.95	12
D.J.Shepherd	1950-72	47302	**2218**	21.32	12
E.G.Dennett	1903-26	42571	**2147**	19.82	12
T.Richardson	1892-1905	38794	**2104**	18.43	10
T.E.Bailey	1945-67	48170	**2082**	23.13	9
R.Illingworth	1951-83	42023	**2072**	20.28	10
F.E.Woolley	1906-38	41066	**2068**	19.85	8
N.Gifford	1960-88	48731	**2068**	23.56	4
G.Geary	1912-38	41339	**2063**	20.03	11
D.V.P.Wright	1932-57	49307	**2056**	23.98	10
J.A.Newman	1906-30	51111	**2032**	25.15	9
A.Shaw	1864-97	24580	**2026+1**	12.12	9
S.Haigh	1895-1913	32091	**2012**	15.94	11

ALL-ROUND RECORDS
THE 'DOUBLE'

3000 runs and 100 wickets: J.H.Parks (1937)

2000 runs and 200 wickets: G.H.Hirst (1906)

2000 runs and 100 wickets: F.E.Woolley (4), J.W.Hearne (3), W.G.Grace (2), G.H.Hirst (2), W.Rhodes (2), T.E.Bailey, D.E.Davies, G.L.Jessop, V.W.C.Jupp, J.Langridge, F.A.Tarrant, C.L.Townsend, L.F.Townsend

1000 runs and 200 wickets: M.W.Tate (3), A.E.Trott (2), A.S.Kennedy

Most Doubles: 16 – W.Rhodes; 14 – G.H.Hirst; 10 – V.W.C.Jupp

Double in Debut Season: D.B.Close (1949) – aged 18, the youngest to achieve this feat.

The feat of scoring 1000 runs and taking 100 wickets in a season has been achieved on 305 occasions, R.J.Hadlee (1984) and F.D.Stephenson (1988) being the only players to complete the 'double' since the reduction of County Championship matches in 1969.

WICKET-KEEPING RECORDS
EIGHT DISMISSALS IN AN INNINGS

9	(8ct, 1st)	Tahir Rashid	Habib Bank v PACO	Gujranwala	1992-93
9	(7ct, 2st)	W.R.James	Matabeleland v Mashonaland CD	Bulawayo	1995-96
8	(8ct)	A.T.W.Grout	Queensland v W Australia	Brisbane	1959-60
8	(8ct)	D.E.East	Essex v Somerset	Taunton	1985
8	(8ct)	S.A.Marsh	Kent v Middlesex	Lord's	1991
8	(6ct, 2st)	T.J.Zoehrer	Australians v Surrey	The Oval	1993
8	(7ct, 1st)	D.S.Berry	Victoria v South Australia	Melbourne	1996-97
8	(7ct, 1st)	Y.S.S.Mendis	Bloomfield v Kurunegala Youth	Colombo	2000-01
8	(7ct, 1st)	S.Nath	Assam v Tripura (*on debut*)	Gauhati	2001-02
8	(8ct)	J.N.Batty	Surrey v Kent	The Oval	2004
8	(8ct)	Golam Mabud	Sylhet v Dhaka	Dhaka	2005-06

TWELVE DISMISSALS IN A MATCH

13	(11ct, 2st)	W.R.James	Matabeleland v Mashonaland CD	Bulawayo	1995-96
12	(8ct, 4st)	E.Pooley	Surrey v Sussex	The Oval	1868
12	(9ct, 3st)	D.Tallon	Queensland v NSW	Sydney	1938-39
12	(9ct, 3st)	H.B.Taber	NSW v South Australia	Adelaide	1968-69

MOST DISMISSALS IN A SEASON

128	(79ct, 49st)	L.E.G.Ames		1929

1000 DISMISSALS IN A CAREER

	Career	Dismissals	Ct	St
R.W.Taylor	1960-88	**1649**	1473	176
J.T.Murray	1952-75	**1527**	1270	257
H.Strudwick	1902-27	**1497**	1242	255
A.P.E.Knott	1964-85	**1344**	1211	133
R.C.Russell	1981-2004	**1320**	1192	128
F.H.Huish	1895-1914	**1310**	933	377
B.Taylor	1949-73	**1294**	1083	211
S.J.Rhodes	1981-2004	**1263**	1139	124
D.Hunter	1889-1909	**1253**	906	347
H.R.Butt	1890-1912	**1228**	953	275
J.H.Board	1891-1914/15	**1207**	852	355
H.Elliott	1920-47	**1206**	904	302
J.M.Parks	1949-76	**1181**	1088	93
R.Booth	1951-70	**1126**	948	178
L.E.G.Ames	1926-51	**1121**	703	418
D.L.Bairstow	1970-90	**1099**	961	138
G.Duckworth	1923-47	**1096**	753	343
H.W.Stephenson	1948-64	**1082**	748	334
J.G.Binks	1955-75	**1071**	895	176
T.G.Evans	1939-69	**1066**	816	250
A.Long	1960-80	**1046**	922	124
G.O.Dawkes	1937-61	**1043**	895	148
R.W.Tolchard	1965-83	**1037**	912	125
W.L.Cornford	1921-47	**1017**	675	342

FIELDING RECORDS

MOST CATCHES IN AN INNINGS

7	M.J.Stewart	Surrey v Northamptonshire	Northampton	1957
7	A.S.Brown	Gloucestershire v Nottinghamshire	Nottingham	1966

MOST CATCHES IN A MATCH

10	W.R.Hammond	Gloucestershire v Surrey	Cheltenham	1928

MOST CATCHES IN A SEASON

78	W.R.Hammond	1928	77	M.J.Stewart	1957

750 CATCHES IN A CAREER

1018	F.E.Woolley	1906-38	784	J.G.Langridge	1928-55
887	W.G.Grace	1865-1908	764	W.Rhodes	1898-1930
830	G.A.R.Lock	1946-70/71	758	C.A.Milton	1948-74
819	W.R.Hammond	1920-51	754	E.H.Hendren	1907-38
813	D.B.Close	1949-86			

UNIVERSITY MATCH RESULTS

Played: 162. Wins: Cambridge 56; Oxford 53. Drawn: 53. Abandoned: 1

In 2001, for the very first time, Cambridge hosted the University Match, cricket's oldest surviving first-class fixture, after the ECB's re-organisation of university cricket around six centres of excellence had removed it from Lord's. Dating from 1827 it has, wartime interruptions apart, been played annually since 1838. With the exception of five matches played in the area of Oxford (1829, 1843, 1846, 1848 and 1850), all the previous fixtures had been staged at Lord's. Since 2001 it has been played over four days rather than three.

In 2003, Oxford (with Brookes), Cambridge (with Anglia) and Durham were joined by Loughborough in playing three first-class matches against counties. The other two centres – Cardiff (with UWIC and Glamorgan), and Leeds (with Bradford and Leeds Metropolitan) – also play three counties apiece but without first-class status.

Year	Result	Year	Result	Year	Result	Year	Result
1827	Drawn	1876	Cambridge	1921	Cambridge	1968	Drawn
1829	Oxford	1877	Oxford	1922	Cambridge	1969	Drawn
1836	Oxford	1878	Cambridge	1923	Oxford	1970	Drawn
1838	Oxford	1879	Cambridge	1924	Cambridge	1971	Drawn
1839	Cambridge	1880	Cambridge	1925	Drawn	1972	Cambridge
1840	Cambridge	1881	Oxford	1926	Cambridge	1973	Drawn
1841	Cambridge	1882	Cambridge	1927	Cambridge	1974	Drawn
1842	Cambridge	1883	Cambridge	1928	Drawn	1975	Drawn
1843	Cambridge	1884	Oxford	1929	Drawn	1976	Oxford
1844	Drawn	1885	Cambridge	1930	Cambridge	1977	Drawn
1845	Cambridge	1886	Oxford	1931	Oxford	1978	Drawn
1846	Oxford	1887	Oxford	1932	Drawn	1979	Cambridge
1847	Cambridge	1888	Drawn	1933	Drawn	1980	Drawn
1848	Oxford	1889	Cambridge	1934	Drawn	1981	Drawn
1849	Cambridge	1890	Cambridge	1935	Cambridge	1982	Cambridge
1850	Oxford	1891	Cambridge	1936	Cambridge	1983	Drawn
1851	Cambridge	1892	Oxford	1937	Oxford	1984	Oxford
1852	Oxford	1893	Cambridge	1938	Drawn	1985	Drawn
1853	Oxford	1894	Oxford	1939	Oxford	1986	Cambridge
1854	Oxford	1895	Cambridge	1946	Oxford	1987	Drawn
1855	Oxford	1896	Oxford	1947	Drawn	1988	Abandoned
1856	Cambridge	1897	Cambridge	1948	Oxford	1989	Drawn
1857	Oxford	1898	Oxford	1949	Cambridge	1990	Drawn
1858	Oxford	1899	Drawn	1950	Drawn	1991	Drawn
1859	Cambridge	1900	Drawn	1951	Oxford	1992	Cambridge
1860	Cambridge	1901	Drawn	1952	Drawn	1993	Oxford
1861	Cambridge	1902	Cambridge	1953	Cambridge	1994	Drawn
1862	Cambridge	1903	Oxford	1954	Drawn	1995	Oxford
1863	Oxford	1904	Drawn	1955	Drawn	1996	Drawn
1864	Oxford	1905	Cambridge	1956	Drawn	1997	Drawn
1865	Oxford	1906	Cambridge	1957	Cambridge	1998	Cambridge
1866	Oxford	1907	Cambridge	1958	Cambridge	1999	Drawn
1867	Cambridge	1908	Oxford	1959	Oxford	2000	Drawn
1868	Cambridge	1909	Drawn	1960	Drawn	2001	Oxford
1869	Cambridge	1910	Oxford	1961	Drawn	2002	Drawn
1870	Cambridge	1911	Oxford	1962	Drawn	2003	Oxford
1871	Oxford	1912	Cambridge	1963	Drawn	2004	Oxford
1872	Cambridge	1913	Cambridge	1964	Drawn	2005	Oxford
1873	Oxford	1914	Oxford	1965	Drawn	2006	Oxford
1874	Oxford	1919	Oxford	1966	Oxford	2007	Drawn
1875	Oxford	1920	Drawn	1967	Drawn		

CAMBRIDGE UNIVERSITY RECORDS
ALL FIRST-CLASS MATCHES

Highest Total	For 703-9d		v	Sussex	Hove	1890
	V 730-3		by	W Indians	Cambridge	1950
Lowest Total	For 30		v	Yorkshire	Cambridge	1928
	V 32		by	Oxford U	Lord's	1878
Highest Innings	For 254*	K.S.Duleepsinhji	v	Middlesex	Cambridge	1927
	V 304*	E.de C.Weekes	for	W Indians	Cambridge	1950
Highest Partnership						
(2nd wicket)	429*	J.G.Dewes/G.H.G.Doggart	v	Essex	Cambridge	1949
Best Innings Bowling	10-69	S.M.J.Woods	v	Thornton's XI	Cambridge	1890
Best Match Bowling	15-88	S.M.J.Woods	v	Thornton's XI	Cambridge	1890
Most Runs – Season	1581	D.S.Sheppard		(av 79.05)		1952
Most Runs – Career	4310	J.M.Brearley		(av 38.48)		1961-68
Most 100s – Season	7	D.S.Sheppard				1952
Most 100s – Career	14	D.S.Sheppard				1950-52
Most Wkts – Season	80	O.S.Wheatley		(av 17.63)		1958
Most Wkts – Career	208	G.Goonesena		(av 21.82)		1954-57

UNIVERSITY MATCH RECORDS

Highest Total	604		Oxford	2002
Lowest Total	39		Lord's	1858
Highest Innings	211	G.Goonesena	Lord's	1957
Best Innings Bowling	8-44	G.E.Jeffery	Lord's	1873
Best Match Bowling	13-73	A.G.Steel	Lord's	1878

Hat Tricks: F.C.Cobden (1870), A.G.Steel (1879), P.H.Morton (1880), J.F.Ireland (1911), R.G.H.Lowe (1926)

OXFORD UNIVERSITY RECORDS
ALL FIRST-CLASS MATCHES

Highest Total	For 651		v	Sussex	Hove	1895
	V 679-7d		by	Australians	Oxford	1938
Lowest Total	For 12		v	MCC	Oxford	1877
	V 24		by	MCC	Oxford	1846
Highest Innings	For 281	K.J.Key	v	Middlesex	Chiswick Park	1887
	V 338	W.W.Read	for	Surrey	The Oval	1888
Highest Partnership						
(3rd wicket)	408	S.Oberoi/D.R.Fox	v	Cambridge U	Cambridge	2005
Best Innings Bowling	10-38	S.E.Butler	v	Cambridge U	Lord's	1871
Best Match Bowling	15-65	B.J.T.Bosanquet	v	Sussex	Oxford	1900
Most Runs – Season	1307	Nawab of Pataudi sr		(av 93.35)		1931
Most Runs – Career	3319	N.S.Mitchell-Innes		(av 47.41)		1934-37
Most 100s – Season	6	Nawab of Pataudi sr				1931
Most 100s – Career	9	A.M.Crawley				1927-30
	9	Nawab of Pataudi sr				1928-31
	9	N.S.Mitchell-Innes				1934-37
	9	M.P.Donnelly				1946-47
Most Wkts – Season	70	I.A.R.Peebles		(av 18.15)		1930
Most Wkts – Career	182	R.H.B.Bettington		(av 19.38)		1920-23

UNIVERSITY MATCH RECORDS

Highest Total	610-5d		Cambridge	2005
Lowest Total	32		Lord's	1878
Highest Innings	247	S.Oberoi	Cambridge	2005
Best Innings Bowling	10-38	S.E.Butler	Lord's	1871
Best Match Bowling	15-95	S.E.Butler	Lord's	1871

Match Doubles: P.R.le Couteur (160 and 11-66 in 1910); G.J.Toogood (149 and 10-93 in 1985)

LIMITED-OVERS INTERNATIONALS RESULTS

1970-71 to 23 February 2008

These records exclude all matches involving multinational teams, as well as any abandoned without a ball bowled, regardless of the toss having been made.

	Opponents	Matches	Won											Tied	NR
			E	A	SA	WI	NZ	I	P	SL	Z	B	Ass		
England	Australia	93	37	52	–	–	–	–	–	–	–	–	–	2	2
	South Africa	35	11	–	22	–	–	–	–	–	–	–	–	1	1
	West Indies	75	32	–	–	39	–	–	–	–	–	–	–	–	4
	New Zealand	64	28	–	–	–	31	–	–	–	–	–	–	2	3
	India	65	30	–	–	–	–	33	–	–	–	–	–	–	2
	Pakistan	63	35	–	–	–	–	–	26	–	–	–	–	–	2
	Sri Lanka	43	22	–	–	–	–	–	–	21	–	–	–	–	–
	Zimbabwe	30	21	–	–	–	–	–	–	–	8	–	–	–	1
	Bangladesh	8	8	–	–	–	–	–	–	–	–	0	–	–	–
	Associates	11	11	–	–	–	–	–	–	–	–	–	0	–	–
Australia	South Africa	67	–	36	28	–	–	–	–	–	–	–	–	3	–
	West Indies	114	–	53	–	57	–	–	–	–	–	–	–	2	2
	New Zealand	112	–	78	–	–	30	–	–	–	–	–	–	1	3
	India	93	–	56	–	–	–	30	–	–	–	–	–	–	7
	Pakistan	74	–	43	–	–	–	–	27	–	–	–	–	1	3
	Sri Lanka	67	–	46	–	–	–	–	–	19	–	–	–	–	2
	Zimbabwe	27	–	25	–	–	–	–	–	–	1	–	–	–	1
	Bangladesh	13	–	12	–	–	–	–	–	–	–	1	–	–	–
	Associates	12	–	12	–	–	–	–	–	–	–	–	0	–	–
S Africa	West Indies	45	–	–	32	12	–	–	–	–	–	–	–	–	1
	N Zealand	50	–	–	29	–	17	–	–	–	–	–	–	–	4
	India	57	–	–	35	–	–	20	–	–	–	–	–	–	2
	Pakistan	52	–	–	35	–	–	–	16	–	–	–	–	1	–
	Sri Lanka	45	–	–	22	–	–	–	–	21	–	–	–	1	1
	Zimbabwe	27	–	–	24	–	–	–	–	–	2	–	–	–	1
	Bangladesh	8	–	–	7	–	–	–	–	–	–	1	–	–	–
	Associates	15	–	–	15	–	–	–	–	–	–	–	0	–	–
W Indies	New Zealand	45	–	–	–	23	18	–	–	–	–	–	–	–	4
	India	90	–	–	–	53	–	35	–	–	–	–	–	1	1
	Pakistan	110	–	–	–	64	–	–	44	–	–	–	–	1	1
	Sri Lanka	43	–	–	–	24	–	–	–	18	–	–	–	–	1
	Zimbabwe	36	–	–	–	27	–	–	–	–	8	–	–	–	1
	Bangladesh	13	–	–	–	11	–	–	–	–	–	0	–	–	2
	Associates	12	–	–	–	10	–	–	–	–	–	–	1	–	1
N Zealand	India	75	–	–	–	–	35	36	–	–	–	–	–	1	3
	Pakistan	78	–	–	–	–	29	–	47	–	–	–	–	1	1
	Sri Lanka	67	–	–	–	–	34	–	–	30	–	–	–	1	2
	Zimbabwe	28	–	–	–	–	19	–	–	–	7	–	–	1	1
	Bangladesh	11	–	–	–	–	11	–	–	–	–	0	–	–	–
	Associates	9	–	–	–	–	9	–	–	–	–	–	0	–	–
India	Pakistan	113	–	–	–	–	–	43	66	–	–	–	–	–	4
	Sri Lanka	98	–	–	–	–	–	50	–	38	–	–	–	–	10
	Zimbabwe	49	–	–	–	–	–	39	–	–	8	–	–	–	2
	Bangladesh	17	–	–	–	–	–	15	–	–	–	2	–	–	–
	Associates	21	–	–	–	–	–	19	–	–	–	–	2	–	–
Pakistan	Sri Lanka	110	–	–	–	–	–	–	67	39	–	–	–	1	3
	Zimbabwe	40	–	–	–	–	–	–	36	–	2	–	–	1	1
	Bangladesh	18	–	–	–	–	–	–	17	–	–	1	–	–	–
	Associates	16	–	–	–	–	–	–	15	–	–	–	1	–	–
Sri Lanka	Zimbabwe	37	–	–	–	–	–	–	–	30	6	–	–	–	1
	Bangladesh	22	–	–	–	–	–	–	–	21	–	1	–	–	–
	Associates	12	–	–	–	–	–	–	–	11	–	–	1	–	–
Zimbabwe	Bangladesh	33	–	–	–	–	–	–	–	–	18	15	–	–	–
	Associates	26	–	–	–	–	–	–	–	–	20	–	3	1	2
Bangladesh	Associates	23	–	–	–	–	–	–	–	–	–	15	8	–	–
Associates	Associates	55	–	–	–	–	–	–	–	–	–	–	53	–	2
		2672	235	413	249	320	233	320	361	248	80	36	69	23	85

MERIT TABLE OF ALL L-O INTERNATIONALS
1970-71 to 23 February 2008

	Matches	Won	Lost	Tied	No Result	% Won (exc NR)
South Africa	401	249	136	5	11	63.84
Australia	672	413	230	8	21	63.44
West Indies	583	320	241	5	17	56.53
Pakistan	674	361	292	6	15	54.77
England	487	235	232	5	15	49.78
India	678	320	325	3	30	49.38
Sri Lanka	544	248	273	3	20	47.32
New Zealand	539	233	278	5	23	45.15
Associate Members	267	69	190	1	7	26.53
Zimbabwe	333	80	239	5	9	24.69
Bangladesh	166	36	128	–	2	21.95

TEAM RECORDS
HIGHEST TOTALS

443-9	(50 overs)	Sri Lanka v Holland	Amstelveen	2006
438-9	(49.5 overs)	South Africa v Australia	Johannesburg	2005-06
434-4	(50 overs)	Australia v South Africa	Johannesburg	2005-06
418-5	(50 overs)	South Africa v Zimbabwe	Potchefstroom	2006-07
413-5	(50 overs)	India v Bermuda	Port-of-Spain	2006-07
398-5	(50 overs)	Sri Lanka v Kenya	Kandy	1995-96
397-5	(44 overs)	New Zealand v Zimbabwe	Bulawayo	2005
392-6	(50 overs)	South Africa v Pakistan	Pretoria	2006-07
391-4	(50 overs)	England v Bangladesh	Nottingham	2005
377-6	(50 overs)	Australia v South Africa	Basseterre	2006-07
376-2	(50 overs)	India v New Zealand	Hyderabad, India	1999-00
373-6	(50 overs)	India v Sri Lanka	Taunton	1999
371-9	(50 overs)	Pakistan v Sri Lanka	Nairobi	1996-97
368-5	(50 overs)	Australia v Sri Lanka	Sydney	2005-06
363-3	(50 overs)	South Africa v Zimbabwe	Bulawayo	2001-02
363-5	(50 overs)	New Zealand v Canada	Gros Islet	2006-07
363-7	(55 overs)	England v Pakistan	Nottingham	1992
360-4	(50 overs)	West Indies v Sri Lanka	Karachi	1987-88
359-2	(50 overs)	Australia v India	Johannesburg	2002-03
359-5	(50 overs)	Australia v India	Sydney	2003-04
358-5	(50 overs)	Australia v Holland	Basseterre	2006-07
356-4	(50 overs)	South Africa v West Indies	St George's	2006-07
356-9	(50 overs)	India v Pakistan	Vishakhapatnam	2004-05
354-3	(50 overs)	South Africa v Kenya	Cape Town	2001-02
353-3	(40 overs)	South Africa v Holland	Basseterre	2006-07
353-5	(50 overs)	India v New Zealand	Hyderabad, India	2003-04
353-6	(50 overs)	Pakistan v England	Karachi	2005-06
351-3	(50 overs)	India v Kenya	Paarl	2001-02
351-4	(50 overs)	Pakistan v South Africa	Durban	2006-07
350-6	(50 overs)	India v Sri Lanka	Nagpur	2005-06
350-9	(49.3 overs)	New Zealand v Australia	Hamilton	2006-07

The highest for Zimbabwe is 340-2 (v Namibia, Harare, 2002-03), and for Bangladesh 301-7 (v Kenya, Bogra, 2005-06).

HIGHEST TOTALS BATTING SECOND

WINNING:	438-9	(49.5 overs)	South Africa v Australia	Johannesburg	2005-06
LOSING:	344-8	(50.0 overs)	Pakistan v India	Karachi	2003-04

HIGHEST MATCH AGGREGATE

872-13	(99.5 overs)	South Africa v Australia	Johannesburg	2005-06

LARGEST RUNS MARGINS OF VICTORY

257 runs	India beat Bermuda	Port-of-Spain	2006-07
256 runs	Australia beat Namibia	Potschefstroom	2002-03
245 runs	Sri Lanka beat India	Sharjah	2000-01
243 runs	Sri Lanka beat Bermuda	Port-of-Spain	2006-07
233 runs	Pakistan beat Bangladesh	Dhaka	1999-00
232 runs	Australia beat Sri Lanka	Adelaide	1984-85
229 runs	Australia beat Holland	Basseterre	2006-07
224 runs	Australia beat Pakistan	Nairobi	2002
221 runs	South Africa beat Holland	Basseterre	2006-07
217 runs	Pakistan beat Sri Lanka	Sharjah	2001-02
215 runs	Australia beat New Zealand	St George's	2006-07
210 runs	New Zealand beat USA	The Oval	2004
209 runs	South Africa beat West Indies	Cape Town	2003-04
208 runs	South Africa beat Kenya	Cape Town	2001-02
208 runs	Australia beat India	Sydney	2003-04
206 runs	New Zealand beat Australia	Adelaide	1985-86
206 runs	Sri Lanka beat Holland	Colombo (RPS)	2002-03
203 runs	Australia beat Scotland	Basseterre	2006-07
202 runs	England beat India	Lord's	1975
202 runs	South Africa beat Kenya	Nairobi	1996-97
202 runs	Zimbabwe beat Kenya	Dhaka	1998-99
200 runs	India beat Bangladesh	Dhaka	2002-03

LOWEST TOTALS (Excluding reduced innings)

35	(18.0 overs)	Zimbabwe v Sri Lanka	Harare	2003-04
36	(18.4 overs)	Canada v Sri Lanka	Paarl	2002-03
38	(15.4 overs)	Zimbabwe v Sri Lanka	Colombo (SSC)	2001-02
43	(19.5 overs)	Pakistan v West Indies	Cape Town	1992-93
45	(40.3 overs)	Canada v England	Manchester	1979
45	(14.0 overs)	Namibia v Australia	Potschefstroom	2002-03
54	(26.3 overs)	India v Sri Lanka	Sharjah	2000-01
54	(23.2 overs)	West Indies v South Africa	Cape Town	2003-04
55	(28.3 overs)	Sri Lanka v West Indies	Sharjah	1986-87
63	(25.5 overs)	India v Australia	Sydney	1980-81
64	(35.5 overs)	New Zealand v Pakistan	Sharjah	1985-86
65	(24.0 overs)	USA v Australia	Southampton	2004
65	(24.3 overs)	Zimbabwe v India	Harare	2005
68	(31.3 overs)	Scotland v West Indies	Leicester	1999
69	(28.0 overs)	South Africa v Australia	Sydney	1993-94
69	(22.5 overs)	Zimbabwe v Kenya	Harare	2005-06
70	(25.2 overs)	Australia v England	Birmingham	1977
70	(26.3 overs)	Australia v New Zealand	Adelaide	1985-86

The lowest for England is 86 (v A, Manchester, 2001), and for Bangladesh 76 (v SL, Colombo (SSC), 2002, and v I, Dhaka, 2002-03).

LOWEST MATCH AGGREGATES

73-11	(23.2 overs)	Canada (36) v Sri Lanka (37-1)	Paarl	2002-03
75-11	(27.2 overs)	Zimbabwe (35) v Sri Lanka (40-1)	Harare	2003-04
78-11	(20.0 overs)	Zimbabwe (38) v Sri Lanka (40-1)	Colombo (SSC)	2001-02

BATTING RECORDS
HIGHEST INDIVIDUAL INNINGS

194	Saeed Anwar	Pakistan v India	Madras	1996-97
189*	I.V.A.Richards	West Indies v England	Manchester	1984
189	S.T.Jayasuriya	Sri Lanka v India	Sharjah	2000-01
188*	G.Kirsten	South Africa v UAE	Rawalpindi	1995-96
186*	S.R.Tendulkar	India v New Zealand	Hyderabad	1999-00
183*	M.S.Dhoni	India v Sri Lanka	Jaipur	2005-06
183	S.C.Ganguly	India v Sri Lanka	Taunton	1999

181*	M.L.Hayden	Australia v New Zealand	Hamilton	2006-07
181	I.V.A.Richards	West Indies v Sri Lanka	Karachi	1987-88
175*	Kapil Dev	India v Zimbabwe	Tunbridge Wells	1983
175	H.H.Gibbs	South Africa v Australia	Johannesburg	2005-06
173	M.E.Waugh	Australia v West Indies	Melbourne	2000-01
172*	C.B.Wishart	Zimbabwe v Namibia	Harare	2002-03
172	A.C.Gilchrist	Australia v Zimbabwe	Hobart	2003-04
172	L.Vincent	New Zealand v Zimbabwe	Bulawayo	2005
171*	G.M.Turner	New Zealand v East Africa	Birmingham	1975
169*	D.J.Callaghan	South Africa v New Zealand	Pretoria	1994-95
169	B.C.Lara	West Indies v Sri Lanka	Sharjah	1995-96
167*	R.A.Smith	England v Australia	Birmingham	1993
164	R.T.Ponting	Australia v South Africa	Johannesburg	2005-06
161	A.C.Hudson	South Africa v Holland	Rawalpindi	1995-96
160	Imran Nazir	Pakistan v Zimbabwe	Kingston	2006-07
159*	D.Mongia	India v Zimbabwe	Gauhati	2001-02
158	D.I.Gower	England v New Zealand	Brisbane	1982-83
158	M.L.Hayden	Australia v West Indies	North Sound	2006-07
157	S.T.Jayasuriya	Sri Lanka v Holland	Amstelveen	2006
156	B.C.Lara	West Indies v Pakistan	Adelaide	2004-05
156	A.Symonds	Australia v New Zealand	Wellington	2005-06
154	A.C.Gilchrist	Australia v Sri Lanka	Melbourne	1998-99
153*	I.V.A.Richards	West Indies v Australia	Melbourne	1979-80
153*	M.Azharuddin	India v Zimbabwe	Cuttack	1997-98
153*	S.C.Ganguly	India v New Zealand	Gwalior	1999-00
153*	C.H.Gayle	West Indies v Zimbabwe	Bulawayo	2003-04
153	B.C.Lara	West Indies v Pakistan	Sharjah	1993-94
153	R.Dravid	India v New Zealand	Hyderabad	1999-00
153	H.H.Gibbs	South Africa v Bangladesh	Potchefstroom	2002-03
152*	D.L.Haynes	West Indies v India	Georgetown	1988-89
152*	C.H.Gayle	West Indies v South Africa	Johannesburg	2003-04
152	C.H.Gayle	West Indies v Kenya	Nairobi	2001-02
152	S.R.Tendulkar	India v Namibia	Pietermaritzburg	2002-03
152	A.J.Strauss	England v Bangladesh	Nottingham	2005
152	S.T.Jayasuriya	Sri Lanka v England	Leeds	2006
151*	S.T.Jayasuriya	Sri Lanka v India	Bombay	1996-97
151	A.Symonds	Australia v Sri Lanka	Sydney	2005-06
150	S.Chanderpaul	West Indies v South Africa	East London	1998-99

The highest for Bangladesh is 134* by Shakib Al Hasan (v Canada, St John's, 2006-07).

HUNDRED ON DEBUT

D.L.Amiss	103	England v Australia	Manchester	1972
D.L.Haynes	148	West Indies v Australia	St John's	1977-78
A.Flower	115*	Zimbabwe v Sri Lanka	New Plymouth	1991-92
Salim Elahi	102*	Pakistan v Sri Lanka	Gujranwala	1995-96

Shahid Afridi scored 102 for P v SL, Nairobi, 1996-97, in his second match having not batted in his first.

Fastest 100	37 balls	Shahid Afridi (102)	P v SL	Nairobi	1996-97
Fastest 50	17 balls	S.T.Jayasuriya (76)	SL v P	Singapore	1995-96

CARRYING BAT THROUGH INNINGS (SIDE ALL OUT)

G.W.Flower	84*	Zimbabwe (205) v England	Sydney	1994-95
Saeed Anwar	103*	Pakistan (219) v England	Harare	1994-95
N.V.Knight	125*	England (246) v Pakistan	Nottingham	1996
R.D.Jacobs	49*	West Indies (110) v Australia	Manchester	1999
D.R.Martyn	116*	Australia (191) v New Zealand	Auckland	1999-00
H.H.Gibbs	59*	South Africa (101†) v Pakistan	Sharjah	1999-00
A.J.Stewart	100*	England (192) v West Indies	Nottingham	2000
Javed Omar	33*	Bangladesh (103) v Zimbabwe	Harare	2000-01

† One batsman retired hurt.

5000 RUNS IN A CAREER

		LOI	I	NO	HS	Runs	Avge	100	50
S.R.Tendulkar	I	413	403	37	186*	16088	43.95	41	87
S.T.Jayasuriya	SL	404	393	18	189	12187	32.49	25	64
Inzamam-ul-Haq	P	375	348	52	137*	11701	39.53	10	83
S.C.Ganguly	I	308	297	23	183	11221	40.95	22	71
R.T.Ponting	A	290	281	35	164	10627	43.19	24	61
R.Dravid	I	329	304	39	153	10464	39.48	12	80
B.C.Lara	WI	294	285	32	169	10348	40.90	19	62
J.H.Kallis	SA	269	255	49	139	9512	46.17	16	65
M.Azharuddin	I	334	308	54	153*	9378	36.92	7	58
A.C.Gilchrist	A	279	271	11	172	9307	35.79	15	54
P.A.de Silva	SL	308	296	30	145	9284	34.90	11	64
Saeed Anwar	P	247	244	19	194	8823	39.21	20	43
Mohd Yousuf Youhana	P	249	237	37	141*	8707	43.53	14	59
D.L.Haynes	WI	238	237	28	152*	8648	41.37	17	57
M.S.Atapattu	SL	267	259	32	132*	8529	37.57	11	59
M.E.Waugh	A	244	236	20	173	8500	39.35	18	50
S.P.Fleming	NZ	277	268	21	134*	8007	32.41	8	49
S.R.Waugh	A	325	288	58	120*	7569	32.90	3	45
A.Ranatunga	SL	269	255	47	131*	7454	35.83	4	49
H.H.Gibbs	SA	224	217	16	175	7383	36.73	20	33
Javed Miandad	P	233	218	41	119*	7381	41.70	8	50
S.Chanderpaul	WI	228	215	31	150	7291	39.62	8	49
Salim Malik	P	283	256	38	102	7171	32.89	5	47
D.P.M.D.Jayawardena	SL	261	244	26	128	7124	32.67	9	41
N.J.Astle	NZ	221	217	14	145*	7090	34.92	16	41
M.G.Bevan	A	232	196	67	108*	6912	53.58	6	46
G.Kirsten	SA	185	185	19	188*	6798	40.95	13	45
A.Flower	Z	213	208	16	145	6786	35.34	4	55
I.V.A.Richards	WI	187	167	24	189*	6721	47.00	11	45
Ijaz Ahmed	P	250	232	29	139*	6564	32.33	10	37
G.W.Flower	Z	219	212	18	142*	6536	33.69	6	40
A.R.Border	A	273	252	39	127*	6524	30.62	3	39
R.B.Richardson	WI	224	217	30	122	6248	33.41	5	44
C.H.Gayle	WI	172	169	12	153*	6189	39.42	15	33
D.M.Jones	A	164	161	25	145	6068	44.61	7	46
K.C.Sangakkara	SL	206	190	22	138*	6040	35.95	7	39
D.C.Boon	A	181	177	16	122	5964	37.04	5	37
M.L.Hayden	A	157	151	15	181*	5940	43.67	10	33
J.N.Rhodes	SA	245	220	51	121	5935	35.11	2	33
Ramiz Raja	P	198	197	15	119*	5841	32.09	9	31
C.L.Hooper	WI	227	206	43	113*	5761	35.34	7	29
Yuvraj Singh	I	197	179	25	109	5594	36.32	8	35
W.J.Cronje	SA	188	175	31	112	5565	38.64	2	39
A.Jadeja	I	196	179	36	119	5359	37.47	6	30
Shahid Afridi	P	248	235	14	109	5332	24.12	4	29
D.R.Martyn	A	205	179	51	144*	5259	41.08	5	36
A.D.R.Campbell	Z	188	184	14	131*	5185	30.50	7	30
R.S.Mahanama	SL	213	198	23	119*	5162	29.49	4	35
C.G.Greenidge	WI	128	127	13	133*	5134	45.03	11	31
V.Sehwag	I	172	167	7	130	5017	31.35	8	24

The most for England is 4677 in 162 innings by A.J.Stewart, and for Bangladesh 2168 (105) by Habibul Bashar.

15 HUNDREDS

		Inns	100	E	A	SA	WI	NZ	I	P	SL	Z	B	Ass
S.R.Tendulkar	I	403	41	1	7	3	4	4	–	5	7	5	–	5
S.T.Jayasuriya	SL	393	25	4	2	–	1	5	3	–	1	1	1	
R.T.Ponting	A	281	24	3	–	2	1	6	4	1	4	1	1	1
S.C.Ganguly	I	297	22	1	1	3	–	3	–	2	4	3	1	4

249

		Inns	100	E	A	SA	WI	NZ	I	P	SL	Z	B	Ass
H.H.Gibbs	SA	217	20	2	2	–	5	2	2	2	1	2	1	1
Saeed Anwar	P	244	20	–	1	–	2	4	4	–	7	2	–	–
B.C.Lara	WI	285	19	1	3	3	–	2	–	5	2	1	1	1
M.E.Waugh	A	236	18	1	–	2	3	3	3	1	1	3	–	1
D.L.Haynes	WI	237	17	2	6	–	–	2	2	4	1	–	–	
J.H.Kallis	SA	255	16	1	1	–	4	3	1	1	3	1	–	1
D.L.Haynes	WI	237	17	2	6	–	–	2	2	4	1	–	–	
C.H.Gayle	WI	169	15	2	–	3	–	–	4	1	–	2	1	2
A.C.Gilchrist	A	271	15	2	–	2	–	2	1	1	6	1	–	–

The most for England is 12 by M.E.Trescothick (in 122 innings), for Zimbabwe 7 by A.D.R.Campbell (184), and for Bangladesh 4 by Shahriar Nafis (49).

HIGHEST PARTNERSHIP FOR EACH WICKET

1st	286	W.U.Tharanga/S.T.Jayasuriya	Sri Lanka v England	Leeds	2006
2nd	331	S.R.Tendulkar/R.Dravid	India v New Zealand	Hyderabad (Ind)	1999-00
3rd	237*	R.Dravid/S.R.Tendulkar	India v Kenya	Bristol	1999
4th	275*	M.Azharuddin/A.Jadeja	India v Zimbabwe	Cuttack	1997-98
5th	223	M.Azharuddin/A.Jadeja	India v Sri Lanka	Colombo (RPS)	1997-98
6th	165	M.E.K.Hussey/B.J.Haddin	Australia v West Indies	Kuala Lumpur	2006-07
	165	C.D.McMillan/B.B.McCullum	New Zealand v Australia	Hamilton	2006-07
7th	130	A.Flower/H.H.Streak	Zimbabwe v England	Harare	2001-02
8th	138*	J.M.Kemp/A.J.Hall	South Africa v India	Cape Town	2006-07
9th	126*	Kapil Dev/S.M.H.Kirmani	India v Zimbabwe	Tunbridge Wells	1983
10th	106*	I.V.A.Richards/M.A.Holding	West Indies v England	Manchester	1984

BOWLING RECORDS
SIX WICKETS IN AN INNINGS

8-19	W.P.U.C.J Vaas	Sri Lanka v Zimbabwe	Colombo (SSC)	2001-02
7-15	G.D.McGrath	Australia v Namibia	Potschefstroom	2002-03
7-20	A.J.Bichel	Australia v England	Port Elizabeth	2002-03
7-30	M.Muralitharan	Sri Lanka v India	Sharjah	2000-01
7-36	Waqar Younis	Pakistan v England	Leeds	2001
7-37	Aqib Javed	Pakistan v India	Sharjah	1991-92
7-51	W.W.Davis	West Indies v Australia	Leeds	1983
6-12	A.Kumble	India v West Indies	Calcutta	1993-94
6-14	G.J.Gilmour	Australia v England	Leeds	1975
6-14	Imran Khan	Pakistan v India	Sharjah	1984-85
6-14	M.F.Maharoof	Sri Lanka v West Indies	Bombay	2006-07
6-15	C.E.H.Croft	West Indies v England	Kingstown	1980-81
6-16	Shoaib Akhtar	Pakistan v New Zealand	Karachi	2001-02
6-18	Azhar Mahmood	Pakistan v West Indies	Sharjah	1999-00
6-19	H.K.Olonga	Zimbabwe v England	Cape Town	1999-00
6-19	S.E.Bond	New Zealand v Zimbabwe	Harare	2005
6-20	B.C.Strang	Zimbabwe v Bangladesh	Nairobi	1997-98
6-22	F.H.Edwards	West Indies v Zimbabwe	Harare	2003-04
6-22	M.Ntini	South Africa v Australia	Cape Town	2005-06
6-23	A.A.Donald	South Africa v Kenya	Nairobi	1996-97
6-23	A.Nehra	India v England	Durban	2002-03
6-23	S.E.Bond	New Zealand v Australia	Port Elizabeth	2002-03
6-25	S.B.Styris	New Zealand v West Indies	Port-of-Spain	2002
6-25	W.P.U.C.J Vaas	Sri Lanka v Bangladesh	Pietermaritzburg	2002-03
6-26	Waqar Younis	Pakistan v Sri Lanka	Sharjah	1989-90
6-26	Mashrafe Mortaza	Bangladesh v Kenya	Nairobi	2006
6-27	Naved-ul-Hasan	Pakistan v India	Jamshedpur	2004-05
6-27	M.Kartik	India v Australia	Bombay	2007-08
6-27	C.R.D.Fernando	Sri Lanka v England	Colombo (RPS)	2007-08
6-28	H.K.Olonga	Zimbabwe v Kenya	Bulawayo	2002-03
6-29	B.P.Patterson	West Indies v India	Nagpur	1987-88
6-29	S.T.Jayasuriya	Sri Lanka v England	Moratuwa	1992-93
6-30	Waqar Younis	Pakistan v New Zealand	Auckland	1993-94
6-31	P.D.Collingwood	England v Bangladesh	Nottingham	2005

6-35	S.M.Pollock	South Africa v West Indies	East London	1998-99
6-35	Abdul Razzaq	Pakistan v Bangladesh	Dhaka	2001-02
6-39	K.H.MacLeay	Australia v India	Nottingham	1983
6-41	I.V.A.Richards	West Indies v India	Delhi	1989-90
6-42	A.B.Agarkar	India v Australia	Melbourne	2003-04
6-44	Waqar Younis	Pakistan v New Zealand	Sharjah	1996-97
6-49	L.Klusener	South Africa v Sri Lanka	Lahore	1997-98
6-50	A.H.Gray	West Indies v Australia	Port-of-Spain	1990-91
6-55	S.Sreesanth	India v England	Indore	2005-06
6-59	Waqar Younis	Pakistan v Australia	Nottingham	2001
6-59	A.Nehra	India v Sri Lanka	Colombo (RPS)	2005

150 WICKETS IN A CAREER

		LOI	Balls	R	W	Avge	Best	5w	R/Over
Wasim Akram	P	356	18186	11812	502	23.52	5-15	6	3.89
M.Muralitharan	SL	295	16046	10318	450	22.92	7-30	8	3.85
Waqar Younis	P	262	12698	9919	416	23.84	7-36	13	4.68
W.P.U.C.J.Vaas	SL	309	15211	10596	391	27.09	8-19	4	4.17
S.M.Pollock	SA	294	15430	9410	387	24.31	6-35	5	3.65
G.D.McGrath	A	247	12850	8315	377	22.05	7-15	7	3.88
A.Kumble	I	269	14376	10300	334	30.83	6-12	2	4.29
J.Srinath	I	229	11935	8847	315	28.08	5-23	3	4.44
S.T.Jayasuriya	SL	404	13985	11065	304	36.39	6-29	4	4.74
S.K.Warne	A	193	10600	7514	291	25.82	5-33	1	4.25
Saqlain Mushtaq	P	169	8770	6275	288	21.78	5-20	6	4.29
A.B.Agarkar	I	191	9484	8021	288	27.85	6-42	2	5.07
B.Lee	A	161	8213	6439	281	22.91	5-22	7	4.70
A.A.Donald	SA	164	8561	5926	272	21.78	6-23	2	4.15
M.Ntini	SA	164	8249	6119	255	23.99	6-22	4	4.45
Kapil Dev	I	225	11202	6945	253	27.45	5-43	1	3.72
Abdul Razzaq	P	227	9707	7546	245	30.80	6-35	3	4.66
H.H.Streak	Z	187	9414	7065	237	29.81	5-32	1	4.50
J.H.Kallis	SA	269	9276	7424	235	31.59	5-30	2	4.80
D.Gough	E	158	8421	6154	234	26.29	5-44	2	4.38
C.A.Walsh	WI	205	10822	6915	227	30.46	5- 1	1	3.83
C.E.L.Ambrose	WI	176	9353	5430	225	24.13	5-17	4	3.48
D.L.Vettori	NZ	209	9948	6932	215	32.24	5- 7	2	4.18
Shahid Afridi	P	248	10060	7759	215	36.08	5-11	2	4.62
Shoaib Akhtar	P	133	6303	4864	213	22.83	6-16	4	4.63
C.J.McDermott	A	138	7460	5018	213	24.71	5-44	1	4.03
C.Z.Harris	NZ	248	10667	7613	203	37.50	5-42	1	4.28
C.L.Cairns	NZ	214	8132	6557	200	32.78	5-42	1	4.83
B.K.V.Prasad	I	161	8129	6332	196	32.30	5-27	1	4.67
S.R.Waugh	A	325	8883	6764	195	34.68	4-33	–	4.56
C.L.Hooper	WI	227	9573	6957	193	36.04	4-34	–	4.36
L.Klusener	SA	171	7336	5751	192	29.95	6-49	6	4.70
Z.Khan	I	138	6931	5711	188	30.37	5-42	1	4.94
Aqib Javed	P	163	8012	5721	182	31.43	7-37	4	4.28
Imran Khan	P	175	7462	4845	182	26.62	6-14	1	3.90
Harbhajan Singh	I	165	8767	6085	181	33.61	5-31	2	4.16
Mushtaq Ahmed	P	144	7543	5361	161	33.29	5-36	1	4.26
R.J.Hadlee	NZ	115	6182	3407	158	21.56	5-25	5	3.31
M.Prabhakar	I	130	6360	4534	157	28.87	5-33	2	4.27
M.D.Marshall	WI	136	7175	4233	157	26.96	4-18	–	3.54
C.R.D.Fernando	SL	122	5244	4536	154	29.45	6-27	1	5.18
S.R.Tendulkar	I	413	8009	6795	154	44.12	5-32	2	5.09
G.B.Hogg	A	120	5408	4055	153	26.50	5-32	2	4.49
U.D.U.Chandana	SL	147	6136	4809	151	31.84	5-61	1	4.70

The most for Bangladesh is 119 by Mohammad Rafique (123 LOI).

HAT-TRICKS

Jalaluddin	Pakistan v Australia	Hyderabad	1982-83
B.A.Reid	Australia v New Zealand	Sydney	1985-86
C.Sharma	India v New Zealand	Nagpur	1987-88

Wasim Akram	Pakistan v West Indies	Sharjah	1989-90
Wasim Akram	Pakistan v Australia	Sharjah	1989-90
Kapil Dev	India v Sri Lanka	Calcutta	1990-91
Aqib Javed	Pakistan v India	Sharjah	1991-92
D.K.Morrison	New Zealand v India	Napier	1993-94
Waqar Younis	Pakistan v New Zealand	East London	1994-95
Saqlain Mushtaq	Pakistan v Zimbabwe	Peshawar	1996-97
E.A.Brandes	Zimbabwe v England	Harare	1996-97
A.M.Stuart	Australia v Pakistan	Melbourne	1996-97
Saqlain Mushtaq	Pakistan v Zimbabwe	The Oval	1999
W.P.U.C.J Vaas	Sri Lanka v Zimbabwe	Colombo (SSC)	2001-02
Mohammad Sami	Pakistan v West Indies	Sharjah	2001-02
W.P.U.C.J Vaas	Sri Lanka v Bangladesh	Pietermaritzburg	2002-03
B.Lee	Australia v Kenya	Durban	2002-03
J.M.Anderson	England v Pakistan	The Oval	2003
S.J.Harmison	England v India	Nottingham	2004
C.K.Langeveldt	South Africa v West Indies	Bridgetown	2004-05
Shahadat Hossain	Bangladesh v Zimbabwe	Harare	2006
J.E.Taylor	West Indies v Australia	Bombay	2006-07
S.E.Bond	New Zealand v Australia	Hobart	2006-07
S.L.Malinga	Sri Lanka v South Africa	Providence	2006-07

[1] The first three balls of the match. Took four wickets in opening over (W W W 4 wide W 0).

WICKET-KEEPING RECORDS
SIX DISMISSALS IN AN INNINGS

6	(6ct)	A.C.Gilchrist	Australia v South Africa	Cape Town	1999-00
6	(6ct)	A.J.Stewart	England v Zimbabwe	Manchester	2000
6	(5ct/1st)	R.D.Jacobs	West Indies v Sri Lanka	Colombo (RPS)	2001-02
6	(5ct/1st)	A.C.Gilchrist	Australia v England	Sydney	2002-03
6	(6ct)	A.C.Gilchrist	Australia v Namibia	Potchefstroom	2002-03
6	(6ct)	A.C.Gilchrist	Australia v Sri Lanka	Colombo (RPS)	2003-04
6	(6ct)	M.V.Boucher	South Africa v Pakistan	Cape Town	2006-07
6	(5ct/1st)	M.S.Dhoni	India v England	Leeds	2007
6	(6ct)	A.C.Gilchrist	Australia v India	Baroda	2007-08

100 DISMISSALS IN A CAREER

Total			LOI	Ct	St
461‡	A.C.Gilchrist	Australia	274	408	53
377	M.V.Boucher	South Africa	258	360	17
287‡	Moin Khan	Pakistan	211	214	73
233	I.A.Healy	Australia	168	194	39
223†‡	K.C.Sangakkara	Sri Lanka	164	172	51
220‡	Rashid Latif	Pakistan	164	182	38
207‡	R.S.Kaluwitharana	Sri Lanka	187	132	75
204‡	P.J.L.Dujon	West Indies	167	183	21
187	R.D.Jacobs	West Indies	146	159	28
165	D.J.Richardson	South Africa	122	148	17
165†‡	A.Flower	Zimbabwe	185	133	32
163†‡	A.J.Stewart	England	138	148	15
154‡	N.R.Mongia	India	139	110	44
153†‡	B.B.McCullum	New Zealand	120	140	13
136†‡	A.C.Parore	New Zealand	148	111	25
126	Khaled Masud	Bangladesh	125	91	35
124	R.W.Marsh	Australia	92	120	4
122	M.S.Dhoni	India	99	94	28
103	Salim Yousuf	Pakistan	86	81	22

† Excluding catches taken in the field. ‡ Excluding matches when not wicket-keeper.

FIELDING RECORDS
FIVE CATCHES IN AN INNINGS

5	J.N.Rhodes	South Africa v West Indies	Bombay	1993-94

100 CATCHES IN A CAREER

Total			LOI
156	M.Azharuddin	India	334
132	D.P.M.D.Jayawardena	Sri Lanka	261
132	S.P.Fleming	New Zealand	277
127	A.R.Border	Australia	273
127	R.T.Ponting	Australia	290
122	R.Dravid	India	329
122	S.R.Tendulkar	India	413
120	C.L.Hooper	West Indies	227
117	B.C.Lara	West Indies	294
116	M.Muralitharan	Sri Lanka	295
116	S.T.Jayasuriya	Sri Lanka	404
113	Inzamam-ul-Haq	Pakistan	375
111	S.R.Waugh	Australia	325
109	R.S.Mahanama	Sri Lanka	213
108	M.E.Waugh	Australia	244
105	J.N.Rhodes	South Africa	245
104	S.M.Pollock	South Africa	294
101	I.V.A.Richards	West Indies	187
101	J.H.Kallis	South Africa	269
100	S.C.Ganguly	India	308

The most for England 85 by P.D.Collingwood (141), for Zimbabwe 86 by G.W.Flower (219), and for Bangladesh 28 by Mohammad Rafique (123).

ALL-ROUND RECORDS
50 RUNS AND 5 WICKETS IN A MATCH

I.V.A.Richards	119	5-41	West Indies v New Zealand	Dunedin	1986-87
K.Srikkanth	70	5-27	India v New Zealand	Vishakhapatnam	1988-89
M.E.Waugh	57	5-24	Australia v West Indies	Melbourne	1992-93
L.Klusener	54	6-49	South Africa v Sri Lanka	Lahore	1997-98
Abdul Razzaq	70*	5-48	Pakistan v India	Hobart	1999-00
G.A.Hick	80	5-33	England v Zimbabwe	Harare	1999-00
Shahid Afridi	61	5-40	Pakistan v England	Lahore	2000-01
S.C.Ganguly	71*	5-34	India v Zimbabwe	Kanpur	2000-01
S.B.Styris	63*	6-25	New Zealand v West Indies	Port-of-Spain	2002
R.C.Irani	53	5-26	England v India	The Oval	2002
C.H.Gayle	60	5-46	West Indies v Australia	St George's	2002-03
P.D.Collingwood	112*	6-31	England v Bangladesh	Nottingham	2005

1000 RUNS AND 100 WICKETS

England	I.T.Botham (2113/145), A.Flintoff (2989/145).
Australia	S.P.O'Donnell (1242/108); A.Symonds (4645/122); S.K.Warne (1016/291); S.R.Waugh (7569/195).
South Africa	W.J.Cronje (5565/114); J.H.Kallis (9512/235); L.Klusener (3576/192); S.M.Pollock (3193/387).
West Indies	C.H.Gayle (6189/142); C.L.Hooper (5761/193); I.V.A.Richards (6721/118)
New Zealand	C.L.Cairns (4881/200); R.J.Hadlee (1751/158); C.Z.Harris (4379/203); J.D.P.Oram (1764/119); S.B.Styris (3488/119); D.L.Vettori (1322/215)
India	A.B.Agarkar (1268/288); S.C.Ganguly (11221/100); Kapil Dev (3782/253); I.K.Pathan (1221/134); M.Prabhakar (1858/157); R.J.Shastri (3108/129); S.R.Tendulkar (16088/154)
Pakistan	Abdul Razzaq (4417/245); Azhar Mahmood (1521/123); Imran Khan (3709/182); Mudassar Nazar (2654/111); Shahid Afridi (5332/215); Shoaib Malik (4142/120); Wasim Akram (3717/502)
Sri Lanka	U.D.U.Chandana (1627/151); P.A.de Silva (9284/106); H.D.P.K.Dharmasena (1222/138); S.T.Jayasuriya (12187/304); W.P.U.C.J.Vaas (1946/391)
Zimbabwe	G.W.Flower (6536/104); H.H.Streak (2901/237)
Bangladesh	Mohammad Rafique (1190/119)
Kenya	T.M.Odoyo (1842/103)

413	S.R.Tendulkar	India	290	R.T.Ponting	Australia
404	S.T.Jayasuriya	Sri Lanka	283	Salim Malik	Pakistan
375	Inzamam-ul-Haq	Pakistan	279	A.C.Gilchrist	Australia
356	Wasim Akram	Pakistan	273	A.R.Border	Australia
334	M.Azharuddin	India	269	A.Kumble	India
329	R.Dravid	India	269	A.Ranatunga	Sri Lanka
325	S.R.Waugh	Australia	269	J.H.Kallis	South Africa
309	W.P.U.C.J.Vaas	Sri Lanka	268	M.S.Atapattu	Sri Lanka
308	P.A.de Silva	Sri Lanka	262	D.P.M.D.Jayawardena	Sri Lanka
308	S.C.Ganguly	India	262	Waqar Younis	Pakistan
295	M.Muralitharan	Sri Lanka	258	M.V.Boucher	South Africa
294	B.C.Lara	West Indies	250	Ijaz Ahmed	Pakistan
294	S.M.Pollock	South Africa			

The most for England is 170 by A.J.Stewart, for Zimbabwe 219 by G.W.Flower, and for Bangladesh 126 by Khaled Masud.

The most consecutive appearances is 172 by A.Flower for Zimbabwe (Feb 1992-Apr 2001).

100 MATCHES AS CAPTAIN

LOI			W	L	T	NR	% Won (exc NR)
216	S.P.Fleming	New Zealand	98	106	1	11	48.27
193	A.Ranatunga	Sri Lanka	89	95	1	8	48.10
178	A.R.Border	Australia	107	67	1	3	61.14
174	M.Azharuddin	India	90	76	2	6	53.57
159	R.T.Ponting	Australia	121	28	2	8	80.13
146	S.C.Ganguly	India	76	65	–	5	53.90
139	Imran Khan	Pakistan	75	59	1	4	55.55
138	W.J.Cronje	South Africa	99	35	1	3	73.33
124	B.C.Lara	West Indies	59	59	–	6	50.42
118	S.T.Jayasuriya	Sri Lanka	66	47	2	3	57.39
109	Wasim Akram	Pakistan	66	41	2	–	60.55
108	I.V.A.Richards	West Indies	68	36	–	4	65.38
107	G.C.Smith	South Africa	63	38	1	5	61.76
106	S.R.Waugh	Australia	67	35	3	1	63.80

The most for England is 60 by M.P.Vaughan, for Zimbabwe 86 by A.D.R.Campbell, and for Bangladesh 69 by Habibul Bashar.

100 LOI UMPIRING APPEARANCES

186	R.E.Koertzen	South Africa	09.12.1992	to	22.02.2008
171	D.R.Shepherd	England	09.06.1983	to	12.07.2005
167	S.A.Bucknor	Jamaica	18.03.1989	to	08.10.2007
147	D.J.Harper	Australia	14.01.1994	to	15.02.2008
133	D.B.Hair	Australia	14.12.1991	to	15.07.2007
122	B.F.Bowden	New Zealand	23.03.1995	to	23.02.2008
118	S.J.A.Taufel	Australia	13.01.1999	to	22.02.2008
107	D.L.Orchard	South Africa	02.12.1994	to	07.12.2003
101	Alim Dar	Pakistan	16.02.2000	to	02.02.2008
100	R.S.Dunne	New Zealand	06.02.1989	to	26.02.2002
100	R.B.Tiffin	Zimbabwe	25.10.1992	to	07.12.2007

INTERNATIONAL TWENTY20 RECORDS

These records exclude matches abandoned without a ball bowled, regardless of the toss having been made.

MATCH RESULTS

Matches completed by 23 February 2008

	Opponents	Matches	Won	Lost	Tied		Opponents	Matches	Won	Lost	Tied
Australia	Bangladesh	1	1	–	–		Kenya	1	1	–	–
	England	3	2	1	–		Pakistan	1	–	1	–
	India	3	1	2	–		South Africa	3	1	2	–
	New Zealand	2	2	–	–		Sri Lanka	3	1	2	–
	Pakistan	1	–	1	–		West Indies	1	–	–	1
	South Africa	2	1	1	–	**Pakistan**	Australia	1	1	–	–
	Sri Lanka	1	1	–	–		Bangladesh	2	2	–	–
	Zimbabwe	1	–	1	–		England	1	–	1	–
Bangladesh	Australia	1	–	1	–		India	2	–	1	1
	Kenya	1	1	–	–		Kenya	1	1	–	–
	Pakistan	2	–	2	–		New Zealand	1	1	–	–
	South Africa	1	–	1	–		Scotland	1	1	–	–
	Sri Lanka	1	–	1	–		South Africa	1	1	–	–
	West Indies	1	1	–	–		Sri Lanka	1	1	–	–
	Zimbabwe	1	1	–	–	**Scotland**	Pakistan	1	–	1	–
England	Australia	3	1	2	–	**South Africa**	Australia	2	1	1	–
	India	1	–	1	–		Bangladesh	1	1	–	–
	New Zealand	3	2	1	–		England	1	–	1	–
	Pakistan	1	1	–	–		India	2	–	2	–
	South Africa	1	–	1	–		New Zealand	3	2	1	–
	Sri Lanka	1	–	1	–		Pakistan	1	–	1	–
	West Indies	2	1	1	–		West Indies	3	2	1	–
	Zimbabwe	1	1	–	–	**Sri Lanka**	Australia	1	–	1	–
India	Australia	3	2	1	–		Bangladesh	1	1	–	–
	England	1	1	–	–		England	1	1	–	–
	New Zealand	1	–	1	–		Kenya	1	1	–	–
	Pakistan	2	1	–	1		New Zealand	3	2	1	–
	South Africa	2	2	–	–		Pakistan	1	–	1	–
Kenya	Bangladesh	1	–	1	–	**West Indies**	Bangladesh	1	–	1	–
	New Zealand	1	–	1	–		England	2	1	1	–
	Pakistan	1	–	1	–		New Zealand	1	–	–	1
	Sri Lanka	1	–	1	–		South Africa	3	1	2	–
New Zealand	Australia	2	–	2	–	**Zimbabwe**	Australia	1	1	–	–
	England	3	1	2	–		Bangladesh	1	–	1	–
	India	1	1	–	–		England	1	–	1	–

MATCH RESULTS SUMMARY

	Matches	Won	Lost	Tied		Matches	Won	Lost	Tied
Australia	14	8	6	0	**Pakistan**	11	8	2	1
Bangladesh	8	3	5	0	**Scotland**	1	0	1	0
England	13	5	8	0	**South Africa**	13	8	5	0
India	9	6	2	1	**Sri Lanka**	8	5	3	0
Kenya	4	0	4	0	**West Indies**	7	2	4	1
New Zealand	15	5	9	1	**Zimbabwe**	3	1	2	0

INTERNATIONAL TWENTY20 RECORDS

(To 23 February 2008)

TEAM RECORDS

HIGHEST INNINGS TOTALS

† Batting Second

260-6	Sri Lanka v Kenya	Johannesburg	2007-08
221-5	Australia v England	Sydney	2006-07
218-4	India v England	Durban	2007-08
214-5	Australia v New Zealand	Auckland	2004-05
209-3	Australia v South Africa	Brisbane	2005-06
208-2†	South Africa v West Indies	Johannesburg	2007-08
208-8	West Indies v England	The Oval	2007
205-6	West Indies v South Africa	Johannesburg	2007-08
201-4	South Africa v Australia	Johannesburg	2005-06
200-6†	England v India	Durban	2007-08

LOWEST COMPLETED INNINGS TOTALS

† Batting Second

73 (16.5)	Kenya v New Zealand	Durban	2007-08
74 (17.3)	India v Australia	Melbourne	2007-08
79† (14.3)	Australia v England	Southampton	2005
83† (15.5)	Bangladesh v Sri Lanka	Johannesburg	2007-08
88† (19.3)	Kenya v Sri Lanka	Johannesburg	2007-08
92 (19.4)	Kenya v Pakistan	Nairobi	2007-08
101 (19.3)	Sri Lanka v Australia	Cape Town	2007-08
114† (18.3)	South Africa v Australia	Brisbane	2005-06
115 (18.2)	Sri Lanka v New Zealand	Auckland	2006-07

BATTING RECORDS

MOST RUNS IN A CAREER

Runs			M	I	NO	HS	Avge	50	R/100B
361	G.C.Smith	SA	12	12	2	89*	36.10	3	127.5
337	A.Symonds	A	12	10	4	85*	56.16	2	170.2
330	P.D.Collingwood	E	13	13	–	79	25.38	2	140.4
321	K.P.Pietersen	E	13	13	–	79	24.69	1	158.1
315	R.T.Ponting	A	10	10	2	98*	39.37	2	138.1
308	M.L.Hayden	A	9	9	3	73*	51.33	4	143.9
299	G.Gambhir	I	8	8	–	75	37.37	4	128.3
299	B.B.McCullum	NZ	15	15	2	45	23.00	–	121.5
278	Shoaib Malik	P	11	11	2	57	30.88	2	123.0
272	A.C.Gilchrist	A	13	13	1	48	22.66	–	141.6
251	Misbah-ul-Haq	P	9	9	4	66*	50.20	2	127.4

HIGHEST INDIVIDUAL INNINGS

Score	Balls				
117	57	C.H.Gayle	WI v SA	Johannesburg	2007-08
98*	55	R.T.Ponting	A v NZ	Auckland	2004-05
96	56	D.R.Martyn	A v SA	Brisbane	2005-06
90*	55	H.H.Gibbs	SA v WI	Johannesburg	2007-08
89*	58	G.C.Smith	SA v A	Johannesburg	2005-06
89*	56	J.M.Kemp	SA v NZ	Durban	2007-08
88	44	S.T.Jayasuriya	SL v K	Johannesburg	2007-08
85*	46	A.Symonds	A v NZ	Perth	2007-08
81	50	Nazimuddin	B v P	Nairobi	2007-08
79	41	P.D.Collingwood	E v WI	The Oval	2007
79	37	K.P.Pietersen	E v Z	Cape Town	2007-08
76	53	RT.Ponting	A v I	Bombay	2007-08
75	54	G.Gambhir	I v P	Johannesburg	2007-08

HIGHEST PARTNERSHIP FOR EACH WICKET

1st	145	C.H.Gayle/D.S.Smith	WI v SA	Johannesburg	2007-08
2nd	111	G.C.Smith/H.H.Gibbs	SA v A	Johannesburg	2005-06
3rd	120*	H.H.Gibbs/J.M.Kemp	SA v WI	Johannesburg	2007-08
4th	101	Younus Khan/Shoaib Malik	P v SL	Johannesburg	2007-08
5th	119*	Shoaib Malik/Misbah-ul-Haq	P v A	Johannesburg	2007-08
6th	77*	R.T.Ponting/M.E.K.Hussey	A v NZ	Auckland	2004-05
7th	91	P.D.Collingwood/M.H.Yardy	E v WI	The Oval	2007
8th	40	S.B.Styris/J.W.Wilson	NZ v A	Auckland	2004-05
	40	J.Mubarak/W.P.U.C.J.Vaas	SL v A	Cape Town	2007-08
9th	44	S.L.Malinga/C.R.D.Fernando	SL v NZ	Auckland	2006-07
10th	28	J.D.P.Oram/J.S.Patel	NZ v A	Perth	2007-08

BOWLING RECORDS
MOST WICKETS IN A CAREER

Wkts			Matches	Overs	Mdns	Runs	Avge	Best	R/Over
15	N.W.Bracken	A	12	38.5	1	253	16.86	3-11	6.52
14	Shahid Afridi	P	10	37.3	1	261	18.64	4-19	6.96
14	P.M.Pollock	SA	11	36.3	1	290	20.71	3-28	7.94
13	Umar Gul	P	8	30.4	1	162	12.46	4-25	5.28
13	D.L.Vettori	NZ	8	32	0	176	13.53	4-20	5.50
13	Abdur Razzak	B	8	31	1	178	13.69	3-17	5.74
13	R.P.Singh	I	7	28	0	190	14.61	4-13	6.79
13	S.R.Clark	A	9	36	0	237	18.23	4-20	6.58
12	P.D.Collingwood	E	13	23	0	220	18.33	4-22	9.57
12	J.S.Patel	NZ	9	27.1	0	223	18.58	3-20	8.21
12	I.K.Pathan	I	9	33	1	231	19.25	3-16	7.00
12	S.E.Bond	NZ	9	34.3	1	244	20.33	2-12	7.07
12	Mohammad Asif	P	9	34.5	1	269	22.41	4-18	7.72
12	B.Lee	A	12	44.1	0	308	25.66	3-27	6.97

MOST WICKETS IN AN INNINGS

4- 7	M.R.Gillespie	NZ v K	Durban	2007-08
4- 9	D.W.Steyn	SA v WI	Port Elizabeth	2007-08
4-13	R.P.Singh	I v SA	Durban	2007-08
4-17	M.Morkel	SA v NZ	Durban	2007-08
4-18	Mohammad Asif	P v I	Durban	2007-08
4-19	Shahid Afridi	P v Scotland	Durban	2007-08
4-20	D.L.Vettori	NZ v I	Johannesburg	2007-08
4-20	S.R.Clark	A v SL	Cape Town	2007-08
4-22	P.D.Collingwood	E v SL	Southampton	2006
4-24	J.Lewis	E v A	Southampton	2005
4-25	Umar Gul	P v Scotland	Durban	2007-08
4-29	M.S.Kasprowicz	A v NZ	Auckland	2004-05
4-31	E.Chigumbura	Z v E	Cape Town	2007-08
4-34	Shakib Al Hasan	B v WI	Johannesburg	2007-08

HAT-TRICK

B.Lee	Australia v Bangladesh	Melbourne	2007-08

WICKET-KEEPING RECORDS

MOST DISMISSALS IN A CAREER

Dis			Matches	Ct	St
17	A.C.Gilchrist	Australia	13	17	0
12	B.B.McCullum	New Zealand	15	9	3
11	Mushfiqur Rahim	Bangladesh	8	4	7
10	Kamran Akmal	Pakistan	11	6	4

MOST DISMISSALS IN AN INNINGS

4 (4 ct)	A.C.Gilchrist	Australia v Zimbabwe	Cape Town	2007-08
4 (4 ct)	M.J.Prior	England v South Africa	Cape Town	2007-08
4 (4 ct)	A.C.Gilchrist	Australia v New Zealand	Perth	2007-08

MOST STUMPINGS IN AN INNINGS

3	Kamran Akmal	Pakistan v Kenya	Nairobi	2007-08

FIELDING RECORDS

MOST CATCHES IN A CAREER

Total			Matches
11	L.R.P.L.Taylor	New Zealand	12
8	A.B.de Villiers	South Africa	11
8	M.E.K.Hussey	Australia	12
8	G.C.Smith	South Africa	12
7	Younus Khan	Pakistan	11

MOST CATCHES IN AN INNINGS

3	K.P.Pietersen	England v Australia	Southampton	2005
3	B.Lee	Australia v Sri Lanka	Cape Town	2007-08
3	L.R.P.L.Taylor	New Zealand v Australia	Perth	2007-08

WOMEN'S TEST CRICKET RECORDS

RESULTS SUMMARY

	Opponents	Tests				Won by							Drawn
			E	A	NZ	SA	WI	I	P	SL	Ire	H	
England	Australia	43	8	10	–	–	–	–	–	–	–	–	25
	New Zealand	23	6	–	0	–	–	–	–	–	–	–	17
	South Africa	6	2	–	–	0	–	–	–	–	–	–	4
	West Indies	3	2	–	–	–	0	–	–	–	–	–	1
	India	12	1	–	–	–	–	1	–	–	–	–	10
Australia	New Zealand	13	–	4	1	–	–	–	–	–	–	–	8
	West Indies	2	–	0	–	–	0	–	–	–	–	–	2
	India	9	–	4	–	–	–	0	–	–	–	–	5
New Zealand	South Africa	3	–	–	1	0	–	–	–	–	–	–	2
	India	6	–	–	0	–	–	0	–	–	–	–	6
South Africa	India	1	–	–	–	0	–	1	–	–	–	–	–
	Holland	1	–	–	–	1	–	–	–	–	–	0	–
West Indies	India	6	–	–	–	–	1	1	–	–	–	–	4
	Pakistan	1	–	–	–	–	0	–	0	–	–	–	1
Pakistan	Sri Lanka	1	–	–	–	–	–	–	0	1	–	–	–
	Ireland	1	–	–	–	–	–	–	0	–	1	–	–
		131	19	18	2	1	1	3	0	1	1	0	85

	Tests	Won	Lost	Drawn	Toss Won
England	87	19	11	57	51
Australia	67	18	9	40	22
New Zealand	45	2	10	33	21
South Africa	11	1	4	6	6
West Indies	12	1	3	8	6†
India	34	3	6	25	16†
Pakistan	3	–	2	1	1
Sri Lanka	1	1	–	–	1
Ireland	1	1	–	–	1
Holland	1	–	1	–	1

† Results of tosses in five of the six India v West Indies Tests in 1976-77 are not known

TEAM RECORDS

HIGHEST INNINGS TOTALS

569-6d	Australia v England	Guildford	1998
525	Australia v India	Ahmedabad	1983-84
517-8	New Zealand v England	Scarborough	1996
503-5d	England v New Zealand	Christchurch	1934-35
497	England v South Africa	Shenley	2003
467	India v England	Taunton	2002
455	England v South Africa	Taunton	2003
440	West Indies v Pakistan	Karachi	2003-04
427-4d	Australia v England	Worcester	1998
426-7d	Pakistan v West Indies	Karachi	2003-04
426-9d	India v England	Blackpool	1986
414	England v New Zealand	Scarborough	1996

414	England v Australia	Guildford	1998
404-9d	India v South Africa	Paarl	2001-02
403-8d	New Zealand v India	Nelson	1994-95

The highest totals for countries not included above are:

316	South Africa v England	Shenley	2003
193-3d	Ireland v Pakistan	Dublin	2000
108	Holland v South Africa	Rotterdam	2007

LOWEST INNINGS TOTALS

35	England v Australia	Melbourne	1957-58
38	Australia v England	Melbourne	1957-58
44	New Zealand v England	Christchurch	1934-35
47	Australia v England	Brisbane	1934-35
50	Holland v South Africa	Rotterdam	2007
53	Pakistan v Ireland	Dublin	2000

The lowest innings totals for countries not included above are:

65	India v West Indies	Jammu	1976-77
67	West Indies v England	Canterbury	1979
89	South Africa v New Zealand	Durban	1971-72

BATTING RECORDS
1000 RUNS IN TESTS

			M	I	NO	HS	Avge	100	50
1935	J.A.Brittin	England	27	44	5	167	49.61	5	11
1594	R.Heyhoe-Flint	England	22	38	3	179	45.54	3	10
1317	C.M.Edwards	England	17	31	2	117	45.41	3	7
1301	D.A.Hockley	New Zealand	19	29	4	126*	52.04	4	7
1164	C.A.Hodges	England	18	31	2	158*	40.13	2	6
1110	S.Agarwal	India	13	23	4	190	50.45	4	4
1078	E.Bakewell	England	12	22	4	124	59.88	4	7
1007	M.E.Maclagan	England	14	25	1	119	41.95	2	6

HIGHEST INDIVIDUAL INNINGS ‡ *On debut*

242	Kiran Baluch	P v WI	Karachi	2003-04
214	M.Raj	I v E	Taunton	2002
209*	K.L.Rolton	A v E	Leeds	2001
204	K.E.Flavell	NZ v E	Scarborough	1996
204‡	M.A.J.Goszko	A v E	Shenley	2001
200	J.Broadbent	A v E	Guildford	1998
193	D.A.Annetts	A v E	Collingham	1987
190	S.Agarwal	I v E	Worcester	1986
189	E.A.Snowball	E v NZ	Christchurch	1934-35
179	R.Heyhoe-Flint	E v A	The Oval	1976
177	S.C.Taylor	E v SA	Shenley	2003
176*	K.L.Rolton	A v E	Worcester	1998
167	J.A.Brittin	E v A	Harrogate	1998
161*	E.C.Drumm	E v A	Christchurch	1994-95
160	B.A.Daniels	E v NZ	Scarborough	1996
158*	C.A.Hodges	E v NZ	Canterbury	1984
155*	P.F.McKelvey	NZ v E	Wellington	1968-69

FIVE HUNDREDS

		M	I	E	A	NZ	Opponents SA	WI	IND	P	SL	IRE
5	J.A.Brittin (E)	27	44	–	3	1	–	–	1	–	–	–

HIGHEST PARTNERSHIP FOR EACH WICKET

1st	241	Kiran Baluch/Sajjida Shah	P v WI	Karachi	2003-04
2nd	235	E.A.Snowball/M.E.Hide	E v NZ	Christchurch	1934-35
3rd	309	L.A.Reeler/D.A.Annetts	A v E	Collingham	1987
4th	253	K.L.Rolton/L.C.Broadfoot	A v E	Leeds	2001
5th	138	J.Logtenberg/C.van der Westhuizen	SA v E	Shenley	2003
6th	132	B.A.Daniels/K.M.Leng	E v NZ	Scarborough	1996
7th	157	M.Raj/J.Goswami	I v E	Taunton	2002
8th	181	S.J.Griffiths/D.L.Wilson	A v NZ	Auckland	1989-90
9th	107	B.Botha/M.Payne	SA v NZ	Cape Town	1971-72
10th	119	S.Nitschke/C.R.Smith	A v E	Hove	2005

BOWLING RECORDS

50 WICKETS IN TESTS

Wkts			M	Balls	Runs	Avge	Best	5wI	10wM
77	M.B.Duggan	E	17	3734	1039	13.49	7- 6	5	–
68	E.R.Wilson	A	11	2885	803	11.80	7- 7	4	2
63	D.F.Edulji	I	20	5098†	1624	25.77	6- 64	1	–
60	M.E.Maclagan	E	14	3432	935	15.58	7- 10	3	–
60	C.L.Fitzpatrick	A	13	3603	1147	19.11	5-292	–	–
60	S.Kulkarni	I	19	3320†	1647	27.45	6- 99	5	–
57	R.H.Thompson	A	16	4304	1040	18.24	5- 33	1	–
55	J.Lord	NZ	15	3108	1049	19.07	6-119	4	1
50	E.Bakewell	E	12	2697	831	16.62	7- 61	3	1

† *Excludes balls bowled in Sixth Test v West Indies 1976-77*

TEN WICKETS IN A TEST

13-226	Shaiza Khan	P v WI	Karachi	2003-04
11- 16	E.R.Wilson	A v E	Melbourne	1957-58
11- 63	J.M.Greenwood	E v WI	Canterbury	1979
11-107	L.C.Pearson	E v A	Sydney	2002-03
10- 65	E.R.Wilson	A v NZ	Wellington	1947-48
10- 75	E.Bakewell	E v WI	Birmingham	1979
10- 78	J.Goswami	I v E	Taunton	2006
10-107	K.Price	A v I	Lucknow	1983-84
10-118	D.A.Gordon	A v E	Melbourne	1968-69
10-137	J.Lord	NZ v A	Melbourne	1978-79

SEVEN WICKETS IN AN INNINGS

8-53	N.David	I v E	Jamshedpur	1995-96
7- 6	M.B.Duggan	E v A	Melbourne	1957-58
7- 7	E.R.Wilson	A v E	Melbourne	1957-58
7-10	M.E.Maclagan	E v A	Brisbane	1934-35
7-18	A.Palmer	A v E	Brisbane	1934-35
7-24	L.Johnston	A v NZ	Melbourne	1971-72
7-34	G.E.McConway	E v I	Worcester	1986
7-41	J.A.Burley	NZ v E	The Oval	1966
7-51	L.C.Pearson	E v A	Sydney	2002-03
7-59	Shaiza Khan	P v WI	Karachi	2003-04
7-61	E.Bakewell	E v WI	Birmingham	1979

HAT-TRICKS

E.R.Wilson	Australia v England	Melbourne	1957-58
Shaiza Khan	Pakistan v West Indies	Karachi	2003-04

WICKET-KEEPING, FIELDING AND APPEARANCE RECORDS

25 DISMISSALS IN TESTS

Total			*Tests*	*Ct*	*St*
58	C.Matthews	Australia	20	46	12
43	J.Smit	England	21	39	4
36	S.A.Hodges	England	11	19	17
28	B.A.Brentnall	New Zealand	10	16	12

EIGHT DISMISSALS IN A TEST

9 (8ct, 1st)	C.Matthews	A v I	Adelaide	1990-91
8 (6ct, 2st)	L.Nye	E v NZ	New Plymouth	1991-92

SIX DISMISSALS IN AN INNINGS

8 (6ct, 2st)	L.Nye	E v NZ	New Plymouth	1991-92
6 (2ct, 4st)	B.A.Brentnall	NZ v SA	Johannesburg	1971-72

20 CATCHES IN THE FIELD IN TESTS

Total			*Tests*
25	C.A.Hodges	England	18
21	S.Shah	India	20
20	L.A.Fullston	Australia	12

25 TEST MATCH APPEARANCES

27	J.A.Brittin	England	1979-98

12 MATCHES AS CAPTAIN

			Won	*Lost*	*Drawn*	
14	P.F.McKelvey	NZ	2	3	9	1966–79
12	R.Heyhoe-Flint	E	2	–	10	1966–76
12	S.Rangaswamy	I	1	2	9	1976–84

INTERNATIONAL TEST MATCH RESULTS

Matches completed by 23 February 2008

	Opponents	Tests	E	A	SA	WI	NZ	I	P	SL	Z	B	Tied	Drawn
England	Australia	316	97	131	–	–	–	–	–	–	–	–	–	88
	South Africa	130	54	–	26	–	–	–	–	–	–	–	–	50
	West Indies	138	41	–	–	52	–	–	–	–	–	–	–	45
	New Zealand	88	41	–	–	–	7	–	–	–	–	–	–	40
	India	97	34	–	–	–	–	18	–	–	–	–	–	45
	Pakistan	67	19	–	–	–	–	–	12	–	–	–	–	36
	Sri Lanka	21	8	–	–	–	–	–	–	6	–	–	–	7
	Zimbabwe	6	3	–	–	–	–	–	–	–	0	–	–	3
	Bangladesh	4	4	–	–	–	–	–	–	–	–	0	–	–
Australia	South Africa	77	–	44	15	–	–	–	–	–	–	–	–	18
	West Indies	102	–	48	–	32	–	–	–	–	–	–	1	21
	New Zealand	46	–	22	–	–	7	–	–	–	–	–	–	17
	India	72	–	34	–	–	–	16	–	–	–	–	1	21
	Pakistan	52	–	24	–	–	–	–	11	–	–	–	–	17
	Sri Lanka	20	–	13	–	–	–	–	–	1	–	–	–	6
	Zimbabwe	3	–	3	–	–	–	–	–	–	0	–	–	–
	Bangladesh	4	–	4	–	–	–	–	–	–	–	0	–	–
South Africa	West Indies	22	–	–	14	3	–	–	–	–	–	–	–	5
	New Zealand	35	–	–	20	–	4	–	–	–	–	–	–	11
	India	19	–	–	9	–	–	4	–	–	–	–	–	6
	Pakistan	16	–	–	8	–	–	–	3	–	–	–	–	5
	Sri Lanka	17	–	–	8	–	–	–	–	4	–	–	–	5
	Zimbabwe	7	–	–	6	–	–	–	–	–	0	–	–	1
	Bangladesh	4	–	–	4	–	–	–	–	–	–	0	–	–
West Indies	New Zealand	35	–	–	–	10	9	–	–	–	–	–	–	16
	India	82	–	–	–	30	–	11	–	–	–	–	–	41
	Pakistan	44	–	–	–	14	–	–	15	–	–	–	–	15
	Sri Lanka	10	–	–	–	2	–	–	–	5	–	–	–	3
	Zimbabwe	6	–	–	–	4	–	–	–	–	–	–	–	2
	Bangladesh	4	–	–	–	3	–	–	–	–	–	0	–	1
New Zealand	India	44	–	–	–	–	9	14	–	–	–	–	–	21
	Pakistan	45	–	–	–	–	6	–	21	–	–	–	–	18
	Sri Lanka	24	–	–	–	–	9	–	–	5	–	–	–	10
	Zimbabwe	13	–	–	–	–	7	–	–	–	0	–	–	6
	Bangladesh	6	–	–	–	–	6	–	–	–	–	0	–	–
India	Pakistan	59	–	–	–	–	–	9	12	–	–	–	–	38
	Sri Lanka	26	–	–	–	–	–	10	–	3	–	–	–	13
	Zimbabwe	11	–	–	–	–	–	7	–	–	2	–	–	2
	Bangladesh	5	–	–	–	–	–	4	–	–	–	0	–	1
Pakistan	Sri Lanka	32	–	–	–	–	–	–	15	7	–	–	–	10
	Zimbabwe	14	–	–	–	–	–	–	8	–	2	–	–	4
	Bangladesh	6	–	–	–	–	–	–	6	–	–	0	–	–
Sri Lanka	Zimbabwe	15	–	–	–	–	–	–	–	10	0	–	–	5
	Bangladesh	10	–	–	–	–	–	–	–	10	–	0	–	–
Zimbabwe	Bangladesh	8	–	–	–	–	–	–	–	–	4	1	–	3
		1862	301	323	110	150	64	93	103	51	8	1	2	656

	Tests	Won	Lost	Drawn	Tied	Toss Won
England	867	301	252	314	–	418
Australia	692	323	179	188	2	346
South Africa	327	110	116	101	–	158
West Indies	443	150	143	149	1	235
New Zealand	336	64	133	139	–	170
India	415	93	133	188	1	214
Pakistan	335	103	89	143	–	158
Sri Lanka	175	51	65	59	–	91
Zimbabwe	83	8	49	26	–	49
Bangladesh	51	1	45	5	–	23

INTERNATIONAL TEST CRICKET RECORDS

(To 23 February 2008)

TEAM RECORDS

HIGHEST INNINGS TOTALS

952-6d	Sri Lanka v India	Colombo (RPS)	1997-98
903-7d	England v Australia	The Oval	1938
849	England v West Indies	Kingston	1929-30
790-3d	West Indies v Pakistan	Kingston	1957-58
758-8d	Australia v West Indies	Kingston	1954-55
756-5d	Sri Lanka v South Africa	Colombo (SSC)	2006
751-5d	West Indies v England	St John's	2003-04
747	West Indies v South Africa	St John's	2004-05
735-6d	Australia v Zimbabwe	Perth	2003-04
729-6d	Australia v England	Lord's	1930
713-3d	Sri Lanka v Zimbabwe	Bulawayo	2003-04
708	Pakistan v England	The Oval	1987
705-7d	India v Australia	Sydney	2003-04
701	Australia v England	The Oval	1934
699-5	Pakistan v India	Lahore	1989-90
695	Australia v England	The Oval	1930
692-8d	West Indies v England	The Oval	1995
687-8d	West Indies v England	The Oval	1976
682-6d	South Africa v England	Lord's	2003
681-8d	West Indies v England	Port-of-Spain	1953-54
679-7d	Pakistan v India	Lahore	2005-06
676-7	India v Sri Lanka	Kanpur	1986-87
675-5d	India v Pakistan	Multan	2003-04
674-6	Pakistan v India	Faisalabad	1984-85
674	Australia v India	Adelaide	1947-48
671-4	New Zealand v Sri Lanka	Wellington	1990-91
668	Australia v West Indies	Bridgetown	1954-55
660-5d	West Indies v New Zealand	Wellington	1994-95
659-8d	Australia v England	Sydney	1946-47
658-8d	England v Australia	Nottingham	1938
658-9d	South Africa v West Indies	Durban	2003-04
657-7d	India v Australia	Calcutta	2000-01
657-8d	Pakistan v West Indies	Bridgetown	1957-58
656-8d	Australia v England	Manchester	1964
654-5	England v South Africa	Durban	1938-39
653-4d	England v India	Lord's	1990
653-4d	Australia v England	Leeds	1993

652-7d	England v India	Madras	1984-85
652-7d	Australia v South Africa	Johannesburg	2001-02
652-8d	West Indies v England	Lord's	1973
652	Pakistan v India	Faisalabad	1982-83
650-6d	Australia v West Indies	Bridgetown	1964-65

The highest for Zimbabwe is 563-9d (v WI, Harare, 2001), and for Bangladesh 488 (v Z, Chittagong, 2004-05).

LOWEST INNINGS TOTALS

†One batsman absent

26	New Zealand v England	Auckland	1954-55
30	South Africa v England	Port Elizabeth	1895-96
30	South Africa v England	Birmingham	1924
35	South Africa v England	Cape Town	1898-99
36	Australia v England	Birmingham	1902
36	South Africa v Australia	Melbourne	1931-32
42	Australia v England	Sydney	1887-88
42	New Zealand v Australia	Wellington	1945-46
42†	India v England	Lord's	1974
43	South Africa v England	Cape Town	1888-89
44	Australia v England	The Oval	1896
45	England v Australia	Sydney	1886-87
45	South Africa v Australia	Melbourne	1931-32
46	England v West Indies	Port-of-Spain	1993-94
47	South Africa v England	Cape Town	1888-89
47	New Zealand v England	Lord's	1958
47	West Indies v England	Kingston	2003-04

The lowest for Pakistan is 53† (v A, Sharjah, 2002-03), for Sri Lanka 71 (v P, Kandy, 1994-95), for Zimbabwe 54 (v SA, Cape Town, 2004-05), and for Bangladesh 62 (v SL, Colombo PPS, 2006-07).

BATTING RECORDS

5000 RUNS IN A TEST CAREER

Runs			M	I	NO	HS	Avge	100	50
11912	B.C.Lara	WI	130	230	6	400*	53.17	34	48
11782	S.R.Tendulkar	I	146	237	25	248*	55.57	39	49
11174	A.R.Border	A	156	265	44	205	50.56	27	63
10927	S.R.Waugh	A	168	260	46	200	51.06	32	50
10122	S.M.Gavaskar	I	125	214	16	236*	51.12	34	45
9897	R.Dravid	I	118	203	25	270	55.60	24	51
9676	R.T.Ponting	A	115	191	26	257	58.64	34	38
9331	J.H.Kallis	SA	113	192	31	189*	57.95	29	47
8900	G.A.Gooch	E	118	215	6	333	42.58	20	46
8832	Javed Miandad	P	124	189	21	280*	52.57	23	43
8829	Inzamam-ul-Haq	P	119	198	22	329	50.16	25	46
8540	I.V.A.Richards	WI	121	182	12	291	50.23	24	45
8463	A.J.Stewart	E	133	235	21	190	39.54	15	45
8231	D.I.Gower	E	117	204	18	215	44.25	18	39
8114	G.Boycott	E	108	193	23	246*	47.72	22	42
8032	G.St A.Sobers	WI	93	160	21	365*	57.78	26	30
8029	M.E.Waugh	A	128	209	17	153*	41.81	20	47
8054	M.L.Hayden	A	93	165	13	380	52.98	29	26
7728	M.A.Atherton	E	115	212	7	185*	37.70	16	46

Runs			M	I	NO	HS	Avge	100	50
7674	J.L.Langer	A	104	180	12	250	45.67	23	30
7624	M.C.Cowdrey	E	114	188	15	182	44.06	22	38
7558	C.G.Greenidge	WI	108	185	16	226	44.72	19	34
7525	M.A.Taylor	A	104	186	13	334*	43.49	19	40
7515	C.H.Lloyd	WI	110	175	14	242*	46.67	19	39
7487	D.L.Haynes	WI	116	202	25	184	42.29	18	39
7429	S.Chanderpaul	WI	107	183	26	203*	47.31	17	45
7422	D.C.Boon	A	107	190	20	200	43.65	21	32
7289	G.Kirsten	SA	101	176	15	275	45.27	21	34
7271	D.P.M.D.Jayawardena	SL	93	151	11	374	51.93	21	30
7249	W.R.Hammond	E	85	140	16	336*	58.45	22	24
7110	G.S.Chappell	A	87	151	19	247*	53.86	24	31
6996	D.G.Bradman	A	52	80	10	334	99.94	29	13
6973	S.T.Jayasuriya	SL	110	188	14	340	40.07	14	31
6971	L.Hutton	E	79	138	15	364	56.67	19	33
6875	S.P.Fleming	NZ	108	183	10	274*	39.73	9	43
6868	D.B.Vengsarkar	I	116	185	22	166	42.13	17	35
6806	K.F.Barrington	E	82	131	15	256	58.67	20	35
6770	Mohd Yousuf Youhana	P	79	134	12	223	55.49	23	28
6744	G.P.Thorpe	E	100	179	28	200*	44.66	16	39
6581	S.C.Ganguly	I	103	169	14	239	42.45	15	32
6361	P.A.de Silva	SL	93	159	11	267	42.97	20	22
6227	R.B.Kanhai	WI	79	137	6	256	47.53	15	28
6215	M.Azharuddin	I	99	147	9	199	45.03	22	21
6167	H.H.Gibbs	SA	90	154	7	228	41.95	14	26
6149	R.N.Harvey	A	79	137	10	205	48.41	21	24
6080	G.R.Viswanath	I	91	155	10	222	41.93	14	35
6032	K.C.Sangakkara	SL	71	116	9	287	56.37	16	24
5949	R.B.Richardson	WI	86	146	12	194	44.39	16	27
5825	M.E.Trescothick	E	76	143	10	219	43.79	14	29
5807	D.C.S.Compton	E	78	131	15	278	50.06	17	28
5768	Salim Malik	P	103	154	22	237	43.69	15	29
5764	N.Hussain	E	96	171	16	207	37.19	14	33
5762	C.L.Hooper	WI	102	173	15	233	36.46	13	27
5658	V.V.S.Laxman	I	90	148	20	281	44.20	12	32
5502	M.S.Atapattu	SL	90	156	15	249	39.02	16	17
5475	A.C.Gilchrist	A	95	135	20	204*	47.60	17	25
5444	M.D.Crowe	NZ	77	131	11	299	45.36	17	18
5410	J.B.Hobbs	E	61	102	7	211	56.94	15	28
5357	K.D.Walters	A	74	125	14	250	48.26	15	33
5345	I.M.Chappell	A	75	136	10	196	42.42	14	26
5334	J.G.Wright	NZ	82	148	7	185	37.82	12	23
5312	M.J.Slater	A	74	131	7	219	42.84	14	21
5248	Kapil Dev	I	131	184	15	163	31.05	8	27
5234	W.M.Lawry	A	67	123	12	210	47.15	13	27
5200	I.T.Botham	E	102	161	6	208	33.54	14	22
5138	J.H.Edrich	E	77	127	9	310*	43.54	12	24
5105	A.Ranatunga	SL	93	155	12	135*	35.69	4	38
5062	Zaheer Abbas	P	78	124	11	274	44.79	12	20
5356	M.P.Vaughan	E	73	132	9	197	43.54	17	17

The most for Zimbabwe is 4794 (63 innings) by A.Flower, and for Bangladesh 3013 by Habibul Bashar (97 innings).

750 RUNS IN A SERIES

Runs			Series	M	I	NO	HS	Avge	100	50
974	D.G.Bradman	A v E	1930	5	7	–	334	139.14	4	–
905	W.R.Hammond	E v A	1928-29	5	9	1	251	113.12	4	–
839	M.A.Taylor	A v E	1989	6	11	1	219	83.90	2	5
834	R.N.Harvey	A v SA	1952-53	5	9	–	205	92.66	4	3
829	I.V.A.Richards	WI v E	1976	4	7	–	291	118.42	3	2
827	C.L.Walcott	WI v A	1954-55	5	10	–	155	82.70	5	2
824	G.St A.Sobers	WI v P	1957-58	5	8	2	365*	137.33	3	3
810	D.G.Bradman	A v E	1936-37	5	9	–	270	90.00	3	1
806	D.G.Bradman	A v SA	1931-32	5	5	1	299*	201.50	4	–
798	B.C.Lara	WI v E	1993-94	5	8	–	375	99.75	2	2
779	E.de C.Weekes	WI v I	1948-49	5	7	–	194	111.28	4	2
774	S.M.Gavaskar	I v WI	1970-71	4	8	3	220	154.80	4	3
765	B.C.Lara	WI v E	1995	6	10	1	179	85.00	3	3
761	Mudassar Nazar	P v I	1982-83	6	8	2	231	126.83	4	1
758	D.G.Bradman	A v E	1934	5	8	–	304	94.75	2	1
753	D.C.S.Compton	E v SA	1947	5	8	–	208	94.12	4	2
752	G.A.Gooch	E v I	1990	3	6	–	333	125.33	3	2

HIGHEST INDIVIDUAL INNINGS

400*	B.C.Lara	WI v E	St John's	2003-04
380	M.L.Hayden	A v Z	Perth	2003-04
375	B.C.Lara	WI v E	St John's	1993-94
374	D.P.M.D.Jayawardena	SL v SA	Colombo (SSC)	2006
365*	G.St A.Sobers	WI v P	Kingston	1957-58
364	L.Hutton	E v A	The Oval	1938
340	S.T.Jayasuriya	SL v I	Colombo (RPS)	1997-98
337	Hanif Mohammed	P v WI	Bridgetown	1957-58
336*	W.R.Hammond	E v NZ	Auckland	1932-33
334*	M.A.Taylor	A v P	Peshawar	1998-99
334	D.G.Bradman	A v E	Leeds	1930
333	G.A.Gooch	E v I	Lord's	1990
329	Inzamam-ul-Haq	P v NZ	Lahore	2001-02
325	A.Sandham	E v WI	Kingston	1929-30
317	C.H.Gayle	WI v SA	St John's	2004-05
311	R.B.Simpson	A v E	Manchester	1964
310*	J.H.Edrich	E v NZ	Leeds	1965
309	V.Sehwag	I v P	Multan	2003-04
307	R.M.Cowper	A v E	Melbourne	1965-66
304	D.G.Bradman	A v E	Leeds	1934
302	L.G.Rowe	WI v E	Bridgetown	1973-74
299*	D.G.Bradman	A v SA	Adelaide	1931-32
299	M.D.Crowe	NZ v SL	Wellington	1990-91
291	I.V.A.Richards	WI v E	The Oval	1976
287	R.E.Foster	E v A	Sydney	1903-04
287	K.C.Sangakkara	SL v SA	Colombo (SSC)	2006
285*	P.B.H.May	E v WI	Birmingham	1957
281	V.V.S.Laxman	I v A	Calcutta	2000-01
280*	Javed Miandad	P v I	Hyderabad	1982-83
278	D.C.S.Compton	E v P	Nottingham	1954
277	B.C.Lara	WI v A	Sydney	1992-93
277	G.C.Smith	SA v E	Birmingham	2003
275*	D.J.Cullinan	SA v NZ	Auckland	1998-99
275	G.Kirsten	SA v E	Durban	1999-00
274*	S.P.Fleming	NZ v SL	Colombo (SSC)	2002-03

274	R.G.Pollock	SA v A	Durban	1969-70
274	Zaheer Abbas	P v E	Birmingham	1971
271	Javed Miandad	P v NZ	Auckland	1988-89
270*	G.A.Headley	WI v E	Kingston	1934-35
270	D.G.Bradman	A v E	Melbourne	1936-37
270	R.Dravid	I v P	Rawalpindi	2003-04
270	K.C.Sangakkara	SL v Z	Bulawayo	2003-04
268	G.N.Yallop	A v P	Melbourne	1983-84
267*	B.A.Young	NZ v SL	Dunedin	1996-97
267	P.A.de Silva	SL v NZ	Wellington	1990-91
267	Younus Khan	P v I	Bangalore	2004-05
266	W.H.Ponsford	A v E	The Oval	1934
266	D.L.Houghton	Z v SL	Bulawayo	1994-95
262*	D.L.Amiss	E v WI	Kingston	1973-74
262	S.P.Fleming	NZ v SA	Cape Town	2005-06
261*	R.R.Sarwan	WI v B	Kingston	2004
261	F.M.M.Worrell	WI v E	Nottingham	1950
260	C.C.Hunte	WI v P	Kingston	1957-58
260	Javed Miandad	P v E	The Oval	1987
259	G.M.Turner	NZ v WI	Georgetown	1971-72
259	G.C.Smith	SA v E	Lord's	2003
258	T.W.Graveney	E v WI	Nottingham	1957
258	S.M.Nurse	WI v NZ	Christchurch	1968-69
257*	Wasim Akram	P v Z	Sheikhupura	1996-97
257	R.T.Ponting	A v I	Melbourne	2003-04
256	R.B.Kanhai	WI v I	Calcutta	1958-59
256	K.F.Barrington	E v A	Manchester	1964
255*	D.J.McGlew	SA v NZ	Wellington	1952-53
254	D.G.Bradman	A v E	Lord's	1930
254	V.Sehwag	I v P	Lahore	2005-06
253	S.T.Jayasuriya	SL v P	Faisalabad	2004-05
251	W.R.Hammond	E v A	Sydney	1928-29
250	K.D.Walters	A v NZ	Christchurch	1976-77
250	S.F.A.F.Bacchus	WI v I	Kanpur	1978-79
250	J.L.Langer	A v E	Melbourne	2002-03

The highest for Bangladesh is 158* by Mohammad Ashraful (v I, Chittagong, 2004-05).

20 HUNDREDS

								Opponents					
			200	Inn	E	A	SA	WI	NZ	I	P	SL	Z	B
39	S.R.Tendulkar	I	4	237	6	9	3	3	3	–	2	7	3	3
34	R.T.Ponting	A	4	191	7	–	7	6	2	5	4	1	1	1
34	S.M.Gavaskar	I	4	214	4	8	–	13	2	–	5	2	–	–
34	B.C.Lara	WI	8	230	7	9	4	–	1	2	4	5	1	1
32	S.R.Waugh	A	1	260	10	–	2	7	2	2	3	3	1	2
29	D.G.Bradman	A	12	80	19	–	4	2	–	4	–	–	–	–
29	M.L.Hayden	A	2	165	5	–	6	5	1	6	1	3	2	–
29	J.H.Kallis	SA	–	192	5	3	–	7	5	1	4	–	3	1
27	A.R.Border	A	2	265	8	–	–	3	5	4	6	1	–	–
26	G.St A.Sobers	WI	2	160	10	4	–	–	1	8	3	–	–	–
25	Inzamam-ul-Haq	P	2	198	5	1	–	4	3	3	–	5	2	2
24	G.S.Chappell	A	4	151	9	–	–	5	3	1	6	–	–	–
24	I.V.A.Richards	WI	3	182	8	5	–	–	1	8	2	–	–	–
24	R.Dravid	I	5	203	3	2	1	3	4	–	5	1	3	2
23	Mohd Yousuf Youhana	P	4	134	6	1	–	7	1	4	–	–	2	2
23	J.L.Langer	A	3	180	5	–	2	3	4	3	4	2	–	–

268

Opponents

			200	Inn	E	A	SA	WI	NZ	I	P	SL	Z	B
23	Javed Miandad	P	6	189	2	6	–	2	7	5	–	1	–	–
22	W.R.Hammond	E	7	140	–	9	6	1	4	2	–	–	–	–
22	M.Azharuddin	I	–	147	6	2	4	–	2	–	3	5	–	–
22	M.C.Cowdrey	E	–	188	–	5	3	6	2	3	3	–	–	–
22	G.Boycott	E	1	193	–	7	1	5	2	4	3	–	–	–
21	R.N.Harvey	A	2	137	6	–	8	3	–	4	–	–	–	–
21	G.Kirsten	SA	3	176	5	2	–	3	2	3	2	1	1	2
21	D.P.M.D.Jayawardena	SL	4	151	6	1	5	–	2	3	–	–	1	3
21	D.C.Boon	A	1	190	7	–	3	3	6	1	1	–	–	–
20	K.F.Barrington	E	1	131	–	5	2	3	3	3	4	–	–	–
20	P.A.de Silva	SL	2	159	2	1	–	–	2	5	8	–	1	1
20	M.E.Waugh	A	–	209	6	–	4	4	1	1	3	1	–	–
20	G.A.Gooch	E	2	215	–	4	–	5	4	5	1	1	–	–

The most for New Zealand is 17 by M.D.Crowe (131 innings), for Zimbabwe 12 by A.Flower (112), and for Bangladesh 4 by Mohammad Ashraful (78).

The most double hundreds by batsmen not included above is 6 by M.S.Atapattu (16 hundreds for Sri Lanka), 4 by L.Hutton (19 for England), 4 by C.G.Greenidge (19 for West Indies) and 4 by Zaheer Abbas (12 for Pakistan).

HIGHEST PARTNERSHIP FOR EACH WICKET

1st	413	V.Mankad/Pankaj Roy	I v NZ	Madras	1955-56
2nd	576	S.T.Jayasuriya/R.S.Mahanama	SL v I	Colombo (RPS)	1997-98
3rd	624	K.C.Sangakkara/D.P.M.D.Jayawardena	SL v SA	Colombo (SSC)	2006
4th	411	P.B.H.May/M.C.Cowdrey	E v WI	Birmingham	1957
5th	405	S.G.Barnes/D.G.Bradman	A v E	Sydney	1946-47
6th	346	J.H.W.Fingleton/D.G.Bradman	A v E	Melbourne	1936-37
7th	347	D.St E.Atkinson/C.C.Depeiza	WI v A	Bridgetown	1954-55
8th	313	Wasim Akram/Saqlain Mushtaq	P v Z	Sheikhupura	1996-97
9th	195	M.V.Boucher/P.L.Symcox	SA v P	Johannesburg	1997-98
10th	151	B.F.Hastings/R.O.Collinge	NZ v P	Auckland	1972-73
	151	Azhar Mahmood/Mushtaq Ahmed	P v SA	Rawalpindi	1997-98

BOWLING RECORDS

200 WICKETS IN TESTS

Wkts			M	Balls	Runs	Avge	5 wI	10 wM
718	M.Muralitharan	SL	117	38878	15585	21.70	62	20
702	S.K.Warne	A	144	40518	17924	25.53	37	10
604	A.Kumble	I	125	38864	17428	28.85	35	8
560	G.D.McGrath	A	123	29140	12144	21.68	29	3
519	C.A.Walsh	WI	132	30019	12688	24.45	22	3
434	Kapil Dev	I	131	27740	12867	29.64	23	2
431	R.J.Hadlee	NZ	86	21918	9612	22.30	36	9
421	S.M.Pollock	SA	108	24453	9733	23.11	16	1
414	Wasim Akram	P	104	22627	9779	23.62	25	5
405	C.E.L.Ambrose	WI	98	22104	8500	20.98	22	3
383	I.T.Botham	E	102	21815	10878	28.40	27	4
376	M.D.Marshall	WI	81	17584	7876	20.94	22	4
373	Waqar Younis	P	87	16224	8788	23.56	22	5
362	Imran Khan	P	88	19458	8258	22.81	23	6
355	D.K.Lillee	A	70	18467	8493	23.92	23	7
331	W.P.U.C.J.Vaas	SL	102	21786	9744	29.43	11	2
330	A.A.Donald	SA	72	15519	7344	22.25	20	3
329	M.Ntini	SA	82	17143	9214	28.00	17	4

Wkts			M	Balls	Runs	Avge	5 wI	10 wM
325	R.G.D.Willis	E	90	17357	8190	25.20	16	
309	L.R.Gibbs	WI	79	27115	8989	29.09	18	2
307	F.S.Trueman	E	67	15178	6625	21.57	17	3
297	D.L.Underwood	E	86	21862	7674	25.83	17	6
291	C.J.McDermott	A	71	16586	8332	28.63	14	2
269	B.Lee	A	64	13860	8027	29.84	8	
266	B.S.Bedi	I	67	21364	7637	28.71	14	1
259	J.Garner	WI	58	13169	5433	20.97	7	–
259	J.N.Gillespie	A	71	14234	6770	26.13	8	–
256	Harbhajan Singh	I	63	17003	8039	31.40	20	4
252	J.B.Statham	E	70	16056	6261	24.84	9	1
249	M.A.Holding	WI	60	12680	5898	23.68	13	2
248	R.Benaud	A	63	19108	6704	27.03	16	1
247	M.J.Hoggard	E	66	13681	7413	30.01	7	1
246	G.D.McKenzie	A	60	17681	7328	29.78	16	3
242	B.S.Chandrasekhar	I	58	15963	7199	29.74	16	2
237	D.L.Vettori	NZ	76	18073	8034	33.89	13	3
236	A.V.Bedser	E	51	15918	5876	24.89	15	5
236	Abdul Qadir	P	67	17126	7742	32.80	15	5
236	J.Srinath	I	67	15104	7196	30.49	10	1
235	G.St A.Sobers	WI	93	21599	7999	34.03	6	–
234	A.R.Caddick	E	62	13558	6999	29.91	13	1
229	D.Gough	E	58	11821	6503	28.39	9	–
228	R.R.Lindwall	A	61	13650	5251	23.03	12	–
223	J.H.Kallis	SA	113	14969	6979	31.29	4	–
220	Danish Kaneria	P	51	14994	7458	33.90	12	2
218	C.L.Cairns	NZ	62	11698	6410	29.40	13	1
216	C.V.Grimmett	A	37	14513	5231	24.21	21	7
216	H.H.Streak	Z	65	13559	6079	28.14	7	–
212	M.G.Hughes	A	53	12285	6017	28.38	7	1
208	Saqlain Mushtaq	P	49	14070	6206	29.83	13	3
207	S.J.Harmison	E	55	12060	6433	31.07	8	1
202	A.M.E.Roberts	WI	47	11136	5174	25.61	11	2
202	J.A.Snow	E	49	12021	5387	26.66	8	1
200	J.R.Thomson	A	51	10535	5601	28.00	8	–

The most for Bangladesh is 94 in 31 Tests by Mohammad Rafique.

35 WICKETS IN A SERIES

Wkts		Series	M	Balls	Runs	Avge	5 wI	10 wM
49	S.F.Barnes	E v SA	1913-14	4	1356	536	10.93	7	3
46	J.C.Laker	1956	5	1703	442	9.60	4	2
44	C.V.Grimmett	A v SA	1935-36	5	2077	642	14.59	5	3
42	T.M.Alderman	A v E	1981	6	1950	893	21.26	4	–
41	R.M.Hogg	A v E	1978-79	6	1740	527	12.85	5	2
41	T.M.Alderman	A v E	1989	6	1616	712	17.36	6	1
40	Imran Khan	P v I	1982-83	6	1339	558	13.95	4	2
40	S.K.Warne	A v V	2005	5	1517	797	19.92	3	2
39	A.V.Bedser	E v A	1953	5	1591	682	17.48	5	1
39	D.K.Lillee	A v E	1981	6	1870	870	22.30	2	1
38	M.W.Tate	E v A	1924-25	5	2528	881	23.18	5	1
37	W.J.Whitty	A v SA	1910-11	5	1395	632	17.08	2	–
37	H.J.Tayfield	SA v E	1956-57	5	2280	636	17.18	4	1
36	A.E.E.Vogler	SA v E	1909-10	5	1349	783	21.75	4	1
36	A.A.Mailey	A v E	1920-21	5	1465	946	26.27	4	2

Wkts		Series	M	Balls	Runs	Avge	5 wI	10 wM
36	G.D.McGrath	A v E	1997	6	1499	701	19.47	2	–
35	G.A.Lohmann	E v SA	1895-96	3	520	203	5.80	4	2
35	B.S.Chandrasekhar	I v E	1972-73	5	1747	662	18.91	4	–
35	M.D.Marshall	WI v E	1988	5	1219	443	12.65	3	1

The most for New Zealand is 33 by R.J.Hadlee (3 Tests v A, 1985-86), for Sri Lanka 30 by M.Muralitharan (3 Tests v Z, 2001-02), for Zimbabwe 22 by H.H.Streak (3 Tests v P, 1994-95), and for Bangladesh 18 by Enamul Haque II (2 Tests v Z, 2004-05).

15 WICKETS IN A TEST († On debut)

19- 90	J.C.Laker	E v A	Manchester	1956
17-159	S.F.Barnes	E v SA	Johannesburg	1913-14
16-136†	N.D.Hirwani	I v WI	Madras	1987-88
16-137†	R.A.L.Massie	A v E	Lord's	1972
16-220	M.Muralitharan	SL v E	The Oval	1998
15- 28	J.Briggs	E v SA	Cape Town	1888-89
15- 45	G.A.Lohmann	E v SA	Port Elizabeth	1895-96
15- 99	C.Blythe	E v SA	Leeds	1907
15-104	H.Verity	E v A	Lord's	1934
15-123	R.J.Hadlee	NZ v A	Brisbane	1985-86
15-124	W.Rhodes	E v A	Melbourne	1903-04
15-217	Harbhajan Singh	I v A	Madras	2000-01

The best analysis for South Africa is 13-132 by M.Ntini (v WI, Port-of-Spain, 2004-05), for West Indies 14-149 by M.A.Holding (v E, The Oval, 1976), for Pakistan 14-116 by Imran Khan (v SL, Lahore, 1981-82), for Zimbabwe 11-257 by A.G.Huckle (v NZ, Bulawayo, 1997-98), and for Bangladesh 12-200 by Enamul Haque II (v Z, Dhaka, 2004-05).

NINE WICKETS IN AN INNINGS

10- 53	J.C.Laker	E v A	Manchester	1956
10- 74	A.Kumble	I v P	Delhi	1998-99
9- 28	G.A.Lohmann	E v SA	Johannesburg	1895-96
9- 37	J.C.Laker	E v A	Manchester	1956
9- 51	M.Muralitharan	SL v Z	Kandy	2001-02
9- 52	R.J.Hadlee	NZ v A	Brisbane	1985-86
9- 56	Abdul Qadir	P v E	Lahore	1987-88
9- 57	D.E.Malcolm	E v SA	The Oval	1994
9- 65	M.Muralitharan	SL v E	The Oval	1998
9- 69	J.M.Patel	I v A	Kanpur	1959-60
9- 83	Kapil Dev	I v WI	Ahmedabad	1983-84
9- 86	Sarfraz Nawaz	P v A	Melbourne	1978-79
9- 95	J.M.Noreiga	WI v I	Port-of-Spain	1970-71
9-102	S.P.Gupte	I v WI	Kanpur	1958-59
9-103	S.F.Barnes	E v SA	Johannesburg	1913-14
9-113	H.J.Tayfield	SA v E	Johannesburg	1956-57
9-121	A.A.Mailey	A v E	Melbourne	1920-21

The best analysis for Zimbabwe is 8-109 by P.A.Strang (v NZ, Bulawayo, 2000-01), and for Bangladesh 7-95 by Enamul Haque II (v Z, Dhaka, 2004-05).

HAT-TRICKS

F.R.Spofforth	Australia v England	Melbourne	1878-79
W.Bates	England v Australia	Melbourne	1882-83
J.Briggs	England v Australia	Sydney	1891-92
G.A.Lohmann	England v South Africa	Port Elizabeth	1895-96
J.T.Hearne	England v Australia	Leeds	1899

H.Trumble	Australia v England	Melbourne	1901-02
H.Trumble	Australia v England	Melbourne	1903-04
T.J.Matthews (2)[2]	Australia v South Africa	Manchester	1912
M.J.C.Allom[1]	England v New Zealand	Christchurch	1929-30
T.W.J.Goddard	England v South Africa	Johannesburg	1938-39
P.J.Loader	England v West Indies	Leeds	1957
L.F.Kline	Australia v South Africa	Cape Town	1957-58
W.W.Hall	West Indies v Pakistan	Lahore	1958-59
G.M.Griffin	South Africa v England	Lord's	1960
L.R.Gibbs	West Indies v Australia	Adelaide	1960-61
P.J.Petherick[1]	New Zealand v Pakistan	Lahore	1976-77
C.A.Walsh[3]	West Indies v Australia	Brisbane	1988-89
M.G.Hughes[3]	Australia v West Indies	Perth	1988-89
D.W.Fleming[1]	Australia v Pakistan	Rawalpindi	1994-95
S.K.Warne	Australia v England	Melbourne	1994-95
D.G.Cork	England v West Indies	Manchester	1995
D.Gough	England v Australia	Sydney	1998-99
Wasim Akram[4]	Pakistan v Sri Lanka	Lahore	1998-99
Wasim Akram[4]	Pakistan v Sri Lanka	Dhaka	1998-99
D.N.T.Zoysa[5]	Sri Lanka v Zimbabwe	Harare	1999-00
Abdul Razzaq	Pakistan v Sri Lanka	Galle	2000-01
G.D.McGrath	Australia v West Indies	Perth	2000-01
Harbhajan Singh	India v Australia	Calcutta	2000-01
Mohammad Sami	Pakistan v Sri Lanka	Lahore	2001-02
J.J.C.Lawson	West Indies v Australia	Bridgetown	2002-03
Alok Kapali	Bangladesh v Pakistan	Peshawar	2003
A.M.Blignaut	Zimbabwe v Bangladesh	Harare	2003-04
M.J.Hoggard	England v West Indies	Bridgetown	2003-04
J.E.C.Franklin	New Zealand v Bangladesh	Dhaka	2004-05
I.K.Pathan[6]	India v Pakistan	Karachi	2005-06

[1] On debut. [2] Hat-trick in each innings. [3] Involving both innings. [4] In successive Tests.
[5] His first 3 balls (second over of the match). [6] The fourth, fifth and sixth balls of the match.

WICKET-KEEPING RECORDS

100 DISMISSALS IN TESTS†

Total			Tests	Ct	St
411	M.V.Boucher	South Africa	108	392	19
409	A.C.Gilchrist	Australia	95	374	35
395	I.A.Healy	Australia	119	366	29
355	R.W.Marsh	Australia	96	343	12
270†	P.J.L.Dujon	West Indies	79	265	5
269	A.P.E.Knott	England	95	250	19
241†	A.J.Stewart	England	82	227	14
228	Wasim Bari	Pakistan	81	201	27
219	R.D.Jacobs	West Indies	65	207	12
219	T.G.Evans	England	91	173	46
201†	A.C.Parore	New Zealand	67	194	7
198	S.M.H.Kirmani	India	88	160	38
189	D.L.Murray	West Indies	62	181	8
187	A.T.W.Grout	Australia	51	163	24
176	I.D.S.Smith	New Zealand	63	168	8
174	R.W.Taylor	England	57	167	7
165	R.C.Russell	England	54	153	12
152	D.J.Richardson	South Africa	42	150	2
151†	A.Flower	Zimbabwe	55	142	9
147†	Moin Khan	Pakistan	66	127	20

Total			Tests	Ct	St
146†	K.C.Sangakkara	Sri Lanka	49	126	20
142	Kamran Akmal	Pakistan	38	123	19
141	J.H.B.Waite	South Africa	49	124	17
133	G.O.Jones	England	34	128	5
130	Rashid Latif	Pakistan	37	119	11
130	K.S.More	India	49	110	20
130	W.A.S.Oldfield	Australia	54	78	52
119	R.S.Kaluwitharana	Sri Lanka	49	93	26
112†	J.M.Parks	England	43	101	11
107	N.R.Mongia	India	44	99	8
104	Salim Yousuf	Pakistan	32	91	13
101†	J.R.Murray	West Indies	31	98	3

The most for Bangladesh is 87 (78 ct, 9 st) by Khaled Masud in 44 Tests.

† Excluding catches taken in the field

25 DISMISSALS IN A SERIES

28	R.W.Marsh	Australia v England	1982-83
27 (inc 2st)	R.C.Russell	England v South Africa	1995-96
27 (inc 2st)	I.A.Healy	Australia v England (6 Tests)	1997
26 (inc 3st)	J.H.B.Waite	South Africa v New Zealand	1961-62
26	R.W.Marsh	Australia v West Indies (6 Tests)	1975-76
26 (inc 5st)	I.A.Healy	Australia v England (6 Tests)	1993
26 (inc 1st)	M.V.Boucher	South Africa v England	1998
26 (inc 2st)	A.C.Gilchrist	Australia v England	2001
26 (inc 2st)	A.C.Gilchrist	Australia v England	2006-07
25 (inc 2st)	I.A.Healy	Australia v England	1994-95
25 (inc 2st)	A.C.Gilchrist	Australia v England	2002-03

TEN DISMISSALS IN A TEST

11	R.C.Russell	England v South Africa	Johannesburg	1995-96
10	R.W.Taylor	England v India	Bombay	1979-80
10	A.C.Gilchrist	Australia v New Zealand	Hamilton	1999-00

SEVEN DISMISSALS IN AN INNINGS

7	Wasim Bari	Pakistan v New Zealand	Auckland	1978-79
7	R.W.Taylor	England v India	Bombay	1979-80
7	I.D.S.Smith	New Zealand v Sri Lanka	Hamilton	1990-91
7	R.D.Jacobs	West Indies v Australia	Melbourne	2000-01

FIVE STUMPINGS IN AN INNINGS

5	K.S.More	India v West Indies	Madras	1987-88

FIELDING RECORDS

100 CATCHES IN TESTS

Total			Tests	Total			Tests
181	M.E.Waugh	Australia	128	122	G.S.Chappell	Australia	87
166	S.P.Fleming	New Zealand	108	122	I.V.A.Richards	West Indies	121
165	R.Dravid	India	118	120	I.T.Botham	England	102
164	B.C.Lara	West Indies	130	120	M.C.Cowdrey	England	114
157	M.A.Taylor	Australia	104	115	C.L.Hooper	West Indies	102
156	A.R.Border	Australia	156	115	J.H.Kallis	South Africa	113
132	R.T.Ponting	Australia	115	112	S.R.Waugh	Australia	168
128	D.P.M.D.Jayawardena	Sri Lanka	93	110	R.B.Simpson	Australia	62
125	S.K.Warne	Australia	144	110	W.R.Hammond	England	85

Total			Tests		Total			Tests
109	G.St A.Sobers	West Indies	93		105	M.Azharuddin	India	99
108	S.M.Gavaskar	India	125		105	G.P.Thorpe	England	100
105	I.M.Chappell	Australia	75		103	G.A.Gooch	England	118

The most for Pakistan is 93 by Javed Miandad (124), for Zimbabwe 60 by A.D.R.Campbell (60) and for Bangladesh 21 by Habibul Bashar (49).

15 CATCHES IN A SERIES

15	J.M.Gregory		Australia v England		1920-21

SEVEN CATCHES IN A TEST

7	G.S.Chappell	Australia v England	Perth	1974-75
7	Yajurvindra Singh	India v England	Bangalore	1976-77
7	H.P.Tillekeratne	Sri Lanka v New Zealand	Colombo (SSC)	1992-93
7	S.P.Fleming	New Zealand v Zimbabwe	Harare	1997-98
7	M.L.Hayden	Australia v Sri Lanka	Galle	2003-04

FIVE CATCHES IN AN INNINGS

5	V.Y.Richardson	Australia v South Africa	Durban	1935-36
5	Yajurvindra Singh	India v England	Bangalore	1976-77
5	M.Azharuddin	India v Pakistan	Karachi	1989-90
5	K.Srikkanth	India v Australia	Perth	1991-92
5	S.P.Fleming	New Zealand v Zimbabwe	Harare	1997-98

APPEARANCE RECORDS

100 TEST MATCH APPEARANCES

							Opponents					
			E	A	SA	WI	NZ	I	P	SL	Z	B
168	S.R.Waugh	Australia	46	–	16	32	23	18	20	8	3	2
156	A.R.Border	Australia	47	–	6	31	23	20	22	7	–	–
146	S.R.Tendulkar	India	22	25	19	16	16	–	18	16	9	5
144	S.K.Warne	Australia	36	–	24	19	20	14	15	13	1	2
133	A.J.Stewart	England	–	33	23	24	16	9	13	9	6	–
132	C.A.Walsh	West Indies	36	38	10	–	10	15	18	3	2	–
131	Kapil Dev	India	27	20	4	25	10	–	29	14	2	–
130	B.C.Lara	West Indies	30	30	18	–	11	17	12	8	2	2
128	M.E.Waugh	Australia	29	–	18	28	14	14	15	9	1	–
125	S.M.Gavaskar	India	38	20	–	27	9	–	24	7	–	–
125	A.Kumble	India	19	18	19	17	11	–	15	15	7	4
124	Javed Miandad	Pakistan	22	24	–	17	18	28	–	12	3	–
123	G.D.McGrath	Australia	30	–	17	23	14	11	17	8	1	2
121	I.V.A.Richards	West Indies	36	34	–	–	7	28	16	–	–	–
119	I.A.Healy	Australia	33	–	12	28	11	9	14	11	1	–
119	Inzamam-ul-Haq	Pakistan	19	13	13	15	12	10	–	20	11	6
119	R.Dravid	India	15	22	15	17	9	–	15	11	9	5
118	G.A.Gooch	England	–	42	3	26	15	19	10	3	–	–
117	D.I.Gower	England	–	42	–	19	13	24	17	2	–	–
117	M.Muralitharan	Sri Lanka	16	12	15	10	12	15	14	–	14	9
116	D.L.Haynes	West Indies	36	33	1	–	10	19	16	1	–	–
116	D.B.Vengsarkar	India	26	24	–	25	11	–	22	8	–	–
115	M.A.Atherton	England	–	33	18	27	11	7	11	4	4	–
115	R.T.Ponting	Australia	26	–	15	15	11	19	10	12	3	4
114	M.C.Cowdrey	England	–	43	14	21	18	8	10	–	–	–
113	J.H.Kallis	South Africa	20	17	–	21	14	8	13	12	6	2

274

		Opponents									
		E	A	SA	WI	NZ	I	P	SL	Z	B
110 S.T.Jayasuriya	Sri Lanka	14	13	15	10	13	10	17	–	13	5
110 C.H.Lloyd	West Indies	34	29	–	–	8	28	11	–	–	–
108 M.V.Boucher	South Africa	17	12	–	21	14	7	13	14	6	4
108 G.Boycott	England	–	38	7	29	15	13	6	–	–	–
108 S.P.Fleming	New Zealand	16	14	15	11	–	13	9	13	11	6
108 C.G.Greenidge	West Indies	29	32	–	–	10	23	14	–	–	–
108 S.M.Pollock	South Africa	23	13	–	16	11	12	12	13	5	3
107 D.C.Boon	Australia	31	–	6	22	17	11	11	9	–	–
107 S.Chanderpaul	West Indies	23	12	18	–	11	18	13	2	6	4
104 M.A.Taylor	Australia	33	–	11	20	11	9	12	8	–	–
104 J.L.Langer	Australia	21	–	11	18	14	14	13	8	3	2
104 Wasim Akram	Pakistan	18	13	4	17	9	12	–	19	10	2
103 S.C.Ganguly	India	12	20	14	12	8	–	12	11	9	5
103 Salim Malik	Pakistan	19	15	1	7	18	22	–	15	6	–
102 I.T.Botham	England	–	36	–	20	15	14	14	3	–	–
102 C.L.Hooper	West Indies	24	25	10	–	2	19	14	6	2	–
102 W.P.U.C.J.Vaas	Sri Lanka	15	12	11	7	10	11	16	–	15	5
101 G.Kirsten	South Africa	22	18	–	13	13	10	11	9	3	2
100 G.P.Thorpe	England	–	16	16	27	13	5	8	9	2	4

The most for Zimbabwe is 67 by G.W.Flower, and for Bangladesh 49 by Habibul Bashar.

100 CONSECUTIVE TEST APPEARANCES

153	A.R.Border	Australia	March 1979 to March 1994
107	M.E.Waugh	Australia	June 1993 to October 2002
106	S.M.Gavaskar	India	January 1975 to February 1987

50 TESTS AS CAPTAIN

			Won	Lost	Drawn	Tied
93	A.R.Border	Australia	32	22	38	1
80	S.P.Fleming	New Zealand	28	27	25	–
74	C.H.Lloyd	West Indies	36	12	26	–
57	S.R.Waugh	Australia	41	9	7	–
56	A.Ranatunga	Sri Lanka	12	19	25	–
54	M.A.Atherton	England	13	21	20	–
53	W.J.Cronje	South Africa	27	11	15	–
52	G.C.Smith	South Africa	24	15	13	–
50	I.V.A.Richards	West Indies	27	8	15	–
50	M.A.Taylor	Australia	26	13	11	–

The most for India is 49 by S.C.Ganguly, for Pakistan 48 by Imran Khan, for Zimbabwe 21 by A.D.R.Campbell and H.H.Streak, and for Bangladesh 18 by Habibul Bashar.

50 TEST UMPIRING APPEARANCES

120	S.A.Bucknor	(Jamaica)	28.04.1989 to 06.01.2008
92	D.R.Shepherd	(England)	01.08.1985 to 07.06.2005
87	R.E.Koertzen	(South Africa)	26.12.1992 to 12.12.2007
76	D.B.Hair	(Australia)	25.01.1992 to 20.08.2006
73	S.Venkataraghavan	(India)	29.01.1993 to 20.01.2004
69	D.J.Harper	(Australia)	28.11.1998 to 22.12.2007
66	H.D.Bird	(England)	05.07.1973 to 24.06.1996

TEST MATCH SCORES AND SERIES AVERAGES
ENGLAND v WEST INDIES (1st Test)

At Lord's, London, on 17, 18, 19, 20, 21 May 2007.
Toss: West Indies. Result: **MATCH DRAWN**.
Debuts: England – M.J.Prior.

ENGLAND

*A.J.Strauss	c Smith b Powell	33	c Morton b Collymore	24
A.N.Cook	c Bravo b Taylor	105	c Ramdin b Collymore	65
O.A.Shah	c Smith b Powell	6	c Ramdin b Collymore	4
K.P.Pietersen	c Smith b Collymore	26	lbw b Gayle	109
P.D.Collingwood	b Powell	111	c Morton b Bravo	34
I.R.Bell	not out	109	c Ganga b Bravo	3
†M.J.Prior	not out	126	c Bravo b Gayle	21
L.E.Plunkett			st Ramdin b Gayle	0
S.J.Harmison			not out	11
M.S.Panesar			not out	3
M.J.Hoggard				
Extras	(B 8, LB 17, W 9, NB 3)	37	(B 1, LB 3, W 1, NB 5)	10
Total	(5 wickets declared)	**553**	(8 wickets declared)	**284**

WEST INDIES

C.H.Gayle	b Plunkett	30	not out	47
D.Ganga	lbw b Panesar	49	not out	31
D.S.Smith	b Panesar	21		
*R.R.Sarwan	lbw b Panesar	35		
S.Chanderpaul	lbw b Panesar	74		
R.S.Morton	lbw b Panesar	14		
D.J.Bravo	c Cook b Collingwood	56		
†D.Ramdin	c Collingwood b Plunkett	60		
D.B.L.Powell	not out	36		
J.E.Taylor	c sub (L.J.Hodgson) b Harmison	21		
C.D.Collymore	lbw b Panesar	1		
Extras	(B 4, LB 17, W 16, NB 3)	40	(B 4, LB 3, W 3, NB 1)	11
Total		**437**	(0 wickets)	**89**

WEST INDIES	O	M	R	W		O	M	R	W
Powell	37	9	113	2		9	0	44	0
Taylor	24	4	114	1	(5)	4	0	21	0
Collymore	32	5	110	1	(2)	15	1	58	3
Bravo	32	8	106	1		18	2	91	2
Gayle	10	0	48	0	(3)	20.5	4	66	3
Morton	1	0	4	0					
Sarwan	6	0	33	0					
ENGLAND									
Hoggard	10.1	3	29	0					
Harmison	28	2	117	1	(1)	8	1	21	0
Plunkett	30	7	107	2	(2)	11	1	48	0
Collingwood	11.5	2	34	1					
Panesar	36.1	3	129	6	(3)	3	0	13	0

FALL OF WICKETS

	E	WI	E	WI
Wkt	1st	1st	2nd	2nd
1st	88	38	35	–
2nd	103	83	51	–
3rd	162	151	139	–
4th	219	165	241	–
5th	363	187	248	–
6th	–	279	264	–
7th	–	362	264	–
8th	–	387	271	–
9th	–	424	–	–
10th	–	437	–	–

Umpires: Asad Rauf (*Pakistan*) (10) and R.E.Koertzen (*South Africa*) (80).
Referee: A.G.Hurst (*Australia*) (12).   **Test No. 1830/135 (E858/WI437)**

ENGLAND v WEST INDIES (2nd Test)

At Headingley, Leeds, on 25, 26, 27 (*no play*), 28 May 2007.
Toss: England. Result: **ENGLAND** won by an innings and 283 runs.
Debuts: None.

ENGLAND

A.J.Strauss	c Ramdin b Powell	15
A.N.Cook	lbw b Gayle	42
*M.P.Vaughan	c Morton b Taylor	103
K.P.Pietersen	c Taylor b Bravo	226
P.D.Collingwood	c Gayle b Collymore	29
I.R.Bell	c Ramdin b Collymore	5
†M.J.Prior	b Powell	75
L.E.Plunkett	not out	44
S.J.Harmison		
R.J.Sidebottom		
M.S.Panesar		
Extras	(B 1, LB 15, W 9, NB 6)	31
Total	(7 wickets declared)	**570**

WEST INDIES

C.H.Gayle	lbw b Sidebottom	11		c Prior b Plunkett	13
D.Ganga	lbw b Sidebottom	5		lbw b Sidebottom	9
D.S.Smith	c Cook b Plunkett	26	(4)	c Strauss b Sidebottom	16
S.C.Joseph	c Strauss b Harmison	13	(5)	lbw b Sidebottom	1
R.S.Morton	c Prior b Harmison	5	(6)	c Prior b Harmison	25
D.J.Bravo	b Sidebottom	23	(7)	c Plunkett b Panesar	52
†D.Ramdin	c Prior b Plunkett	6	(8)	lbw b Harmison	5
D.B.L.Powell	c Collingwood b Plunkett	8	(3)	lbw b Sidebottom	0
J.E.Taylor	not out	23		b Harmison	0
C.D.Collymore	c Strauss b Sidebottom	3		not out	0
*R.R.Sarwan	absent hurt	–		absent hurt	–
Extras	(LB 13, W 3, NB 7)	23		(B 1, LB 14, NB 5)	20
Total		**146**			**141**

WEST INDIES	O	M	R	W		O	M	R	W		FALL OF WICKETS			
Powell	33	5	153	2								E	WI	WI
Collymore	29	1	110	2							*Wkt*	*1st*	*1st*	*2nd*
Taylor	22	4	116	1							1st	38	17	20
Bravo	24.3	3	97	1							2nd	91	23	22
Gayle	14	1	78	1							3rd	254	68	30
											4th	316	74	47
ENGLAND											5th	329	82	57
Sidebottom	12	2	42	4		15	4	44	4		6th	489	94	120
Harmison	12	0	55	2	(3)	13.1	3	37	3		7th	570	114	141
Plunkett	12	1	35	3	(2)	8	2	25	1		8th	–	124	141
Panesar	1	0	1	0		6	1	20	1		9th	–	146	141
											10th	–	–	–

Umpires: Asad Rauf (*Pakistan*) (11) and R.E.Koertzen (*South Africa*) (81).
Referee: A.G.Hurst (*Australia*) (13). **Test No. 1831/136 (E859/WI438)**

ENGLAND v WEST INDIES (3rd Test)

At Old Trafford, Manchester, on 7, 8, 9, 10, 11 June 2007.
Toss: England. Result: **ENGLAND** won by 60 runs.
Debuts: West Indies – D.J.G.Sammy.

ENGLAND

A.J.Strauss	lbw b Taylor	6	lbw b Edwards		0
A.N.Cook	c Bravo b Sammy	60	lbw b Gayle		106
*M.P.Vaughan	b Collymore	41	c and b Sammy		40
K.P.Pietersen	c Bravo b Collymore	9	hit wicket b Bravo		68
P.D.Collingwood	lbw b Taylor	10	c Ganga b Sammy		42
I.R.Bell	c Ramdin b Collymore	97	c Ramdin b Sammy		2
†M.J.Prior	c Morton b Bravo	40	c Ramdin b Sammy		0
L.E.Plunkett	b Edwards	13	c Bravo b Sammy		0
S.J.Harmison	c Ramdin b Edwards	18	c Morton b Sammy		16
R.J.Sidebottom	b Edwards	15	not out		8
M.S.Panesar	not out	14	c Gayle b Sammy		0
Extras	(B 15, LB 8, W 6, NB 18)	47	(B 2, LB 6, W 6, NB 12, Pen 5)		31
Total		**370**			**313**

WEST INDIES

C.H.Gayle	c Cook b Plunkett	23	c Collingwood b Harmison		16
*D.Ganga	lbw b Harmison	5	lbw b Harmison		0
D.S.Smith	c Bell b Panesar	40	c Cook b Panesar		42
R.S.Morton	c Strauss b Harmison	35	lbw b Panesar		54
S.Chanderpaul	c Pietersen b Sidebottom	50	not out		116
D.J.Bravo	c Prior b Sidebottom	24	c Cook b Panesar		49
†D.Ramdin	c Pietersen b Sidebottom	5	c Collingwood b Panesar		34
D.J.G.Sammy	c Collingwood b Panesar	1	c and b Panesar		25
J.E.Taylor	c Strauss b Panesar	6	c Cook b Harmison		11
C.D.Collymore	c Collingwood b Panesar	4 (11)	c Bell b Panesar		0
F.H.Edwards	not out	0 (10)	c Bell b Harmison		0
Extras	(B 20, LB 10, W 9, NB 3)	42	(B 14, LB 21, W 8, NB 4)		47
Total		**229**			**394**

WEST INDIES	O	M	R	W		O	M	R	W
Taylor	20	1	67	2	(2)	10	—	42	0
Edwards	20.1	2	94	3	(1)	12	1	54	1
Collymore	25	5	60	3		7	2	24	0
Bravo	23	4	94	1	(6)	8	2	14	1
Sammy	17	7	32	1	(4)	21.3	6	66	7
Chanderpaul					(5)	11	1	43	0
Gayle						16	0	57	1
ENGLAND									
Sidebottom	12	3	48	3		27	8	53	0
Harmison	11	2	53	2		33	8	95	4
Plunkett	12	0	43	1	(4)	16	2	57	0
Panesar	16.4	5	50	4	(3)	51.5	13	137	6
Collingwood	1	0	5	0					
Pietersen					(5)	5	2	17	0

FALL OF WICKETS				
	E	WI	E	WI
Wkt	1st	1st	2nd	2nd
1st	13	17	1	4
2nd	117	49	99	35
3rd	132	116	221	88
4th	132	157	265	161
5th	166	216	272	249
6th	264	224	272	311
7th	285	225	272	348
8th	324	225	300	385
9th	338	225	313	385
10th	370	229	313	394

Umpires: Alim Dar (*Pakistan*) (38) and B.F.Bowden (*New Zealand*) (40).
Referee: A.G.Hurst (*Australia*) (14).   **Test No. 1832/137 (E860/WI439)**

ENGLAND v WEST INDIES (4th Test)

At Riverside, Chester-le-Street, on 15 (no play), 16, 17, 18, 19 June 2007.
Toss: England. Result: **ENGLAND** won by seven wickets.
Debuts: None.

WEST INDIES

*D.Ganga	c Cook b Sidebottom	0	(3) c Prior b Hoggard		6
C.H.Gayle	lbw b Hoggard	28	(1) c Prior b Hoggard		52
D.S.Smith	b Sidebottom	4	(2) lbw b Hoggard		0
R.S.Morton	c Sidebottom b Harmison	6	b Panesar		7
S.Chanderpaul	not out	136	b Panesar		70
D.J.Bravo	b Hoggard	44	c Sidebottom b Panesar		43
M.N.Samuels	b Sidebottom	19	c Collingwood b Panesar		2
†D.Ramdin	c Collingwood b Sidebottom	13	b Panesar		4
D.B.L.Powell	c Prior b Harmison	1	c Vaughan b Harmison		4
F.H.Edwards	b Sidebottom	5	b Harmison		0
C.D.Collymore	lbw b Panesar	13	not out		16
Extras	(B 4, LB 13, NB 1)	18	(B 1, LB 12, W 2, NB 3)		18
Total		**287**			**222**

ENGLAND

A.J.Strauss	c Ramdin b Edwards	77	b Powell		13
A.N.Cook	c Ramdin b Edwards	13	c Bravo b Powell		7
*M.P.Vaughan	c Bravo b Edwards	19	not out		48
M.J.Hoggard	c Gayle b Collymore	0			
K.P.Pietersen	c Ramdin b Edwards	0	(4) c Samuels b Gayle		28
P.D.Collingwood	b Collymore	128	(5) not out		5
I.R.Bell	c Morton b Powell	11			
†M.J.Prior	c Smith b Edwards	62			
S.J.Harmison	c Ganga b Powell	9			
R.J.Sidebottom	not out	26			
M.S.Panesar	b Powell	4			
Extras	(B 5, LB 8, W 15, NB 23)	51	(B 4, NB 6)		10
Total		**400**	(3 wickets)		**111**

ENGLAND	O	M	R	W	O	M	R	W		FALL OF WICKETS			
										WI	E	WI	E
Sidebottom	29	10	88	5	15	4	40	0	Wkt	1st	1st	2nd	2nd
Hoggard	26	8	58	2	11	4	28	3	1st	0	37	7	16
Harmison	25	4	78	2	20	2	92	2	2nd	32	110	15	29
Panesar	13.1	2	34	1	16	2	46	5	3rd	34	119	38	105
Collingwood	4	1	12	0					4th	55	121	94	–
Pietersen					(5) 2	0	3	0	5th	141	133	162	
									6th	199	165	169	
WEST INDIES									7th	219	334	175	
Edwards	23	1	112	5	7	0	46	0	8th	220	369	188	
Powell	32	6	89	3	7	0	38	2	9th	229	369	194	
Collymore	29	5	116	2					10th	287	400	222	
Gayle	9	3	25	0	3.4	0	11	1					
Bravo	2	0	10	0									
Samuels	5	0	35	0	(3) 4	0	12	0					

Umpires: Alim Dar (*Pakistan*) (39) and B.F.Bowden (*New Zealand*) (41).
Referee: A.G.Hurst (*Australia*) (15).   **Test No. 1833/138 (E861/WI440)**

ENGLAND v WEST INDIES 2007

ENGLAND – BATTING AND FIELDING

	M	I	NO	HS	Runs	Avge	100	50	Ct/St
K.P.Pietersen	4	7	–	226	466	66.57	2	1	2
M.J.Prior	4	6	1	126*	324	64.80	1	2	8
M.P.Vaughan	3	5	1	103	251	62.75	1	–	1
P.D.Collingwood	4	7	1	128	359	59.83	2	–	8
A.N.Cook	4	7	–	106	398	56.85	2	2	7
R.J.Sidebottom	3	3	2	26*	49	49.00	–	–	2
I.R.Bell	4	6	1	109*	227	45.40	1	1	3
A.J.Strauss	4	7	–	77	168	24.00	–	1	5
L.E.Plunkett	3	4	1	44*	57	19.00	–	–	1
S.J.Harmison	4	4	1	18	54	18.00	–	–	–
M.S.Panesar	4	4	2	14*	21	10.50	–	–	1
M.J.Hoggard	2	1	–	0	0	0.00	–	–	–

Played in one Test: O.A.Shah 6, 4.

ENGLAND – BOWLING

	O	M	R	W	Avge	Best	5wI	10wM
M.S.Panesar	143.5	26	430	23	18.69	6-129	3	1
R.J.Sidebottom	110	31	315	16	19.68	5- 88	1	–
M.J.Hoggard	47.1	15	115	5	23.00	3- 28	–	–
S.J.Harmison	150.1	22	548	16	34.25	4- 95	–	–
L.E.Plunkett	89	13	315	7	45.00	3- 35	–	–

Also bowled: P.D.Collingwood 16.5-3-51-1; K.P.Pietersen 7-2-20-0.

WEST INDIES – BATTING AND FIELDING

	M	I	NO	HS	Runs	Avge	100	50	Ct/St
S.Chanderpaul	3	5	2	136*	446	148.66	2	3	–
D.J.Bravo	4	7	–	56	291	41.57	–	2	7
R.R.Sarwan	2	1	–	35	35	35.00	–	–	–
C.H.Gayle	4	8	1	52	220	31.42	–	1	3
D.S.Smith	4	7	–	42	149	21.28	–	–	4
R.S.Morton	4	7	–	54	146	20.85	–	1	6
D.Ramdin	4	7	–	60	127	18.14	–	1	11/1
D.Ganga	4	8	1	49	105	15.00	–	–	3
J.E.Taylor	3	5	1	23*	55	13.75	–	–	1
D.B.L.Powell	3	5	1	36*	49	12.25	–	–	–
C.D.Collymore	4	7	2	16*	37	7.40	–	–	–
F.H.Edwards	2	4	1	5	5	1.66	–	–	–

Played in one Test: S.C.Joseph 13, 1; D.J.G.Sammy 1, 25 (1 ct); M.N.Samuels 19, 2 (1 ct).

WEST INDIES – BOWLING

	O	M	R	W	Avge	Best	5wI	10wM
D.J.G.Sammy	38.3	9	98	8	12.25	7- 66	1	–
F.H.Edwards	62.1	3	306	9	34.00	5-112	1	–
C.D.Collymore	137	19	478	11	43.45	3- 58	–	–
C.H.Gayle	73.3	8	285	6	47.50	3- 66	–	–
D.B.L.Powell	118	20	437	9	48.55	3- 89	–	–
D.J.Bravo	107.3	19	412	6	68.66	2- 91	–	–
J.E.Taylor	80	9	360	4	90.00	2- 67	–	–

Also bowled: S.Chanderpaul 11-1-43-0; R.S.Morton 1-0-4-0; M.N.Samuels 9-0-47-0; R.R.Sarwan 6-0-33-0.

BANGLADESH v INDIA (1st Test)

At Bir Shrestha Shahid Ruhul Amin Stadium, Chittagong, on 18, 19, 20, 21, 22 May 2007.
Toss: India. Result: **MATCH DRAWN**.
Debuts: Bangladesh – Shakib Al Hasan; India – R.R.Powar.

INDIA

W.Jaffer	b Mortaza	0	c Bashar b Shahadat		0
K.D.Karthik	c Ashraful b Mortaza	56	c Nafees b Mortaza		22
*R.Dravid	c Masud b Shahadat	61	c Saleh b Shahadat		2
S.R.Tendulkar	c Ashraful b Shahadat	101	b Rafique		31
S.C.Ganguly	c Rafique b Mortaza	100	c Nafees b Rafique		13
†M.S.Dhoni	c Javed b Mortaza	36	not out		17
R.R.Powar	b Rafique	7	st Masud b Rafique		6
A.Kumble	retired hurt	1			
Z. Khan	c Masud b Shahadat	0	(8) not out		2
V.R.Singh	not out	1			
R.P.Singh					
Extras	(B 2, LB 8, W 2, NB 12)	24	(LB 1, W 2, NB 4)		7
Total	(8 wickets declared)	**387**	(6 wickets declared)		**100**

BANGLADESH

Javed Omar	lbw b R.P.Singh	7	not out		52
Shahriar Nafees	c Tendulkar b Khan	32	c Dhoni b R.P.Singh		1
*Habibul Bashar	c Tendulkar b R.P.Singh	0	c R.P.Singh b Powar		37
Rajin Saleh	c Ganguly b Powar	41	not out		7
Mohammad Ashraful	c Karthik b R.P.Singh	5			
Shakib Al Hasan	b V.R.Singh	27			
†Khaled Masud	lbw b V.R.Singh	2			
Mashrafe Mortaza	b V.R.Singh	79			
Mohammad Rafique	st Dhoni b Powar	9			
Shahadat Hossain	b Tendulkar	31			
Enamul Haque II	not out	0			
Extras	(LB 1, W 3, NB 1)	5	(LB 6, NB 1)		7
Total		**238**	(2 wickets)		**104**

BANGLADESH	O	M	R	W		O	M	R	W		FALL OF WICKETS			
Mashrafe Mortaza	24.5	5	97	4	(2)	8	1	36	1			I		B
Shahadat Hossain	18	1	76	2	(1)	7	3	30	2			I	B	I
Mohammad Rafique	24	3	99	1		8	0	27	3		*Wkt*	*1st*	*1st*	*2nd*	*2nd*
Enamul Haque II	15	0	59	0		1	0	6	0		1st	0	20	0	12
Shakib Al Hasan	13	2	29	0							2nd	124	20	6	82
Mohammad Ashraful	1	0	5	0							3rd	132	47	60	–
Rajin Saleh	3	1	12	0							4th	321	58	64	–
											5th	366	114	78	–
											6th	381	116	93	–
INDIA											7th	384	122	–	–
Khan	15	1	63	1		7	0	24	0		8th	387	149	–	–
R.P.Singh	17	2	45	3		6	0	29	1		9th	–	226	–	–
V.R.Singh	15.2	5	48	3		5	1	22	0		10th	–	238	–	–
Powar	17	1	66	2		7	2	16	1						
Tendulkar	4	0	15	1		3	0	7	0						

Umpires: B.R.Doctrove (*West Indies*) (12) and D.J.Harper (*Australia*) (64).
Referee: R.S.Mahanama (*Sri Lanka*) (14).
In the first innings, Kumble (1) retired hurt at 384-6.   **Test No. 1834/4 (B45/I404)**

BANGLADESH v INDIA (2nd Test)

At Shere Bangla National Stadium, Mirpur, on 25, 26, 27 May 2007.
Toss: Bangladesh. Result: **INDIA** won by an innings and 239 runs.
Debuts: India – I. Sharma.

INDIA

K.D.Karthik	c Bashar b Mortaza	129
W.Jaffer	retired hurt	138
*R.Dravid	c Javed b Rafique	129
S.R.Tendulkar	not out	122
S.C.Ganguly	c Saleh b Rafique	15
†M.S.Dhoni	not out	51
R.R.Powar		
Z.Khan		
A.Kumble		
R.P.Singh		
I.Sharma		
Extras	(B 7, LB 7, W 5, NB 7)	26
Total	(3 wickets declared)	**610**

BANGLADESH

Javed Omar	c Karthik b Khan	0	c Dhoni b Khan		0
Shahriar Nafees	b Khan	2	c Dhoni b Singh		4
*Habibul Bashar	c Dhoni b Singh	4	c Dravid b Khan		5
Rajin Saleh	c Jaffer b Kumble	20	c Ganguly b Powar		42
Mohammad Ashraful	lbw b Khan	0	c Tendulkar b Kumble		67
Shakib Al Hasan	lbw b Khan	30	c Dravid b Powar		15
Mohammad Sharif	lbw b Kumble	13	(9) c and b Kumble		17
†Khaled Masud	c Dhoni b Kumble	25	(7) c Tendulkar b Powar		8
Mashrafe Mortaza	c Kumble b Sharma	2	(8) c Dhoni b Tendulkar		70
Mohammad Rafique	b Khan	12	lbw b Tendulkar		11
Syed Rasel	not out	2	not out		1
Extras	(LB 2, NB 6)	8	(LB 1, W 3, NB 9)		13
Total		**118**			**253**

BANGLADESH	O	M	R	W	O	M	R	W
Mashrafe Mortaza	31.4	4	100	1				
Syed Rasel	23.4	0	109	0				
Mohammad Sharif	25.4	2	109	0				
Mohammad Rafique	45	4	181	2				
Shakib Al Hasan	19	1	62	0				
Mohammad Ashraful	8	0	35	0				
INDIA								
Khan	10	1	34	5	8	1	54	2
Singh	9	2	28	1	6	1	28	1
Kumble	9.2	3	32	3	(4) 15	1	72	2
Sharma	7	1	19	1	(3) 6	1	30	0
Powar	2	1	3	0	16	4	33	3
Tendulkar					6.3	1	35	2

FALL OF WICKETS			
	I	B	B
Wkt	1st	1st	2nd
1st	408	0	0
2nd	493	5	10
3rd	525	7	10
4th	–	7	91
5th	–	40	135
6th	–	58	150
7th	–	85	154
8th	–	93	208
9th	–	110	223
10th	–	118	253

Umpires: B.R.Doctrove (*West Indies*) (13) and D.J.Harper (*Australia*) (65).
Referee: R.S.Mahanama (*Sri Lanka*) (15).
Karthik (82) retired hurt at 175 and resumed at 408; Jaffer (138) retired hurt at 281.

Test No. 1835/5 (B46/I405)

SRI LANKA v BANGLADESH (1st Test)

At Sinhalese Sports Club, Colombo, on 25, 26, 27, 28 June 2007.
Toss: Sri Lanka. Result: **SRI LANKA** won by an innings and 234 runs.
Debuts: Sri Lanka – B.S.M.Warnapura.

BANGLADESH

Javed Omar	c HAPW Jayawardena b Vaas	8	lbw b Malinga		62
Shahriar Nafees	c HAPW Jayawardena b Malinga	15	c and b Muralitharan		38
Rajin Saleh	lbw b Muralitharan	3	c DPMD Jayawardena b Dilshan		51
Habibul Bashar	lbw b Fernando	2	c HAPW Jayawardena b Vaas		17
*Mohammad Ashraful	c Warnapura b Fernando	7	c Vaas b Muralitharan		37
Shakib Al Hasan	lbw b Muralitharan	16	c Warnapura b Malinga		8
†Khaled Masud	not out	12	b Malinga		1
Shahadat Hossain	c Muralitharan b Fernando	1	(10) st HAPW Jayawardena b Muralitharan		1
Mashrafe Mortaza	st HAPW Jayawardena b Muralitharan	1	(8) lbw b Muralitharan		9
Mohammad Rafique	lbw b Muralitharan	11	(9) b Malinga		0
Abdur Razzak	st HAPW Jayawardena b Muralitharan	4	not out		0
Extras	(LB 2, NB 7)	9	(B 2, LB 10, W 1, NB 17)		30
Total		**89**			**254**

SRI LANKA

M.G.Vandort	c Nafees b Rafique	117
B.S.M.Warnapura	lbw b Shahadat	0
K.C.Sangakkara	c Masud b Shahadat	6
*D.P.M.D.Jayawardena	c Shakib b Mortaza	127
L.P.C.Silva	c Mortaza b Razzak	1
T.M.Dilshan	run out	79
†H.A.P.W.Jayawardena	not out	120
W.P.U.C.J.Vaas	not out	100
S.L.Malinga		
M.Muralitharan		
C.R.D.Fernando		
Extras	(B 6, LB 7, W 2, NB 12)	27
Total	(6 wickets declared)	**577**

SRI LANKA	O	M	R	W	O	M	R	W
Vaas	7	3	8	1	12	3	36	1
Malinga	7	0	31	1	17	2	80	4
Fernando	11	2	33	3	(4) 15	5	28	0
Muralitharan	7.3	3	15	5	(3) 36.1	12	87	4
Dilshan					7	3	11	1

BANGLADESH	O	M	R	W
Mashrafe Mortaza	19	2	72	1
Shahadat Hossain	18	0	102	2
Abdur Razzak	30	2	109	1
Mohammad Rafique	28.5	1	138	1
Shakib Al Hasan	16	0	57	0
Mohammad Ashraful	13	0	52	0
Rajin Saleh	3	0	12	0
Habibul Bashar	8	0	22	0

FALL OF WICKETS

	B	SL	B
Wkt	1st	1st	2nd
1st	28	1	86
2nd	28	14	126
3rd	32	187	160
4th	43	304	227
5th	50	321	231
6th	61	354	238
7th	64	–	250
8th	69	–	252
9th	85	–	253
10th	89	–	254

Umpires: Asad Rauf (*Pakistan*) (12) and S.L.Shastri (*India*) (1).
Referee: J.J.Crowe (*New Zealand*) (19).
D.P.M.D. Jayawardena (93) retired at 184 and resumed at 304.

Test No. 1836/8 (SL168/B47)

SRI LANKA v BANGLADESH (2nd Test)

At P.Saravanamuttu Stadium, Colombo, on 3, 4, 5 July 2007.
Toss: Sri Lanka. Result: **SRI LANKA** won by an innings and 90 runs.
Debuts: Bangladesh – Mehrab Hossain II.

BANGLADESH

Javed Omar	c HAPW Jayawardena b Malinga	8		lbw b Vaas	28
Shahriar Nafees	lbw b Malinga	0		c HAPW Jayawardena b Vaas	20
Rajin Saleh	c DPMD Jayawardena b Muralitharan	21		c DPMD Jayawardena b Fernando	0
Habibul Bashar	c DPMD Jayawardena b Malinga	5	(5)	b Fernando	12
*Mohammad Ashraful	c Warnapura b Malinga	0	(6)	not out	129
Mehrab Hossain II	b Fernando	6	(4)	b Fernando	8
†Mushfiqur Rahim	c HAPW Jayawardena b Muralitharan	9		c and b Muralitharan	80
Mashrafe Mortaza	c DPMD Jayawardena b Fernando	0	(9)	lbw b Vaas	0
Mohammad Rafique	c Vaas b Muralitharan	2	(10)	run out	3
Mohammad Sharif	not out	4	(8)	lbw b Vaas	2
Shahadat Hossain	b Muralitharan	1		run out	2
Extras	(LB 1, W 1, NB 4)	6		(B 2, LB 2, W 2, NB 9)	15
Total		**62**			**299**

SRI LANKA

M.G.Vandort	b Mortaza	14
B.S.M.Warnapura	c Nafees b Shahadat	82
K.C.Sangakkara	not out	200
*D.P.M.D.Jayawardena	c Nafees b Shahadat	49
L.P.C.Silva	c Mortaza b Mehrab	33
T.M.Dilshan	b Mehrab	0
†H.A.P.W.Jayawardena	c Javed b Mortaza	14
W.P.U.C.J.Vaas	not out	30
S.L.Malinga		
M.Muralitharan		
C.R.D.Fernando		
Extras	(B 6, LB 7, W 3, NB 13)	29
Total	(6 wickets declared)	**451**

SRI LANKA	O	M	R	W	O	M	R	W	FALL OF WICKETS		
										B	SL	B
Vaas	5	1	6	0	20.2	8	55	4	Wkt	1st	1st	2nd
Malinga	9	1	25	4	15	1	86	0	1st	3	41	48
Fernando	6	1	16	2	17	2	60	3	2nd	14	169	51
Muralitharan	5.2	1	14	4	28	6	84	1	3rd	22	267	55
Dilshan					6	1	10	0	4th	22	359	59
									5th	33	359	78
BANGLADESH									6th	45	395	269
Mashrafe Mortaza	30	7	77	2					7th	48	–	276
Shahadat Hossain	21	3	81	2					8th	51	–	276
Mohammad Sharif	24	4	86	0					9th	59	–	286
Mohammad Rafique	35	3	134	0					10th	62	–	299
Mohammad Ashraful	7	0	31	0								
Mehrab Hossain	7.5	0	29	2								

Umpires: Asad Rauf (*Pakistan*) (13) and R.E.Koertzen (*South Africa*) (82).
Referee: J.J.Crowe (*New Zealand*) (20).   **Test No. 1837/9 (SL169/B48)**

SRI LANKA v BANGLADESH (3rd Test)

At Asgiriya Stadium, Kandy, on 11, 12, 13, 14 July 2007.
Toss: Sri Lanka. Result: **SRI LANKA** won by an innings and 193 runs.
Debuts: None.

BANGLADESH

Javed Omar	lbw b Malinga	8		c Sangakkara b Malinga	22
Shahriar Nafees	c De Silva b Muralitharan	29		c DPMD Jayawardena b Muralitharan	64
Habibul Bashar	c HAPW Jayawardena b Maharoof	18		b Muralitharan	15
Rajin Saleh	c DPMD Jayawardena b Muralitharan	0	(7)	c DPMD Jayawardena b De Silva	0
*Mohammad Ashraful	c HAPW Jayawardena b De Silva	26	(4)	lbw b Muralitharan	19
Tushar Imran	c DPMD Jayawardena b De Silva	17		c DPMD Jayawardena b Malinga	17
†Mushfiqur Rahim	not out	11	(5)	c Tharanga b De Silva	1
Mashrafe Mortaza	c and b Muralitharan	5		c sub (BSM Warnapura) b Muralitharan	8
Mohammad Rafique	c and b Muralitharan	5		not out	0
Shahadat Hossain	c Dilshan b Muralitharan	0		b Muralitharan	5
Syed Rasel	c Silva b Muralitharan	0		c Maharoof b Muralitharan	4
Extras	(B 4, LB 2, W 1, NB 5)	12		(B 4, LB 1, W 3, NB 13)	21
Total		**131**			**176**

SRI LANKA

M.G.Vandort	b Rasel	43
W.U.Tharanga	lbw b Rasel	12
K.C.Sangakkara	not out	222
*D.P.M.D.Jayawardena	c Ashraful b Rasel	165
L.P.C.Silva	run out	25
T.M.Dilshan	not out	17
†H.A.P.W.Jayawardena		
S.L.Malinga		
W.R.S. de Silva		
M.Muralitharan		
M.F.Maharoof		
Extras	(B 4, LB 2, W 2, NB 8)	16
Total	(4 wickets declared)	**500**

SRI LANKA	O	M	R	W	O	M	R	W
Malinga	10	2	41	1	10	0	46	2
De Silva	12	3	29	2	12	4	34	2
Maharoof	8	4	21	1	16	7	37	0
Muralitharan	14.5	6	28	6	21	5	54	6
Dilshan	4	1	6	0				

BANGLADESH	O	M	R	W
Mashrafe Mortaza	24	2	125	0
Syed Rasel	31	1	104	3
Shahadat Hossain	16	1	71	0
Mohammad Rafique	14	1	72	0
Mohammad Ashraful	12	0	74	0
Tushar Imran	10	0	48	0

FALL OF WICKETS

	B	SL	B
Wkt	1st	1st	2nd
1st	10	47	47
2nd	50	74	98
3rd	61	385	123
4th	64	445	138
5th	98	–	138
6th	111	–	142
7th	118	–	166
8th	130	–	167
9th	131	–	172
10th	131	–	176

Umpires: R.E.Koertzen (*South Africa*) (83) and S.L.Shastri (*India*) (2).
Referee: J.J.Crowe (*New Zealand*) (21).   **Test No. 1838/10 (SL170/B49)**

SRI LANKA v BANGLADESH 2007

SRI LANKA – BATTING AND FIELDING

	M	I	NO	HS	Runs	Avge	100	50	Ct/St
K.C.Sangakkara	3	3	2	222*	428	428.00	2	–	1
H.A.P.W.Jayawardena	3	2	1	120*	134	134.00	1	–	8/3
W.P.U.C.J.Vaas	2	2	2	100*	130	–	1	–	2
D.P.M.D.Jayawardena	3	3	–	165	341	113.66	2	–	10
M.G.Vandort	3	3	–	117	174	58.00	1	–	–
T.M.Dilshan	3	3	1	79	96	48.00	–	1	1
B.S.M.Warnapura	2	2	–	82	82	41.00	–	1	3
L.P.C.Silva	3	3	–	33	59	19.66	–	–	1

Played in one Test: W.U.Tharanga 12 (1 ct). Did not bat: W.R.S. de Silva (1 match – 1 ct); C.R.D.Fernando (2); M.F.Maharoof (1 – 1 ct); S.L.Malinga (3); M.Muralitharan (3 – 5ct).

SRI LANKA – BOWLING

	O	M	R	W	Avge	Best	5wI	10wM
M Muralitharan	112.5	33	282	26	10.84	6-28	3	1
W.R.S. de Silva	24	7	63	4	15.75	2-29	–	–
C.R.D.Fernando	49	10	137	8	17.12	3-33	–	–
W.P.U.C.J.Vaas	44.2	15	105	6	17.50	4-55	–	–
S.L.Malinga	68	6	309	12	25.75	4-25	–	–

Also bowled: T.M.Dilshan 17-5-27-1; M.F.Maharoof 24-11-58-1.

BANGLADESH – BATTING AND FIELDING

	M	I	NO	HS	Runs	Avge	100	50	Ct/St
Mohammad Ashraful	3	6	1	129*	218	43.60	1	–	1
Mushfiqur Rahim	2	4	1	80	101	33.66	–	1	–
Shahriar Nafees	3	6	–	64	166	27.66	–	1	3
Javed Omar	3	6	–	62	136	22.66	–	1	1
Rajin Saleh	3	6	–	51	75	12.50	–	1	–
Habibul Bashar	3	6	–	18	69	11.50	–	–	–
Mohammad Rafique	3	6	1	11	21	4.20	–	–	–
Mashrafe Mortaza	3	6	–	9	23	3.83	–	–	2
Shahadat Hossain	3	6	–	5	10	1.66	–	–	–

Played in one Test: Abdur Razzak 4, 0*; Khaled Masud 12*, 1 (1 ct); Mehrab Hossain II 6, 8; Mohammad Sharif 4*, 2; Shakib Al Hasan 16, 8 (1 ct); Syed Rasel 0, 4; Tushar Imran 17, 17.

BANGLADESH – BOWLING

	O	M	R	W	Avge	Best	5wI	10wM
Mehrab Hossain II	7.5	0	29	2	14.50	2- 29	–	–
Syed Rasel	31	1	104	3	34.66	3-104	–	–
Shahadat Hossain	55	4	254	4	63.50	2- 81	–	–
Mashrafe Mortaza	73	11	274	3	91.33	2- 77	–	–

Also bowled: Abdur Razzak 30-2-109-1; Habibul Bashar 8-0-22-0; Mohammad Ashraful 32-0-157-0; Mohammad Rafique 77.5-5-344-1; Mohammad Sharif 24-4-86-0; Rajin Saleh 3-0-12-0; Shakib Al Hasan 16-0-57-0; Tushar Imran 10-0-48-0.

ENGLAND v INDIA (1st Test)

At Lord's, London, on 19, 20, 21, 22, 23 July 2007
Toss: England. Result: **MATCH DRAWN**.
Debuts: England – C.T.Tremlett.

ENGLAND

A.J.Strauss	c Dravid b Kumble	96		c Tendulkar b Khan	18
A.N.Cook	lbw b Ganguly	36		lbw b Khan	17
*M.P.Vaughan	c Dhoni b Singh	79		b Singh	30
K.P.Pietersen	c Dhoni b Khan	37		b Singh	134
P.D.Collingwood	lbw b Kumble	0		c Laxman b Singh	4
R.J.Sidebottom	b Singh	1	(9)	c Dravid b Kumble	9
I.R.Bell	b Khan	20	(6)	b Singh	9
†M.J.Prior	lbw b Sreesanth	1	(7)	c Dhoni b Khan	42
C.T.Tremlett	lbw b Sreesanth	0	(8)	b Khan	0
M.S.Panesar	lbw b Sreesanth	0		lbw b Singh	3
J.M.Anderson	not out	0		not out	4
Extras	(B 9, LB 10, W 7, NB 2)	28		(B 9, LB 1, W 2)	12
Total		**298**			**282**

INDIA

K.D.Karthik	lbw b Sidebottom	5	(2)	c Collingwood b Anderson	60
W.Jaffer	c and b Tremlett	58	(1)	c Pietersen b Anderson	8
*R.Dravid	c Prior b Anderson	2		lbw b Tremlett	9
S.R.Tendulkar	lbw b Anderson	37		lbw b Panesar	16
S.C.Ganguly	b Anderson	34		lbw b Sidebottom	40
R.P.Singh	c Anderson b Sidebottom	17	(10)	b Panesar	2
V.V.S.Laxman	c Prior b Sidebottom	15		b Tremlett	39
†M.S.Dhoni	c Bell b Anderson	0	(7)	not out	76
A.Kumble	lbw b Sidebottom	11	(8)	lbw b Sidebottom	3
Z.Khan	c Strauss b Anderson	7	(9)	c Prior b Tremlett	0
S.Sreesanth	not out	0		not out	4
Extras	(B 4, LB 7, NB 4)	15		(B 13, LB 5, W 6, NB 1)	25
Total		**201**		**(9 wickets)**	**282**

INDIA	O	M	R	W	O	M	R	W		FALL OF WICKETS			
Khan	18.2	4	62	2	28	6	79	4			E	I	E	I
Sreesanth	22	8	67	3	16	3	62	0		Wkt	1st	1st	2nd	2nd
Singh	17	6	58	2	16.3	2	59	5		1st	76	18	40	38
Ganguly	9	3	24	1						2nd	218	27	43	55
Kumble	23	2	60	2	(4) 17	3	70	1		3rd	252	106	102	84
Tendulkar	2	0	8	0	(5) 1	0	2	0		4th	255	134	114	143
										5th	272	155	132	145
ENGLAND										6th	286	173	251	231
Sidebottom	22	5	65	4	19	4	42	2		7th	287	175	251	247
Anderson	24.2	8	42	5	25	4	83	2		8th	287	192	266	254
Tremlett	20	8	52	1	21	5	52	3		9th	297	197	275	263
Collingwood	3	1	9	0	(5) 1	0	4	0		10th	298	201	282	–
Panesar	8	3	22	0	(4) 26	7	63	2						
Vaughan					4	0	18	0						

Umpires: S.A.Bucknor (*West Indies*) (118) and S.J.A.Taufel (*Australia*) (41).
Referee: R.S.Madugalle (*Sri Lanka*) (94).   Test No. 1839/95 (E862/I406)

ENGLAND v INDIA (2nd Test)

At Trent Bridge, Nottingham, on 27, 28, 29, 30, 31 July 2007.
Toss: India. Result: **INDIA** won by seven wickets.
Debuts: None.

ENGLAND

A.J.Strauss	c Tendulkar b Khan	4	c Dhoni b Khan		55
A.N.Cook	lbw b Ganguly	43	lbw b Khan		23
*M.P.Vaughan	c Tendulkar b Khan	9	b Khan		124
K.P.Pietersen	lbw b Singh	13	lbw b Singh		19
P.D.Collingwood	b Sreesanth	28	c Karthik b Khan		63
I.R.Bell	lbw b Khan	31	lbw b Khan		0
†M.J.Prior	c Dravid b Kumble	11	b Singh		7
C.T.Tremlett	b Kumble	20	c Singh b Kumble		5
R.J.Sidebottom	not out	18	not out		25
M.S.Panesar	c Laxman b Khan	1	c Karthik b Kumble		4
J.M.Anderson	b Kumble	1	b Kumble		1
Extras	(B 8, LB 7, W 1, NB 3)	19	(B 7, LB 6, W 9, NB 7)		29
Total		**198**			**355**

INDIA

K.D.Karthik	c Cook b Panesar	77	c Prior b Tremlett		22
W.Jaffer	c Prior b Tremlett	62	c Pietersen b Tremlett		22
*R.Dravid	c Bell b Panesar	37	not out		11
S.R.Tendulkar	lbw b Collingwood	91	c Cook b Tremlett		1
S.C.Ganguly	c Prior b Anderson	79	not out		2
V.V.S.Laxman	c Prior b Tremlett	54			
†M.S.Dhoni	c Prior b Sidebottom	5			
A.Kumble	c Prior b Tremlett	30			
Z. Khan	not out	10			
R.P.Singh	lbw b Panesar	0			
S.Sreesanth	lbw b Panesar	2			
Extras	(B 16, LB 16, W 1, NB 1)	34	(B 4, LB 6, W 2, NB 3)		15
Total		**481**	(3 wickets)		**73**

INDIA	O	M	R	W		O	M	R	W	FALL OF WICKETS				
Khan	21	5	59	4		27	10	75	5		E	I	E	I
Sreesanth	12	7	16	1		21	2	60	0	Wkt	1st	1st	2nd	2nd
Singh	10	1	56	1		18	5	52	2	1st	4	147	49	47
Ganguly	8	4	11	1	(5)	6	0	22	0	2nd	24	149	130	55
Kumble	12.3	2	32	3	(4)	25	4	104	3	3rd	47	246	175	62
Tendulkar	2	0	9	0		7	4	29	0	4th	101	342	287	–
										5th	109	409	287	–
ENGLAND										6th	147	414	304	–
Sidebottom	36	11	75	1	(2)	8	0	28	0	7th	157	464	323	–
Anderson	33	4	134	1	(1)	9	2	23	0	8th	186	473	329	–
Tremlett	40	13	80	3		7.1	2	12	3	9th	195	474	333	–
Collingwood	16	3	59	1						10th	198	481	355	–
Panesar	33.5	8	101	4										

Umpires: I.L.Howell (*South Africa*) (8) and S.J.A.Taufel (*Australia*) (42).
Referee: R.S.Madugalle (*Sri Lanka*) (95).　　　　**Test No. 1840/96 (E863/I407)**

ENGLAND v INDIA (3rd Test)

At Kennington Oval, London, on 9, 10, 11, 12, 13 August 2007.
Toss: India. Result: **MATCH DRAWN**.
Debuts: None.

INDIA

K.D.Karthik	c Prior b Sidebottom	91	c Collingwood b Tremlett		8
W.Jaffer	c Pietersen b Anderson	35	lbw b Anderson		0
*R.Dravid	b Anderson	55	c Strauss b Collingwood		12
S.R.Tendulkar	c Strauss b Anderson	82	b Anderson		1
S.C.Ganguly	lbw b Collingwood	37	c Strauss b Collingwood		57
V.V.S.Laxman	c Prior b Tremlett	51	not out		46
†M.S.Dhoni	c Cook b Pietersen	92	c Prior b Tremlett		36
A.Kumble	not out	110	not out		8
Z.Khan	c Anderson b Panesar	11			
R.P.Singh	c and b Anderson	11			
S.Sreesanth	c Vaughan b Panesar	35			
Extras	(B 33, LB 13, W 2, NB 6)	54	(B 1, LB 5, NB 6)		12
Total		**664**	(6 wickets declared)		**180**

ENGLAND

A.J.Strauss	c Sreesanth b Khan	6	c Laxman b Singh		32
A.N.Cook	c Singh b Kumble	61	c Laxman b Kumble		43
J.M.Anderson	lbw b Singh	16			
*M.P.Vaughan	c and b Kumble	11	(3) c Dhoni b Sreesanth		42
K.P.Pietersen	c Dravid b Tendulkar	41	(4) c Karthik b Sreesanth		101
P.D.Collingwood	lbw b Sreesanth	62	(5) b Sreesanth		40
I.R.Bell	c Dhoni b Khan	63	(6) lbw b Kumble		67
†M.J.Prior	c Tendulkar b Sreesanth	0	(7) not out		12
R.J.Sidebottom	c and b Khan	2	(8) not out		3
C.T.Tremlett	not out	25			
M.S.Panesar	lbw b Kumble	9			
Extras	(B 16, LB 12, W 10, NB 11)	49	(B 2, LB 4, W 9, NB 14)		29
Total		**345**	(6 wickets)		**369**

ENGLAND	O	M	R	W		O	M	R	W
Sidebottom	32	8	93	1					
Anderson	40	5	182	4	(1)	15	8	34	2
Tremlett	40	6	132	1	(2)	15	2	58	2
Panesar	45	5	159	2		18	1	58	0
Collingwood	7	1	11	1	(3)	10	1	24	2
Pietersen	6	0	41	1					
INDIA									
Khan	22	13	32	3		20	3	59	0
Sreesanth	21	2	80	2		21	7	53	3
Kumble	29.1	9	94	3		37	9	123	2
Singh	18	3	72	1		13	2	50	1
Ganguly	5	1	8	0					
Tendulkar	7	0	26	1	(5)	19	0	78	0
Laxman	1	0	5	0					

FALL OF WICKETS				
	I	E	I	E
Wkt	1st	1st	2nd	2nd
1st	62	12	10	79
2nd	189	78	10	86
3rd	199	119	11	152
4th	276	124	76	266
5th	354	202	89	289
6th	417	288	158	363
7th	508	303	–	–
8th	570	305	–	–
9th	591	305	–	–
10th	664	345	–	–

Umpires: S.A.Bucknor (*West Indies*) (119) and I.L.Howell (*South Africa*) (9).
Referee: R.S.Madugalle (*Sri Lanka*) (96).   Test No. 1841/97 (**E864/I408**)

ENGLAND v INDIA 2007

ENGLAND – BATTING AND FIELDING

	M	I	NO	HS	Runs	Avge	100	50	Ct/St
K.P.Pietersen	3	6	–	134	345	57.50	2	–	3
M.P.Vaughan	3	6	–	124	295	49.16	1	1	1
A.N.Cook	3	6	–	61	223	37.16	–	1	3
A.J.Strauss	3	6	–	96	211	35.16	–	2	4
P.D.Collingwood	3	6	–	63	197	32.83	–	2	2
I.R.Bell	3	6	–	67	190	31.66	–	2	2
R.J.Sidebottom	3	6	3	25*	58	19.33	–	–	–
M.J.Prior	3	6	1	42	73	14.60	–	–	12
C.T.Tremlett	3	5	1	25*	50	12.50	–	–	1
J.M.Anderson	3	5	2	16	22	7.33	–	–	3
M.S.Panesar	3	5	–	9	17	3.40	–	–	–

ENGLAND – BOWLING

	O	M	R	W	Avge	Best	5wI	10wM
P.D.Collingwood	37	6	109	4	27.25	2- 24	–	–
C.T.Tremlett	143.1	36	386	13	29.69	3- 12	–	–
J.M.Anderson	146.2	31	498	14	35.57	5- 42	1	–
R.J.Sidebottom	117	28	303	8	37.87	4- 65	–	–
M.S.Panesar	130.5	24	403	8	50.37	4-101	–	–

Also bowled: K.P.Pietersen 6-0-41-1; M.P.Vaughan 4-0-18-0.

INDIA – BATTING AND FIELDING

	M	I	NO	HS	Runs	Avge	100	50	Ct/St
A.Kumble	3	5	2	110*	162	54.00	1	–	1
M.S.Dhoni	3	5	1	92	209	52.25	–	2	6
V.V.S.Laxman	3	5	1	54	205	51.25	–	2	4
S.C.Ganguly	3	6	1	79	249	49.80	–	2	–
K.D.Karthik	3	6	–	91	263	43.83	–	3	3
S.R.Tendulkar	3	6	–	91	228	38.00	–	2	4
W.Jaffer	3	6	–	62	185	30.83	–	2	–
R.Dravid	3	6	1	55	126	25.20	–	1	4
S.Sreesanth	3	4	2	35	41	20.50	–	–	1
Z.Khan	3	4	1	11	28	9.33	–	–	1
R.P.Singh	3	4	–	17	30	7.50	–	–	2

INDIA – BOWLING

	O	M	R	W	Avge	Best	5wI	10wM
Z.Khan	136.2	41	366	18	20.33	5-75	1	–
R.P.Singh	92.5	20	347	12	28.91	5-59	1	–
S.C.Ganguly	28	8	65	2	32.50	1-11	–	–
A.Kumble	143.4	25	483	14	34.50	3-32	–	–
S.Sreesanth	113	29	338	9	37.55	3-53	–	–

Also bowled: V.V.S.Laxman 1-0-5-0; S.R.Tendulkar 38-0-152-1.

SOUTH AFRICA v PAKISTAN (1st Test)

At National Stadium, Karachi, on 1, 2, 3, 4, 5 October 2007.
Toss: South Africa. Result: **SOUTH AFRICA** won by 160 runs.
Debuts: Pakistan – Abdur Rehman.

SOUTH AFRICA

H.H.Gibbs	c Hafeez b Gul	54	(2)	c Faisal b Kaneria	18
*G.C.Smith	lbw b Hafeez	42	(1)	c Akmal b Rehman	25
H.M.Amla	b Asif	71		st Akmal b Rehman	0
J.H.Kallis	c Akmal b Kaneria	155		not out	100
A.G.Prince	c and b Kaneria	36		b Kaneria	45
A.B. de Villiers	b Gul	77		b Rehman	1
†M.V.Boucher	c Akmal b Rehman	1		c Misbah b Kaneria	29
A.Nel	c Misbah b Rehman	2		c Misbah b Rehman	33
P.L.Harris	c Akmal b Rehman	1		not out	1
D.W.Steyn	b Rehman	0			
M.Ntini	not out	0			
Extras	(B 1, LB 6, NB 4)	11		(B 10, LB 2)	12
Total		**450**		(7 wickets declared)	**264**

PAKISTAN

Mohammad Hafeez	c Kallis b Harris	34		b Steyn	1
†Kamran Akmal	lbw b Harris	42	(8)	c Boucher b Harris	9
Younus Khan	b Nel	6		b Steyn	126
Faisal Iqbal	b Kallis	7		c Kallis b Harris	44
Misbah-ul-Haq	c Boucher b Steyn	23	(6)	lbw b Nel	23
*Shoaib Malik	st Boucher b Harris	73	(7)	c Nel b Ntini	30
Abdur Rehman	c Boucher b Nel	9	(9)	lbw b Steyn	0
Salman Butt	lbw b Harris	24	(2)	c Amla b Steyn	3
Umar Gul	st Boucher b Harris	12	(10)	c Nel b Steyn	8
Danish Kaneria	not out	26	(11)	not out	0
Mohammad Asif	b Steyn	10	(5)	c Amla b Nel	6
Extras	(B 15, LB 7, W 1, NB 2)	25		(B 8, LB 4, NB 1)	13
Total		**291**			**263**

PAKISTAN	O	M	R	W		O	M	R	W
Mohammad Asif	26	6	83	1		6	1	14	0
Umar Gul	21.3	6	60	2		12	1	35	0
Danish Kaneria	36	3	124	2	(4)	28	3	85	3
Abdur Rehman	31	3	105	4	(3)	38	6	105	4
Shoaib Malik	8	2	31	0					
Mohammad Hafeez	14	0	40	1	(5)	9	0	13	0

SOUTH AFRICA	O	M	R	W		O	M	R	W
Steyn	13.3	2	50	2	(2)	15	3	56	5
Ntini	11	2	48	0	(1)	12.5	4	34	1
Harris	36	13	73	5	(4)	30	8	58	2
Nel	20	4	59	2	(3)	19	5	59	2
Kallis	11	3	21	1	(6)	4	3	4	0
Smith	6	1	18	0	(5)	3	0	33	0
Amla					(7)	1	0	7	0

FALL OF WICKETS

	SA	P	SA	P
Wkt	1st	1st	2nd	2nd
1st	87	71	41	1
2nd	109	82	43	20
3rd	279	84	43	134
4th	352	97	131	161
5th	373	120	132	197
6th	392	149	188	230
7th	408	233	251	239
8th	412	238	–	249
9th	448	259	–	257
10th	450	291	–	263

Umpires: M.R.Benson (*England*) (16) and S.J.A.Taufel (*Australia*) (43).
Referee: A.G.Hurst (*Australia*) (16).   **Test No. 1842/15 (SA321/P331)**

SOUTH AFRICA v PAKISTAN (2nd Test)

At Gaddafi Stadium, Lahore, on 8, 9, 10, 11, 12 October 2007.
Toss: South Africa. Result: **MATCH DRAWN**.
Debuts: None.

SOUTH AFRICA

H.H.Gibbs	c Misbah b Gul	13	(2) c Akmal b Gul		16
*G.C.Smith	b Kaneria	46	(1) c sub (Yasir Hamid) b Kaneria		133
H.M.Amla	b Asif	10	b Rehman		17
J.H.Kallis	lbw b Kaneria	59	not out		107
A.G.Prince	b Rehman	63	b Rehman		11
A.B. de Villiers	run out	45	not out		8
†M.V.Boucher	c Rehman b Kaneria	54			
A.Nel	c Misbah b Gul	0			
P.L.Harris	c Malik b Gul	46			
D.W.Steyn	b Kaneria	0			
M.Ntini	not out	0			
Extras	(LB 2, W 7, NB 7, Pen 5)	21	(B 12, NB 1)		13
Total		**357**	(4 wickets declared)		**305**

PAKISTAN

Salman Butt	c Smith b Harris	40	c sub (S.M.Pollock) b Ntini		6
†Kamran Akmal	c Smith b Harris	52	b Harris		71
Younus Khan	b Nel	3	c Boucher b Kallis		130
Mohd Yousuf Youhana	lbw b Steyn	25	not out		63
Inzamam-ul-Haq	c Boucher b Kallis	14	st Boucher b Harris		3
Misbah-ul-Haq	c Boucher b Ntini	41			
*Shoaib Malik	c Amla b Steyn	1	(6) not out		20
Abdur Rehman	not out	25			
Umar Gul	lbw b Ntini	0			
Danish Kaneria	c Boucher b Ntini	0			
Mohammad Asif	c Amla b Harris	4			
Extras	(LB 1)	1	(B 3, LB 14, W 5, NB 1)		23
Total		**206**	(4 wickets)		**316**

PAKISTAN	O	M	R	W	O	M	R	W
Mohammad Asif	34	9	83	1	4	1	14	0
Umar Gul	29	4	103	3	16	3	48	1
Danish Kaneria	43.1	5	114	4	44.3	11	99	1
Abdur Rehman	14	5	30	1	42	7	112	2
Shoaib Malik	5	0	20	0				
Younus Khan					(5) 4	0	20	0

SOUTH AFRICA	O	M	R	W	O	M	R	W
Ntini	8	1	42	3	(2) 17	3	60	1
Steyn	12	3	60	2	(1) 15	2	56	0
Nel	16	3	39	1	(4) 20	1	75	0
Harris	20	5	57	3	(5) 40	14	60	2
Kallis	7	3	7	1	(3) 15	0	48	1

FALL OF WICKETS				
	SA	P	SA	P
Wkt	1st	1st	2nd	2nd
1st	24	90	34	15
2nd	47	93	66	176
3rd	100	99	273	265
4th	160	123	290	272
5th	243	149	–	–
6th	259	150	–	–
7th	259	189	–	–
8th	347	189	–	–
9th	350	189	–	–
10th	357	206	–	–

Umpires: M.R.Benson (*England*) (17) and S.J.A.Taufel (*Australia*) (44).
Referee: A.G.Hurst (*Australia*) (17). **Test No. 1843/16 (SA322/P332)**

AUSTRALIA v SRI LANKA (1st Test)

At Wooloongabba, Brisbane, on 8, 9, 10, 11, 12 November 2007.
Toss: Sri Lanka. Result: **AUSTRALIA** won by an innings and 40 runs.
Debuts: Australia – M.G.Johnson.

AUSTRALIA

P.A.Jaques	st HAPW Jayawardena b Muralitharan	100
M.L.Hayden	c Muralitharan b Vaas	43
*R.T.Ponting	st HAPW Jayawardena b Muralitharan	56
M.E.K.Hussey	c Atapattu b Fernando	133
M.J.Clarke	not out	145
A.Symonds	not out	53
†A.C.Gilchrist		
B.Lee		
M.G.Johnson		
S.R.Clark		
S.C.G.MacGill		
Extras	(B 4, LB 12, W 1, NB 4)	21
Total	**(4 wickets declared)**	**551**

SRI LANKA

M.S.Atapattu	c Jaques b Johnson	51	c Gilchrist b Symonds	16
S.T.Jayasuriya	c Gilchrist b Lee	7	c Ponting b Lee	39
M.G.Vandort	c Gilchrist b Lee	0	b MacGill	82
*D.P.M.D.Jayawardena	c Gilchrist b Clark	14	c Gilchrist b Johnson	49
T.T.Samaraweera	c Gilchrist b Johnson	13	c Hussey b Johnson	20
L.P.C.Silva	c Clarke b Clark	40	c Hussey b Lee	43
†H.A.P.W.Jayawardena	lbw b Lee	37	lbw b Clark	1
M.F.Maharoof	b Symonds	21	b Lee	18
W.P.U.C.J.Vaas	b MacGill	8	not out	11
C.R.D.Fernando	c Johnson b Lee	7	b Lee	4
M.Muralitharan	not out	6	b Clark	4
Extras	(LB 1, NB 6)	7	(B 4, LB 3, NB 6)	13
Total		**211**		**300**

SRI LANKA	O	M	R	W	O	M	R	W
Vaas	28	6	102	1				
Maharoof	34	6	107	0				
Fernando	34	3	130	1				
Muralitharan	50	4	170	2				
Jayasuriya	4	0	18	0				
Samaraweera	1	0	8	0				
AUSTRALIA								
Lee	17.5	9	26	4	27	7	86	4
Johnson	18	2	49	2	19	5	47	2
MacGill	25	5	79	1	(5) 25	5	64	1
Clark	16	4	46	2	(3) 22.3	3	75	2
Symonds	5	3	10	4	(4) 6	1	21	1

FALL OF WICKETS				
		A	SL	SL
Wkt	1st	1st	2nd	
1st	69	7	53	
2nd	183	11	65	
3rd	216	45	167	
4th	461	65	213	
5th	–	119	215	
6th	–	153	226	
7th	–	181	259	
8th	–	198	281	
9th	–	198	290	
10th	–	211	300	

Umpires: A.L.Hill (*New Zealand*) (5) and R.E.Koertzen (*South Africa*) (84).
Referee: M.J.Procter (*South Africa*) (42).   **Test No. 1844/19 (A687/SL171)**

AUSTRALIA v SRI LANKA (2nd Test)

At Bellerive Oval, Hobart, on 16, 17, 18, 19, 20 November 2007.
Toss: Australia. Result: **AUSTRALIA** won by 96 runs.
Debuts: None.

AUSTRALIA

P.A.Jaques	c Fernando b Jayasuriya	150	c Vandort b Malinga	68
M.L.Hayden	c HAPW Jayawardena b Fernando	17	lbw b Muralitharan	33
*R.T.Ponting	c DPMD Jayawardena b Muralitharan	31	not out	53
M.E.K.Hussey	lbw b Fernando	132	not out	34
M.J.Clarke	c HAPW Jayawardena b Malinga	71		
A.Symonds	not out	50		
†A.C.Gilchrist	not out	67		
B.Lee				
M.G.Johnson				
S.R.Clark				
S.C.G.MacGill				
Extras	(B 5, LB 1, W 1, NB 17)	24	(B 2, LB 1, NB 19)	22
Total	(5 wickets declared)	**542**	(2 wickets declared)	**210**

SRI LANKA

M.S.Atapattu	c Clarke b Lee	25	c Jaques b Lee	80
M.G.Vandort	b Lee	14	c sub (R.J.G.Lockyear) b Johnson	4
K.C.Sangakkara	c Hussey b Johnson	57	c Ponting b Clark	192
*D.P.M.D.Jayawardena	c Clarke b Lee	104	b Lee	0
S.T.Jayasuriya	b MacGill	3	c Gilchrist b Lee	45
L.P.C.Silva	c Gilchrist b MacGill	4	c Ponting b Johnson	0
†H.A.P.W.Jayawardena	c Gilchrist b Clark	0	lbw b Johnson	0
M.F.Maharoof	run out	19	c Lee b MacGill	4
C.R.D.Fernando	c Gilchrist b Lee	2	run out	2
S.L.Malinga	b Clark	1	not out	42
M.Muralitharan	not out	1	b Lee	15
Extras	(LB 7, NB 9)	16	(B 1, LB 6, W 6, NB 13)	26
Total		**246**		**410**

SRI LANKA	O	M	R	W	O	M	R	W	FALL OF WICKETS				
Malinga	35	6	156	1	12	0	61	1		A	SL	A	SL
Maharoof	23	4	82	0					Wkt	1st	1st	2nd	2nd
Fernando	26	4	134	2	(2) 12	1	50	0	1st	48	41	83	15
Muralitharan	46	4	140	1	(3) 20	1	90	1	2nd	133	54	154	158
Jayasuriya	9	1	24	1	(4) 2	0	6	0	3rd	285	127	–	158
									4th	410	134	–	265
AUSTRALIA									5th	447	152	–	272
Lee	23.2	4	82	4	26.3	3	87	4	6th	–	163	–	272
Johnson	17	3	44	1	28	4	101	3	7th	–	196	–	284
Clark	16	6	32	2	24	5	103	1	8th	–	207	–	290
MacGill	25	5	81	2	20	1	102	1	9th	–	243	–	364
Clarke					6	1	10	0	10th	–	246	–	410

Umpires: Alim Dar (*Pakistan*) (40) and R.E.Koertzen (*South Africa*) (85).
Referee: M.J.Procter (*South Africa*) (43).   **Test No. 1845/20 (A688/SL172)**

SOUTH AFRICA v NEW ZEALAND (1st Test)

At The Wanderers, Johannesburg, on 8, 9, 10, 11 November 2007.
Toss: South Africa. Result: **SOUTH AFRICA** won by 358 runs.
Debuts: New Zealand – L.R.P.L.Taylor.

SOUTH AFRICA

*G.C.Smith	b Martin	1	(2)	b Martin	9
H.H.Gibbs	c Fleming b Martin	63	(1)	c Papps b Bond	8
H.M.Amla	c McCullum b Bond	12		not out	176
J.H.Kallis	c McCullum b O'Brien	29		c McCullum b Oram	186
A.G.Prince	c Fleming b Bond	1		not out	25
A.B.de Villiers	c Oram b Bond	33			
†M.V.Boucher	c Papps b Vettori	43			
A.Nel	c McCullum b Bond	15			
P.L.Harris	lbw b Vettori	3			
D.W.Steyn	c McCullum b Martin	13			
M.Ntini	not out	0			
Extras	(LB 6, W 1, NB 6)	13		(B 9, LB 7, W 1, NB 1)	18
Total		**226**		(3 wickets declared)	**422**

NEW ZEALAND

C.D.Cumming	lbw b Steyn	12		c Smith b Steyn	7
M.H.W.Papps	c De Villiers b Ntini	2	(7)	c De Villiers b Kallis	5
S.P.Fleming	c De Villiers b Ntini	40	(2)	c Smith b Nel	17
S.E.Bond	b Steyn	0	(11)	absent hurt	
S.B.Styris	c Smith b Kallis	11	(3)	c Boucher b Steyn	16
L.R.P.L.Taylor	c Gibbs b Kallis	15	(4)	c Kallis b Nel	4
J.D.P.Oram	c Kallis b Steyn	1	(6)	c Nel b Harris	40
†B.B.McCullum	lbw b Steyn	9	(5)	c Gibbs b Steyn	26
*D.L.Vettori	c Harris b Ntini	7	(8)	not out	46
I.E.O'Brien	not out	14	(9)	c Amla b Steyn	0
C.S.Martin	c Harris b Steyn	0	(10)	b Steyn	0
Extras	(LB 5, NB 1)	6		(B 7, LB 1, W 2, NB 1)	11
Total		**118**			**172**

NEW ZEALAND	O	M	R	W	O	M	R	W		FALL OF WICKETS			
Bond	17	1	73	4	16	1	60	1			SA	NZ	SA	NZ
Martin	17.3	3	67	3	24	6	55	1	Wkt	1st	1st	2nd	2nd
Oram	12	3	31	0	16.4	2	49	1	1st	1	16	8	12
O'Brien	10	4	23	1	23	5	91	0	2nd	20	40	20	34
Vettori	18	6	26	2	37	3	116	0	3rd	73	54	350	39
Styris					6	2	25	0	4th	92	64	–	60
Taylor					3.2	0	10	0	5th	141	83	–	90
									6th	162	84	–	109
SOUTH AFRICA									7th	182	88	–	154
Steyn	14.3	3	34	5	17	1	59	5	8th	195	102	–	170
Ntini	14	3	47	3	13	0	42	0	9th	219	118	–	172
Nel	9	1	21	0	12	1	37	2	10th	226	118	–	
Kallis	4	0	11	2	9	0	15	1					
Harris					6	2	11	1					

Umpires: M.R.Benson (*England*) (18) and D.J.Harper (*Australia*) (66).
Referee: J.Srinath (*India*) (5).   **Test No. 1846/34 (SA323/NZ333)**

SOUTH AFRICA v NEW ZEALAND (2nd Test)

At Centurion Park (Verwoerdburg), Pretoria, on 16, 17, 18 November 2007.
Toss: New Zealand. Result: **SOUTH AFRICA** won by an innings and 59 runs.
Debuts: New Zealand – M.R.Gillespie.

NEW ZEALAND

C.D.Cumming	retired hurt	48		absent hurt	–
M.H.W.Papps	c Gibbs b Ntini	9		lbw b Steyn	1
L.Vincent	c Harris b Steyn	33	(1)	lbw b Steyn	4
S.P.Fleming	c Prince b Kallis	43	(3)	lbw b Steyn	54
S.B.Styris	lbw b Steyn	3	(4)	c De Villiers b Kallis	29
L.R.P.L.Taylor	c Prince b Nel	17	(5)	run out	8
†B.B.McCullum	c De Villiers b Nel	13	(6)	c Smith b Steyn	21
*D.L.Vettori	not out	17	(7)	c De Villiers b Ntini	8
M.R.Gillespie	lbw b Steyn	0	(8)	c Kallis b Steyn	0
I.E.O'Brien	c Gibbs b Steyn	0	(9)	b Steyn	0
C.S.Martin	c Kallis b Ntini	0	(10)	not out	0
Extras	(LB 2, NB 3)	5		(B 1, LB 9, NB 1)	11
Total		**188**			**136**

SOUTH AFRICA

*G.C.Smith	b Martin	2
H.H.Gibbs	b Martin	25
H.M.Amla	c Papps b O'Brien	103
J.H.Kallis	lbw b Gillespie	131
A.G.Prince	c sub (J.M.How) b Gillespie	13
A.B.de Villiers	c McCullum b Gillespie	33
†M.V.Boucher	b Gillespie	1
P.L.Harris	c McCullum b Gillespie	0
A.Nel	lbw b Vettori	25
D.W.Steyn	c Papps b O'Brien	25
M.Ntini	not out	0
Extras	(B 6, LB 4, W 2, NB 13)	25
Total		**383**

SOUTH AFRICA	O	M	R	W		O	M	R	W	FALL OF WICKETS			
Steyn	14	5	42	4		10.3	1	49	6		NZ	SA	NZ
Ntini	15.4	4	52	2		12	4	39	1	Wkt	1st	1st	2nd
Kallis	11	2	35	1	(4)	5	2	18	1	1st	26	2	4
Nel	13	3	42	2	(3)	7	2	20	0	2nd	88	31	9
Harris	3	0	15	0						3rd	105	251	69
										4th	147	282	78
NEW ZEALAND										5th	165	312	117
Martin	22	6	81	2						6th	184	325	128
Gillespie	30	7	136	5						7th	187	332	128
O'Brien	21.3	6	78	2						8th	187	332	136
Vettori	20	2	61	1						9th	188	383	136
Styris	4	0	17	0						10th	–	383	–

Umpires: M.R.Benson (*England*) (19) and D.J.Harper (*Australia*) (67).
Referee: J.Srinath (*India*) (6).
In the first innings Cumming (48) retired hurt at 101. **Test No. 1847/35 (SA324/NZ334)**

INDIA v PAKISTAN (1st Test)

At Feroz Shah Kotla, Delhi, on 22, 23, 24, 25, 26 November 2007.
Toss: Pakistan. Result: **INDIA** won by six wickets.
Debuts: Pakistan – Sohail Tanvir.

PAKISTAN

Batsman	1st innings		2nd innings	
Salman Butt	b Khan	1	c Dravid b Kumble	67
Yasir Hamid	b Kumble	29	c Laxman b Kumble	36
Younus Khan	c Patel b Khan	7	lbw b Kumble	23
Mohd Yousuf Youhana	lbw b Ganguly	27	c and b Harbhajan	18
Misbah-ul-Haq	run out	82	(7) c Karthik b Ganguly	45
*Shoaib Malik	c Dhoni b Patel	0	(5) b Harbhajan	11
†Kamran Akmal	b Kumble	30	(6) c sub (Yuvraj Singh) b Khan	21
Sohail Tanvir	lbw b Harbhajan	4	c Harbhajan b Khan	13
Shoaib Akhtar	b Kumble	2	(10) not out	0
Mohammad Sami	not out	28	(9) c Jaffer b Ganguly	5
Danish Kaneria	b Kumble	0	run out	0
Extras	(B 6, LB 12, W 2, NB 1)	21	(LB 6, NB 2)	8
Total		**231**		**247**

INDIA

Batsman	1st innings		2nd innings	
W.Jaffer	lbw b Akhtar	32	(2) c Butt b Akhtar	53
K.D.Karthik	c Akmal b Akhtar	9	(1) c Akmal b Akhtar	1
R.Dravid	b Tanvir	38	b Akhtar	34
S.R.Tendulkar	run out	1	not out	56
S.C.Ganguly	b Tanvir	8	c Tanvir b Akhtar	48
V.V.S.Laxman	not out	72	not out	6
†M.S.Dhoni	c Akmal b Kaneria	57		
*A.Kumble	c Younis b Kaneria	24		
Harbhajan Singh	b Tanvir	1		
Z.Khan	c Akhtar b Kaneria	9		
M.M.Patel	lbw b Kaneria	0		
Extras	(B 11, LB 8, W 1, NB 5)	25	(B 1, LB 3, NB 1)	5
Total		**276**	(4 wickets)	**203**

INDIA	O	M	R	W	O	M	R	W
Khan	20	5	45	2	18	4	45	2
Patel	24	5	61	1	10	2	48	0
Kumble	21.2	6	38	4	27.1	8	68	3
Ganguly	14	5	28	1	9	2	20	2
Harbhajan	15	1	37	1	17	4	56	2
Tendulkar	2	0	4	0	2	0	4	0

PAKISTAN	O	M	R	W		O	M	R	W
Shoaib Akhtar	16	2	44	2		18.1	4	58	4
Sohail Tanvir	24	5	83	3		12	4	26	0
Mohammad Sami	17	1	71	0	(4)	15	1	65	0
Danish Kaneria	21.4	3	59	4	(3)	16	2	50	0

FALL OF WICKETS

Wkt	P	I	P	I
1st	13	15	71	2
2nd	35	71	114	84
3rd	59	73	149	93
4th	76	88	155	181
5th	83	93	161	
6th	122	208	213	
7th	137	262	229	
8th	142	263	243	
9th	229	276	247	
10th	231	276	247	

Umpires: B.R.Doctrove (*West Indies*) (14) and S.J.A.Taufel (*Australia*) (45).
Referee: R.S.Madugalle (*Sri Lanka*) (97). Test No. 1848/57 (I409/P333)

INDIA v PAKISTAN (2nd Test)

At Eden Gardens, Calcutta, on 30 November, 1, 2, 3, 4 December 2007.
Toss: India. Result: **MATCH DRAWN**.
Debuts: None.

INDIA

W.Jaffer	c Akmal b Tanvir	202	b Kaneria		56
K.D.Karthik	c Younis b Tanvir	1	c Misbah b Kaneria		28
R.Dravid	c Akmal b Kaneria	50	(5) not out		8
S.R.Tendulkar	b Kaneria	82			
S.C.Ganguly	c Tanvir b Butt	102	(4) b Akhtar		46
V.V.S.Laxman	not out	112			
†M.S.Dhoni	not out	50	(3) b Akhtar		37
*A.Kumble					
Harbhajan Singh					
Z.Khan					
M.M.Patel					
Extras	(B 8, LB 5, W 1, NB 3)	17	(LB 3, NB 6)		9
Total	(5 wickets declared)	**616**	(4 wickets declared)		**184**

PAKISTAN

Salman Butt	c Dravid b Harbhajan	42	(3) lbw b Kumble		11
Yasir Hamid	lbw b Kumble	21	(1) c and b Khan		14
*Younus Khan	c Dhoni b Patel	43	(4) not out		107
Mohd Yousuf Youhana	b Harbhajan	6	(6) not out		44
Misbah-ul-Haq	not out	161	b Patel		6
Faisal Iqbal	lbw b Kumble	0			
†Kamran Akmal	b Harbhajan	119	(2) b Kumble		14
Mohammad Sami	c Jaffer b Laxman	38			
Sohail Tanvir	c Dravid b Kumble	0			
Shoaib Akhtar	c Dravid b Harbhajan	0			
Danish Kaneria	b Harbhajan	0			
Extras	(B 8, LB 7, W 1, NB 10)	26	(B 8, LB 6, NB 4)		18
Total		**456**	(4 wickets)		**214**

PAKISTAN	O	M	R	W		O	M	R	W	FALL OF WICKETS				
Shoaib Akhtar	24	2	84	0		12.4	0	46	2		I	P	I	P
Sohail Tanvir	39	6	166	2		9	0	41	0	Wkt	1st	1st	2nd	2nd
Mohammad Sami	29	2	99	0		5	1	28	0	1st	2	38	75	22
Danish Kaneria	50	7	194	2		15	0	61	2	2nd	138	77	95	37
Yasir Hamid	4	0	24	0						3rd	313	85	166	65
Salman Butt	6.5	0	36	1	(5)	1	0	5	0	4th	375	134	184	78
										5th	538	150	–	–
INDIA										6th	–	357	–	–
Khan	25.2	8	69	0		8	0	32	0	7th	–	448	–	–
Patel	21	4	85	1	(3)	10	3	21	1	8th	–	449	–	–
Harbhajan Singh	45.5	9	122	5	(4)	31	5	67	0	9th	–	452	–	–
Kumble	47	14	122	1	(2)	25	4	73	2	10th	–	456	–	–
Tendulkar	7	1	32	0		3	0	7	0					
Ganguly	4	0	9	0										
Laxman	1	0	2	1										

Umpires: B.R.Doctrove (*West Indies*) (15) and R.E.Koertzen (*South Africa*) (86).
Referee: R.S.Madugalle (*Sri Lanka*) (98). **Test No. 1849/58 (I410/P334)**

INDIA v PAKISTAN (3rd Test)

At M.Chinnaswamy Stadium, Bangalore, on 8, 9, 10, 11, 12 December 2007.
Toss: India. Result: **MATCH DRAWN**.
Debuts: Pakistan – Yasir Arafat.

INDIA

W.Jaffer	lbw b Arafat	17	lbw b Arafat		18
G.Gambhir	c Akmal b Sami	5	b Akhtar		3
R.Dravid	c Misbah b Arafat	19	lbw b Kaneria		42
S.C.Ganguly	b Kaneria	239	c Faisal b Sami		91
V.V.S.Laxman	b Arafat	5	retired hurt		14
Yuvraj Singh	c Faisal b Sami	169	c Akmal b Sami		2
†K.D.Karthik	c Akmal b Arafat	24	c Akmal b Arafat		52
I.K.Pathan	c Akmal b Kaneria	102	not out		21
*A.Kumble	lbw b Kaneria	4			
Harbhajan Singh	b Arafat	4			
I.Sharma	not out	0			
Extras	(B 13, LB 19, NB 6)	38	(B 9, LB 24, W 1, NB 7)		41
Total		**626**	(6 wickets declared)		**284**

PAKISTAN

Salman Butt	c Karthik b Ganguly	68	c Karthik b Kumble		8
Yasir Hamid	lbw b Kumble	19	b Kumble		39
*Younus Khan	b Harbhajan	80	c and b Kumble		0
Mohd Yousuf Youhana	c Yuvraj b Pathan	24	(7) not out		10
Misbah-ul-Haq	not out	133	b Yuvraj		37
Faisal Iqbal	c Gambhir b Sharma	22	(4) c Sharma b Kumble		51
†Kamran Akmal	st Karthik b Harbhajan	65	(6) b Kumble		0
Yasir Arafat	b Sharma	44	b Yuvraj		0
Mohammad Sami	b Sharma	1	not out		4
Shoaib Akhtar	c Gambhir b Sharma	1			
Danish Kaneria	c and b Sharma	4			
Extras	(B 35, LB 26, NB 15)	76	(B 12, LB 1)		13
Total		**537**	(7 wickets)		**162**

PAKISTAN	O	M	R	W		O	M	R	W
Shoaib Akhtar	10	3	23	0		17	6	43	1
Mohammad Sami	36	5	149	2		20	2	63	2
Yasir Arafat	39	5	161	5		13.3	3	49	2
Danish Kaneria	46.2	8	168	3		26	2	96	1
Younus Khan	2	0	14	0					
Salman Butt	10	1	36	0					
Yasir Hamid	7	0	43	0					

INDIA	O	M	R	W		O	M	R	W
Pathan	37	14	80	1		7	4	30	0
Sharma	33.1	12	118	5		6	3	22	0
Kumble	44	12	116	1		14	2	60	5
Ganguly	10	2	20	1					
Harbhajan Singh	38	7	131	2	(4)	6	1	28	0
Yuvraj Singh	6	2	11	0	(5)	3	0	9	2

FALL OF WICKETS

	I	P	I	P
Wkt	1st	1st	2nd	2nd
1st	8	59	17	44
2nd	44	149	26	44
3rd	51	221	178	73
4th	61	227	178	144
5th	361	288	184	144
6th	427	432	284	148
7th	605	525	–	154
8th	615	527		
9th	620	529	–	–
10th	626	537	–	–

Umpires: R.E.Koertzen (*South Africa*) (87) and S.J.A.Taufel (*Australia*) (46).
Referee: R.S.Madugalle (*Sri Lanka*) (99).
In the second innings, Laxman (14) retired hurt at 225.   **Test No. 1850/59 (I411/P335)**

299

INDIA v PAKISTAN 2007-08

INDIA – BATTING AND FIELDING

	M	I	NO	HS	Runs	Avge	100	50	Ct/St
V.V.S.Laxman	3	5	4	112*	209	209.00	1	1	1
S.C.Ganguly	3	6	–	239	534	89.00	2	1	–
M.S.Dhoni	2	3	1	57	144	72.00	–	2	2
S.R.Tendulkar	2	3	1	82	139	69.50	–	2	–
W.Jaffer	3	6	–	202	378	63.00	1	2	2
R.Dravid	3	6	1	50	191	38.20	–	1	4
K.D.Karthik	3	6	–	52	115	19.16	–	1	3/1
A.Kumble	3	2	–	24	28	14.00	–	–	1
Z.Khan	2	1	–	9	9	9.00	–	–	1
Harbhajan Singh	3	2	–	4	5	2.50	–	–	2
M.M.Patel	2	1	–	0	0	0.00	–	–	1

Played in one Test: G.Gambhir 5, 3 (2 ct); I.K.Pathan 102, 21*; I.Sharma 0* (2 ct); Yuvraj Singh 169, 2 (1 ct).

INDIA – BOWLING

	O	M	R	W	Avge	Best	5wI	10wM
S.C.Ganguly	37	10	77	4	19.25	2- 20	–	–
A.Kumble	178.3	46	477	18	26.50	5- 60	1	–
I.Sharma	39.1	13	140	5	28.00	5-118	1	–
Z.Khan	71.2	17	191	5	38.20	2- 45	–	–
Harbhajan Singh	152.5	27	441	10	44.10	5-122	1	–
M.M.Patel	65	14	215	3	71.66	1- 21	–	–

Also bowled: V.V.S.Laxman 1-0-2-1; I.K.Pathan 44-18-110-1; S.R.Tendulkar 14-1-47-0; Yuvraj Singh 9-2-20-2.

PAKISTAN – BATTING AND FIELDING

	M	I	NO	HS	Runs	Avge	100	50	Ct/St
Misbah-ul-Haq	3	6	2	161*	464	116.00	2	1	2
Younus Khan	3	6	1	107*	260	52.00	1	1	2
Kamran Akmal	3	6	–	119	249	41.50	1	1	10
Salman Butt	3	6	–	68	197	32.83	–	2	1
Mohd Yousuf Youhana	3	6	2	44*	129	32.25	–	–	–
Yasir Hamid	3	6	–	39	158	26.33	–	–	–
Mohammad Sami	3	5	2	38	76	25.33	–	–	–
Faisal Iqbal	2	3	–	51	73	24.33	–	1	2
Sohail Tanvir	2	3	–	13	17	5.66	–	–	2
Danish Kaneria	3	4	–	4	4	1.00	–	–	–
Shoaib Akhtar	3	4	1	2	3	1.00	–	–	1

Played in one Test: Shoaib Malik 0, 11; Yasir Arafat 44, 0.

PAKISTAN – BOWLING

	O	M	R	W	Avge	Best	5wI	10wM
Yasir Arafat	52.3	8	210	7	30.00	5-161	1	–
Shoaib Akhtar	97.5	17	298	9	33.11	4- 58	–	–
Danish Kaneria	175	22	628	12	52.33	4- 59	–	–
Sohail Tanvir	84	15	316	5	63.20	3- 83	–	–
Mohammad Sami	122	12	475	4	118.75	2- 63	–	–

Also bowled: Salman Butt 17.5-1-77-1; Yasir Hamid 11-0-67-0; Younus Khan 2-0-14-0.

SRI LANKA v ENGLAND (1st Test)

At Asgiriya Stadium, Kandy, on 1, 2, 3, 4, 5 December 2007.
Toss: Sri Lanka. Result: **SRI LANKA** won by 88 runs.
Debuts: England – R.S.Bopara.

SRI LANKA

Batsman	Dismissal	R	Dismissal	R
M.G.Vandort	c Vaughan b Hoggard	8	c Bell b Anderson	49
S.T.Jayasuriya	c Pietersen b Sidebottom	10	lbw b Hoggard	78
K.C.Sangakkara	c Collingwood b Anderson	92	c Vaughan b Collingwood	152
*D.P.M.D.Jayawardena	c Prior b Hoggard	1	c Prior b Hoggard	65
L.P.C.Silva	c Prior b Hoggard	2	lbw b Panesar	37
J.Mubarak	c Prior b Hoggard	0	c sub (G.P.Swann) b Panesar	9
†H.A.P.W.Jayawardena	c Cook b Panesar	51	b Collingwood	20
W.P.U.C.J.Vaas	b Panesar	12	not out	6
C.R.D.Fernando	c Vaughan b Panesar	0	(10) not out	9
S.L.Malinga	not out	1	(9) b Panesar	2
M.Muralitharan	run out	1		
Extras	(LB 8, NB 2)	10	(B 5, LB 10)	15
Total		**188**	(8 wickets declared)	**442**

ENGLAND

Batsman	Dismissal	R	Dismissal	R
A.N.Cook	lbw b Vaas	0	c Silva b Vaas	4
*M.P.Vaughan	c Silva b Muralitharan	37	c HAPW Jayawardena b Vaas	5
I.R.Bell	c Silva b Muralitharan	83	(4) b Muralitharan	74
K.P.Pietersen	lbw b Muralitharan	31	(5) b Fernando	18
P.D.Collingwood	b Muralitharan	45	(6) c Sangakkara b Fernando	16
R.S.Bopara	c HAPW Jayawardena b Muralitharan	8	(7) lbw b Jayasuriya	34
†M.J.Prior	c Mubarak b Fernando	0	(8) b Muralitharan	63
R.J.Sidebottom	c HAPW Jayawardena b Malinga	31	(9) lbw b Muralitharan	1
M.J.Hoggard	st HAPW Jayawardena b Muralitharan	15	(10) b Malinga	8
J.M.Anderson	lbw b Vaas	9	(3) b Vaas	11
M.S.Panesar	not out	2	not out	2
Extras	(B 6, LB 1, W 2, NB 11)	20	(B 5, LB 9, NB 11)	25
Total		**281**		**261**

ENGLAND	O	M	R	W		O	M	R	W
Sidebottom	15	1	58	1	(2)	25	5	65	0
Hoggard	14	3	29	4	(1)	18	5	55	2
Anderson	15.4	3	39	1	(4)	23	4	128	1
Bopara	1	0	8	0	(5)	8	3	16	0
Panesar	14	4	46	3	(3)	45	5	132	3
Vaughan						3	0	6	0
Collingwood						8	0	25	2

SRI LANKA	O	M	R	W		O	M	R	W
Vaas	18.1	3	76	2		17	3	56	3
Malinga	20	2	86	1		15	3	39	1
Muralitharan	35	14	55	6		36	12	85	3
Jayasuriya	2	0	9	0		14	6	28	1
Fernando	18	2	48	1		12	1	39	2

FALL OF WICKETS

	SL	E	SL	E
Wkt	1st	1st	2nd	2nd
1st	11	0	113	4
2nd	29	107	166	22
3rd	40	132	288	27
4th	42	170	359	55
5th	42	182	387	90
6th	148	185	423	139
7th	180	242	426	248
8th	182	266	429	249
9th	186	272	–	253
10th	188	281	–	261

Umpires: Alim Dar (*Pakistan*) (41) and Asad Rauf (*Pakistan*) (14).
Referee: J.J.Crowe (*New Zealand*) (22). Test No. 1851/19 (SL173/E865)

SRI LANKA v ENGLAND (2nd Test)

At Sinhalese Sports Ground, Colombo, on 9, 10, 11, 12, 13 December 2007.
Toss: England. Result: **MATCH DRAWN**.
Debuts: England – S.C.J.Broad.

ENGLAND

A.N.Cook	lbw b Malinga	81	c D.P.M.D.Jayawardena b Silva	62
*M.P.Vaughan	c Mubarak b Muralitharan	87	c and b Fernando	61
I.R.Bell	c Mubarak b Muralitharan	15	c Vandort b Muralitharan	54
K.P.Pietersen	c Sangakkara b Vaas	7	not out	45
P.D.Collingwood	lbw b Vaas	52	not out	23
R.S.Bopara	b Malinga	0		
†M.J.Prior	c and b Muralitharan	79		
S.C.J.Broad	lbw b Malinga	2		
R.J.Sidebottom	c D.P.M.D.Jayawardena b Muralitharan	17		
S.J.Harmison	c Silva b Muralitharan	0		
M.S.Panesar	not out	0		
Extras	(B 8, LB 2, NB 7)	17	(NB 5)	5
Total		**351**	**(3 wickets)**	**250**

SRI LANKA

M.G.Vandort	lbw b Sidebottom	138
W.U.Tharanga	c Prior b Sidebottom	10
K.C.Sangakkara	c Prior b Sidebottom	1
*D.P.M.D.Jayawardena	c Collingwood b Panesar	195
L.P.C.Silva	c Bopara b Harmison	49
J.Mubarak	c Bell b Harmison	9
†H.A.P.W.Jayawardena	c Prior b Harmison	79
W.P.U.C.J.Vaas	c Bell b Broad	4
S.L.Malinga	lbw b Panesar	9
C.R.D.Fernando	not out	36
M.Muralitharan		
Extras	(B 7, LB 9, W 1, NB 1)	18
Total	**(9 wickets declared)**	**548**

SRI LANKA	O	M	R	W		O	M	R	W
Vaas	32	8	68	2		16	2	56	0
Malinga	24	3	78	3		8	1	37	0
Fernando	23	3	79	0		10	0	30	1
Muralitharan	47.2	9	116	5	(5)	27	5	58	1
Mubarak					(4)	1	0	8	0
D.P.M.D.Jayawardena						2	1	4	0
Silva						13	1	57	1

ENGLAND	O	M	R	W
Sidebottom	36	4	100	3
Broad	36	5	95	1
Harmison	41.5	9	111	3
Panesar	50	7	151	2
Pietersen	15	0	57	0
Collingwood	1	1	0	0
Bopara	7	2	18	0

FALL OF WICKETS

	E	SL	E
Wkt	1st	1st	2nd
1st	133	20	107
2nd	168	22	152
3rd	171	249	204
4th	237	377	–
5th	237	399	–
6th	269	420	–
7th	272	425	–
8th	346	450	–
9th	350	548	–
10th	351	–	–

Umpires: Alim Dar (*Pakistan*) (42) and D.J.Harper (*Australia*) (68).
Referee: J.J.Crowe (*New Zealand*) (23). Test No. 1852/20 (SL174/E866)

SRI LANKA v ENGLAND (3rd Test)

At Galle International Stadium on 18, 19, 20, 21, 22 December 2007.
Toss: England. Result: **MATCH DRAWN**.
Debuts: Sri Lanka – U.W.M.B.C.A.Welegedara.

SRI LANKA

M.G.Vandort	lbw b Sidebottom	18
W.U.Tharanga	lbw b Harmison	16
K.C.Sangakkara	c Panesar b Harmison	46
*D.P.M.D.Jayawardena	not out	213
L.P.C.Silva	c Bell b Harmison	1
T.M.Dilshan	run out	84
†H.A.P.W. Jayawardena	c Prior b Bopara	0
W.P.U.C.J.Vaas	c Vaughan b Hoggard	90
S.L.Malinga	b Collingwood	5
U.W.M.B.C.A.Welegedara		
M.Muralitharan		
Extras	(B 1, LB 14, W 8, NB 3)	26
Total	(8 wickets declared)	**499**

ENGLAND

A.N.Cook	c HAPW Jayawardena b Welegedara	13	c HAPW Jayawardena b Welegedara	118
*M.P.Vaughan	lbw b Vaas	1	c DPMD Jayawardena b Welegedara	24
I.R.Bell	run out	1	b Muralitharan	34
K.P.Pietersen	c HAPW Jayawardena b Malinga	1	c DPMD Jayawardena b Muralitharan	30
P.D.Collingwood	b Welegedara	29	st HAPW Jayawardena b Muralitharan	0
R.S.Bopara	c Welegedara b Vaas	0	run out	0
†M.J.Prior	b Vaas	4	not out	19
R.J.Sidebottom	c Dilshan b Muralitharan	11	not out	0
S.J.Harmison	not out	9		
M.J.Hoggard	c DPMD Jayawardena b Welegedara	0		
M.S.Panesar	not out	0		
Extras	(B 4, NB 8)	12	(B 6, LB 5, W 1, NB 14)	26
Total		**81**	(6 wickets)	**251**

ENGLAND	O	M	R	W	O	M	R	W		FALL OF WICKETS		
											SL	E	E
Sidebottom	34	8	95	1						Wkt	1st	1st	2nd
Hoggard	32	4	121	1						1st	34	5	67
Harmison	34	4	104	3						2nd	44	9	128
Panesar	26	3	76	0						3rd	132	22	200
Bopara	10	1	39	1						4th	138	22	200
Collingwood	9.5	2	38	1						5th	287	25	200
Pietersen	3	0	11	0						6th	287	33	250
										7th	470	70	–
SRI LANKA										8th	499	72	–
Vaas	9.5	2	28	4	(2) 18	7	37	0		9th	–	72	–
Malinga	9	2	26	1	(3) 20	3	42	0		10th	–	81	–
Welegedara	8	1	17	2	(4) 14	1	59	2					
Muralitharan	4	2	6	1	(1) 38	8	91	3					
Dilshan					3	1	8	0					
Silva					2	1	3	0					

Umpires: Asad Rauf (*Pakistan*) (15) and D.J.Harper (*Australia*) (69).
Referee: J.J.Crowe (*New Zealand*) (24).   **Test No. 1853/21 (SL175/E867)**

SRI LANKA v ENGLAND 2007-08

SRI LANKA – BATTING AND FIELDING

	M	I	NO	HS	Runs	Avge	100	50	Ct/St
D.P.M.D.Jayawardena	3	4	1	213*	474	158.00	2	1	5
K.C.Sangakkara	3	4	–	152	291	72.75	1	1	2
M.G.Vandort	3	4	–	138	213	53.25	1	–	1
C.R.D.Fernando	2	3	2	36*	45	45.00	–	–	1
H.A.P.W.Jayawardena	3	4	–	79	150	37.50	–	2	6/2
W.P.U.C.J.Vaas	3	4	1	90	112	37.33	–	1	–
L.P.C.Silva	3	4	–	49	89	22.25	–	–	4
W.U.Tharanga	2	2	–	16	26	13.00	–	–	–
J.Mubarak	2	3	–	9	18	6.00	–	–	3
S.L.Malinga	3	4	1	9	17	5.66	–	–	–
M.Muralitharan	3	1	–	1	1	1.00	–	–	1

Played in one Test: T.M.Dilshan 84 (1 ct); S.T.Jayasuriya 10, 78. U.W.M.B.C.A.Welegedara did not bat (1 ct).

SRI LANKA – BOWLING

	O	M	R	W	Avge	Best	5wI	10wM
U.W.M.B.C.A.Welegedara	22	2	76	4	19.00	2-17	–	–
M.Muralitharan	187.2	50	411	19	21.63	6-55	2	–
W.P.U.C.J.Vaas	111	25	321	11	29.18	4-28	–	–
C.R.D.Fernando	63	6	196	4	49.00	2-39	–	–
S.L.Malinga	96	14	308	6	51.33	3-78	–	–

Also bowled: T.M.Dilshan 3-1-8-0; S.T.Jayasuriya 16-6-37-1; D.P.M.D.Jayawardena 2-1-4-0; J.Mubarak 1-0-8-0; L.P.C.Silva 15-2-60-1.

ENGLAND – BATTING AND FIELDING

	M	I	NO	HS	Runs	Avge	100	50	Ct/St
A.N.Cook	3	6	–	118	278	46.33	1	2	1
I.R.Bell	3	6	–	83	261	43.50	–	3	4
M.J.Prior	3	5	1	79	165	41.25	–	2	8
M.P.Vaughan	3	6	–	87	215	35.83	–	2	4
P.D.Collingwood	3	6	1	52	165	33.00	–	1	2
K.P.Pietersen	3	6	1	45*	126	25.20	–	–	1
R.J.Sidebottom	3	5	1	31	60	15.00	–	–	–
S.J.Harmison	2	2	1	9*	9	9.00	–	–	–
R.S.Bopara	3	5	–	34	42	8.40	–	–	1
M.J.Hoggard	2	3	–	15	23	7.66	–	–	–
M.S.Panesar	3	4	3	2*	4	4.00	–	–	1

Played in one Test: J.M.Anderson 9, 11; S.C.J.Broad 2.

ENGLAND – BOWLING

	O	M	R	W	Avge	Best	5wI	10wM
P.D.Collingwood	18.5	3	63	3	21.00	2- 25	–	–
M.J.Hoggard	64	12	205	7	29.28	4- 29	–	–
S.J.Harmison	75.5	13	215	6	35.83	3-104	–	–
M.S.Panesar	135	19	405	8	50.62	3- 46	–	–
R.J.Sidebottom	110	18	318	5	63.60	3-100	–	–

Also bowled: J.M.Anderson 38.4-7-167-2; R.S.Bopara 26-6-81-1; S.C.J.Broad 36-5-95-1; K.P.Pietersen 18-0-68-0; M.P.Vaughan 3-0-6-0.

LEADING TEST AGGREGATES 2007

1000 RUNS IN 2007

	M	I	NO	HS	Runs	Avge	100	50
J.H.Kallis (SA)	9	17	3	186	1210	86.42	5	6
S.C.Ganguly (I)	10	19	1	239	1106	61.44	3	4
K.P.Pietersen (E)	11	21	1	226	1007	50.35	4	1

RECORD CALENDAR YEAR RUNS AGGREGATE

	M	I	NO	HS	Runs	Avge	100	50
Mohd Yousuf Youhana (P) (2006)	11	19	1	202	1788	99.33	9	3

RECORD CALENDAR YEAR RUNS AVERAGE

	M	I	NO	HS	Runs	Avge	100	50
G.St A. Sobers (WI) (1958)	7	12	3	365*	1193	132.55	5	3

1000 RUNS IN DEBUT CALENDAR YEAR

	M	I	NO	HS	Runs	Avge	100	50
M.A.Taylor (A) (1989)	11	20	1	219	1219	64.15	4	5
A.N.Cook (E) (2006)	13	24	2	127	1013	46.04	4	3

MOST WICKETS IN 2007

	M	O	R	W	Avge	Best	5wI	10wM
M.Muralitharan (SL)	8	416.1	1093	49	22.30	6-28	5	1
A.Kumble (I)	10	464	1441	49	29.40	5-60	2	–

RECORD CALENDAR YEAR WICKETS AGGREGATE

	M	O	R	W	Avge	Best	5wI	10wM
M.Muralitharan (SL) (2006)	11	588.4	1521	90	16.90	8-70	9	5
S.K.Warne (A) (2005)	14	691.4	2043	90	22.70	6-46	6	2

MOST WICKET-KEEPING DISMISSALS IN 2007

	M	Dis	Ct	St
M.V.Boucher (SA)	9	29	24	5

RECORD CALENDAR YEAR DISMISSALS AGGREGATE

	M	Dis	Ct	St
I.A.Healy (A) (1993)	16	67	58	9
M.V.Boucher (SA) (1998)	13	67	65	2

15 CATCHES BY FIELDERS IN 2007

	M	Ct
H.H.Gibbs (SA)	8	16
D.P.M.D.Jayawardena (SL)	8	15
J.H.Kallis (SA)	9	15

RECORD CALENDAR YEAR CATCHES AGGREGATE (Non wicket-keepers)

	M	Ct
S.P.Fleming (NZ) (1997)	10	28

TEST MATCH CHAMPIONSHIP SCHEDULE

Months indicate the start of a series. Number of Tests in brackets.
All series involving Zimbabwe are subject to confirmation.

2008	**Mar**	**New Zealand host England (3)**
		Pakistan host Australia (3)
		India host South Africa (3)
		West Indies host Sri Lanka (3)
	May	West Indies host Australia (4)
		England host New Zealand (3)
	Jun	Zimbabwe host India (2)
	Jul	**England host South Africa (4)**
		Australia host Bangladesh (2)
		Sri Lanka host India (3)
	Oct	India host Australia (4)
		Bangladesh host New Zealand (2)
	Nov	**India host England (3)**
		Australia host New Zealand (3)
		South Africa host Bangladesh (2)
		Sri Lanka host Zimbabwe (2)
	Dec	Australia host South Africa (3)
2009	**Jan**	Pakistan host India (3)
		New Zealand host West Indies (3)
		Bangladesh host Sri Lanka (2)
	Feb	**West Indies host England (4)**
		South Africa host Australia (3)
	Mar	New Zealand host India (3)
		Zimbabwe host Sri Lanka (2)
	Apr	Bangladesh host West Indies (2)
	May	**England host Zimbabwe (2)**
	Jul	**England host Australia (5)**
		Sri Lanka host Pakistan (3)
		Zimbabwe host New Zealand (2)
	Aug	Sri Lanka host New Zealand (3)
		Zimbabwe host Bangladesh (2)
	Oct	Bangladesh host Zimbabwe (2)
	Nov	**South Africa host England (4)**
		Australia host Pakistan (3)
		India host Sri Lanka (3)
	Dec	Australia host West Indies (3)
		Bangladesh host India (2)
		Pakistan host New Zealand (3)
2010	**Jan**	New Zealand host Bangladesh (2)
	Feb	**Pakistan host England (4)**
		New Zealand host Australia (3)
		India host South Africa (3)
	Mar	West Indies host Zimbabwe (2)
	May	**England host Bangladesh (2)**
		West Indies host South Africa (4)
		Zimbabwe host India (2)
	Jul	**England host West Indies (4)**
	Sep	Pakistan host Bangladesh (2)
		South Africa host Zimbabwe (2)
	Oct	Bangladesh host New Zealand (2)
		Pakistan host South Africa (2)
	Nov	**Australia host England (5)**
		India host New Zealand (3)
		Sri Lanka host West Indies (3)
	Dec	South Africa host India (3)

		New Zealand host Pakistan (3)
		Bangladesh host Zimbabwe (2)
2011	**Apr**	Bangladesh host Australia (2)
		West Indies host India (4)
	May	**England host Sri Lanka (3)**
		West Indies host Pakistan (2)
	Jun	Australia host Zimbabwe (2)
	Jul	**England host India (4)**
		Zimbabwe host Bangladesh (2)
	Aug	Sri Lanka host Australia (3)
	Sep	South Africa host Australia (3)
		Zimbabwe host Pakistan (2)
	Oct	Pakistan host Sri Lanka (3)
		Bangladesh host West Indies (2)
	Nov	Australia host New Zealand (3)
		India host West Indies (3)
	Dec	Australia host India (4)
		New Zealand host Zimbabwe (2)
		Bangladesh host Pakistan (2)
		South Africa host Sri Lanka (3)
2012	**Jan**	**Bangladesh host England (2)**
	Feb	**Zimbabwe host England (2)**
		New Zealand host South Africa (3)
	Mar	West Indies host Australia (4)
		India host Pakistan (3)
	Apr	West Indies host New Zealand (3)

TEST MATCH CHAMPIONSHIP TABLE

(As at 28 January 2008)

		Rating
1	Australia (1)	141
2	India (4)	111
3	Sri Lanka (5)	109
4	South Africa (6)	108
5	England (2)	107
6	Pakistan (3)	94
7	New Zealand (7)	93
8	West Indies (8)	73
9	Bangladesh (9)	2

May 2007 positions in brackets.
Zimbabwe has a rating of 12 but does not currently qualify for inclusion in this table.

MAJOR ICC EVENTS

Sep 2008	Champions Trophy
Jun 2009	20/20 World Championship
Apr/May 2010	Champions Trophy
Feb/Mar 2011	World Cup

SECOND XI CHAMPIONSHIP FIXTURES 2008

3-DAY MATCHES (* 4-DAY)

APRIL

Wed 16	Hove	Sussex v Hampshire
	High Wycombe	MCC YC v Glos
	Derby	Derbys v Lancs
Tue 22	*Southend	Essex v Surrey
	Hinckley	Leics v Yorks
Wed 23	Horsham	Sussex v Durham
	Radlett CC	MCC YC v Middx
	Ombersley	Worcs v Lancs
Tue 29	Taunton Vale CC	Somerset v Glos
	Pontarddulais	Glam v Yorks
Wed 30	Belper Meadows	Derbys v Leics
	Bromsgrove	Worcs v MCC YC
	Radlett CC	Middx v Northants
	Reigate Priory CC	Surrey v Hants

MAY

Mon 5	Chester-le-Street	Durham v Somerset
Tue 6	Hinckley	Leics v Glam
	Bristol	Glos v Lancs
	*Cheam	Surrey v Warwks
Wed 7	Stamford Bridge	Yorks v Notts
Mon 12	Derby	Derbys v Sussex
Tue 13	Notts SC	Notts v Glam
	*Leeds	Yorks v Lancs
	*Taunton Vale CC	Somerset v Surrey
Wed 14	Finedon CC	Northants v Leics
	Ealing	Middx v Hants
Tue 20	Notts SC	Notts v Scotland
	Moseley	Warwks v Worcs
	Milton Keynes	Northants v Durham
	Todmorden	Yorks v Somerset
Wed 21	Uxbridge (VL)	Middx v Essex
Tue 27	Derby	Derbys v Yorks
	Southampton (RB)	Hants v Surrey
	Stowe S	Northants v Essex
	Sedbergh S	Durham v Worcs
Wed 28	Stirlands CC	Sussex v Kent
	Birmingham	Warwks v Lancs
	Notts Sports Club	Notts v Glos
	Radlett CC	MCC YC v Leics

JUNE

Tue 3	tba	Warwks v Hants
	Denby	Derbys v MCC YC
	Himley	Worcs v Leics
	*Wimbledon	Surrey v Durham
	Blackpool	Lancs v Scotland
Wed 4	Winchmore Hill	Middx v Glam
	Horsham	Sussex v Glos
Tue 10	Belper Meadows	Derbys v Scotland
	*Ombersley	Worcs v Surrey
	Chelmsford	Essex v Lancs
	Abergavenny	Glam v Glos
	Hinckley	Leics v Durham
	Radlett CC	MCC YC v Northants
Wed 11	Richmond	Middx v Kent
	Stirlands CC	Sussex v Warwks
Tue 17	Radlett CC	MCC YC v Glam
	Merchant Taylors S	Middx v Warwks

	Sheffield	Yorks v Scotland
	Alderley Edge	Lancs v Durham
Wed 18	Hinckley	Leics v Derbys
Mon 23	Norton CC	Durham v Scotland
Wed 25	Liverpool	Lancs v Notts

JULY

Tue 15	Dunstall CC	Derbys v Warwks
Wed 16	Coggleshall	Essex v Glam
	Canterbury (King's S)	Kent v MCC YC
Mon 21	Darlington	Durham v MCC YC
	The Oval	Surrey v Sussex
Tue 22	*Stamford Bridge	Yorks v Warwks
Wed 23	Notts SC	Notts v Worcs
	Hinckley	Leics v Northants
	Taunton Vale CC	Somerset v Essex
	Bristol U	Glos v Middx
Tue 29	Cardiff	Glam v Somerset
	Notts SC	Notts v MCC YC
	*Bristol	Glos v Surrey
Wed 30	Beckenham	Kent v Sussex
	Northampton	Northants v Warwks

AUGUST

Tue 5	*Bristol	Glos v Somerset
Wed 6	Denby	Derbys v Durham
	Leeds	Yorks v Worcs
	Stirlands CC	Sussex v Surrey
	Stratford-upon-Avon	Warwks v Notts
	Billericay	Essex v MCC YC
	Barnes (St Paul's S)	Middx v Lancs
	Cardiff	Glam v Hants
Tue 12	Uxbridge (VL)	MCC YC v Durham
	Chester (Boughton H)	Lancs v Derbys
	Bournemouth SC	Hants v Kent
	Chelmsford	Essex v Middx
	Panteg	Glam v Sussex
	*York	Yorks v Surrey
Wed 13	Barnt Green	Worcs v Northants
Mon 18	Basingstoke	Hants v Glos
Tue 19	Notts SC	Notts v Derbys
	*Worcester	Worcs v Warwks
	*Whitgift S	Surrey v Middx
	Hinckley	Leics v Scotland
	Taunton	Somerset v MCC YC
	Southport	Lancs v Northants
Mon 25	Derby	Derbys v Northants
Tue 26	tba	Warwks v Leics
Wed 27	Horsham	Sussex v Yorks
	Sth North CC	Durham v Lancs
	Halstead	Essex v Hants
	Guildford	Surrey v Kent

SEPTEMBER

Wed 3	Todmorden	Lancs v Yorks
	Taunton Vale CC	Somerset v Hants
	Radlett CC	Middx v Durham
	Milton Keynes	Northants v Notts
	Knowle & Dorridge	Warwks v Derbys
Tue 9	*Uxbridge (VL)	MCC YC v Surrey
Wed 10	Kidderminster	Worcs v Somerset

Oakham S	Leics v Notts	
Leeds	Yorks v Derbys	
Southampton (RB)	Hants v Sussex	
Beckenham	Kent v Essex	
Swallwell CC	Durham v Glam	

Mon 15	Seaton Carew	Durham v Yorks
Tue 16	Crosby (Northern CC)	Lancs v Surrey
	Bristol	Glos v MCC YC
	Uxbridge	Middx v Worcs
Wed 17	Horsham	Sussex v Somerset

SECOND XI TROPHY FIXTURES 2008

1-DAY MATCHES

JUNE

Mon 9	Southampton (RB)	Hants v MCC YC
Wed 18	Southampton (RB)	Hants v Kent
Thu 19	Dunstable CC	Minor Co v Essex
Mon 23	Hinckley	Leics v Derbys
	Uxbridge (VL)	MCC YC v Sussex
	Billericay	Essex v Middx
Tue 24	Sutton	Surrey v MCC YC
	Dorridge CC	Warwks v Worcs
Wed 25	Milton Keynes	Minor Co v Northants
	Bradford & Bingley	Yorks v Leics
Thu 26	Southampton (RB)	Hants v Surrey
	Milton Keynes	Minor Co v Middx
	Tonbridge S	Kent v MCC YC
	Barnt Green	Worcs v Warwks
Fri 27	Seaton Carew	Durham v Yorks
	Usk	Glam v Somerset
	Alvaston & Boulton	Derbys v Leics
	Uxbridge (VL)	MCC YC v Surrey
Mon 30	Cardiff	Glam v Glos
	Wellbeck Colliery	Notts v Minor Co
	Northampton	Northants v Essex
	Horsham	Sussex v MCC YC

JULY

Tue 1	Haydock CC	Lancs v Durham
	Denby	Derbys v Yorks
	Beckenham	Kent v Surrey
	Malvern C	Worcs v Glos
Wed 2	Milton Keynes	Northants v Middx
	Bishop's Stortford	Essex v Notts
	Hinckley	Leics v Hants
	Uxbridge (VL)	MCC YC v Hants
	Cardiff	Glam v Worcs
	North Perrott	Somerset v Warwks
Thu 3	Cardiff	Glam v Warwks
	Middleton	Lancs v Derbys
	Beckenham	Kent v Sussex
	Hartlepool	Durham v Leics
	Winchmore Hill	Middx v Essex
	Purley	Surrey v Hants
Fri 4	tba	Warwks v Somerset
	Bristol U	Glos v Worcs
	Glossop	Derbys v Lancs

	Radlett CC	MCC YC v Kent
	Uxbridge (VL)	Middx v Northants
Mon 7	Canterbury (King's S)	Kent v Hants
	North Perrott	Somerset v Glos
	Dulwich C	Surrey v Sussex
	Caythorpe CC	Notts v Middx
	Wickford	Essex v Northants
	Stockton	Durham v Derbys
Tue 8	Sheffield United	Yorks v Derbys
	Taunton Vale CC	Somerset v Worcs
	tba	Glos v Warwks
	Worksop C	Notts v Essex
	Stockton	Durham v Lancs
Wed 9	Charterhouse S	Surrey v Kent
Thu 10	Ealing	Middx v Minor Co
	Hastings	Sussex v Kent
	Moseley	Warwks v Glam
	Belper Meadows	Derbys v Durham
	Bristol CC	Glos v Somerset
	Leeds (Weetwood)	Yorks v Lancs
Fri 11	Leicester	Leics v Durham
	Manchester	Lancs v Yorks
	tba	Warwks v Glos
	Stirlands CC	Sussex v Surrey
	Cuckney CC	Notts v Northants
	Billericay	Essex v Minor Co
	Taunton Vale CC	Somerset v Glam
Mon 14	Leeds (Weetwood)	Yorks v Durham
	Horsham	Sussex v Hants
	Worcester (RGS)	Worcs v Somerset
	Bristol (WICC)	Glos v Glam
Tue 15	Manchester	Lancs v Leics
	Worcester (RGS)	Worcs v Glam
	tba	Northants v Minor Co
	Barnes (St Paul's S)	Middx v Notts
Wed 16	Southampton (RB)	Hants v Sussex
	Milton Keynes	Minor Co v Notts
Thu 17	Rugby S	Northants v Notts
	Hinckley	Leics v Lancs

AUGUST

Mon 4	tba	Semi-Finals

SEPTEMBER

Mon 1	tba	FINAL

3-DAY COMBINED XI MATCHES (* 4-DAY)

APRIL

Mon 28	Beckenham	Kent/Essex v Durham

MAY

Wed 7	Southend	Kent/Essex v Middx

Wed 21	Southampton (RB)	Hants v Kent/Sussex

JUNE

Tue 3	*Beckenham	Kent/Northants v Yorks

MINOR COUNTIES FIXTURES 2008

Sun 27 April   **KNOCK-OUT TROPHY**

Wem	Shropshire v Oxfordshire (1)
Ampthill	Bedfordshire v Cheshire (1)
Norwich (Manor Park)	Norfolk v Hertfordshire (2)
Gosforth (S Northumberland)	Northumberland v Suffolk (2)
Henley	Berkshire v Herefordshire (3)
Devizes	Wiltshire v Cornwall (3)
Woodhall Spa	Lincolnshire v Cambridgeshire (4)
St Fagans	Wales v Dorset (4)

Sun 4 May   **KNOCK-OUT TROPHY**

Neston	Cheshire v Shropshire (1)
Netherfield	Cumberland v Bedfordshire (1)
Woodbridge School	Suffolk v Norfolk (2)
Leek	Staffordshire v Northumberland (2)
Camborne	Cornwall v Berkshire (3)
Exmouth	Devon v Wiltshire (3)
Sherborne School	Dorset v Lincolnshire (4)
Slough	Buckinghamshire v Wales (4)

Sun 11 May   **KNOCK-OUT TROPHY**

Shrewsbury	Shropshire v Cumberland (1)
Great & Little Tew	Oxfordshire v Cheshire (1)
Norwich (Manor Park)	Norfolk v Staffordshire (2)
Welwyn Garden City	Hertfordshire v Suffolk (2)
Falkland	Berkshire v Devon (3)
Colwall	Herefordshire v Cornwall (3)
Bracebridge Heath	Lincolnshire v Buckinghamshire (4)
March	Cambridgeshire v Dorset (4)

Sun 18 May   **KNOCK-OUT TROPHY**

Flitwick	Bedfordshire v Shropshire (1)
Workington	Cumberland v Oxfordshire (1)
Morpeth (Longhirst Hall)	Northumberland v Norfolk (2)
Leek	Staffordshire v Hertfordshire (2)
Trowbridge	Wiltshire v Berkshire (3)
Budleigh Salterton	Devon v Herefordshire (3)
Abergavenny	Wales v Lincolnshire (4)
Wing (Ascott Park)	Buckinghamshire v Cambridgeshire (4)

Sun 25 – Tue 27 May   **MCCA CHAMPIONSHIP**

Dunstable	Bedfordshire v Suffolk
Banbury	Oxfordshire v Devon

Sun 1 June   **KNOCK-OUT TROPHY**

Bramhall	Cheshire v Cumberland (1)
Challow & Childrey	Oxfordshire v Bedfordshire (1)
Mildenhall	Suffolk v Staffordshire (2)
Long Marston	Hertfordshire v Northumberland (2)
St Just	Cornwall v Devon (3)
Kington	Herefordshire v Wiltshire (3)
Sherborne School	Dorset v Buckinghamshire (4)
Wisbech	Cambridgeshire v Wales (4)

Sun 8 – Tue 10 June	MCCA CHAMPIONSHIP
Trowbridge	Wiltshire v Cheshire
Falkland	Berkshire v Cornwall
Shifnal	Shropshire v Herefordshire
Jesmond	Northumberland v Norfolk
Sleaford	Lincolnshire v Staffordshire
Bishop's Stortford	Hertfordshire v Cambridgeshire

Mon 9 – Wed 11 June	
Sedbergh School	Cumberland v Buckinghamshire

Sun 15 or Wed 18 June	K-O TROPHY Quarter-Finals
	Winner 1 v Runner-Up 3
	Winner 2 v Runner-Up 1
	Winner 4 v Runner-Up 2
	Winner 3 v Runner-Up 4

Sun 22 – Tue 24 June	MCCA CHAMPIONSHIP
Brockhampton	Herefordshire v Dorset
Torquay	Devon v Berkshire
Truro	Cornwall v Shropshire
Challow & Childrey	Oxfordshire v Wiltshire
Chester Boughton Hall	Cheshire v Wales
Ipswich (Ransomes)	Suffolk v Cumberland
Longton	Staffordshire v Hertfordshire
Benwell Hill	Northumberland v Lincolnshire
Gerrards Cross	Buckinghamshire v Cambridgeshire

Sun 6 – Tue 8 July	MCCA CHAMPIONSHIP
Bournemouth (Dean Park)	Dorset v Devon
Pontardulais	Wales v Berkshire
St Austell	Cornwall v Herefordshire
Alderley Edge	Cheshire v Oxfordshire
Bridgnorth	Shropshire v Wiltshire
Radlett	Hertfordshire v Norfolk
Ipswich School	Suffolk v Buckinghamshire
Barrow	Cumberland v Bedfordshire
March	Cambridgeshire v Lincolnshire
Stone	Staffordshire v Northumberland

Sun 13 July	K-O TROPHY Semi-Finals
	Winner Match 2 v Winner Match 4
	Winner Match 3 v Winner Match 1

Sun 20 – Tue 22 July	MCCA CHAMPIONSHIP
Corsham	Wiltshire v Dorset
Whitchurch	Shropshire v Oxfordshire
Finchampstead	Berkshire v Herefordshire
Falmouth	Cornwall v Wales
Exmouth	Devon v Cheshire
Cleethorpes	Lincolnshire v Hertfordshire
Bedford Modern School	Bedfordshire v Cambridgeshire
Jesmond	Northumberland v Suffolk
Slough	Buckinghamshire v Staffordshire

Mon 21 – Wed 23 July	MCCA CHAMPIONSHIP
Norwich (Manor Park)	Norfolk v Cumberland

Sun 27 – Tue 29 July	MCCA CHAMPIONSHIP
Norwich (Manor Park)	Norfolk v Bedfordshire

Sun 3 – Tue 5 August	MCCA CHAMPIONSHIP
Salisbury (South Wilts)	Wiltshire v Devon
Banbury	Oxfordshire v Berkshire
Abergavenny	Wales v Shropshire
Bournemouth (Dean Park)	Dorset v Cornwall
Eastnor	Herefordshire v Cheshire
Norwich (Manor Park)	Norfolk v Suffolk
Knypersley	Staffordshire v Bedfordshire
Cambridge (Fenner's)	Cambridgeshire v Northumberland
Long Marston	Hertfordshire v Cumberland
Grantham	Lincolnshire v Buckinghamshire

Wed 6 August	KNOCK-OUT TROPHY FINAL
Lord's	

Thur 14 August	REPRESENTATIVE MATCH
Gerrards Cross	MCC v MCCA

Sun 17-Tue 19 August	MCCA CHAMPIONSHIP
Colwall	Herefordshire v Wales
Falkland	Berkshire v Wiltshire
Bournemouth (Dean Park)	Dorset v Oxfordshire
Nantwich	Cheshire v Cornwall
Instow	Devon v Shropshire
Bury St Edmunds	Suffolk v Hertfordshire
Keswick	Cumberland v Northumberland
March	Cambridgeshire v Staffordshire
Burnham	Buckinghamshire v Norfolk
Luton Town	Bedfordshire v Lincolnshire

Sun 31 August	KNOCK-OUT TROPHY FINAL
Reserve Day	

Sun 7 – Wed 10 September	MCCA CHAMPIONSHIP
West Div Winner	FINAL

MCCA KNOCK-OUT TROPHY GROUPS

Group 1	*Group 2*	*Group 3*	*Group 4*
Cheshire	Bedfordshire	Berkshire	Buckinghamshire
Cumberland	Lincolnshire	Cornwall	Cambridgeshire
Herefordshire	Norfolk	Devon	Hertfordshire
Northumberland	Northumberland	Dorset	Oxfordshire
Shropshire	Staffordshire	Wales	Wiltshire

PRINCIPAL FIXTURES 2008

CC1	LV County Championship (1st Div)	
CC2	LV County Championship (2nd Div)	
F	Floodlit	
FCF	First-Class Friendly	
FPT	Friends Provident Trophy	
LOI	NatWest Limited-Overs International	

P40[1]	NatWest Pro40 League (1st Div)	
P40[2]	NatWest Pro40 League (2nd Div)	
T20	Twenty20 Cup	
[T20]	Other Twenty20 game	
TM	npower Test Match	
UCCE	Univ Centre of Cricketing Excellence	

Thu 10 – Sun 13 April

FCF	Lord's	MCC v Sussex

Sat 12 – Mon 14 April

FCF	Derby	Derbyshire v Durham UCCE
	Southampton	Hampshire v Cardiff UCCE
	Canterbury	Kent v Leeds/Brad UCCE
FCF	The Oval	Surrey v Loughboro' UCCE
FCF	Cambridge	Cambridge UCCE v Essex
FCF	Oxford	Oxford UCCE v Middlesex

Wed 16 – Sat 19 April

CC2	Chelmsford	Essex v Northants
CC2	Bristol	Glos v Derbyshire
CC1	Southampton	Hampshire v Sussex
CC1	Canterbury	Kent v Notts
CC2	Leicester	Leics v Middlesex
CC1	The Oval	Surrey v Lancashire
CC2	Birmingham	Warwicks v Worcs

Wed 16 – Fri 18 April

FCF	Chester-le-St	Durham v Durham UCCE
	Leeds	Yorkshire v Leeds/Brad UCCE
FCF	Cambridge	Cambridge UCCE v Somerset
FCF	Oxford	Oxford UCCE v Glamorgan

Sun 20 April

FPT	Chester-le-St	Durham v Yorkshire
FPT	Bristol	Glos v Worcs
FPT	Canterbury	Kent v Essex
FPT	Manchester	Lancashire v Derbyshire
FPT	Leicester	Leics v Northants
FPT	Taunton	Somerset v Hampshire
FPT	The Oval	Surrey v Middlesex
FPT	Birmingham	Warwicks v Notts

Wed 23 – Sat 26 April

CC2	Derby	Derbyshire v Essex
CC1	Chester-le-St	Durham v Surrey
CC1	Manchester	Lancashire v Somerset
CC2	Lord's	Middlesex v Glamorgan
CC2	Northampton	Northants v Warwicks
CC1	Hove	Sussex v Kent
CC2	Worcester	Worcs v Leics
CC1	Leeds	Yorkshire v Hampshire

Wed 23 – Fri 25 April

FCF	Bristol	Glos v Loughboro' UCCE
FCF	Oxford	Oxford UCCE v Notts

Sun 27 April

	Arundel	MCC v New Zealanders

Thu 10 – Sun 13 April (continued)

FPT	Chelmsford	Essex v Sussex
FPT	Bristol	Glos v Glamorgan
FPT	Lord's	Middlesex v Kent
FPT	Northampton	Northants v Warwicks
FPT	Worcester	Worcs v Somerset
FPT	Leeds	Yorkshire v Derbyshire
FPT	Dublin	Ireland v Notts
FPT	Edinburgh	Scotland v Lancashire

Mon 28 – Wed 30 April

FCF	Canterbury	Kent v New Zealanders

Tue 29 Apr – Fri 2 May

CC2	Bristol	Glos v Glamorgan
CC2	Birmingham	Warwicks v Leics

Wed 30 Apr – Sat 3 May

CC2	Northampton	Northants v Worcs
CC1	Hove	Sussex v Surrey
CC1	Leeds	Yorkshire v Notts

Wed 30 Apr – Fri 2 May

	Richmond	Middlesex v Cardiff UCCE
FCF	Durham	Durham UCCE v Lancashire

Fri 2 – Mon 5 May

FCF	Chelmsford	Essex v New Zealanders

Fri 2 May

FPT	F Derby	Derbyshire v Durham
FPT	F Southampton	Hampshire v Somerset

Sun 4 May

FPT	Derby	Derbyshire v Scotland
FPT	Southampton	Hampshire v Glos
FPT	Manchester	Lancashire v Durham
FPT	Leicester	Leics v Ireland
FPT	Lord's	Middlesex v Surrey
FPT	Nottingham	Notts v Northants
FPT	Taunton	Somerset v Glamorgan
FPT	Hove	Sussex v Kent

Mon 5 May

FPT	Manchester	Lancashire v Scotland
FPT	Northampton	Northants v Ireland
FPT	The Oval	Surrey v Kent
FPT	Hove	Sussex v Middlesex
FPT	Birmingham	Warwicks v Leics
FPT	Worcester	Worcs v Glamorgan
FPT	Leeds	Yorkshire v Durham

Wed 7 – Sat 10 May

CC2	Derby	Derbyshire v Warwicks

CC2	Chelmsford	Essex v Middlesex
CC1	Manchester	Lancashire v Durham
CC1	Nottingham	Notts v Kent
CC1	Taunton	Somerset v Hampshire

Wed 7 – Fri 9 May

	Northampton	Northants v Cardiff UCCE
FCF	Kidderminster	Worcs v Loughboro' UCCE

Thu 8 – Sun 11 May

FCF	Southampton	England Lions v New Zealanders

Thu 8 May

FPT	^FHove	Sussex v Surrey

Fri 9 May

FPT	^FCardiff	Glamorgan v Glos

Sat 10

FPT	Northampton	Northants v Leics

Sun 11 May

FPT	Bristol	Glos v Somerset
FPT	Canterbury	Kent v Lancashire
FPT	Manchester	Lancashire v Yorkshire
FPT	Nottingham	Notts v Leics
FPT	The Oval	Surrey v Essex
FPT	Birmingham	Warwicks v Northants
FPT	Worcester	Worcs v Hampshire
FPT	Edinburgh	Scotland v Durham

Mon 12 – Wed 14 May

FCF	Cambridge	Cambridge UCCE v Warwicks

Tue 13 – Fri 16 May

CC2	Leicester	Leics v Northants

Wed 14 – Sat 17 May

CC1	Chester-le-St	Durham v Yorkshire
CC2	Cardiff	Glamorgan v Derbyshire
CC1	Southampton	Hampshire v Surrey
CC1	Nottingham	Notts v Lancashire
CC1	Taunton	Somerset v Sussex
CC2	Worcester	Worcs v Glos

Thu 15 – Mon 19 May

TM1	Lord's	ENGLAND v NEW ZEALAND

Fri 16 May

FPT	^FChelmsford	Essex v Kent
FPT	Belfast	Ireland v Warwicks

Sun 18 May

FPT	Chester-le-St	Durham v Lancashire
FPT	Chelmsford	Essex v Middlesex
FPT	Cardiff	Glamorgan v Hampshire
FPT	Canterbury	Kent v Surrey
FPT	Nottingham	Notts v Warwicks
FPT	Taunton	Somerset v Worcs
FPT	Belfast	Ireland v Leics
FPT	Edinburgh	Scotland v Yorkshire

Tue 20 – Fri 23 May

CC1	Nottingham	Notts v Sussex

Tue 20 May

FPT	^FSouthampton	Hampshire v Worcs

Wed 21 – Sat 24 May

CC2	Chelmsford	Essex v Leics
CC2	*Tba*	Glamorgan v Northants
CC1	Tunbridge W	Kent v Somerset
CC1	The Oval	Surrey v Yorkshire
CC2	Birmingham	Warwicks v Middlesex

Thu 22 May

FPT	^FDerby	Derbyshire v Lancashire

Fri 23 – Tue 27 May

TM2	Manchester	ENGLAND v NEW ZEALAND

Sun 25 May

FPT	Derby	Derbyshire v Yorkshire
FPT	Chester-le-St	Durham v Scotland
FPT	Chelmsford	Essex v Surrey
FPT	*Tba*	Glamorgan v Worcs
FPT	Bristol	Glos v Hampshire
FPT	Southgate	Middlesex v Sussex
FPT	Northampton	Northants v Notts
FPT	Birmingham	Warwicks v Ireland

Mon 26 May

FPT	Chester-le-St	Durham v Derbyshire
FPT	Southampton	Hampshire v Glamorgan
FPT	Tunbridge W	Kent v Middlesex
FPT	Oakham	Leics v Warwicks
FPT	Nottingham	Notts v Ireland
FPT	Bath	Somerset v Glos
FPT	Hastings	Sussex v Essex
FPT	Leeds	Yorkshire v Scotland

Wed 28 May

FPT	Cardiff	Glamorgan v Somerset
FPT	Oakham	Leics v Notts
FPT	Lord's	Middlesex v Essex
FPT	Croydon	Surrey v Sussex
FPT	Worcester	Worcs v Glos
FPT	Leeds	Yorkshire v Lancashire
FPT	Dublin	Ireland v Northants
FPT	Glasgow	Scotland v Derbyshire

Fri 30 May – Mon 2 June

CC2	Gloucester	Glos v Warwicks
CC1	Southampton	Hampshire v Kent
CC2	Leicester	Leics v Glamorgan
CC2	Lord's	Middlesex v Derbyshire
CC1	Croydon	Surrey v Somerset
CC1	Hove	Sussex v Durham
CC2	Worcester	Worcs v Essex
CC1	Leeds	Yorkshire v Lancashire

Fri 30 May – Sun 1 June

FCF	Northampton	Northants v New Zealanders

Wed 4 June *(No Reserve Days)*

FPT	Quarter-Finals	

Thu 5 – Mon 9 June

TM3	Nottingham	ENGLAND v NEW ZEALAND

Fri 6 – Mon 9 June

CC2	Chesterfield	Derbyshire v Worcs

CC1	Chester-le-St	Durham v Hampshire
CC2	Cardiff	Glamorgan v Warwicks
CC1	Canterbury	Kent v Sussex
CC1	Manchester	Lancashire v Notts
CC2	Lord's	Middlesex v Essex
CC2	Northampton	Northants v Glos
CC2	Taunton	Somerset v Yorkshire

Fri 6 – Sun 8 June
	Leeds (Weetwood)	Leeds/Bradford UCCE v Leics

Wed 11 June
	Worcester	Worcs v New Zealanders
T20	Chester-le-St	Durham v Derbyshire
T20	F Cardiff	Glamorgan v Warwicks
T20	F Southampton	Hampshire v Middlesex
T20	Canterbury	Kent v Sussex
T20	Leicester	Leics v Lancashire
T20	Taunton	Somerset v Northants
T20	The Oval	Surrey v Essex

Thu 12 June
T20	Lord's	Middlesex v Essex
T20	Worcester	Worcs v Glos
T20	Leeds	Yorkshire v Derbyshire

Fri 13 June
[T20]	Manchester	England v New Zealand
T20	F Derby	Derbyshire v Lancashire
T20	F Cardiff	Glamorgan v Somerset
T20	Bristol	Glos v Warwicks
T20	Leicester	Leics v Durham
T20	Northampton	Northants v Worcs
T20	The Oval	Surrey v Kent
T20	F Hove	Sussex v Hampshire
T20	Leeds	Yorkshire v Notts

Sat 14 June
T20	F Southampton	Hampshire v Kent
T20	Nottingham	Notts v Durham
T20	Taunton	Somerset v Warwicks

Sun 15 June
LOI	Chester-le-St	England v New Zealand
T20	Chesterfield	Derbyshire v Yorkshire
T20	Chelmsford	Essex v Middlesex
T20	Cardiff	Glamorgan v Worcs
T20	Bristol	Glos v Northants
T20	Manchester	Lancs v Leics
T20	The Oval	Surrey v Sussex

Mon 16 June
T20	Canterbury	Kent v Hampshire
T20	Lord's	Middlesex v Surrey
T20	Nottingham	Notts v Derbyshire

Tue 17 June
T20	Manchester	Lancashire v Durham
T20	Leicester	Leics v Yorkshire
T20	Milton Keynes	Northants v Glos
T20	Taunton	Somerset v Glamorgan
T20	F Hove	Sussex v Essex

T20	Worcester	Worcs v Warwicks
	Lord's	Cambridge U v Oxford U

Wed 18 June
LOI	Birmingham	England v New Zealand
T20	Chester-le-St	Durham v Notts
T20	F Chelmsford	Essex v Kent
T20	F Cardiff	Glamorgan v Glos
T20	The Oval	Surrey v Hampshire
T20	Leeds	Yorkshire v Lancashire

Thu 19 June
T20	Lord's	Middlesex v Sussex
T20	Milton Keynes	Northants v Warwicks
T20	Nottingham	Notts v Leics
T20	Worcester	Worcs v Somerset

Fri 20 June
T20	F Derby	Derbyshire v Notts
T20	Chester-le-St	Durham v Leics
T20	F Chelmsford	Essex v Surrey
T20	F Cardiff	Glamorgan v Northants
T20	F Southampton	Hampshire v Sussex
T20	Beckenham	Kent v Middlesex
T20	Manchester	Lancashire v Yorks
T20	Taunton	Somerset v Glos
T20	Birmingham	Warwicks v Worcs

Sat 21 June
LOI	Bristol	England v New Zealand

Sun 22 June
T20	Derby	Derbyshire v Leics
T20	Beckenham	Kent v Essex
T20	Richmond	Middlesex v Hampshire
T20	Northampton	Northants v Glam
T20	Nottingham	Notts v Lancashire
T20	Taunton	Somerset v Worcs
T20	Hove	Sussex v Surrey
T20	Birmingham	Warwicks v Glos
T20	Leeds	Yorkshire v Durham

Mon 23 June
T20	F Southampton	Hampshire v Surrey
T20	Manchester	Lancashire v Derbyshire

Tue 24 June
T20	Chester-le-St	Durham v Yorkshire
T20	F Chelmsford	Essex v Sussex
T20	Bristol	Glos v Glamorgan
T20	Leicester	Leics v Notts
T20	Uxbridge	Middlesex v Kent
T20	Birmingham	Warwicks v Somerset
T20	Worcester	Worcs v Northants

Wed 25 June
LOI	The Oval	England v New Zealand
T20	F Derby	Derbyshire v Durham
T20	Bristol	Glos v Worcs
T20	F Southampton	Hampshire v Essex
T20	Canterbury	Kent v Surrey
T20	Manchester	Lancashire v Notts

T20	[F]Hove	Sussex v Middlesex

Thu 26 June

T20	Northampton	Northants v Somerset
T20	Birmingham	Warwicks v Glamorgan
T20	Leeds	Yorkshire v Leics

Fri 27 June

T20	Chester-le-St	Durham v Lancashire
T20	Chelmsford	Essex v Hampshire
T20	Bristol	Glos v Somerset
T20	Leicester	Leics v Derbyshire
T20	Nottingham	Notts v Yorkshire
T20	The Oval	Surrey v Middlesex
T20	Hove	Sussex v Kent
T20	Birmingham	Warwicks v Northants
T20	Worcester	Worcs v Glamorgan

Sat 28 June

LOI	Lord's	**England v New Zealand**

Sun 29 – Tue 1 July

FCF	Taunton	Somerset v South Africans

Sun 29 June – Wed 2 July

CC2	Chelmsford	Essex v Derbyshire
CC1	Southampton	Hampshire v Notts
CC2	Leicester	Leics v Worcs
CC2	Uxbridge	Middlesex v Northants
CC1	The Oval	Surrey v Kent
CC1	Hove	Sussex v Lancashire
CC2	Birmingham	Warwicks v Glos
CC1	Leeds	Yorkshire v Durham

Tue 1 – Fri 4 July

FCF	Oxford	Oxford U v Cambridge U

Thu 3 July

[T20]	The Oval	International XI v Asia XI

Fri 4 – Sun 6 July

FCF	Uxbridge	Middlesex v South Africans

Fri 4 July *(No Reserve Day)*

FPT		Semi-Final

Sat 5 July *(No Reserve Day)*

FPT		Semi-Final

Mon 7 July

T20		Quarter-Finals 1 & 2

Tue 8 July

T20		Quarter-Final 3

Wed 9 July

T20		Quarter-Final 4

Thu 10 – Mon 14 July

TM1	Lord's	**ENGLAND v SOUTH AFRICA**

Thu 10 – Sun 13 July

CC2	Worcester	Worcs v Northants

Fri 11 – Sun 13 July

FCF	Birmingham	Warwicks v Bangladesh A

Fri 11 – Mon 14 July

CC2	Derby	Derbyshire v Leics
CC1	Chester-le-St	Durham v Somerset

CC2	Cardiff	Glamorgan v Essex
CC2	Bristol	Glos v Middlesex
CC1	Southampton	Hampshire v Lancashire
CC1	Canterbury	Kent v Yorkshire
CC1	Nottingham	Notts v Surrey

Tue 15 July

P40	[F]Worcester	Worcs v Notts

Wed 16 – Fri 18 July

FCF	Leicester	Leics v Bangladesh A

Wed 16 – Sat 19 July

CC2	Uxbridge	Middlesex v Warwicks
CC2	Northampton	Northants v Derbyshire
CC1	Taunton	Somerset v Kent
CC1	Guildford	Surrey v Durham
CC1	Arundel	Sussex v Hampshire

Wed 16 July

P40[2]	[F]Chelmsford	Essex v Yorkshire

Thu 17 – Sun 20 July

CC2	Worcester	Worcs v Glamorgan

Thu 17 July

P40[1]	[F]Manchester	Lancashire v Glos

Fri 18 – Tue 22 July

TM2	Leeds	**ENGLAND v SOUTH AFRICA**

Sun 20 July

P40[2]	Leicester	Leics v Essex
P40[1]	Uxbridge	Middlesex v Durham
P40[2]	Northampton	Northants v Derbyshire
P40[1]	Nottingham	Notts v Hampshire
P40[2]	Guildford	Surrey v Yorkshire
P40[1]	Arundel	Sussex v Somerset
P40[2]	Birmingham	Warwicks v Kent

Mon 21 – Wed 23 July

FCF	Derby	Derbyshire v Bangladesh A

Tue 22 – Fri 25 July

CC2	Chelmsford	Essex v Glos
CC1	Manchester	Lancashire v Hampshire
CC2	Lord's	Middlesex v Worcs
CC2	Northampton	Northants v Leics
CC1	Nottingham	Notts v Yorkshire

Wed 23 July

P40[1]	[F]Chester-le-St	Durham v Somerset

Thu 24 July

P40[2]	[F]Cardiff	Glamorgan v Surrey

Fri 25 – Sun 27 July

FCF	Worcester	South Africans v Bangladesh A

Fri 25 July

	Birmingham	England XI v R.A.Woolmer World XI

Sat 26 July

T20	Southampton	Semi-Finals & [F]Final

Mon 28 July

P40[2]	[F]Derby	Derbyshire v Essex

Tue 29 July

P40[2]	[F]Leicester	Leics v Warwicks

Wed 30 July – Sun 3 August

TM3	Birmingham	**ENGLAND v SOUTH AFRICA**

Wed 30 July – Sat 2 August

CC2	Chesterfield	Derbyshire v Northants
CC2	Southend	Essex v Glamorgan
CC2	Cheltenham	Glos v Worcs
CC1	Canterbury	Kent v Hampshire
CC2	Leicester	Leics v Warwicks
CC1	Nottingham	Notts v Durham
CC1	Horsham	Sussex v Somerset
CC1	Leeds	Yorkshire v Surrey

Wed 30 July

	Alderley Edge	Lancashire v Bangladesh A

Fri 1 August

	Durham	MCC v Bangladesh A

Sun 3 August

	Chester-le-St	Durham v Bangladesh A
P40²	Chesterfield	Derbyshire v Surrey
P40²	Southend	Essex v Northants
P40¹	Cheltenham	Glos v Notts
P40¹	Southampton	Hampshire v Lancashire
P40²	Canterbury	Kent v Glamorgan
P40¹	Horsham	Sussex v Worcs
P40²	Leeds	Yorkshire v Leics

Mon 4 August

P40¹	ᶠLord's	Middlesex v Somerset

Tue 5 August

P40²	ᶠChelmsford	Essex v Surrey
P40¹	Cheltenham	Glos v Sussex

Wed 6 – Sat 9 August

CC1	Chester-le-St	Durham v Kent
CC2	Colwyn Bay	Glamorgan v Middlesex
CC2	Cheltenham	Glos v Leics
CC1	Southampton	Hampshire v Yorkshire
CC1	Manchester	Lancashire v Sussex
CC1	Taunton	Somerset v Notts
CC2	Worcester	Worcs v Derbyshire

Wed 6 August

P40²	ᶠBirmingham	Warwicks v Northants

Thu 7 – Mon 11 August

TM4	The Oval	ENGLAND v SOUTH AFRICA

Thu 7 – Sun 10 August

CC2	Birmingham	Warwicks v Northants

Sun 10 August

P40¹	Chester-le-St	Durham v Sussex
P40²	Colwyn Bay	Glamorgan v Leics
P40¹	Cheltenham	Glos v Hampshire
P40¹	Manchester	Lancashire v Worcs
P40¹	Taunton	Somerset v Notts

Tue 12 – Fri 15 August

CC2	Derby	Derbyshire v Middlesex
CC1	Chester-le-St	Durham v Notts
CC2	Cardiff	Glamorgan v Glos
CC1	Manchester	Lancashire v Yorkshire

Wed 12 August

CC1	Taunton	Somerset v Surrey
CC2	Birmingham	Warwicks v Essex

Tue 12 August

P40²	ᶠCanterbury	Kent v Leics

Wed 13 August

P40¹	ᶠSouthampton	Hampshire v Sussex

Thu 14 August

	Leicester	England Lions v South Africans

Sat 16 August

FPT	Lord's	Final (Reserve 17 August)
	Derby	England Lions v South Africans

Sun 17 August

P40²	Canterbury	Kent v Derbyshire
P40¹	Manchester	Lancashire v Middlesex
P40¹	Taunton	Somerset v Hampshire
P40²	The Oval	Surrey v Northants

Tue 19 – Fri 22 August

CC2	Bristol	Glos v Northants
CC1	Southampton	Hampshire v Somerset

Tue 19 August

P40¹	ᶠNottingham	Notts v Durham

Wed 20 – Sat 23 August

CC2	Colchester	Essex v Worcs
CC1	Canterbury	Kent v Lancashire
CC2	Lord's	Middlesex v Leics
CC1	The Oval	Surrey v Sussex

Wed 20 August

[T20]	Chester-le-St	**England v South Africa**

Thu 21 August

P40²	ᶠDerby	Derbyshire v Yorkshire

Fri 22 August

LOI	ᶠLeeds	**England v South Africa**
P40²	ᶠCardiff	Glamorgan v Warwicks

Sat 23 August

P40¹	Taunton	Somerset v Glos

Sun 24 August

P40²	Colchester	Essex v Glamorgan
P40¹	Lord's	Middlesex v Hampshire
P40¹	Worcester	Worcs v Durham

Mon 25 August

P40²	Leicester	Leics v Derbyshire
P40²	Northampton	Northants v Glamorgan
P40¹	ᶠHove	Sussex v Lancashire
P40²	Birmingham	Warwicks v Surrey
P40²	Scarborough	Yorkshire v Kent

Tue 26 August

LOI	ᶠNottingham	**England v South Africa**

Wed 27 – Sat 30 August

CC1	Southampton	Hampshire v Durham
CC1	Blackpool	Lancashire v Surrey
CC2	Leicester	Leics v Essex
CC2	Northampton	Northants v Glamorgan
CC1	Hove	Sussex v Notts

316

CC2	Birmingham	Warwicks v Derbyshire
CC1	Scarborough	Yorkshire v Kent

Wed 27 August

P40[1]	FBristol	Glos v Middlesex

Thu 28 August

P40[1]	FTaunton	Somerset v Worcs

Fri 29 August

LOI	The Oval	**England v South Africa**

Sat 30 August

P40[1]	Worcester	Worcs v Glos

Sun 31 August

LOI	Lord's	**England v South Africa**
P40[2]	Northampton	Northants v Kent
P40[2]	Scarborough	Yorkshire v Glamorgan

Mon 1 September

P40[1]	FSouthampton	Hampshire v Durham

Tue 2 – Fri 5 September

CC2	Derby	Derbyshire v Glamorgan
CC2	Worcester	Worcs v Warwicks

Tue 2 September

P40[2]	FThe Oval	Surrey v Kent

Wed 3 – Sat 6 September

CC1	Chester-le-St	Durham v Lancashire
CC2	Lord's	Middlesex v Glos
CC1	Nottingham	Notts v Somerset
CC1	Scarborough	Yorkshire v Sussex

Wed 3 September

LOI	FCardiff	**England v South Africa**
[T20]	Southampton	Hampshire v Essex

Thu 4 – Sun 7 September

CC1	Canterbury	Kent v Surrey

Fri 5 September

[T20]	Chelmsford	Essex v Hampshire

Sat 6 September

P40[1]	Southampton	Hampshire v Worcs

Sun 7 September

P40[1]	Chester-le-St	Durham v Lancashire
P40[2]	Leicester	Leics v Northants
P40[1]	Lord's	Middlesex v Notts
P40[2]	Birmingham	Warwicks v Essex

Mon 8 September

P40[2]	FCardiff	Glamorgan v Derbyshire

Tue 9 – Fri 12 September

CC2	Leicester	Leics v Glos
CC2	Northampton	Northants v Essex
CC1	Taunton	Somerset v Durham
CC1	The Oval	Surrey v Hampshire

Tue 9 September

P40[2]	FLeeds	Yorkshire v Warwicks

Wed 10 – Sat 13 September

CC2	Cardiff	Glamorgan v Worcs

Wed 10 September

P40[1]	FNottingham	Notts v Lancashire

Thu 11 September

P40[1]	FHove	Sussex v Middlesex

Sat 13 September

P40[2]	Derby	Derbyshire v Warwicks
P40[2]	Canterbury	Kent v Essex
P40[2]	Northampton	Northants v Yorkshire
P40[2]	The Oval	Surrey v Leics

Sun 14 September

P40[1]	Chester-le-St	Durham v Glos
P40[1]	Liverpool	Lancashire v Somerset
P40[1]	Nottingham	Notts v Sussex
P40[1]	Worcester	Worcs v Middlesex

Wed 17 – Sat 20 September

CC2	Derby	Derbyshire v Glos
CC1	Chester-le-St	Durham v Sussex
CC2	Chelmsford	Essex v Warwicks
CC2	Cardiff	Glamorgan v Leics
CC1	Liverpool	Lancashire v Kent
CC1	The Oval	Surrey v Notts
CC2	Worcester	Worcs v Middlesex
CC1	Leeds	Yorkshire v Somerset

Sun 21 September

P40	Play-Off	

Wed 24 – Sat 27 September

CC2	Bristol	Glos v Essex
CC1	Canterbury	Kent v Durham
CC2	Leicester	Leics v Derbyshire
CC2	Northampton	Northants v Middlesex
CC1	Nottingham	Notts v Hampshire
CC1	Taunton	Somerset v Lancashire
CC1	Hove	Sussex v Yorkshire
CC2	Birmingham	Warwicks v Glamorgan

INTERNATIONAL UNDER-19 CRICKET

Sun 6 – Tue 8 July
    Loughborough England v Bangladesh A

TEST MATCH SERIES
England v New Zealand
| TM1 | Taunton | Sat 26 – Tue 29 July |
| TM2 | Worcester | Fri 1 – Mon 4 August |

LIMITED-OVERS INTERNATIONALS
England v New Zealand
LOI	Canterbury	Fri 8 August
LOI	Canterbury	Sat 9 August
LOI	^FHove	Mon 11 August
LOI	Northampton	Thu 14 August
LOI	Northampton	Fri 15 August

WOMEN'S INTERNATIONAL FIXTURES

England v South Africa
LOI	Canterbury	Wed 6 August
LOI	Lord's	Fri 8 August
TM1	Shenley	Mon 11 – Thu 14 August
LOI	Chesterfield	Mon 18 August
T20	Chesterfield	Wed 20 August
T20	Northampton	Fri 22 August
T20	Northampton	Sat 23 August

England v India
LOI	Bath CC	Sat 30 August
LOI	Shenley	Mon 1 September
LOI	Taunton	Thu 4 September
T20	Taunton	Fri 5 September
LOI	Arundel	Sun 7 September
LOI	^FHove	Tue 9 September

MCC UCCE CHALLENGE

Tue 22, Wed 23 April
| Weetwood | Leeds/Bradford v Cambridge |
| *Tba* | Cardiff v Durham |

Tue 29, Wed 30 April
| Cambridge | Cambridge v Loughborough |
| Oxford | Oxford v Leeds/Bradford |

Sat 3, Sun 4 May
| Loughborough | Loughborough v Leeds/Bradford |

Thu 8, Fri 9 May
| Durham | Durham v Cambridge |

Mon 12, Tue 13 May
| *Tba* | Cardiff v Loughborough |

Thu 15, Fri 16 May
| Oxford | Oxford v Cardiff |

Thu 29, Fri 30 May
| Durham | Durham v Oxford |

Fri 13, Sat 14 June
Oxford	Oxford v Cambridge
Weetwood	Leeds/Bradford v Cardiff
Loughborough	Loughborough v Durham

Sat 21, Sun 22 June
Tba	Cardiff v Cambridge
Weetwood	Leeds/Bradford v Durham
Loughborough	Loughborough v Oxford

Mon 30 June
| Lord's | Final |

FIELDING CHART

(For a right-handed batsman)

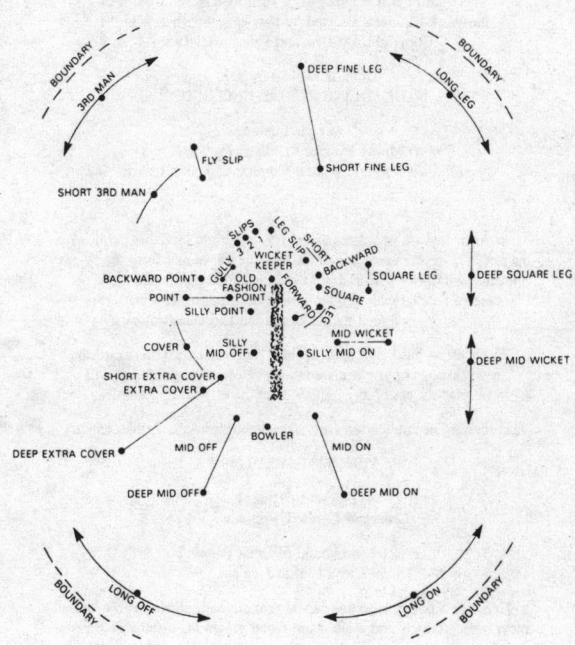

First published in 2008
by HEADLINE PUBLISHING GROUP

Cover photographs:
(*Front*) Monty Panesar © Allstar Picture Library
(*Back and Spine*) Stephen Fleming © Action Images

1

Cataloguing in Publication Data is available from the British Library

ISBN 978 0 7553 1745 5

Typeset in Times by
Letterpart Limited, Reigate, Surrey

Printed and bound in Great Britain by
Clays Ltd, St Ives plc

Headline's policy is to use papers that are natural, renewable and
recyclable products and made from wood grown in sustainable forests.
The logging and manufacturing processes are expected to conform
to the environmental regulations of the country of origin.

HEADLINE PUBLISHING GROUP
An Hachette Livre UK Company
338 Euston Road
London NW1 3BH
www.headline.co.uk
www.hachettelivre.co.uk